BASIC IGNITION & ELECTRICAL SYSTEMS

BASIC IGNITION & ELECTRICAL SYSTEMS NO. 6

INTRODUCTION

When the original edition of this book was published some fifteen years ago, its intent was to present a basic text/reference guide to automotive ignition and electrical systems...a volume that would explain all the electrical components on a car and their interrelationships in simple, practical terms.

Many changes have emerged in the intervening years—worldwide gas shortages, inflation, the downsizing of cars, sticker shock, the virtual exile of the V-8 in favor of turbocharged 4-bangers, to name but a few—and many more will materialize in the years ahead. As a result, Americans are hanging onto their cars longer and taking better care of them.

Space-age electronic wizardry was introduced in American cars by the Chrysler Corp. in 1972, and the emergence of stringent emissions legislation virtually forced *all* automakers to follow suit. The result has been the emergence of the "black box" (which isn't black) as the controlling genius of today's automobile. Electronics are increasingly taking over the operation of our automobiles, relegating the owner who doesn't understand his or her car to the side of the road—waiting for the tow truck.

Today, more than ever, you need a good, basic, and up-to-date reference book on automotive ignitions and electrical systems—and this is still the one! In this, our latest edition, we introduce you to state-of-the-art electronic ignitions/electronic engine controls and show you how they work, while refreshing your background in the other links in the chain of electricity that makes our cars run. Thus, you'll still find chapters on batteries, starters, alternators, solenoids, switches, instruments, lights, and accessories, as well as the more esoteric subjects such as generators.

The subject is timeless, and although automotive ignitions and electrical systems may take differing forms, the basics remain just that—basic. If you understand how something works, you have a much better chance of coping with the inevitable malfunction or component failure. So turn the page and delve into the fascinating world of auto electricity and electronics—you just may find it easier than you think.

Copyright © 1985 by Green Hill Publishers.
All rights reserved.

Green Hill Publishers
722 Columbus Street
Ottawa, Illinois 61350

(815) 434-7905

Printed in the United States of America

Distributed by Kampmann & Company, New York City.

BASIC IGNITION & ELECTRICAL SYSTEMS

CONTENTS

- SPARK PLUGS 4
  - **HOW-TO:** READING PLUGS 12
- PLUG WIRES 14
  - **HOW-TO:** PLUG WIRE REPLACEMENT 20
- COILS 22
- CONVENTIONAL DISTRIBUTORS 30
  - **HOW-TO:** BREAKER POINT REPLACEMENT 40
  - **HOW-TO:** DISTRIBUTOR CARE 42
- BREAKERLESS DISTRIBUTORS 44
  - **HOW-TO:** ACCEL CONVERSION 56
  - **HOW-TO:** MALLORY LED CONVERSION 58
- TROUBLESHOOTING ELECTRONIC IGNITIONS 60
- ELECTRONIC ENGINE CONTROLS 65
- ELECTRICAL TEST EQUIPMENT 74
- IGNITION TUNING 81
  - **HOW-TO:** IGNITION TUNE-UP 90
- BATTERIES 94
  - **HOW-TO:** BATTERY CARE 104
- STARTERS 106
  - **HOW-TO:** STARTER REBUILD 116
- SOLENOIDS & SWITCHES 120
- GENERATORS 126
  - **HOW-TO:** GENERATOR OVERHAUL 132
- ALTERNATORS 134
  - **HOW-TO:** ALTERNATOR OVERHAUL 142
- REGULATORS 146
- LIGHTS 153
- INSTRUMENTS 159
- WIRING 165
- ELECTRICAL TROUBLESHOOTING 172
- ACCESSORIES 178
- WIRING GUIDE 185
- NOTES 187

SPARK PLUGS

The modern internal combustion engine is a highly refined source of automotive power, yet its ability to operate is totally dependent upon a component with no moving parts—the spark plug. The major function of a spark plug is to provide a gap for high voltage from the coil to jump, creating a spark to ignite the air-fuel mixture in the combustion chamber. All ignition systems are designed with this end in mind, and for that reason, it's the most appropriate point with which to begin our look at *Basic Ignition & Electrical Systems*. Before examining spark plugs in detail, let's take a quick look at how they do their job.

HOW SPARK PLUGS WORK

An automotive ignition system is divided into two circuits—primary and secondary. When the ignition switch is turned on, low voltage travels from the battery through the switch to the primary windings of the coil. This is the primary circuit. As this low incoming voltage moves from the primary to the secondary windings of the coil, it is transformed into a high outgoing or secondary voltage.

Leaving the coil, the high voltage goes through a short secondary lead to the distributor cap. A rotor directly under the cap connected to the distributor shaft conducts the voltage to each of the cap electrodes in a sequence to match the predetermined firing order of the engine. These electrodes connect to the individual towers on the cap where the spark-plug wires are plugged in. From this point, the voltage travels through the plug wire and down the center electrode of the plug. At the bottom of the plug, it jumps the gap between the center and side electrodes, creating a spark inside the combustion chamber which fires the mixture.

The voltage then returns through the engine to the chassis and up the ground cable to the ground terminal of the battery, making a complete electrical circuit. Secondary wiring usually has heavy insulation to contain the high voltage, whereas the primary wire carrying low voltage requires only a thin covering.

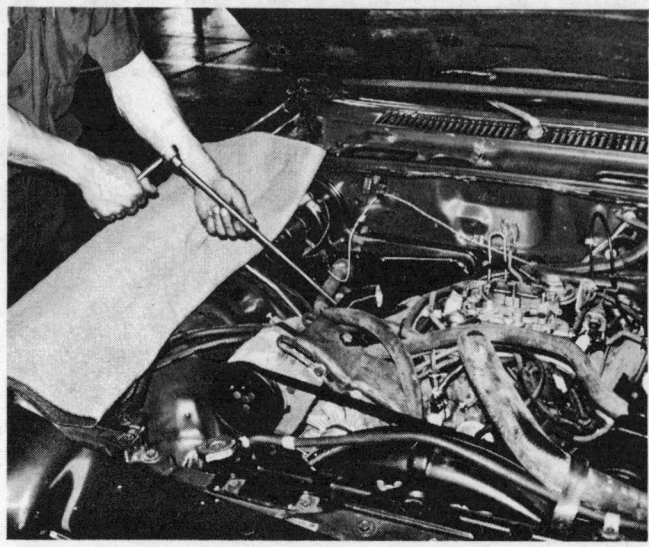

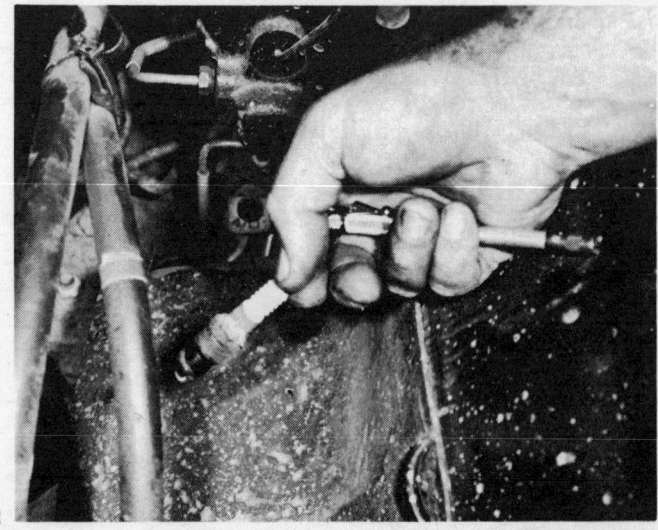

SPARK-PLUG CONSTRUCTION

Spark plugs consist of three principal components—an insulator, electrodes, and the shell. The ceramic insulator must withstand great physical, chemical, and electrical stress during combustion while offering rapid heat conductivity. Plug electrodes are also stressed by high combustion chamber temperatures, corrosion, and sparking erosion. To keep gap increase to a minimum, electrodes are made of a wear-resistant nickel alloy.

The steel shell is the spark plug's main structural part. It not only grips the insulator in a gasproof seal that can withstand pressure up to 600 psi, but also absorbs the stresses of being threaded into the engine's cylinder head by a socket. The lower part of the shell has rolled threads. This allows torque applied on the seat to provide the leakproof seal.

The threaded part of the shell is made in a number of different sizes: 18 mm, 14 mm, 12 mm, and 10 mm. The 14-mm thread is the most widely used, although many domestic Ford products employ the 18-mm size. The 12-mm and 10-mm sizes are presently found only in motorcycles, some foreign models, and

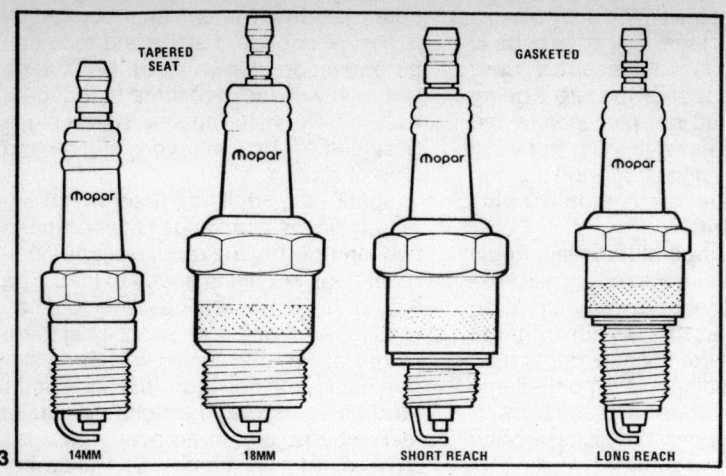
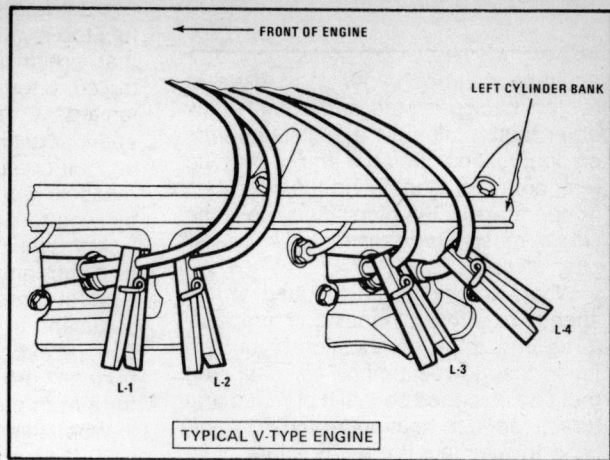

some older cars. Plugs may be installed with a gasket or designed with a tapered seat.

To place the high-voltage spark exactly where it's required in the combustion chamber, the plug's threaded portion must match the dimensional requirements of the cylinder head precisely. The length of this threaded portion is called the plug's *reach*. Common reaches used are 3/8-inch, 7/16-inch, .460-inch, 1/2-inch, and 3/4-inch.

Each spark-plug manufacturer has incorporated into its plugs patented design features that it claims make its product a little better than the others. It would require too much space to discuss all of these in detail, but the two or three basic types made by *most* manufacturers deserve special description.

Resistance plugs contain an electrical resistor located inside the insulator. First made by the Electric Autolite Co. for use in Chrysler products, resistor plugs have been around for many years. The resistor's original purpose was to produce a better idle. An engine idles smoother with wide plug gaps, but wide plug gaps are not possible when there is no resistance in the secondary circuit. Without resistance, current flow burns metal off the plug electrodes at a rapid rate. If you start with wide plug gaps, they will increase so greatly that the engine won't run.

Secondary resistance is still used to control electrode erosion, but it's also necessary to minimize radio and TV interference. Late-model engines use both resistor plugs and suppression-type spark-plug leads. Since the electrodes last longer on resistor plugs, a wider-than-standard gap of .035-inch can be used, resulting in better engine performance.

Series-gap plugs are available from several major plug producers. The series- or booster-gap plug has an additional air gap in the center electrode located *inside* the ceramic insulator. Series-gap plugs are able to keep firing in spite of semiconductive carbon or oil deposits on the plug's firing tip.

Spark voltage requires time to build up in a conventional ignition system, and much of the useful spark energy can leak away through plug deposits before the voltage peak is reached. For this reason, the voltage may never attain a level sufficient to fire the plug.

By incorporating an additional gap inside the plug, the voltage does not reach the plug electrodes until it has built up sufficient energy to jump across both the booster gap and the firing gap. If you have a problem with plug fouling, the series-gap plugs may be an answer.

Copper-core plugs are sold under the NGK brand. Since copper has better heat conductivity than nickel-steel, it is able to carry heat away from the plug tip more effectively. This extends the plug's useful heat range by keeping its firing tip cooler at high speeds and under heavy loads.

HEAT RANGE

The efficiency and life expectancy of spark plugs are strongly influenced by the conditions existing inside the engine's combustion chambers. Fuel-air ratios, compression ratios, emissions

1. Periodic spark plug replacement is important. Always work on a cool engine to avoid the possibility of a bad burn, especially if clearances are close.

2. On some engines, it may be necessary to use a magnet to remove and install the plugs. Ford V-8's are bad in this respect, followed closely by GM.

3. Various types of plugs have been used. The most popular ones use either 14mm or 18mm diameter threads. Some plugs have a tapered seat; others use gaskets. Thread reach is important—installing a long reach plug in a short reach cylinder head can result in piston/valve damage. A short reach plug in a long reach head reduces combustion efficiency.

4. To prevent mixing up the plug wires when replacing spark plugs, use masking tape or numbered clothes pins to identify each wire before removing it. This saves a lot of time and trouble if you're not familiar with your engine.

5. Inspect each plug carefully as it's removed. A flashlight magnifier comes in very handy for this job.

6. Make yourself a plug holder by punching holes in a cardboard box or by drilling holes in a block of wood. This will let you keep the plugs in the order removed. If one of them has excessive oil or carbon, this method lets you remember which cylinder has the problem.

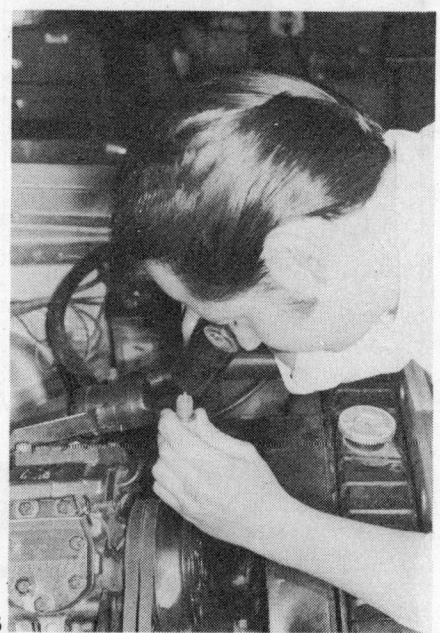
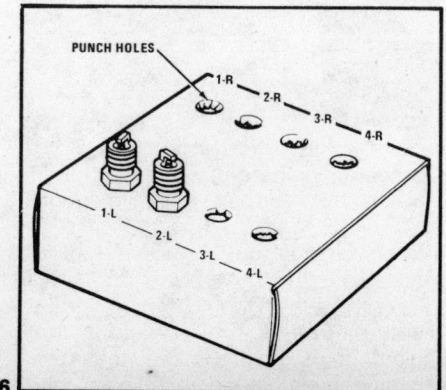

equipment, turbocharger boost, exhaust system back pressure, and a great many other factors all have a definite bearing on combustion chamber *and* spark-plug temperatures. Controlling the operating temperature of the plug's firing tip *is the single most important factor in spark-plug design.*

When an engine is operated at low speeds or with light loads, the temperatures inside the combustion chambers fall to their lowest point. The spark plug must be designed so that it picks up and retains enough heat under these conditions to maintain the temperature of its firing tip *above* 750 degrees. If it falls below this point, deposits will begin to accumulate on the plug tips which cannot be burned off. This condition is called *fouling,* and if allowed to continue, will prevent the plug from firing at all, resulting in engine misfire.

If the same engine is operated at high speeds or with heavy loads, the combustion chamber temperatures start to climb. Should the plugs be designed to retain too much of this heat, they may begin to cause preignition. Preignition becomes a danger at about 1750 degrees, the temperature where plug tips start to become incandescent.

At low speeds with heavy loads, preignition causes the engine to ping or knock very much like that caused by an overadvanced spark timing or by using a fuel too low in octane. The difference is that preignition is not as easily controlled, since the air-fuel mixture is being ignited by the red-hot plug *before* the spark actually fires. With the pistons still on their compression stroke, the burning mass is squeezed rather than being allowed to expand.

At this point, temperatures really begin to climb, and on successive compression strokes, the heat may become sufficient to start the air-fuel charge burning everywhere at once, rather than normally proceeding in a smooth flame front from the spark-plug electrodes.

When this happens, the piston is once again rising in the cylinder, making its compression stroke. The burning mass is compressed, and an explosion called detonation results, forcing the piston and rod down in the cylinder while it is still traveling upward. Plugs are often destroyed by overheating. If detonation is severe enough, pistons and rods can be broken and blown apart. Detonation is a highly destructive force that can be avoided by installing the spark plugs designed for use with your engine and type of driving.

Spark plugs must be used which will operate in the heat range between these two limits—fouling and preignition—regardless of engine speed or load. The type of driving or engine condition may require a change in spark-plug heat range from that specified for your particular engine. Slow city driving is hard on spark plugs, as long periods of idle in traffic create an overly rich gas mixture. At idle, combustion chamber temperature isn't high enough, and the engine isn't running fast enough to burn the gas completely. As a result, the plugs become fouled with unburned gas, and idle becomes rough. If the majority of driving is done in slow city traffic rather than at freeway speeds, or the engine uses oil, plug deposits can be burned off by changing to only slightly hotter plugs.

The hotter plug would be ideal for just city driving, but occasional freeway driving can produce dangerous preignition. A solution to this problem is to change to a projected-nose plug design having the same heat range as the standard plug specified for your engine. The projected-nose plug has a longer nose, which extends farther into the combustion chamber. This type of plug runs hotter in slow traffic and cooler at highway speeds, reducing the chances of plug fouling in the city and preignition at higher speeds. The projected-nose plug is discussed at length later in the chapter, and should be read about before making a change.

If the car is used almost exclusively for high-speed freeway driving, or if the engine has been modified, the specified plugs might be too hot, resulting in rapid electrode wear and dangerous preignition. In this case, it is always safer to

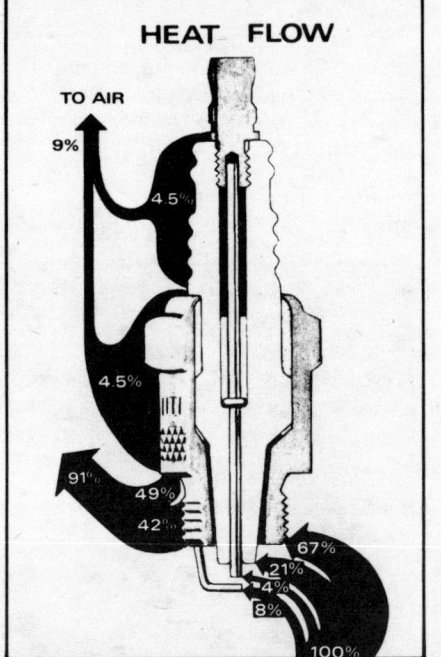

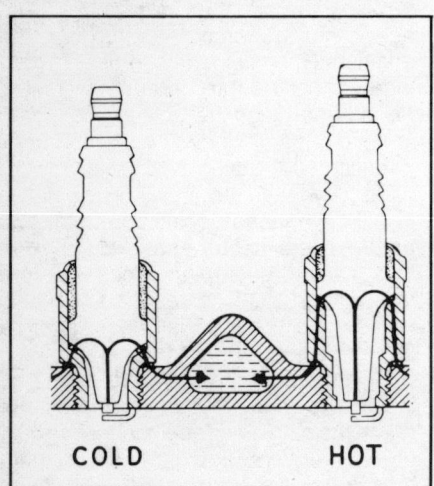

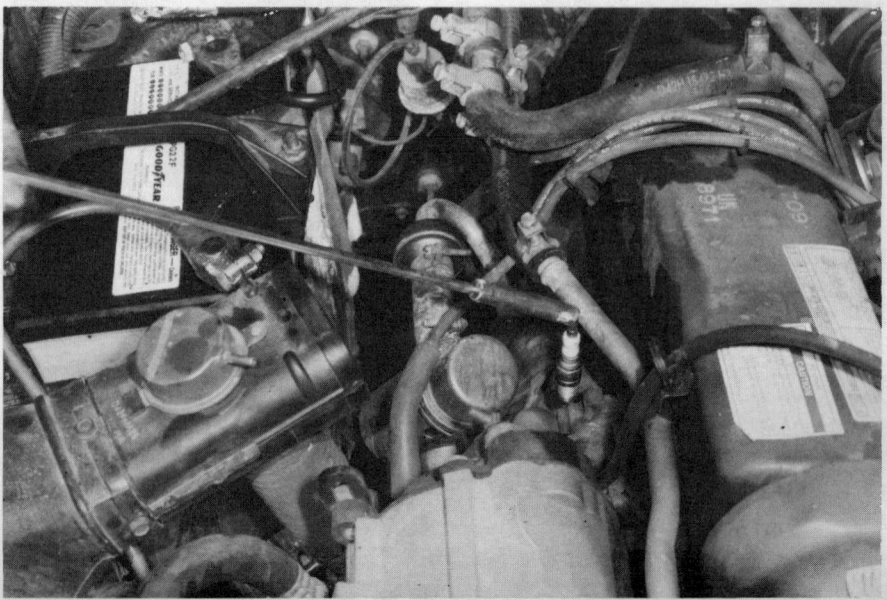

7. *The longer the insulator, the hotter the plug, since the heat has a longer path to travel.*

8. *Heat generally reaches the plug through its shell nose and insulator tip, then dissipates through the plug shell threads and seat. Smaller amounts of heat enter through the electrodes and exit into the surrounding air.*

9. *This AC resistor plug does away with the spring by using seals that will conduct electricity. The ACniter plug has been standard equipment on GM cars and trucks since 1969.*

change to a slightly colder plug or the projected-nose type.

The speed at which a spark plug can transfer combustion chamber heat to the cylinder head determines its *heat range*. Heat range is controlled by the length of the porcelain insulator nose and/or by the size and shape of the area between the nose and the outer metal shell—the threaded portion. The ceramic insulator nose of the plug extends into the combustion chamber and absorbs its heat, passing it on to the plug's outer metal shell. The heat then moves along the shell to the cylinder head, where it escapes into the air.

A *hot* plug is made with a longer insulator nose (and/or more space between the nose and the outer metal shell) than is a cold plug. For this reason, the hot plug has more area to hold heat and is slower to dissipate it. The plug thus remains hot enough even at low speeds to burn off fouling deposits.

Cold plugs have a short insulator nose and more contact between the insulator nose and the outer shell, and that enables it to transfer combustion chamber heat faster. At high speeds and under heavy loads, the cold plug will transfer heat well enough to avoid preignition.

VOLTAGE REQUIREMENT

Spark plugs do not make the spark; they merely provide a gap for the voltage from the coil to arc across. The shape and material of the electrodes, the gap width, and the existing pressures and temperatures determine the amount of voltage necessary to produce a spark. This is called the spark plug's voltage requirement.

An ignition coil produces only enough voltage to jump any gaps in the secondary circuit. As an example, suppose a coil is capable of producing 25,000 volts, but only 10,000 volts are required to jump the plug gap. In this case, the coil will only produce 10,000 volts. Now suppose the plug requires 30,000 volts to produce a spark. The coil will not be able to produce enough voltage to jump the gap. The result is no spark at the plug and an engine that either misses or won't run at all.

The space between the plug electrodes is filled with millions of air molecules, and air is a good electrical insulator. When a sufficient voltage is delivered to the electrodes, the air molecules become ions—molecules with an electrical charge. Placed in an electrical field—as between the electrodes of a spark plug—ions are capable of movement, allowing a spark to jump the plug gap. In short, a spark plug's voltage requirement is simply the electrical pressure necessary to produce ionization of the air-fuel mixture within the spark plug's gap.

Sharp edges on the electrodes tend to concentrate ionization and lower the voltage requirement, but spark-plug electrodes begin to erode away with use, rounding the electrodes and widening the gap at an average rate of .001-inch every 1000-2000 miles. Both of these changes increase the plug's voltage requirement, and when the voltage required to produce a spark finally exceeds the output of the ignition system, the plug will no longer fire.

Worn plugs are most noticeable while accelerating. A plug requires three times as much voltage to be fired during acceleration as that during idle speeds. As engine rpm increases, however, the coil has less time to produce voltage. This means that its output drops as engine speed rises. For this reason, a plug with an enlarged or wider than specified gap may require more voltage to fire during acceleration than the coil is able to provide. As a result, the engine will misfire and sputter until you let up on the accelerator pedal. Reducing acceleration has the effect of reducing the plug's voltage requirement, causing the engine to run smoother.

Spark-plug voltage requirements are also raised by deposits on the plug, high cylinder pressures, low temperatures (which separate the air molecules), lean mixtures, and overheated electrodes.

PLUG SPECIFICATIONS

The numbers and letters used to designate a particular spark plug indicate the heat range, thread size, reach, and gap configuration of the plug. All plug makers use numbers to indicate the relative heat range of their spark plugs. American companies such as Champion, Autolite, and AC use lower numbers to indicate colder plugs and higher numbers to indicate hotter plugs. Foreign manufacturers like Bosch, Lodge, NGK, and KLG use higher numbers to designate colder plugs, and lower numbers for hotter heat ranges.

An Autolite AG 2, for example, is a step colder than an Autolite AG 3, but an NGK B-6E is a step hotter than an NGK B-7E. Letters are used to indicate the thread reach and size, with the exception of Bosch plugs, which use numbers instead. Additional letters and/or numbers found in spark-plug designations indicate such special features as internal resistors and series gaps.

When a car maker brings out a new engine or makes important modifications in an older one, the design is referred to the engineering department of the auto manufacturer's spark-plug supplier for proper "plugging." Champion handles this for Chrysler, American Motors, and a large number of overseas manufacturers. Ford has its own company, Motorcraft, and GM has its AC division.

In addition, all plug makers list replacement sizes for cars that do not carry their brand as original equipment. The spark-plug companies go to great lengths to compete in the replacement market, and do a great deal of research to ensure that the plugs listed in their charts are the best possible choice for

SPARK PLUGS

the cars for which they are recommended.

SPARK-PLUG APPLICATIONS

There are many different spark-plug and electrode designs, including special racing types. Most motorists simply replace the plugs in their engine with the same type installed at the factory. If their driving is average, with no excessive high-speed travel or prolonged idling, this is a satisfactory procedure. But special conditions in the engine, such as excessive oil in the combustion chamber, require the use of a special plug.

J-Gap Plugs

These are sometimes called cutback-gap plugs. Autolite uses the letter "X" after the plug number to indicate this modification, Champion uses the letter "J" and AC uses the prefix "M." For example, a Champion J-6 plug is a regular-gap ⅜-inch-reach plug, whereas a J-6J indicates the same plug with a side electrode that extends only midway out over the center electrode.

The big advantage of the J-gap design is that the sharp edge of the cutback side electrode aids ionization of the air gap and thus requires less voltage to fire. J-gap plugs are therefore more suitable to high rpm and less likely to be shorted out by carbon particles in the combustion chamber. This makes them ideal for a street/strip car, competition sports car, or any racing engine short of an all-out fuel-burning blown dragster or Indy car.

Projected-Nose Plugs

Sometimes called self-cleaning plugs, these were developed in the late 1950s for the high-compression V-8 and six-cylinder overhead-valve engines of that era. The firing tip of the projected-nose plug protrudes beyond the end of the plug shell, extending down into the combustion chamber. The longer insulator tip on the plug provides a longer fouling path for cleaning by combustion chamber gases.

During light-load, low-speed operation, the extreme tip temperature of the projected-nose plug allows it to burn off fouling combustion deposits. At high speeds, the insulator is cooled by the incoming air-fuel mixture, which helps prevent preignition. In fact, a projected-nose plug actually runs cooler than a regular-gap plug at engine speeds above 2000 rpm.

You should not install projected-nose plugs in an engine unless the engine or plug manufacturer specifically recommends their use. To do so may result in both plug and engine damage if the nose projects into the combustion chamber enough to tough the piston head on its

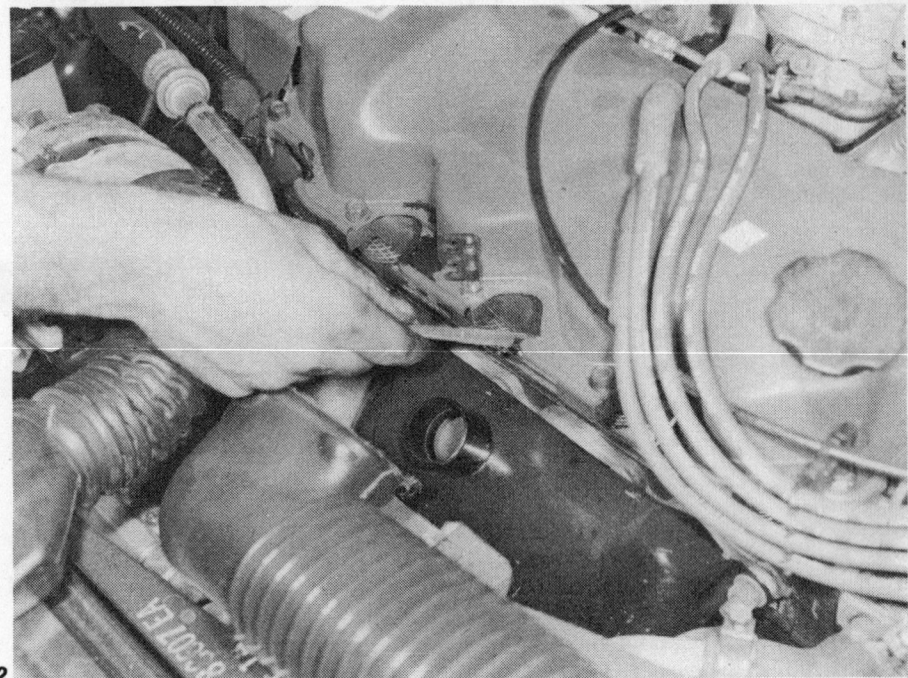

11. Never pull plug wires off—always twist them off. If possible, use a plug wire remover. It's almost a necessity on some engines like the Ford 1.6L Escort/Lynx powerplant.

12. Deeply recessed plugs on the Ford 1.6L engine require the use of a pencil magnet to get them out.

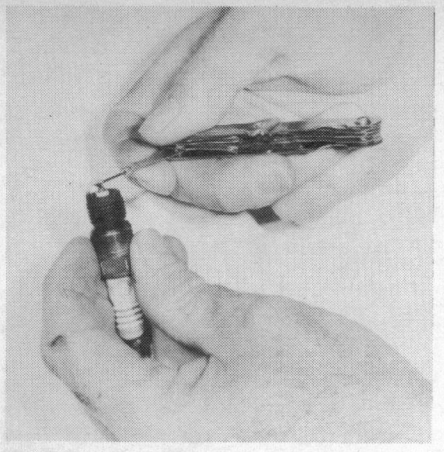
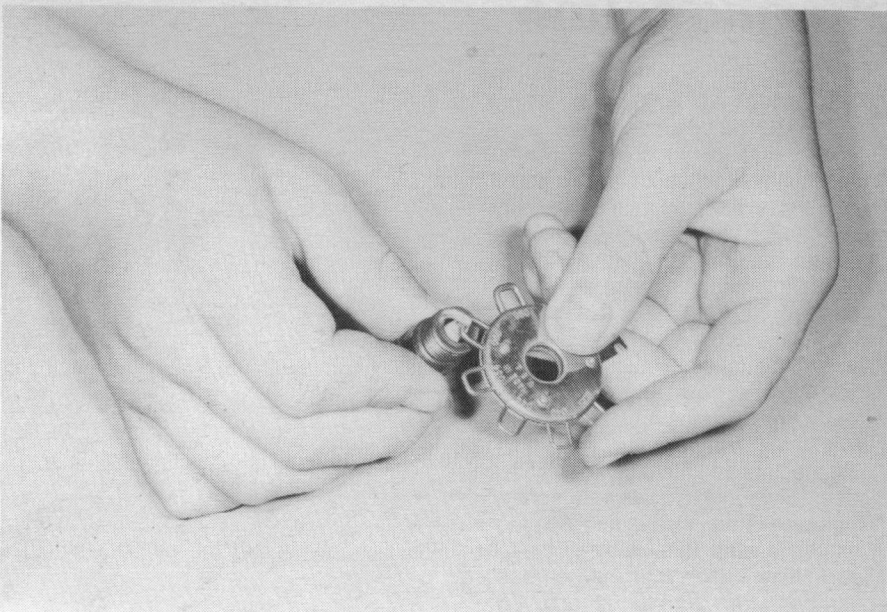

13A and 13B. Always check the plug gap with a round wire feeler gauge. A shows one popular type; B shows the use of another type.

upward stroke. Champion identifies its projected-nose plugs by adding the letter "Y" to their number, and Autolite uses the number "2" and calls its plug a "Power Tip." AC adds the suffix "S," and NGK inserts the letter "P" in its designation.

Series-Gap Plugs

Discussed in detail earlier, this plug design increases the frequency of the spark discharge and isolates the coil buildup from the conductive firing and deposits. This results in protection from misfiring caused by plug fouling. Many series-gap plugs also have a vented terminal to release ozone produced when the spark jumps the series gap.

Platinum-Gap Plugs

Before ceramic engineers found a way to make projected-nose plugs, platinum electrodes were the only means of extending spark-plug heat ranges. The fine-wire platinum electrodes retain their shape even when heated to incandescence, and they burn away fouling deposits. On the intake stroke, they're cooled by the incoming air-fuel mixture.

If clearance problems will not permit the use of a projected-nose plug in your engine, and you need an extended heat-range plug to prevent low-speed fouling, platinum-gap plugs are worth a try. Champion HO-3, UJ-64P and UL-60P platinum plugs have been widely used in racing 327 Corvettes for this reason.

Retracted-Gap Plugs

These have been designed for high-horsepower engines that have been converted for racing. Since the side electrode is located in a hole bored into the plug shell, these spark plugs are sometimes known as push-wire type. A special tool is required to move the side electrode back and forth in its hole for gap adjustments. Some designs, however, permit no adjustment.

Retracted-gap plugs have the least resistance to fouling of any plug type and are not really suitable for street use. They are intended for all-out racing engines or highly modified, supercharged fuel burners which are never operated at low rpm and which demand very cold plugs.

In general, any electrode design that features sharp edges has a lower voltage requirement than one with flat or rounded surfaces. The sharper the edge, however, the sooner it erodes away. If inspected under a magnifying glass, a new spark-plug electrode appears to have many sharp little irregularities. Each time a spark jumps from one of these, it is burned smooth until the electrodes of an old, worn plug merely have a smoothly pitted appearance.

Since projected-nose plugs place the spark gap deeper in the combustion chamber, a change to these from standard-gap plugs can have two immediate effects on engine operation. The first is more efficient burning of the air-fuel mixture; the other is that the spark-plug timing is effectively advanced. The spark does not fire sooner, but changing its location in the combustion chamber causes the mixture to ignite earlier. For this reason, it may be necessary to retard the ignition from one to four degrees when projected-nose plugs are installed in place of standard-gap plugs.

Spark plugs that may normally be of the same heat range may have different preignition levels because of electrode design. A thin, overheated electrode is much more likely to go into preignition than a heavier, cooler one—unless, of course, it is made from some metal like platinum. Keep this in mind the next time you see bargain plugs that claim to be an exact replacement for a name-brand/heat-range plug.

PLUG CARE & MAINTENANCE

Spark-plug replacement and maintenance are one job that even the most unskilled driver can do. Most engines need new plugs every 10,000 to 12,000 miles, despite claims by automakers that new plugs will last for 30,000 or more miles because of leaner mixtures and the use of high-voltage electronic ignition systems.

A properly gapped spark plug requires between 5000 and 8000 volts to fire when new. After 10,000 miles of average driving, the electrode has worn sufficiently to increase the gap by about .008-inch, effectively doubling the voltage necessary to fire the plug. In addition, it takes about twice as much voltage to fire a plug at cruising speed as it does at idle, and three times the voltage under hard acceleration. If the engine cuts out when you floor the accelerator, it's a sign that the plug gaps have probably eroded.

When spark plugs misfire noticeably under such heavy loads, they are probably misfiring or tracking unnoticeably during the rest of the speed range. This means that they are wasting fuel and power—the most important reason for replacing plugs every 10,000 miles, even though the old ones "look" all right.

When it's time to replace the plugs, remove and install only one plug wire and plug at a time before moving on to the next. This prevents mixing plug wires and gives you an opportunity to read each plug. Compare them to a plug chart such as the one provided at the end of this chapter. This will tell you a good deal about what's going on inside your engine.

Allow the engine sufficient time to cool down before pulling the plugs—it will make the job easier. If you attempt to replace plugs in some of the new four-cylinder engines (such as Ford's 1.6 L)

SPARK PLUGS

when they are hot, you'll run a high risk of stripping the plug aluminum hole threads or cross-threading the plugs. When this happens special tools are required to restore the plug hole. If it happens a second time to the same plug hole, the cylinder head must be replaced.

A stuck plug can sometimes be loosened by tightening it a bit before trying to unscrew it, or by applying penetrating oil or Liquid Wrench. Fit a socket wrench over the plug and apply steady pressure to break the plug loose. When this happens, dirt which has collected around the plug will also break loose. Blow or brush this debris from the plug port before unscrewing the plug the rest of the way. This will keep the loose debris from falling into the combustion chamber when the plug is removed.

Once seized plugs are out, check the threads in the cylinder heads for dirt and damage. Clean them with a spark-plug thread chaser, a tool available at most auto-supply stores. This will remove any carbon that has accumulated in the threaded area of the cylinder head and make plug installation easier. It will also ensure better contact between the head and plug shell for heat transfer.

Check new plugs with a gapping tool to make sure that the electrode gap is the same as factory specs. Use the bending bar on the gap gauge to bend the side electrode. Never close the gap by banging the plug against a hard surface—this can crack the ceramic insulator. For complete accuracy, gap spark plugs with a round wire gauge—not a flat feeler gauge. The wire gauge should pass through the gap with a solid snap, but don't force it.

Keeping your plugs clean is important, since a heavy accumulation of deposits can eventually ruin a plug. Your engine makes a pretty good plug cleaner but you've got to be careful. If the plugs are loaded with deposits from lots of slow driving, you can ruin them by simply flooring the accelerator. Such an approach can fuse soft deposits into a permanent conductive glaze.

The right way to remove deposits by using the engine is to accelerate to the speed where the engine begins to miss, then back off the gas until the engine smooths out. You've got to keep the cylinders firing if you're going to do any good. Hold this speed for a few miles, then repeat the process several times. If the miss occurs at a higher speed each time, you're getting the cleaning job done.

Sandblast cleaning increases a plug's voltage requirement rather than lowers it. Why? Because sandblasting not only removes the conductive deposits from the electrodes, but also rounds off the electrodes by its abrasive action. Spark plugs should always have their electrodes filed to a sharp, square shape

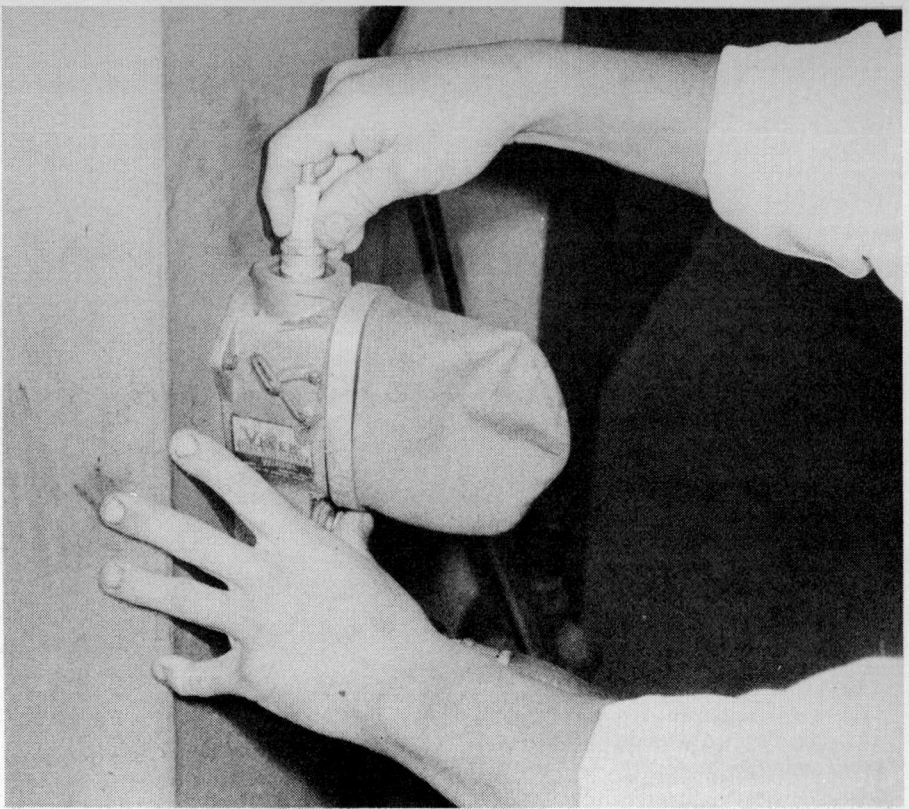

14. Sandblast cleaning is popular but it increases the plug's voltage requirement.

15. Once the plugs are cleaned and the electrodes filed, open the gap by moving the side electrode away from the center one. Use a special bending tool like that shown to prevent damage.

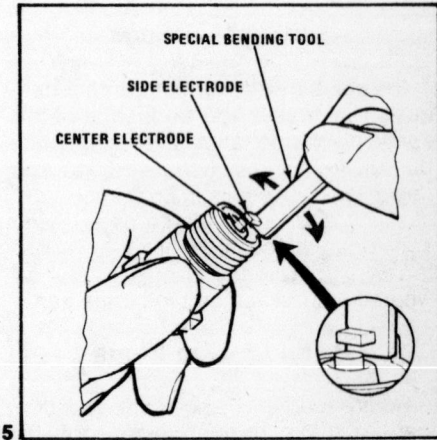

after sandblasting. First sandblast, then file. You'll return the plug almost to its original voltage requirement.

Sandblast cleaning is no substitute for new plugs. If you have a fast buildup of fouling deposits, it's worth cleaning the plugs at 5000-mile intervals between changes. Sandblasting will not completely remove heavy deposits, nor will filing the electrodes by hand restore their condition to that of a new plug. Cleaning spark plugs just isn't economical after 10,000 miles—it's cheaper, easier, and better for your engine if you replace plugs with this mileage with new ones.

When replacing plugs, replace them as a set. Installing only one or two at a time to replace fouled plugs, for example, means that the remaining ones will probably have to be replaced within a few thousand miles. One-by-one plug replacement will never give you the benefits and economy of new-plug performance. Remember, a chain is only as strong as its weakest link, and an engine is no more efficient than its oldest plug.

Installing spark plugs carelessly can wreck a cylinder head—especially an aluminum one. Lubricate the plug threads with a thin film of oil from the dipstick before screwing it in the plug hole. If the engine has an aluminum head, it's a good idea to coat the threads with an antiseize compound. Cadmium-plated plugs, such as Champions, help prevent plug-seizing problems.

When tightening the spark plugs, be careful not to overtighten them. Tapered-seat plugs must be installed according to torque specs—about 15 ft.-lb. for 14-mm plugs and 20 ft.-lb. for 18-mm plugs. If a torque wrench is not available, tighten the plugs finger-tight and then an additional one-sixth turn. If you go any tighter, you'll have real problems when removal time comes around again.

Overtightening gasket-type plugs can crush the gasket and make it useless. Crimped-on gaskets such as those used by Champion need be tightened only about a one-half turn with the wrench after the plug has been seated by hand. Most car makers, however, specify a torque-wrench reading for spark-plug installation. Gaskets also work best

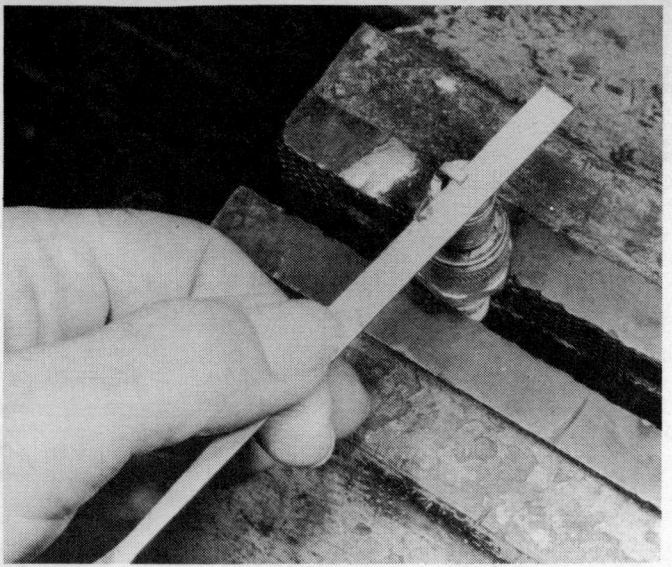
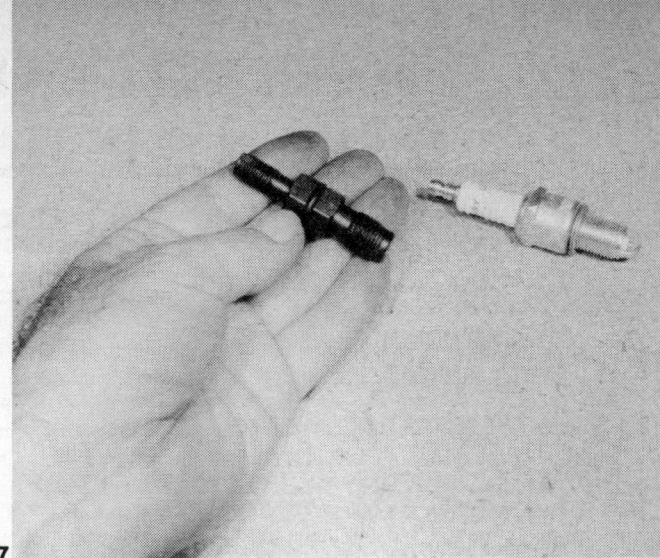

16. If you do clean a spark plug, resurface the electrodes with a flat file to restore their sharp edges.

17. A plug chaser is a handy way to clean up plug hole threads. It removes contamination and makes plug installation easier and surer.

18. This shows three areas of concern—the insulator, electrode flatness and gap. Make sure all are in good shape when reusing plugs.

when a torque wrench is used. Check your car's specs and if a certain plug torque is listed, use it.

PLUGS TELL A STORY

A close reading of your plugs will tell you much about the internal condition of an engine. When two consecutive plugs in an inline engine are fouled, look for a blown head gasket between the two cylinders. If the two center plugs in an inline engine are fouled, there's a good chance that gas is boiling out of the carburetor into the intake manifold when the engine is shut off. This condition will foul plugs quickly when the car is subjected to heavy stop-and-start usage or short trips. Check the float level and look for a good seal at the needle valve seat. If these check out satisfactorily, the use of an insulating gasket between the carburetor and manifold may be necessary.

When the rear four plugs in a V-8 or rear two plugs in a V-6 show signs of overheating, engine coolant isn't reaching the back of the engine. Check and clean the cooling system to restore circulation throughout the engine. A single overheated plug may result from an intake manifold leak near that cylinder. If this is not the case, check the firing order of the plugs. When the bad plug is located next to a plug that fires just before or after it, the overheated condition may be the result of a crossfire. Separate the plug leads to prevent any potential crossfire from induced voltage.

When large V-8 engines are mainly used for stop-and-go driving, the two rear plugs may become oil-fouled. This happens when the oil drain holes at the back of the head plug up with excessive sludge, and oil is drawn up around the intake-valve stems.

PLUG MYTHS

Many myths and misconceptions have grown up about spark plugs. The "spark-plug intensifiers" are a good example. These devices prey on the popular assumption that a hotter spark will improve a car's fuel economy and power. Actually, it doesn't matter if the spark is hot, cold, or lukewarm, as long as it manages to ignite the air-fuel mixture in the combustion chamber. Such devices can be helpful when used with some older engines in poor condition, but only because they are nothing more than electrical resistances or auxiliary gaps. Their effect is identical to that of ordinary series-gap plugs. Unfortunately, the intensifier is sold at a price far greater than the cost of a set of resistor or series-gap plugs.

Another misconception is that hot plugs produce a hotter spark than do cold plugs. As we have seen, hot and cold plugs have nothing to do with the power of the spark itself, but only refer to the relative ability of the plug to conduct heat away from the firing tip. When you remember that racing engines require colder, not hotter, plugs, this idea seems even more ludicrous.

"Gimmick" plugs can be spotted by their advertisements, which are elaborate and exaggerated. The gimmick plug makers will often offer "scientific proof" of benefits offered by their product, such as increased rpm with a closed throttle. Of course, they neglect to point out that the design of their plugs changes the effective spark advance at low engine

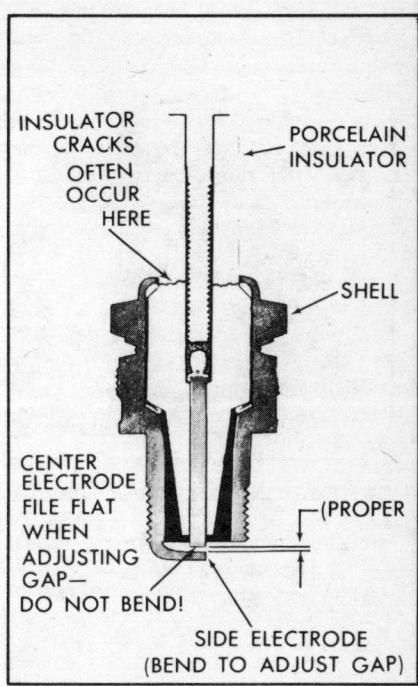

speeds. This may very well speed up the idle, but it will generally result in a power loss at higher speeds!

You should also avoid those engine-operated abrasive spark-plug cleaning devices sold in department stores. These claim to offer your plugs the same benefits as sandblasting them in a regular shop cleaner, but about all they really do is dust the firing end with a fine abrasive that does little to remove deposits.

For most drivers, the spark plugs recommended by the automaker, or their equivalent, are the best choice when it comes to replacing the plugs in your engine. For special engines or special driving situations, however, one of the specialized kinds of plugs can be a real boon to driveability and performance.

Plug size and type don't tell the whole story. You must "read" the plug.

One of the most valuable skills which you can acquire is the ability to determine engine operating conditions from the appearance of its spark plugs. An inspection of the firing tips of the old plugs at each spark plug change can often be a tip-off that there is something in need of attention that has not yet become a serious problem. Also, when a serious problem does suddenly turn up, a look at the spark plugs will often pinpoint the trouble. By carefully studying the following photos you can familiarize yourself with the most common abnormal plug conditions and their causes. Remember that most of these conditions are caused by engine trouble, not plug trouble. The idea is not to change — for example — to a hotter plug when the type that has served the engine previously begins to oil foul, but to replace the piston rings, valve guides, or whatever, to correct the trouble that's making your plugs look like a petroleum-based fudgesicle.

NORMAL PLUG / Description: Insulator light tan or gray. Few deposits. Indicates proper type and heat range for engine and use. Recommendation: Replace plug at regular intervals with same type and heat range. Plugs showing this reading indicate good longevity and will give acceptable performance.

DETONATION CLUE/ Description: Side electrode snapped off. Plug appears more carbon coated than overheated. Cause: Overheated carbon deposits have begun to cause detonation. Treatment: Remove cylinder head, clean away carbon deposits and check closely for hot spots in the combustion chamber.

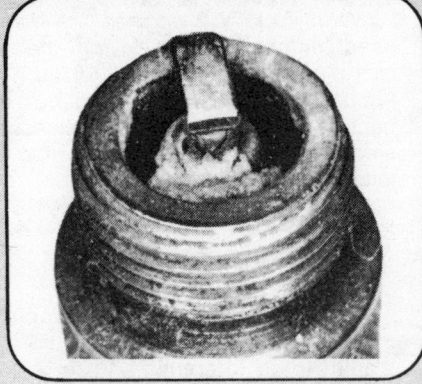

CORE BRIDGING/ Description: Combustion chamber deposits build up between the insulator and plug shell. Cause: Excessive carbon build-up, poor oil, bad oil control, long idling — then rapid acceleration. Treatment: Use good oil, check rings, valve guides, avoid extended idling in traffic if possible.

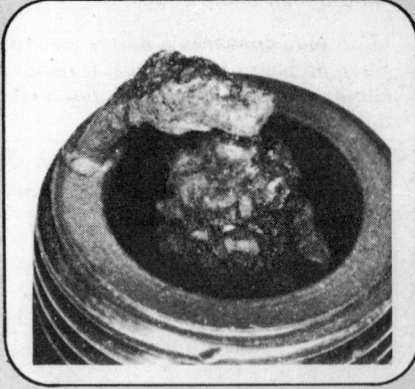

SILICA DEPOSITS/ Description: Hard conductive deposits of fused sand, lead and fuel additives. Cause: Dirt, dust and sand entering with the air/fuel mixture. Treatment: Repair or replace air cleaner on carburetor. Check for any loose bolts, leaks and bad intake gaskets or poorly fitting air cleaners.

SPLASHED DEPOSITS/ Description: Dark spots flecking insulator nose. Cause: Recent tune-up is clearing up old combustion chamber deposits which are splashing onto insulator. Treatment: Condition will soon disappear; however, rapid acceleration could prove harmful by loosening up deposits in the chamber.

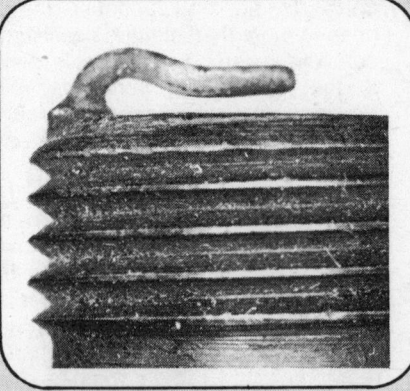

BENT ELECTRODE/ Description: Side electrode has peculiar "question mark" shape. Cause: Using pliers-type gapping tool — especially on filed plugs or worn center electrode. Treatment: Regap plugs or replace those that can't be brought up to specs without deforming the electrode or bending it excessively.

GAP BRIDGING/ Description: Combustion chamber deposits lodged between electrode. Cause: Too much carbon build-up in cylinders, poor oil control or long idling — then all-out acceleration. Treatment: Check your engine for the above trouble then clean and reinstall your plugs with proper gapping.

TOO WIDE GAP/ Description: Excessive gap width between insulator nose and electrode. Cause: The action of intense heat, combustion chamber pressures, corrosive gases and spark discharge cause gap to widen. Treatment: Regap plug and then check for adequate secondary resistance in circuit.

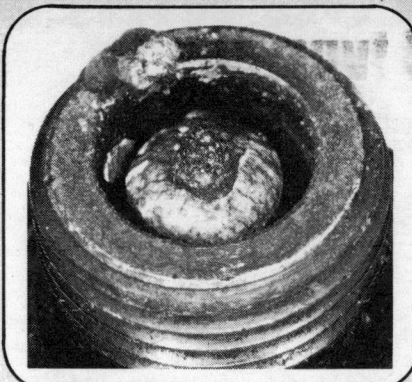

INITIAL PRE-IGNITION/ Description: Electrodes burned away, insulator tip blistered or deformed. Cause: Excessive spark advance, plug too hot, inferior fuel being used. Treatment: Bring timing up to specs, check advance, switch to better gas and try using a colder plug, with a booster gap if available.

SCAVENGE DEPOSITS/ Description: Yellow, white or brownish crust-like deposits over electrodes and insulator. Cause: Typical of chemical make-up of some gasolines, but usually a result of "old fogey" driving. Treatment: Clean and file electrodes, go out and "stand-on-it" to clean out combustion chamber.

ALUMINUM THROW-OFF/ Description: Molten chunks of aluminum imbedded between electrode and insulator. Cause: Pre-ignition causes hot spots on aluminum piston heads. Treatment: Check timing, ignition advance, change to a top grade of gasoline and install colder plugs. Be sure plug is right reach.

OIL FOULED PLUG/ Description: Soft, wet, oily deposits covering insulator and nose of plug. Cause: Excess oil reaching combustion chamber. Treatment: Check or repair worn oil control rings, valve guides, crankcase vent, oil level, oil bath air cleaners. Use hotter plugs. Booster gap plugs will fire longer.

GLAZING/ Description: Hard, glassy, brown coating on insulator tip and electrode. Cause: Fast acceleration after low-speed driving. Treatment: Accelerate slowly after long periods of in-town driving. Glaze is conductive and can ruin plugs, so don't squirrel around the pits. Don't idle engine for long periods.

CARBON FOULED PLUG/ Description: Dry, fluffy black carbon deposits over the entire firing end. Cause: Plug too cold, choke not open, over-rich mixture, low voltage, weak condenser, sticking valves. Treatment: End richness, free the valves, raise voltage, use hotter plug. Check carb float level.

WORN PLUG/ Description: Electrodes are obviously rounded and thinned, insulator pitted and encrusted with old deposits. Cause: Plug has been in service for an extremely long time. Treatment: Be sure to replace your old plugs with a set of new ones after driving approximately 8000 to 12,000 miles.

MECHANICAL DAMAGE/ Description: Insulator nose broken, electrode bent. Cause: Loose object or inadequate piston/valve-to-plug clearance. Treatment: Look for loose parts, check for engine damage, see proper clearance between plugs and engine's moving parts is maintained. Use correct reach plug.

PLUG WIRES

Secondary ignition cables are probably the most overlooked part of the entire ignition system. The best spark plugs money can buy are worthless if the secondary or plug cables can't deliver voltage to them. Yet even the most reliable system can often be improved by incorporating better components, or by devoting more care to it.

RESISTANCE CABLES

Spark-plug wires aren't wires at all. If you cut through the insulation of most cables used on production cars, you'll find that there is actually no metallic wire inside them. Instead, there is some form of semiconductive synthetic core that transmits the spark from the distributor to the plugs. Automakers use a high-carbon-impregnated string or braided linen-nylon core instead of metallic wire. This is usually identified by the words "Radio Resistance" or "Radio-GM TVRS" printed at intervals on the insulation.

If you connect one of these cables to a battery, it won't carry the current needed to light a flashlight bulb, but it is conductive enough to provide a path for the high-voltage spark impulse to race along. The idea behind resistance cables is to eliminate radio and TV interference. Without them, your car radio as well as the television sets in residences you drive past will be affected by ignition noise.

Resistance-type wires have been condemned as sources of ignition trouble and poor gas mileage. If your car is regularly driven on the street, you should be using them to comply with federal communications laws, but that's not the only reason. Resistor wires were not tossed into the picture at the last minute; there's a good reason for their use.

Resistance wires were designed into the car's system, and the resistance they provide is there because the coil, condenser, and plugs all work best with that amount of secondary resistance in the system. An engineer could design an ignition system that would put out a more reliable spark if he didn't have to use resistor wires, but he would probably change other parts so the system would work well without the secondary resistance provided by the wires.

Some kinds of resistance wire certainly are troublesome, but there are also types available that not only are as efficient as metallic-core cables, but can also take rough use. Resistance cables that cause trouble are those that have broken or burned-out conductors. This is nearly always the result of the cable having been bent sharply, stretched, or poorly connected to its terminal.

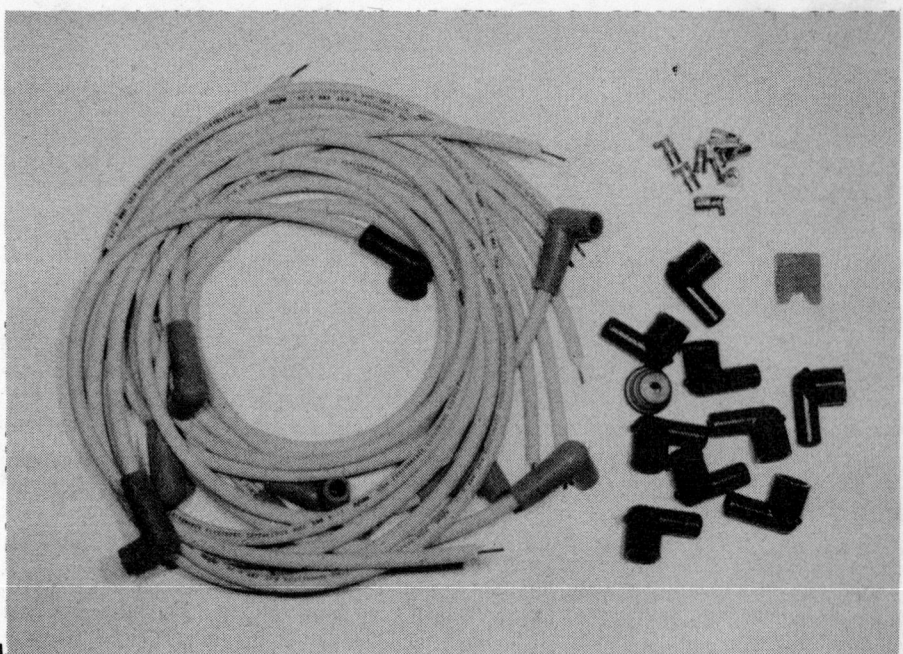

One way to locate faulty wiring, a cracked distributor cap, and any bad connections is to observe engine operation at night. The absence of any light makes it easy to see stray sparks. If everything is tight and in proper condition, no sparks should be visible.

Some aftermarket resistance cables use a solid piece of graphite-impreg-

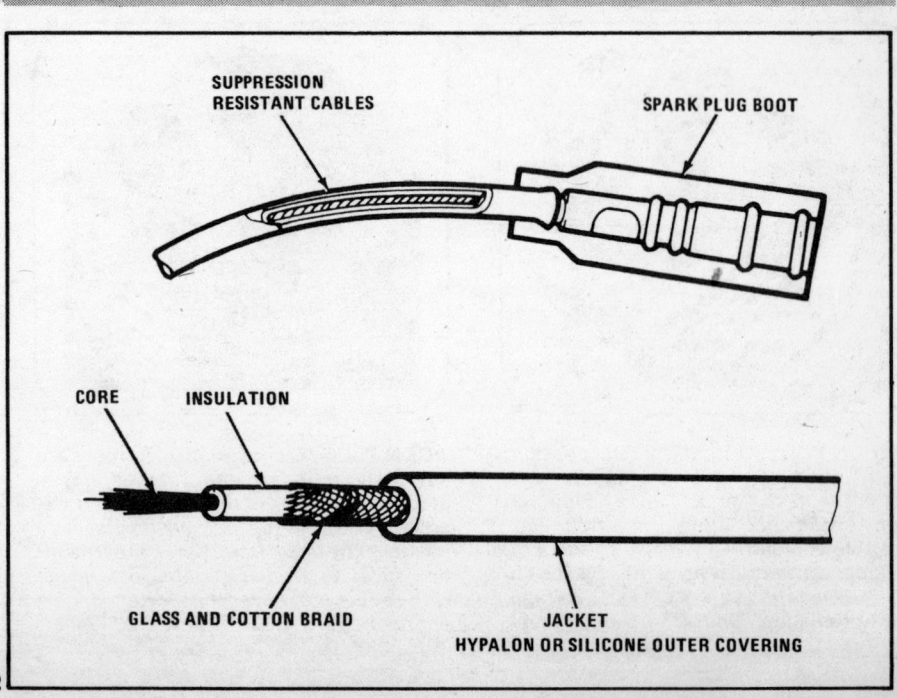

nated nylon. These work fine until the first time they are bent or pulled, particularly in cold weather. Like nylon-cord tires that tend to get a flat spot after being parked overnight, the core of these cables takes a rigid set. When bent, as in removing the leads for a plug change, the nylon core cracks. Every time the plug fires after this happens, the spark has to jump this crack. The burning-out process has started. After only a few hundred miles, the interior of the cable is so eaten away that a chronic engine miss develops.

Another type of resistance cable uses many very fine strands of graphite-impregnated nylon or plastic, and a second type has a core of braided textile material that is saturated with carbon. These types resist damage from rough handling, but since the core is so flimsy, it is difficult to guarantee solid contact between it and the terminal attachments. Eventually, a spark begins to arc between the cable core and its terminal, and the connection is soon burned away. The heat of the spark usually destroys the cable's insulation as well, and in some cases it goes so far as to ruin the distributor cap.

The best type of resistance cable has a tube-shaped core that is both flexible and elastic. This type of conductor not only resists breakage even when stretched moderately or tied in a knot, but also provides the best possible

1. Spark plug wires are expensive these days. You can save money with a kit such as this one by Mallory. It lets you tailor each wire length correctly for proper wire installation.

2. Since yesterday's spark plug wires cause RFI interference, today's wires no longer contain wire. A typical design contains a glass filament carbon-impregnated core inside a specially formulated insulation. Stretch control is provided by a basket weave of glass and cotton. Everything is housed in a hypalon or silicone outer jacket to ward off heat.

3. Plug cables must be routed away from hot engine parts or they'll be damaged. The headers did a number (arrow) on these wires.

4. To prevent cross-firing, plug wires are usually routed in a sequence different from plug installation. In this example with a firing order of 1-5-4-2-6-3-7-8, the No. 7 and No. 8 cables are located in opposite sides of the bracket.

5. You have fewer routing options on 4-cylinder engines. Cross-firing is caused by high voltage induced from one cable to another. If the engine runs rough for no apparent reason, check the firing order (usually 1-3-4-2) to see if the cables for consecutive firing cylinders are properly separated in the wire brackets (arrows).

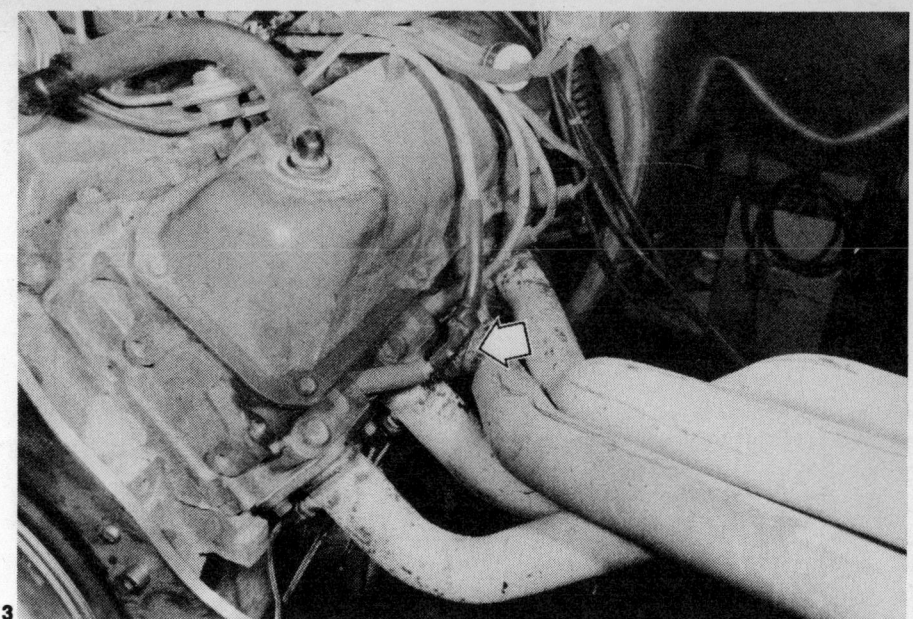
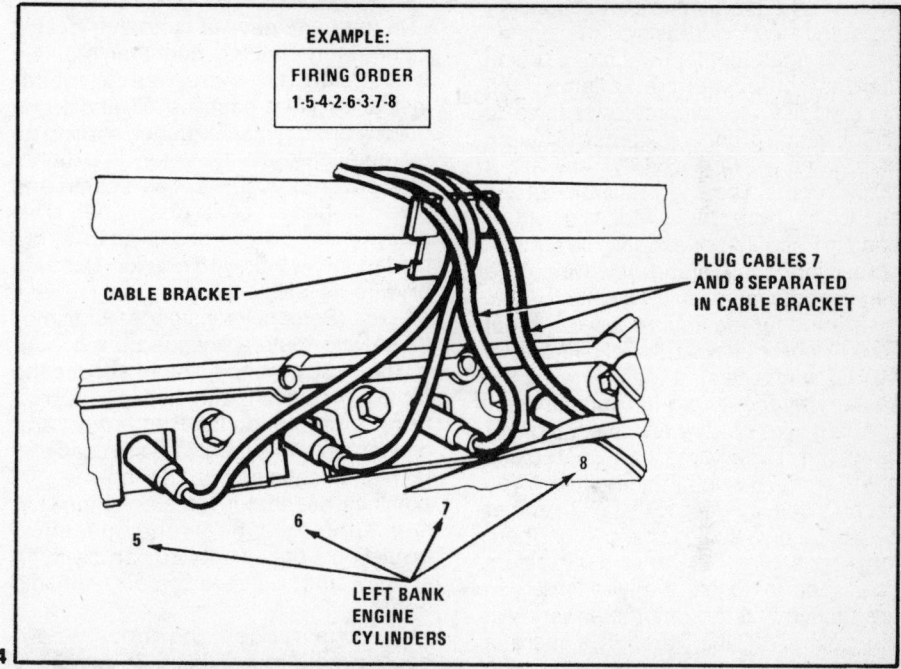
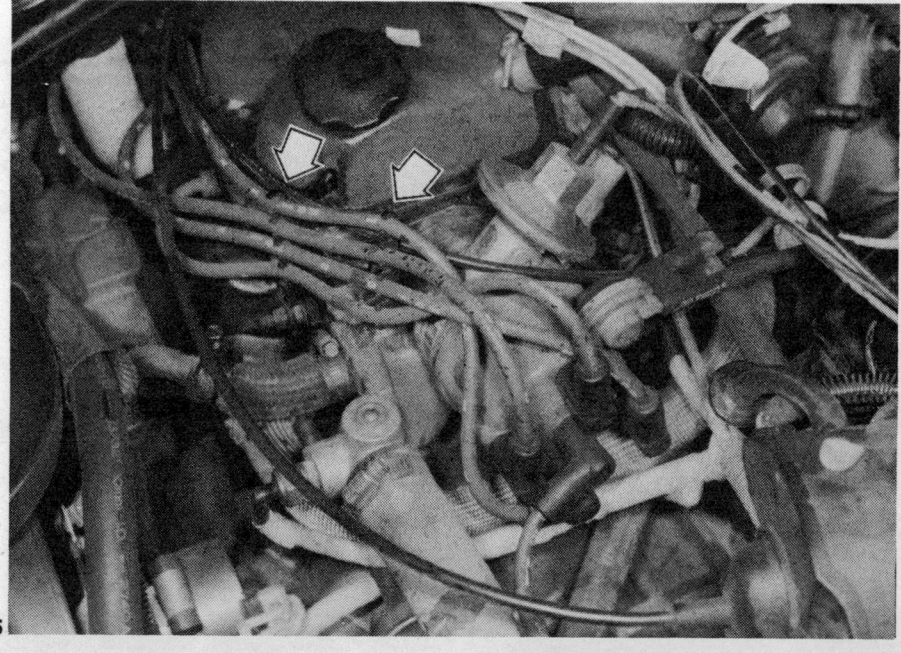

PLUG WIRES

contact between the semiconductor and its terminal attachments. If the terminals are carefully and properly installed on this type of cable, it is just as reliable as the metallic conductor types.

WIRE-RESISTANCE VALUES

Resistance in the spark-plug wires, or in any part of the ignition system that conducts the spark, is called secondary resistance. It is there primarily to reduce the current flow as an aid to prolonging plug life. Without the resistance, the spark creates radio and TV interference. It can even give an airplane problems in getting through to the local airport tower.

Secondary resistance is a good thing—when designed into the ignition system. The problem is that secondary resistance can increase as the ignition system ages until one cold morning there is not enough fire to light up the car's engine. An ohmmeter is used to check for the proper resistance values in plug wires. A wire usually runs about 20,000 ohms. The total resistance of any spark-plug wire, no matter how old or handled, should not exceed the amount of resistance in a brand-new wire of the same length, at least not by much. Total resistance for most wires will run about 20,000 ohms. If you have one that is 40,000 ohms, test a new wire of the same type and length for comparison.

A bad wire usually tests very high for its length. Long wires can go 150,000 ohms or more when they are bad. If you get an infinity reading with the ohmmeter set on the high scale, it means that there must be a break in the wire. It's also a good idea to wiggle the wire while you are testing it. If the ohmmeter varies at all, get rid of the wire. The more a carbon-impregnated wire is handled, the greater the resistance, as flexing the wire separates the carbon particles slightly. This will eventually result in a break in the cable's continuity.

METALLIC CABLES

The number of strands of wire used in metallic-core ignition cable has little to do with its electrical efficiency. However, cables that feature many fine strands have a somewhat more limp feel than those with a few heavy ones. The "softies" are a bit easier to push through tubular wire looms, whereas the stiff ones hold their shape better when unsupported. This helps keep them from dangling against the exhaust headers and hot cylinder heads.

Three wire materials are commonly used in metallic-core ignition cables— steel (stiff and durable), copper and copper alloys (soft, low resistance), and silver-plated copper (maximum conductivity). Your best guide in buying a high-quality cable is to stick with the well-known, reliable brand names like Motorcraft, Belden, Delco, and Packard. Packard 440, which has a silver-plated copper core, has long been a favorite with hot rodders, sports car racers, and top racing engine builders. Another Packard wire, 430, is identical to it in construction but has a steel wire core.

Metallic cables have proved to be most reliable, especially when soldered to their end terminals. Soldering not only provides a better connection, but also ensures that the connection will transmit electricity better. If you use metallic-core wires on a combination street/strip vehicle, keep a piece of resistance wire for substitution between the coil and distributor when you go back on the street to prevent any possible radio or TV interference.

INSULATION

In the early days of motoring, ignition cables were nothing more than ordinary wires with an extra-heavy rubber insulation. Heat, gasoline, oil, and ozone quickly destroyed the rubber, making for extreme unreliability. Later, the rubber was covered with a cotton sheath and given a heavy coat of lacquer. This delayed the oil and ozone attacks, but the lacquer developed cracks. This kind of wire is still available from several makers (Belden, for instance) for use by those who restore antique cars.

The next advance was to encase the rubber insulation with a thick layer of neoprene, which is fuel-, oil-, and ozoneproof. This method is still used and is highly satisfactory. Its only shortcomings are that it remains somewhat susceptible to heat and the inner insulation core of rubber can become spongy and water-absorbent with old age.

Silicone rubber, the most recent development in insulation, is extremely heat-resistant and is used on all production cars with electronic ignitions. Many aftermarket cables also use this type of insulation, but it's a good idea to stay with name brands. There are many bargain specials on the market using cheap plastic insulation. Always check the outside of the cable; if it's not stamped with a recognizable and reputable brand name and type designation, pass it by.

BOOTS & NIPPLES

The rubberlike shields that cover the spark-plug terminals are commonly referred to as plug boots. Those that slip over the wires to cover the distributor cap towers are called nipples. This is another area where unbranded wire sets usually fail. Some inexpensive plug boots are nothing more than synthetic rubber, which melts and cracks after just a few hours on a sizzling plug insulator. The best plug boots are molded from silicone material, but most of those supplied by reputable ignition cable makers are satisfactory.

Distributor cap nipples face an entirely different set of conditions. Comparatively speaking, it is cooler around the distributor, but there is often a considerable amount of gasoline and oil vapors. For this reason, neoprene makes the best nipple material. Take your distributor cap along for a trial fitting so that you can be sure the nipples you buy will fit tightly and stay waterproof when installed.

TERMINAL ATTACHMENTS

Ignition cables are no better than the terminals attached to them. Wire sets used on many production cars simply have a wire clip that presses into the end and side of their resistance-type cables. Poor contact between the terminal attachments and the cable's resistance

16/IGNITION & ELECTRICAL SYSTEMS

core is one of the major causes of burnouts.

Two methods of attaching terminals to resistance cables provide relatively trouble-free service. One system employs on the terminal itself a small screw that threads directly into the core of the cable. The other is a simple U-shaped prong, one side of which inserts into the center of the cable while the other lies flat along its outside. A brass outer terminal can be inserted into the metal sockets inside the distributor cap towers. As a general rule, terminal attachments that pierce a resistance cable's insulation should be avoided. In a great many instances, these have caused resistance cables to burn off at the point where the insulation has been punctured.

The terminals used with metallic-core cables come in a much greater variety and range in quality from good to excellent. Available for metallic-core cables are many patented spark-plug connectors that provide good insulator shielding and will not vibrate off. The British Lucas plug connectors are very popular with sports car racers, and many of the hot-rod set choose the famous Rajah connectors, which are available in several different styles.

Metallic cable terminal attachments that fit into the distributor cap come in two basic styles. The most common is the familiar brass clip, which squeezes together to grip the wire as it is pressed into the distributor cap. British cars with Lucas distributors have screw-in distributor cap terminals, which require that a washerlike fitting be attached to the wire core. Even if you are only wiring the family sedan, you can pick up some welcome gains in starting reliability by soldering the terminal attachments in place.

When the secondary cables begin to show signs of wear and tear, there's always the temptation to purchase a prepackaged wiring set, but you'll profit in the long run if you spend a little additional time assembling your own wiring set and making it as permanent, durable, and reliable as any other part of the car. High-quality ready-made wiring sets are available, but they will cost you about twice as much as one you assemble yourself. On the other hand, if it's a relatively inexpensive set, you'll find that parts of it are not all they should be in quality.

A major complaint with most inexpensive wire sets is that the cables have the nipples molded right onto them. If the nipple goes bad, you must replace the entire wire. But even the best sets are only made to "stock" specifications. The terminals are not soldered on, and the plug connectors are a type that may vibrate off. Obviously, if you want the very best in secondary wiring, the most satisfactory approach is to select the individual components yourself and assemble them in the best way.

If it's a street job, you'd better narrow your choice to a resistance-type cable. This in turn dictates the type of terminals you'll have to use. If the cable manufacturer also makes terminals, it's a good bet that these will best match the cable's design. With wire-core cable, the best material for the terminals is brass, not only because brass resists corrosion better than most other materials, but also because it is easier to solder.

Whether you're using resistance or metallic cable, your plug connectors must be selected to fit the spark plug being used and to suit the plug location of your engine. Some plug connectors

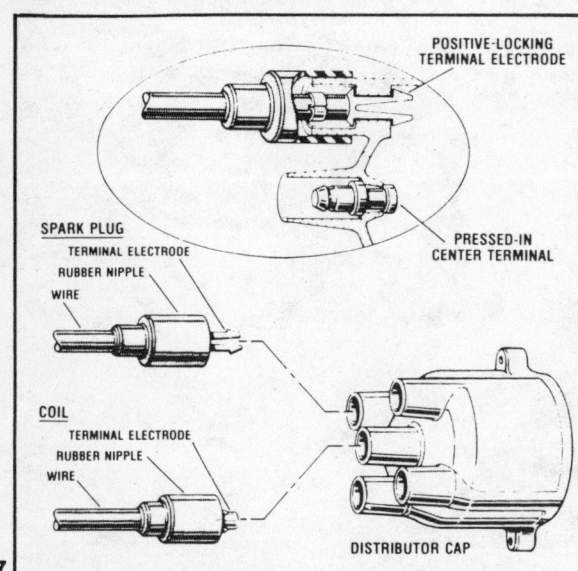

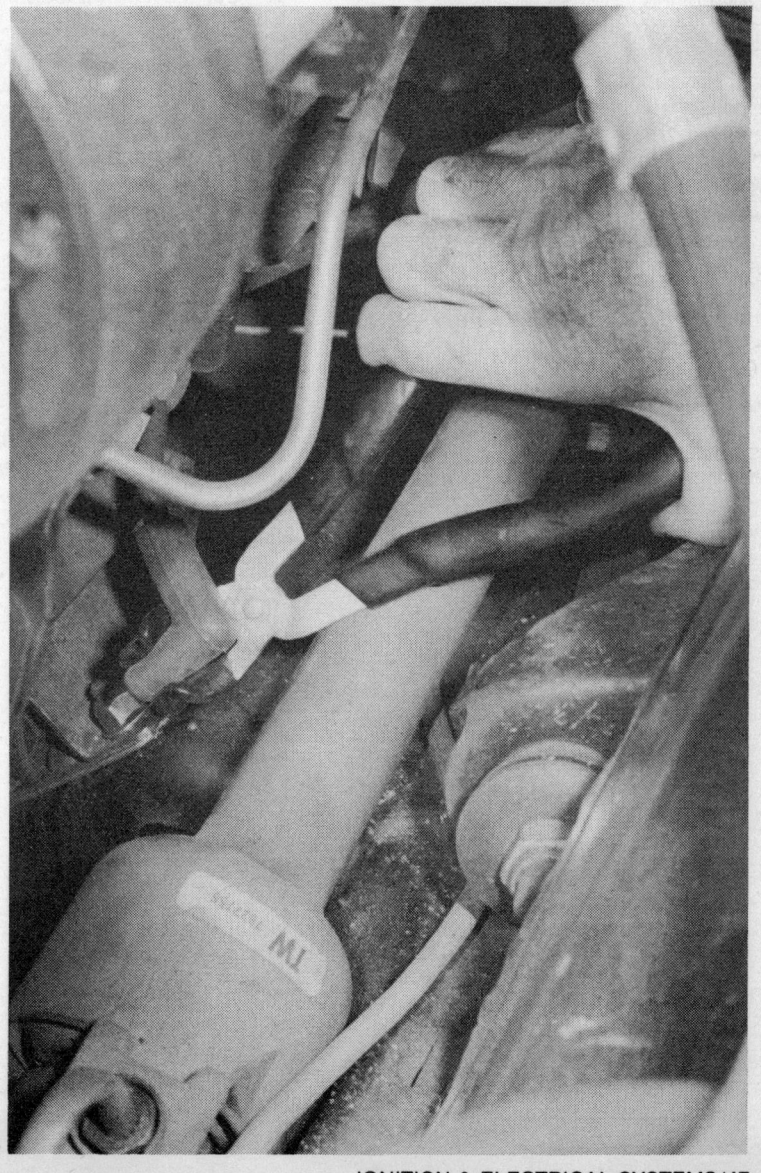

6. Here's a handy tool when replacing the wire set or pulling the plugs. When the wire is removed from the plug, it's inserted in the tool slot bearing the proper cylinder number, keeping confusion to a minimum.

7. Chrysler pioneered the use of plug wires with terminals that lock in the distributor cap to form the cap electrodes. These wires cannot be pulled from the cap as in the past; the cap must be removed and the terminals squeezed together to free the wire.

8. Pulling plug wires off the plugs can damage the suppression cable inside. Wires must be TWISTED off by their boot, preferably with plug wire pliers.

PLUG WIRES

require that the spark-plug terminal nut be removed. If you select these but the plug you intend to use comes only with a solid terminal, you've neatly painted yourself into a corner.

WIRE ROUTING

The first step is to cut the wires to the proper length. On inline engines, this isn't usually much of a problem, since wire routing is simple and there aren't many heated or moving parts for the cables to rub against. On V-8s things can be a bit more complicated. One way is to fit each wire into the distributor first, route it over the engine, then cut it off at the individual plug locations. Another procedure that works well—particularly on engines where the cables are routed under the exhaust manifold or headers—is to cut the plug terminal off the old cable, butt the end of the new one against it, and bind them together with electrical tape. All you have to do is start pulling the old wire from the distributor end and it will snake the new cable right into place.

In all cases, take your time and do not forcibly pull on the wires. Always make sure that the cables are as short as possible without causing them to make any sharp bends or to come into contact with heated, vibrating, or moving parts. After the cables have been cut to length, including the high-tension lead that fits between the coil and the distributor, it's time to install the boots and nipples. Boots and nipples that do not slip easily onto the cables can be lubricated lightly with glycerine, brake fluid, a small amount of petroleum jelly, soapy water, or silicone—never use grease or oil.

If you're going to solder the terminals in place, here's the best way to go about it. Install the distributor terminals first. Strip about 3/16-inch of insulation from the end of the cables and lightly coat the end of each terminal attachment with solder before installing it on the wire. The projecting end of the metallic wire can then be passed through the hole in the center of the terminal attachment. Individual strands of wire should be bent over so that they radiate across the end of the terminal. After doing this, the wire can be bonded to the terminal with just a quick touch of the soldering iron. Never use a torch or try to make the solder joint without first having tinned the terminal, for that will apply far too much heat to the cable itself and damage the insulation.

Some patented plug connectors like the Rajah require no soldering since they have a built-in screw that firmly grips the wire core of the ignition cable. The simpler sleeve-type connectors that are commonly sold in parts stores may require a slight modification to make them suitable for soldered connections. One way is to drill a small hole in the side of the terminal so that the metallic wire can be slipped through it and soldered to the outside of the connector. Always use rosin-core solder.

LOOMS

Chromed tubular wire looms look sharp but can be a headache. The problems occur when they are able to pick up a lot of heat and are solidly grounded to the engine block. They not only overheat the cable's insulation but also can cause electrical interference and induction or crossfiring. The best wire looms and supports are the type that carries the wires in neoprene insulating rings.

Induction or crossfiring is a phenomenon that occurs when long ignition cables are allowed to lie closely against one another. Spark energy passing through one cable can induce a current in the other which will cause both cylinders to fire at the same time. This can result in mechanical damage or even a carburetor fire. When routing your wires, allow as much space between them as is practical and avoid having them run parallel for long distances.

Needless to say, ignition cables must be connected between the distributor and the spark plugs according to the firing order of the engine. The No. 1 terminal of the distributor is usually marked in some way. The cable leading from this terminal must connect to the spark plug of the No. 1 cylinder. Your car's manual will list the firing order of the engine, or it will be cast in raised numbers on the intake manifold or engine block. The remaining cables are connected in succession around the cap from the No. 1 terminal in the direction of distributor rotation, and run to each cylinder in turn according to the firing order.

PERIODIC WIRING SERVICE

Assuming that you now have a good set of ignition cables installed, simply inspecting them at periodic intervals will tell you much about the condition of the ignition system. Check the cable

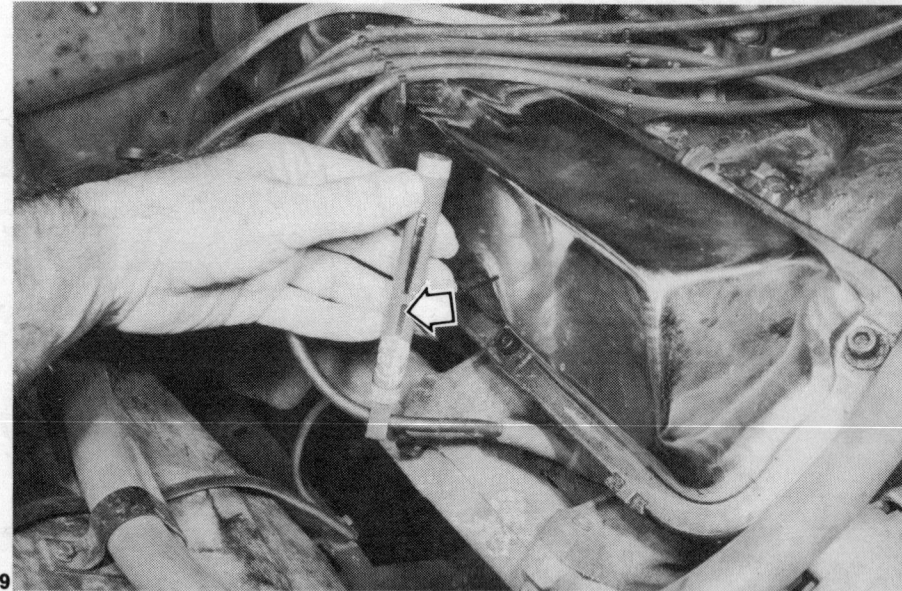

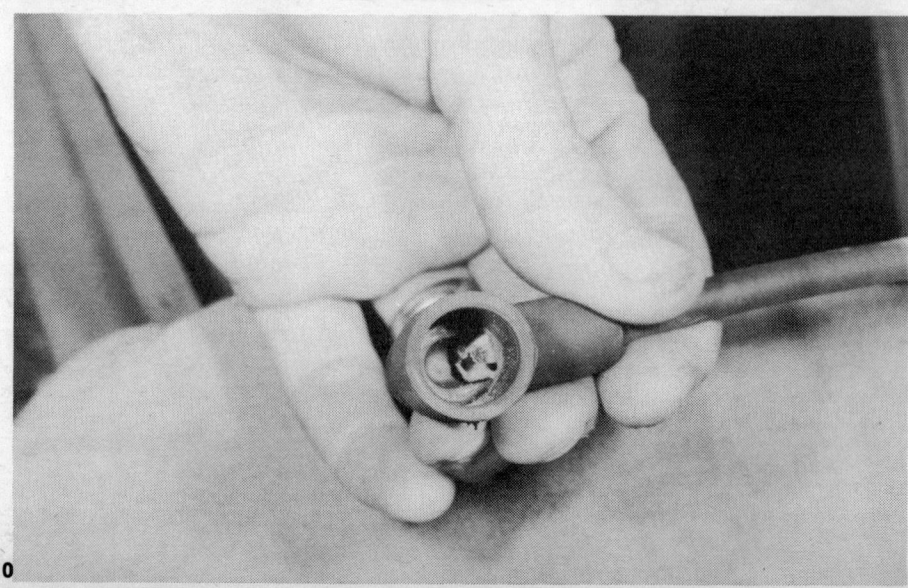

insulation; if it is oil-soaked and spongy, hard or brittle, cracked or worn through by abrasion, replace it. Look for loose or corroded connections, grease- or oil-soaked cable boots or nipples. These conditions will allow leakage to ground and result in low ignition voltage.

To remove the cable from the spark plug without causing internal damage to the core, grasp the boot and twist it slightly to break the seal, then lift up with a steady, straight pull. Spark-plug cable pliers are very useful in reaching out-of-the-way plugs, especially if the engine is still warm. When replacing the cable, make sure that the boot fits snugly around the plug terminal; if not, replace it.

To remove the cable from the distributor cap or coil tower, twist the nipple first to loosen it, then grasp the upper part of the nipple and cable. Pull straight up without bending or kinking the cable. To replace it, push the cable straight down into the tower to fully seat the terminal. Slide the nipple down in place on the cap or coil tower. If the cable is not fully seated, it will create an additional gap in the circuit, causing the spark to jump and corrode the terminal.

Magnetic induction test equipment leads will not damage the cable and should be used when possible. Older test equipment requires the use of an adapter between the plug and cable terminal, but many people (and mechanics) simply pierce the cable insulation with alligator clamps or insert a nail between the cable and boot to make contact. This is a destructive practice, as it can damage the resistor wire core or boot and allow moisture to pass through the insulation to the core.

9. This little gadget will locate broken wires or damaged insulation. Just clip it over the wire with the engine running and watch the intensity of the light inside the tube (arrow). If the light is bright and strong, the cable is good.

10. This plug cable terminal was broken off inside the boot, causing a misfire for no apparent reason.

11. A secondary cable that's not fully seated in the distributor cap will arc, corroding the tower terminal. A tower cleaning tool can be used to remove the corrosion and restore satisfactory contact, if arcing damage is not too great.

12. Here's the hook-up for testing plug cable resistance. Check the manufacturer's specs (they differ) and compare to your reading.

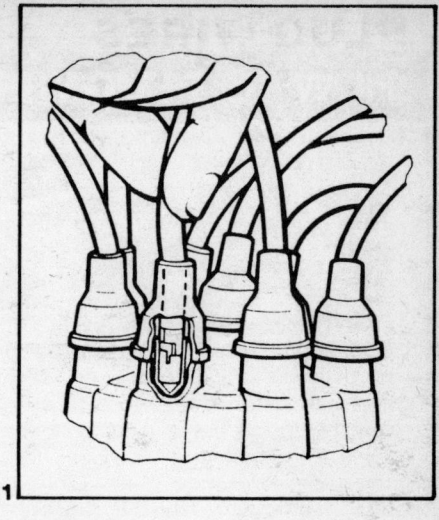

Replace the cable if resistance is excessive.

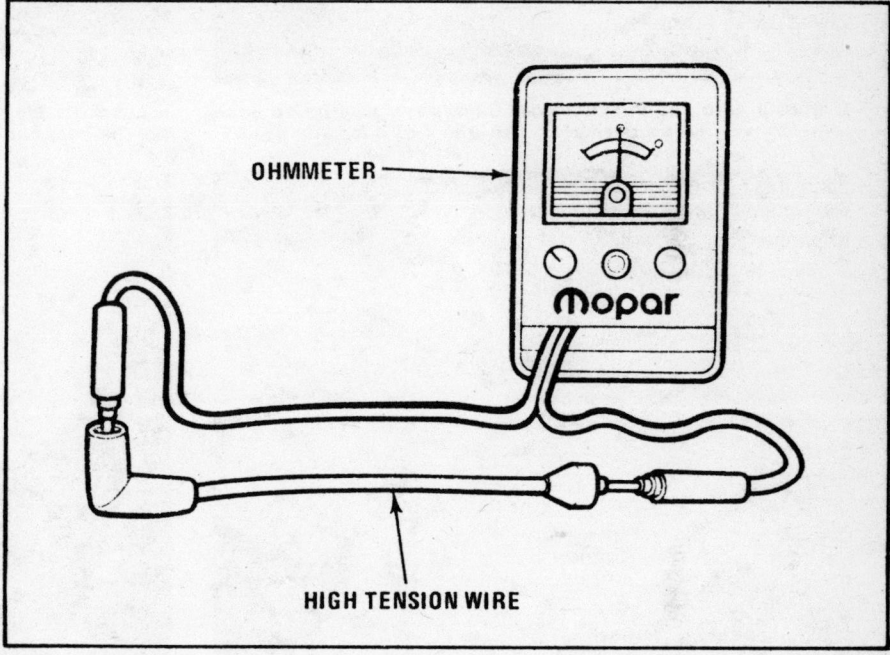

IGNITION & ELECTRICAL SYSTEMS/19

Plug Wires

HOW-TO: PLUG WIRE REPLACEMENT

1. Nobu's Auto Lab in Hollywood, Calif. swears by Delco suppression wire, so we decided to use a reel of it for this car.

2. Lubricate the tip of the cable with a silicone spray first so that the boot can slide on easily. Don't use motor oil.

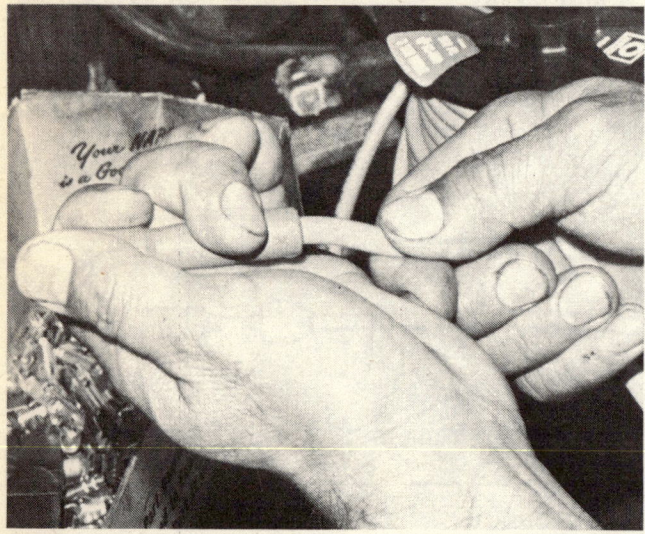

3. Now the spark plug rubber boot slips on. It's amazing how many mechanics forget to put on the boot before the terminal.

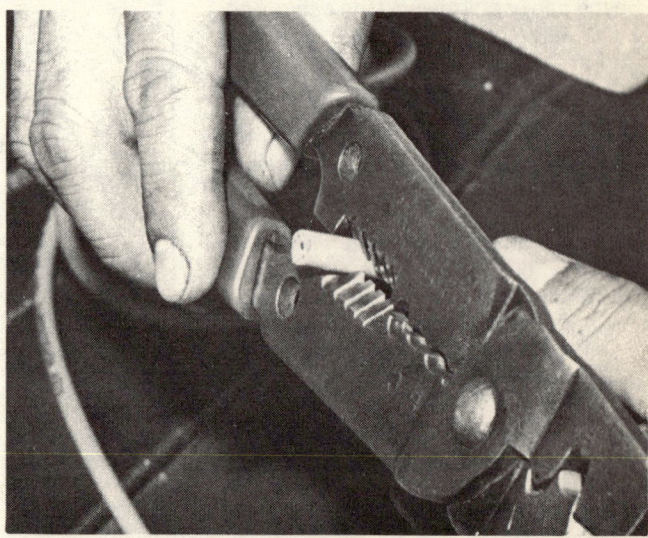

4. Using these special, extremely handy automotive wiring pliers, a little more than ¼-in. of insulation is stripped off.

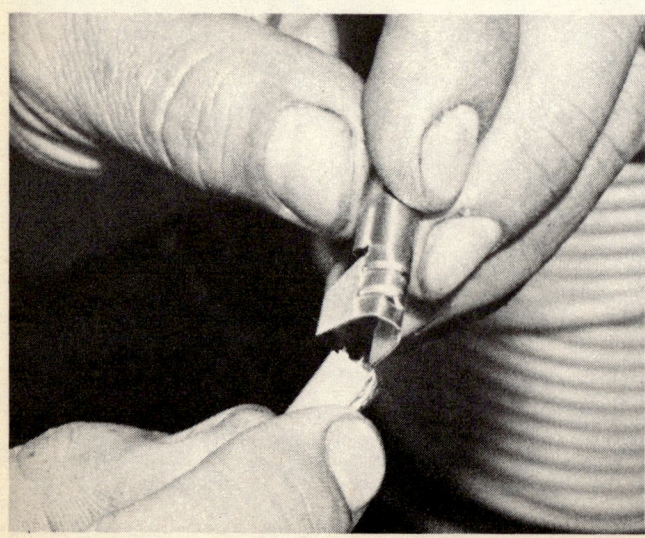

5. The end of the wire is then bent back up and over the insulation to provide a good contact with the metal terminal.

6. The special pliers are used again to crimp the terminal. Pliers like these can be purchased at most auto parts stores.

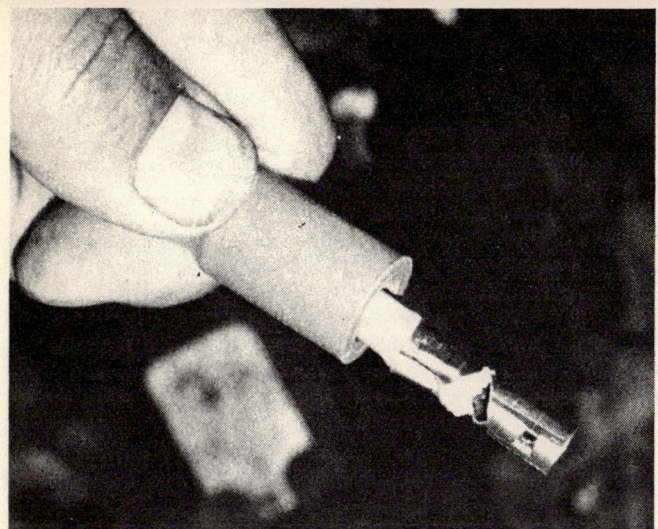
7. Note how the tabs of the terminal are folded inward to grasp the cable. It's difficult to do this with plain pliers.

8. With one terminal attached, next measure for proper length by using the old wire as a guide. Do only one wire at a time.

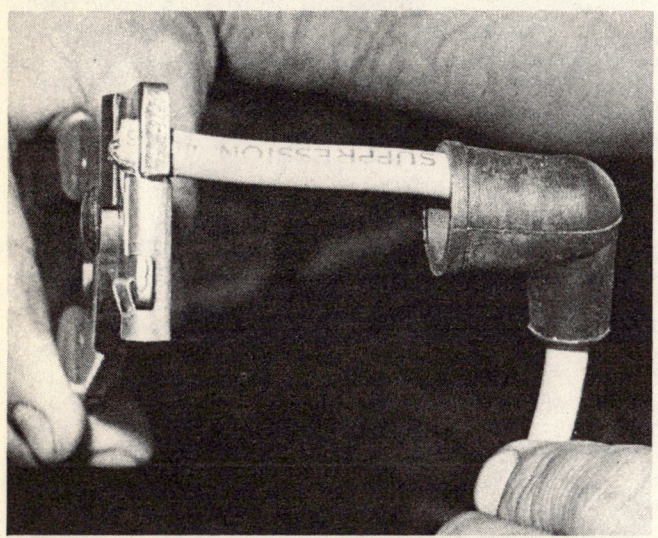
9. The distributor on this car required 90° terminals, so the auto pliers are used again to attach the special terminal.

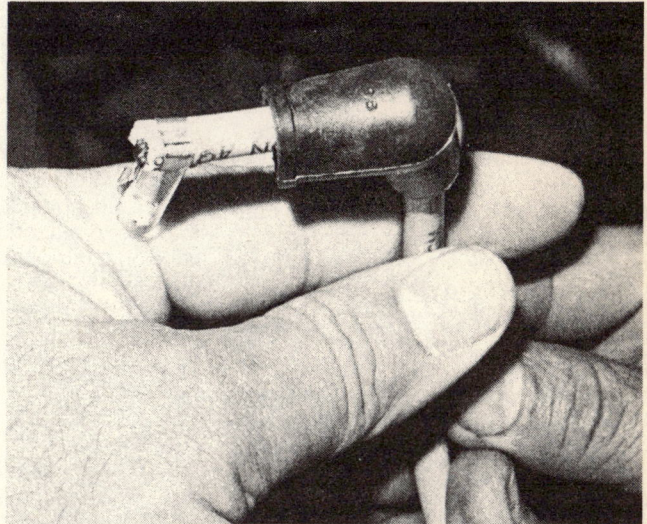
10. This type of terminal is one of the two kinds commonly used for 90° installations. Note the type of boot it requires.

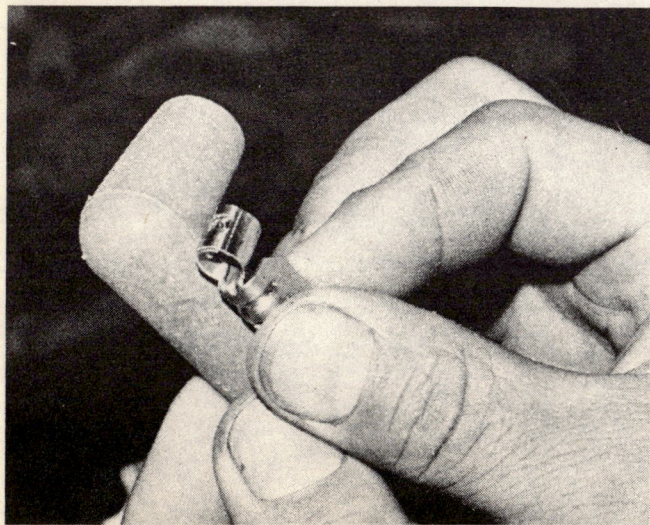
11. The other kind of 90° terminal is just as satisfactory, but it takes a different boot, which is usually red in color.

12. Use the correct terminal. The one on the left is a straight terminal that's been bent to 90°; you'll break wires that way.

COILS

One of the most trouble-free parts of the modern automobile, the ignition coil has only one job: to produce the high-voltage current needed to fire the spark plugs. An auto battery alone will produce a good spark, but 12 volts just aren't sufficient pressure to ionize the plug gaps and push an electrical current across them. The coil transforms the battery's low or primary voltage into a very high secondary voltage for firing the spark plugs.

HOW IT WORKS

Electricity is measured in two ways: amperage for amount and voltage for pressure. When electricity comes from a controlled source, such as a car's alternator, or from a nonvariable source, such as a battery, it's just like water running from a garden hose. You can adjust the nozzle for great pressure, but you lose on the amount of water coming out. If you turn the nozzle so that a lot of water comes out, the pressure falls off to almost nothing. The pressure produced by the battery is small (only 12 volts), but very high (comparably) in its rate of flow—amperage. The battery's voltage is our starting point in understanding how the coil works.

A negative-ground system, which is almost universally used today, is one in which the negative (-) battery cable is grounded to the chassis and the positive (+) battery pole is wired to the starter motor solenoid and the car's switches, the most important of which is the ignition switch. The path of the electrical current is circular. It exits from the positive battery terminal, travels through the car to operate its components, and then returns through the chassis to the negative or grounded side of the battery. This circuit is a continuous cycle until a wire is cut or shorted, a battery cable is disconnected, or the battery goes completely dead.

In a negative-ground system, the positive battery cable is connected directly to a terminal on the starter motor solenoid. The ignition switch usually picks up its voltage from this same terminal by a "hot" wire running from the terminal to the switch. In some older cars, the hot wire may be attached directly to the battery cable. At the ignition switch, the car's electrical components are sorted out according to their sequence of operation. Many components like the heater blower motor and the radio are often wired so that they will operate regardless of the position of the ignition switch. These tap power from the switch's "hot" terminal. For all the others, the switch position determines which components receive battery voltage.

It's important to remember that this hot wire to the ignition switch always has voltage, regardless of the position of the switch. For this reason, it's also wise to disconnect either this wire or the battery cable itself while working around electrical wiring.

The operation of the ignition switch can be understood by comparing it to a drawbridge, and the current from the battery to a car waiting to cross that bridge. When the switch is in its off position, an electrical conductor (the bridge) within the switch is raised and makes no contact with the rest of the switch's conductors. In electrical terminology, this is an open circuit. In this position, the current (the car) from the battery can't cross or go any farther. Turning the ignition switch on physically moves the conductor (lowers the bridge) to contact another conductor within the switch, thus allowing the current to cross over and continue on until an accessor switch is encountered. If a particular accessory switch is on, then the current can enter the switch and the accessory to operate it. After passing through all the on accessories, the current returns through the chassis and up the ground cable to complete the circuit.

The starting solenoid and ignition switch are both involved with the coil in operating the starting system of any car. Battery voltage from the ignition switch is needed at only two places to start the engine—at the "hot" side of the coil and at the starter solenoid. The ignition switch and the wiring system are designed so that they can supply coil voltage only, or coil plus solenoid, but not solenoid only. Remember, one terminal of the ignition switch always has voltage, even when the ignition key is in the off position.

When the ignition key is turned on, current is sent through a special resistor wire from the ignition switch to the coil—we'll explain why resistor wire is used later. In the usual negative-ground electrical system, this wire is attached to the coil terminal marked with a "+"; on some coils, this terminal is marked instead with an "SW" for switch or a "BATT" for battery. However it is labeled, this is the coil terminal in the primary or low-voltage system which receives battery voltage. There is one other coil primary terminal, which is marked with a "-" or "CB" for contact

breakers, or "DIST" for distributor. The wire from this terminal leads to the distributor's breaker points or their electronic equivalent, and from there to ground. With voltage now supplied to the coil, the engine will run if the starter motor turns it over.

When you turn the ignition key to "start," the ignition switch momentarily interrupts the current that's going directly to the coil and diverts it instead into another primary wire running to the starter solenoid. Three other wires are attached to this solenoid. One is another primary wire to the coil—to the same coil terminal as the hot wire coming from the ignition switch. This solenoid-to-coil wire is called the bypass wire; it picks up battery voltage from the solenoid and delivers it to the coil. Its purpose is to bypass the ignition switch-to-coil resistance wire so that during and only during starting, the coil receives the full 12 volts of current from the battery.

The two other wires attached to the solenoid are really two parts of the same wire—the heavy battery cable. One part runs up to the positive post on the battery so that it is always hot. The other runs down to the starter motor. The solenoid is really nothing more than an electromagnetic switch that connects these two parts of the battery cable. When current flows from the ignition switch to the solenoid, the many turns of fine wire in the solenoid's case create a magnetic field, which pulls forward an iron plunger inside the solenoid. This plunger connects the two cable terminals on the solenoid's case, completing the battery-to-starter-motor circuit. Heavy current then flows from the battery, the starter motor goes into operation, and the engine turns over.

As soon as the engine starts running, the ignition key is released and it returns to the on position. Current to the starter solenoid is then cut off, the solenoid's magnetic field collapses, and a spring inside the solenoid pushes back the plunger to break the battery cable circuit. This shuts off power to the starter motor, which immediately disengages

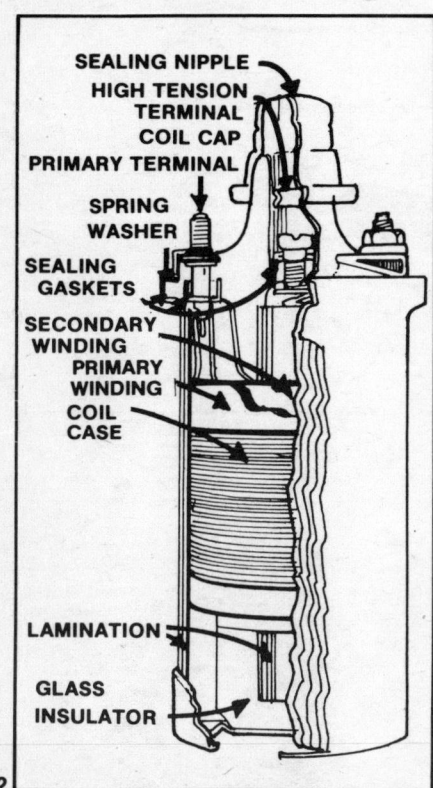

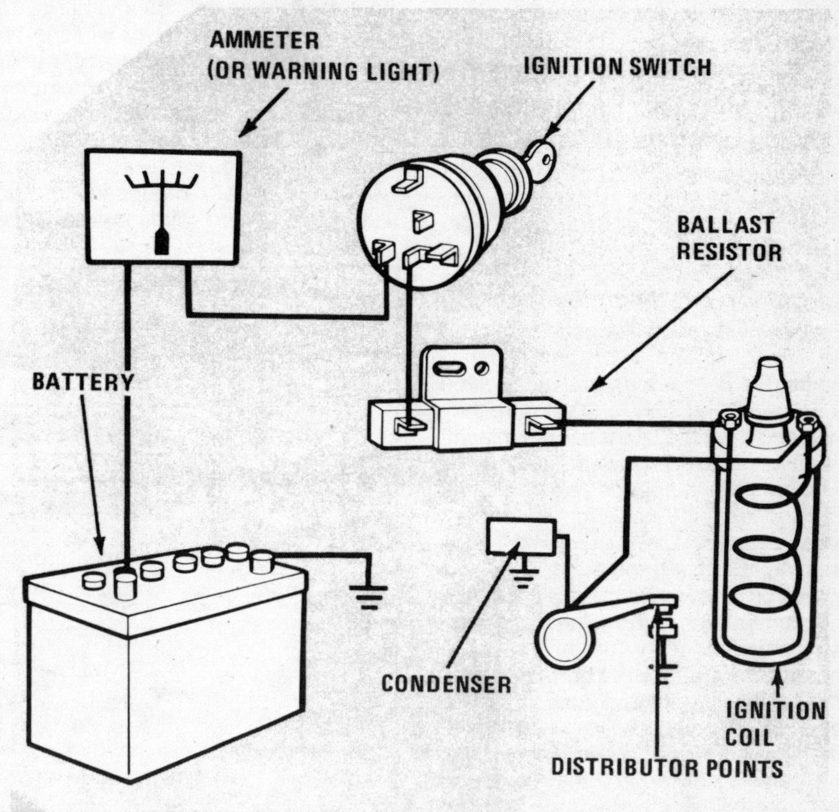

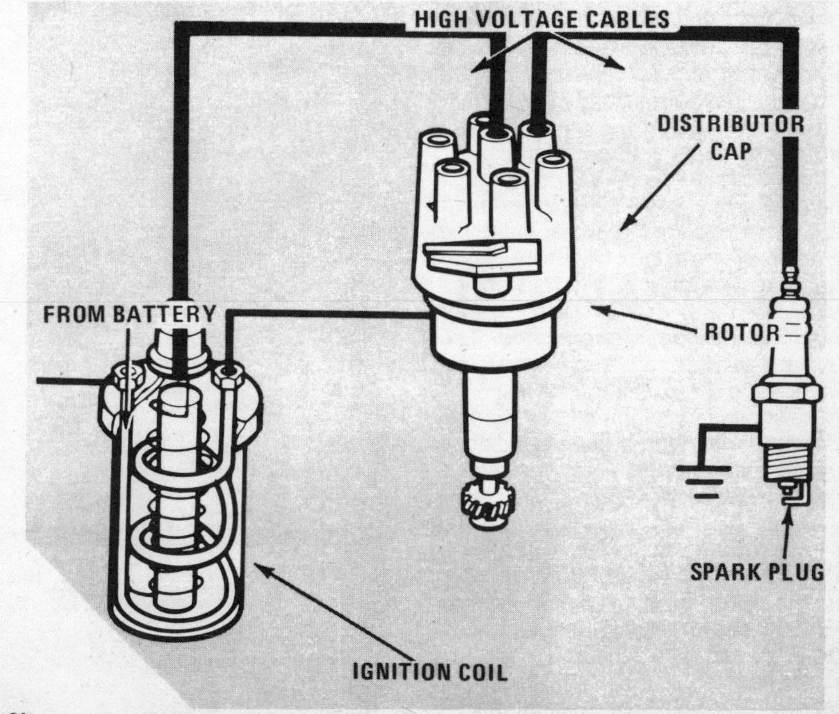

1. The traditional oil-filled coil is prone to vibration problems when mounted on the engine; many coils are now mounted on the fender apron.

2. Oil or pitch-filled coils surround the windings in traditional coil design. Either is satisfactory if precision-made.

3A and 3B. The ignition system consists of the primary or low voltage circuit (A) and the secondary or high voltage circuit (B). The coil acts as the bridge between the two.

COILS

from the flywheel. The bypass wire current to the coil is also cut off, but this does not matter; the ignition switch is now supplying current to the coil through the normal resistance wire.

The purpose of the resistance wire is to reduce coil voltage once the engine has started. Cranking an engine, especially when it is cold, can quickly discharge a battery. During the starting process, the bypass wire allows a full 12 volts to the coil. Once the engine has started, however, 12 volts would quickly burn the points, so the voltage must be reduced before reaching the points. The resistance wire cuts the 12 volts to approximately 6 volts before the voltage enters the coil. During cranking, point damage is minimal, because the points are exposed to 12 volts for only a very short time and the engine is turning over very slowly. Once the engine has started, the points move faster, and wear increases with engine speed. Even at an idle speed of only 800 rpm in a V-8 engine, the points open and close 3200 times in one minute; at 5000 rpm, they open and close 20,000 times per minute. It's obvious that point wear takes place at higher engine speeds and not during cranking; thus the need for resistance.

Now let's look at the coil itself. It is basically a pulse transformer designed to convert a low voltage (12 volts) into one high enough to jump the spark-plug gap and ignite the air-fuel mixture in the combustion chamber. The inside of a coil consists of a primary and a secondary winding of wire coiled around a vertically mounted soft iron core. Look at a cutaway of the coil and you'll see that the primary or low-voltage winding is a fairly heavy wire connected to the inside bottom half of the incoming primary terminal. On a negative-ground system, this terminal is often marked with a (+); positive-ground systems are marked (-). The sign indicates which terminal receives battery voltage.

The wire is then vertically coiled a few hundred times and its other end attached to the outgoing primary terminal at the other side of the coil. In a negative-ground system, this terminal is signified by a "-" sign, or one of the other markings previously mentioned. The current exits the coil from this terminal and goes to the distributor points.

The secondary (high-voltage) winding is located within the primary winding. It consists of about 200 feet of extremely fine wire wrapped in several insulated layers around the soft iron core. The end of the secondary winding connects internally to the coil's secondary terminal. This is the protruding tower situated between the primary terminals. Connected to it is the large-diameter, high-voltage cable that carries approximately 25,000 volts to the distributor cap for distribution by the rotor to the plugs.

Now that you're familiar with the basic structure of the coil and understand where the current enters and exits, here's what actually goes on inside. The operation of the coil depends upon a complex interaction of induction, magnetism, and electrical transformation. This last principle is the easiest to understand, so we'll discuss it first.

Like the coil, any transformer has primary and secondary windings that are not physically connected to each other. When current flows in the primary winding, the electromagnetic phenomenon of induction causes another current to flow in the secondary winding. The voltage of this secondary current depends upon the ratio of the number of wiring turns in the secondary winding compared to the number of turns in the primary winding. Whereas the primary winding is usually composed of about 200 turns of fine wire, the secondary winding may have as many as 22,000 turns. The resulting ratio is very large, so the secondary voltage is around 25,000 volts in coils used with conventional breaker-point ignitions, and as great as 35,000 volts in electronic ignition coils, even though the primary voltage is only 12 volts.

What happens next depends upon interacting laws of electricity. When a current flows in a wire, a magnetic field is set up around the wire. A very strong magnetic field can be established by wrapping many turns of wire around an iron core and passing a current through the wire. This is exactly what is done with the primary windings in the coil. Whenever the ignition switch is on and the distributor points are closed, the primary circuit is complete. Current then flows through the coil, setting up a strong magnetic field. The magnetic field envelops the thousands of turns of fine

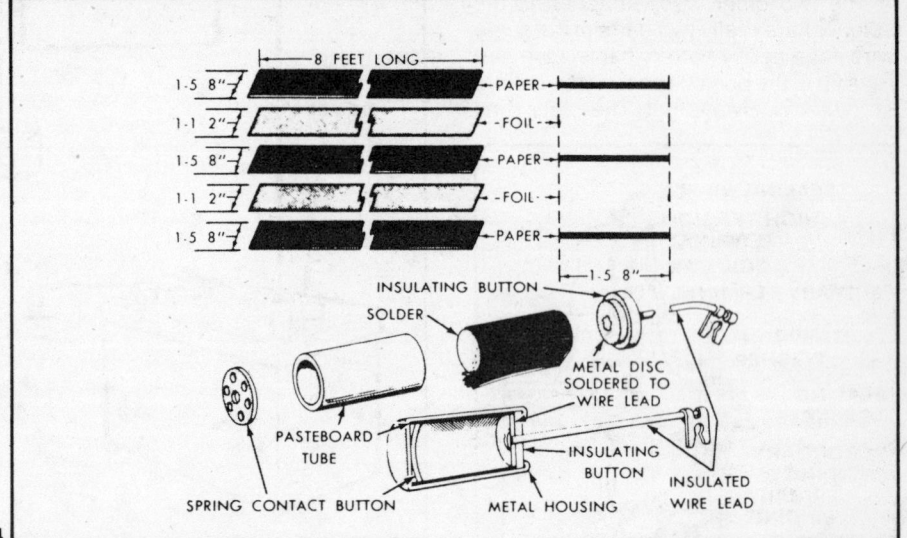

4

5

wire in the secondary windings as well as the soft iron core.

When the points open, however, the primary current is interrupted and the magnetic field instantly collapses. Whenever there is relative movement between a magnetic field and an electrical conductor, a voltage is induced in the conductor. The strength of this voltage depends upon the strength of the magnetic field and the speed of the relative movement. In the coil, the collapse of its magnetic field provides the relative movement, and immediately a very powerful voltage is induced into the secondary windings. This secondary voltage is very high because there are so many secondary windings and because the collapse of the magnetic field is so fast. A heavily insulated thick wire carries the secondary voltage from the coil to the distributor, which distributes it to the spark plugs.

When the distributor points open and the high voltage is induced in the secondary windings, a self-induced voltage also appears in the primary windings, amounting to about 250 volts. The self-induced voltage has no place to go except to the condenser. The condenser is connected into the primary system, usually mounted in the distributor next to the points. After the 250 volts of electrical pressure have rammed into the insulated side of the condenser and filled it to capacity, there is an unbalanced condition in the primary. The result is that the pressure from the condenser fires back through the primary in the opposite direction, charging up the grounded side of the condenser and creating another unbalanced condition. The condenser continues to oscillate through the primary, and these oscillations help "pump" the secondary current across the spark gap at the plug.

Attached at the top of the distributor shaft to rotate with it is the rotor, which is a plastic cap with a metal pointer extending from it. Inside each of the other cap towers is a metal insert that extends into the cap's interior and forms a contact at the bottom. The contacts are evenly spaced from each other (except in some Ford EEC distributors) and form a circle within the cap. The plug wires fit tightly into these towers and contact the inserts. Just as the points in the distributor open (or the air gap increases in a breakerless distributor), the rotor aligns with a cap contact connected to one of the spark-plug wires. The pressure (voltage) behind the secondary current is conducted from the rotor to this contact. From the contact, it goes up the spark-plug wire to energize the plug, ionize the gap, and project the current across the spark-plug gap to ground.

All this happens thousands of times a minute—about 18,000 times per minute at 4500 rpm in an eight-cylinder engine—with perfect timing. To cope with these extreme demands, the ignition coil must be of a very highly specialized design.

CONSTRUCTION

One of the most important things an ignition coil must do is to magnetize and demagnetize itself almost instantaneously. This is why soft iron is used for solenoids, electric motor armatures, relays, and ignition coils. Soft iron has

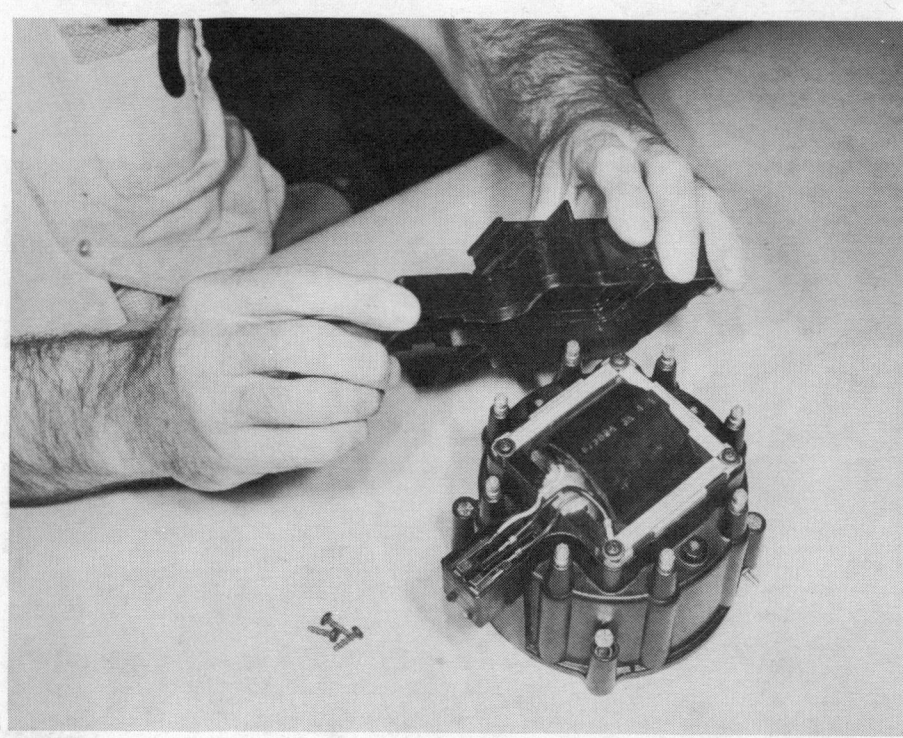

4. A condenser is little more than a tube of tinfoil but it must be precision-made or it can cause a lot of trouble.

5. The coil used with HEI distributors (left) is smaller, lighter in weight and more powerful than the traditional oil-filled coil (right).

6. The HEI coil resembles a small transformer. On V-8 and some 6-cylinder distributors, it's housed inside the distributor cap.

7. HEI coils must be replaced with one bearing the same part number (A). Note the ground lead (B) and insulating washer (C) under the coil inside the cap.

COILS

not only the ability to accept magnetism, but the property of losing it quickly as well. Hard steels and nickel, on the other hand, will retain magnetism for years and are thus used to make permanent magnets.

Coil windings are generally of copper to keep internal resistance as low as possible. The copper wire is insulated by a coating of varnish, which keeps the windings from shorting out against one another and weakening the coil's output. Each layer of windings in the secondary coil is insulated from the next by a sheet of specially impregnated paper. After the windings and their core are assembled, they are slipped into a metal container. Most good-quality stock ignition coils are further sealed and strengthened by filling the can with oil, which also serves as an insulator. The coil's "tower" or "nose" is then fitted to seal the container and provide a terminal for the secondary cable and the two smaller primary leads.

BALLAST RESISTORS

Forcing more current through the primary windings of a coil should result in the production of more secondary voltage when the distributor points open. This is exactly what happens. The way to get more current through the coil windings is to increase the electrical pressure (voltage).

Putting a resistor in the primary wire between the battery and the coil may seem like the wrong thing to do, as resistance results in a voltage drop, which in turn cuts down on the amount of current going through the coil windings. But this is exactly what most domestic car makers have done. The resistance is bypassed during starting so that the coil will receive full voltage, but at other times the resistance is in the circuit so that the coil in a 12-volt system actually runs on 6 volts.

At low engine speeds, the distributor shaft rotates slowly, causing the points to open and close slowly, and to remain closed for a relatively long period of time. This action allows current to flow in the primary circuit for a relatively long period as a result. But with these long current flows, the ballast resistor gets hotter. The hotter a resistor gets, the more resistance it produces, thus lowering the current to the coil.

At high engine speeds, the points open and close very quickly, giving the coil less time to become saturated with current. The reduction of current through the resistor allows it to cool off and permit more current flow to the coil. The ballast resistor is really a means of controlling the spark and lengthening the life of the coil by reducing current flow when it is not needed.

Some ballast resistors are built into

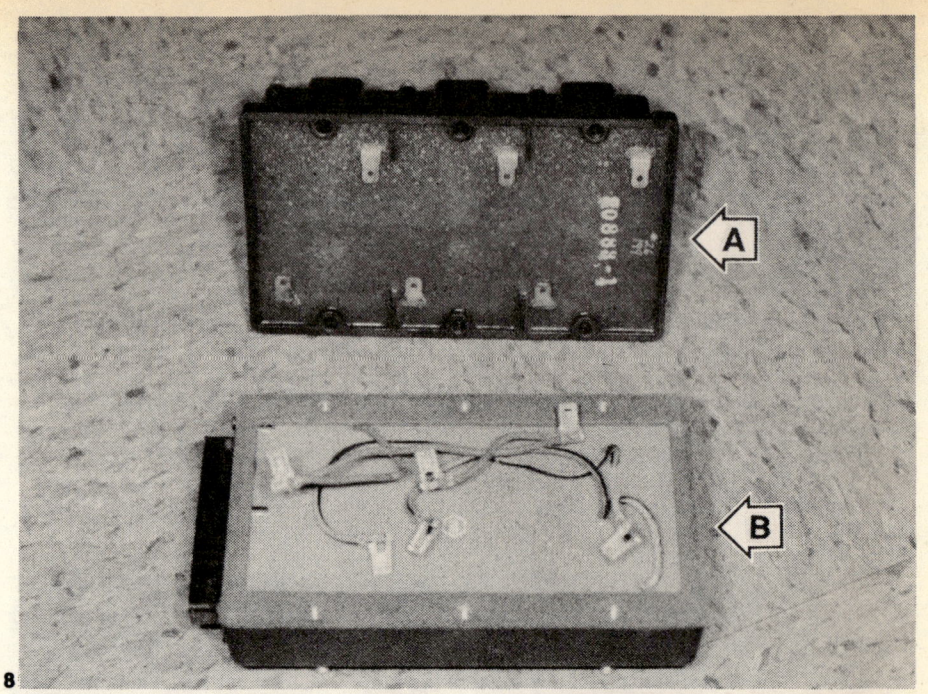

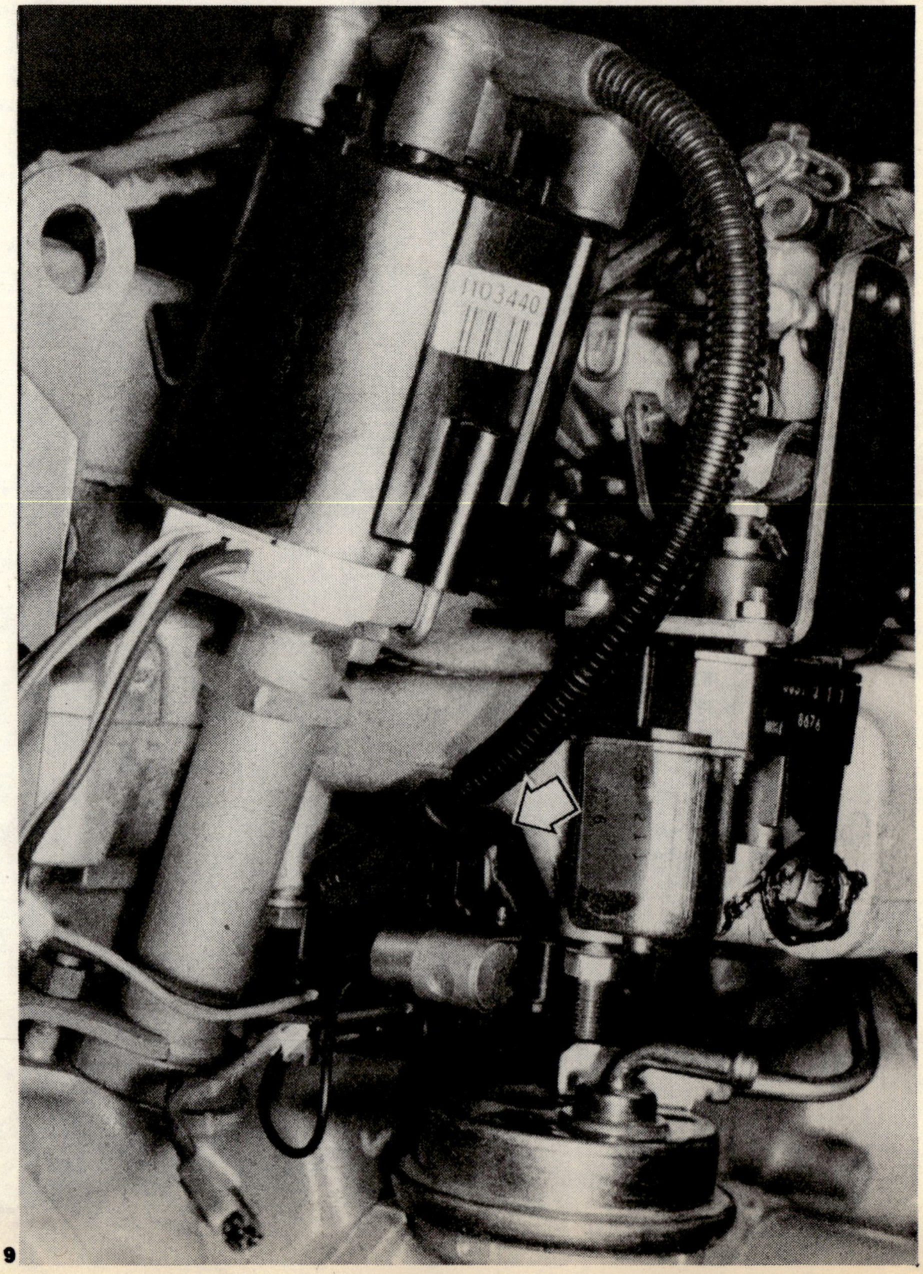

the coil, while others are located outside, often mounted on the firewall. Some are even built into the primary wire itself between the ignition switch and coil. To replace this type, either replace the wire or put in a nonresistor wire with a firewall-mounted resistor.

TROUBLESHOOTING COIL FAILURES

Most coil troubles result from defects in the secondary windings. Either the insulation between the windings breaks down, reducing the spark voltage, or the insulation from ground breaks down, allowing the current to escape internally. Coils subjected to vibration are particularly vulnerable, since shaking the windings against one another can wear away their thin varnish insulation. Broken windings and internal connections are nearly always the cause of complete and sudden coil failure, but such trouble is really quite rare. The most common coil defects result from a gradual deterioration of the internal insulation. Complete failure is usually preceded by many signs of an impending breakdown.

One of the most common signals that a coil needs checking is hard or unreliable starting. Another symptom is chronic high-speed missing and cutting out during acceleration. If the car's battery is up to par, the distributor tuned, and the plugs and cables in good shape, such problems are most likely coil-related. You can perform preliminary coil checks without special equipment. If these indicate that a coil defect does indeed exist, you can replace the coil. If your home tests are not conclusive, don't pronounce the coil healthy until it has been subjected to more elaborate test procedures.

The first test is to remove the high-tension cable that connects the distributor and the coil. Disconnect it at the distributor cap and hold the cable end about 3/16-inch away from a grounded part of the engine while cranking the engine with the ignition switch turned on. A bright blue spark should jump the gap.

A weak, yellowish or red spark indicates insufficient spark voltage. This definitely points to a weak coil—providing the points, condenser, and battery are all in good condition.

If your preliminary test with the high-tension cable produces no spark at all, try to pinpoint the trouble before replacing the coil with a new one. A 12-volt bulb with two test leads attached to it is all that's needed. Start by taking off the distributor cap. Then either turn the engine until the points are open, or separate them with a small piece of cardboard. Turn the ignition switch on and connect one test lamp lead to ground on the engine. Touch the other test lead to first one and then the other of the coil's primary terminals.

If the bulb lights when touched to the primary terminal leading to the distributor, it indicates that the coil is getting current and that the primary windings are all right. If the bulb lights when touched to the other primary terminal, but not when attached to the one leading to the distributor, the primary windings are faulty and the coil is no good. If the light does not go on when connected to either primary connection, the trouble is somewhere else—perhaps in the ignition switch or starter relay.

If your tests show that the coil is receiving current at both primary terminals, remove the high-tension cable from the center distributor cap

10a

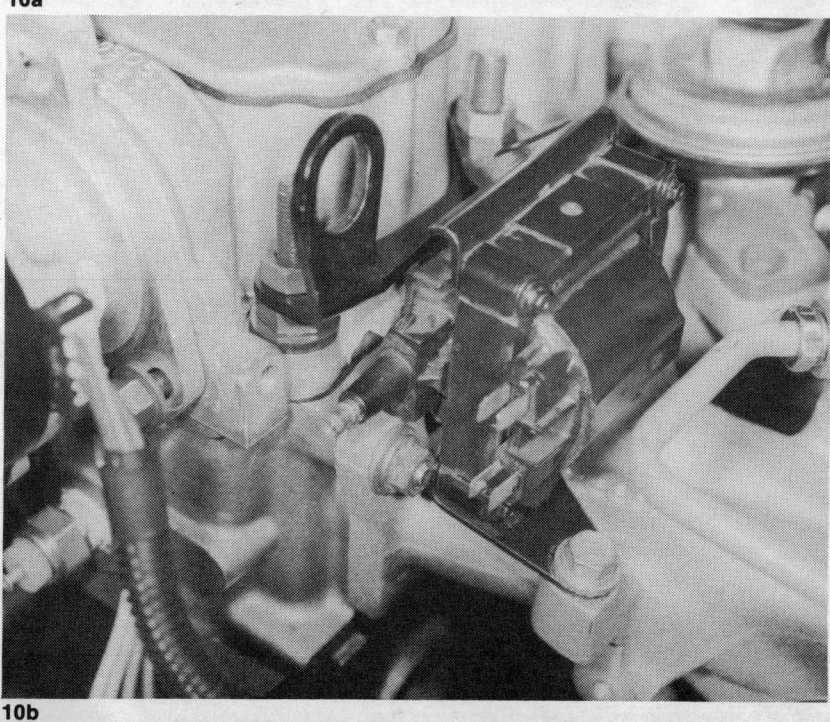
10b

8. The Computer Controlled Coil Ignition on 1984 Turbo V-6 Buicks contains three coils sealed in epoxy (A). Each coil fires two cylinders. The coils connect to the ignition module (B) which serves as the lower half of the "black box."

9. The remote 4-cylinder HEI coil is engine-mounted, often under the intake manifold where servicing it is difficult.

10A and 10B. The HEI coil on GM 2.0L OHC engines is bracket-mounted to the cylinder head and intake manifold (A). Note the push-on secondary (1) and primary (2) terminals used with this design (B).

COILS

tower and try shorting across the open distributor points with the nonoily tip of a screwdriver. If a spark jumps from the coil's high-tension secondary wire to a grounded point on the engine as the screwdriver is removed, the trouble is probably oil, dirt, or water on the points—or simply burned points. If clean and dry, the screwdriver will conduct a spark that wet, dirty, or burned points cannot.

If this last test also fails to produce a spark at the high-tension wire, disconnect the small thin primary lead that passes between the coil and the distributor. Attach a test wire to the coil in its place. Ground the other end of this jumper lead against the engine block and then pull it away. In this case, the test wire is duplicating the job of the points. Grounding the wire does the same thing as closing the points. Pulling the wire away should create the same effect as opening the points—a spark from the coil's high-tension wire.

If a spark jumps from the high-tension cable when the test wire is removed from the ground, the coil is good and the trouble is either grounded points or a shorted condenser. If a spark does not jump during this test, the secondary windings of the coil are probably faulty.

Poor contact between the engine and the ground pole of the battery might also be causing the trouble. Whenever there is a mysterious electrical problem that seems impossible to trace, check the ground strap between the battery and the engine first. While doing all this testing, maintain a healthy respect for the power of the coil's secondary voltage. Use a clean, dry rag carefully to wipe off any part of the secondary wiring that you are going to touch while testing. If you suspect that the wiring insulation is not up to par, wear a rubber glove, or grasp the wire with a piece of rubber. The best bet is to use a pair of special insulated pliers, and don't stand on a damp surface or you'll receive a jolt you'll remember.

In some cases, a coil will test out perfectly, yet the engine remains hard to start and misses at higher speeds, suggesting that there is inadequate spark voltage. If the engine has recently been tuned up, repaired, or newly installed in the car, it's a hint to the real problem—reversed coil polarity. This occurs when the two primary wires leading to the coil have been reversed by incorrect reconnection. When this happens, the spark voltage has positive polarity. It should always be negative, regardless of the way in which the battery is installed in the car. If it isn't, the sparking current has a low pressure in relation to the spark-plug ground electrode to which it must jump. The end result is a weak spark, even though every other part of the ignition system is in perfect condition. Another indication of reversed coil polarity is a "dishing" of the spark plugs' side electrodes.

To test for reversed coil polarity, use a common lead pencil. Simply remove one of the spark-plug leads and hold it about 1/4-inch from the spark-plug terminal or any ground point. Then insert the point of the pencil between the ignition lead and the plug while the engine is running. If the spark flares on the ground or spark-plug side of the pencil, the polarity is correct. If it flares between the ignition lead and the pencil, however, the polarity is wrong and the primary wires should be exchanged at the coil.

If the plug connector terminals are deeply recessed in a boot or insulating shield, the test can still be carried out by straightening all but one bend of a paper clip and inserting the looped end into the plug connector. The polarity test can then be performed between the tip of the paper clip and a grounded place on the engine.

Stock coils are most susceptible to damage from high temperatures and vibration. For this reason, weak coils are most likely to fail completely on a long summer trip. Cars whose coils are mounted in especially hot locations and are subjected to a great deal of vibration often show a repeated tendency to coil failure. If possible, relocate the coil to a cooler, steadier spot in the engine compartment, but make sure the high-tension cable does not exceed 12 inches in length.

When replacing a defective coil, it's very important to make sure that the new one is the correct voltage for the car. It must also be of the correct polarity. If the car has a positive ground, the coil primary terminal marked positive (+) must be connected to the distributor; on cars with a negative ground, it's the other way around. If the original coil is being discarded because of evidence of arcing at the tower, always replace the nipple or boot on the coil end of the high-tension lead. Any arcing at the tower carbonizes the nipple, so placing it on a new coil will invariably cause another coil failure.

HIGH-PERFORMANCE COILS

In most cases, a high-performance coil is unnecessary on a stock engine. If a plug requires only 10,000 volts to jump its gap, then a coil advertised to produce 40,000 volts will produce just the 10,000 volts required by the plug under the same conditions. As the plugs wear, their gaps increase and they require more voltage to fire them. In such a case or when plugs become oil-fouled, a high-performance coil will produce the necessary extra voltage for the firing, but the answer is to find out what is causing the plugs to foul, or to install new plugs with the proper gap setting rather than to try to cure the ill with a hotter coil.

A stock coil is also designed to produce enough voltage to keep an engine firing up to a certain rpm. At high engine speeds, the points are closed for only a very short time. This gives the coil less time to become saturated with current, resulting in lower voltage to the plugs. If an engine has been modified to increase its maximum rpm output, a stock coil may be insufficient at these higher engine speeds and a high-performance coil needed.

If you buy a high-performance coil, be sure that it is made for your engine and that you hook it up exactly according to instructions. A nonstock coil can be designed to operate with or without primary resistance. The instructions with the coil should be very specific on that point. If hooked up incorrectly, the coil will either put out a very weak spark, or overheat and fail. Before buying a new coil of any kind, check the rest of the ignition system pretty thoroughly. Unless you do, you may never obtain any benefit from the replacement. Remember,

11. *The coil can be tested on the engine with an ohmmeter, but such a test cannot pinpoint intermittent problems. This coil tester can, but few garages have one.*

nothing can cure an engine that's in need of a complete tuneup, valve job, or overhaul.

BREAKERLESS IGNITION SYSTEMS

The biggest automotive advance in recent years has been the development of magnetic-pulse breakerless ignitions, often called electronic ignitions. Several different types are in use. In the most common factory installations, the biggest advantage is that the troublesome distributor points are gone and the primary current is switched on and off by the control module. As far as the coil is concerned, however, its function, if not always its shape, has remained unchanged.

The coil used in Ford's various electronic systems has retained its traditional shape and is still mounted in the engine compartment separately from the distributor. Several GM inline engines mount the coil separately and its shape is new—it looks like a little transformer. The GM high-energy ignition (HEI) system used for V-8 and late-model inline engines mounts the coil right in the distributor cap. In the HEI system, the wire from the ignition switch to the coil is not a resistance wire, since the amplifier module automatically controls the dwell period, limiting it at low rpm and extending it at high rpm.

Factory-installed breakerless ignitions tend to be of the inductive-discharge type. This means that they operate like normal ignitions, except for the substitution of electronic components for the points. Many aftermarket systems, however, are of the capacitative-discharge (CD) type. In these, the discharge of a capacitor is what surges through the coil's primary, with its rapid rise and collapse triggering the secondary discharge to the spark plugs.

There are definite advantages to a CD system. The capacitor's discharge is considerably higher voltage than the battery voltage, so the coil's secondary voltage is correspondingly higher. Since the primary voltage is high, the coil does not need a lengthy dwell period to establish the magnetic field, so it can operate efficiently at very high engine rpm.

Many aftermarket CD systems are designed to operate in conjunction with breaker points. They are "bolt-ons," so you will still have some problems with the points, including the need for periodic replacement. Point life is greatly extended, however, since CD systems cut down on the current across the points, preventing them from arcing and burning.

Since the primary current is less, the increased primary voltage does not harm stock ignition components, so your original coil can still be used. If your car is an older model not equipped with factory electronic ignition, it could benefit greatly from the installation of a CD system, or even the conversion to a breakerless distributor.

CONVENTIONAL DISTRIBUTORS

The distributor in an automotive ignition system is nothing more than an electromechanical switching device that is engine-operated. It serves two functions in the ignition system—to switch on and off the current supplying the coil's primary windings, and to distribute the coil's high-voltage secondary output according to the firing order of the engine.

On four-stroke engines, the distributor is customarily driven off the camshaft. In American-production cars this is accomplished by a pair of helical spiral gears—one on the distributor shaft and one on the cam. The ratio of these gears is 1:1. This means that like the camshaft, the distributor shaft turns at one-half engine crankshaft speed.

The switching of the primary circuit in a conventional distributor is accomplished by the breaker points—often simply called points. These are operated by a multilobed cam on the distributor shaft. In eight-cylinder engines this cam has eight lobes or ridges and eight flat spots, one for each cylinder. There are six lobes and six flat spots in the distributor of a six-cylinder engine, four in a four-cylinder distributor, etc. The points have attached to them a nylon or phenolic block that rides against this cam as it rotates.

As each lobe of the cam passes under and contacts this rubbing block, the points are opened. A lobe is immediately followed by a flat spot which allows the points to close by not contacting the rubbing block. At this time the points are kept closed by a spring, whose tension is very important to proper ignition operation. If the point spring is weak, the points will begin to "bounce" at high rpm, causing the timing to become very erratic. A spring that's too heavy promotes rapid wear of the rubbing block and the point gap will decrease with continued operation. This gradually results in a marked falloff in performance, as well as harder starting and a rough idle.

The distributor's high-tension or secondary circuit consists solely of the rotor and the cap into which the coil's high-tension cable and the plug cable leads are connected. The rotor is mounted on the end of the distributor shaft and conducts a spark to every cylinder of the engine with a complete rotation. The rotor is in permanent electrical contact with the center terminal of the distributor cap, which in turn is connected to the high-tension lead from the coil. The cap contains metal inserts cast into the individual plug cable towers to hold the distributor end of the plug cables. These inserts extend down inside the cap where they form a circle of electrical contacts.

The rotor is designed with a strap of metal long enough to reach close to this circle of contacts. Absolute physical contact between the rotor tip and the plug cable terminals in the cap is not necessary. There is always an air gap between the two, but one that requires only about 2000 to 3000 volts to carry the secondary current across the gap to the plug cables. The amount of cam rotation necessary to put the points through one complete closing and opening cycle is just enough to move the rotor tip from one plug cable contact to the next. Thus, a different plug is fired each time the points open.

SPARK ADVANCE

Just sending a spark to each cylinder is not enough—it has to get there at precisely the right time. At low engine speeds, the spark plug fires at approximately 3 to 10 degrees of crankshaft

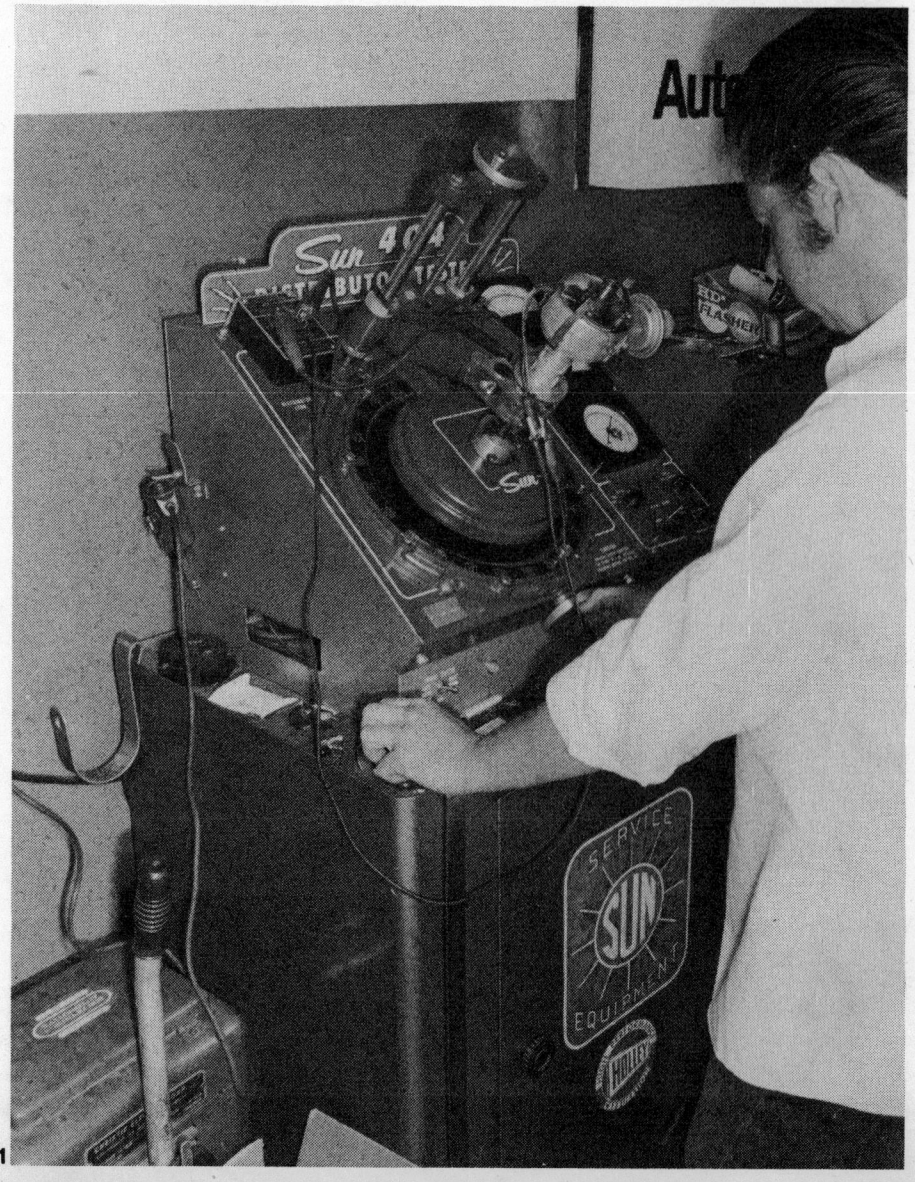
1

rotation *before* the piston reaches the top of its compression stroke. This gives the air-fuel mixture an instant to "light up" before it starts to expand and drive the piston down on its power stroke. The air-fuel mixture takes just about the same time to start burning at high engine speeds, but since the engine is turning faster, the piston has already started down before the expanding gases have developed their "push." An engine operating under these circumstances will definitely have a steady loss of power as engine speed increases. For this reason, the spark must be fired earlier at high rpm than at an idle. By moving the cam ahead of the distributor shaft, the cam lobes will open/close the points earlier, thus advancing the spark. Doing this is the job of the distributor's advance mechanisms.

There are currently three spark advances in common use. The first is the pure centrifugal type, found in special high-performance distributors. Ford high-performance cars, 1968-69 L88 427 Corvettes, VW transporters of the same vintage, and early VW Beetles, Porsches, and Formula Vee race cars were fitted with pure centrifugal-advance distributors. This unit operates quite simply by advancing the spark as engine rpm increases, and retarding it as rpm approaches idle. Its chief disadvantages are relatively poor low-speed economy, the possibility of excessive advance under certain full-throttle conditions, and high emissions.

The pure vacuum-advance distributor has had wide use both in the U.S. and abroad, but in recent years its only significant application was Ford's economy sixes fitted with Loadomatic distributors, and some VW passenger cars. Vacuum advances on VWs functioned well enough under most everyday driving conditions, but tended to limit top-speed and full-throttle acceleration. For this reason they are generally replaced with centrifugal-advance distributors when VW engines are installed in race cars or off-road buggies.

The third type of distributor uses both centrifugal and vacuum advances. This "dual-advance" distributor is found on virtually all domestic and foreign cars. The vacuum-advance unit receives its vacuum supply from one of two sources— either from *below* the throttle valves (intake manifold vacuum) or from a location *above* the carburetor throttle valves (spark-ported vacuum).

Manifold vacuum is highest at idle and decreases as the throttle valves open, but spark-ported vacuum functions differently. It is lowest at idle and increases with throttle opening. During idle and part-throttle running, manifold vacuum advances the spark for more economical operation, but when the throttle is opened, vacuum advance is not provided. This reduces the chances of engine "ping" or damaging detona-

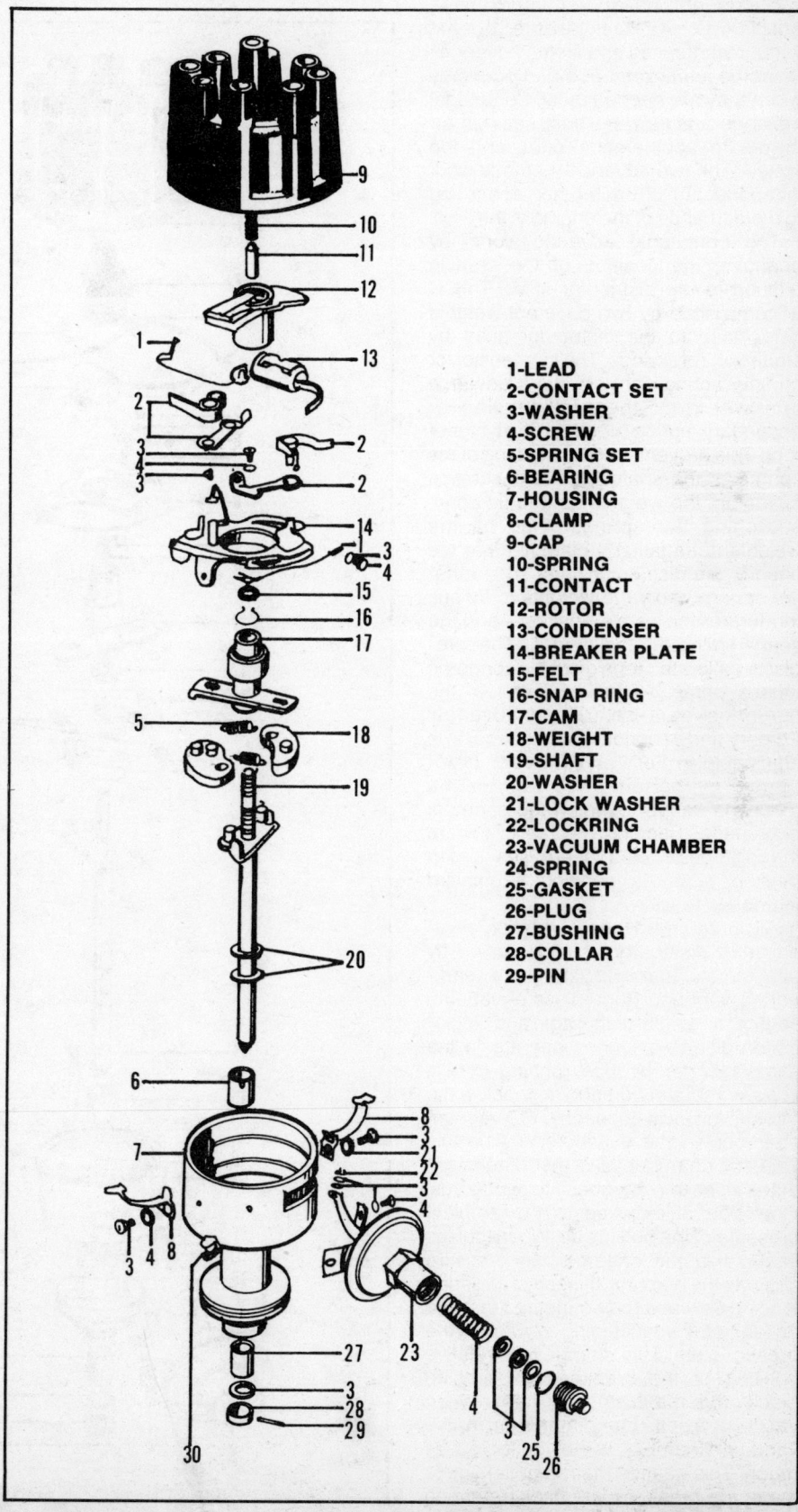

1-LEAD
2-CONTACT SET
3-WASHER
4-SCREW
5-SPRING SET
6-BEARING
7-HOUSING
8-CLAMP
9-CAP
10-SPRING
11-CONTACT
12-ROTOR
13-CONDENSER
14-BREAKER PLATE
15-FELT
16-SNAP RING
17-CAM
18-WEIGHT
19-SHAFT
20-WASHER
21-LOCK WASHER
22-LOCKRING
23-VACUUM CHAMBER
24-SPRING
25-GASKET
26-PLUG
27-BUSHING
28-COLLAR
29-PIN

1. *The best way to set up a breaker point distributor is to remove it from the engine and run it on a distributor tester. This will show up any shaft/bushing wear and determine whether the advance curve is correct.*

2. *This dual-point distributor was used on many Chrysler high-performance engines. Dual points increase dwell time, giving more coil saturation time. While one point is breaking the circuit, the other is closing it. After 1973, this unit was replaced by Chrysler's breakerless distributor.*

CONVENTIONAL DISTRIBUTORS

tion.

Spark-ported vacuum has been used since 1966 for emission reasons. Spark-ported vacuum is better tailored to the performance and economy demands of the engine. It is not available at idle or any other time the throttle closes, so the spark is not advanced under such conditions. As the throttle opens, vacuum increases and timing advances to increase performance and economy when they are needed most. Centrifugal advance ensures the best settings for maximum acceleration rates and top speed. The two advance methods work independently of each other, according to the demands of the engine at the time.

The centrifugal advance works by changing the position of the cam in relation to the distributor shaft. This is accomplished by two governor weights held close to the distributor shaft by small control springs. The low-tension or primary spring controls spark advance at lower rpm; the high-tension or secondary spring controls it at higher rpm. This prevents overadvancing of the spark. As the shaft's speed of rotation builds up, the weights tend to fly apart, stretching the springs. Pins on the weights act against a plate fitted to the base of the distributor cam. The further the springs allow the weights to fly out, the further the cam's position—and the spark timing—is advanced. The precisely calibrated tension of the springs is thus a prime controlling factor in the operation of a centrifugal advance. Primary and secondary spring tension is adjustable in Ford and Chrysler distributors by bending the tab on the mounting flange to which the spring is connected. Bending the tab in toward the distributor cam decreases spring tension, whereas bending it outward increases tension.

All vacuum-advance units on dual-advance distributors are controlled by either intake manifold vacuum or spark-ported vacuum. Regardless of vacuum source, all single-diaphragm and single-action-diaphragm units operate in the same manner. A tube running from a special vacuum port above or below the throttle valves is connected to a vacuum chamber on the distributor. Inside this vacuum chamber is a thin diaphragm that divides the chamber into two halves. One side is exposed to the ambient pressure of the outside air. When there is vacuum in the chamber, air pressure deflects the diaphragm against its spring loading so that a rod connected to it can advance the spark timing by rotating the breaker plate. This changes the relative position of the breaker-point rubbing block and the distributor cam. When vacuum drops, the diaphragm in the vacuum chamber is not deflected as much. This causes the rod or linkage to move the breaker plate back, retarding the spark timing slightly. The only significant departure from this system was the distributor used on older Chevrolet six-cylinder engines. On these engines, the vacuum unit moved the entire distributor body, not just the breaker plate.

Automakers provide accurate data on advance curves in the factory shop manual for a particular make and model car. Applying this information, however, requires special testing equipment not generally available to the home mechanic. The important thing to remember is that any defects that machine testing might uncover are usually the direct result of dirt, lack of lubrication, wear, or faulty parts in the distributor.

POINTS

The breaker points are the key electrical part of the distributor. They

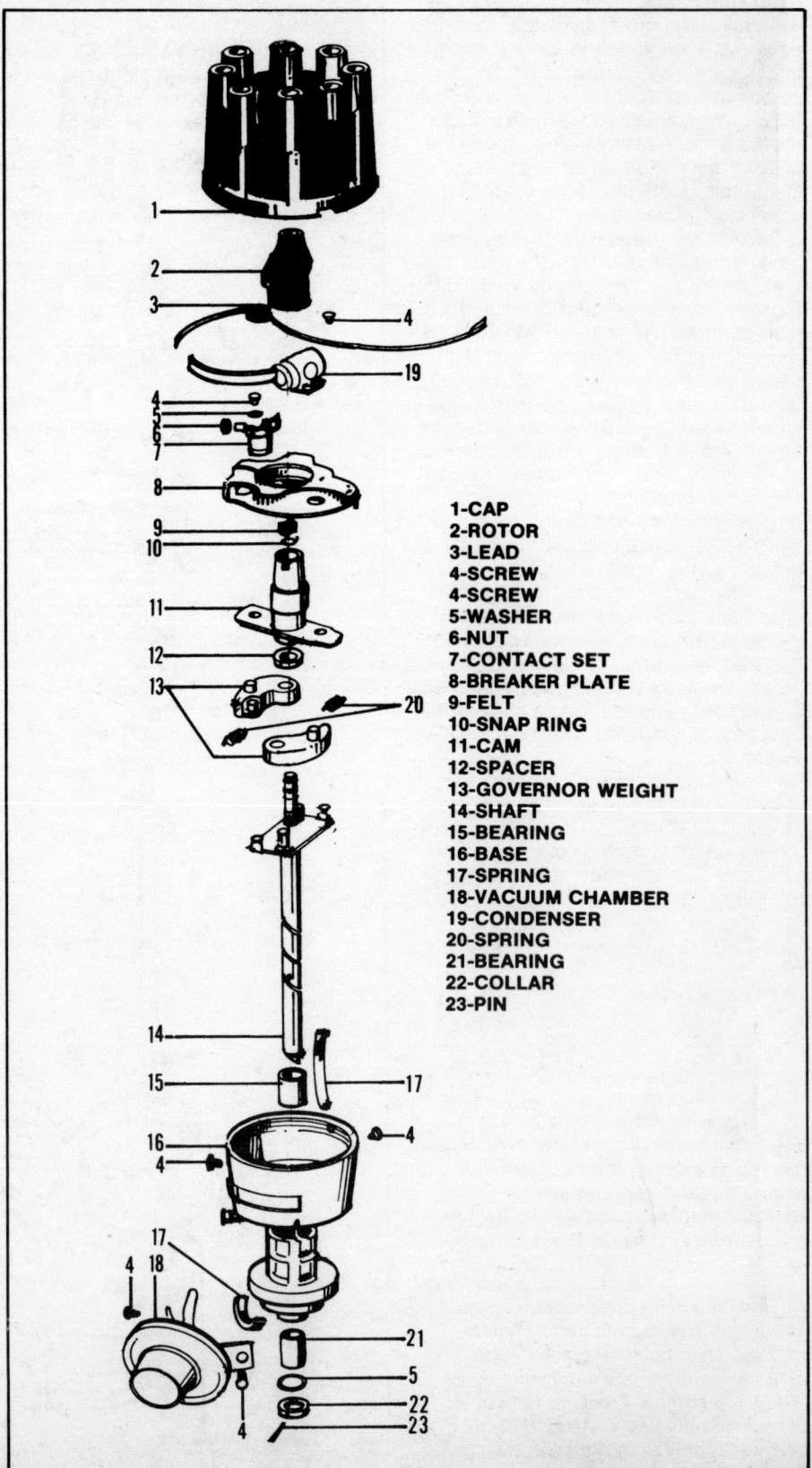

1-CAP
2-ROTOR
3-LEAD
4-SCREW
4-SCREW
5-WASHER
6-NUT
7-CONTACT SET
8-BREAKER PLATE
9-FELT
10-SNAP RING
11-CAM
12-SPACER
13-GOVERNOR WEIGHT
14-SHAFT
15-BEARING
16-BASE
17-SPRING
18-VACUUM CHAMBER
19-CONDENSER
20-SPRING
21-BEARING
22-COLLAR
23-PIN

control not only the primary current flow in the ignition system, but ultimately the engine's spark timing as well. How long the points stay closed has a very important relationship to coil "saturation." The longer the points feed battery current into the coil's primary windings, the stronger the magnetic field becomes. As a result, greater spark voltages are produced.

There is a limit, however, to how long the points can remain closed effectively, because of the design of the distributor cam. The time during which the points remain together is called the *cam angle* or *dwell.* Both terms refer to the number of degrees of distributor rotation during which the points remain closed. The initial gap to which the points are adjusted determines dwell. Although there is a specific tolerance for these settings, efficiency is lost beyond a certain point. If the points are set too wide, they will open gradually. This can cause excessive arcing and burning of the contacts. It also shortens the coil-saturation time. If the points are set too close, dwell time is increased, but point bounce often occurs at higher speeds, the idle becomes rough, and starting is more difficult.

Dual or two sets of breaker points have been used in distributors to overcome the problem of coil saturation vs. efficient point operation. The dual points accomplish their purpose by being wired into the primary circuit in such a way that battery current flows to the coil when either set is closed. Their position relative to the cam is staggered, so that one set opens before the other. The spark isn't fired, however, until the second set opens to break finally the primary connection. But the first set is already starting to close when the second set fires the spark. The first set will thus have been closed for many degrees before the set of points that actually initiated the spark.

The result is a greatly increased total dwell time over that available from a single-point distributor. This increased dwell lengthens the coil-saturation time to produce a hotter spark. In addition, the breaker-arm spring tension is greater, reducing the possibility of point bounce at high engine rpm.

Traditionally, the point set has been designed in two parts—the stationary contact assembly and the movable contact assembly. The stationary assembly is grounded to the breaker plate in the distributor and includes the breaker-point pivot post. The movable assembly is insulated from ground and connected to both the condenser lead and the primary wire from the coil. The movable contact assembly also includes the rubbing block that rides against the cam, as well as the spring that closes the contacts. To simplify point installation, most manufacturers now preassemble the two into a single contact set assembly.

CONDENSER

The consenser does several things in the ignition system. Its primary purpose is to create a clean cutoff of current flow when the points open. Current that might arc across the space between the points finds the condenser more attractive and rushes into it to create an unbalanced condition. Without the condenser, induced current in the primary would flow across the point gap, bleeding off the energy in the coil and resulting in no spark at the plug. Reducing arcing at the points in this way results in longer point life.

The condenser is a very rugged and reliable part of the ignition system. There is absolutely no reason to replace it unless actual testing proves it to be weak. Nor is there any need to replace the condenser with each change of points, although this is a routine practice by tuneup mechanics. The construction of the condenser has a definite bearing on its efficiency and resistance to failure. Inside the sealed case are two rolled strips of foil separated from each other in sandwich fashion by strips of thin paper impregnated with an insulating compound (waxed paper or mica). One strip is pressed into contact with the condenser case, while the other presses against a metal disc soldered to the condenser's lead wire.

Two problems can develop with the condenser, both of which are typical with inexpensive, off-brand types. Poor contact of the foil with either the condenser case or the lead-in wire will cause failure, as vibration causes interrupted contact that results in erratic ignition. The use of a low-quality dielectric (insulation) will permit moisture absorption or rapid current leakage. A high-quality condenser combined with a clean, tight installation should prevent condenser troubles.

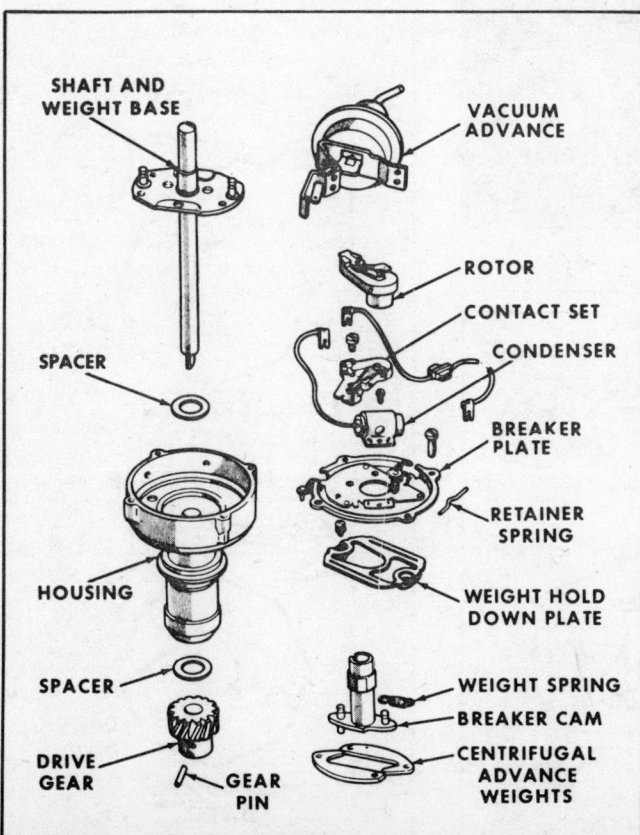

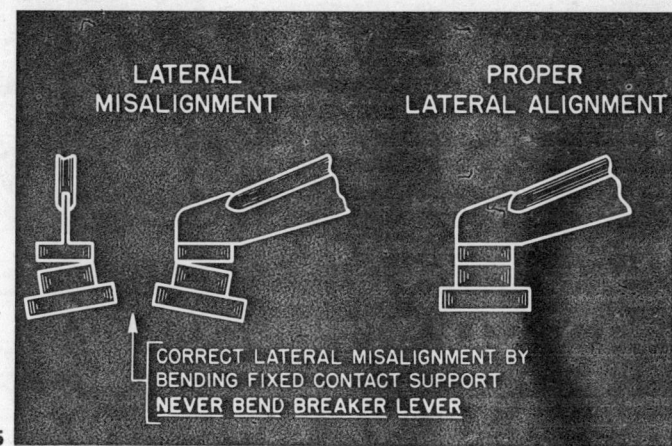

3. An exploded view of a typical Chrysler 8-cylinder distributor shows the centrifugal advance weights located below the breaker plate. The "bearings" are actually bronze bushings.

4. A typical GM 6-cylinder distributor with its centrifugal advance weights located under the breaker plate in the distributor bowl.

5. Bad point alignment shortens point life considerably. The result of insufficient point contact is a poor spark.

CONVENTIONAL DISTRIBUTORS

The condenser is often suspected when an engine misfires at high speed, or if the breaker points become burned and pitted after only a short time in service. Simply changing the condenser, however, may not solve the problem. The misfiring could be caused by spark plugs or high-tension cables that have an excess voltage requirement, and oil on the points may be responsible for the burning and pitting of the contacts.

Contact-point pitting, however, generally results from an out-of-balance condition in the ignition system, causing transfer of tungsten from one contact point to the other. The result is a "mountain" on one contact and a "valley" in the other. The direction in which the material transfer occurs can be used as a basis for analysis and correction of the pitting. For example, if the material transfers from the negative contact point to the positive (the movable point on negative-ground cars), either the condenser capacity needs to be increased within the specifications given by the car maker, or the condenser has become weak and must be replaced. If the material transfer takes place in the opposite direction—from positive to negative—the condenser is over the proper capacity and must be replaced by one with a lower rating.

When testing for capacity, the condenser should be tapped lightly to show up poor internal contact and hidden weaknesses. Some service garages have condenser testers and can check the unit in your car if it is suspected of malfunctioning, but if this equipment is not available, a test condenser is a handy substitute. This is simply a standard ignition condenser with two leads equipped with test clips soldered onto it. One clip can be placed on a good ground somewhere on the distributor housing and the other snapped onto the distributor's primary terminal. This hookup replaces or augments the condenser in the system.

If the original condenser is causing the trouble, attaching the test condenser will immediately clear things up, unless the old one is grounded. In that case, you must disconnect it to allow the test condenser to do its job. Before throwing out the old condenser, make certain that the real trouble is not simply a loose or high-resistance connection.

In many cases, apparent condenser trouble is caused by a poor ground contact. A high percentage of condenser problems can be eliminated by simply making sure that all external connections are clean and tight. This applies particularly to the condenser mounting strap, which must be in good electrical contact with the distributor. When installing a new condenser or replacing one after testing, the mounting strap and the part of the distributor to which it attaches should be brightened with emery paper to ensure a perfect ground for the case.

POINT ALIGNMENT

For maximum efficiency and minimum deterioration, the breaker-point contacts must meet accurately, both horizontally and vertically as well as at 0-degree angle. If the mismatching is severe, you should probably return the points to the dealer, but in most cases, a little judicious bending of the stationary contact mount will correct minor alignment problems. Any major bending is of questionable merit when weighed against the possibility of irreparable damage. Point alignment problems are seldom encountered with single contact assemblies manufactured by reputable companies.

The points supplied for many foreign cars may have a fiber washer installed on the breaker-point pivot post between the stationary and movable point assemblies. This washer can be filed to correct the vertical alignment errors, since the construction of the movable point arm is such that bending it is impossible.

INSTALLING BREAKER POINTS

Many troubles experienced with ignition points can be avoided by proper installation and maintenance. Breaker points can be removed and replaced with the distributor in the car provided the location of the distributor provides easy access and an uninterrupted line of sight. Unfortunately, many distributors are hard to reach when installed on the engine. It's a good idea to remove the distributor from the engine when replacing the points. This provides an opportunity to clean the housing and the inside of the distributor bowl, properly lubricate the unit, and check advance operation. A typical breaker-point installation with the distributor removed from the engine is shown in a pictorial sequence following this chapter.

Remove the distributor cap and aim the rotor at the No. 1 cylinder. Mark the position of the distributor body relative to the engine so that lines and wires will

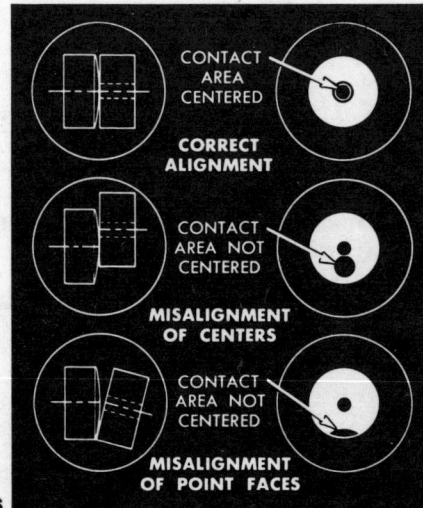

6

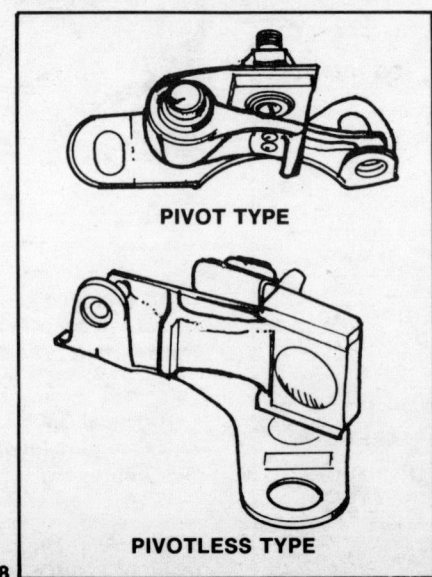

8

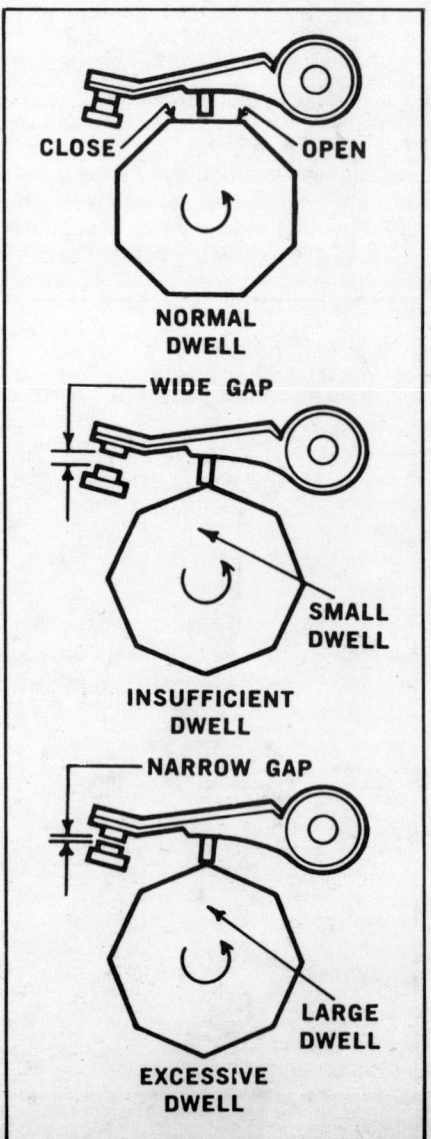

7

hook up easily when you put it back. Remove the distributor holddown clamp and pull the distributor straight up and out of the engine. One of two things will happen when you do this. The rotor may not move at all, or it may rotate just a small amount as the helical gears disengage.

If the distributor is the type driven by the oil pump gear, the rotor will not turn. When you remove the unit, you will see no gear on the end of the distributor shaft. If it does turn, remember or mark the rotor's final position relative to its original location. When reinstalling the unit, all that is necessary is to place the rotor in the final position and insert it into the engine. The gears should engage

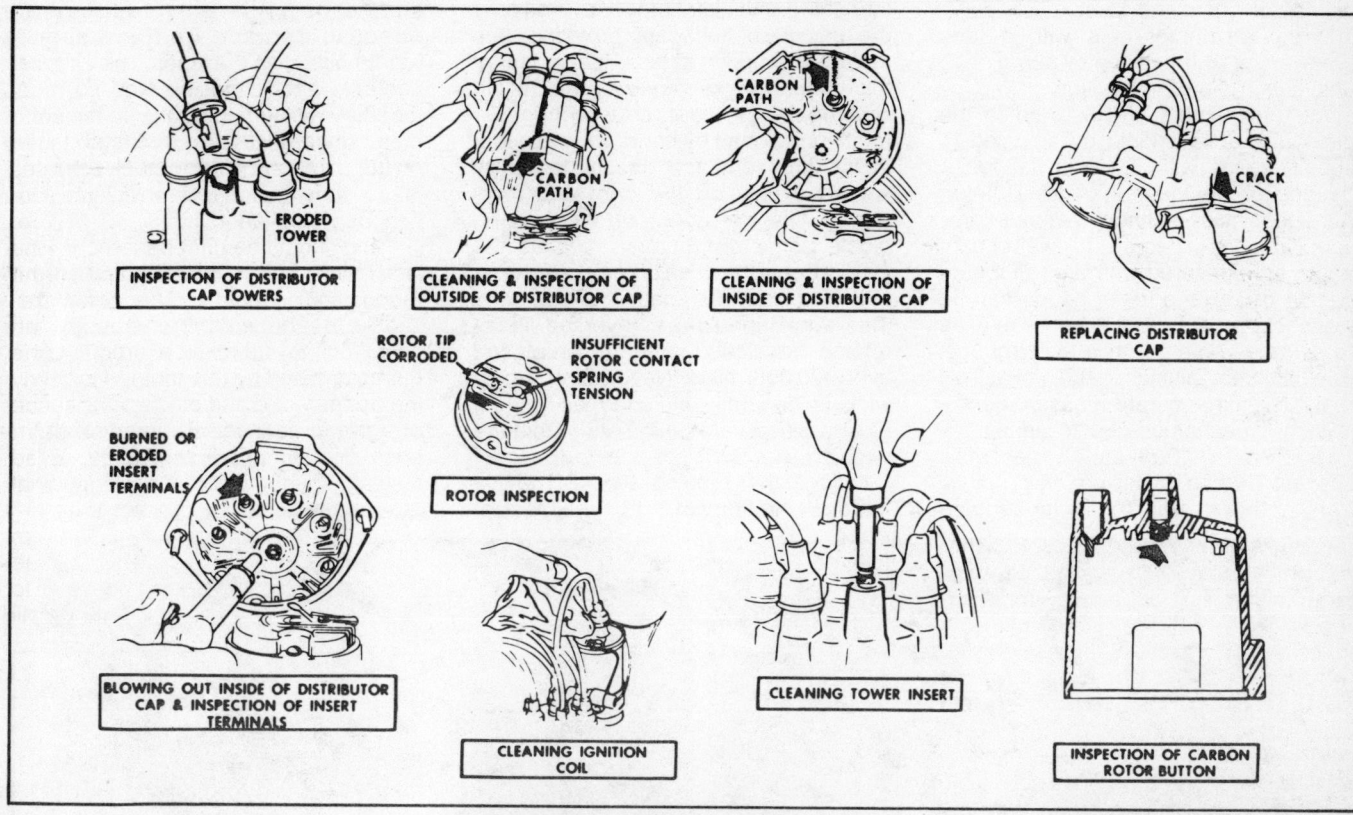

6. Points should be aligned by bending the stationary contact only. Don't worry about breaking it off; it's made of metal that will take quite a bit of flexing.

7. Dwell is small with a wide gap, but as the rubbing block begins to wear, the gap closes and dwell increases.

8. Autolite-Ford points come in two types. The regular pivot type can be used if you don't care for the pivotless kind.

9. Visual inspection of the distributor cap, rotor and coil can reveal numerous trouble spots. Early detection and correction will prevent more serious problems down the road.

10. Late model Delco 8-cylinder distributors use a 2-piece RFI shield to reduce radio interference from the condenser wire.

IGNITION & ELECTRICAL SYSTEMS/35

CONVENTIONAL DISTRIBUTORS

and turn the rotor back to its initial position. On some cars, the oil pump drive may not align with the tang on the distributor shaft end. Just reach down into the distributor hole with a long screwdriver and turn the oil pump drive until it is in the right position.

After the points are installed in the distributor, they should be adjusted to specifications with a set of flat feeler gauges or an electronic dwell meter. Although most service manuals give specifications in degrees of dwell or cam angle as measured with a dwell meter, setting gap with a feeler gauge can be just about as accurate. But don't ever try to set used points with a feeler gauge. The slightest pitting of the points will result in an inaccurate measurement.

Some mechanics like to adjust the gap .002- to .003-inch wider than specified when installing new points. This compensates for initial rubbing block wear. If you want top performance from the new set of points immediately, it's a better practice simply to recheck the gap after a few hundred miles or so.

Rubbing block wear can be a real problem unless the cam is properly lubricated with distributor cam grease or the packet of lubricant provided with replacement point sets. A light smear of this grease works very well for limiting rubbing block wear and friction. By rotating the shaft by hand, you can work in the lubricant and ensure that it is spread evenly on the cam and thoroughly fills the pores of the rubbing block. Some distributors, such as the Delco-Remy, have an oil-saturated wick that distributes lubrication to the cam. This wick should be reversed in its retainer at 12,000 miles and replaced every 20,000 miles. Never oil it. A new wick is generally included as part of most replacement point sets. Avoid the circular files sold for the purpose of "seating" the rubbing block. The file removes the burnish put on the block at the factory and leaves a rough surface that wears out much faster.

Smoothing used points with a point file is of little value. While badly pitted points can be made reusable by filing them, the surfaces are left rougher than they should be. This only reduces the effective contact area and speeds further pitting on the faces. The tungsten contacts should not be filed so much that they will burn through into the softer metal underneath. The tungsten facing on the contacts of many stock point sets is so thin that even one filing can seriously weaken it.

Filing should be undertaken only as a last resort, and is only the first step in reconditioning points. After filing, they should be honed mirror-smooth with either a fine stone or a crocus cloth. Points dressed by this method will have the appearance and efficiency (almost) of a brand-new set. Be very careful to hone the surfaces absolutely flat. A bulging, rounded contour will severely reduce the effective contact area and

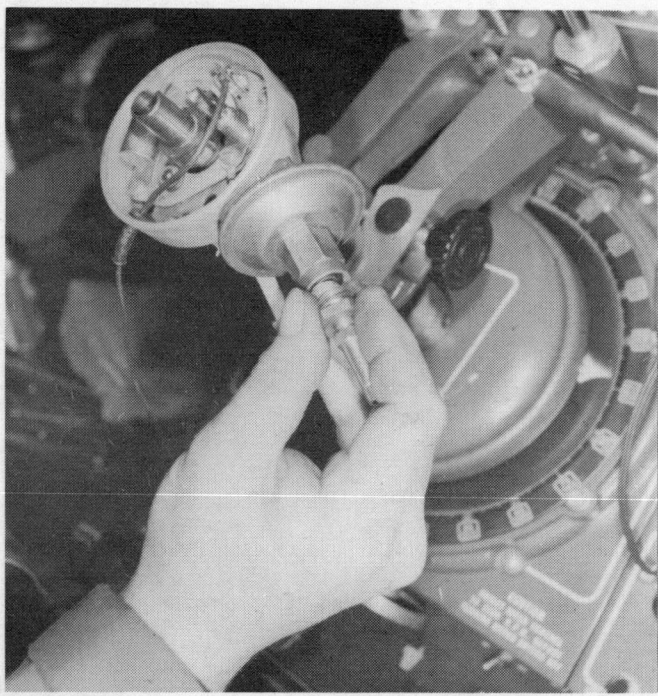
11

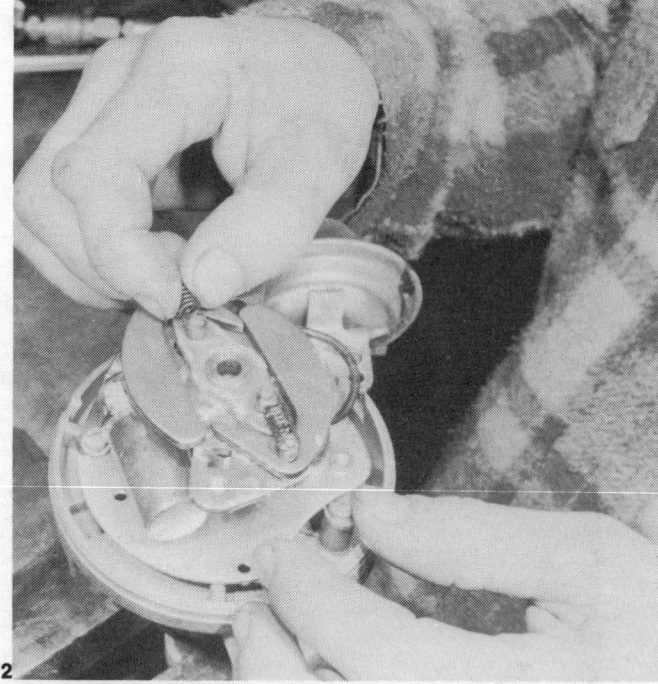
12

13

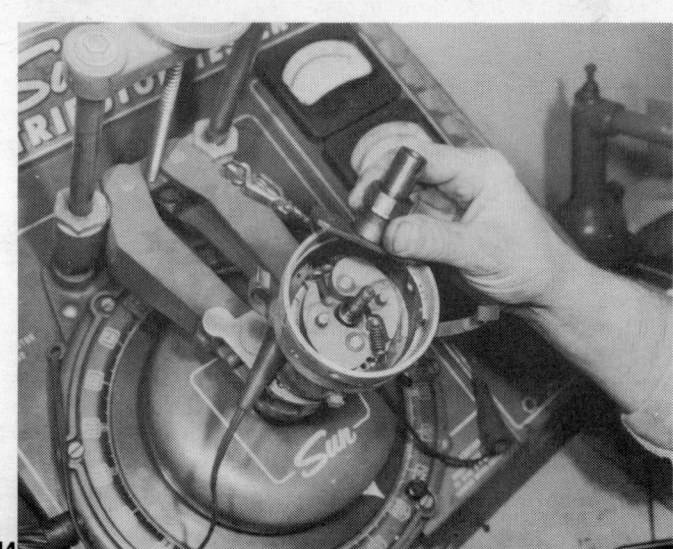
14

result in excessive localized burning. After filing, honing, and polishing, the points may require a slight realignment as described earlier. Remember, points that show signs of severe burning and discoloration, or that have developed deep pits, indicate an imbalance in the ignition system which must be corrected or the trouble will soon recur.

Contact-point burning may result from an abnormally high primary voltage or the presence of oil or other foreign matter on the point surfaces. Oil or crankcase vapors that work up around the distributor shaft are a frequent cause of point burning, but one that is easy to detect since the oil produces a smudgy line on the distributor's breaker plate directly under the contacts. Overoiled parts, clogged engine breather pipes, or a plugged PCV valve is the usual cause of this. Anything other than a lightly frosted appearance of the contacts should be considered abnormal.

TIMING THE ENGINE

If you accidentally rotate the engine while the distributor is out, remove the spark plug from the No. 1 cylinder. Hold your thumb over the plug hole while an assistant turns the engine over. Stop when the piston is at top dead center (TDC) on the compression stroke, as evidenced by the compressed air pushing your thumb away from the hole. Practice this several times until you are certain that the piston is on top dead center of the compression stroke. If it is, the slash or mark on the crankshaft pulley or flywheel should align with the

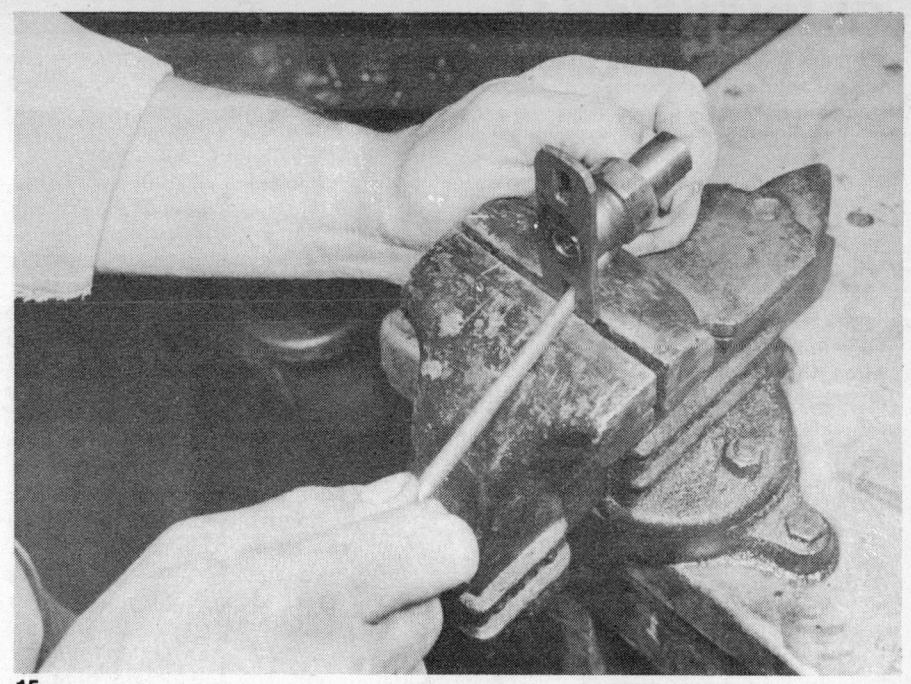
15

11. Some Ford vacuum advance mechanisms can be adjusted by changing the washer thickness on the plunger shaft.

12. Delco V-8 distributors carry the centrifugal advance weights on top of the distributor shaft where they can be easily inspected and cleaned.

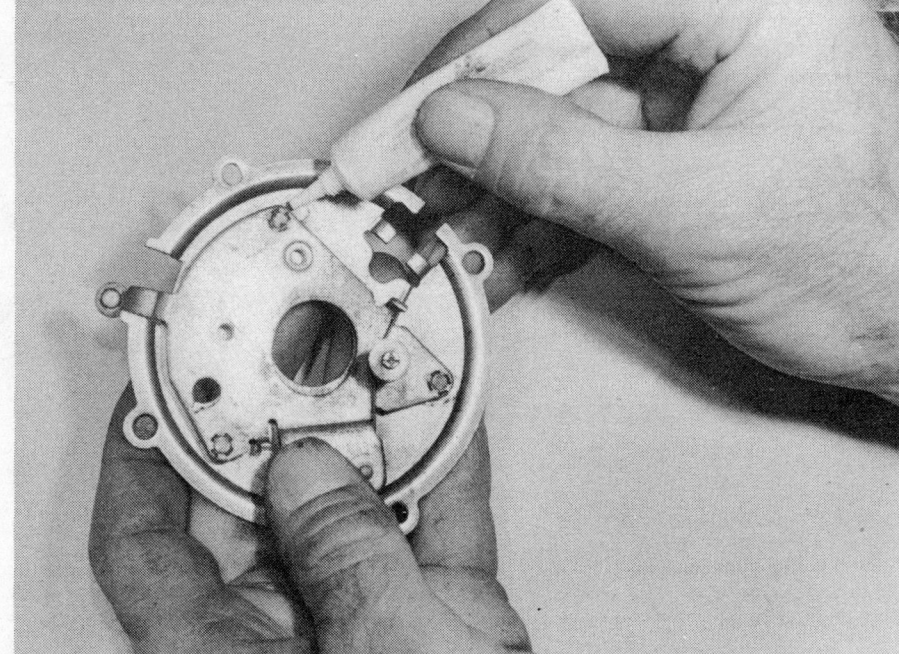
16

13. Other distributor designs place the centrifugal advance weights under the cam breaker plate. A tiny lock ring must be taken out of the cam assembly before it can be removed.

14. Once the lock ring is removed, you can get to the centrifugal advance mechanism for cleaning and inspection.

15. The centrifugal advance curve can be changed by filing out or brazing in the cam assembly slots. This increases or restricts advance weight movement.

16. Clean the breaker plate, then check it for wear. Lubricate with cam grease before reinstalling it.

17. The pivot shafts should also be lubricated before installing the weights.

17

IGNITION & ELECTRICAL SYSTEMS/37

CONVENTIONAL DISTRIBUTORS

stationary mark on the engine. If the stationary mark is calibrated in degrees, then the slash should align with 0 degrees—this is TDC. If you can see the piston through the hole or feel it with a broom straw, the TDC positioning is completely verified.

Once you have the piston at TDC in the No. 1 cylinder, find out which wire goes to that cylinder. It will be easy if the wires and cap are still in position on the engine. Now insert the distributor so that the rotor points directly to the No. 1 cylinder wire tower in the cap (in an installed position) and position the distributor body so that the points are just about to open. To determine exactly when the points open, place a piece of tissue or thin paper between them. The instant the points start to open, the paper will come loose.

If you keep the rotor pointing to the correct wire tower and are sure that the points are just about to open, you can insert the distributor in any position relative to the engine block. It makes no difference to the timing of the engine, but only the original stock position will let you put the cap on the distributor without twisting the wires into a pretzel. If you put the distributor body back in its original position, any vacuum lines or wires can be properly connected without difficulty.

Snug down the distributor holddown bolt and connect all the wires and cap. The engine should fire up. If it won't, you made one of two common mistakes: (1) you thought the points were positioned about to open when they were actually about to close, (2) the piston was on the exhaust stroke instead of the compression stroke.

Suppose someone not only turned the engine over with the distributor out but also pulled all the wires out of the cap? To solve this problem, you must know the firing order and cylinder numbering sequence of the engine. The firing order is usually stamped on the intake manifold or other visible engine location. Many distributor caps also have the No. 1 cylinder wire tower marked with a "1." If the cap is not so marked, time any one cap tower to the No. 1 cylinder. Then connect the next segment in the distributor cap to the next cylinder in the firing order until you have worked your way around the cap in the direction of rotation. Be sure to position the distributor body to allow easy hookup of any vacuum lines, tach drives, etc.

TROUBLESHOOTING THE DISTRIBUTOR

In many cases, you can detect improper distributor operation by the way the car behaves. Slow cranking when the engine is warm, backfiring, noticeable losses in performance, ragged idling, "breaking up" at high speeds—these are some of the usual symptoms. If the compression is good, the carburetor properly adjusted and not leaking, and the ignition system in othewise perfect shape, the distributor and its advance mechanisms deserve a close inspection. Just by checking, cleaning, and lubricating the distributor each time you install new points, you can usually prevent most trouble before it ever affects the engine's operation.

On many cars, you can check the condition of the diaphragm in the vacuum-advance mechanism quite easily without even removing the distributor from the engine. Just disconnect the vacuum line from the distributor to the carburetor and take the cap off the distributor. Move the breaker plate by hand until the full-advanced position is reached. Place your finger over the vacuum port and release the breaker plate. It should move only very slightly and then stop. After a few seconds, remove your finger from the vacuum port. The advance mechanism should now snap back to the full-retarded position.

If placing your finger over the vacuum port will not hold the plate in the advanced position, the diaphragm is leaking and the entire vacuum chamber unit will have to be replaced. If the plate does not snap back to the retard position when the vacuum port is uncovered, the advance parts are binding or the spring is broken. If the advance plate is binding or sticking, it can usually be put back into serviceable condition by taking it out, cleaning it, and lubricating it—a broken spring will require a new vacuum chamber unit.

Three things can impair the efficiency of centrifugal-advance mechanisms. The most common is dirt and lack of lubrication. After a year's service, the average centrifugal advance should be removed, cleaned, checked for wear, and properly lubricated. This is absolutely necessary if precise action is to be obtained. The weights and linkage of the centrifugal advance must be completely clean and lightly lubricated with engine

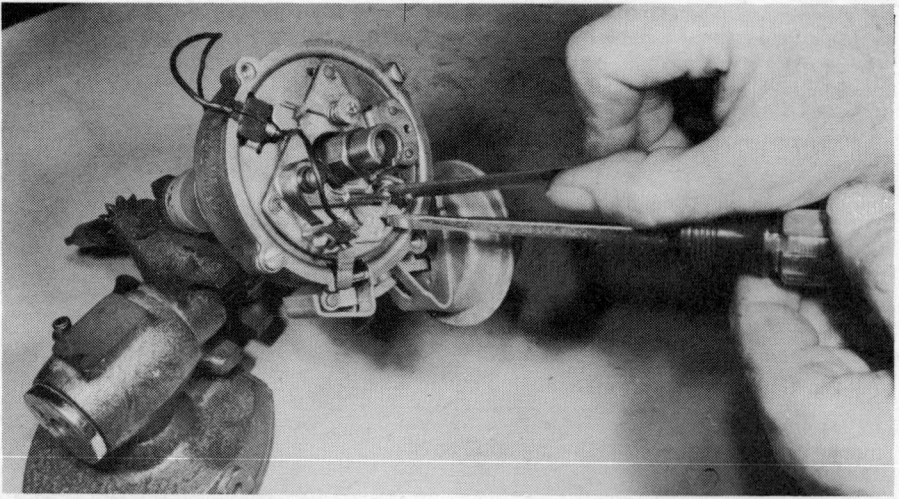

18

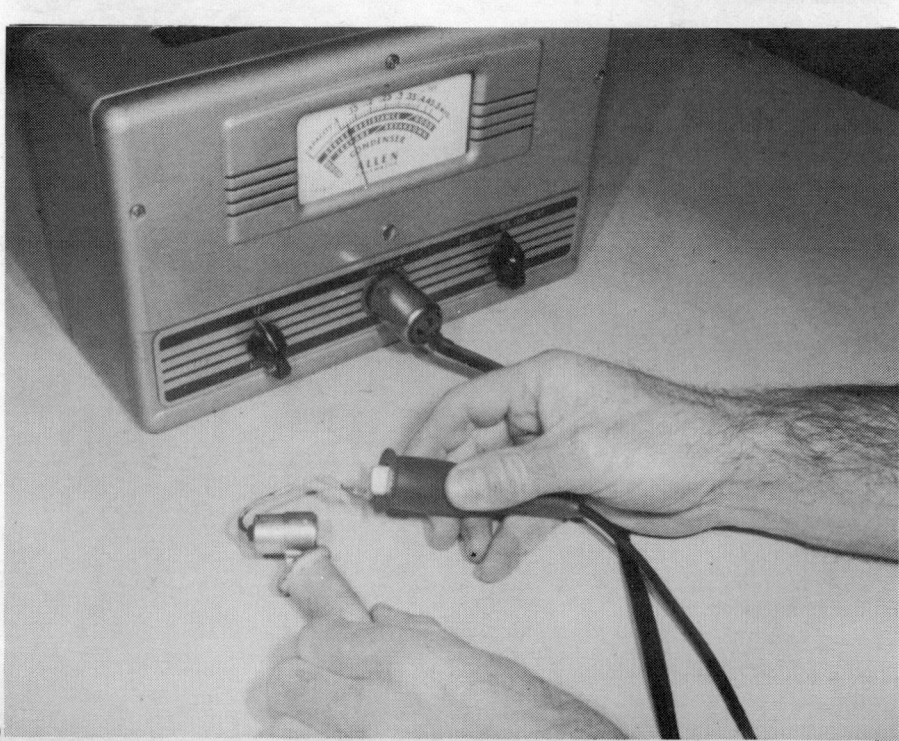

19

oil. Most distributors have a felt wick in the center of the distributor cam which needs to be regularly given a few drops of oil to keep the centrifugal-advance mechanism properly oiled. Also check the weights to see that they are free from rust or burrs, which tend to hinder their smooth movement.

Second, wear in the distributor shaft, its bearings, thrust washers, or cam can seriously disrupt the timing and functioning of the centrifugal advance. If the distributor shaft can be shaken noticeably from side to side (with the holddown clamp removed), the shaft or its bearings are worn. Shaft end play should be no greater than .012- to .015-inch. Removing the clamp permits the distributor to move, so timing should be checked after testing for end play. Older distributors have replaceable bushings in their housing. When replaceable, the bushings or bearings can be removed with a bushing driver or an arbor press. It's best to have this work done at an automotive machine shop.

Excessive end play can usually be corrected by installing new thrust washers on the shaft. The repair is made by driving out the pin that holds the drive gear and removing the gear from the shaft. Withdraw the shaft from the housing and roll it on a flat surface to check for straightness. If satisfactory, reinsert the shaft into the housing, slip the washers on, and press the gear in position to be pinned.

If the distributor cam shows any visible wear, it is seriously affecting the engine's timing. In most cases, this is a very inexpensive part that can be installed in a few minutes. Proper cam lubrication usually prevents such trouble. A badly lubed cam can also affect the operation of both the centrifugal and vacuum advances by slowing the motion of the cam and breaker plate. To function perfectly, a distributor must be kept as friction-free as possible.

One final factor that can affect the accuracy of centrifugal-advance units is incorrect point spring tension. Like a poorly lubricated cam, this may also affect the operation of the vacuum-advance system to some degree. The point spring tension should be adjusted if possible, but incorrect spring tension is often the result of installing the wrong points in the distributor.

Incorrect springs installed in the centrifugal advance can also affect its precision. When replacing any distributor parts, make certain they are the correct ones for your particular distributor, since the same distributor may be used in many different makes and models but with different advance rates. Each time you change the points, mark the exact location of the distributor to ensure correct reinstallation and then remove it. Clean the unit thoroughly, inspect it for wear and lubricate it properly. You'll not only save yourself the cost of many repairs; your engine will run better.

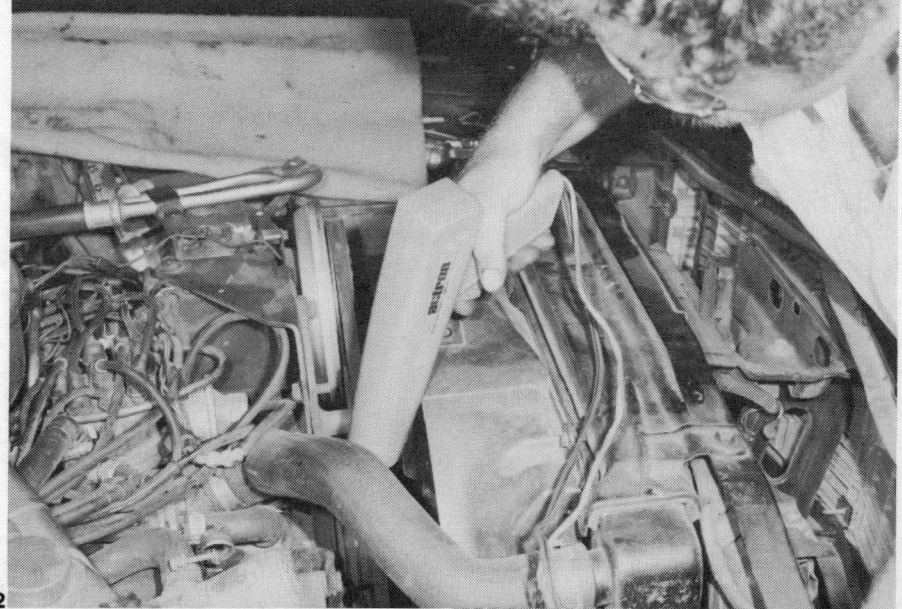

18. You can set point gap with the distributor out of the car, but you'll probably have to reset it once you've installed the distributor.

19. Most people simply throw the condenser away and install a new one whenever they change the points. A condenser tester is most useful for troubleshooting a condenser suspected of being defective.

20. Delco came out with its Uniset combined points and condenser in 1972 but were forced to take them off the market for awile. They came back with the Uniset in 1974, just before points were eliminated entirely. Static shields are unnecessary with the Uniset.

21. Cracks or splits in the distributor cap allow moisture and contamination inside the unit. Replace such caps before you have an ignition failure.

22. Initial timing must always be checked and reset whenever you make any ignition adjustments.

HOW-TO: BREAKER POINT REPLACEMENT

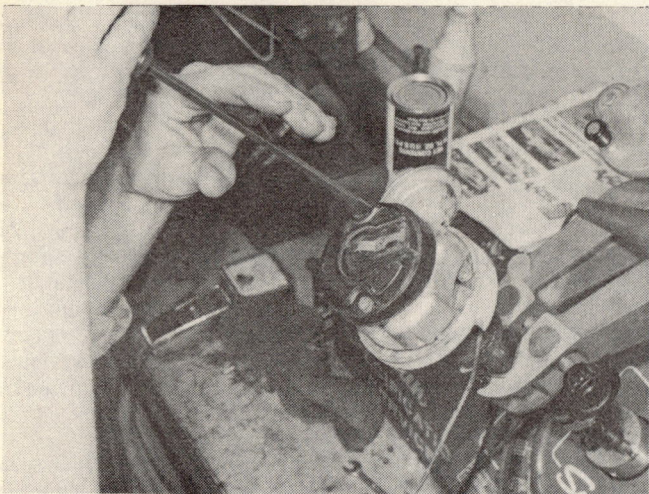

1. To replace breaker points on a Delco-Remy V-8 distributor, remove the distributor cap. Loosen rotor attaching screws and lift the rotor up and off the advance mechanism.

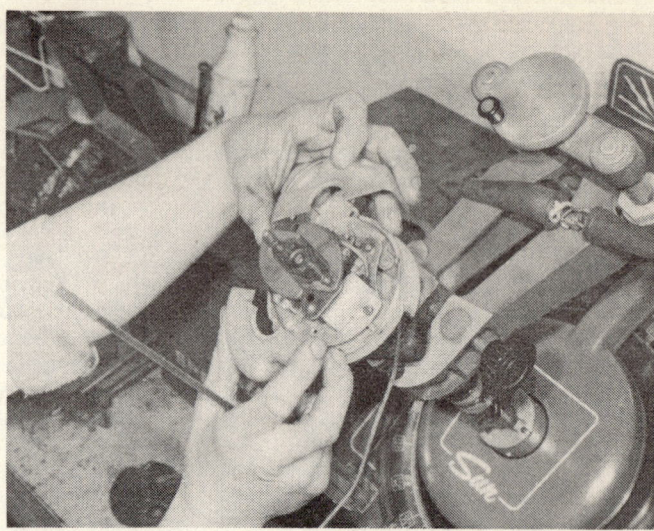

2. Unless previously discarded, an RFI shield is positioned over the breaker points on non-Uni-Set distributors. Remove attaching shield screws, separate shield and remove.

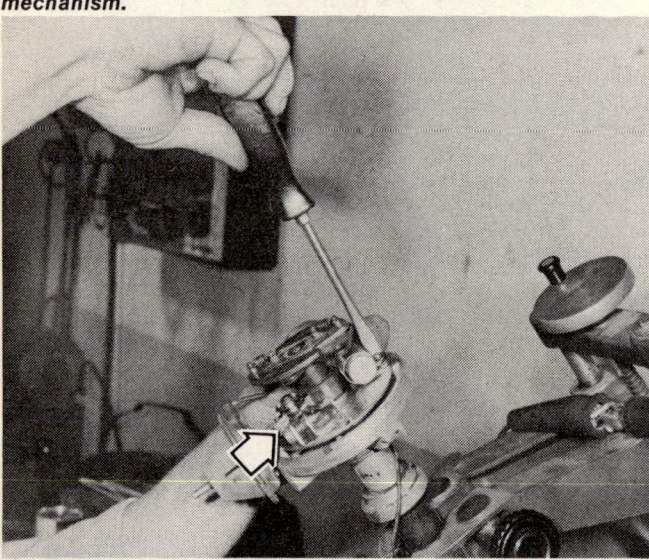

3. Disconnect breaker point and condenser leads from push-in terminal (arrow). Loosen condenser bracket screw and slide condensor out of bracket.

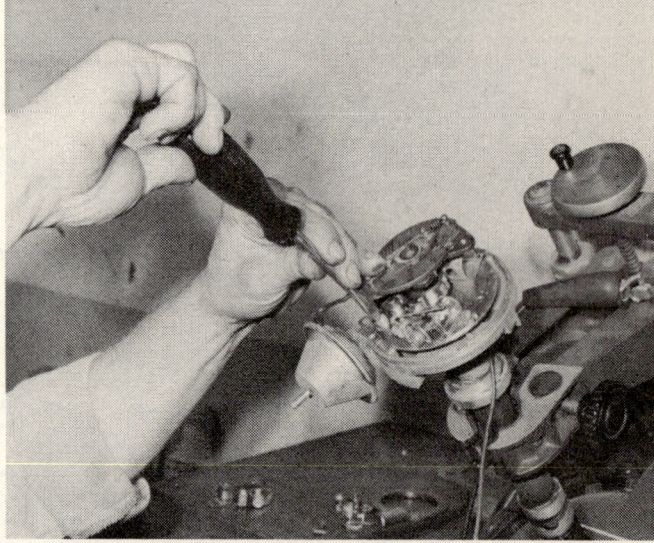

4. Breaker point set is held to breaker plate with a single screw and a pivot pin which fits into slot on breaker plate. Remove screw and lift off point assembly.

5. Since the advance weights are on top, it's easy to keep this distributor design clean and functioning well. Remove dirt and grease with solvent and a brush.

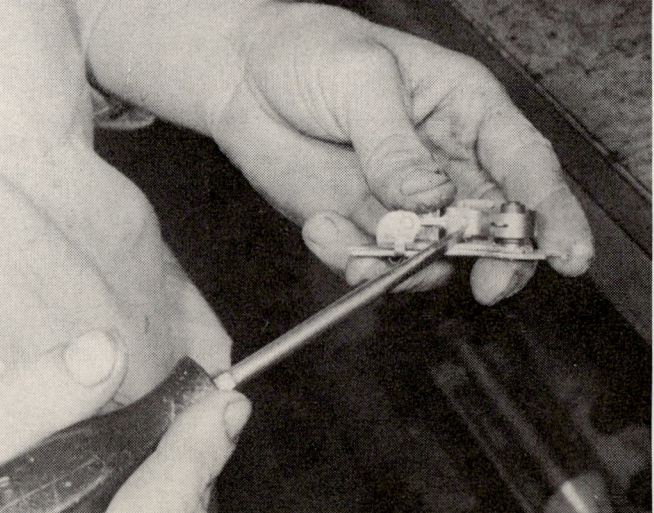

6. Check new point set to make sure that points are in proper vertical and horizontal alignment. If not, get another set—do not try to bend this type into adjustment.

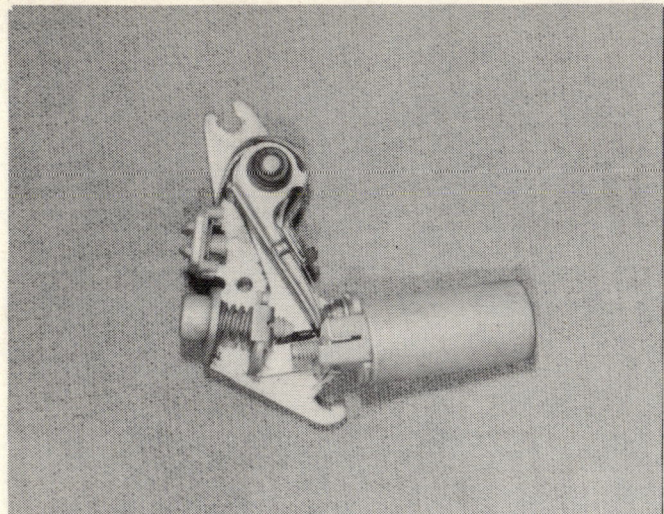

7. This is the point set for a Uni-set distributor used in the mid-Seventies. It combines the points, condenser and dwell adjusting screw in one unit—and was loved by none.

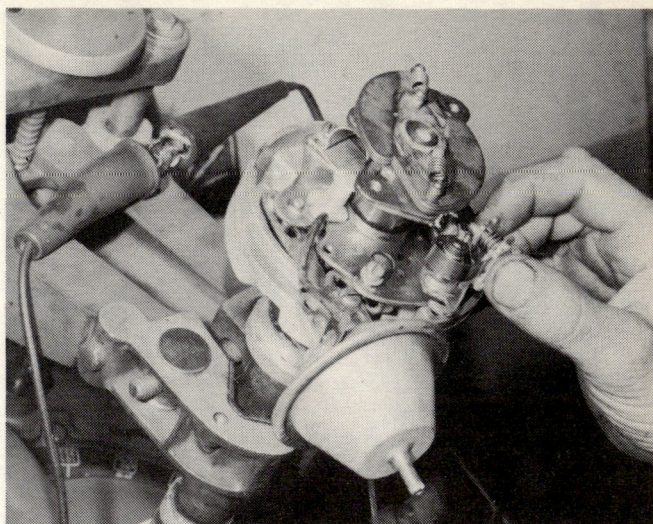

8. Install breaker point set on breaker plate. Place pivot pin of new point set in plate cutout and swing into place under the attaching screw, then tighten screw.

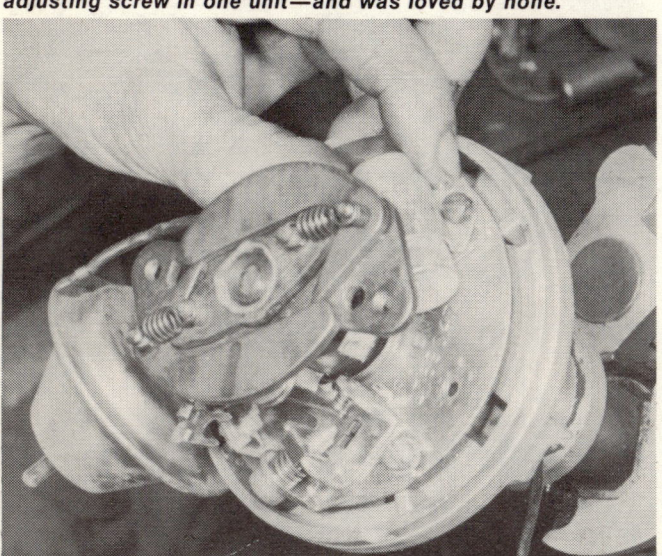

9. Install the new condenser by slipping it into the bracket with the lead on the left side until it's centered, then tightening the hold-down screw.

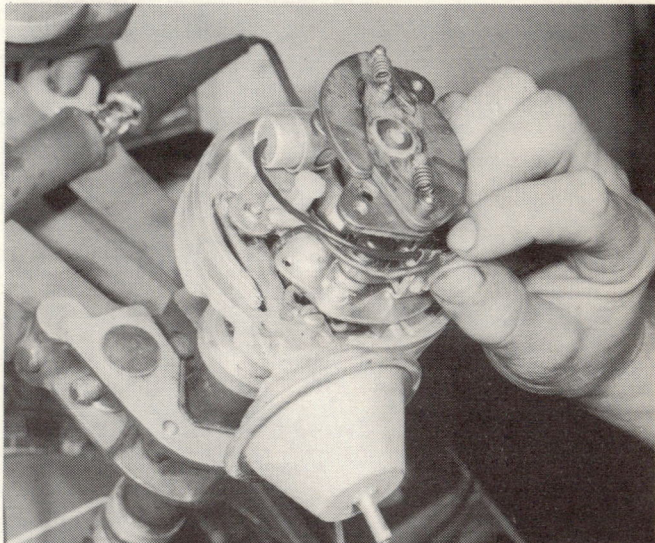

10. Fold point set and condenser leads around distributor to push-in terminal connector as shown. Make sure leads will not contact RFI shield when it's reinstalled.

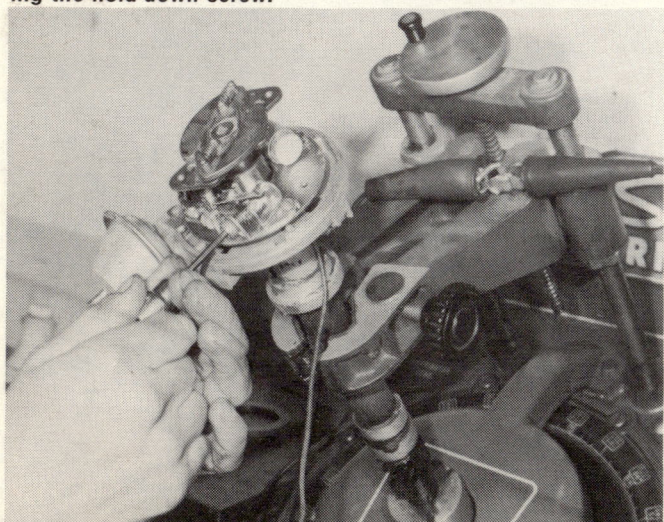

11. If distributor is in car, replace cap, open its metal window and set point dwell with engine running. Here, we set dwell to provide specified gap before installing it in car.

12. It's also a good idea to run the distributor on a tester to check the operation of the advance mechanisms and the advance curves. When everything's right, reinstall in car.

HOW-TO: DISTRIBUTOR CARE

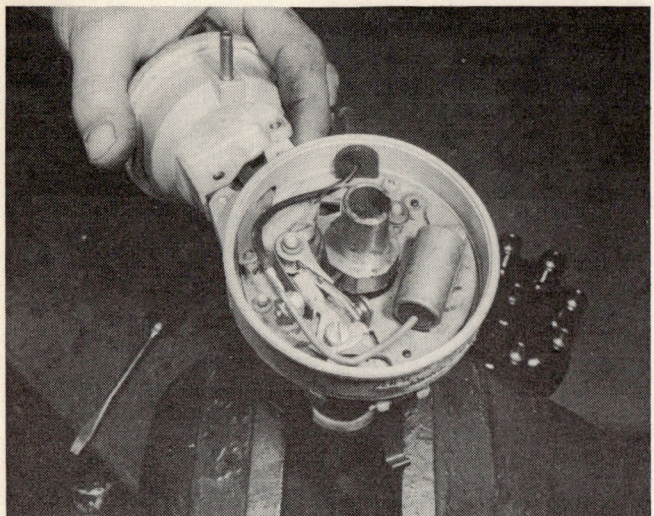

1. To strip down Motorcraft, Chrysler or comparable breaker point distributor, remove vacuum advance attaching screws, lift advance arm from pivot (arrow) and remove from housing.

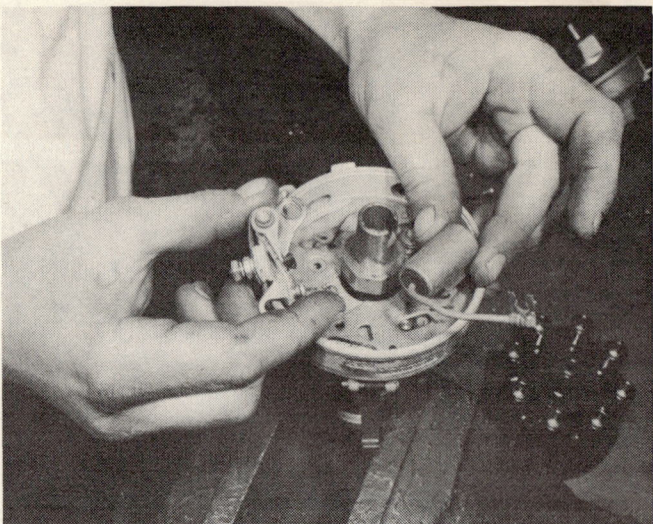

2. Loosen primary terminal nut holding condenser and primary lead wire in place. Remove point set/condenser attaching screws and lift each from breaker plate.

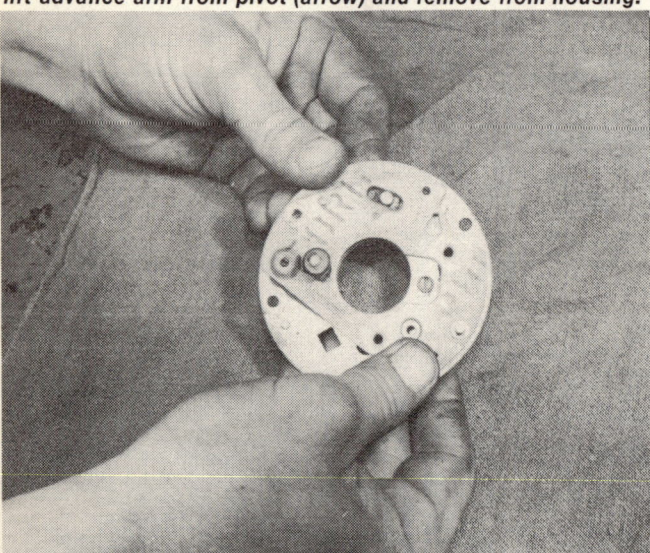

3. Pry breaker plate from distributor bowl. Do not remove ground lead attached to it. Check plate for signs of wear or missing support button between upper and lower plate.

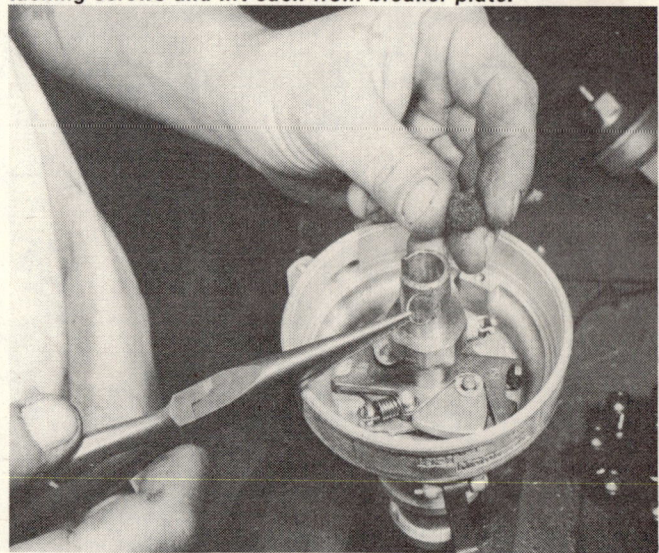

4. Remove self-lubricating wick from cam assembly shaft. Reach inside shaft with needle nose pliers and carefully pull out tiny wire retaining clip.

5. Centrifugal advance spring size/length may vary, so note which goes where, then remove carefully to avoid stretching. Remove circlips holding weights in place and remove weights.

6. Reverse distributor in vise and carefully tap out drive gear/collar retaining pins with a suitable drift. Remove the gear, collar and shaft.

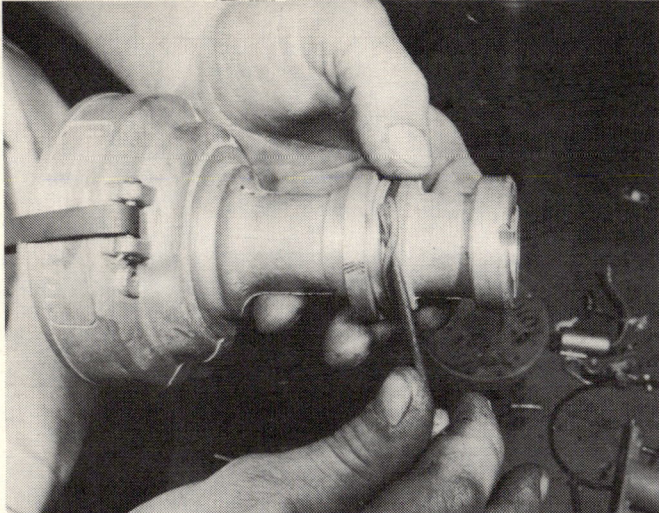

7. Slip a small screwdriver blade under the O-ring seal, remove and discard it. Install a new O-ring with a little lubricant to help fit it in place.

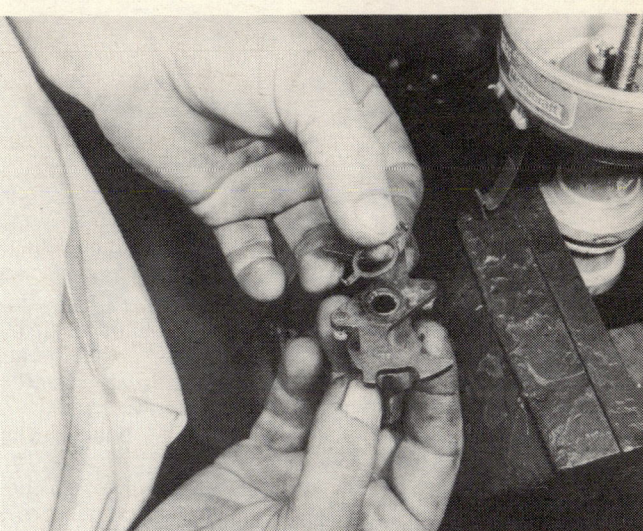

8. Reinstall distributor shaft, drive gear and collar. Make sure this tanged washer is fitted in place on Motorcraft distributors before replacing cam assembly.

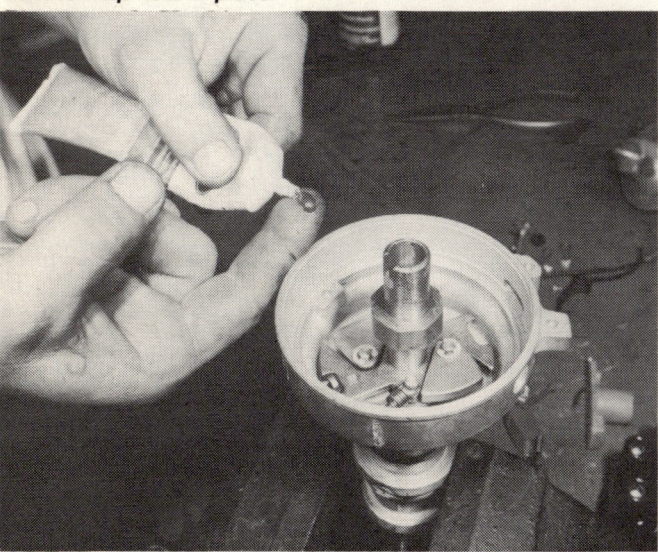

9. Clean distributor bowl and reinstall advance weights and springs. Check weight operation by revolving shaft, then apply a little cam lube to the cam assembly.

10. Reinstall wire clip and felt wick in cam assembly. Install breaker plate, then remove and clean ground connection. Install primary wire and grommet in bowl.

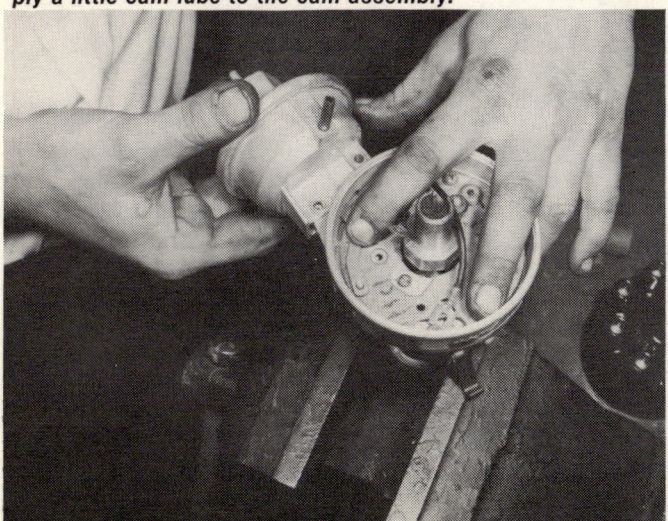

11. Insert vacuum advance arm and reconnect to breaker plate pivot pin. Hold arm in place and reinstall attaching screws. Install new points/condenser and connect ground lead.

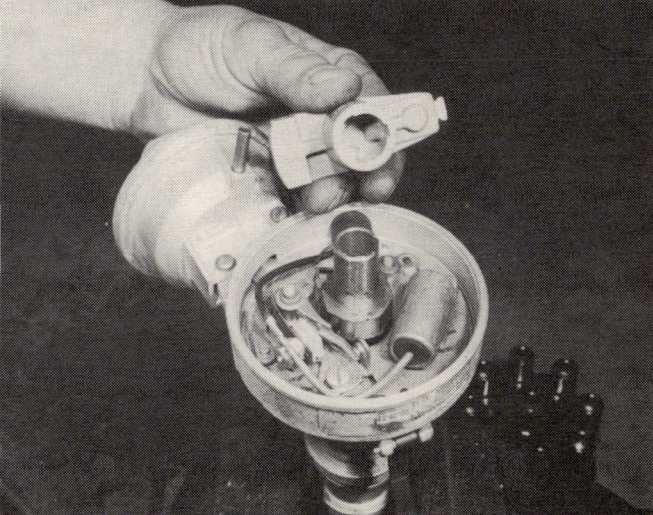

12. Replace rotor. Note cutout in shaft and plastic tang in rotor. Tang must fit into cutout before rotor can be seated properly. Reinstall distributor cap.

BREAKERLESS DISTRIBUTORS

Before Detroit arrived at breakerless ignition across the board in 1975, the auto companies offered various transistorized and breakerless systems as options. GM and Chrysler eliminated the breaker points, using transistors instead to make and break the primary current. Ford also used transistors, but kept the points by inserting a resistor into the wiring harness. This permitted only a very small voltage (3.9) to pass through the points, resulting in minimal point wear.

A considerable improvement over breaker points, transistors do not wear out, can handle much higher voltage, and operate much faster than points. However, the early transistorized control boxes were much more expensive to produce. As an option, the systems were not very profitable and so GM (except for Pontiac) and Ford discontinued their production until stringent emission requirements forced them to reconsider the alternatives in the early seventies.

CAPACITOR-DISCHARGE IGNITION

Initiated by Oldsmobile and Pontiac, the CDI system consisted of a magnetic-pulse distributor, a transistorized ignition pulse amplifier, and a special coil design. This coil cannot be tested on a conventional tester. Aside from the red coil and distributor cap, the distributor appeared quite conventional from the outside, but removing the cap exposed a rather unconventional unit. Like standard Delco-Remy distributors, the rotor and centrifugal-advance weights were situated at the top, but the conventional contact cam was no longer present beneath them. In its place was an iron timer core, which was mounted on the shaft and rotated with it. On the outside rim of the timer core were equally spaced projections or teeth, one for each engine cylinder.

A round magnetic pickup assembly took the place of the breaker plate, points, and condenser. This assembly consisted of a round ceramic permanent magnet, a metal pole piece and a pickup coil. The magnet was sandwiched between a mounting plate at its base and the pole piece on top, while the coil was situated between the two. The pole piece also had the same number of equally spaced teeth as the timer core. The pickup assembly, like the conventional breaker plate, was actuated by the vacuum control unit to provide vacuum advance. The centrifugal-advance weights operated in their usual manner and moved the timer core for mechanical advance. The pickup coil was connected to the pulse amplifier by two wires. Within the amplifier was a circuit board with electronic components but no moving parts.

The battery was connected to the pulse amplifier through the ignition switch. When the ignition switch is turned on, 12 volts of DC battery current travel through a primary wire to the amplifier, where the current is converted to AC for use by an AC transformer within the amplifier. The transformer raises the 12 volts to 300 and sends them on to a capacitor where the power is momentarily stored. A zener diode in the amplifier circuit prevents overloading by limiting capacitor voltage to 300.

Once the teeth on the pole piece align with the teeth on the timer core, a current pulse resulting from magnetic attraction is picked up by the pickup coil and sent to the pulse amplifier. When the amplifier is signaled by the pickup coil, a thyristor in the amplifier is triggered by a series of transistors. The 300 volts are released through a primary wire to the primary side of the ignition coil. The voltage travels through the primary winding and out the negative terminal to ground. Since the capacitor is part of the primary circuit, the circuit is broken when all 300 volts have been drained from it. Breaking the circuit in this manner has the same

1a

1b

effect as breaking it by opening conventional contact points.

The transformer within the CDI system is responsible for providing the coil's primary winding with a much greater voltage than the 12 volts provided by the breaker-point system. In the conventional ignition, the 12 volts in the coil are multiplied to about 20,000 by the secondary winding. The CDI coil is constructed to handle higher voltage—when 300 volts enter the primary, a voltage much higher than 20,000 leaves the secondary. Other transistorized systems don't contain a transformer, so a greater strain is imposed upon the battery. Since the CDI transformer multiplies voltage to the required amount, the system makes only a minimum draw on the battery.

DELCO-REMY MAGNETIC-PULSE IGNITION

This consisted of a special distributor, an ignition pulse amplifier, and a coil with a special primary winding. A second resistance wire was also used from the coil's negative terminal to ground. The Delco-Remy Magnetic-Pulse distributor contained the same parts as the CDI system and operated in the same way. Both included an amplifier unit, but only the CDI contained a transformer and a capacitor. This was the major difference between the two systems.

DELCO-REMY UNIT IGNITION

This system used the same components as the magnetic-pulse system and operated in the same way. It differed mainly in that the coil and the electronic module or amplifier were combined into a single unit.

FOR TRANSISTOR IGNITION

Ford's system was used on the 427 CID engine from 1963 to 1967. Unlike its competitors, the Ford system used conventional breaker points but no

1A and 1B. "Electronic" ignitions use a breakerless distributor. The brains of the system may be contained within the distributor as in the GM HEI ignition (1A) or in a separate ignition module as used by Ford (1B).

2. Pontiac's Unit Ignition combined the magnetic pulse components with the electronic module and coil in one assembly within the distributor.

3. Oldsmobile's capacitive discharge system contained a capacitor and transformer within the amplifier. The transformer converts 12 battery volts into approximately 300 volts, which is stored by the capacitor and released to the coil's primary when triggered by the distributor.

condenser. The system differed from a conventional ignition by the presence of a ballast resistor block, a tachometer connecting block, a cold-start relay, and a transistor control box or amplifier. If the breaker points were closed and the ignition switch was turned on, current flowed from the battery through the ignition switch and through the resistor block to the amplifier. The amplifier was mounted under the dash away from engine heat and contained the main or PNP transistor, a zener diode, and a toroid.

The PNP transistor consisted of three parts: the top was called the collector, the middle the base, and the lower part the emitter. When the current passed through the PNP transistor, it was broken into two circuits—high and low voltage. The high voltage was the power circuit and went through the primary winding of the coil to ground. The low voltage was the switching circuit and went through the closed breaker points to ground.

The resistor block in the Ford system was actually two separate resistors—the collector and emitter resistor. Both were connected in series to the collector/emitter circuit of the transistor. There was also a 7.9-ohm base resistor wire between the base part of the transistor and the distributor. This wire limited the voltage across the points to 3.9 volts for long point life. Breaker-point rubbing block wear was also minimal because the contact cam was highly polished, resulting in little change to the

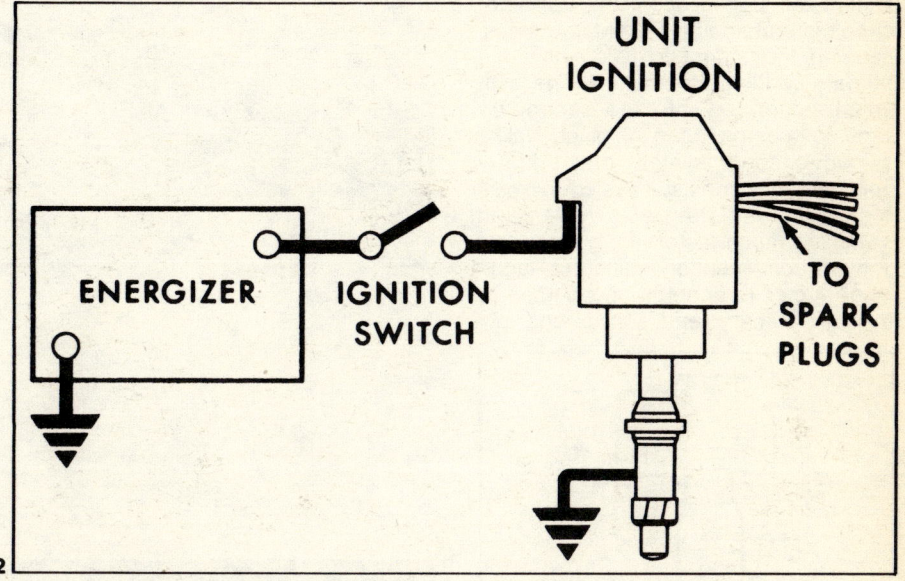

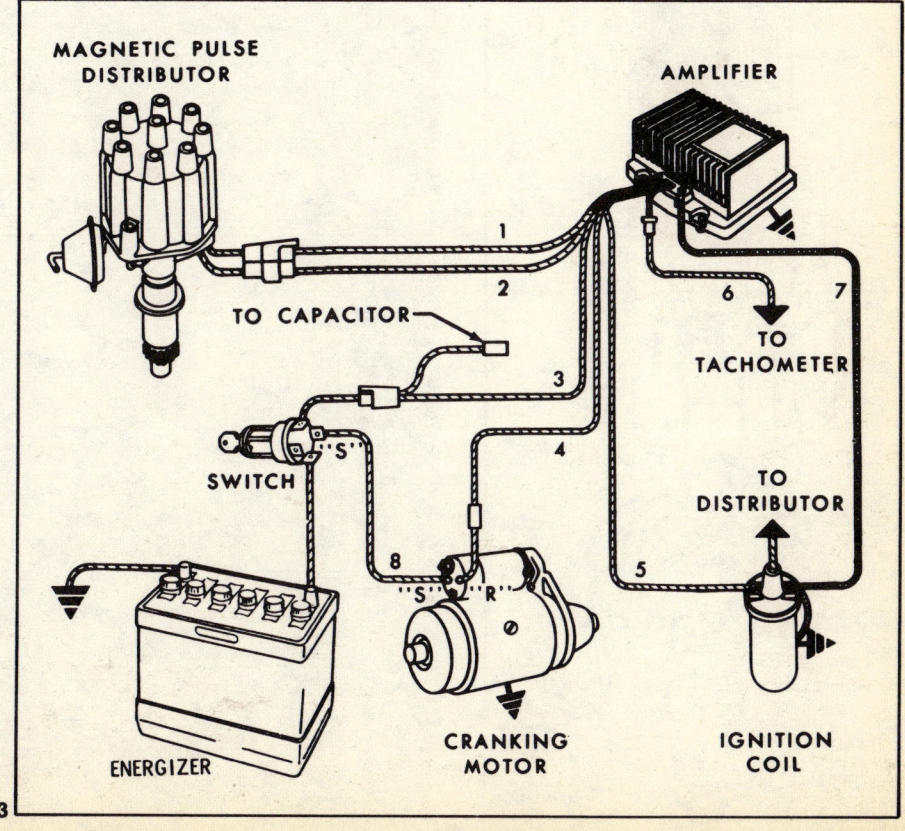

BREAKERLESS DISTRIBUTORS

.020-inch point gap. It's important to realize that replacing this resistor wire with anything but a duplicate will destroy the transistor. The emitter resistor was also in series with the base resistor in the base/emitter circuit. Combining the resistances in each circuit produced a 1-amp base current, which was further reduced by the base wire to 0.5 amp at the points and a collector current to the coil of about 12 amps.

Current will not pass through the transistor if the points are open, or if the primary winding is not grounded. When the points are closed, current builds up in the primary winding of the coil. The instant the points open, the transistor circuit is broken and current flow stops, causing the magnetic field within the primary winding to collapse. The high voltage induced into the secondary winding goes on to fire the plugs. Unlike a conventional system, the primary voltage of the transistor system is much higher as resistance is lower and switching much faster.

In a conventional ignition, a tach/dwell meter is generally connected to the coil primary lead and ground, but with the transistor system, this would cause inaccurate readings and burn out the transistor. A tach block was installed in the system solely to provide a place to attach test leads. The red meter lead connects to the red tach block terminal, and the black lead to the black block terminal.

A cold-start relay is placed in the Ford circuit at the starter relay. It provides full battery current for the coil primary when the starter draw is high. While the engine is running, the relay contacts are closed. They open during cranking except when

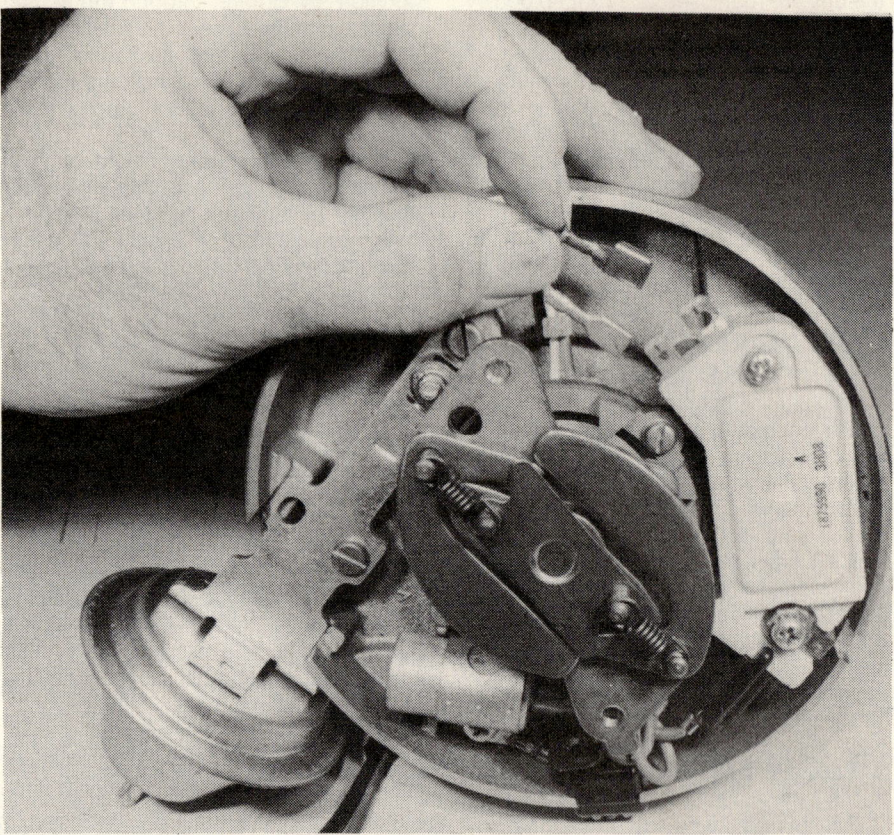
5

4
6

46/IGNITION & ELECTRICAL SYSTEMS

battery voltage drops below a certain level. At that time, the points close again and the ignition resistor is bypassed to permit full battery current for cold-weather starting.

ELECTRONIC IGNITIONS

As emission requirements became more difficult to comply with, automakers took a different approach to ignition systems in the early seventies. The heart of the so-called electronic ignitions offered as standard equipment since 1975 is a special distributor using no breaker points. Conventional breaker points burn easily because they are capable of handling only a limited amount of primary voltage. In addition, breaker-point wear causes engine timing to change, gradually affecting engine performance. If the primary voltage can be increased, secondary voltage will also be much higher, resulting in cleaner, longer-lasting spark plugs, higher voltage at higher rpm, less engine misfiring, and lower emissions.

By eliminating the breaker points, the breakerless distributor provides these benefits, along with stable ignition timing. To do this, the distributor creates magnetic pulses that trigger an electronic control module to create high voltage in a special coil. This was made possible by replacing the distributor cam, breaker plate, points, and condenser of the conventional distributor with an armature (trigger wheel, reluctor, etc.) and a pickup coil (sensor, stator assembly, etc.). The armature and pickup coil physically replace the points and cam but do their job quite differently. A condenser is not necessary in electronic systems.

HOW THEY WORK

Just as with a conventional ignition system, the electronic ignition consists of two electrical circuits—the primary or low-voltage and the secondary or high-voltage. In general terms, electronic ignitions operate as follows: when the ignition switch is turned on, current from the battery flows through the switch and to the coil primary windings. This energizes the coil. As each tooth or leg of the revolving armature approaches the magnetic pickup coil, it induces a voltage. This voltage signals the electronic control module to turn off the coil primary current.

A timing circuit built into the module turns the current on again once the coil field has collapsed. When the current is on, it travels from the battery through the ignition switch to the primary windings of the coil and then through the module's circuits to ground. Once the current is shut off by the module, the magnetic field in the coil collapses, inducing a high voltage into the coil's secondary windings. High voltage is produced this way each time the coil is built up and collapsed. Secondary current flow is exactly like that of a conventional ignition. It travels from the coil high-tension lead to the distributor cap, where the rotor distributes it to the proper spark-plug terminal in the distributor

4. The GM High Energy Ignition (HEI) is a far more sophisticated version of the early Unit Ignition.

5. There are now several versions of the basic HEI design. The 1974-1980 models used an ignition module with two terminals on each end.

6. Current HEI distributors with electronic spark timing (EST) use a seven-terminal module. This cutaway of the two modules shows the greater degree of electronic complexity in the EST module compared to the standard one.

7. Regardless of how many terminals an HEI module has, it must be installed with a coating of silicone grease to absorb heat or module life is extremely short (and expensive).

8. The GM centrifugal advance weights tend to wear down their pivot pins (arrows). When this happens, timing becomes erratic. Keep the pivot pins well lubricated to prevent this.

9. The Computer Controlled Coil Ignition used on 1984 Turbo V-6 Buicks has no distributor as such, but the basic distributor housing/shaft design forms the basis for the Hall-Effect crankshaft position sensor.

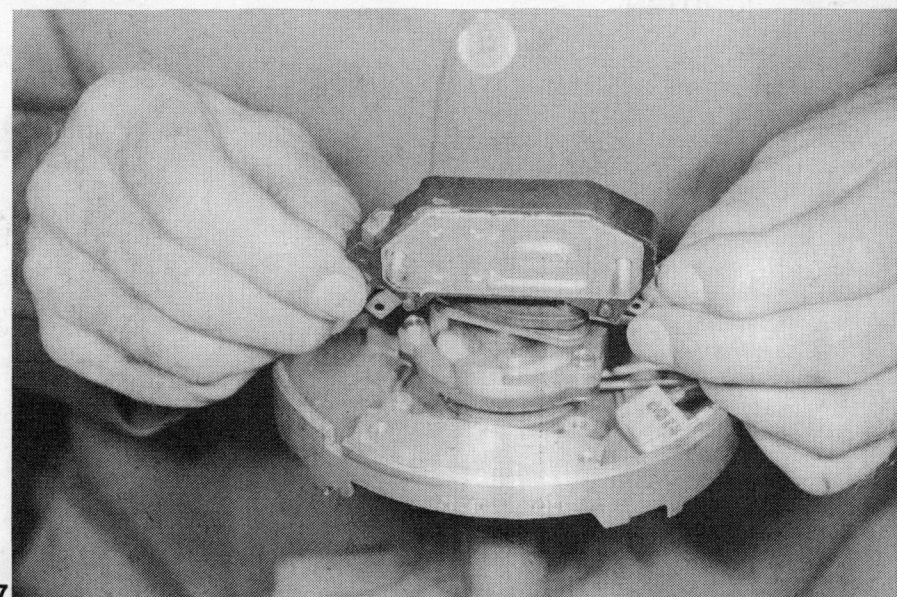

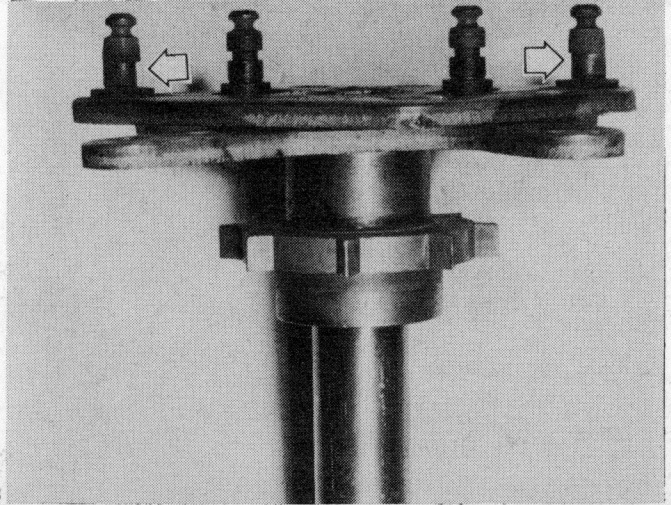

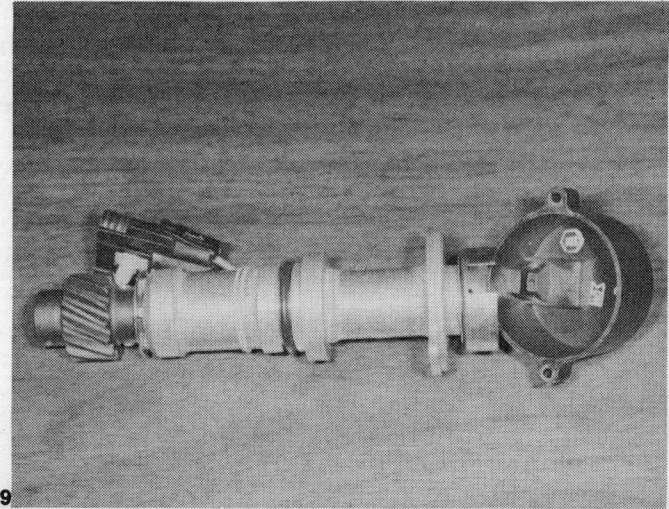

IGNITION & ELECTRICAL SYSTEMS/47

BREAKERLESS DISTRIBUTORS

cap.

Minor differences in system operation and major ones in component design exist among the electronic ignitions offered by automakers. However, you should realize that the spark advance mechanisms, the entire secondary circuit, and that part of the primary circuit from the battery to the BAT terminal of the coil are identical with those in a conventional ignition system. The same troubleshooting tests used with conventional ignitions also apply to the electronic ones—except for that part of the primary circuit between the BAT terminal of the coil and the final ground at the distributor housing. Since dwell affects ignition timing and dwell is not adjustable on an electronic ignition, periodic adjustment of timing is no longer necessary once basic timing has been set. After correctly establishing timing, there is no need to bother with it unless the distributor is removed for testing or service.

CHRYSLER ELECTRONIC IGNITION

The breakerless distributor in the Chrysler system is very similar in external appearance to that of the conventional Chrysler breaker-point distributor. The housing, cap, rotor, and advance mechanisms have been the same since Chrysler introduced the system as standard equipment in 1973. Late-model distributors used in Chrysler Electronic Spark Control systems have no centrifugal- or vacuum-advance units, as the function of spark timing has been taken over by the spark control computer.

The difference between the conventional and breakerless distributors can be seen after removing the distributor cap. A toothed reluctor and magnetic pickup coil assembly replace the cam and breaker points. The gearlike reluctor is attached to the distributor shaft and has one tooth for each cylinder in the engine—six teeth for six-cylinder engines and eight teeth for V-8s. The pickup assembly is mounted to the breaker plate and contains a pickup coil, pole piece, and permanent magnet.

As a reluctor tooth moves into alignment with the pole piece, the normally weak magnetic field created by the permanent magnet is strengthened. This increase in the field strength induces a positive voltage in the pickup coil. This pickup voltage is a precisely timed signal sent to the electronic control unit, which cuts off primary current flow in the coil. When this happens, the primary field collapses, inducing high voltage in the coil secondary to fire the spark plug. As the reluctor tooth rotates away from the pole piece, pickup coil voltage becomes negative and the control unit switches primary current back on. The rapid increase and decrease of the magnetic field create the tiny electrical impulses that trigger the switching transistor in the control unit to interrupt the flow of primary circuit current.

Some Chrysler electronic distributors used in the Electronic Lean Burn and Spark Control systems contain dual pickup coils. One provides a signal with a fixed advance for plug firing during cranking, the other supplies the signal once the engine starts and varies advance according to the control unit. A second-generation spark control computer controls these functions, and the distributor used with it contains only one pickup coil.

The electronic control unit or ECU contains the power switching transformer which controls primary current flow. This switching transistor is located on top of the control unit and should not be touched when the ignition switch is on. It contains sufficient voltage at this time to produce a nasty shock. The ECU determines how long the ignition coil primary current flows before it is interrupted. This means that the control unit determines dwell, which is not adjustable.

A dual-ballast resistor was used in Chrysler electronic ignitions through 1979. The compensating side played the same role as that in a conventional ignition by maintaining constant primary current regardless of engine speed. During starting, it was bypassed to allow full battery voltage to be applied to the coil. The auxiliary side limited current flow in the electronic part of the circuit to protect the control unit. A single resistor has been used since 1980; the function of the auxiliary side of the dual resistor is now incorporated in the spark control computer.

Hall-Effect Distributor

The electronic ignition fitted to Omni/Horizon and Reliance/Aries models with four-cylinder engines differs considerably from the system described above. The distributor contains a Hall-Effect pickup assembly which signals the spark control module when to fire the spark plugs. There is no

10

11

advance mechanism inside the distributor, and since the Hall-Effect assembly is permanently mounted, a fixed amount of advance is available during the start mode. When the engine starts, the control module switches into run mode and determines the required advance electronically based on sensor data.

10. *Chrysler introduced the first magnetic pulse breakerless ignition in 1972. It was made standard in 1973 but other auto makers didn't catch up until 1974-1975. With all of these units, you must use a brass or plastic (non-magnetic) feeler gauge to check the reluctor-to-pickup air gap.*

11. *The control unit is generally mounted on the firewall or fender apron. Periodically check the tightness of the retaining screw on the plug-in harness (1). Don't touch the switching transistor (2) with the key on. Ground is provided by the mounting screws (3).*

12. *The rear of the Chrysler control unit is completely sealed with epoxy, so no repairs can be made. The unit is serviced by replacement if it malfunctions. Have your dealer check it out with his factory tester before blaming the control unit.*

13. *Chrysler also pioneered the use of the Hall-Effect pickup with its Omni/Horizon distributors. GM and Ford are making increasing use of the Hall-Effect switch, as it's less expensive and more reliable than the older pickup coil/reluctor systems.*

14. *The Ford contact-controlled transistor circuit is nothing more than a conventional ignition with a transistorized switching device inserted between the points and the primary circuit. Points only tell the transistor when to turn the current on and off.*

15. *The Prestolite BID ignition system was used briefly on AMC cars. It suffered from vacuum advance and sensor problems.*

FORD SOLID-STATE IGNITION SYSTEM

Introduced on California cars in 1974 and nationwide the following year, Ford's original electronic ignition closely resembled the Chrysler system. A magnetic pickup coil assembly called a stator is located inside the distributor bowl along with an armature that rotates with the distributor shaft. Like the Chrysler reluctor, Ford's armature has one spoke for each cylinder. As a spoke nears the stator pickup, an electrical signal is generated in the signal coil. When the spoke and magnet align, a zero signal is generated in the pickup. The zero signal tells the electronic amplifier module to turn off the primary circuit in the coil. A timing circuit in the module turns the current back on after the coil field has collapsed. This timing period is comparable to dwell in a breaker-point distributor, but is not adjustable.

When the current is on, it flows from the battery through the ignition swtich, through the primary windings of the ignition coil, and through the amplifier module circuits on its way to ground. Once the current is shut off, the magnetic field built up in the coil is allowed to collapse, inducing a high voltage into the secondary windings of the coil. High voltage is thus produced each time the field builds up and collapses. The high voltage flows through the coil high-tension lead to the distributor cap, where the rotor distributes it first to one of the spark-plug terminals and then to the plug itself. The process repeats for each power stroke of the engine.

Although operation of the Ford Solid-State Ignition is similar to that of Chrysler's Electronic Ignition, there are detail differences. The Motorcraft distributor provides a relatively wide, fixed air gap between the armature spokes and the pickup coil piece. Chrysler has a narrower gap which can be adjusted when required. The Ford

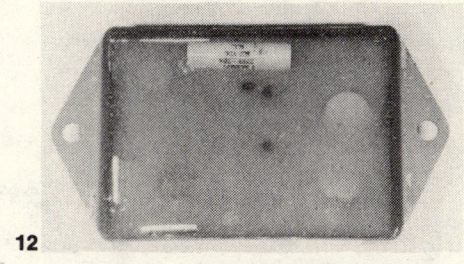
12

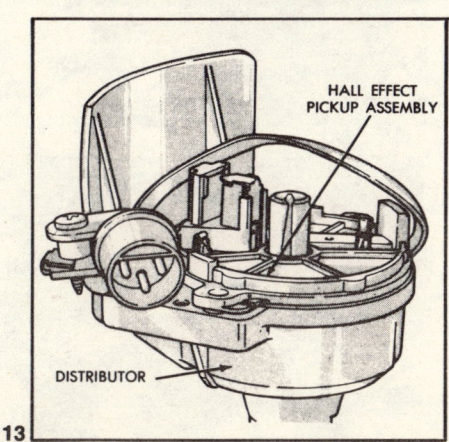
13

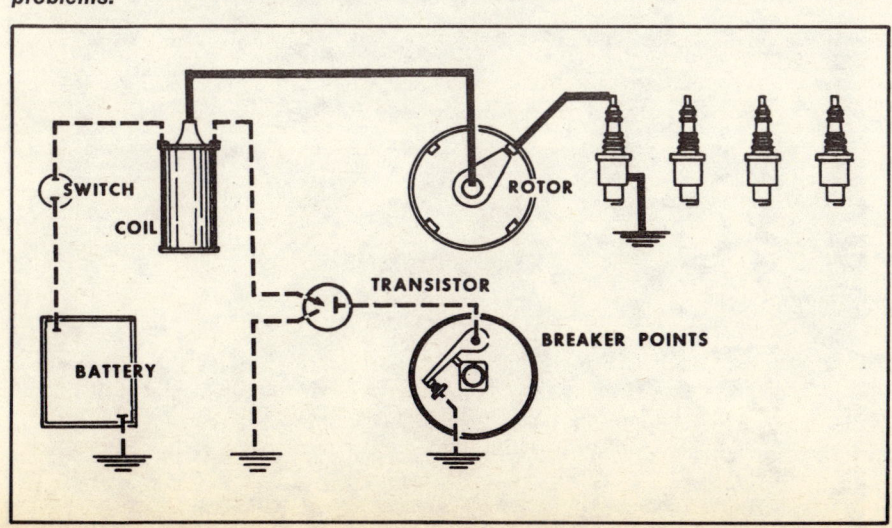
15

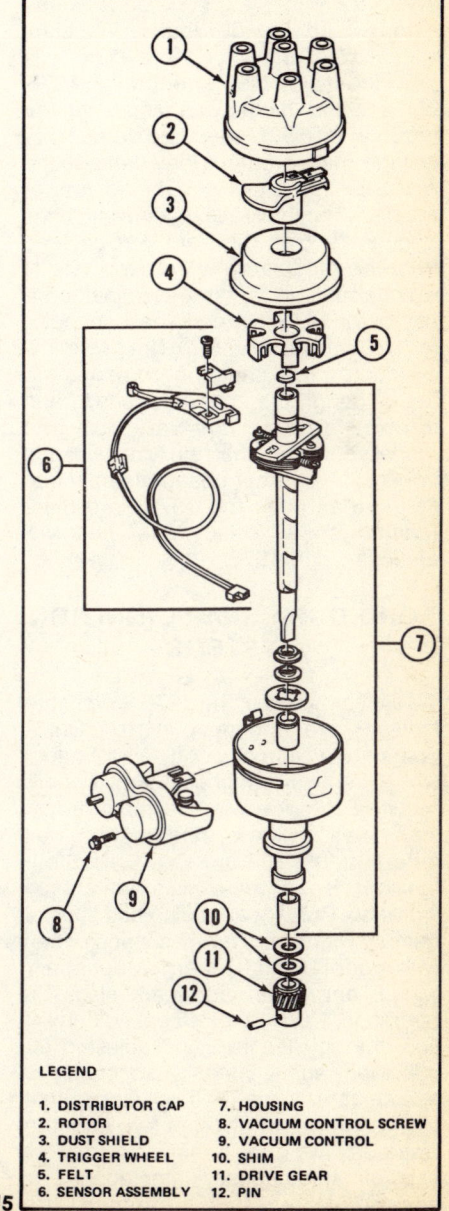

LEGEND
1. DISTRIBUTOR CAP
2. ROTOR
3. DUST SHIELD
4. TRIGGER WHEEL
5. FELT
6. SENSOR ASSEMBLY
7. HOUSING
8. VACUUM CONTROL SCREW
9. VACUUM CONTROL
10. SHIM
11. DRIVE GEAR
12. PIN

BREAKERLESS DISTRIBUTORS

ignition coil has a higher output and provides considerably higher voltage than the Chrysler coil.

Ford's module contains protective circuitry in addition to the detector, timer, and power switching circuits; Chrysler uses a dual-ballast resistor to protect its module. Internal circuitry changes in the Ford module during 1975-76 complicate system diagnosis, as test equipment connections and procedures differ. For this reason, modules and wiring harnesses cannot be interchanged between model years.

Wire color coding is important to servicing the Solid-State Ignition. Battery current reaches the electronic module from the ignition switch through the white wire during cranking, but through the red wire after the engine is running. Distributor signals are transmitted through the orange and purple wires. Primary current from the coil is carried to the module by the green wire. The black wire is a ground between the module and the distributor. Transient voltage protection for the system was provided by the blue wire through 1975, but a zener diode was added to the module in 1976 to dump temporary voltage surges before they damage the module; the blue wire is no longer needed. These wires (seven in systems through 1975 and six from 1976 on) feed from the module in two groups, one of which ends in a three-terminal connector for 1975 (two-terminal connector for 1976) and the other in a four-terminal connector. It is important to remember that although the connector shape and terminal arrangement vary from one model year to another, the wire color and continuity have not changed. American Motors has used the 1976 Solid-State Ignition on all six-cylinder and V-8 engines since 1978.

FORD DURA-SPARK IGNITION SYSTEMS

Two variations of the 1976 Solid-State Ignition were introduced in 1977: Dura-Spark I and Dura-Spark II. Dura-Spark I was essentially a higher-energy system required to cope with California emission laws. A new module and coil differentiated it from the Solid-State Ignition. Since there was an energy increase, Dura-Spark I also had special primary wiring, a different distributor cap with adapter, high-energy secondary wiring, and wide-gap spark plugs. In operation, Dura-Spark I sensed current flow through the coil and adjusted for maximum spark intensity according to engine rpm. If the module sensed that the ignition switch was on and the distributor was not turning, coil current shut off automatically after about one second. When this happened, the ignition key had to be turned to the start or off position, then on again. The system was discontinued at the end of the 1979 model year.

To boost energy output, Dura-Spark II uses a ballast resistor value of 1.10 instead of the 1.35 ohms of the Solid-State Ignition. It also uses the Dura-Spark I rotor, distributor cap with adapter, new secondary wiring, and wide-gap spark plugs. The Dura-Spark II amplifier module also works differently. Both the module and coil are on when the ignition switch is on. For this reason, the ignition system will generate a spark when the switch is turned off. When doing underhood work on a Dura-Spark

16a

16b

II ignition, make sure that the ignition switch remains off—just removing the distributor cap with the switch on can cause the system to fire.

Dura-Spark II is still current at this writing but has been joined by Dura-Spark III. With some Dura-Spark II applications, the module's sophistication has been increased to incorporate cranking retard, altitude compensation and/or economy modes. You'll find more about these electronic engine control systems in the next chapter.

16A and 16B. The BID trigger wheel had to be removed with a puller (A) and installed with a socket (B). Owners were well-advised to carry a spare sensor with them. Voltage limiting function.

17. Trigger wheel-to-sensor gap was critical on the BID ignition and required a special gauge to set the gap correctly.

18A and 18B. The Ford Dura-Spark (A) and Dura-Spark III distributors show how many distributor functions were incorporated within the vehicle's on-board computer in a very short time. Dura-Spark III had no vacuum or centrifugal advance mechanism.

Thick Film Integrated Distributor

Introduced as part of a Dura-Spark II system on the 1.6L Escort/Lynx powerplant, this new distributor design has evolved into a separate ignition type. The unusual-looking distributor mounts horizontally on the rear of the cylinder head and is driven directly by the camshaft by an offset tang on the distributor shaft which fits into a corresponding slot on the rear of the cam. Unlike all previous Ford distributors, it uses top-mounted centrifugal-advance weights and a circular rotor held in place by two screws.

The 1982 version saw several substantial changes in ignition component and distributor design. A new Thick Film Integrated (TFI) module attaches directly to a mounting pad on the side of the

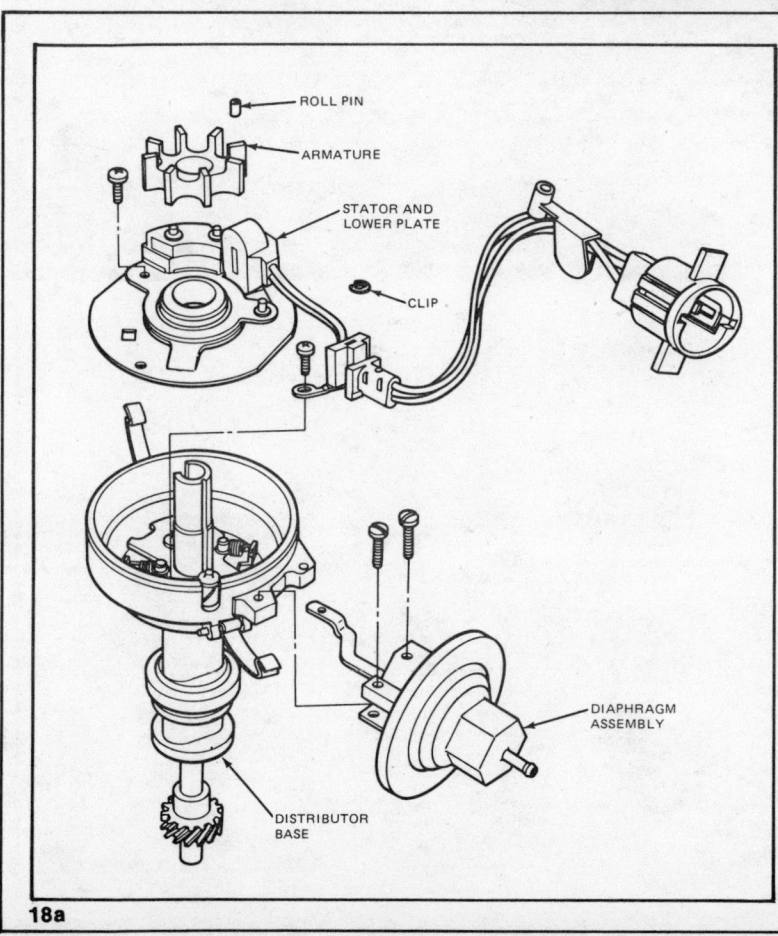

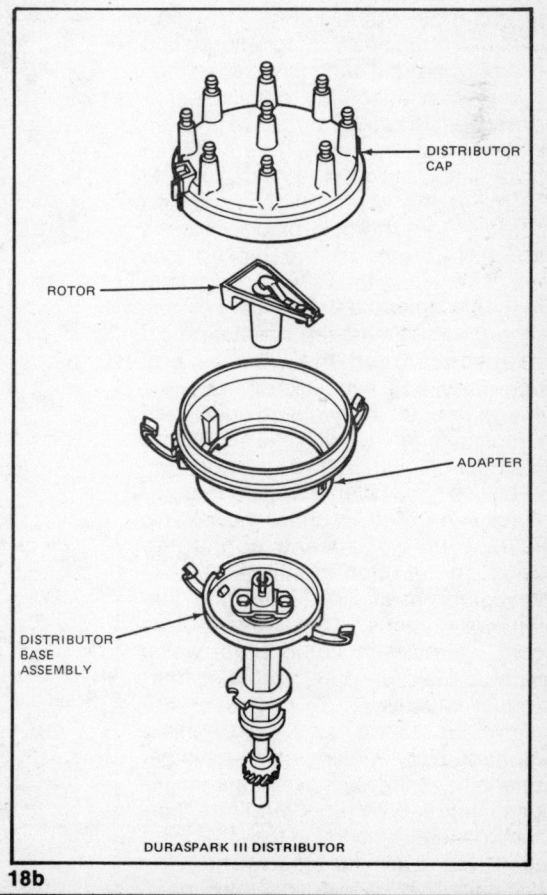

IGNITION & ELECTRICAL SYSTEMS/51

BREAKERLESS DISTRIBUTORS

distributor housing. A new low-resistance "E" core coil was added and used without a ballast resistor. Similar in appearance to the GM HEI coil used with late-model four-cylinder engines, the new Ford coil is potted in plastic and laminated much like a toy-train transformer.

Further evolution of the distributor and ignition system occurred in 1983, when the module was made smarter and integrated into the EEC-IV system. Its TFI module is programmed to permit a "push-start" mode to permit push starting of the car; the 1982 module required a crank mode signal to restart the engine.

Centrifugal- and vacuum-advance functions are now incorporated into the module, with an octane rod taking the place of the vacuum advance. Under certain specified conditions, the length of this rod can be changed by a service technician to change the advance slightly. A Hall-Effect switch replaced the previously used stator assembly and the distributor acquired a new name—the Universal distributor.

GM HIGH-ENERGY (HEI) SYSTEM

A third-generation outgrowth of the original Delco-Remy Magnetic-Pulse ignition described earlier, the HEI distributor contains a magnetic pickup assembly around the distributor shaft. This pickup assembly consists of a permanent magnet, stationary pole piece with internal teeth, and a pickup coil. A timer core rotates inside the pole piece. As its teeth align and then separate from the pole-piece teeth, an induced voltage in the pickup coil transmits a signal to the electronic module to open the coil primary circuit. When this happens, the magnetic field collapses around the primary and secondary coil windings, inducing a voltage in both. The voltage developed in the secondary windings is sent to the proper spark plug by the distributor rotor.

Physically smaller than other automotive coils, the HEI coil is mounted in the distributor cap and connected directly to the rotor on all but 1975-77 distributors used with four- and six-cylinder engines. These distributors have externally mounted coils, which are also used on 1982 and later four-cylinder engines.

The HEI coil contains more primary and secondary windings than do other automotive coils. A conventional coil is constructed with the windings surrounding the iron core; in the HEI coil, a laminated iron core surrounds the windings. The HEI coil operates basically the same as other coils, but can produce a voltage as high as 35,000 volts when the primary circuit is broken.

The HEI electronic control module delivers full battery voltage to the coil. Located inside the distributor bowl, it contains five complete circuits to control spark timing, switching, current limitation, dwell, and distributor pickup.

A "tach" terminal is provided on the distributor cap connector for easy test equipment connection. On some 1980 and later engines, the HEI distributor is so difficult to reach that a "tach" pigtail is provided for easier test lead connection. Don't ground this terminal or you can damage the expensive HEI module.

Electronic sophistication has also been applied to the HEI system, creating several variations incorporated in the new GM electronic engine controls. These are discussed in the following chapter.

PRESTOLITE BID IGNITION SYSTEM

A breakerless inductive discharge system, the BID ignition was used by American Motors on its 1974-77 six- and eight-cylinder engines. The BID distributor is conventional in design and function, except for the sensor and trigger wheel which replace the breaker points, condenser, and distributor cam. When the ignition switch is turned to start or on, the control unit is activated and alternating current is sent to the distributor sensor, where an electromagnetic field develops. As the leading edge of the trigger-wheel leg enters the sensor field, it causes a reduction in the sensor's oscillation strength, which continues to diminish as the leg nears alignment with the sensor.

Once the oscillation strength is

19

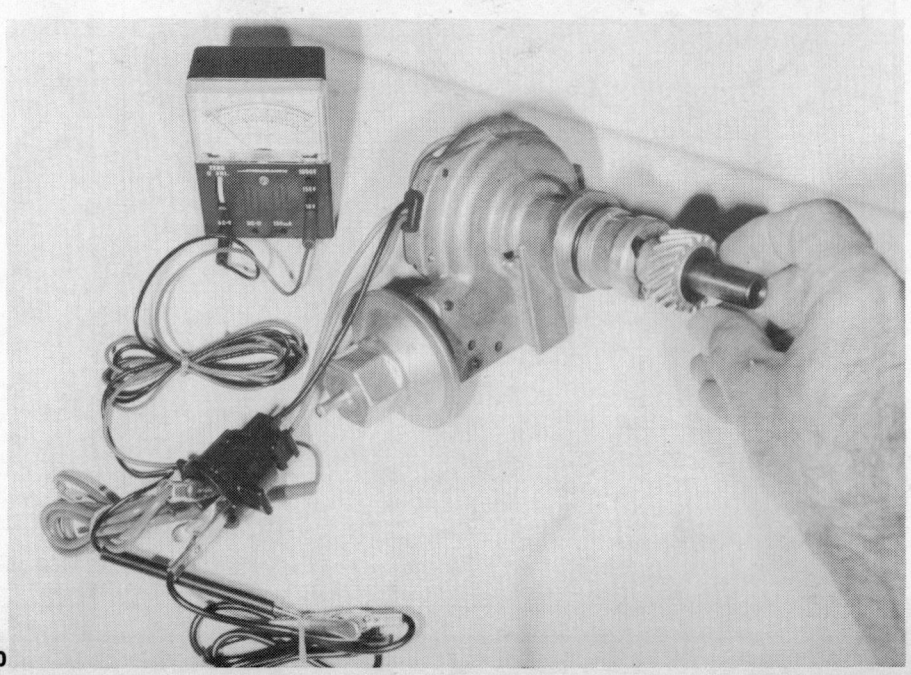

20

19. The most basic troubleshooting test with a Ford Solid-State distributor is to check out the stator's permanent magnet for magnetism. If it doesn't attract your screwdriver, the stator should be replaced.

20. Test the Solid-State distributor to see if it produces any voltage when the shaft is turned by hand. Use the low AC scale of your voltmeter for this test. Hook the meter to the orange and purple wire prongs. This can also be done in the car with the engine cranking and the coil secondary wire grounded.

21. Checking for resistance between the orange and purple wires, we get 700 ohms, right in the specified range of 600-800 ohms.

22. Ford's latest is the Universal Distributor introduced on the 1981 Escort/Lynx 1.6L engine.

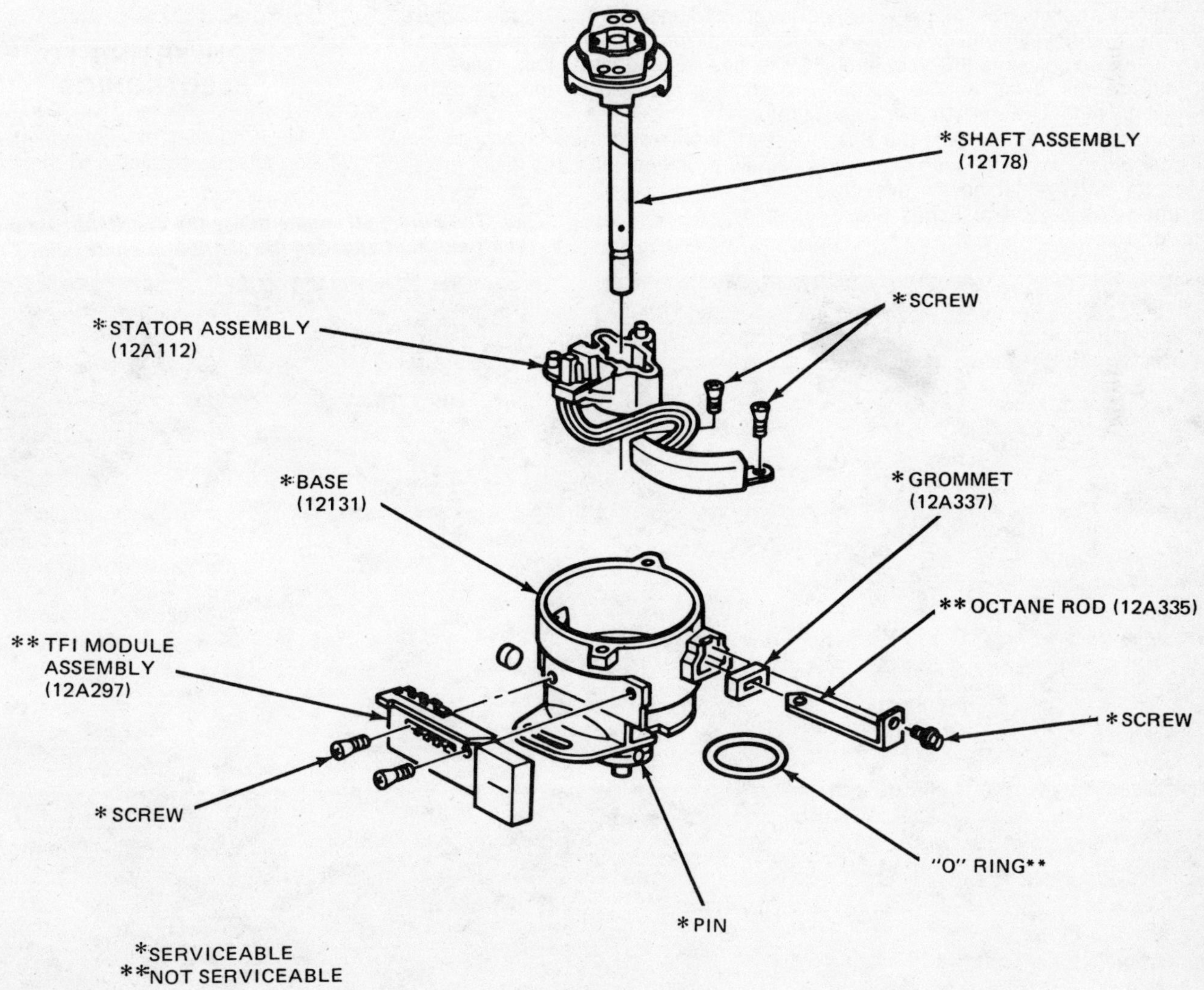

1.6 EFI UNIVERSAL DISTRIBUTOR

BREAKERLESS DISTRIBUTORS

reduced to a predetermined level, a demodulator circuit switches. This activates a power transistor in series with the coil primary circuit to switch off the circuit, inducing high voltage in the secondary coil windings. The high voltage is then distributed to the spark plugs in a conventional manner by the rotor, distributor cap, and secondary cables.

The BID control unit contains built-in reverse polarity protection, transient voltage protection, and current regulation features. As a result, no resistance wire or ballast resistor is necessary in the primary circuit. Since full battery voltage is present at the coil positive terminal when the ignition switch is in the on or start position, a bypass is not required during cranking.

A small coil wound of fine wire, the sensor receives an AC signal from the electronic control unit. There are no wear surfaces between the trigger wheel and sensor, so dwell remains constant and requires no adjustment. The control unit determines dwell as the angle between the trigger-wheel legs. Sensors gave considerable trouble with the BID ignitions, which may have been a major reason for AMC replacing the system with the 1976 version of Ford's Sold-State Ignition.

PREVENTIVE MAINTENANCE

As we've seen, electronic ignition distributors are not really electronic. Mechanically, they operate in the same manner as conventional breaker-point distributors. Electrically, they perform the same function but with slightly different components. Although there are no breaker points and condenser which require periodic replacement, this does not mean that the breakerless distributor is totally maintenance-free, despite some claims to the contrary by automakers.

The distributor cap and rotor require periodic inspection. The cap should be cleaned and checked for chips, hairline cracks, carbon tracks, etc. The rotor should be inspected for the same defects. If its metal tip is corroded, clean it with crocus cloth to restore a bright finish and good electrical contact. This last statement does not apply to Ford rotors, which require an application of a dielectric silicone compound that looks like a crusty deposit of ash after the rotor has been used. A new rotor design introduced on some 1983 models uses a multipoint rotor, which has two or three wire tips instead of a solid blade. No silicone is required on the tips of this rotor.

Dirt, wear, and lack of lubrication remain problems with any distributor—breaker-point or breakerless. Dirt can inhibit free movement of the centrifugal advance weights; wear can disrupt both the ignition timing and the centrifugal-advance operation, and lack of proper lubrication will cause or further complicate the wear problem. Only the HEI distributor is self-lubricating—engine oil lubes the lower bushing and an oil-filled reservoir lubes the upper bushing.

Incidentally, bushing wear can be an expensive problem. With most conventional distributors, bushings could be removed and replaced, but the economies of manufacturing now prevent bushing replacement on breakerless distributors. You can remove the bushing, but you can't buy a replacement for it. Bushings are now sold only as integral parts of a new distributor housing. This means that if the bushing is worn enough to permit excessive shaft movement, you'll have to buy the entire distributor housing to correct the problem. It's a very good reason to remove a breakerless distributor every year (just as you should a conventional one) to clean, check for wear, and lubricate it properly.

CONVERTING TO ELECTRONICS

A large number of aftermarket conversion kits are available to those who

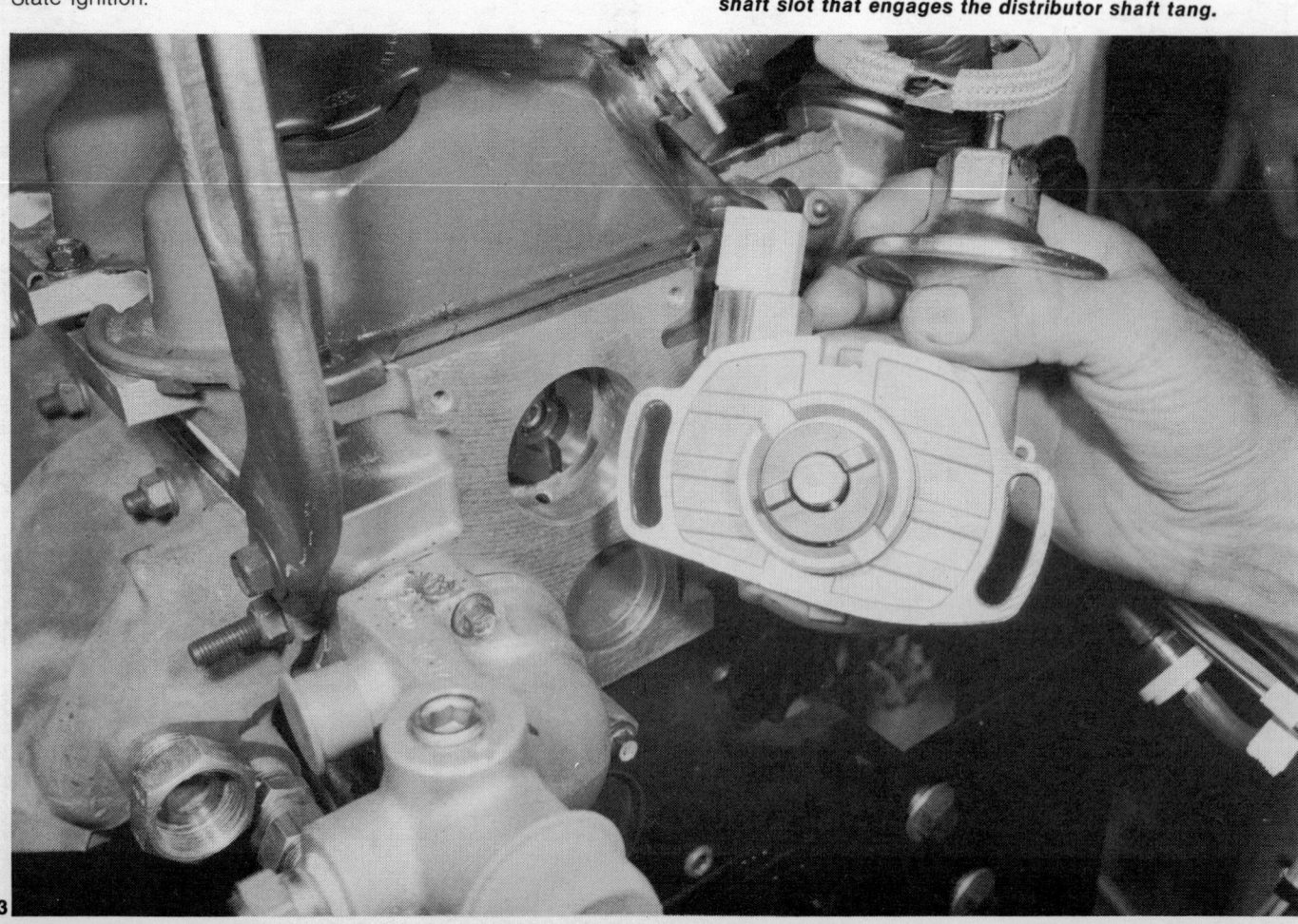

23. The Ford 1.6L engine drives the distributor via a camshaft slot that engages the distributor shaft tang.

would like to exchange their conventional breaker-point distributor for the benefits of a breakerless one. Even the automakers will supply you with the necessary components to convert to a breakerless ignition. A majority of the aftermarket products are patterned after designs that have already proven successful, with only minor changes in voltage output or spark duration.

There's nothing very new as electronic ignitions don't offer too many different combinations with which to work, but the names behind these systems are both established and reliable. Until something revolutionary comes along, most makers are offering either magnetic-pulse or light-emitting diode (LED) systems. For those who are interested in such conversions, a step-by-step how-to section follows on installing on the Accel magnetic-pulse system and a Mallory Unilite LED conversion.

HOW-TO: ACCEL CONVERSION

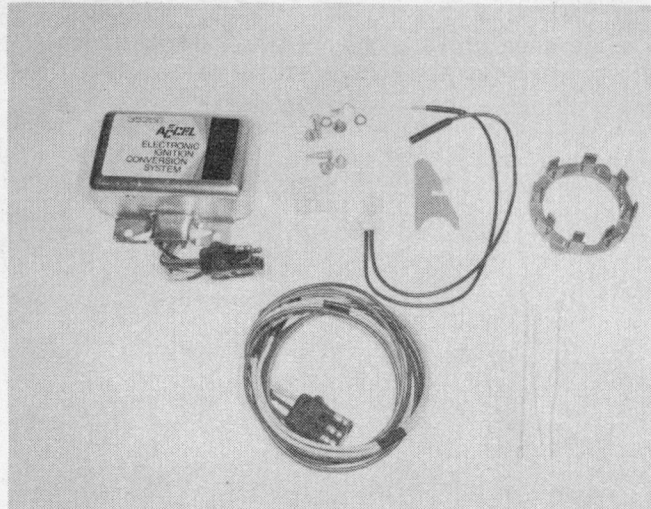

1. The Accel electronic ignition conversion kit comes complete with everything to make the changeover. This is the GM/AMC kit; Chrysler and Ford kits differ in components.

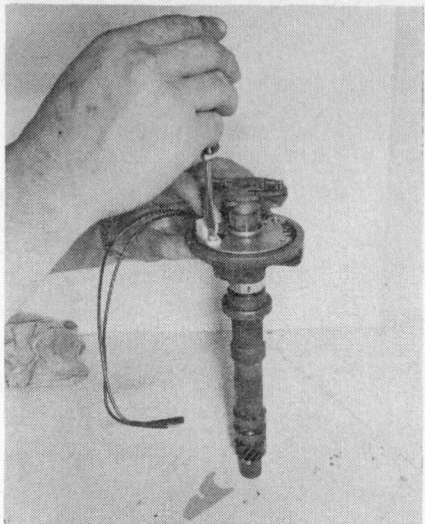

2. Remove points, condenser and primary lead wire from distributor. Clean it thoroughly, then install the sensor but do not tighten the hold-down screw at this point.

3. Use the fiber gauge provided to accurately locate the proper sensor position, then tighten the hold-down screw. Could any adjustment be easier?

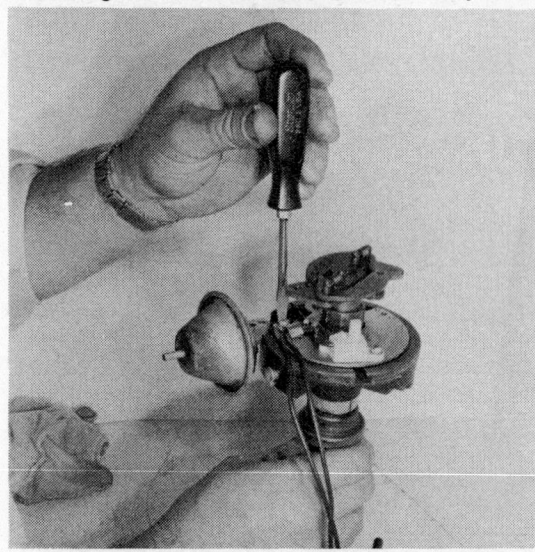

4. Route the sensor leads under this hold-down clip and then tighten it snugly. Conversion is designed to maintain total simplicity of installation.

5. Angle the trigger wheel and slip it over the advance weights. This saves you the trouble of removing and reinstalling the weights.

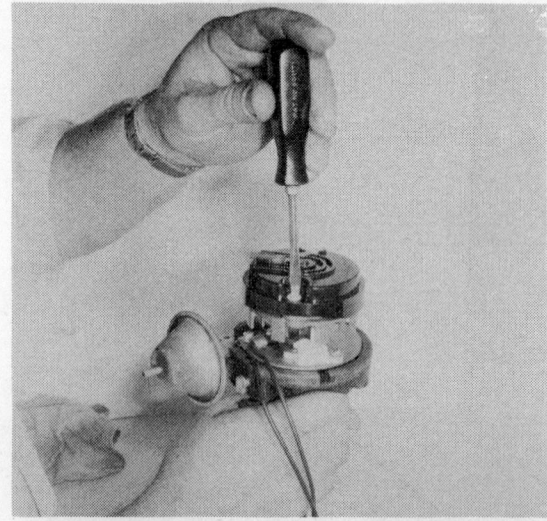

6. Connect the rotor, advance weights and trigger wheel together with the two screws provided in the kit. Check trigger wheel legs for adequate sensor clearance on both sides.

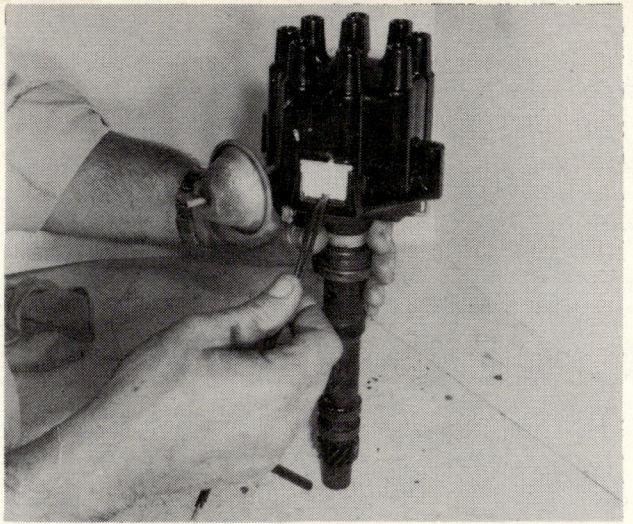

7. Install replacement plastic window in place of the metal one in the distributor cap. Thread sensor leads through window, taking up any slack. Distributor conversion is complete.

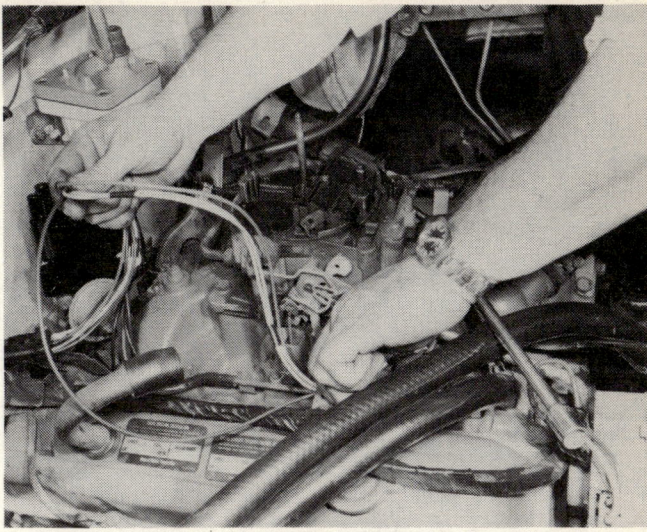

8. Secure the electronic control unit to the firewall and replace the stock coil with an Accel Super Coil. At this point, you can install and connect the wiring harness.

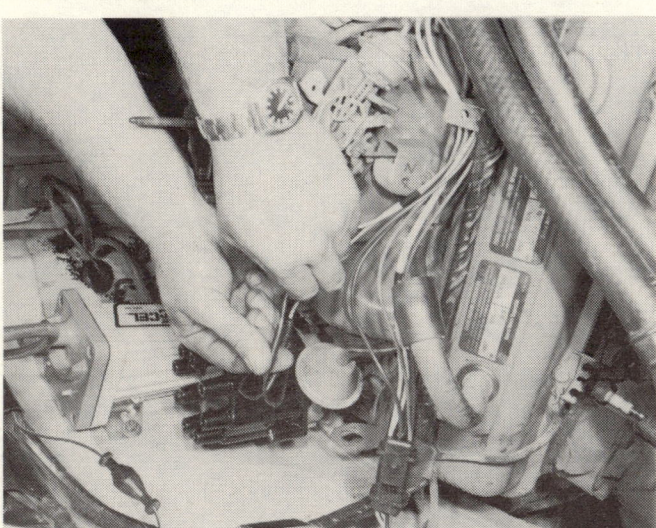

9. Plug the sensor leads into their matching recepticles on the wiring harness, then secure the harness wires neatly in place with the plastic ties provided.

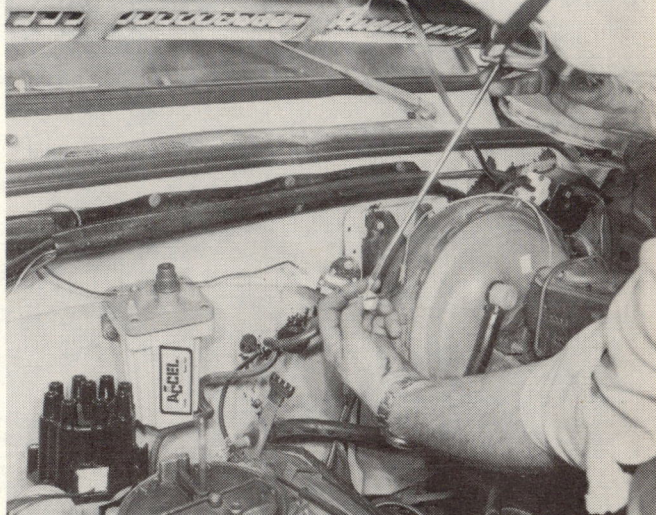

10. A ballast resistor furnished with the Accel coil must be installed. If your vehicle uses a separate ballast resistor, insert this one between yours and the Super Coil.

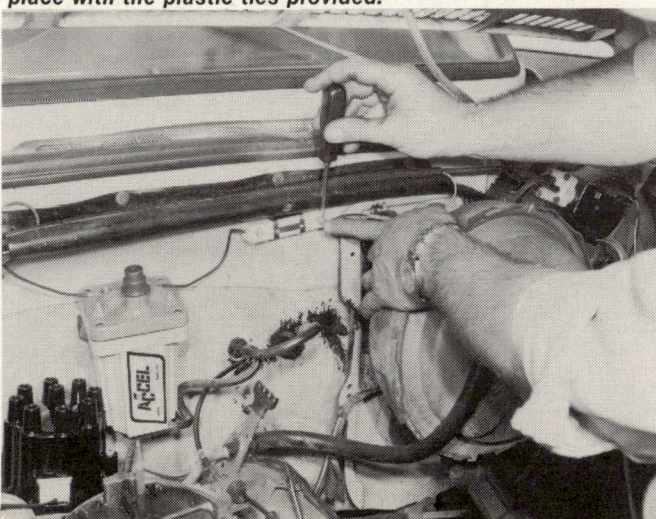

11. Attach the new ballast resistor to the firewall and tighten all connections snugly. Position components to produce as neat an installation as possible.

12. The finishing touch comes with the replacement of the stock plug wires with a custom set of Accel 8mm Silicone Suppression Core wires. You're ready to roll!

HOW-TO: **MALLORY LED CONVERSION**

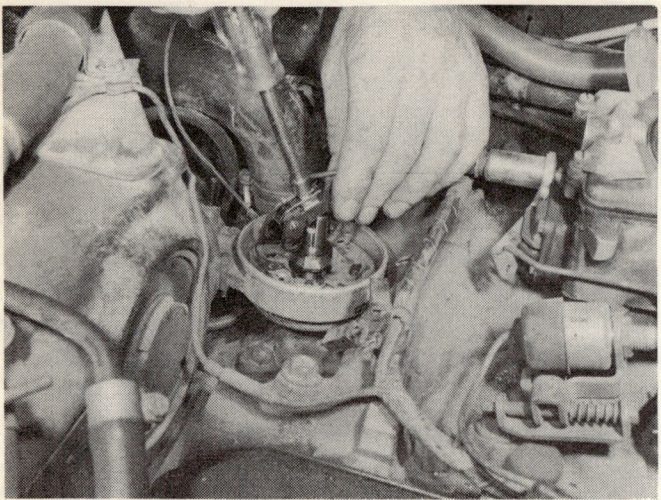

1. Installing Mallory Unilite conversion begins with removal of old breaker point/condenser set. Front-mounted distributors like this make in-vehicle installation easier than rear-mounted ones.

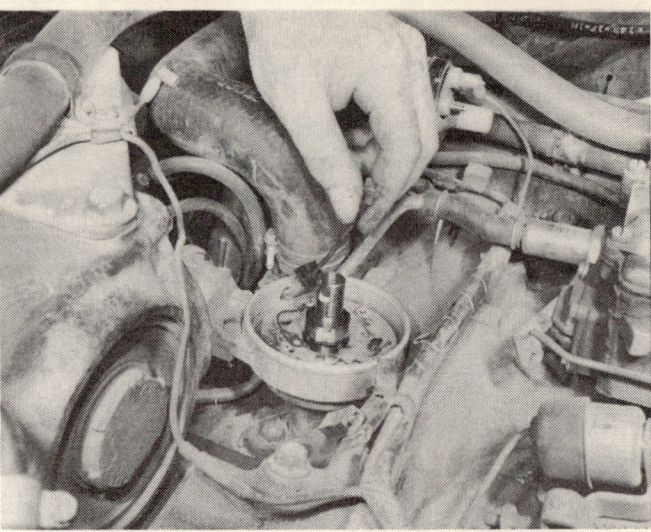

2. Disconnect the primary lead from the coil and pull it through the distributor housing opening. Remove lead with old rubber grommet and discard.

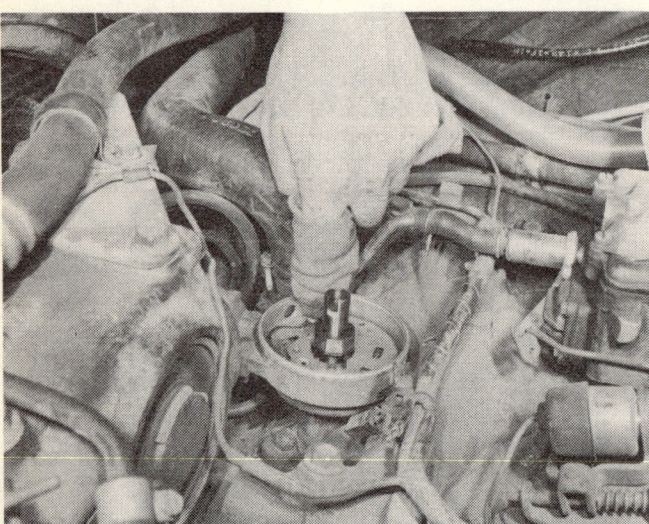

3. Dirt and excess lubricant are the major enemies of distributors. Clean the breaker plate thoroughly with a lint-free cloth moistened with solvent.

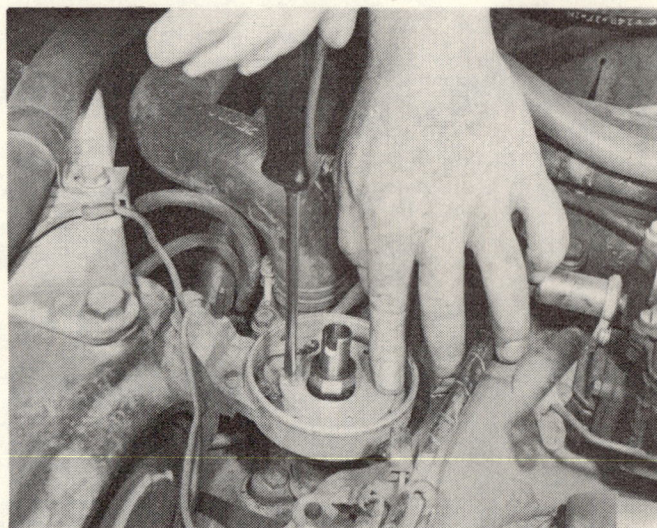

4. Position the lower mounting plate and install with the screws provided in the kit. Make sure all holes are aligned, then snug the screws down tight.

5. Fit the upper mounting plate over the lower one and install the two attaching screws. Tighten snugly to prevent vibration from loosening them.

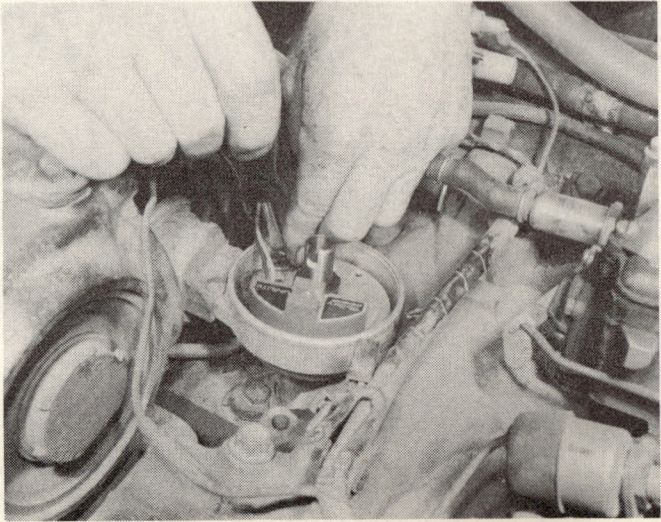

6. Install the optic module with the remaining screws and install the new rubber grommet furnished in the distributor housing hole with a screwdriver blade.

7. Fit module leads through the grommet and install them in the plastic terminal pin housing. Green lead must be installed under the index rib. Seat each lead until it locks in place.

8. Snap module lead connector to the wire harness furnished, then fit the optic interruptor/rotor assembly over the distributor cam and seat, just as you would a new rotor.

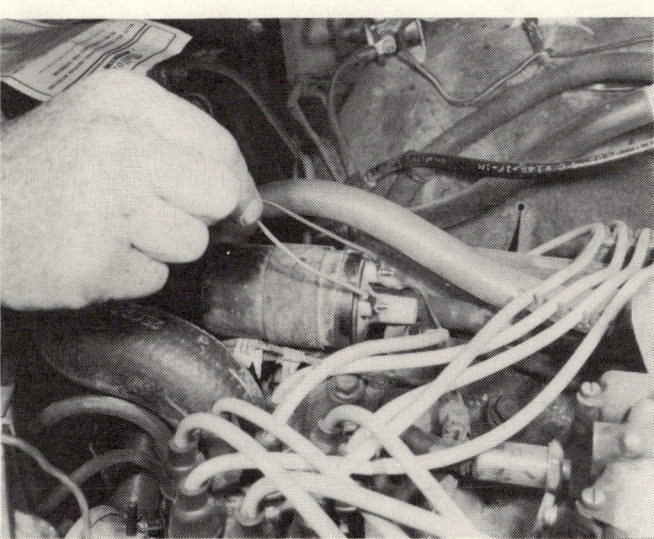

9. If the stock coil is retained, connect red/brown lead to positive terminal and green/brown lead to negative terminal. The brown lead goes to ground.

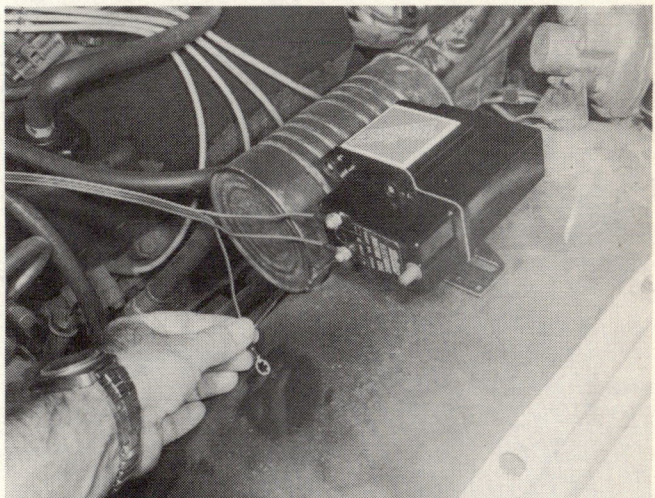

10. If a Mallory Electronic Coil is installed, mount it on the fenderwell or firewall. Drill a hole, scrape a small area around it clean and attach the ground wire shown.

11. Install a new Mallory 7mm silicone wire set. Replace one plug wire at a time to avoid mixups. Use of the numbered heat shrink sleeves included in the kit is shown here.

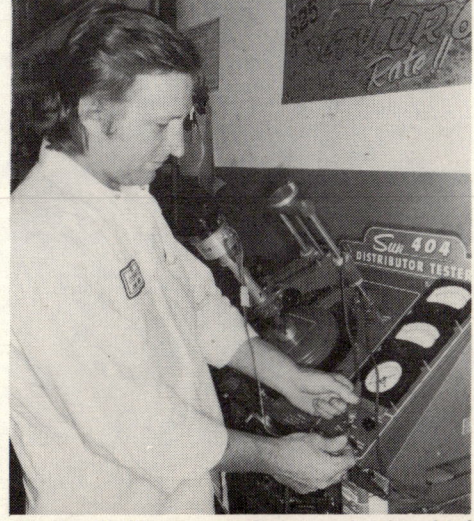

12. The Unilite conversion can also be obtained already installed in a Mallory distributor. If you go this route, have the advance curve checked on a distributor tester.

TROUBLESHOOTING ELECTRONIC IGNITIONS

As we've seen, breakerless or electronic ignitions are really quite similar to the conventional breaker-point ignition—both use many of the same components and do the same job. The difference is in how the primary circuit is interrupted to produce high voltage from the coil that fires the spark plugs. Breaker-point ignitions accomplish this by opening the contact points; breakerless ignitions do it by a transistor that controls primary current flow through the primary side of the coil.

We've already discussed the basic operation of each type of system in previous chapters. Here, we'll give you the information you need to troubleshoot your electronic ignition. Understand that if your engine has electronic controls, you can only troubleshoot the ignition to a certain point without special equipment. And if you want to modify the ignition for any reason, remember that the computer will not allow you to change the distributor timing curve.

PRECAUTIONS

There are several precautions you should take when working with an electronic ignition. Making a goof with a breaker-point ignition is not likely to be expensive; the same goof can blow the computer and other expensive electronic components when you're working on a breakerless ignition. First, remember that the secondary voltage is considerably higher with a breakerless ignition. If you're careless, you can get a very bad shock which can even be lethal to some people.

When you're testing a breakerless ignition, you must make all test connections with the ignition switch off. You should also check for frayed or damaged insulation on wiring. Look for corroded or loose ground connections at the control unit. Any short to ground can destroy electronic components more quickly than you can blink an eye. When you're finished testing, make sure the ignition is off before disconnecting any test equipment. If the engine is running or the ignition switch is on, the high-voltage surge created when you remove the test equipment can also be destructive.

If you're going to run a compression test, be sure to disconnect the pickup connector from the wiring harness at the distributor—with the ignition off. And use a magnetic or induction-type timing light—don't connect a series pickup timing light to a plug wire with the engine running. Whenever you disconnect the battery, make sure the ignition switch is off. If you pull a plug wire or the coil lead for a spark test, be sure to keep the gap the spark has to jump to about ⅜ inch or less. If the gap is too wide and the spark doesn't jump it, you may end up with a damaged control module.

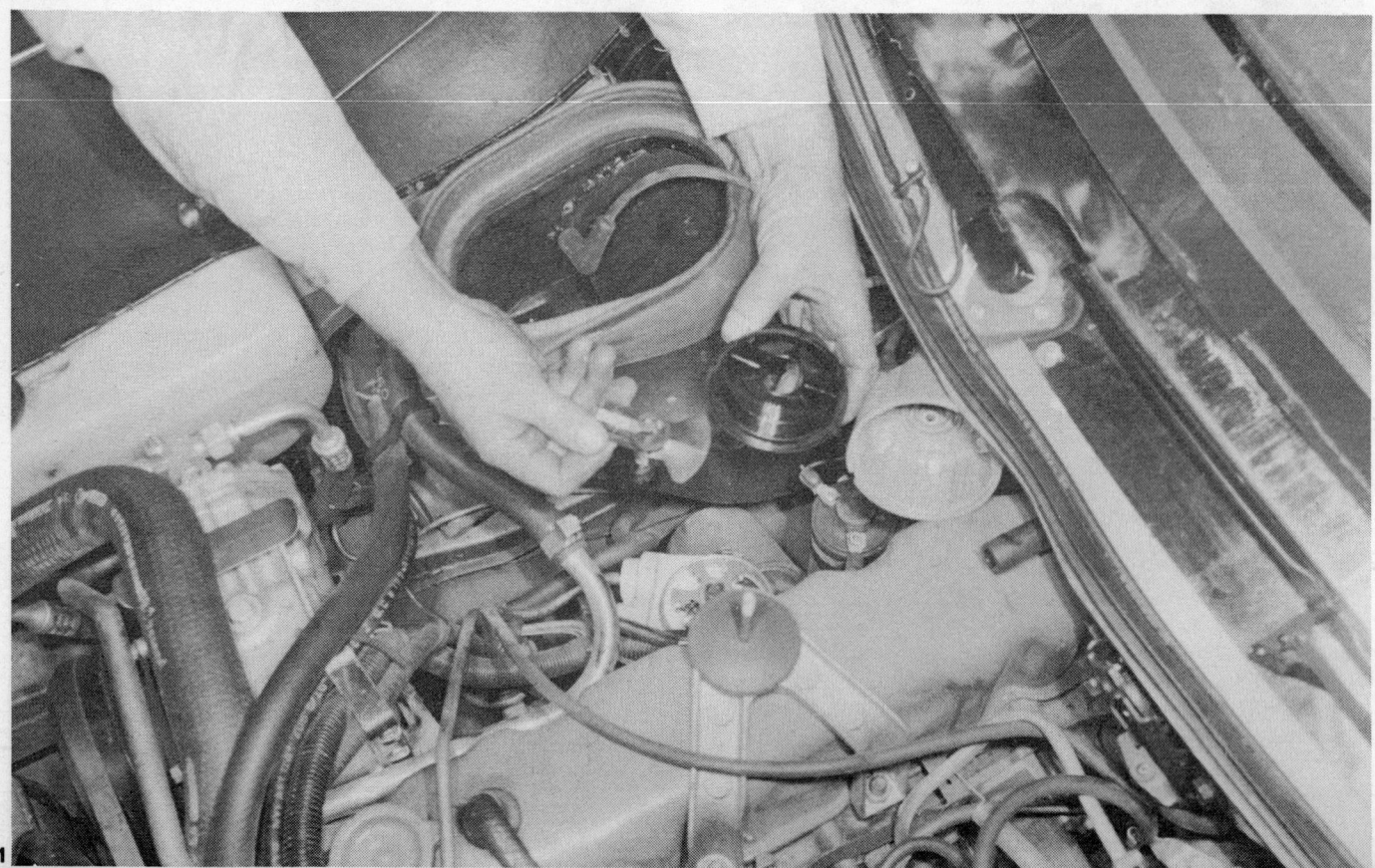

1

Don't use inexpensive off-brand name replacement components unless you are positive that they meet OEM (original equipment manufacturer) specifications. You can buy everything from distributor caps and rotors to electronic control units at a much cheaper price, but you'll pay for it somewhere along the line.

Distributor caps and rotors used with conventional ignitions were made of bakelite and served their purpose very well. Unfortunately, bakelite cannot withstand the high voltages of a breakerless system for very long. Breakerless distributors require a cap made of a material that will not only resist high voltages but also prevent carbon tracking in the secondary system.

The inexpensive control units do not have the same protective circuitry built into them—that's one big reason why they're less expensive. Such units will perform satisfactorily for a while, but eventually you'll end up with one or more problems for which you can find no logical answer—primarily because you assume that the control unit is doing the job it's supposed to do. Stay with name-brand parts and you'll avoid many problems you don't need.

Now, let's look at the peculiarities of each major system used on domestic cars. Unless otherwise specified, the secondary circuit tests you should perform are identical to those of a breaker-point ignition. If no problem shows up in the secondary circuit, you'll have to check the components in the primary circuit. Each test should be performed in the order given, since it is designed to check a particular component. If the test indicates something wrong, make the necessary repairs before continuing the procedure.

PRESTOLITE BID SYSTEM (1974-77 AMC & Jeep)

The BID system used by AMC contains four major components: a trigger wheel and sensor in the distributor, an ignition coil, and the electronic control unit. The trigger wheel and sensor send a timing signal to the control unit, which turns the ignition coil on or off. The sensor and vacuum-advance units proved to be the weak links in the chain.

Air-Gap Check

There must be 0.050-inch clearance between the trigger wheel and sensor. The use of a positioning gauge is necessary whenever the sensor is removed or replaced. Air gap is then checked with an L-shaped 0.050-inch wire gauge.

Ignition Coil Check

Check the coil on the car with an ohmmeter. Warm the engine to operating temperature and turn the ignition off. Disconnect the high-tension lead and both primary leads from the coil. Connect the ohmmeter leads to the primary terminals (– and +). If the ohmmeter does not read between 1 and 2 ohms on the low scale, replace the coil. Now connect the ohmmeter between the coil tower and the + primary terminal. If it does not read 8000–17,500 ohms, replace the coil.

Cranking Voltage Test

To see if the ignition system is getting sufficient voltage, perform a cranking voltage test. Connect your voltmeter to the coil positive (+) terminal and a good engine ground. Turn the ignition switch on. The voltmeter scale should read 12-13 volts. If it reads less, there's high resistance between the battery (through the ignition switch) and the coil. Locate and correct the problem before proceeding. If the voltage reading is okay,

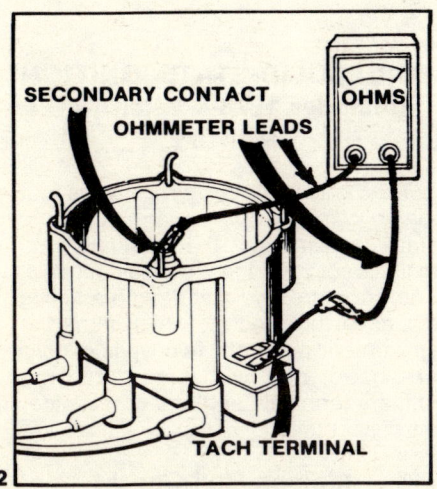

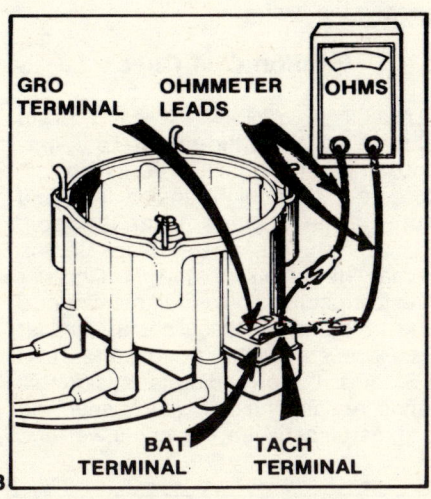

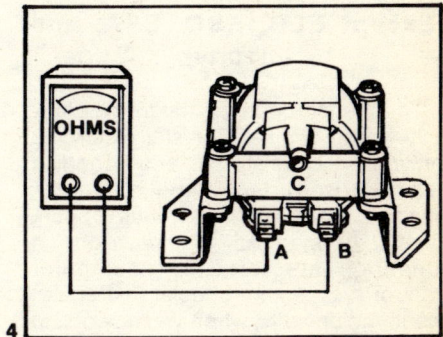

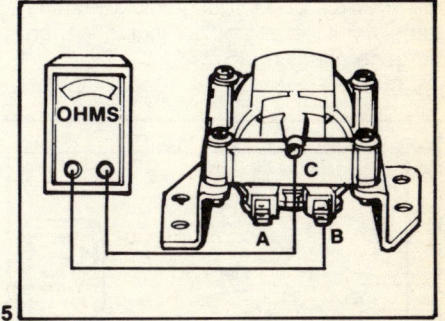

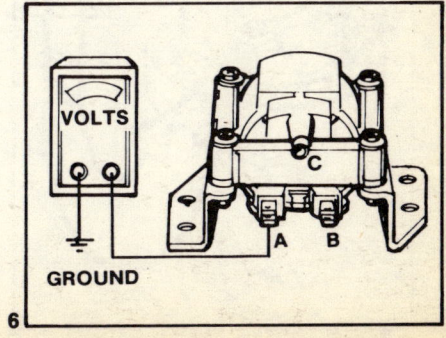

1. Breakerless distributors require the same kind of care as breaker point units. Periodic cap and rotor inspections should be a routine part of any tune-up.

2. V-6/V-8 HEI Primary Resistance Ignition Coil Test
   0.3 to 1.0 ohm reading

3. V-6/V-8 HEI Secondary Resistance Ignition Coil Test
   Prior to May 1975—16,000 to 40,000 ohms
   After May 1975—Infinite reading

4. I4/I6 HEI Primary Resistance Ignition Coil Test
   A to B — 0.3 to 1.0 ohm reading

5. I4/I6 HEI Secondary Resistance Ignition Coil Test
   B to C — 6,000 to 30,000 ohms

6. I4/I6 HEI Cranking Voltage Test
   Ignition switch On—Battery voltage
   Engine cranking—9.6 volts or more

TROUBLESHOOTING ELECTRONIC IGNITIONS

crank the engine over with the ignition switch and read the voltmeter. If it's less than 9.6 volts, don't go any further until you recharge or replace the battery.

Sensor Check

With the ignition off, disconnect the sensor connector from the wiring harness. Connect an ohmmeter across the sensor connector leads. It should read between 1.6 and 2.4 volts on the low scale. Wiggle the sensor wires while you take the reading. If the meter needle does not remain steady, you've got a sensor problem.

Electronic Control Unit

About all you can check is to make sure the electrical connections are clean and tight. If testing to this point does not turn up the cause of the problem, try replacing the control unit to see if the car runs better. If not, head for the dealer.

CHRYSLER ELECTRONIC IGNITION
(Except ELB, ESC, ESA, and Imports)

The test procedures that follow apply only to the original Chrysler electronic ignition (which is still used on Canadian vehicles) used on six- and eight-cylinder engines. Cars with Lean Burn, Spark Control, or Spark Advance have ignition functions integrated with computer control and require special test equipment. Incidentally, when you're working around the control module mounted on the firewall, don't touch the switching transistor if the engine is running—it can be quite shocking.

Air-Gap Check

Use a 0.008-inch (1972-76) or 0.006-inch (1977 on) nonmagnetic feeler gauge for this test. Insert it between a reluctor tooth and the pickup coil. It should fit snugly but move smoothly between the two. If not, loosen the holddown screw on the pickup coil. Set the proper gap and tighten the screw. Rotate the crankshaft a couple of turns and recheck the gap with a 0.010-inch (1972-76) or 0.008-inch (1977 on) nonmagnetic feeler gauge. It should not fit. If it does, there's a good chance that either the distributor shaft is bent or its bushings are worn.

Pickup Coil/Reluctor Check

With the ignition off, remove the distributor cap and check the reluctor visually. If any one of the teeth is cracked, chipped, or corroded, or has rounded edges, replace it before proceeding. Disconnect the distributor connector and connect an ohmmeter across the connector terminals. The resistance should read between 150 and 900 ohms, with between 500 and 700 preferred. Wiggle the wires while watching the ohmmeter needle; it should remain steady unless there's a break or short in the wiring.

Ignition Coil Check

Check the coil on the car with an ohmmeter. Warm the engine to operating temperature and turn the ignition off. Disconnect the high-tension lead and both primary leads from the coil. Connect the ohmmeter leads to the primary terminals (− and +). Chrysler Prestolite coils should read between 1.6 and 1.8 ohms on the low scale; Chrysler Essex coils should read between 1.4 and 1.6 ohms. If the reading is outside this range, replace the coil. Now connect the ohmmeter between the coil tower and the + primary terminal. Prestolite coils should read 9400-11,700 ohms and Essex coils 8000-11,000 ohms. If the secondary reading is not up to par, you need a new coil.

Ballast Resistor Check

This should be performed when the engine is cold. With the ignition switch off, disconnect the ballast resistor leads. Connect an ohmmeter to the auxiliary resistor—you can identify this one by the "5" stamped in the brass connector. It should read between 4.75 and 5.75 ohms. Repeat the procedure to test the remaining two resistor terminals (compensating side). The meter should read 0.5 ohm (1972-78) or 1.2 ohms (1979 on). If you happen to have a 1980-on model equipped with a single resistor, it should read between 1.12 and 1.38 ohms. If any reading is out of spec, replace the resistor.

Most electrical problems with this ignition center around a poor ground on the electronic control unit, a loose or corroded distributor-to-control-unit connection or a bad ballast resistor. Since the control unit cannot be tested, it is reasonable to assume that it is the cause of your problem if other tests have turned up nothing.

FORD SOLID-STATE IGNITION
(Includes 1978 & Later AMC Models)

The Solid-State system contains four major components: an armature and stator assembly in the distributor, the ignition coil, and the electronic module. The armature and stator send a timing signal to the module, which turns the ignition coil on or off. Two types of coils are used: one with screw-and-nut primary terminals and one with a slide-on connector.

Ignition Coil Check

Check the coil on the car with an ohmmeter. Warm the engine to operating temperature and turn the ignition off. Disconnect the high-tension lead and both primary leads from the coil. Connect the ohmmeter leads to the primary terminals (− and +). The primary resistance should be 1-2 ohms on Ford coils and 1.13-1.23 on AMC coils.

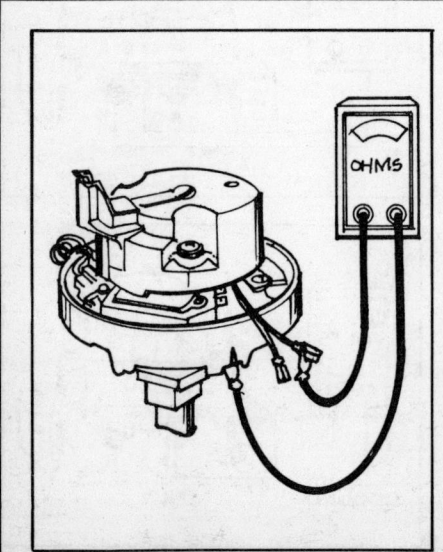
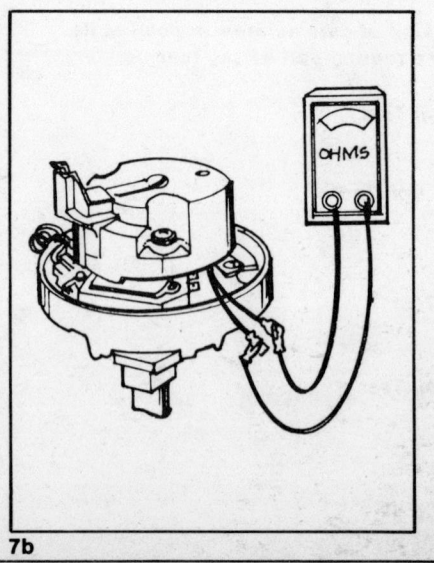

7A. HEI Pick-up Coil Test
Infinite reading if good

7B. HEI Pick-up Coil Test
500 to 1,500 ohms if good

Connect the ohmmeter between the coil tower and the + primary terminal. Secondary resistance should be 7000-13,000 ohms on Ford coils and 7700-9300 ohms on AMC coils. If either reading is not up to specs, you should replace the coil.

Stator Check

With the ignition off, remove the distributor cap and inspect the plastic around the stator winding. Hairline cracks or starlike breaks can cause hard starting in damp weather and may also be responsible for engine backfiring. Check the armature teeth for cracking, chipping, corrosion, or rounded edges. If either the armature or the stator requires replacement, replace each one as a unit.

Disconnect the stator lead from the distributor and connect an ohmmeter between the orange and purple connector wires. If the resistance is outside the 400-800-ohm range, replace the stator and armature. Connect the ohmmeter between the black connector wire and a good ground. Manually operate the vacuum advance and watch the meter needle—it should read zero resistance at all times.

Electronic Module

Make sure all connections are clean and tight, and that the connectors are filled with the recommended silicone grease (Ford Dielectric Compound). Other than this, there is nothing you can do to check the module. If everything else checks out satisfactorily, replace the module with one known to be good. Incidentally, Ford has had one of the highest unnecessary module replacement rates in the industry. By the same token, early Ford module engine compartment mounting was ill chosen in many cases, and modules failed prematurely because of excessive heat or moisture, or both.

GENERAL MOTORS HEI IGNITION SYSTEM

The HEI system also contains four components: a timer core, magnetic pickup, electronic control module, and a unique coil—all mounted in the distributor (1974-77 four- and six-cylinder distributors used a remote coil). The procedures given do not apply to any of the HEI variations, since they are all interactive in one way or another with the computer.

Ignition Coil Check (V-6 and V-8 Engines)

With the ignition off, remove the single terminal battery feed connector and the three-terminal cap-to-distributor connector. Remove the distributor cap and connect the ohmmeter to the terminals on the cap marked "Tach" and "Bat." The ohmmeter should read between 0.3 and 1 ohm.

Leave the ohmmeter lead connected to the "Tach" terminal and connect the other lead to the carbon button in the top of the cap. On systems built before May 1975, the ohmmeter should read 16,000-40,000 ohms. On all others it should read infinity.

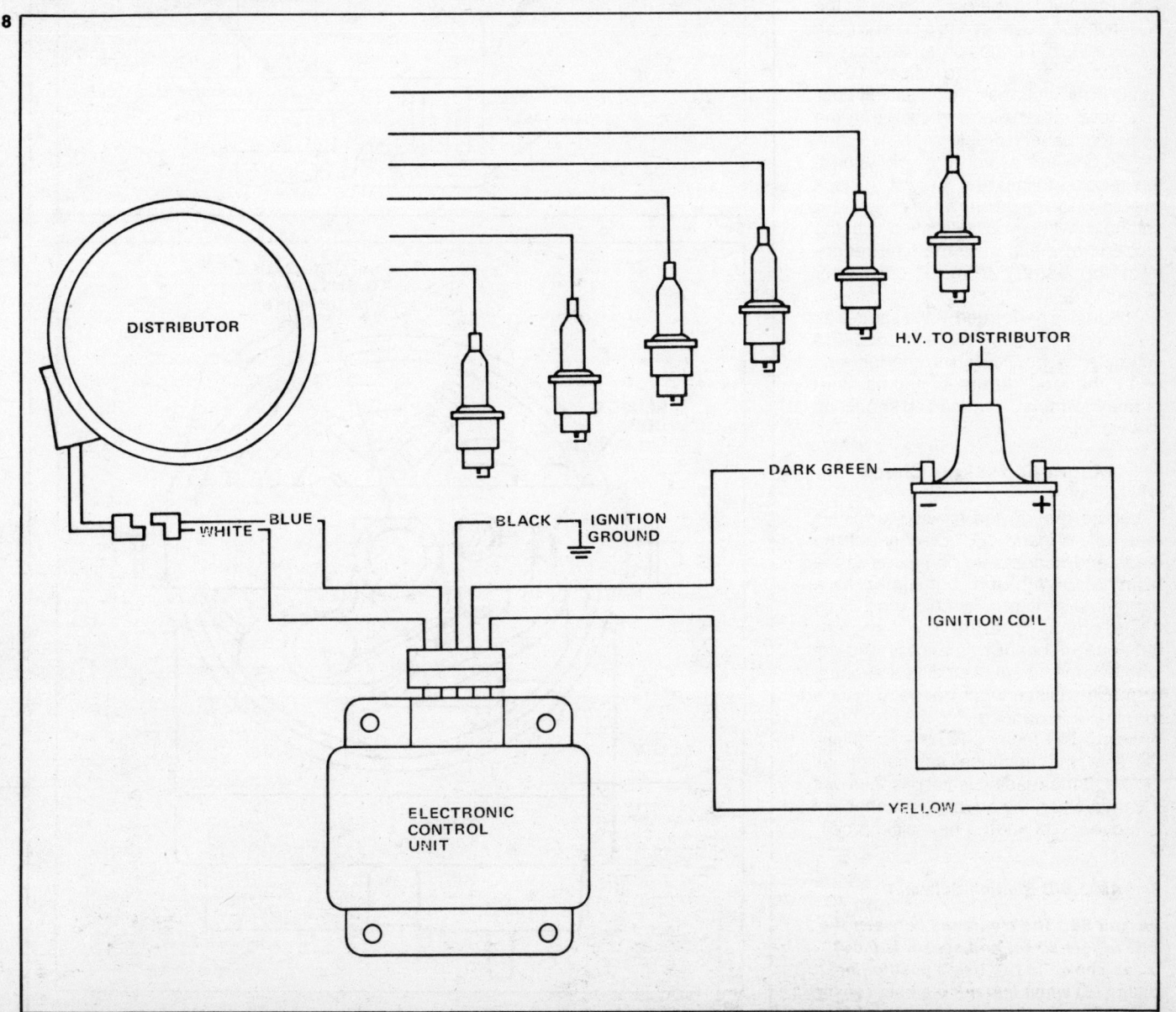

TROUBLESHOOTING ELECTRONIC IGNITIONS

Ignition Coil Check (Four- and Six-Cylinder Engines Through 1977)

Disconnect the coil-to-distributor connector, the battery feed connector, and the high-tension wire from the coil to the distributor cap center tower. Connect an ohmmeter between the primary (blade) terminals. The meter should read 0.3-1.0 ohm. Switch the ohmmeter over to the high scale and connect it between the coil secondary terminal and the righthand primary terminal (with the coil terminals facing toward you). The ohmmeter should read between 6000 and 30,000 ohms. If any reading is out of spec, replace the coil.

Cranking Voltage Check

To perform a cranking voltage test on integral (V-6/V-8) coils, disconnect the battery terminal or feed connector at the distributor cap. Hook the positive voltmeter lead to the connector and the negative voltmeter lead to a good engine ground. Turn the ignition switch on and read the meter—it should indicate 12-13 volts. If the voltage is excessively low, you have either high resistance in the circuit or battery problems. Now crank the engine and watch the voltmeter. If the reading falls under 9.6 volts, check the ignition switch and/or starter solenoid. When you're finished with the procedure, make sure that you reconnect the battery terminal connector properly.

The test is performed in the same way for remote coils, except that the voltmeter is connected to the lefthand (with the coil terminals facing you) primary terminal. The reading should be the same.

Magnetic Pickup Check

Locate the ignition module terminals marked "W" and "G." Disconnect the leads and connect an ohmmeter to the terminals. With the ohmmeter at a midrange setting, it should read 500-1500 ohms. Operate the vacuum-advance mechanism manually and not whether the needle remains stationary or moves. Disconnect one lead from a terminal and connect it to the distributor housing. The meter should read infinity. Operate the advance mechanism as before. If the reading is out of specs or if it varies when the advance mechanism is moved, you need a new pickup coil.

Electronic Control Module

The module is integral to the distributor and cannot be checked. If removed for any reason or replaced, be sure that the base of the module and the mating base of the distributor housing are adequately coated with silicone grease. This absorbs heat, and if it's lacking or not used, the module will fail very quickly.

When All Else Fails

As you can tell, there isn't too much you can do in the way of testing the secondary side of electronic ignitions without special test equipment. This is very expensive and would be a foolish investment for a nonprofessional mechanic. The best advice is to keep the ignition system in good working order, practice good preventive maintenance, and see your trusty shop mechanic if all else fails.

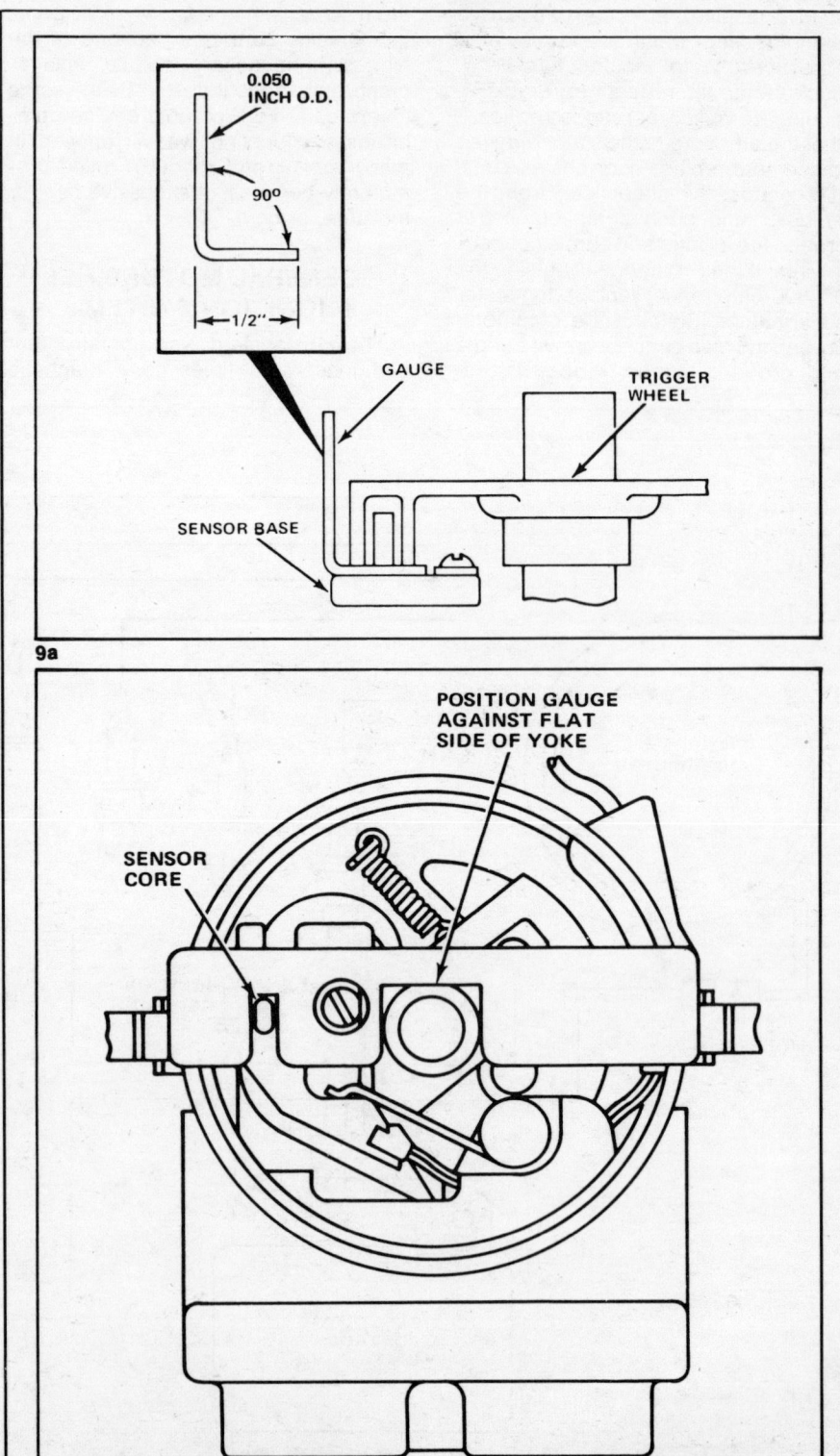

8. *AMC BID Ignition Schematic*

9A and 9B. *The clearance between the BID trigger wheel and sensor is 0.050 in. as shown in (A). Use a positioning gauge (B) when installing a new sensor or trigger wheel.*

ELECTRONIC ENGINE CONTROLS

The distributor has always been the key factor in engine operation, as it routes secondary voltage to the spark plugs. But the breaker points used in a distributor before 1975 were its weakness. They could handle only a limited amount of high voltage and burned easily; but more important, they wore rapidly, causing a slight yet constant change in dwell. To keep a breaker-point distributor working properly, periodic timing adjustments and point service were necessary.

Breakerless distributors came into general use to overcome the disadvantages inherent in the breaker-point ignition system. The transistors, which replaced the breaker points, do not wear out, can handle much higher voltage, and operate more rapidly. The result is longer plug life, less engine misfire, greater efficiency, and lower emissions. Without points to wear and burn, unburned HC from misfiring is eliminated. Without points, ignition timing doesn't fluctuate.

Along the way, control of engine operation was gradually modified. Various components were used to control ignition timing by controlling the vacuum supply to the distributor. Thus, a retard solenoid was used on some Chrysler distributors to retard timing during hot idle. Others used an advance solenoid to advance timing during starting. All automakers used some form of transmission spark control in which ignition timing was determined by the transmission gear or a speed switch mounted on the transmission. These systems were further complicated by thermal switches that activated, deactivated, or overrode them according to coolant temperature. Distributor operation had become dependent upon a large number of variables.

1. Electronic engine controls had their beginning in the Chrysler Lean Burn System.

2. The original analog computer has been discarded in favor of a digital computer now called the Chrysler Spark Control system and mounted on the air cleaner housing. The newest version incorporates electronic engine timing.

ELECTRONIC LEAN BURN SYSTEM (ELB)

Chrysler led the way toward electronic engine control with its introduction of the Lean Burn system on some 1976 models in an effort to reduce emissions and fuel consumption further. The engine's ignition system is controlled by a small on-board computer that receives information from seven engine sensors to instantly calculate changing engine variables. Within milliseconds, it determines the exact amount of spark lead required for optimum engine operation. Igniting the plugs at precisely the right moment, the Lean Burn system produces complete combustion of very lean (up to 18:1) air-fuel mixtures. The spark curve is infinitely and instantly variable to meet different engine operating conditions, instead of the constant curve

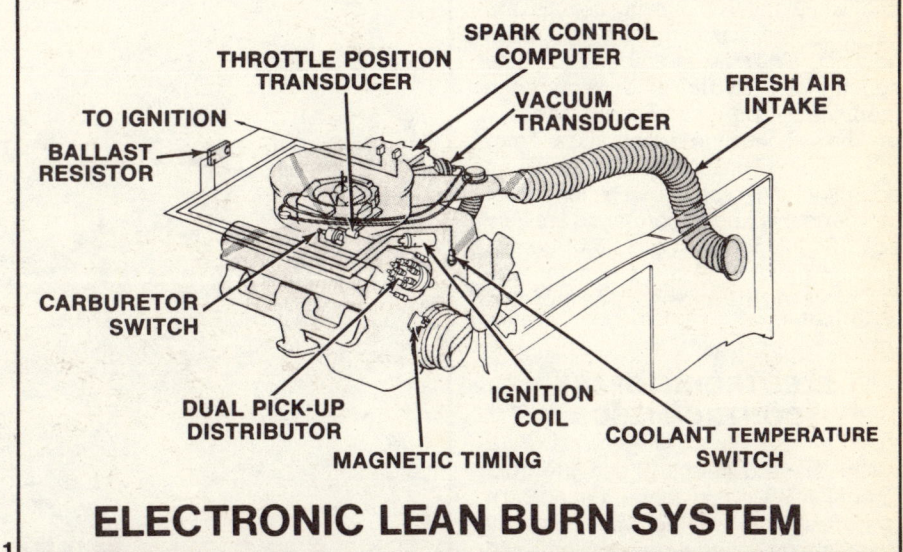

ELECTRONIC LEAN BURN SYSTEM

ELECTRONIC ENGINE CONTROLS

provided by conventional and breakerless systems.

The "start" pickup in the distributor tells the computer when the engine is cranking so that proper timing can be supplied. Once the engine starts, the "run" pickup takes over. This pickup senses both engine speed and the moment when each piston comes up to top dead center (TDC). Other information is provided by the coolant and air cleaner temperature sensors, throttle position transducer, carburetor switch sensor, and a vacuum transducer. The computer provides extra advance during the first 60 seconds of engine operation, which raises the idle for faster warmup. This additional advance is slowly eliminated and the coolant sensor signals the computer to prevent any further advance until the coolant reaches normal operating temperature.

At this point, all sensors are transmitting their information to the computer and while the run pickup signals are used as the basis for the maximum advance available at any given engine speed, inputs from the other sensors can modify it. Computer failure for any reason switches the system into a "limp-in" mode. This permits continued operation until repairs can be made, but fuel economy and performance are very poor. Should the start pickup or control module function of the computer also fail, however, the engine will neither start nor run.

ELECTRONIC SPARK CONTROL (ESC)

Chrysler experienced considerable difficulty with the initial Lean Burn systems. The analog spark control computer gave numerous problems and was replaced on 1978 models by a second-generation computer using a single printed circuit board (instead of two), with all components connected to the computer housing by a single 10-pin wiring connector. The system was renamed Electronic Spark Control and uses a single pickup in the distributor to control both start and run modes. Further modifications were made in the system used in 1980 and later engines by incorporating a feedback carburetion system in which the same computer that controls ignition also controls the air-fuel ratio. This system uses a "combustion computer" consisting of the electronic printed circuit board previously used and a microprocessor. The microprocessor is an electronic module contained within the computer to process signals from engine sensors. Since it uses digital electronic circuitry, the microprocessor offers more operating precision and programming flexibility than the voltage-dependent analog system used in Lean Burn. This latest

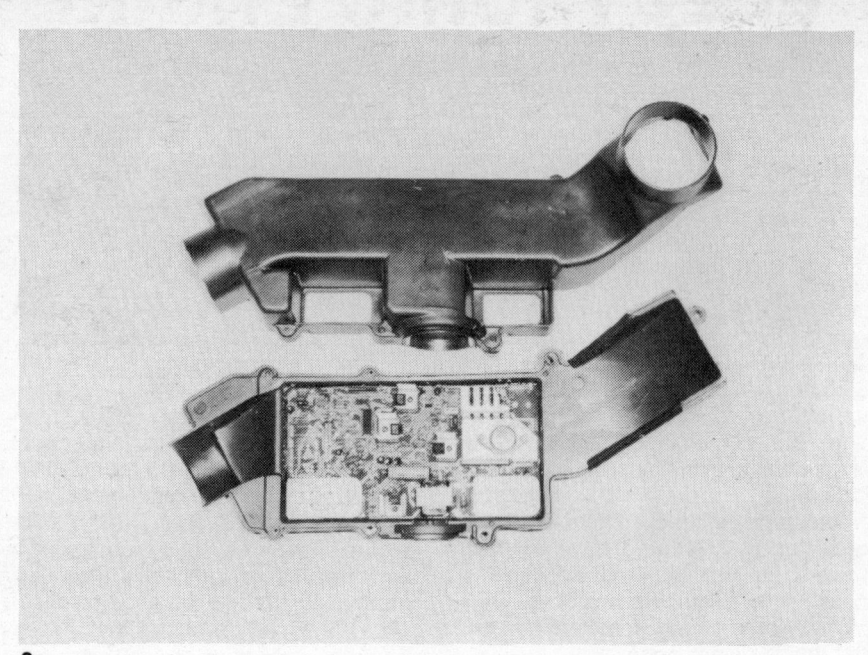
3a

3b

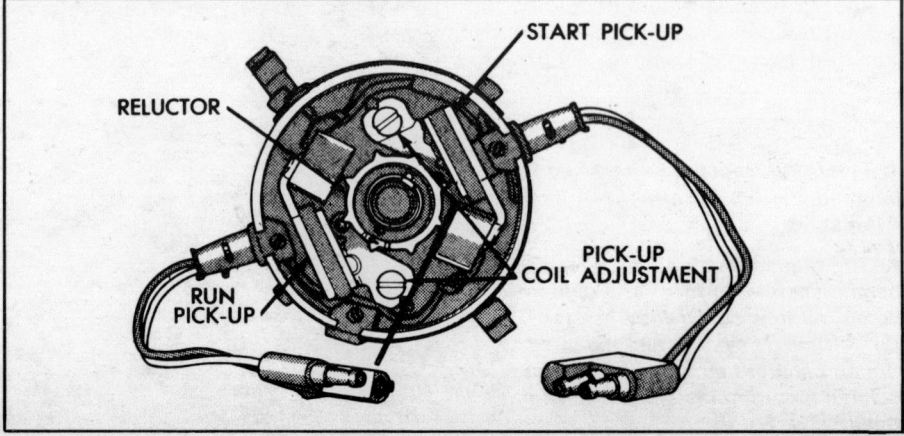
4

version is called Electronic Spark Advance (ESA).

ESA distributors contain dual pickups that function in the same manner as those used in the ELB system. During engine cranking, the start pickup signals the computer, which fires the spark plugs at a fixed amount of advance. Once the engine starts, timing is controlled by the computer based on data received from the run pickup in the distributor, as modified by data from various engine sensors. Two factors determine how much spark advance is provided—engine speed and engine vacuum. Advance from vacuum is provided by the computer when the carburetor switch is open. The amount is programmed into the computer and is proportional to the amount of engine vacuum and rpm. Advance from engine speed is provided when the carburetor switch is open and is programmed to engine rpm. Unlike Lean Burn distributors, those used with ESC and ESA systems contain no centrifugal advance weights. They can be identified by their lack of a vacuum-advance unit on the distributor housing. The computer controls both functions, simplifying the distributor considerably.

CHRYSLER FOUR-CYLINDER SYSTEMS

The systems discussed thus far pertain only to six- and eight-cylinder engines; the electronic ignition fitted to Chrysler four-cylinder engines is an integral part of the ESC system and differs considerably. The distributor contains a Hall-Effect pickup assembly, which tells the ESC module when to fire the spark plugs. There is no advance mechanism within the distributor, and since the Hall-Effect assembly is permanently mounted, only a fixed amount of advance is available in the ignition system during the start mode. Once the engine starts, the run mode takes over and the amount of advance is determined by the ESC according to data received from the sensors.

The four-cylinder distributor caps from 1980 on use special plug wires that have attached terminals and are snapped in place through slots in the cap instead of being plugged into the cap towers. These wires can only be removed by taking off the cap and releasing a snap lock on each wire terminal from inside the cap. The distributor cap coil tower contains a pressed-in terminal to allow easy removal and replacement of the coil lead during servicing.

FORD ELECTRONIC ENGINE CONTROL (EEC) SYSTEM

The first electronic engine control system came from Ford on the 1978 Versailles. This system contains an Electronic Control Assembly or ECA, seven sensors, an air-pressure-operated EGR system, and a Dura-Spark II ignition module/coil with a modified distributor. Since the ECA controls all ignition timing, this EEC distributor has no centrifugal- or vacuum-advance mechanisms. A unique rotor of two-level design and an accompanying distributor cap allow advance from TDC to 60 degrees BTDC.

As the rotor turns, one of its high-voltage pickup arms aligns with a spoke of the center electrode plate in the distributor cap. This carries high voltage from the plate to the proper spark plug. The original distributor cap had two sets of numbers molded into its top. The inner ring was for use with the 302-cubic-inch V-8; the outer ring for the 351 and 400-cubic-inch engines. As a result, Versailles plug cables are not connected to the cap in their actual firing order. Changes were made in the rotor/cap design during the 1979 model year. These second-generation rotors and caps are not interchangeable with the earlier ones.

That same year saw the appearance

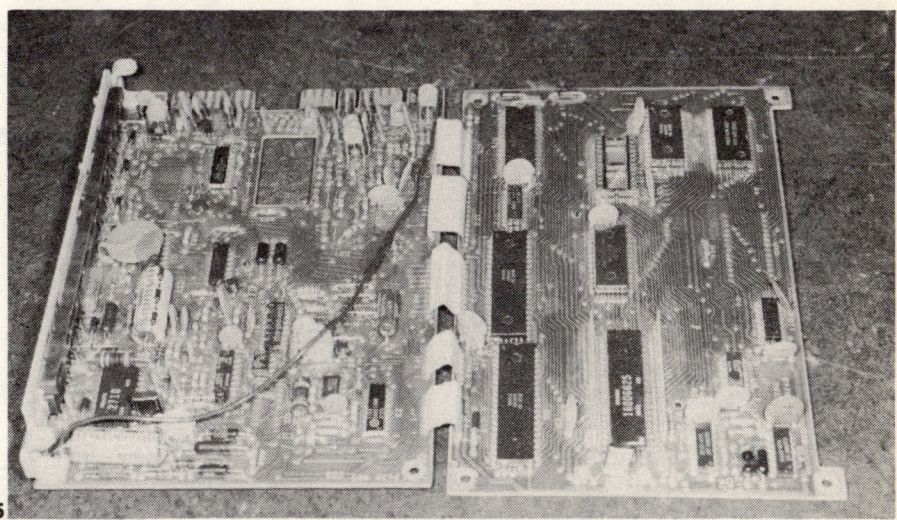

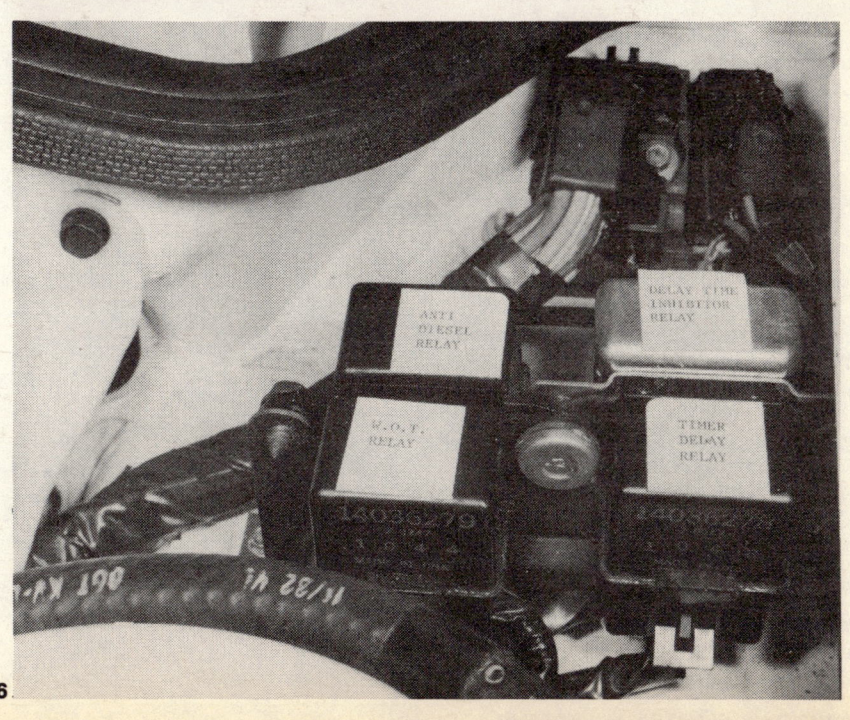

3A and 3B. Here's a peek inside Chrysler's electronic spark control computer (A). This master brain operates the logic module (B) which looks even more complex! The logic module is designed to carry voltages that the master computer cannot handle.
4. The Chrysler Electronic Spark control distributor uses separate magnetic pickup coils for start and run functions.
5. GM's Computer Command Contro or CCC electronic control module (ECM) looks like this inside—and it's getting more complex every year.
6. When GM announced its "J" car to the market, these four relays were necessary. A few months after introduction, two of the relay functions were incorporated in the ECM; by the next model year, all four relays were gone—the computer handled their functions.

IGNITION & ELECTRICAL SYSTEMS/67

ELECTRONIC ENGINE CONTROLS

of EEC-II. This differs from the original system in that it includes the canister purge function and incorporates a feedback carburetion system, similar to the 1980 Chrysler ESC system. In 1980 Ford dropped both EEC-I and EEC-II in favor of EEC-III, a more sophisticated application available in two versions—one for feedback carburetion systems (EEC-FBC) and the other for engines equipped with electronic fuel injection (EEC-EFI). If you think this is fast becoming confusing (1978–80), think of the poor mechanic.

A major difference between EEC-III and its predecessors is a self-test feature used in diagnosing malfunctions. The self-test is programmed into the computer memory of the calibration assembly (a part of the computer which adapts the main memory function for use with a given engine size and car line). Activating the program causes the computer to perform a system test to verify the connection and operation of the various sensors and activators. This self-test feature performs three basic functions:

1. It sends commands to the solenoids concerned and checks for a proper response.
2. It checks sensor readings, compares them with predetermined system parameters, and decides if they are reasonable or unreasonable.
3. It produces a series of numbered codes that tell you if the system is operating properly or if there is a malfunction.

Using the Self-Test Feature

Ford thoughtfully designed the self-test feature so that anyone could activate and interpret it—special equipment is available for this purpose, but is not required. All you need are a pair of self-power test lamps and a hand vacuum pump to troubleshoot the system yourself. Here's how to do it. You must first find the manifold/barometric pressure sensor (MBAR). This is a small oval device of white or black plastic with two nipples protruding from its housings. It is usually located on the right fender apron. One nipple leads to the intake manifold and the other to atmospheric pressure. Close to this sensor you'll find the dual air-control solenoids, also known as the TAD/TAB solenoids. The rear solenoid controls vacuum to the Thermactor air-diverter diaphragm (TAD), and the front one operates the Thermactor air-bypass diaphragm.

Once you've located and identified the two solenoids, you've got the two output points for connecting into the self-test mode. Clip a test lamp lead to the orange wire at one solenoid and ground the other lead. Repeat this with the other solenoid and rear lamp. Start the engine and warm to normal operating temperature. With the engine idling, connect the hand vacuum pump to the nipple marked "Vent" on the MBAR sensor. Pump down the sensor vacuum to 20-inch Hg and hold it for about five seconds. Since this is far below any possible normal barometric pressure, it fools the computer into thinking that something is wrong and the circuitry switches itself into the self-test mode to check the voltage points around the circuit. The results of this testing will be flashed in code on your test lamp.

Interpreting the Codes

The codes shown in the accompanying example are a series of pulses that cause the test lamp to turn on and off. Each pulse has a one-half-second on, one-half-second off duration—a sequence which represents the number "one." A full-second interval separates the code digits. If more than one code results from the self-test, a five-second interval will separate the two-digit codes. This is tricky to catch at first, and you may have to activate the system a second time to make sure you have read the code correctly. Here's an example of how the pattern would look:

A. ½ second on; ½ second off; ½ second on; ½ second off.
B. ½ second on; ½ second off; ½ second on; ½ second off; ½ second on; 5 full seconds off.
C. This equals Code 23—you've got a problem with the throttle position sensor.

DURA-SPARK III AND OTHER FEATURES

This breakerless ignition system appeared in 1979 and is used with all

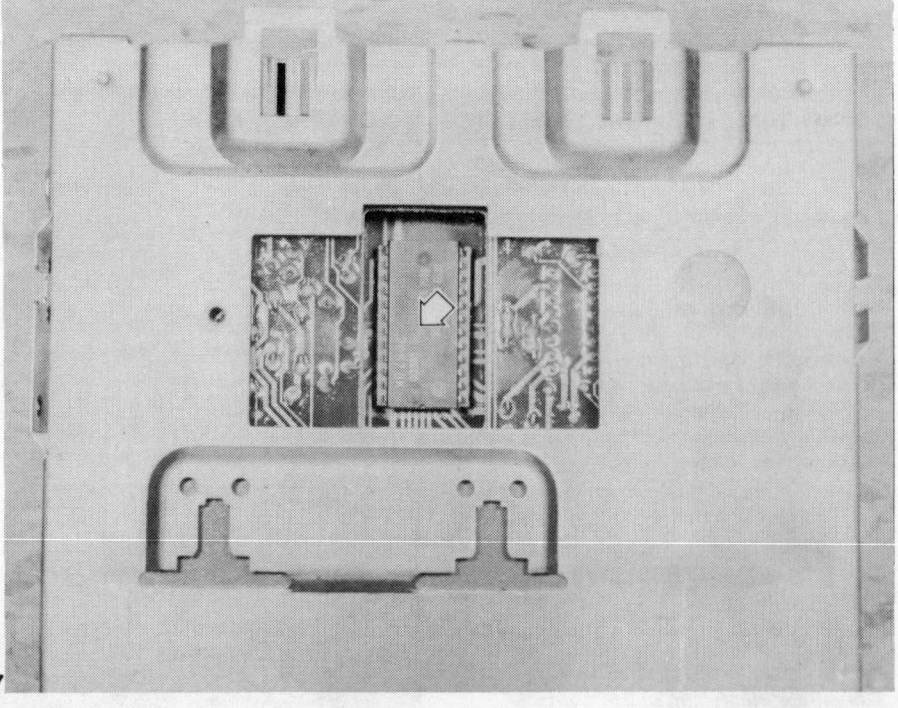

7

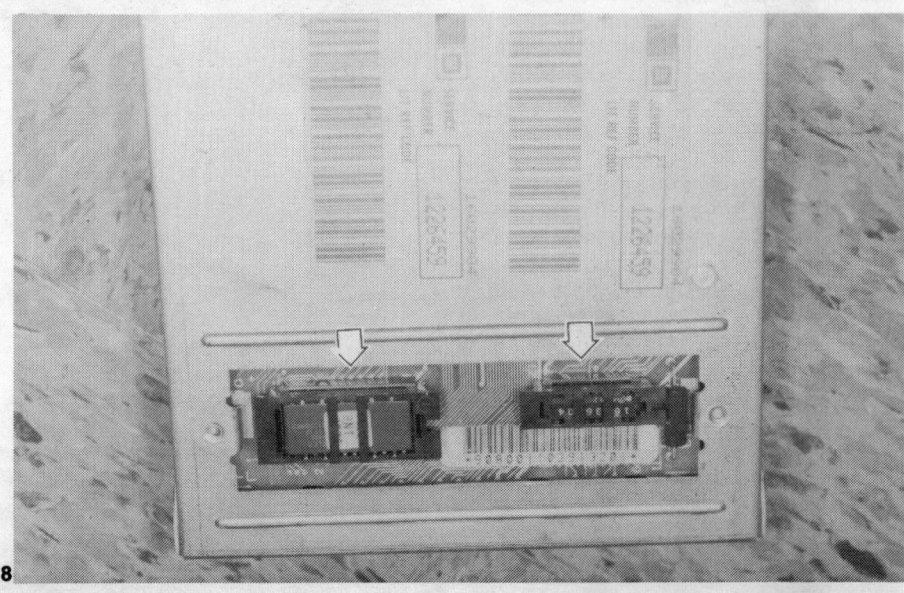

8

68/IGNITION & ELECTRICAL SYSTEMS

1980 and later engines fitted with EEC-III. It uses the same electronic control distributor as the Versailles but the ignition module contains fewer circuits. Those removed from the ignition module are located in the main computer or ECA. You can identify the Dura-Spark III module by the brown wiring grommet at its base.

Some Dura-Spark II ignitions incorporate a cranking retard feature. When the engine is cranking, the slow rpm signal of the distributor magnetic pickup activates a new circuit in the ignition module to retard cranking by 18 degrees. A white four-pin connector and a white wiring grommet at the base of the module identify the cranking retard feature.

Others have a dual-mode timing feature in which the module incorporates either altitude compensation or economy modes. This lets the module modify basic engine timing according to altitude or engine load conditions. A three-wire pigtail at the module connects to either a vacuum switch (economy) or a barometric pressure switch (altitude compensation). Distributor calibration provides the basic timing—the module provides a retard mode when required.

MICROPROCESSOR-CONTROL UNIT (MCU) SYSTEM

But wait, we're not done with Ford—not by a long shot. The MCU system appeared on 1980 California 2.3L engines. It has many of the EEC system features, but is less complicated and thus easier to service. It's also less expensive to manufacture. The other major difference is that it does not control ignition timing. A standard Dura-Spark distributor and ignition module are used.

The heart of the system is the MCU or microprocessor-control unit. Used with a feedback carburetion system and three-way catalytic converter, the MCU receives data input from an exhaust gas oxygen sensor, a cold temperature vacuum switch, an idle tracking switch and an engine rpm signal taken from the coil. Essentially, its job is to control air-fuel ratio to the engine cylinders based on how much oxygen is left in the exhaust gas.

The MCU system also has a self-test feature. A single-pin connector in the wiring harness is grounded and a volt-ohmmeter (VOM) connected across the Thermactor air-bypass solenoid (TAB). When the self-test mode is activated, the MCU module will test the system controls and inputs for proper operation. Voltage is pulsed in an on/off code sequence causing meter needle deflection. Instead of counting light flashes as in EEC-II, you count needle deflections.

ELECTRONIC ENGINE CONTROL-IV (EEC-IV) SYSTEM

This latest (1983) version of electronic engine control promises to make all other Ford systems obsolete in a short time. First introduced with the 1.6L fuel-injected engine in the Escort/Lynx and EXP/LN7 car lines, its use was expanded to other Ford engine applications during 1983, including the Ranger 2.8L, the Turbo T-Bird 2.3L, and the Tempo/Topaz 2.3L HSC engines. It is seeing even wider use on 1984 models.

EEC-IV is a giant leap foward in FoMoCo electronic engine control systems. The microprocessor contains over 300 different strategies programmed into it, is capable of reading seven different engine parameters, and changing each of the seven engine functions in less than 0.03 second—or one revolution of the crankshaft. It can handle one million logic and math operations each second!

In addition, it can determine and compensate for the age of the vehicle. This means that as the vehicle accumulates miles, and tolerances in the moving parts increase from wear, the EEC-IV module will sense this and adjust its operation for the particular characteristics of the car. And if that's not enough, it automatically senses changes in altitude and temperature, and compensates accordingly.

The system controls fuel delivery and

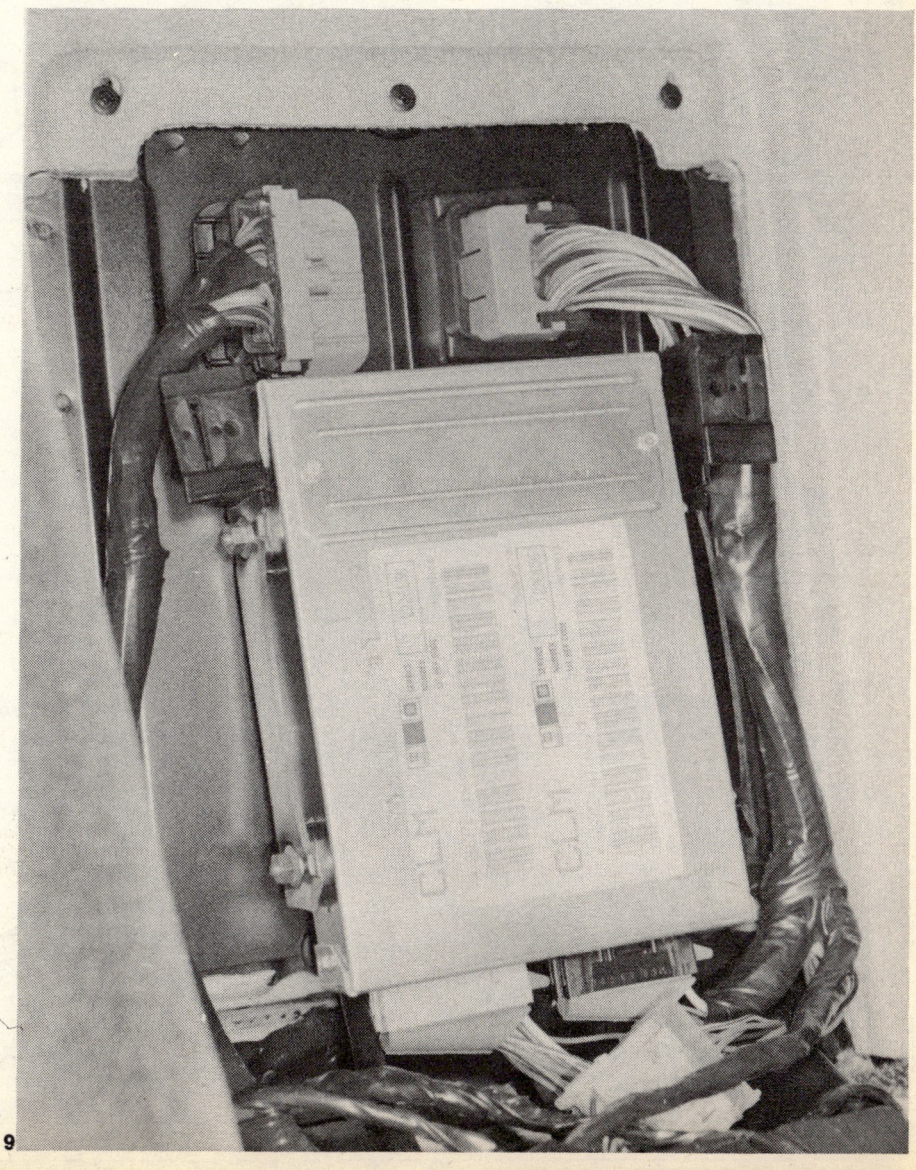

7. The basic GM CCC computer is programmed for a particular engine and car combination by a PROM installed in the computer. The PROM is the calibration or "brain" of the computer.

8. The 1984 Turbo V-6 Buick with Computer Controlled Coil Ignition uses two PROMs. One provides basic system programming; the other controls the multipoint fuel injection.

9. Here's the 1984 Pontiac Fiero's CCC module. Note the complexity of the wire harness hookups, as all of the system functions lead into and out of the computer. The ECM is installed behind the Fiero's console armrest.

ELECTRONIC ENGINE CONTROLS

ignition timing (among many functions) and has a self-test feature similar to that of MCU—pulsing a voltmeter needle to indicate a code number. EEC-III and MCU systems remain in limited use on 1984 models, with virtually all electronically controlled engines using EEC-IV. And Ford engineers tell us that the EEC-IV microprocessor has abilities they haven't even touched to this point. No wonder the Japanese are quietly negotiating with Ford to license the technology.

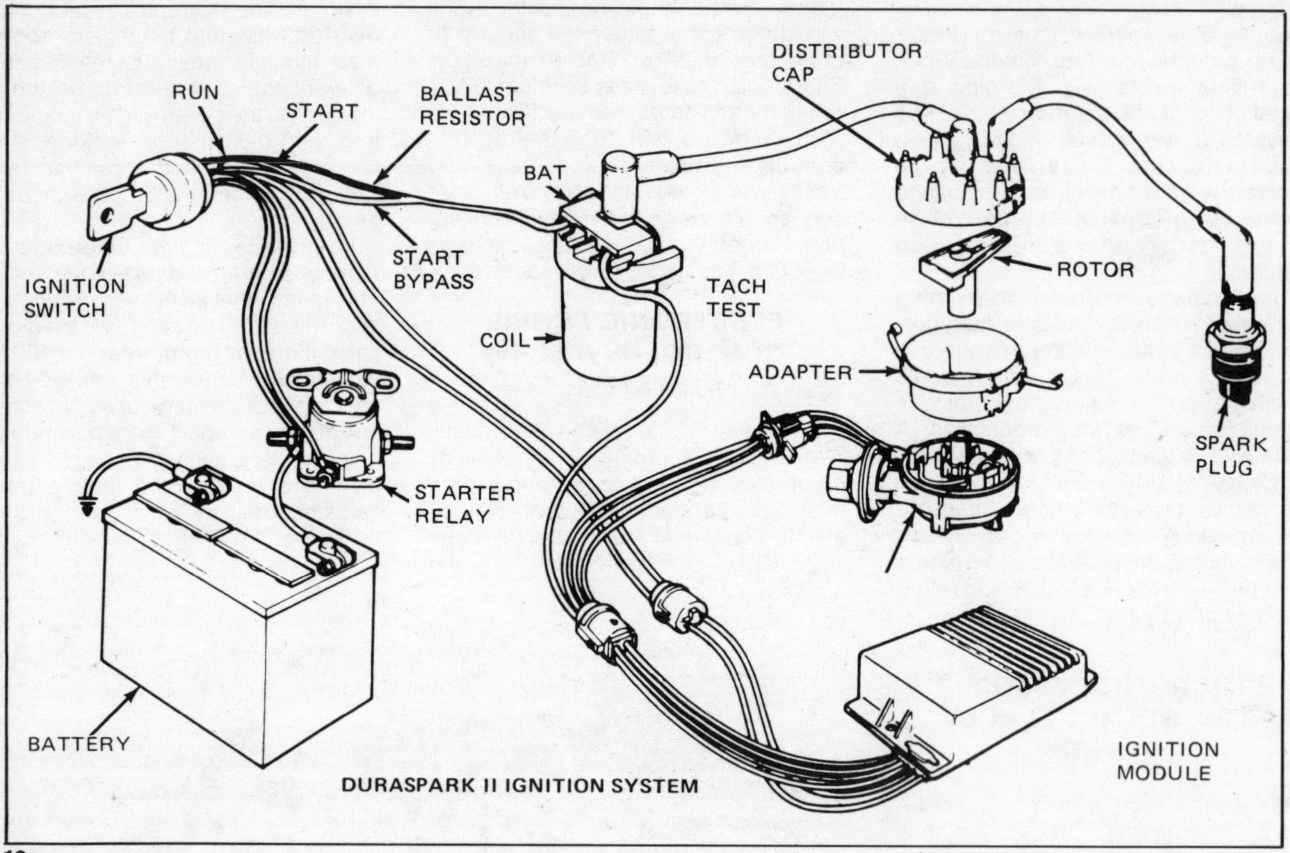

DURASPARK II IGNITION SYSTEM

10a

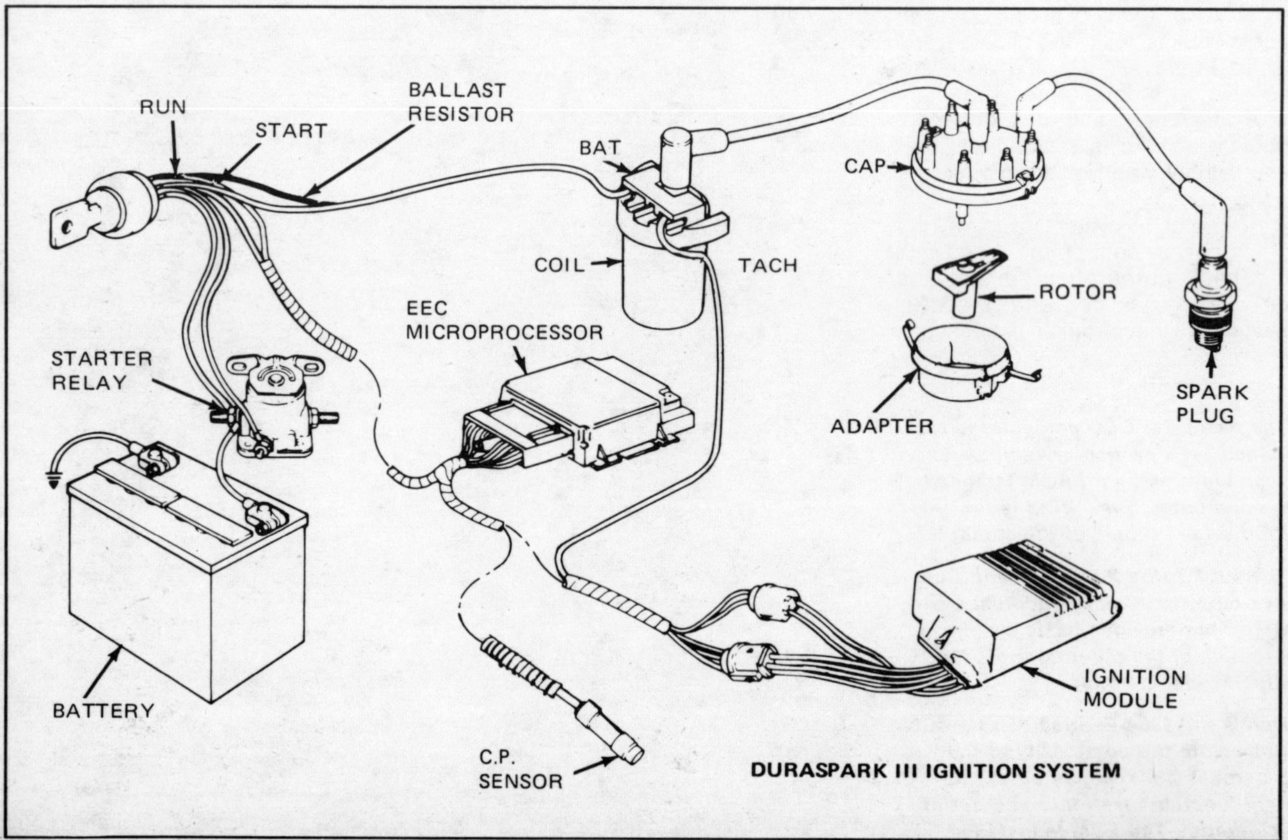

DURASPARK III IGNITION SYSTEM

10b

70/Ignition & Electrical Systems

GM ELECTRONIC ENGINE CONTROLS

The GM feedback carburetion system introduced in 1978-79 evolved into the Computer-Controlled Catalytic Converter or C-4 system the following year. Some applications during 1980 were integrated with electronic spark timing (EST), which uses an HEI distributor without vacuum- or centrifugal-advance mechanisms. A seven-terminal HEI module is used instead of the original four-terminal unit. The wiring harness has an extended pigtail for connection to the new ECM.

A second HEI variation during 1980, electronic spark control, or ESC, uses a modified HEI module which responds to a detonation sensor. Whenever detonation starts to occur, the ECM retards ignition timing electronically by up to 17 degrees. Once the danger of detonation is over, the module returns timing to normal. Other 1980 engines use a five-terminal HEI module to electronically retard ignition timing 10 degrees when the fifth terminal is internally grounded. Called the Electronic Module Retard or EMR system, this HEI variation reduces exhaust emissions under predetermined conditions.

These different applications were brought together in the Computer Command Control (CCC) system introduced in 1981. This electronically controlled system monitors up to 15 different engine/vehicle functions and controls up to nine different operations, depending upon the engine application. The electronic control module (ECM) contains an engine calibration unit called a PROM. Programmed for a particular engine/vehicle combination, the PROM is not interchangeable with other engines having different standards.

The only Computer Command Control function of interest in this chapter is EST. The HEI/EST distributor has no centrifugal or vacuum advance and uses the seven-terminal module. During cranking, the HEI distributor operates independently in a "bypass" mode. Once the engine starts, the ECM takes over and controls advance via a referenced pulse that indicates both engine rpm and crankshaft position. After evaluating this data, the ECM provides the proper amount of advance for the engine operating condition at the moment by transmitting an EST pulse to the distributor. The engine must operate in the bypass mode when setting basic timing. To induce this mode, the four-terminal EST connector lead is disconnected. The HEI module will then assume control while you set the timing. When you're done, reconnecting the EST connector lead returns control to the ECM.

The three terminals not found on standard HEI modules handle reference, EST, and bypass signals. The reference terminal sends rpm and crankshaft position data from the distributor pickup coil to the ECM. Above 200 rpm, the ECM returns a signal to the bypass terminal acknowledging receipt of the reference signal. At the same time, the ECM evaluates sensor data and signals the HEI/EST module of the proper advance through the EST terminal. The module then fires the plugs at the correct time.

Since the HEI/EST module controls base timing, the engine will continue to run if the reference or EST signal is interrupted because of an open circuit or a faulty ECM. Loss of the bypass signal means that the distributor will control timing regardless of engine speed or operating condition. The advance provided by the HEI/EST module is retarded from normal operation, which means that the engine will run, but not as well as it should. Loss of the EST signal with the bypass signal on will stop the engine cold—neither the ECM nor the distributor module is sending a timing signal under these conditions. When restarted, the engine will run for a few seconds, then stop when the bypass signal comes on.

The CCC system has a built-in diagnostic system similar to that used in Ford's EEC-III system. When a problem develops in one of the systems controlled by the CCC system, a "Check Engine" lamp on the instrument panel lights up and a trouble code is stored in the ECM memory. To retrieve the code, you must locate the trouble code "test" terminal and ground it. This is located in the assembly line communication link (ALCL) connector under the dash. Turn the ignition on and connect a jumper lead between the "test" and "ground" terminals in the ALCL connector. The "Check Engine" lamp will start to flash a trouble code that's read in the same manner as the Ford code.

Only two trouble codes refer to problems in the ignition system. Code 12 indicates no reference pulses to the ECM and will flash only while the problem is present—it's not stored in the ECM memory. The problem is generally caused by an open 0 r grounded reference lead from the distributor module to the ECM and requires module replacement. Code 42 indicates that the EST bypass circuit is grounded. If the bypass lead is not grounded, the module is faulty and must be replaced.

The CCC system has undergone constant upgrading and has become increasingly sophisticated. As an example, when the first J-cars rolled off the line, they contained a bank of four relays. By the end of the model year, the function of two of the four relays had already been incorporated into the ECM and the next year saw the same thing happen to the remaining two relays.

10A and 10B. *These wiring and component schematics show the evolution of Ford's Dura-Spark II into the Dura-Spark III. Dura-Spark III has been discontinued in 1984 models in favor of the newer EEC-IV system.*

11. *Dura-Spark rotor design is considerably more complex than the old single blade rotor with which we're all familiar.*

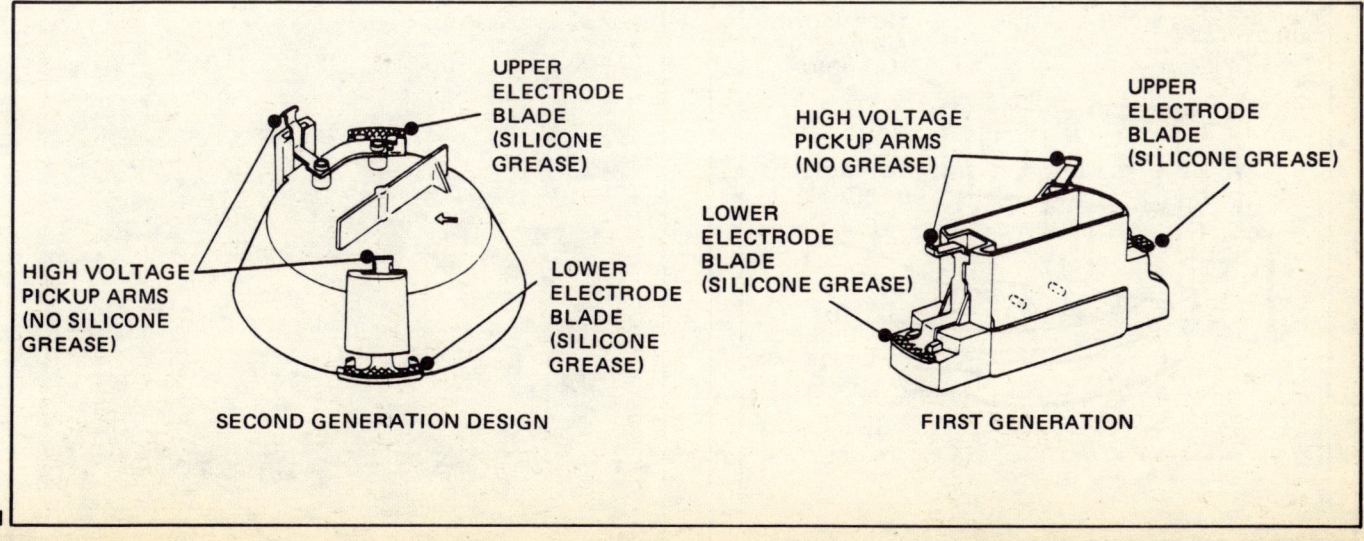

ELECTRONIC ENGINE CONTROLS

Unfortunately, the problem with this is simply that trouble codes have been expanded, revised, and revamped on a running basis. You virtually need a diagnostic manual tailored to the specific car on which you're working to interpret what the system is trying to tell you.

Early systems had no long-term memory, but this has been corrected so that trouble codes are not lost until the problem has been corrected. In addition, the "Check Engine" lamp in early applications had a tendency to come on for what amounted to insignificant problems and owners were soon ignoring it. The circuitry has been revised so that the lamp illuminates only for more serious problems.

Minimum-Function System

Certain 1982 and later Chevette/Pontiac T1000 models are equipped with this minimum-function system. This is a simplified version of CCC, which uses different sensors and an ECM that is internally different from the system just described (which was temporarily known as a "full-function" system during 1982). Minimum function uses a standard HEI ignition system and works with only seven trouble codes, none of which concerns us in this book.

Computer-Controlled Coil Ignition (C3I) System

For 1984, Buick has introduced a radically different ignition system on Regals and Rivieras with the turbocharged V-6 engine—there is no distributor. Instead, three coils are used to fire the spark plugs in pairs. Hall-Effect sensors are used to determine crankshaft and camshaft position. The sensors notify the ECM, which determines the optimum advance and sends a signal to the C3I module. This module then splits the ECM signal into thirds, sending separate signals to each coil when to fire the plugs. Each coil fires the plug twice—once near the end of the compression stroke and again near the end of the exhaust stroke. This means one spark is wasted, but it's necessary, since the plugs in opposing cylinders are fired at the same time.

For example, cylinders 1 and 4 are opposite. When the plugs are fired, cylinder 1 is on its compression stroke while cylinder 4 is on the exhaust stroke. The next time the same two plugs fire, cylinder position is reversed. This eliminates the necessity of having six coils—one to fire each cylinder.

Should the ECM malfunction, a bypass circuit throws timing to a fixed 10 degrees and a warning light illuminates. The car can still be driven, but performance is off enough that its driver will head for the nearest dealer to get the problem solved.

This system is going to be watched very carefully by the industry, since it's tailored to the requirements of fuel injection (where everyone is heading) and offers about as much precision in spark timing as you could possibly imagine. Just as important, it reduces

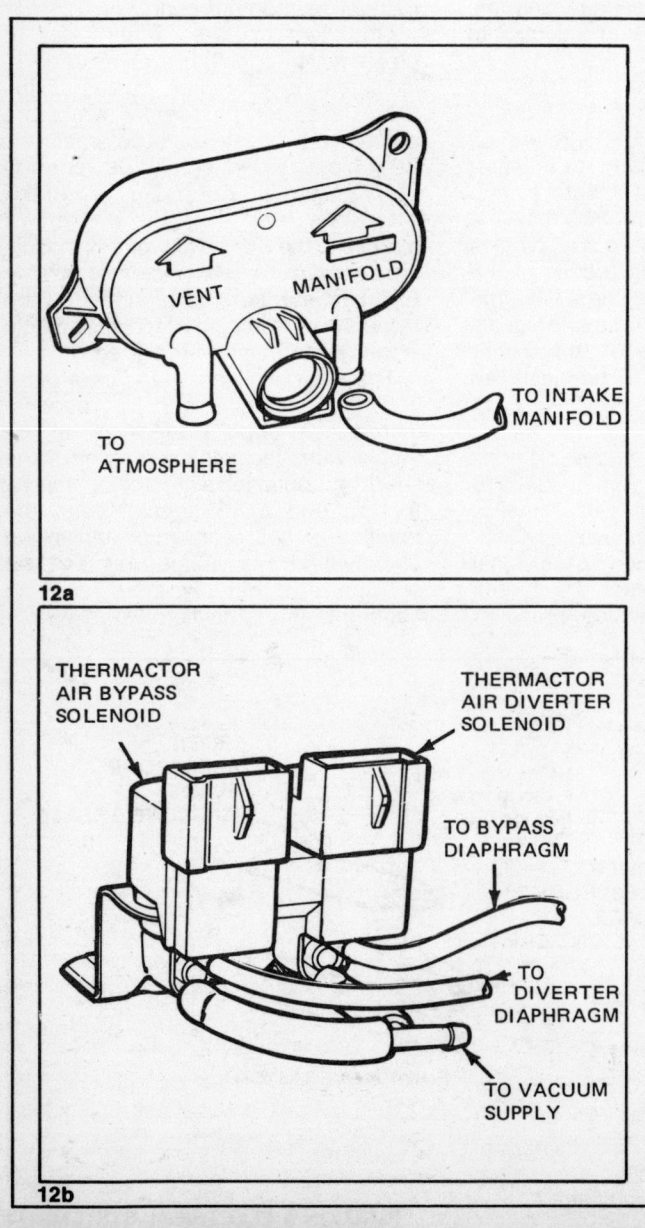

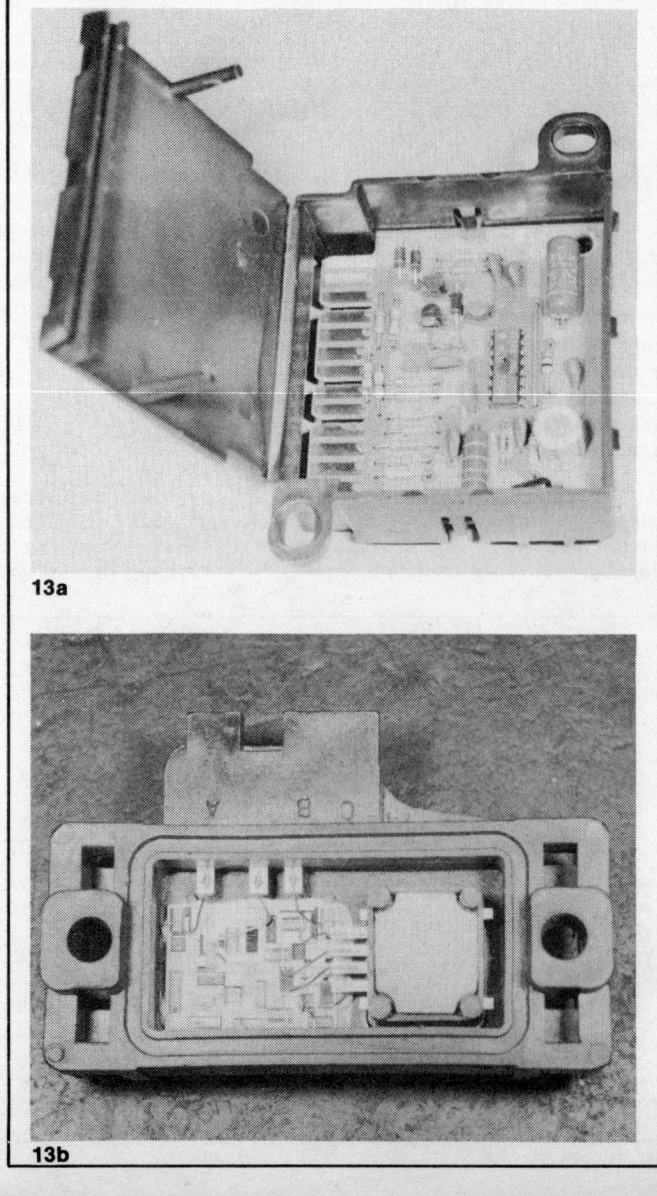

RFI (radio-frequency interference), which has become a genuine nemesis of the electronics in today's cars.

Radio-Frequency Interference (RFI)

Now's the time to introduce this fact of life with modern ignitions. RFI is generally caused by the arcing of the high-voltage spark across the gaps between the distributor cap contacts an the rotor blade. It wasn't really a big problem before the advent of electronic engine controls utilizing on-board computers. If you recall an earlier chapter, RFI was one of the reasons the industry switched to resistor spark plugs and wiring.

With so many electronic controls on modern cars, the amount of magnetism that floats around the engine compartment is considerable, and coupled with the greater arcing from the higher voltage being sent across the plug gaps, there's a great deal of what might be called "electrical garbage" being created under the hood. Look at any new car these days and you'll find not one or two but several grounds in the engine compartment. At first glance, you wonder why so many grounds are necessary when your 1967 Roadrunner had only an engine and a battery ground. RFI and electrical garbage are the reasons.

If you think RFI is not a problem, you just haven't encountered some of the strange things that are happening to drivers these days. One model Cadillac with a certain calibration had the capability of turning signal lights at an intersection into blithering idiots every time the car passed within a certain range. Seems the transformer controlling those lights had a weakness for certain signals emitted by the car's electronics. The only solution to the problem was to replace the transformer, but many heads were scratched nearly bald before the answer became apparent—and believed by all involved!

BOTTOM LINE

As we've seen, sophisticated electronics have reduced the distributor's function to that of a switch—sending secondary voltage to the spark plugs as directed by the ECM—and in the case of some Buicks, eliminated it altogether. The benefits are mixed, so it seems. From a service standpoint, the distributor has never been more trouble-free, provided it is kept clean and properly lubricated.

Troubleshooting the distributor function with an electronically controlled engine is another matter. It's considerably more complicated for the average car owner, who does not have the specialized test equipment or knowledge. All of the systems can be partially checked with a common voltmeter, but locating the source of the problem requires an understanding of the total system and how it works beyond that possessed by most owners—and many mechanics. Lacking the knowledge, they attempt to correct a malfunction in such systems by replacing components until the faulty one is discovered—an expensive and time-consuming process.

If one circuit fails in an ignition or ECM module, the entire unit must be replaced, and that is also expensive. Yet most of these components (especially the computer module) are quite reliable. The big three automakers report that of the modules returned to them as having failed, approximately 40 percent test out as being good. This means that there's an awful lot of modules being replaced in garages across the country when there's nothing really wrong with them.

So how does a new module solve the problem when it is not the cause of the problem? Well, in cases where module replacement takes place, numerous other components are generally also replaced. One of those components, a loose connection, or some other small electrical glitch is usually the cause and it's corrected unknowingly in the process.

You're more likely to have common component failures, such as a stuck thermal switch or a faulty sensor, than a major failure such as a computer. The best way to prevent a breakdown with such systems is to practice preventive maintenance—plugs, wiring, regular service, etc.—just as always. One thing, however, is quite clear: automotive design is heading toward the point where you will be unable to do much more to the ignition system than replace spark plugs and secondary wiring.

12A and 12B. To put an EEC II system into self-test mode as described in the text, locate the MAP sensor (A) and the TAB/TAD solenoids (B). Here's what they look like.

13A and 13B. Even a device as simple as a manifold/barometric pressure sensor has not escaped the electronic revolution. Here's what's inside the Ford (A) and GM (B) sensors.

14. Ford's fourth generation electronic engine control system (EEC-IV) contains 312 operating strategies and will get even smarter. Early computers built by Toshiba had their problems—Ford now builds them itself.

15. The TFI (Thick Film Integrated) ignition module used with EEC-IV and the UFI distributor is another electronic wizard, as this inside view shows. Be careful not to bend the prongs during removal.

14

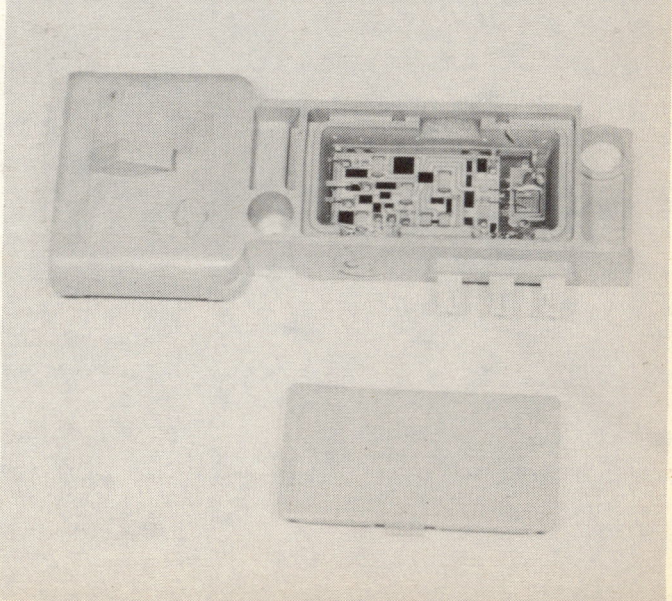
15

ELECTRICAL TEST EQUIPMENT

The tools and test equipment used for electrical system troubleshooting and ignition tuneups range from simple spark-plug gappers and feeler gauges to the elaborate electronic analysis units found in service stations and garages. In this chapter, we'll tell you exactly what you need in the way of equipment to handle any electrical problems you may encounter, as well as provide some useful hints on using it. Let's start with a look at some of the equipment you'll use during an ignition tuneup, and then move on to those units used for troubleshooting.

IGNITION TIMING LIGHT

Since even minute changes in point gap can advance or retard the ignition timing by several degrees, the engine's timing should be readjusted whenever the breaker points are replaced or regapped. A DC-powered timing light is indispensable for setting timing. Such timing lights have three cables, two of which connect to your car's battery for power, and the third connects to the No. 1 cylinder's plug cable. Inexpensive timing lights use an adapter between the spark plug and plug cable to make the No. 1 cylinder connection. Timing lights with an inductive pickup that simply snaps over the No. 1 plug cable are more efficient and easier to use.

The adapter or inductive pickup senses the pulse of current in the plug cable and uses it to trigger the light. When properly connected, the timing light will thus flash every time the No. 1 plug fires. This makes the moving mark on the engine's crankshaft pulley or flywheel appear to stand still when viewed by the timing light. By loosening the distributor holddown and turning the entire distributor housing in the engine, the mark on the pulley can be advanced or retarded until it aligns perfectly with the stationary mark on the engine.

Before using a timing light to set basic timing, be sure that the distributor points and spark plugs are properly cleaned and gapped. Warm the engine to normal operating temperature and set idle speed to specs with a tachometer. If you're using an inductive-type light, the magnetic pickup must fit over the plug cable completely so that the ferrite pole pieces in the pickup touch each other completely. A gap of any size between the pole pieces can cause mistriggering. So can grease, so be sure to wipe the plug cable clean before connecting the pickup unit.

If you have problems with the timing light, try moving the adapter/pickup to another plug wire. If the light now flashes intermittently (as it should), your No. 1 plug cable is either open or shorted in/near the distributor cap. Suppose you see two timing marks instead of one. In this case, the plug cables are crossfiring. This can be caused by poor plug cable insulation, an open plug cable, or two or more cables that are too close to each other. Try separating the cables temporarily and check that all are properly connected to their respective plugs.

The timing light can be used to make a quick check of the distributor's centrifugal-advance mechanism. After basic timing has been set, reconnect all vacuum lines and let the engine idle. Note the position of the timing mark

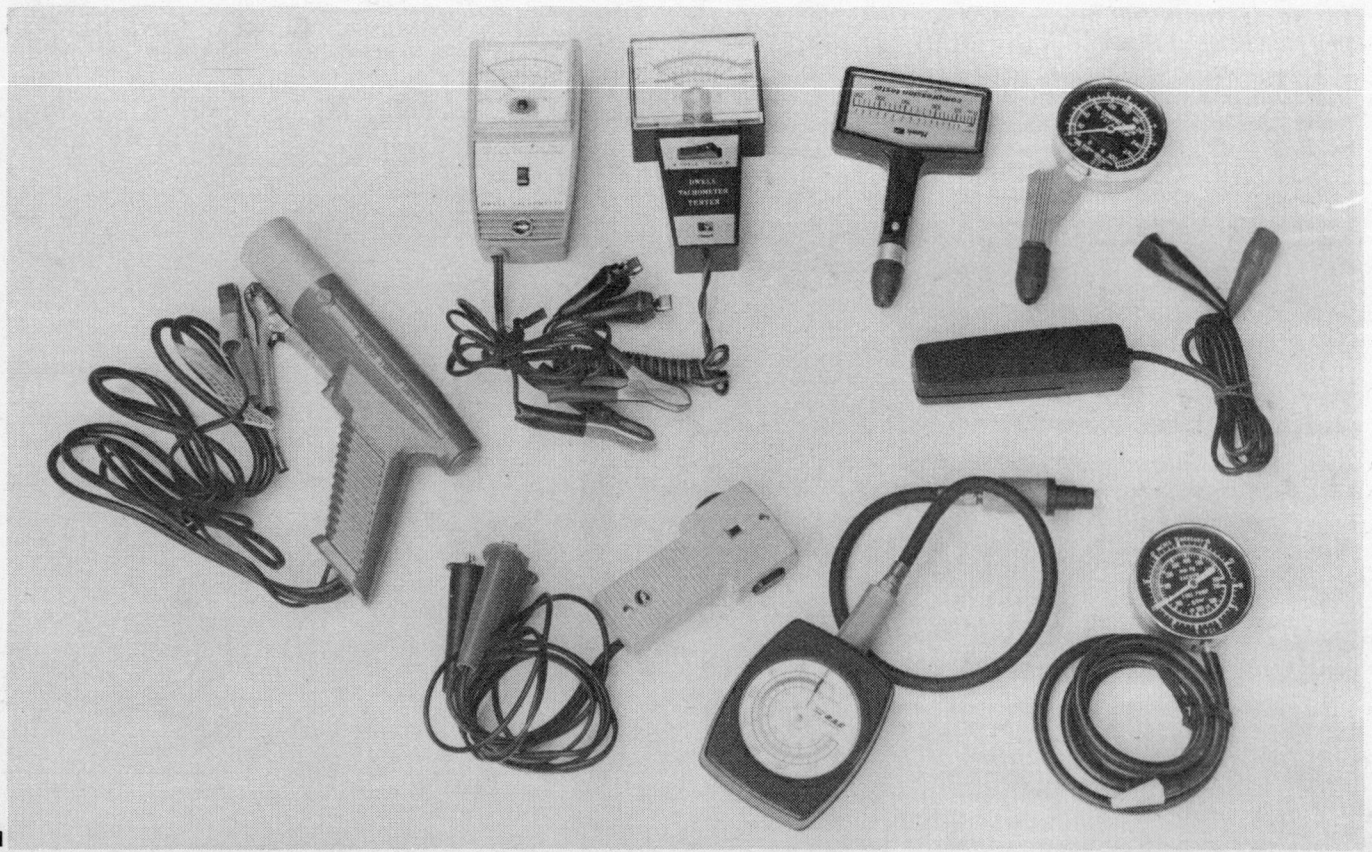

under the light, then gradually increase engine speed. The timing mark should remain stationary until the advance cuts in, then continue to move until engine speed reaches 2000-2500 rpm. The exact cut-in and cutoff points will be found in the distributor specifications for your particular car. If the timing mark does not move smoothly as engine speed increases, the centrifugal-advance mechanism is either sticking or frozen, and requires service.

You can also check the synchronization of dual breaker points in distributors. Set basic timing to specs, then move the timing light to the plug cable of the cylinder indicated at the second timing mark. This mark is usually designated as Syn 2-7 or Ign 2-7, indicating that the No. 2 or No. 7 plug should fire when the timing mark and reference pointer are aligned. If they do not align, the secondary point set should be adjusted until it is in sync with the primary set.

DWELL-TACHOMETER

Breaker-point gap and dwell are inversely proportional. If you set the gap wide, you'll have less dwell; with less gap, you'll have more dwell. Gap is set with a flat feeler gauge; the distributor cap must be off and the engine dead. Dwell is set with the engine running at cranking speed or faster. If you use a dwell meter, you'll probably have to fuss with the adjustment several times, because dwell is different when the engine is running from the way it is while only cranking. The easiest way is to set gap with a feeler gauge, replace the distributor cap, and then check the dwell with a meter. Delco distributors use a cap with a slide-up window. This allows you to set dwell with the cap in place and get it right the first time.

With conventional breaker-point ignitions, one lead of the dwell-tach connects to the DIST. (−) terminal of the coil, and the other to a good engine ground. The unit won't work properly if connected to the coil's BAT. (+) terminal, and may be damaged by such a hookup. The newest in dwell-tach design also includes an inductive pickup which clips over any plug cable. When using these units with a breakerless ignition, the two leads are connected directly to the battery terminal posts.

Your dwell-tach should have both high and low scales that are easy to read. Some tachs also have a point resistance scale. This is really a low-reading voltmeter used with the same connection, but the engine must be off and the points closed. If the points are open, the meter needle will peg itself at the high reading. Just crank the engine a bit until the points close and then read your meter. If it says that the points are bad, it means that they aren't making good contact and should be replaced. If the points look good, but the meter reads bad, there could be a poor contact between the coil post and ground, but this rarely happens. If you install new points and still get a bad reading, check to see if there is paint on the engine where the distributor sets, or a broken ground lead someplace inside the distributor.

The dwell meter can also tell you if the distributor has excessive mechanical wear, such as a worn-out cam, bushings, bearings, or a bent distributor shaft. Watch the indicator needle as you increase engine speed from idle to about 1500 rpm. If the distributor is okay, the change in dwell will not exceed 10 percent or about 3 degrees—unless your distributor has an off-center pivoting breaker plate. In this case, a dwell variation as great as 5 to 7 degrees may be normal. Check your factory shop manual for proper dwell variation specs with this type of distributor.

As we have seen, breakerless ignitions do not have a dwell period in the conventional sense. However, the "on" time of the coil (controlled by the ECM) will give a reading on the dwell meter. Since this "apparent" dwell reading varies with engine rpm, it should increase as engine speed increases. If you suspect ignition problems with a breakerless ignition, you can use a dwell meter to see if the apparent dwell does increase as it should. If it does not, you know that you're on the right track.

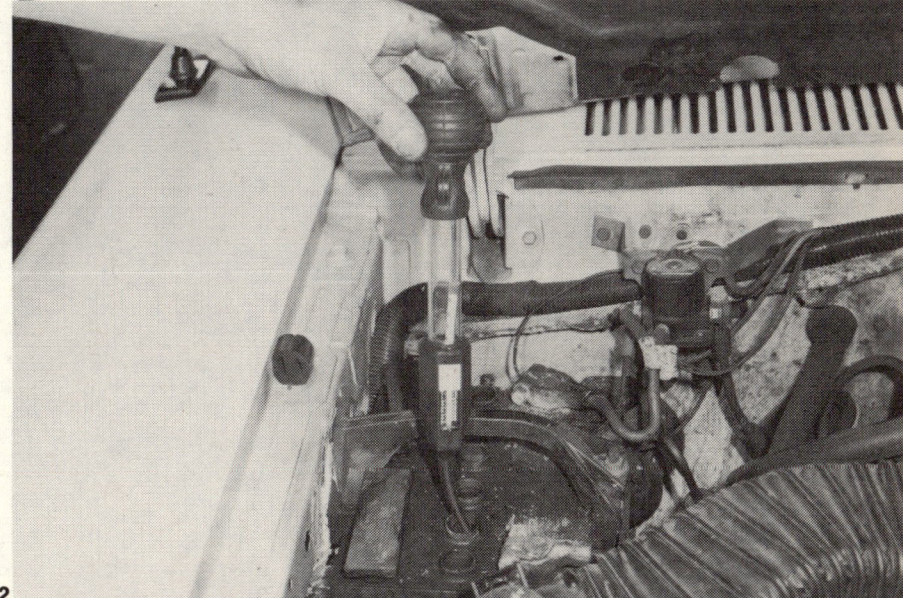

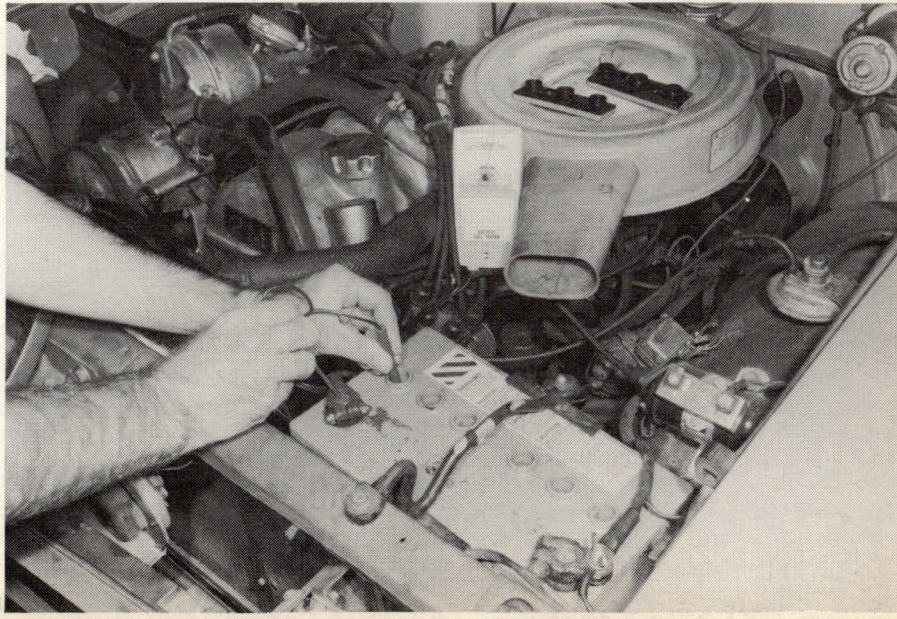

1. Tune-up and test equipment is varied—here's a selection of inexpensive units that can be helpful.

2. A good temperature-compensated hydrometer is probably the best bet for battery care.

3. This battery cell indicator works on the same principle as those used in many garages. Each cell is tested individually with the probes.

VOLTMETER

Voltmeters are used to measure battery voltage while cranking, or charging system voltage while the engine is running. They're also useful in measuring the voltage difference between two given points in an electrical circuit. Voltage in a circuit is measured with the voltmeter connected in parallel with (across) the circuit. The positive voltmeter lead connects to the positive side of the circuit and the negative lead to the negative side.

To check battery voltage while cranking, connect the positive voltmeter lead to the positive battery terminal and the negative lead to the negative battery terminal. Disable the ignition at the coil to prevent the engine from starting and then crank the engine over for 10 to 15 seconds while reading the voltmeter scale. Any reading below 9.6 volts (12-volt system) indicates a problem. Troubleshooting this begins with a check of the battery's state of charge.

Faulty switches, corroded connections or other such problems can affect both current and voltage in an electrical circuit, reducing flow. You can use the voltmeter to check out voltage losses with a voltage drop test. Connect a voltmeter lead to each side of the switch or connection and turn the switch on to allow current to flow. If the voltmeter gives a reading on its scale, that amount of electricity is being prevented from passing through the switch or connection because of resistance. Such losses are generally acceptable up to 0.2 volt. Anything greater is considered excessive in most cases.

A voltmeter can also be used to check for circuit continuity. When connected in series with a part of the circuit and ground, the indicator needle should read battery voltage once power is applied to the circuit. If it does not, there is an open or short to ground in the circuit.

Modern electronic engine controls function on command from a computer or microprocessor. You should be aware of the fact that such electronic brains operate on (very tiny) milliamperes of current. The use of an analog (needle-type) voltmeter is not recommended for such circuitry, as it can pass excessive current and do irreparable damage to the computer. To be on the safe side, use a digital voltmeter with a 10-milliamp impedance on such circuitry. Generally, digital voltmeters are combined with ohmmeters in a multitester called a DVOM (digital volt-ohmmeter), and are no more expensive than a good analog type. They're sensitive enough to read the minute quantities of electricity in the electronic circuit and a good deal safer.

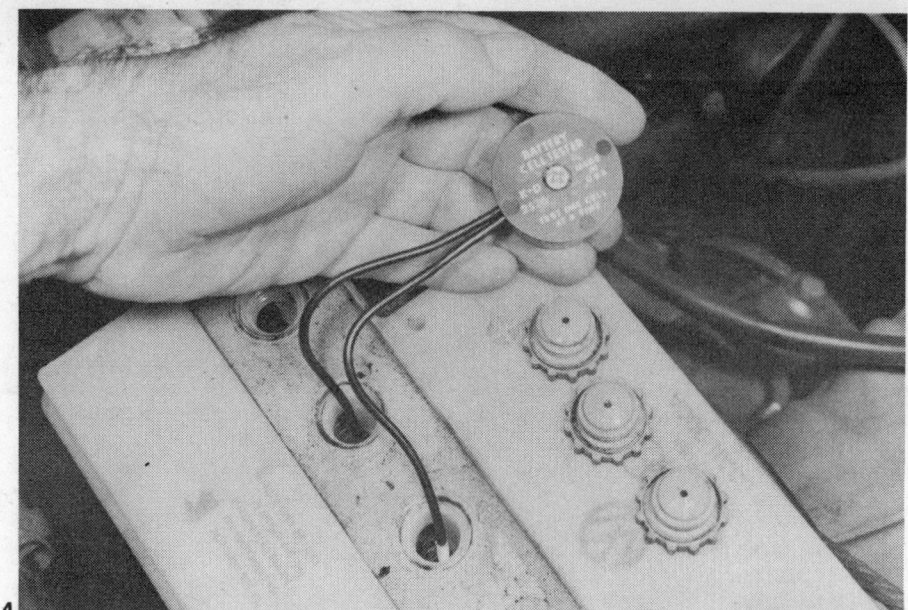
4

5

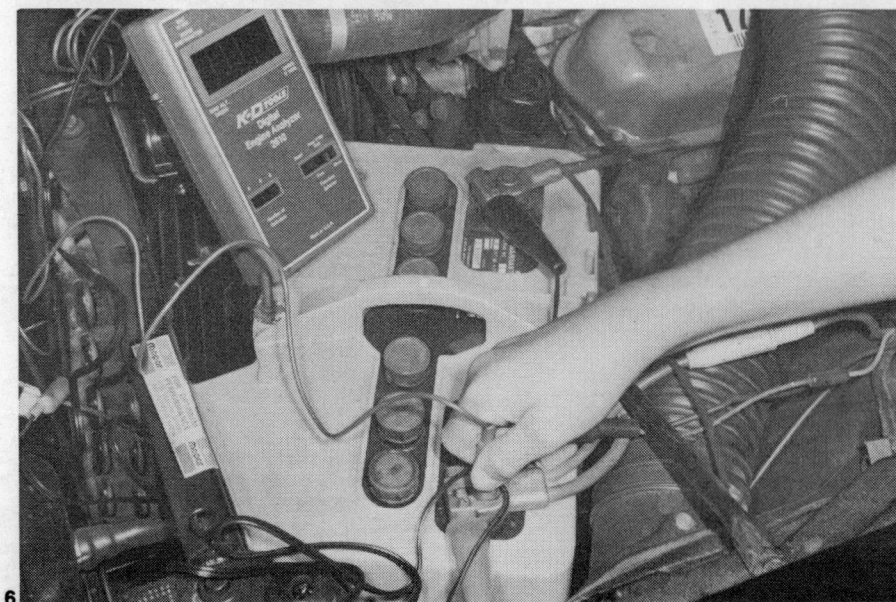
6

AMMETER

An ammeter checks the amount of current or amperes flowing in a given electrical circuit. If you know the current draw specs for a component or a circuit, the ammeter will tell you whether the circuit is grounded or shorted. It'll also detect excessive resistance in a circuit. Since an ammeter has low internal resistance, it must always be connected in series with a circuit. If connected in parallel like a voltmeter, too much current will flow through the meter and cause permanent damage. Ammeters and voltmeters are often combined with a resistance unit in a single piece of test equipment called an alternator-generator tester. Although housed in a single case, you'll have to switch connections to change the unit from a voltmeter to an ammeter.

OHMMETER

A self-powered meter (it contains its own battery), the ohmmeter reads component or circuit resistance directly in ohms, but should never be connected to a live circuit as this will damage the meter. To check the resistance of a component or electrical wire, either isolate it from the circuit, or remove it completely. The ohmmeter will also check for continuity in a circuit.

To use an ohmmeter, isolate or remove the component or wire from the circuit and connect the two test leads across it. A zero reading indicates no measurable resistance, whereas an infinite reading tells you that there is an open in the component or circuit.

4. Avoid inexpensive battery care devices that tell you nothing. This probe-type device has an LED that lights up if the battery cell is low. Unfortunately, it doesn't tell you how low or why.

5. An inexpensive voltmeter will give you battery and cranking voltage—both useful tests when troubleshooting the starting or charging circuits.

6. This more sophisticated digital multimeter performs the same tasks as the voltmeter in 5., but provides a digital LED readout.

7A and 7B. Multimeters come in various sizes, shapes and perform several different functions. Despite what they are called, most are nothing more than a voltmeter, ammeter and ohmmeter housed in one case.

8. Digital analyzers are far more accurate than the analog or needle type readout but they tend to drive some users crazy. While the analog meter gives a steady needle reading which indicates an average reading, the digital type tends to bounce from high to low, requiring some judgment on the user's part.

MULTIMETERS

Several different test meters are often combined in the same housing and are

wired to permit 15, 20, or even more electrical tests to be performed with the single piece of test equipment. These are often called engine analyzers or

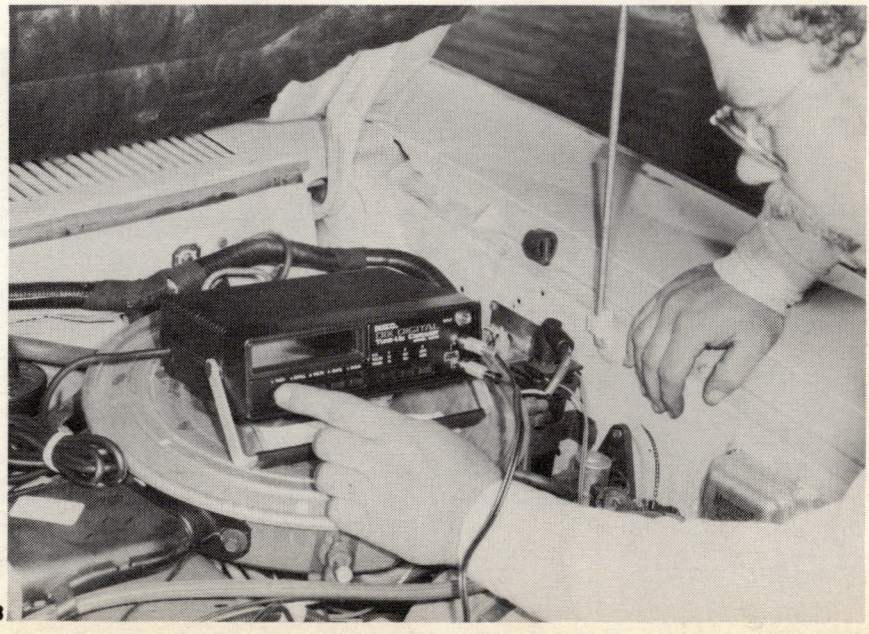

ELECTRICAL TEST EQUIPMENT

ignition analyzers, and such terms often lead the unsuspecting buyer to think he's getting something other than a voltmeter, ammeter, and/or ohmmeter.

In many cases, you are just as well off with the individual pieces of test equipment, since few of the multimeters allow you to use more than one test function at a time, and many require that you switch connections to change functions. One of the more useful combinations that we've seen is the electronic ignition analyzer, such as the Model 1524 offered by Actron.

What makes this particular unit extremely useful is the fact that it has been designed and programmed specifically for troubleshooting breakerless ignition systems. By simply following the test procedures outlined in the instruction manual, you can completely check out any breakerless ignition with a minimum of difficulty. Unlike using individual instruments to perform the various checks and tests, the user does not have to understand what he is doing; if he can read and follow the clearly written steps while making the specified connections and setting the function knob as directed, he can troubleshoot the ignition and locate the problem quickly and easily.

DIAGNOSTIC CONNECTOR TESTER

Discussed in detail in the "Electrical Troubleshooting" chapter, the diagnostic connector is basically a central connection block located in the engine compartment of some GM and Chrysler cars, and it provides easy access to otherwise difficult-to-locate test points. The diagnostic connector tester is a fancy name for a dual-range voltmeter. The example used here is another Actron unit (Model 1509), designed for use with GM cars. Test leads connect it to the battery terminals for power and a separate 10-prong plug is inserted into the diagnostic connector block.

As in the case of the electronic ignition analyzer, the value of this unit lies in the well-written procedure manual that accompanies it. Simply connect the unit, set the switch as directed, and read the meter. Follow the steps specified according to the reading and you can troubleshoot the electrical system as efficiently as Mr. Goodwrench and his expensive GM tester. In addition, the diagnostic connector tester is fitted with individual leads that allow its use as a general-purpose voltmeter.

SINGLE-PURPOSE TEST EQUIPMENT

The advent of light-emitting diodes (LEDs) and digital readouts has lead to a great variety of single-purpose test

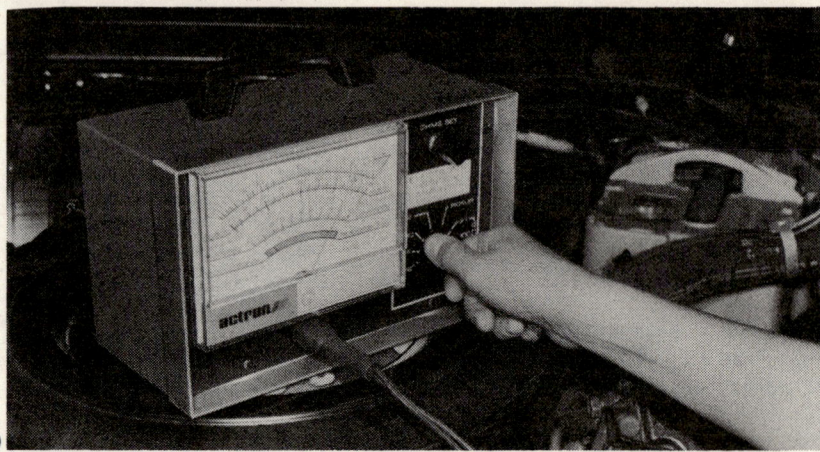
9

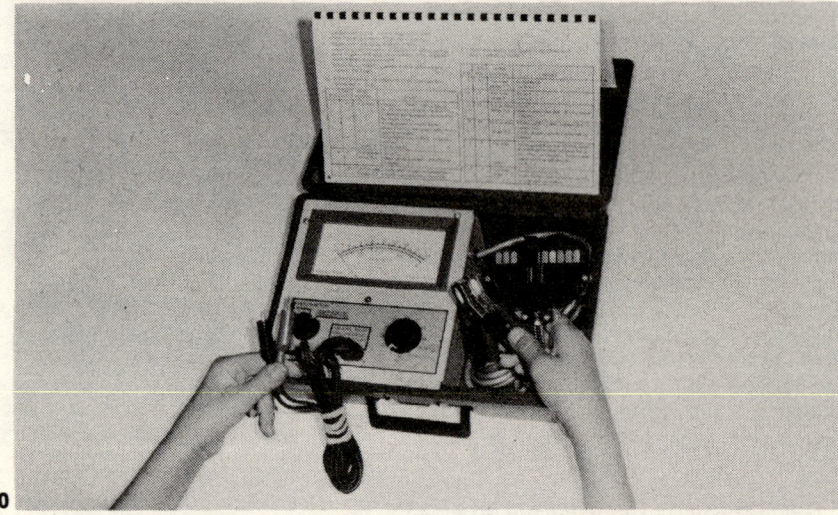
10

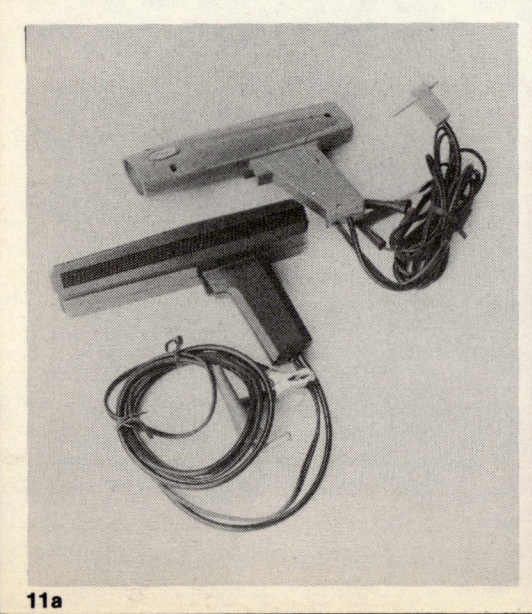
11a

11b

equipment disguised under exotic names. Change the alligator clamps for a set of probes, redesign the meter scale, and the lowly voltmeter is instantly transformed into a battery cell tester. Replace the meter needle with a series of colored LEDs, restore the alligator clamps, and your voltmeter becomes a charging system tester.

Such disguises are often colorful and add a bit of spice to your collection of test equipment, but none will do more than the plain old voltmeter. In many cases, the redesign actually limits what you can do with the equipment. Neither of the examples just cited will perform a voltage drop test, yet both are considerably more expensive than a simple voltmeter.

PROFESSIONAL EQUIPMENT

You may occasionally have need for some test equipment that falls under the heading of professional equipment, such as an oscilloscope or a distributor testing machine. These can be found in most automotive repair facilities.

The oscilloscope can be used to analyze most ignition ills quickly, without taking anything apart. Speed and efficiency are the only real advantages this elaborate testing device has over less sophisticated methods. For example, burned points and a weak condenser can be diagnosed by simply taking out the points for a visual inspection. But this takes more time than to inspect the entire system with a good scope. Various controls on the scope make it possible to change the display to study the spark of each cylinder individually, all cylinders simultaneously for comparison, or in rapid succession to pinpoint cylinder-to-cylinder differences in detail.

Synchrograph-type distributor testers (distributor machines) can not only determine the amount of advance at different speeds, but also pinpoint the number of degrees of rotation between the firing of one cylinder and the next. In addition to a motor that drives the distributor at varying speeds, the testing machine has a vacuum hose. This hose can be connected to the distributor to simulate engine vacuum for checking the vacuum-advance functioning. Most irregularities in timing occur as a result of wear or dirt in the distributor's moving parts. Since the unit can be observed and tested while in actual operation, the particular source of trouble is quickly located. On some distributors, it's possible to adjust the advance mechanism, but on most, it's necessary to replace or perhaps modify the calibrated springs that control the rates of advance.

WHAT DO YOU NEED?

For a very basic or minimum tuneup and troubleshooting kit, we suggest that you have a dwell-tach unit, voltmeter, and DC-powered timing light, preferably with inductive pickup. You can add an ammeter and/or ohmmeter to this basic list as you find need for them. When you shop around, look for quality of construction and legibility of meter scales. Check to see that the test leads furnished are long enough, well insulated, and fitted with spring-loaded alligator clips that will open wide and grip firmly to make a good connection. Stay with name brands that you recognize, read the warranty before buying, and follow the instructions carefully when using the equipment.

9. Actron's Electronic Ignition Analyzer will troubleshoot all early Chrysler, GM HEI and Motorcraft Solid-State ignitions.

10. This Actron diagnostic unit was designed for use with the early GM vehicles equipped with a diagnostic connector and first appeared for use with the 1976 Chevette. It simplified the testing in crowded engine compartments, but automakers soon abandoned the concept.

11A and 11B. Two types of DC timing lights (A). Both use an adapter that must be installed between the No. 1 spark plug and the plug cable. You're better off with an inductive timing light (B) whose magnetic pickup simply slips over the plug cable.

12. A remote start switch of some kind is extremely handy. It connects to the solenoid or relay terminals and allows you to crank the engine from the engine compartment.

13. Since diesel engines have no ignition system, they require special test equipment to determine engine speed accurately.

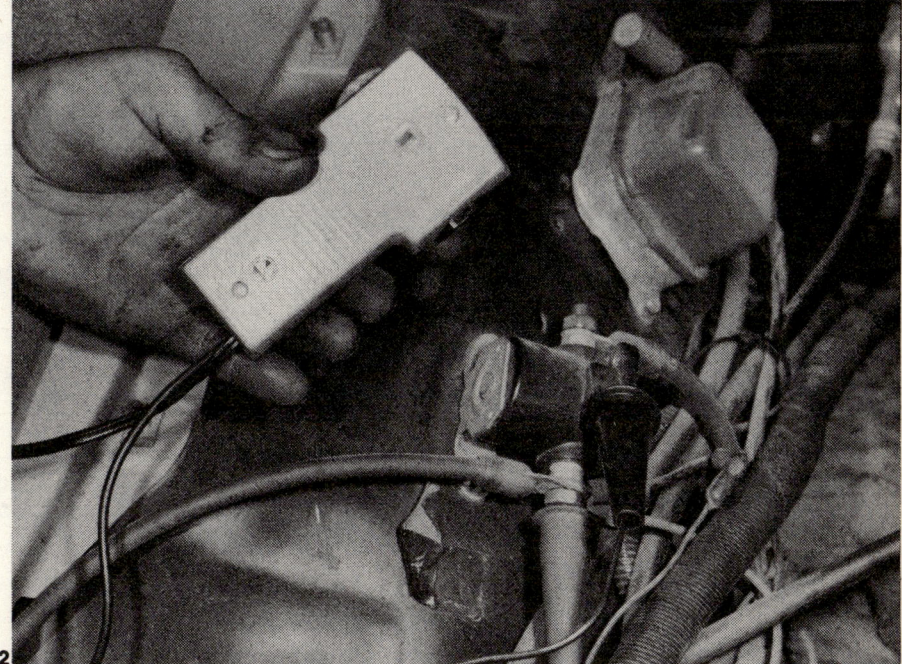
12

13

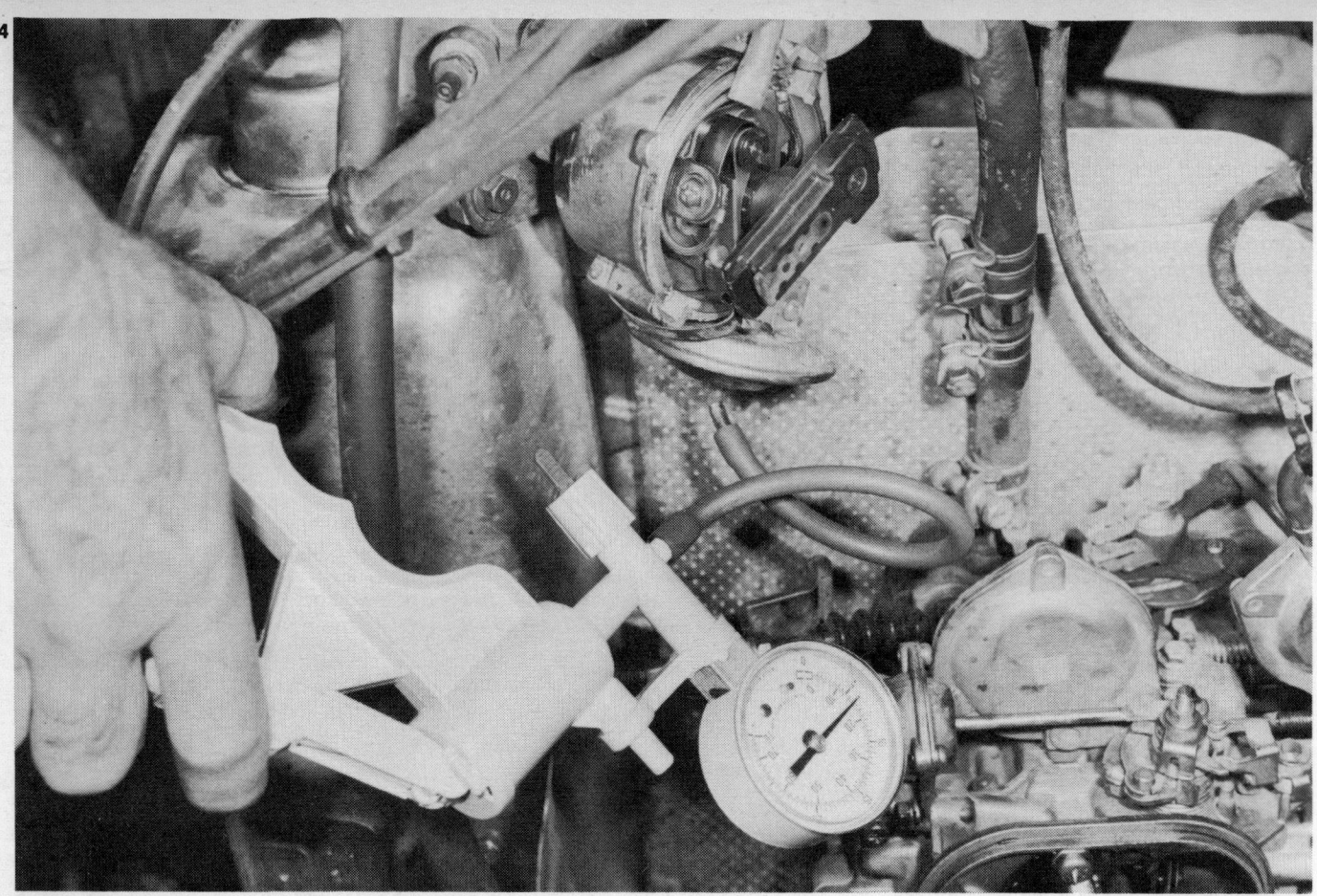

14. The hand vacuum pump is not really a piece of electrical test equipment, but it's very useful in diagnosing such problems as faulty distributor vacuum advance operation.

IGNITION TUNING

Everyone who drives a car should know at least enough about how it works to determine if his mechanic is doing his job properly, even if the driver never expects to lift a screwdriver himself. But the man who does his own tuneups should not make the same mistake that some service garages do—replacing components one by one in hopes that he'll solve the problem. The right way to approach an ignition tuneup is to replace only what needs to be replaced, but to check everything to make sure there are no undiscovered weak spots.

Let's start by taking a grand tour of the ignitions used in different cars, with particular emphasis on some of the finer points deserving special notice during a tuneup. Many are basic points that you'll need to know to do a good tune. In each case, we'll start with the spark plugs and work backward to the ignition switch, describing any special features that may be unique to that particular maker's autos. We'll deal with both the earlier breaker-point ignitions and the later breakerless systems.

GENERAL MOTORS

All GM cars are factory-equipped with 14-mm AC spark plugs. Some use a special tapered-seat 14-mm plug with a 5/8-inch hex rather the usual 13/16-inch, requiring a special wrench. Don't try to put a gasket on any tapered-seat plugs; GM doesn't use them. GM uses different plug reaches in different models, but torque specs for all except tapered-seat plugs are 20 to 25 ft.-lb. in iron heads and about 25 percent less in aluminum heads. Tapered-seat plugs must be tightened to no more than 15 ft.-lb. Any more than that makes it extremely difficult to remove the plugs at the next tuneup. If a torque wrench is not available, tighten the plugs about one-half turn with a plug wrench *after* they are finger-tight in the head.

Spark plugs should be changed each 5000 miles for best service. Packard radio resistance cable is used for the plug and high-tension leads, and the location of the distributor cap terminal serving No. 1 cylinder is usually marked inside the cap. All recent conventional GM V-8 distributors have screwlike distributor cap holddowns that are released by inserting a screwdriver into the slot, pushing down against spring pressure, and turning them 180 degrees in either direction. The rotor used in all eight-cylinder distributors is screwed into place atop the centrifugal-advance mechanism. When replacing the rotor, the round and square lugs molded into its underside must engage the correspondingly shaped holes in the cam flange. The rotors on six-cylinder distributors merely lift off.

Breaker points are a single assembly in late-model conventional ignition GM cars. The Delco points are fitted with a quick-detachment terminal for the primary and condenser wires so as greatly to speed point changes. Care must be taken to reinstall the wires in their original positions or else inter-

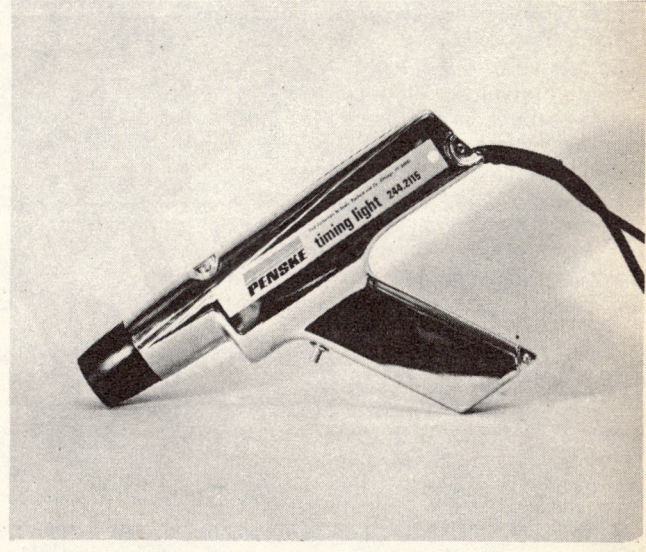

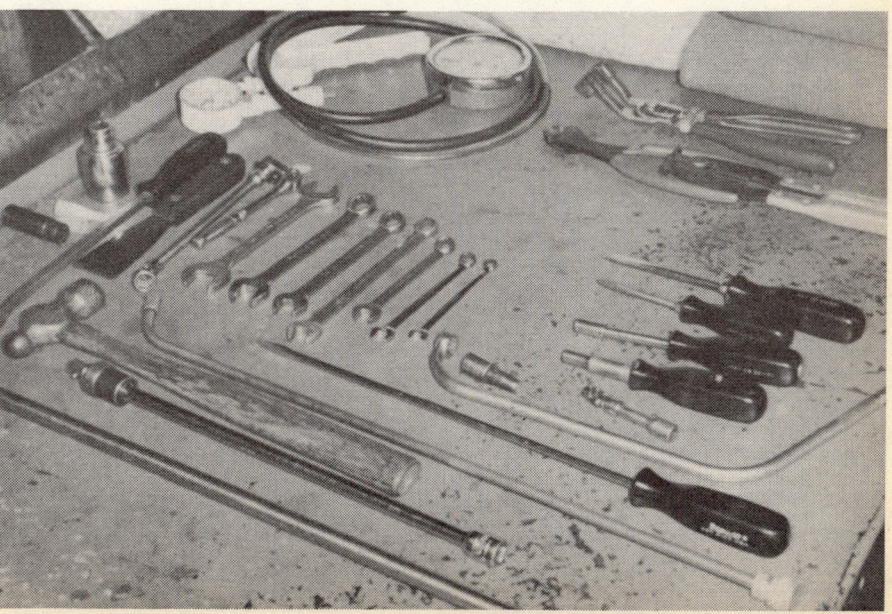

1. Checking ignition timing is the final step of any ignition tune-up. Use a good DC timing light with an inductive pickup to prevent damage to the No. 1 plug wire.
2. Here are some of the tools you'll find handy for an ignition tune-up. While this set will do a full-fledged tuneup on any car, you'll soon discover exactly what your car requires in the way of tools.

IGNITION TUNING

ference with the rotor, cap, and spark advance may occur. GM Delco distributors have a sheet metal radio interference shield over the points. If you buy replacement points with a screw instead of friction-fit leads, the screw head may not clear the metal shield. If it does not, it will ground the points and kill the ignition. Stick with genuine Delco points made to fit under the shield and you won't have that trouble.

The correct point spring tension is 19 to 23 ounces, measured with the hook of a point scale just behind the point surface. Tension is changed by bending the spring, but changes are seldom required. The point assembly has a pilot lug that must engage a matching hole in the breaker plate to prevent incorrect installation. GM shop manuals advise that you set all new points at .003-inch wider than the specified gap setting to allow for initial rubbing block wear.

When fitting new points, wipe the cam clean of all old grease and install a new cam-oiled wick. Do not dip the felt wick that comes with the new point set in oil—it's prelubricated. Six-cylinder distributors have a round, wheel-type lubricator, whereas the eight-cylinder window-type units use a straight felt strip. Remove the old wick by squeezing its base together with a pair of long-nose pliers and pulling it from its loop. The new wick must be positioned so that only its tip brushes against the cam; more contact causes excessive lubrication and eventual contamination of the points.

When checking the distributor with a dwell meter, dwell variation should not exceed 3 degrees. If it does, it indicates that the distributor has an excessively worn breaker plate bushing or shaft bearings. Since dwell meters are relatively inaccurate at high rpm, GM recommends that tests should not be made above 1750 rpm.

Condenser capacity for GM cars should be between .18 and .23 microfarads. If one point picks up material transferred from the other, condensers of slightly higher or lower capacity within the prescribed range can be substituted, according to the direction of the buildup (see "Conventional Distributors" chapter).

Distributor shaft end play should not be more than .002- to .007-inch. Runout—which can be checked by rolling the distributor shaft on a sheet of plate glass or turning it in V-blocks against a dial indicator—should not exceed .002-inch. The distributor shaft is lubricated at its lower end by crankcase vapors and at the top by a reservoir of permanent grease. If the distributor is disassembled or the body washed in solvent, be careful to replenish this grease supply before returning the distributor to service. When replacing the centrifugal advance on the distributor shaft, the top of the shaft should first be coated with Delco Cam & Ball Bearing Grease or its equivalent before assembly. The elimination of external oilers or grease cups has served to extend the service interval for GM autos.

3

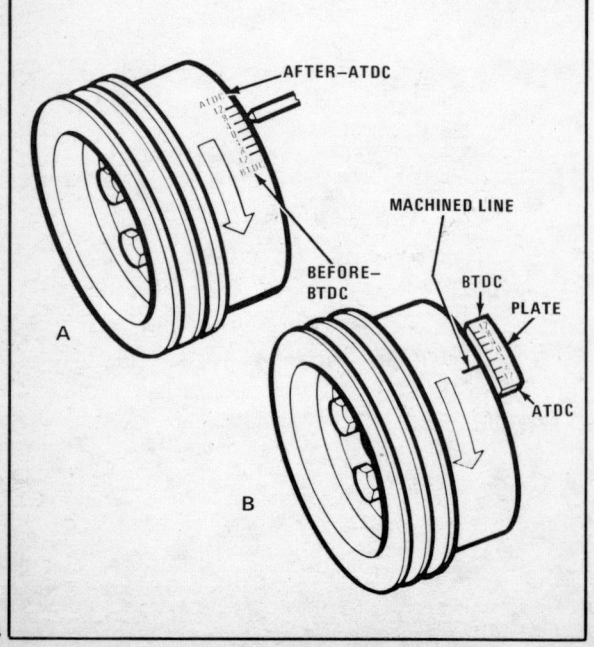
4

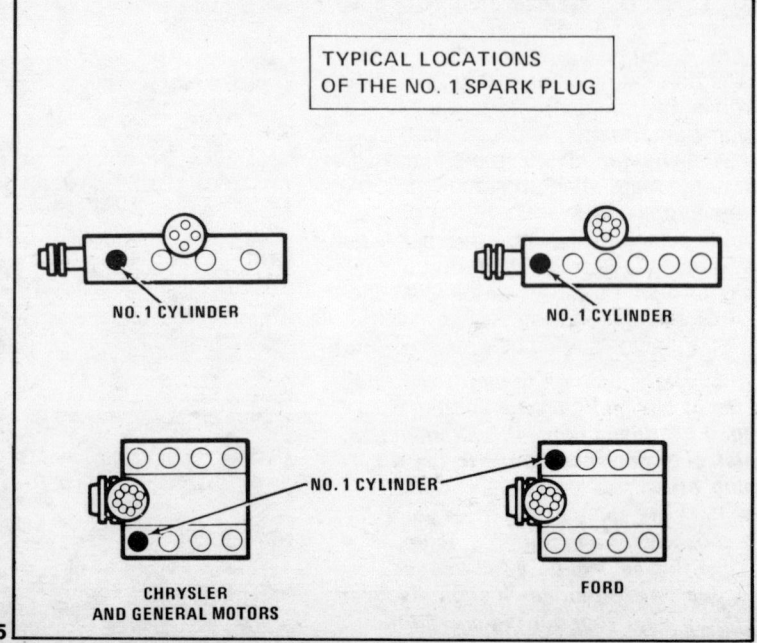
5

The Delco coils found in GM cars have two wires connecting them to the ignition switch. One of these is a normal wire that supplies full battery voltage to the coil when the key is turned to the start position. The other wire is a resistance type of wire used instead of a separate ballast resistor in the primary circuit. The resistance wire supplies current to the coil only when the key is in the on position. When installing custom coils or ignition systems, it is often necessary to locate and remove the stock "ballast." In the case of GM cars, this is done simply by replacing the resistance wire with a regular one.

GM's High-Energy Ignition

Since an HEI system puts out about 10,000 volts more than a conventional GM breaker-point ignition, a larger distributor cap and rotor are required to keep the high voltage from leaking. The new distributor cap is no thicker than the conventional one, so it's prone to giving trouble. Why the extra voltage? When GM engines were set very lean at idle to help meet emission specifications in the early seventies, a phenomenon called "acceleration glazing" reduced spark-plug life by about 50 percent on 1971–73 models. Caused by excessive start-stop driving, this occurred because there was insufficient voltage available to fire the glazed plugs. To extend plug life to its original 10,000–12,000 miles, GM increased the system voltage, and we're right back where we started.

The HEI ignition has proven to be relatively trouble-free, but you should realize that each application uses a different cap-mounted coil. They all look alike and connect in the same way, but system specifications and coil windings differ, not only from GM division to GM division, but also from one engine to another within a division. Don't substitute a coil that does not carry the same part number as the one it replaces or you'll ruin it. You'll also destroy it if you hook up a tach/dwell test unit to the coil terminal marked "tach," if that test unit lacks the circuit capability required to test a transistorized ignition. Most such equipment sold in the past five years is immune to this problem.

You may also have difficulty with the GM pickup coil at times. Occasionally, one overheats and exceeds the stated ohm value. The engine will not restart until the pickup coil cools to less than that stated value. This is a tough one to test for, because the coil is located down in the distributor. By the time you clear a path to it, very likely it will have cooled sufficiently to test out okay. If you suspect pickup coil malfunction, heat it up and cool it down quickly for test purposes with a hair drier and a can of refrigerant.

If you remove the electronic module from the distributor, you'll find a thin coating of grease on its bottom. Don't wipe it off, as the grease is required for proper heat transfer involved in module cooling. When installing a new module, apply the grease included with the replacement to both the metal face of the module and the distributor housing mounting seat.

Until late 1979 models, the pins holding the centrifugal-advance weight springs had a tendency to wear excessively. This gradually elongated the holes in the weights and eventually caused the advance curve to change radically. GM specified no lubrication at these points but service technicians found it necessary to lubricate the pins as a means of holding down wear. Beginning with late 1979 distributors, the pins were changed to stainless steel.

6.

7.

3. You'll find a distributor wrench necessary in most of today's overcrowded engine compartments. Somehow, the distributor hold-down bolt is always buried.

4. Here are the two styles of timing mark arrangements. In (A), the marks on the harmonic balancer should align with the stationary pointer; with (B), the machined line on the balancer or pulley should be aligned with the engine block plate.

5. Where to connect your timing light? To the No. 1 cylinder—and here are typical locations.

6. Remove and inspect the distributor cap. If any cracks, chips or signs of carbon tracking/arcing are noted, replace it AND the rotor.

7. With so much crud on the breaker plate of this distributor, what do you suppose the centrifugal advance weights below the plate look like? Keep all distributor components CLEAN!

IGNITION TUNING

The advance weights are now made of sintered iron impregnated with a special lubricant. GM still maintains that no lubrication is necessary, but it's too early to tell if this will solve the problem.

FORD MOTOR COMPANY

Ford products were unique in having a positive-ground electrical system until 1956, when the 12-volt negative-ground system now standard on all domestic cars was adopted. If you mix parts from old and new Fords, or use older Ford parts in street rods, you must be aware of this difference.

Autolite or Motorcraft spark plugs are standard on all Ford products. All are of the 18-mm tapered-seat variety. Since they have the same 13/16-inch hex as standard 14-mm plugs, you need no special wrench to change them. These plugs use no gaskets and are all of the same 3/8-inch reach. When installing them, it's very important that the tapered seat in the heads and on the plugs be absolutely clean. Tapered-seat plugs must be torqued to 15-20 ft.-lb. Overtightening can make later removal very difficult. Ford manuals make a point of cautioning mechanics that the excessive use of abrasive-type plug cleaners can be very damaging, since the ceramic insulators may be eroded away. This may partially trace to the fact that the larger gas volume of the 18-mm plugs lets more of the cleaning abrasive into the plug's interior. Autolite or Motorcraft radio-resistance cables with molded-on right-angle nipples are standard. The No. 1 terminal on the distributor cap is usually marked on the outside of the cap itself.

Distributor cap removal and rotor removal are conventional on most Ford engines, as is the removal of the breaker-point set. On certain Fords, a one-piece pivotless point assembly is used, which is somewhat quicker to replace. With the earlier types of points, it is possible to adjust contact spring tension by loosening the spring mounting screw and sliding the spring back and forth to achieve the desired load. Dwell variations should not exceed 3 degrees below 2000 rpm, and the distributor cam must be lubricated with a suitable grease during the point installation.

Ford has also marketed a breaker-controlled transistor system using a centrifugal-advance, high-performance distributor equipped with only one set of points and no condenser. When tuning one of these, do not connect a dwell meter or tach to any part of the system other than the tachometer block. This consists of a double ballast resistor, a relay to bypass the resistors for starting and the panel's terminals. Tests of the transistor system should be made as

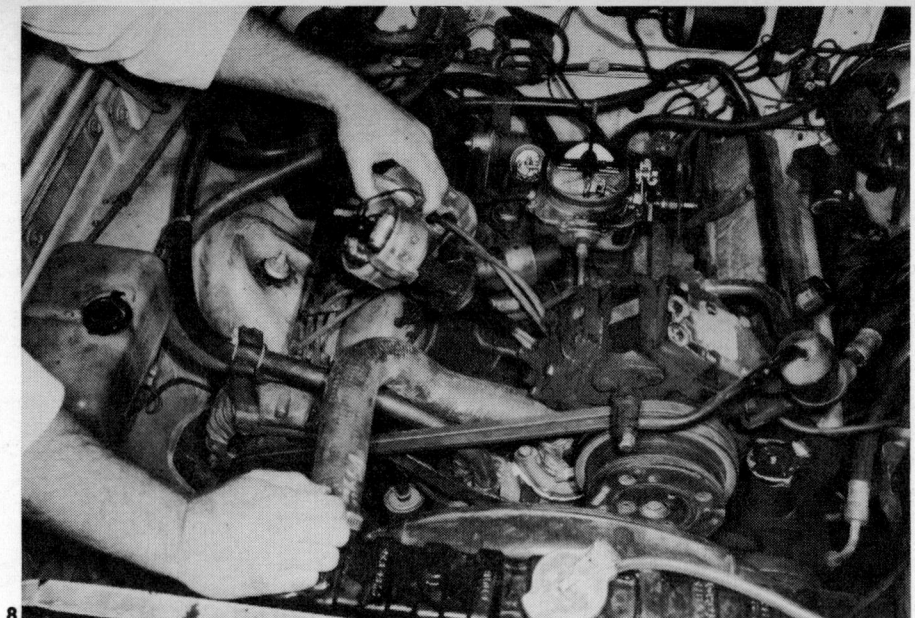

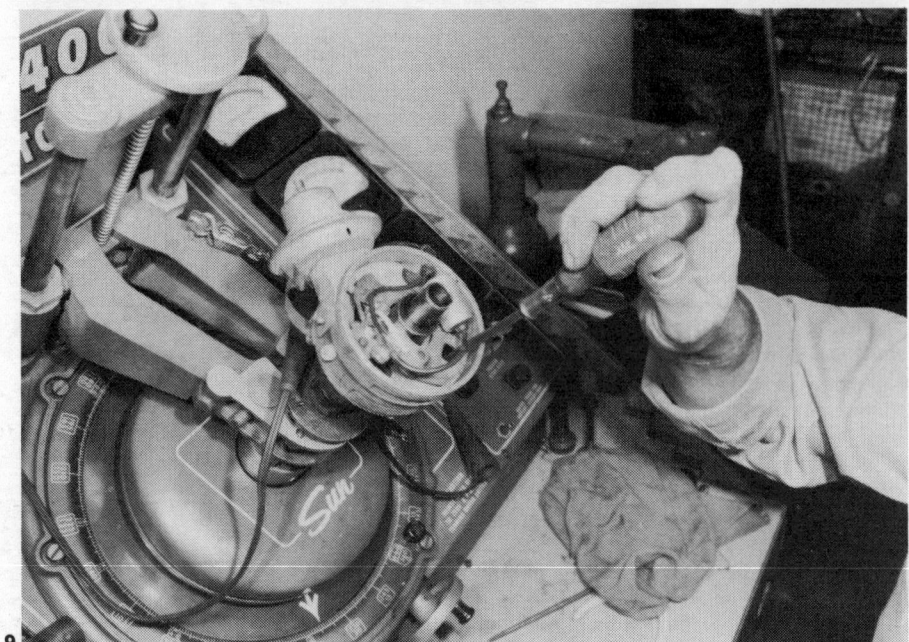

specified in individual Ford shop manuals.

FoMoCo vacuum advances can be adjusted by adding or subtracting washers from the vacuum chamber assembly. The only exception to this is the Loadomatic all-vacuum distributor used in the sixties. This unit is controlled by two calibrated springs—one for high advance and one for low. Adjust the centrifugal advance of dual-advance distributors before checking the vacuum system. This is done by inserting a tool through a hole in the breaker plate and bending the spring mount to increase or decrease spring tension. The greater the tension, the less the advance. Such adjustments must be performed on a distributor testing machine.

The high-performance centrifugal-advance distributor is controlled by calibrated springs only, and advance curve modifications require that the springs be changed or modified. Factory specifications demand that the centrifugal-advance curve of the high-performance unit be within ±1° of the exact figure at all engine rpm.

The standard dual-advance distributors are allowed a maximum of 6 degrees of dwell variation at constant rpm going from 0 to maximum vacuum (not over 25 inches Hg.) on the test machine. If dwell variation exceeds this, there are worn or bent parts in the vacuum-advance mechanism. FoMoCo distributors have oil cups which must be attended to periodically for proper service life.

The coil in conventional Ford ignition systems is served by a resistance wire from the ignition switch and has no separate ballast resistor. The transistor system has a separate ballast resistor unit, as mentioned earlier. The coil of the transistorized system should not be tested on a coil tester as its construction makes such tests inconclusive. Engines used in cars equipped with overdrive have an extra wire on the "Dist." terminal of the coil. This wire serves the overdrive kickdown switch. The current for the ignition system is drawn from a terminal on the starter relay.

Ford's Solid-State Ignition

The early Ford SSI system experienced considerable trouble in the form of poor signal transmission, caused by loose connections between the distributor and the electronic module. A special "DEC" grease (for distributor electronic control) is packed in the ends of the connector plugs to keep moisture out. Whenever you disconnect these plugs, replace the DEC grease. Use enough so that it oozes out when the plugs are reinstalled.

Ford changed the harness wire pin connectors and the wire colors for 1975 and 1976, which is of no interest unless you find it necessary to test the pin connectors while troubleshooting the circuitry. If you do, you'd expect the systems to give the same reading, so if your readings come up a little weird, let that jog your memory—you're testing the wrong circuits for the wrong thing.

The Dura-Spark II distributor, coil, and module are essentially the same as the previously used SSI system except for calibration. The new system has an adapter on the distributor to accommodate the new, larger distributor terminal housing and the larger rotor used with the higher voltage. The terminal housing features spark-plug-type terminal towers. The high-tension spark-plug wires were increased in size to 8 mm and have silicone jacketing for improved insulation. Spark plugs are the new carbon resistor type and have a wider electrode gap. The high voltage and wide spark-plug gap increase plug life and overall engine performance. The system can be readily identified by the large blue distributor cap and high-tension wires.

Like the GM HEI system, the plug wires used with Dura-Spark II are very

8. You can work on the distributor in the car, but it's often much easier to remove it for a thorough cleaning.

9. Have the distributor checked on a distributor machine for shaft or bushing wear, as well as proper advance operation.

10. Many distributors use an O-ring seal (arrow) on the bowl-to-block surface. Be sure to install a new one whenever you pull the distributor.

11A and 11B. Make sure drive belts are properly tensioned if you expect proper electrical operation of your car's systems. Use a belt tensioner gauge (A) when possible, or check for approximately 1/4-3/8 in. deflection when the belt is depressed with about 22 lb. pressure, as shown in (B).

11a

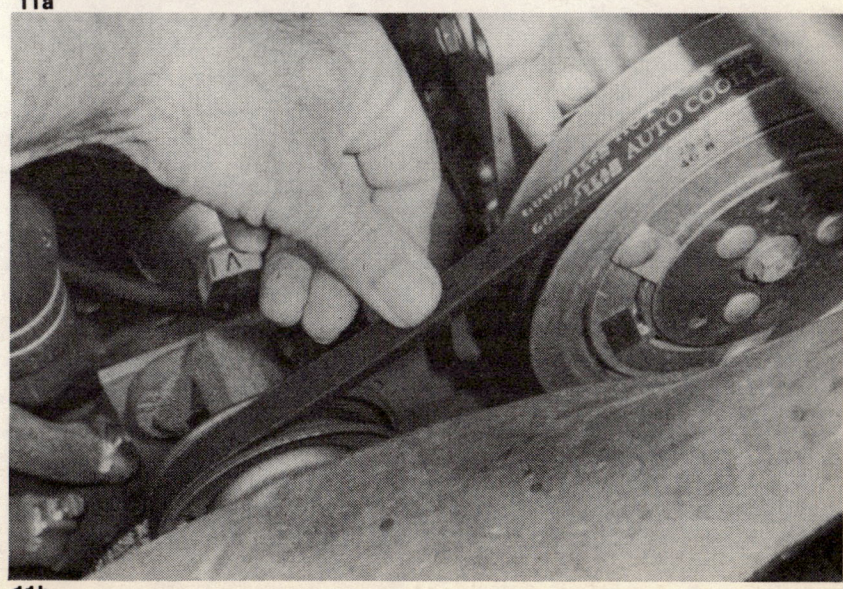
11b

IGNITION & ELECTRICAL SYSTEMS/85

IGNITION TUNING

expensive and should be treated with kid gloves. At approximately $12 per wire, you don't want to pull them off carelessly while checking for spark or changing plugs. Use plug cable pliers to avoid any possible damage. Grasp the insulator and twist it back and forth on the spark plug to free the insulator. Do not pull directly on the wire or it may become separated from the connector inside the insulator.

Two types of Dura-Spark plug cables are used. Both are blue in color and have silicone jacketing to withstand the tremendous heat given off by today's engines. Both types may be found in the same engine compartment, so exercise care when replacing cables. Type SE (identified by letters printed in black) is used where somewhat cooler temperatures are prevalent, and type SS (white printing) where very high engine temperatures are present.

CHRYSLER CORPORATION

Champion supplies the spark plugs used in all Chrysler Corp. cars. All are of the 14-mm size, but various reaches are used in different engines. Chrysler's crimped-on type of plug gaskets does not require a torque wrench for proper seating. About one-third to one-half turn with a plug wrench after making them finger-tight is all that's required. Racing plugs and plugs with other gasket types should be torqued to 30 ft.-lb. The cables used for Chrysler plug leads simply say "radio."

Until 1972 in the introduction of a breakerless electronic ignition, the construction and layout of the Mopar distributors were highly conventional, including the construction and placement of the points, condenser, and advance units. The cam must be greased regularly at each point servicing. There is also an oiler on the distributor body to lubricate the shaft and its bushings. Three drops of SAE 10W engine oil are administered according to the service interval of the particular engine. In addition, there is a felt lubrication wick in the center of the cam which serves the centrifugal advance. This also requires three to five drops of SAE 10W oil.

Maximum shaft end play on either type of distributor should not exceed .006- to .007-inch. If the drive gear is removed to correct excess end play by renewing the thrust washers, be sure it is properly aligned with the rotor when replaced. The bushings of these distributors are fully replaceable, so servicing can return the unit to like-new condition. The advance curve of the high-performance dual-point distributors must fall within ±1° at all rpm.

Chrysler Corp. cars employ a separate ballast resistor in series with the

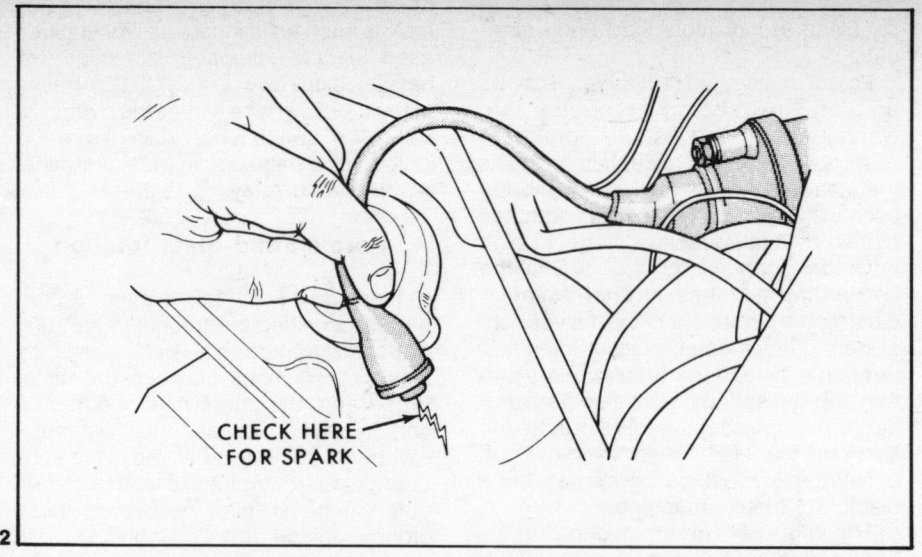

12

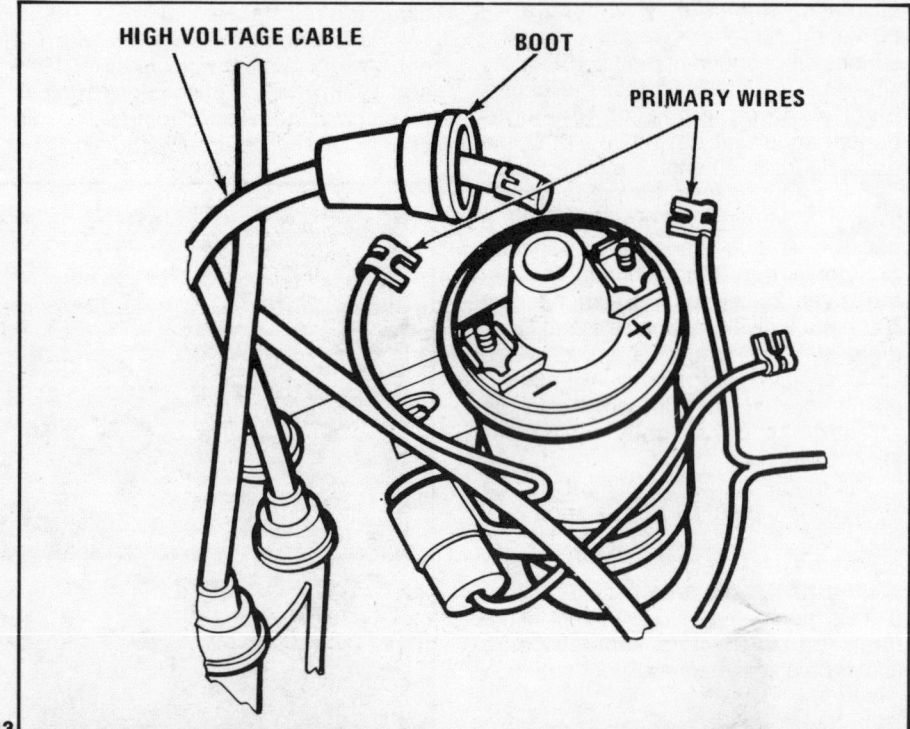

13

14

coil's primary connection. Most models draw ignition current from a terminal on the alternator regulator, but some of the compacts supply the ignition from the starter relay.

Chrysler Electronic Ignition

The most common problem with the Chrysler electronic ignition system proved to be a bad coil that causes a stumble. Chrysler uses an oil-filled coil and since primary buildup time is considerable, the coil tends to overheat consistently and eventually burns out. Placing it horizontally at the rear of V-8 engines is an additional burden for the coil to bear. Chrysler originally used the same switching module for all applications, but in an effort to correct the coil burnout problem, the switching transistor was changed to three different ones, identified by the sticker color on the module—gold, silver, and green.

Because the switching module controls engine firing, you must be careful not to replace a defective module with a new one of the incorrect rating. If you install a six-cylinder module on an eight-cylinder engine, it will fire too slowly and result in a sluggish car. But a six-cylinder engine when incorrectly equipped with an eight-cylinder module will have too rapid a rate of firing; at high engine speeds, the rpm will build up and the engine will blow. Tighten the switching module periodically, as it has a tendency to vibrate loose from its firewall mounting.

If your Chrysler electronic ignition quits dead on the road, check the pickup coil tooth. The Chrysler distributor continues to use the single-pivot connection on the breaker plate, characteristic of the conventional Mopar distributor. With sufficient wear, the breaker plate loosens. When the vacuum advance kicks in, it pulls the pickup coil down. This causes the breaker plate to lean or tilt and eventually brings the coil's tooth into contact with the revolving reluctor teeth, breaking off the coil tooth and stopping the car. A failure to start can often be traced to a defective ballast resistor.

Chrysler Electronic Spark Control systems suffer from spark computer failure. Although a portion of the problem can be traced to manufacturing problems, many spark computers are literally baked by the high underhood temperatures. To alleviate the problem and lengthen the life of the computer, it's a good idea to pop the hood open after a long drive at highway speeds, especially on very hot summer days. This will allow the heat in the engine compartment to escape instead of creating a heat-soak condition as it slowly dissipates with the hood closed. Remember, heat rises and

12. *Here's the standard test for ignition system firing. We suggest you hold the cable with insulated pliers on breakerless ignitions, however, just in case there's a break in the insulation. It can save you finding out the hard way.*

13. *The primary lead from the ignition switch connects to the coil + or BAT terminal; the distributor lead hooks up to the – or DIST terminal. If you reverse them, the engine will run, but about 40 percent more voltage is required to fire the plugs.*

14. *Use care when disconnecting the distributor leads to the HEI distributor cap—it's a snap-in connector that's not the easiest to unsnap.*

15. *Disconnecting the HEI cap from the plug cable loom is a chore. Inspect the cap with a flashlight to avoid the hassle.*

16. *Turning the distributor housing opposite to the direction of rotation advances the timing; turning it in the same direction retards the spark.*

17. *When adjusting the points, move the stationary point arm. If the gap is too great, move the point arm AWAY from the cam. When the gap is too narrow, the arm is moved TOWARD the cam.*

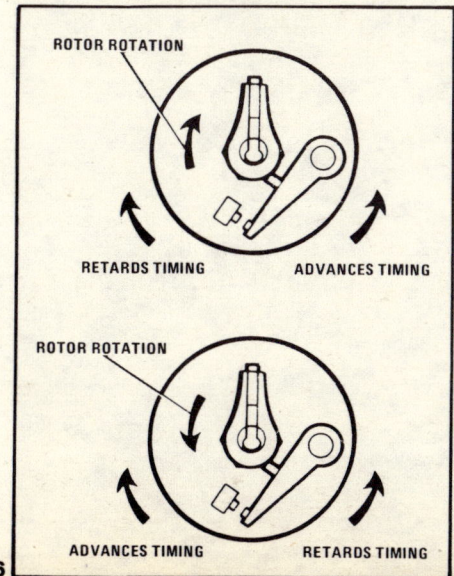

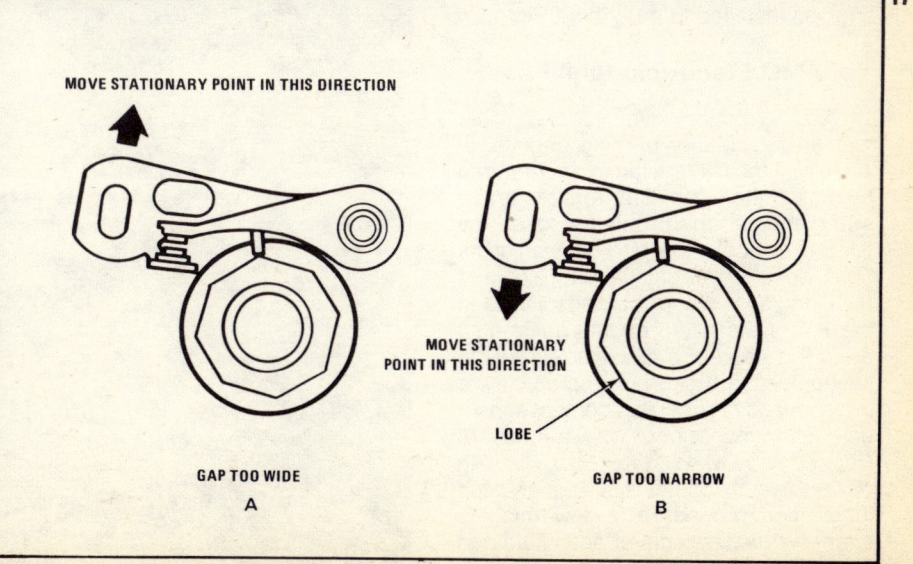

IGNITION TUNING

the insulation under the hood holds it in place.

The final potential problem area lies in the secondary circuitry. Chrysler didn't change it one bit from that used with conventional ignitions, so all the secondary problems you would encounter with a conventional ignition and distributor are still quite possible.

AMERICAN MOTORS

Fourteen-millimeter plugs from Champion are used in all AMC cars. Since 1965, all AMC engines have used a 3/4-inch reach plug, although 7/16-inch reaches predominated in previous years, and were still being used in the 196-cubic-inch ohv AMC six-cylinder in 1965. Since the 232-cubic-inch six was then using 3/4-inch reach plugs, mechanics occasionally have made the mistake of installing these in the "little" six, with disastrous results. Standard Champion plugs require only about one-third to one-half turn with a plug wrench after being seated finger-tight. Racing plugs should be torqued to 25-30 ft.-lb. even in aluminum engines. Radio resistance high-tension cables are standard equipment.

The remainder of the AMC ignition system is of either Autolite-Motorcraft or Delco-Remy manufacture, with all recent six- and eight-cylinder models employing the Delco system. Servicing is identical to that required for Ford products having Autolite-Motorcraft systems, and General Motors products with Delco components. Recent AMC V-8s use the Delco window-type distributor. American Motors differs from GM, however, in choosing to use a separate ballast resistor rather than resistance wire in the primary current source. Ignition current is always picked up at the starter solenoid. Four-cylinder engines in 1977-79 AMC vehicles use the German Bosch system, which has also been used on some 1600-cc engines installed in early Ford Pintos.

AMC Electronic Ignitions

AMC switched over to electronic ignition for cleaner-burning engines in 1975 with the BID system manufactured by Prestolite. The BID ignition gave sufficient sensor problems to cause AMC to switch to the 1976 version of the Ford Solid-State Ignition on 1978 and later engines. When the sensor fails in the BID system, the engine quits—just as in the case of a Chrysler electronic ignition with a broken pickup coil. It's a good idea to carry a replacement sensor unit with you, along with a copy of Petersen's *How to Tune Your Car*, 7th edition, which contains a step-by-step installation procedure. A few minutes spent with a screwdriver and pliers can save you a hefty tow bill.

TUNEUP PROCEDURES

The first step in a good home tuneup is to remove and inspect all the spark plugs. By comparing their appearance with the photos in the "Spark Plugs" chapter, you can often identify engine troubles or ignition weaknesses. If the plugs have been in service for 10,000 miles or more, you'll save time, performance, and fuel by replacing them. Plugs with less than maximum mileage should be inspected to determine if cleaning is necessary. If there are no significant deposits, it's best not to sandblast them. If the electrodes are eroded slightly, they should be squared up with a file and regapped. If their condition is almost like new, a simple regapping is often all that's required.

Wash the distributor cap clean with soapy water and air-dry it thoroughly. Inspect the interior contacts and terminals for wear and erosion. If the contacts show enough wear to widen the rotor gap, the cap needs replacing. Similarly, if the rotor tip is noticeably eroded or worn, it should be discarded in favor of a new one. A special silicone grease is used on the rotor tip and/or distributor cap contacts to improve electrical conductivity in late-model breakerless distributors. This grease gradually turns dark brown or gray-white with age, but the color change does not indicate a problem. It's normal. When servicing the distributor, clean off the residue and apply a 1/32-inch coating of fresh silicone grease available from your dealer's parts department.

The breaker points can be tested in the engine with a voltmeter to determine

18

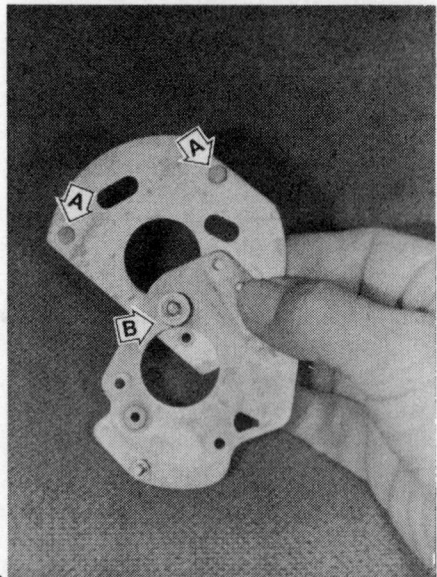
19

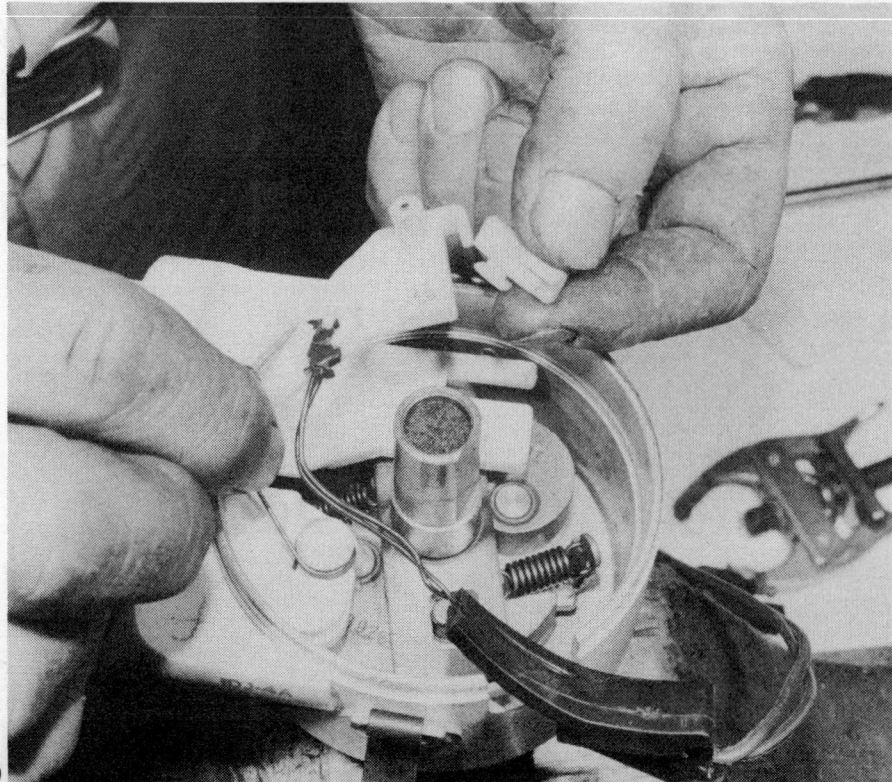
20

if their contact faces are mating adequately. A voltage drop greater than two-tenths of a volt on a sensitive meter indicates poor contact between the points. To do the voltage drop test correctly, you need a voltmeter with a low-reading scale of about one to three volts. A higher scale can be used, but it won't be as accurate, because you want to read in tenths of a volt.

To test the points for voltage drop, remove the center wire from the distributor and ground it to the block so the engine won't start accidentally. Then bump the starter gently until the distributor points are closed. Be sure the points are closed—you should see daylight between the rubbing block and the cam.

Connect one voltmeter clip to the primary terminal on the side of the distributor, if it has one, or to the primary terminal on the distributor side of the coil. Connect the other clip to a good engine ground. Turn the ignition switch on and read the voltage drop on the meter. It

18. Rotors are too often taken for granted, but they suffer from the same potential defects as the distributor cap. When a new rotor is required, replace the cap at the same time.

19. Distributor breaker plate wear can play havoc with point or pick-up coil operation. On the Motorcraft breaker plate, look for worn or damaged nylon inserts (A) as well as a worn pivot (B). Be sure to lubricate the breaker plate before reinstalling it.

20. The Prestolite BID ignition is the only breakerless system that suffers from excessive sensor/pick-up coil problems. If you have one, you've probably already changed a sensor or two.

21. When a ballast resistor burns out, it causes an open circuit in the ignition system. This results in an engine that will not start.

22. The Universal distributor is Ford's first to position the centrifugal advance weights on top of the distributor shaft, like the Delco V-8. Note that its rotor also resembles that used on Delco V-8 distributors.

should be not more than two-tenths of a volt. A higher reading on the voltmeter means that there's excessive resistance somewhere in the circuit between the two voltmeter clips. That would include all connections and ground. Usually the trouble is dirty or worn points that aren't making good contact.

Next, check the distributor cam for wear, and also the advance parts and their bushings. Wiggle the cam back and forth to detect any looseness, then check the condition of the "bumpers" on Delco centrifugal advances. If the distributor has been in service for a year or more, the advance parts should be washed clean with solvent and thoroughly relubricated.

When installing the points and advance parts, make sure that they are lubricated to the manufacturer's specifications. Be sure that the points and condenser are in good ground contact with the breaker plate. The points should be gapped to specs and the cam lubricated with distributor cam grease. Any point misalignment must be corrected. If a protective coating has been applied to the new points, it must be wiped away before they are put into service.

Once the distributor is back on the engine and everything reconnected properly, test the dwell angle with a tach/dwell meter. There's no need to check the dwell if the points were set to specs with a feeler gauge, unless you just want to double-check your work. If the correct point gap should result in a dwell reading that is off by many degrees, it tells you that you have the wrong parts in the distributor, or that something is out of line, such as the points or the breaker plate. Recheck your specs—there's always a chance you misread or used the wrong ones. Remember, changing the dwell (point gap) also changes the timing, but timing changes do not affect dwell. Thus, always adjust the dwell and then the timing.

Adjust the engine idle at the carburetor until the manufacturer's prescribed idle speed is reached. This can be found on a tuneup or emissions decal located

in a conspicuous spot in the engine compartment. It provides idle speed, dwell, and timing specs for that particular engine, and should be consulted during each tuneup. Some decals may even specify the adjustment procedure to be followed.

Switch from the tachometer to the dwell scale and adjust the points until the specified angle is indicated. If the points were gapped to specs, dwell should be within the permissible zone. If not, the gap can be readjusted until dwell is exactly right.

Now connect your timing light. Hook its cables to the proper battery terminals and to the No. 1 spark-plug cable, either at the cap or the plug, and start the engine. Most engines require that the vacuum-advance line be disconnected at the distributor while setting timing. This slows down the engine sufficiently so the timing mark can be seen. Aim the timing light at the engine's timing pointer and move the slightly loosened distributor back and forth until the correct mark aligns with the pointer, then tighten the holddown bolt. It's often helpful to brighten the timing mark with chalk or white paint so that it can be seen more easily.

A complete tuneup includes much more than just spark-plug and distributor work. You should also check the battery, starter, and compression, and adjust the belts and carburetor idle. Additional items that should be checked or serviced are the air cleaner, crankcase breather, smog valve, fuel filter, heat riser valve, cooling system, and engine valves, if adjustable. The idea is to catch the weak points before they break down and cause trouble on the road.

Much of the foregoing can be ignored if your car is equipped with an electronic ignition. All that need be done with these is to gap and change the spark plugs at the indicated intervals, replace spark-plug wires when needed, and check the ignition timing. To help you hit the high points with ease, we've included on the following pages a typical ignition tuneup sequence using a GM V-6 engine in a Citation. Use this as a guide when tuning your engine and you won't go wrong.

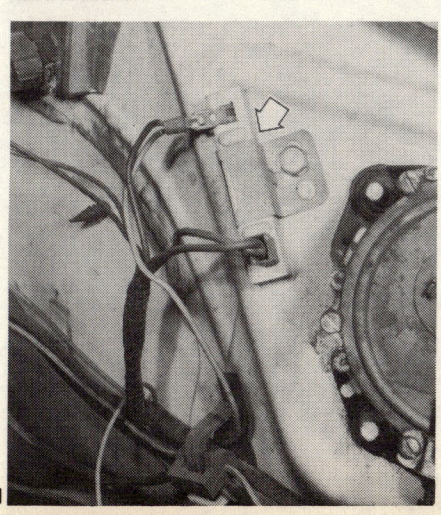

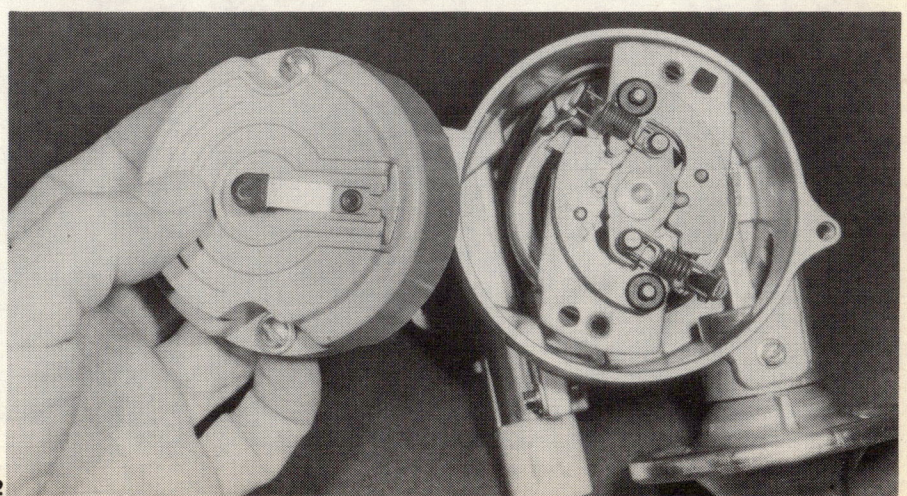

HOW-TO: IGNITION TUNE—UP

1. Remove air cleaner wing nut and cover, disconnect fresh air tube and any tubing, hoses or lines connected to the air cleaner housing. Remove housing from carburetor.

2. Plug cable pliers are a good idea to prevent burning yourself, but may be difficult to use in tight places. Rear bank of plugs on transverse engines may require working by touch.

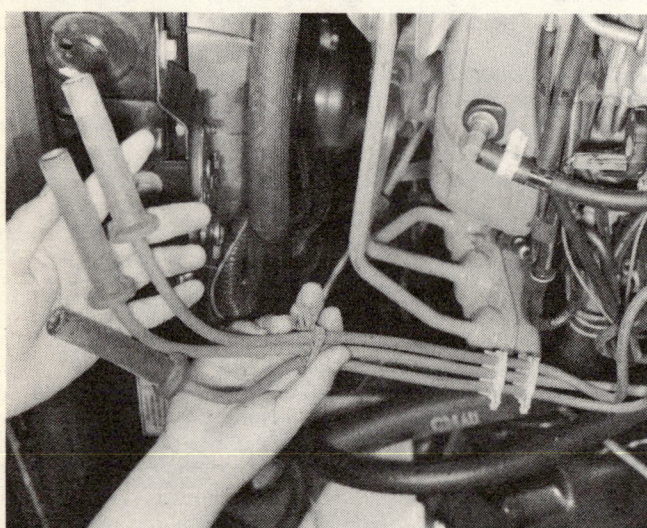

3. Wipe plug cables clean and inspect condition of insulation. Proper cable routing will extend their life, so make sure to reconnect wire looms properly.

4. A speeder wrench with 9-degree angle extension works well to remove plugs on front bank. The rear plugs on transverse engines are more difficult to remove/install.

5. Inspect plug condition closely. The one shown here has a bent side electrode, closing the spark gap completely. Little wonder the engine misfired.

6. Run compression test with plugs out. Disable distributor and crank engine over several times. Lowest cylinder reading should be 75 percent of the highest.

7. To service the HEI distributor or replace the spark plug cables, depress the latches on opposite sides of the cap as shown. This frees the plug wire loom from cap.

8. Remove plug cable loom by lifting straight up and off distributor cap. Individual cables can be replaced at this point if necessary by popping them out of the loom.

9. Four screw locks hold the distributor cap to the housing. To remove cap, depress each screw with a screwdriver and rotate 90 degrees. Screw will turn in only one direction.

10. Lift cap up and off distributor housing. Wipe inside of cap with a clean paper towel and inspect for hairline cracks, burned contacts, carbon tracks or other defects.

11. The HEI distributor rotor is retained by two screws. Loosen screws and remove the rotor. Inspect rotor for same defects as distributor cap. Replace as a set if necessary.

12. Check centrifugal advance action by moving cam to one side and pulling advance weights apart. Let go and watch the motion as weights return. If sluggish, mechanism needs cleaning.

13. When the EGR valve is mounted in a location where it's difficult to watch valve stem action, use a long-handled mirror as shown. Stem should move as engine speed is increased.

14. Pull PCV valve from rocker arm cover and shake. If the valve is satisfactory for reuse, you'll hear a clicking sound when shaken. If not, install a new PCV valve.

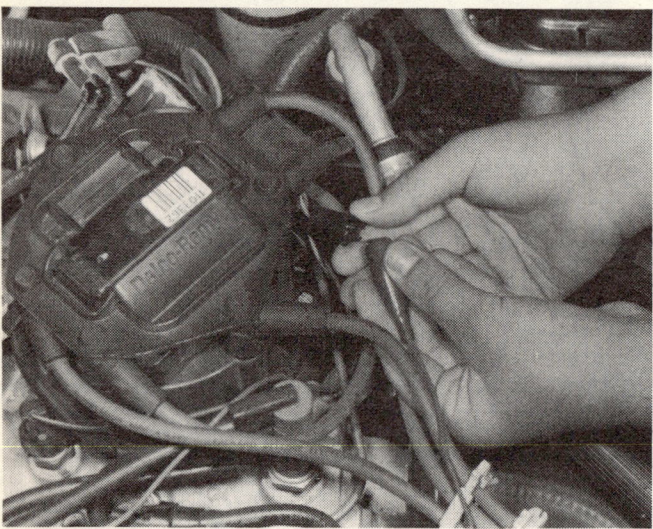

15. An engine tachometer connector is provided to hook up an engine tach for carburetor adjustment/timing. The newer inductive tachs can be used without this connection.

16. It doesn't matter what kind of tach you use, as long as it's accurate and modern. This Cal Custom/Hawk Pocketune is a small, self-contained unit you can carry with you.

17. Check operation of choke butterfly by pushing linkage as shown. The linkage should operate smoothly without binding. Make sure it stays this way with a shot of WD-40.

18. Start engine and spray a can of carb cleaner into the venturi. This will clean the internal passages and reduce the possibility of a carburetor overhaul down the road.

19. Use one wrench to hold the carburetor inlet fitting while breaking the connection loose with a second wrench. Remove fitting and install a new fuel filter.

20. If fuel problems seem apparent, tee a pressure gauge into the fuel line and run a pressure test on the fuel pump to see if it's up to specifications.

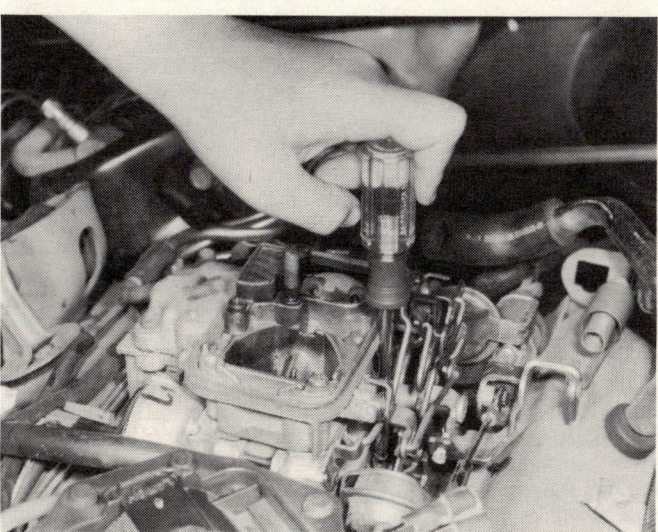
21. The curb idle screw is located under all this linkage at the rear of the carburetor. Set the idle to decal specs. The mixture needle is sealed and cannot be adjusted.

22. Open the throttle wide enough to extend the solenoid plunger, then turn the solenoid screw to adjust the idle to specified rpm. Reconnect the solenoid electrical lead after adjustment.

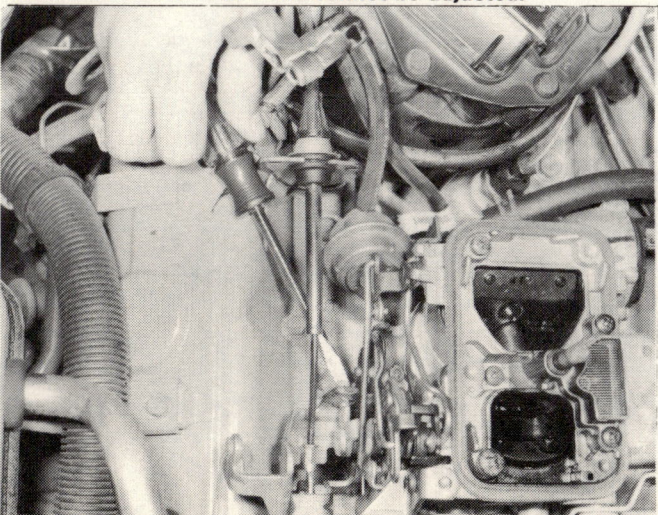
23. Reaching the fast idle screw can be a chore. To set fast idle speed, make sure the screw is on the specified cam step and turn the screw until correct rpm is reached.

24. Connect a timing light and take a look at the ignition timing. If adjustment is needed, loosen distributor hold-down, rotate distributor to align timing marks, and tighten.

BATTERIES

People commonly describe the automotive battery as a "storage" battery, yet this does not accurately describe its true nature. In reality, automotive batteries do not accumulate or store electrical energy at all. Condensers and capacitors are the only true accumulators of electricity. The battery in your car produces electrical energy by means of an electrochemical reaction. The current produced is the direct result of a chemical reaction within the cells—it is not simply the release of a reservoir of current put into the battery in the way that gasoline is poured into the fuel tank.

HOW IT WORKS

The physical design of a battery encompasses many different considerations—size, weight, cost, materials, intended use, resistance to damage, temperature extremes, etc. There are, however, only three electrical conditions that are important: voltage, current-delivering ability, and endurance. Together, these three factors determine practically everything else about a battery. Let's take a look at them and then see how they apply to an automobile battery.

Voltage is determined solely by the materials used in the battery's positive and negative plates. Every metal, metallic compound, as well as some nonmetals—virtually any material that is a conductor of electricity—has an inherent electrical activity when paired with another conductor. Using this activity, scientists have arranged all known conductors into a table called the electromotive series. The farther apart any two materials are in this series, the greater their electrical potential for doing work, or voltage. Voltage can be directly compared to pressure in a hydraulic system. If more voltage is required than can be provided by a single pairing of materials, then each pairing or "cell" is connected in series with more cells until the desired voltage is reached. That is, the positive terminal of one cell is connected to the negative terminal of the next one, and so on. The battery's total voltage is the sum of that produced by the individual cells.

In the automotive battery, the negative material is pure lead, whereas the positive material is lead dioxide, often called lead peroxide since it contains more oxygen than the more usual lead-oxygen compound, lead oxide. Under ideal conditions, this lead–lead peroxide combination yields 2.2 volts per cell. Since conditions are seldom ideal, this is usually rounded off to just 2 volts per cell. A 6-volt battery, then, has three such cells connected in series, and a 12-volt battery has six of them.

The lead and lead peroxide are arranged in parallel plates. Connecting them electrically is the electrolyte, a liquid which is electrically conductive and which also enters into the chemical reaction when the battery is in operation. In the automotive battery, the electrolyte is diluted sulfuric acid, a mixture of sulfuric acid and pure water.

Current-delivering ability depends upon the size of the plates and terminals, but not upon the voltage. For example, the ordinary household dry-cell zinc-carbon flashlight battery is rated at 1½ volts, and connecting eight of them in series would give 12 volts, the same as your car battery. But you could not run your car with eight flashlight batteries. They could not deliver the 25 amps or so needed to operate all the accessories and lights, much less the 125 amps drawn by the starter.

The endurance of the battery also depends upon its size. A large battery can maintain a sizable current for a long time; a small one cannot. The current flow is measured in amperes (amps). It is customary to rate the endurance of auto batteries according to the amp-hour system. A 100-amp-hour battery is capable of delivering 5 amps (a measurement of current flow) for a period of 20 hours. The 20-hour figure is not mentioned in the rating, but is generally understood with auto batteries. The greater the plate area in a battery, the higher the amp-hour rating. There is thus a close relationship between the number of plates in each cell and the rating figure applied to the battery. For example, lower-priced batteries are usually 48-amp-hour units and have four positive plates per cell. Moving up the power scale—and the price range—we find 59-amp-hour batteries with five positive plates, and 70-amp-hour batteries with six positive plates per cell.

The higher the battery's rating, the more work it can do before it becomes discharged. Cars with few accessories can get by satisfactorily on one of the light-duty, low-amp-hour types. But when you start to add accessories like

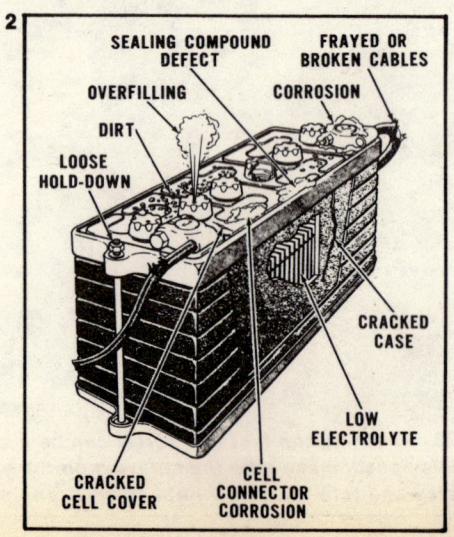

air-conditioning, tape decks, etc., to the battery's normal chores, it requires at least a 70-amp-hour battery to keep up with the demand.

When an auto battery releases electricity so you can operate your car, it does so through the positive post. The current runs through your electrical equipment and completes its circuit when it returns to the battery via the negative post. The plates interact with the acid in such a way that there is a flow of electrons inside each cell from the negative to the positive plates. The acid acts on both positive and negative plate active materials to form a new chemical compound called lead sulfate. The sulfate is supplied by the acid solution (electrolyte), which becomes weaker in concentration as the discharge proceeds. The amount of acid absorbed by the plates is in direct proportion to the amount of electricity removed from the cell. During this process, the battery is being discharged and it will continue to discharge as long as electricity is being drained from it.

Very small amounts of lead and acid are consumed in the discharge process, but since the percentage of acid in the electrolyte is relatively low, the reaction stops long before all the materials are consumed. When all the available sulfuric acid has been absorbed into the chemical structure of the plates, the battery becomes fully discharged. It will then no longer generate electricity, for two reasons. First, the acid content of the electrolyte is depleted. Second, the positive and negative plates have become so much like each other because of their lead sulfate coating that there is practically no voltage difference between them.

This is where charging comes into the picture. Current directed into the battery's cells reverses the chemical reaction by driving sulfuric acid away from the plates and increasing the acid content of the electrolyte. Once this is done, the battery is ready to start producing electrical current once more. In actual practice, the battery electrolyte is kept at a steady state of acidity by the current delivered by the engine's generator or alternator. After running the starter, the amount of acid in the electrolyte is low, since the heavy demand for current has caused it to be absorbed into the plates. The alternator charging system on the car operates the entire electrical system at a constant voltage. When the voltage of the battery is low, as it is after starting, current flows from the alternator into the battery. This is why the ammeter will read higher for several miles after you've run the starter or placed other heavy demands on the battery's current-producing potential.

BATTERY CONSTRUCTION

Automotive batteries consist of either three or six individual cells, depending upon whether they are 6- or 12-volt units. As mentioned earlier, each cell is a battery in itself, producing approximately 2 volts. The cells are connected together in series. The positive pole of the first cell and the negative pole of the last provide the terminals to which the car's battery cables are connected. Each cell has its own "private box" in the battery case, so there is no mixing of the electrolyte from cell to cell.

Battery plates are made with a grid cast from high-purity secondary lead with small amounts of antimony and tin added. The antimony makes the metal hard, and the lead is used because it is the only metal known capable of surviving in sulfuric acid under storage battery conditions. The grid is transformed into a plate by filling the open spaces in it with the more chemically active material. This active material is applied as a paste consisting of lead oxide mixed with water and sulfuric acid.

After the plates have dried, they are immersed in a weak sulfuric acid solution and charged. This converts the active material into sponge lead in the negative plates and lead dioxide (peroxide) in the positive plates. In some dry-charge batteries, a few minutes on the battery charger are necessary for this conversion and to ensure proper polarity of the plates.

If one positive plate were to touch a negative plate, all the plates in that cell would lose their stored energy. To

1. Take good care of your battery and you'll probably never have to use a battery charger.

2. If we ever found a battery like this, we'd send it to an automotive museum. Any one of these conditions should be corrected by replacing the battery, if necessary.

3. Hydrometer testing of the battery's specific gravity is the only sure way to get a true reading of the battery's condition.

4. Hydrometers are calibrated to read accurately at 80 degrees F. At higher or lower electrolyte temperatures, it is necessary to use a temperature-compensated hydrometer or adjust the specific gravity reading of a non-compensated hydrometer by using this chart.

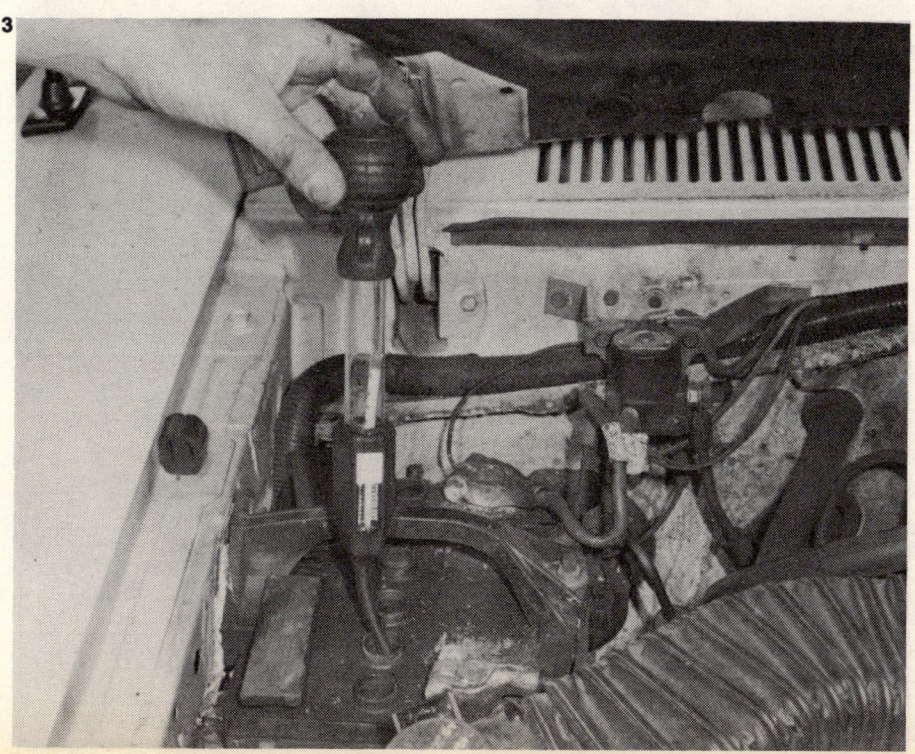

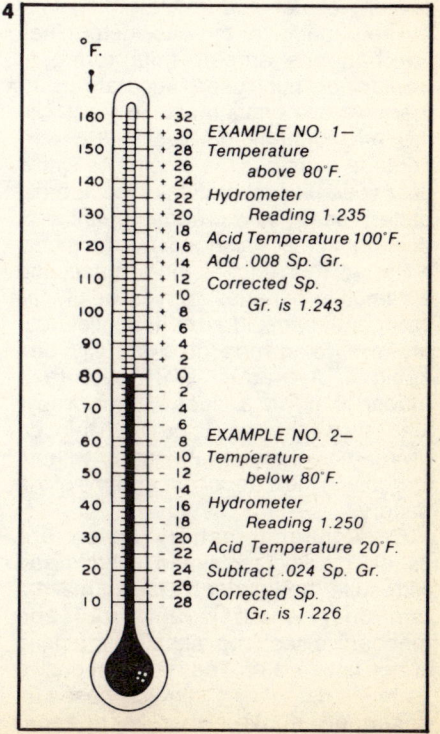

BATTERIES

prevent this from happening, thin sheets of a porous, nonconductive material known as separators are inserted between the plates. Separators have ribs on the side facing the positive plates to provide greater acid volume next to the positives; that will improve efficiency and facilitate acid circulation within the cell. The ribs also minimize the area of contact with the positive plate, which has a highly oxidizing effect on most separators.

Plates of any number and size can be used in a cell, depending upon how much energy is to be stored, but there is always one more negative plate than there are positives, for reasons of improved performance. The greater the plate surface in each cell, the higher the voltage during battery discharge at high rates and low temperatures. Regardless of the size of the cell or the number of plates, the open-circuit voltage of a fully charged cell is only a little over two volts.

Battery cases are formed with narrow rests or bridges at the bottom of each cell compartment, preventing the cells from sitting directly on the bottom of the case. This also creates an area for sediment to settle. Repeated discharging and charging of a battery gradually wear it out. After a time, the active material of the positive plates gradually disintegrates, loses physical contact with its plate, and falls to the bottom of the case.

Battery covers are usually of molded hard-rubber construction to provide an acid-tight seal. They are also provided with vent plugs. These plugs are designed to baffle the gases and any electrolyte that may splash against the underside of the cover. They also prevent loss of acid from the cells.

The capacity of the case determines the battery's ampere-hour rating. It wouldn't be much use to add plate area if there weren't enough acid to react with the additional lead. Raising the percentage of acid in the electrolyte would only speed disintegration of the internal battery parts, so the added quantity of acid must be balanced by additional water. All this requires more space, and automotive batteries conventionally fall into certain limited sizes that allow car makers to standardize battery box designs. A gradual switchover from rubber to plastics, such as polypropylene, allows the case to be much thinner, giving more room on the inside without increasing the exterior dimensions of the battery.

Conventional battery cases are usually made of reclaimed rubber mixed with sulfur and various fillers to make a container which is acidproof and mechanically strong, although cracking is not unheard of. The more expensive batteries use plastic thin-wall cases as described above, whereas cheaper batteries (such as those found in bargain stores and bearing unheard-of brand names) use cases molded with a bituminous binder (asphalt) instead of rubber. These are less expensive, but more brittle and a little less acid-resistant.

Cell connectors are welded to the protruding cell terminal posts. They are heavy enough to carry the high current required for starting without overheating. Various methods are employed to connect the cells in series. The usual method has been to connect the cells by lead straps running along the outside of the case, but that has been virtually abandoned in favor of through-the-partition and over-the-partition internal connections. These both have proved better because they provide an acid-tight seal between cells and are a shorter connection, which ensures minimum voltage loss.

The water in quality batteries is distilled, because distilled water is completely free of any impurities. Water containing iron, chlorides, and manganese is seriously harmful to battery life even in extremely small concentrations. These substances are commonly found in everyday tap water, which should not be used to refill battery cells.

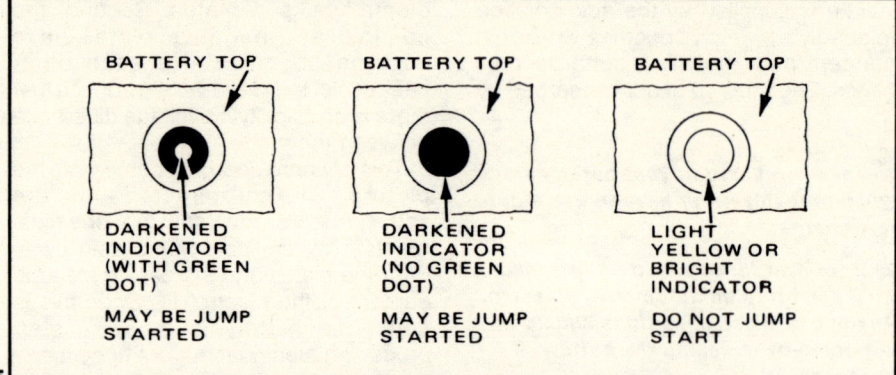

5

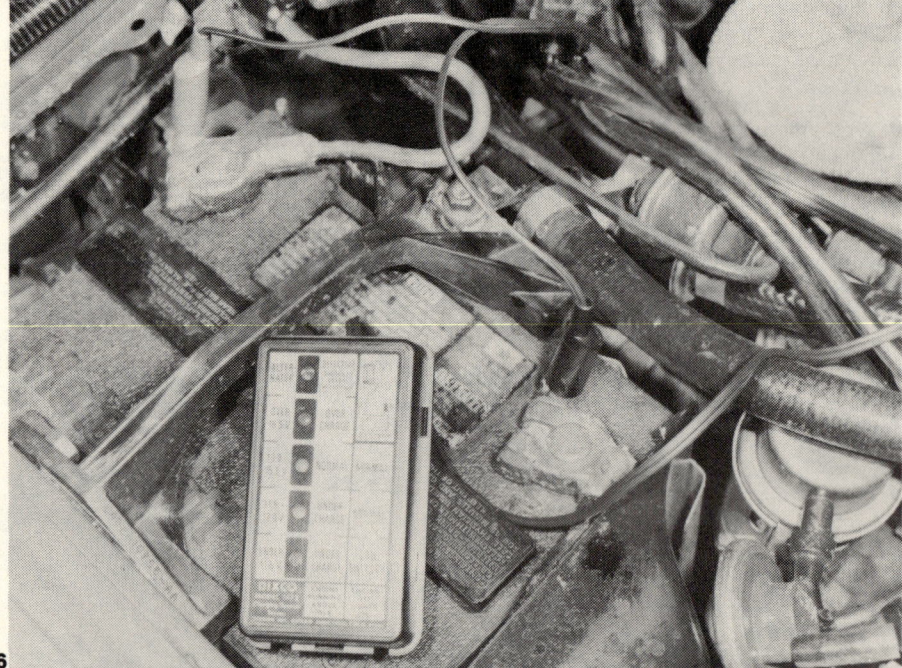

6

Temperature		Starter Power Required	Battery Power Available (Full Charge)
°F	°C		
80	27	100%	100%
50	10	133	82
32	0	165	65
10	−12	210	50
0	−18	250	40
−10	−23	310	33

7

The latest word in battery design is the nonfill or maintenance-free battery pioneered by the Delco Energizer used in some GM cars, and superseded by the Freedom and Freedom II designs. The nonfill feature was achieved by substituting calcium alloy plate grids for the traditional antimony grids. Since less charging current is required, this reduces the amount of internal heat in the battery and minimizes evaporation of the water in the electrolyte. A maintenance-free battery is filled at the factory and permanently sealed; it has no cell openings. The terminals may be located either on the side or top of the case, depending upon its intended application. There are no vent caps for escaping vapors and thus no way to add water. Venting to relieve internal pressure is generally accomplished by the use of two small slits located on the battery case sides at the top. Delco solved this problem by locating a baffled tank in the area above the cells. The vaporized electrolyte gathers in this tank, condenses, and then returns to the liquid electrolyte below. The result is reclaimed electrolyte and no water loss through vapor venting. In addition to requiring no water during its useful life, the maintenance-free battery reduces terminal corrosion, which is nothing more than condensation of normal battery gassing.

HYDROMETER TESTING

Since the percentage of acid in the electrolyte is less when the battery is discharged, the relative acidity of the solution provides a very accurate picture of the battery's state of charge. A device known as a hydrometer measures the specific gravity of the electrolyte solution. Specific gravity is the weight of a solution compared to the weight of an equal volume of pure water. A small float inside the barrel of the hydrometer is weighted in such a way that its scale projects upright through the surface of liquid drawn into the instrument's glass body. If pure water is drawn into a battery hydrometer, the 1.000 line will rest even with the surface of the liquid, showing that the specific gravity is exactly that of water (1 times the weight of water). If there is acid in solution with the water, as in battery electrolyte, the weight of the liquid will be greater than that of pure water, since sulfuric acid is considerably denser than water.

When the battery discharges, sulfuric acid in the electrolyte combines chemically with the plates, so the remaining electrolyte becomes lighter in weight. A

5. Maintenance-free batteries contain a built-in hydrometer in one cell. Battery condition depends upon what you see in the hydrometer "eye."

6. Charging system testers like this Dixco 1472 will pick up defective alternator diodes or stator windings, as well as testing your battery's condition.

7. Starting in cold weather is made much harder due to the fact that available battery power decreases with falling temperatures, while the power required by the starter increases as temperature drops. You must keep your battery in good condition during cold weather.

8. Battery neglect can result in damage to the area around the battery. This one is eating the battery holder as well as the terminals.

9. Periodic battery removal and cleaning with a baking soda/water solution, followed by a clear water rinse, should be a part of normal battery care. This keeps the surface charge to a minimum.

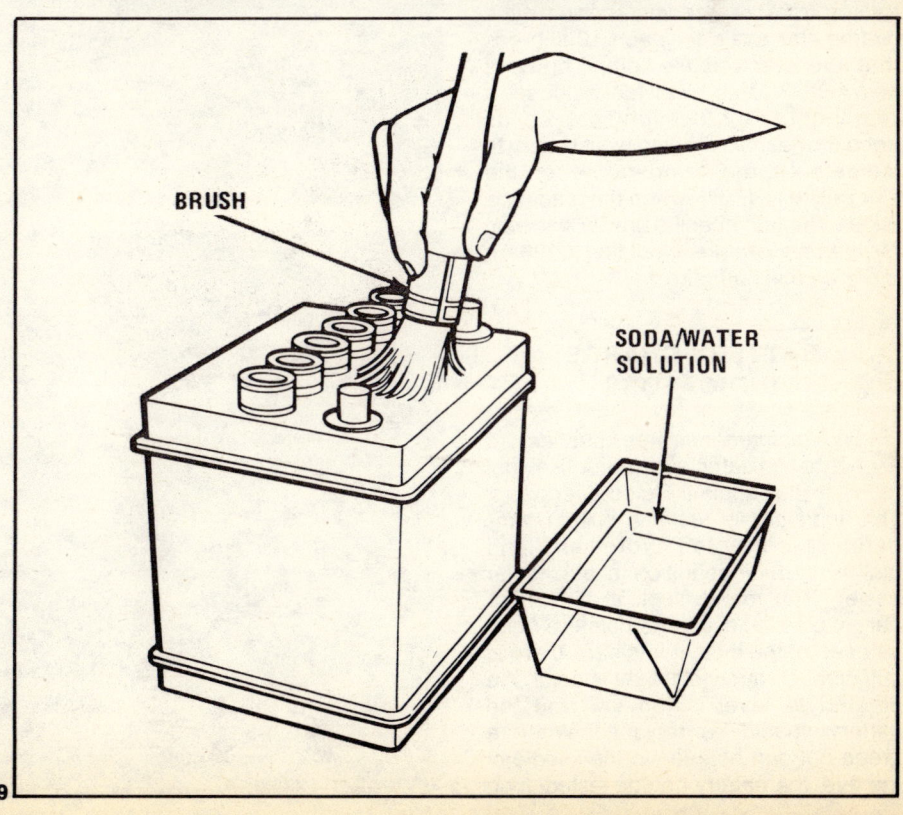

BATTERIES

reading of 1.250 is usually considered good, whereas a fully discharged cell will test only about 1.150. The scale on the average hydrometer extends from 1.300 down to 1.100. A cell in fair condition produces a reading between 1.225 and 1.250. Anything below 1.225 is considered poor. If a cell is found with a specific gravity below 1.150, the battery is dead for all practical purposes. When one or more of the cells produce a reading .050 or more below that of the others, it's a pretty good indication that the low cells are shorted. Also, if charging can't get the battery up to at least a 50 percent charge (about 1.200), it's time to install a new battery in the car. Most auto batteries are designed for discharge cycles of not more than 25 percent. Prolonged or frequent operation with the battery discharged to this level or below can damage it, so try to maintain it at a full charge level.

Electrolyte temperature has a definite effect on the hydrometer reading. In summer when the solution is warmer, lower hydrometer readings will be obtained than in cold weather, when readings are higher. For absolute accuracy, measure electrolyte temperature before hydrometer testing. The more expensive hydrometers have built-in thermometers for this purpose, but a separate immersion thermometer can be used.

Hydrometers are calibrated to be precisely accurate when electrolyte temperature is 80°F. For every 10 degrees above 80 degrees, .004 must be added to the hydrometer's actual reading. Similarly, .004 must be subtracted from the reading shown on the hydrometer scale for each 10 degrees that the electrolyte's temperature is below 80°F. Thus, a cell that produces a reading of 1.220 might not be as unhealthy as this reading would seem to indicate—if the temperature of the electrolyte is 100°F when the reading is taken. The true specific gravity, allowing for the temperature, would be 1.228—a more promising figure.

BATTERY CHARGE INDICATORS

Some maintenance-free batteries use a charge indicator eye much like that found in the original Delco Energizers. This indicator is really a built-in temperature-corrected hydrometer and makes battery condition checking far easier. You merely look at the transparent plastic "eye" and note the color you see. If the indicator is dark, there is sufficient electrolyte; if light in color, the electrolyte level is too low and the battery should be replaced. When a green dot can be seen in the middle of the eye, the battery can be tested. If no green dot is seen, charge the battery until the dot appears; then test it. Should the indicator eye appear clear or yellow in color, the battery is serviceable, but should not be tested, charged, or jump-started.

10

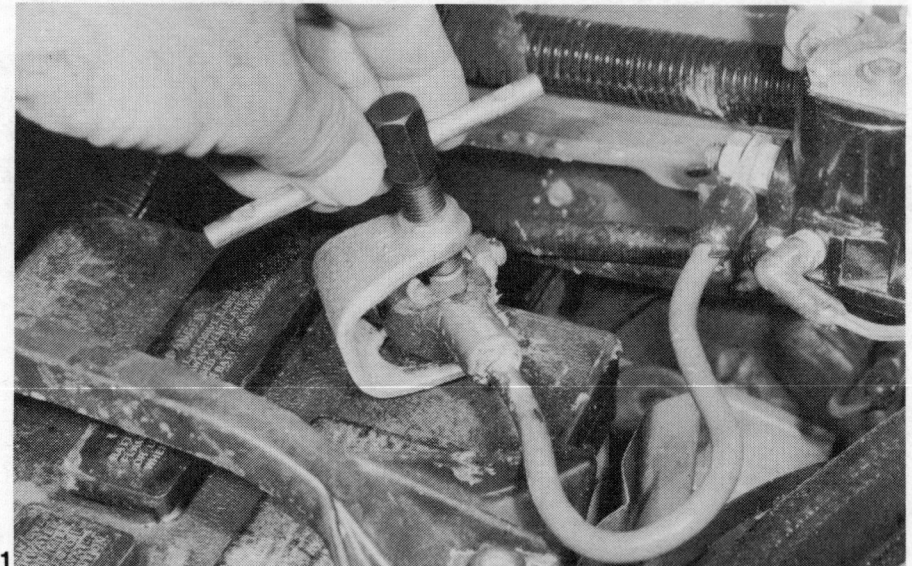
11

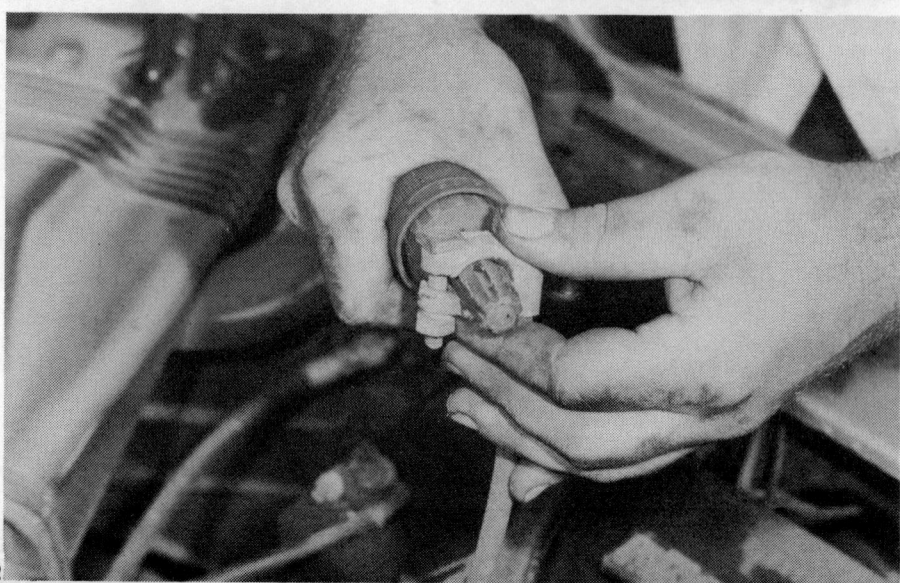
12

BATTERY CHARGING

By passing an electric current through the battery in a direction opposite to that of discharge (from negative to positive), the lead sulfate formed in the battery plates during discharge is made to decompose. As the sulfate is removed from the plates and returns to the electrolyte, the battery is gradually restored to its original strength. This process can be accomplished through the car's alternator, or with a battery charger.

When a storage battery has been severely discharged and you hook a battery charger to it, lead sulfate decomposition in the plates speeds up greatly. As this sulfate is removed from the positive and negative plates through electrical charging, hydrogen and oxygen gases are given off when the plates approach a fully charged condition. These gases result from the decomposition of water, caused by an excess of charging current not used by the plates, and are highly explosive. Small quantities of hydrogen gas are given off at the negative plates even when the cells are not being charged; thus it must be assumed that explosive mixtures of hydrogen gas are present within the cells at all times.

If your battery is low or dead and requires charging, wash all dirt from it and clean the terminals before placing it on charge, taking care to prevent contamination from getting into the cells. Bring the liquid level in the cells to the correct level with distilled water. If the battery is extremely cold, let it warm up before adding water because the water level will rise as it warms up.

To charge your dead battery, properly connect the positive lead from the charger to the positive terminal of the battery, and the negative lead to the negative terminal. Slow-charge the battery at a 4-amp rate for 24 hours or more, as required. As the battery approaches full charge, the electrolyte in each cell will begin to gas or bubble. Once the cells are gassing freely and three temperature-corrected specific gravity readings can be taken at hourly intervals with no increase between them, the battery is fully charged. Most batteries can be recharged at normal rates in 12 to 16 hours. Excessive charging decomposes the water and harms the positive plates.

Many discharged batteries, especially those that are sulphated, can be brought back to good condition by a slow charge. Sulphating is a battery condition that occurs when large areas of the plates become covered with heavy deposits of lead sulphate caused by inadequate charging or old age. The chemical reaction between the lead plates and electrolyte acid changes some of the material into lead sulphate. If the battery is not charged enough to convert the compound back into usable materials,

10. *Some positive battery terminal clamps use a protective cover. Unfortunately, many drivers fail to realize that corrosion can form UNDER the cover.*

11. *Never try to pry off a terminal clamp or knock it loose with a hammer. A terminal puller like this one is the only sure-fire way to free the clamp from the battery post without risking battery damage.*

12. *Keep the terminal clamps clean. Use a terminal cleaning tool to remove any corrosion and renew the surface of the lead clamp to assure a good connection.*

13. *There's a wide variety of terminal cleaning tools available. This design from E-L Tools is a little harder to use than most, but it'll do a good job quickly once you become accustomed to using it.*

14. *If you find this spring clamp on your battery cables instead of the standard bolt/nut clamp type, remove and install it with pliers as shown.*

15. *All GM batteries have their terminals on the side of the case, instead of being top-mounted. Since the attaching bolt hole is blind, be sure to use the correct length bolt and do not overtighten.*

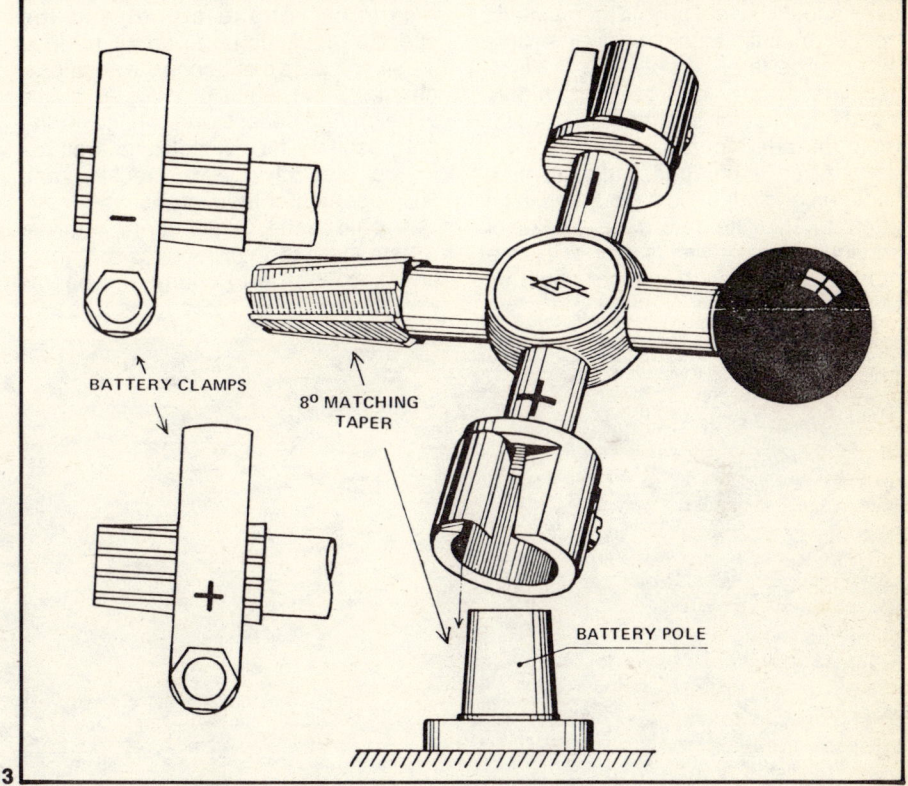

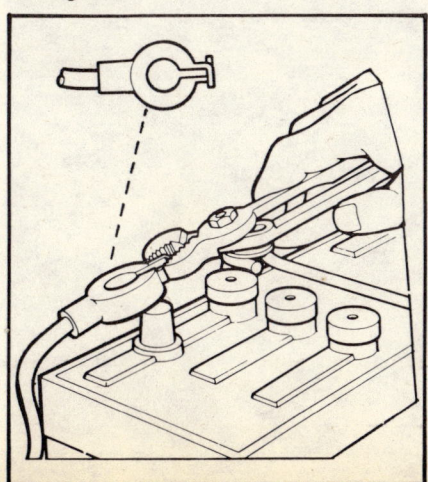

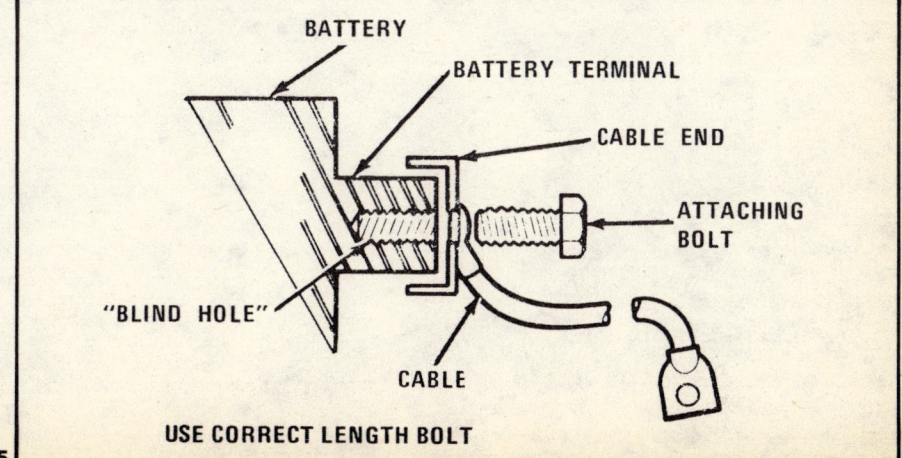

BATTERIES

CARE AND LONGEVITY

sulphating gradually takes place. As sulphated areas tend to harden permanently, their chemical convertibility can be lost. A long slow charge is the only means of completely displacing the acid from the sulphated areas and restoring the battery to its full capacity. A lesser charge will not remove the sulphate, but it can return the battery to temporary service.

A battery can also be quick-charged with a 40- to 50-amp rate for about 1½ hours. Keep an eye on the electrolyte temperature during quick-charging and if it reaches 125°F before the recommended interval is up, either remove the battery from charging temporarily, or reduce the charging rate to prevent battery damage. Quick-charging should be reserved for those rare instances when time is not available for a slow charge. If you intend to use the quick-charging method, the battery charger used should have a built-in thermostatic control to limit automatically the time and charge rate.

Home battery chargers are highly satisfactory as long as they are used for their intended purpose: keeping the battery safely charged under adverse service conditions. Do not buy one in an effort to wring a few more weeks of service from a dying set of cells; the money spent on the charger could be better spent on a new battery.

A properly maintained battery can provide five or more years of flawless service, but if neglected and misused, it can die a sudden death in less than six months. Most battery problems result from improper voltage-regulator functioning or alternator drive belts that are improperly tensioned. Sulfating, for example, is the direct result of the battery being in a constantly undercharged state. There are usually warnings that the battery no longer has its old stamina, and if the cells are given a long slow charge, the battery may be restored to its former vigor, but the cause of such chronic undercharging must be eliminated if you expect continued and uninterrupted service.

Overcharging is as bad for a battery as undercharging. As we have seen, a battery can only accept a charge equal to the amount previously discharged. When the cells are developing their maximum voltage output and the specific gravity is up to about 1.260 to 1.280, the cells can accept no additional charge. If the regulator provides a little extra charge under these conditions, the only result will be elevated temperatures in the electrolyte, and cracking and disintegration of the plates.

A cold battery has more internal resistance and thus requires a higher-charging voltage to charge it properly. For this reason, voltage regulators contain a thermostatic compensator to adjust the charge rate to the prevailing thermal conditions. Yet the battery often gets an overdose on a long-distance trip in the heat of summer, which explains why some motorists switch on their headlights during the day—this practice minimizes the possibility of overheating.

Most batteries have some kind of water-level indicator built into the case. This is usually a tube-shaped filler that extends down into the case. Many have slotted sides or a diamond-shaped bottom to mark the point where the maximum electrolyte level should be. Never fill the cells beyond this point. Generally speaking, the electrolyte level should be kept about one-quarter inch above the tops of the battery plates.

Caring for the outside of the battery is just as important as attending to the inside. Whenever dirt and acid salts are

16. *An inexpensive battery filler makes the messy job of topping up cells easy. Be sure to use distilled, not tap water.*

17A and 17B. *You can prevent terminal corrosion with plain old grease or petroleum jelly, but both are messy. So is the chemical spray (A) used by many garages. The chemically-impregnated washers shown in B are inexpensive, long-lasting and effective in preventing corrosion.*

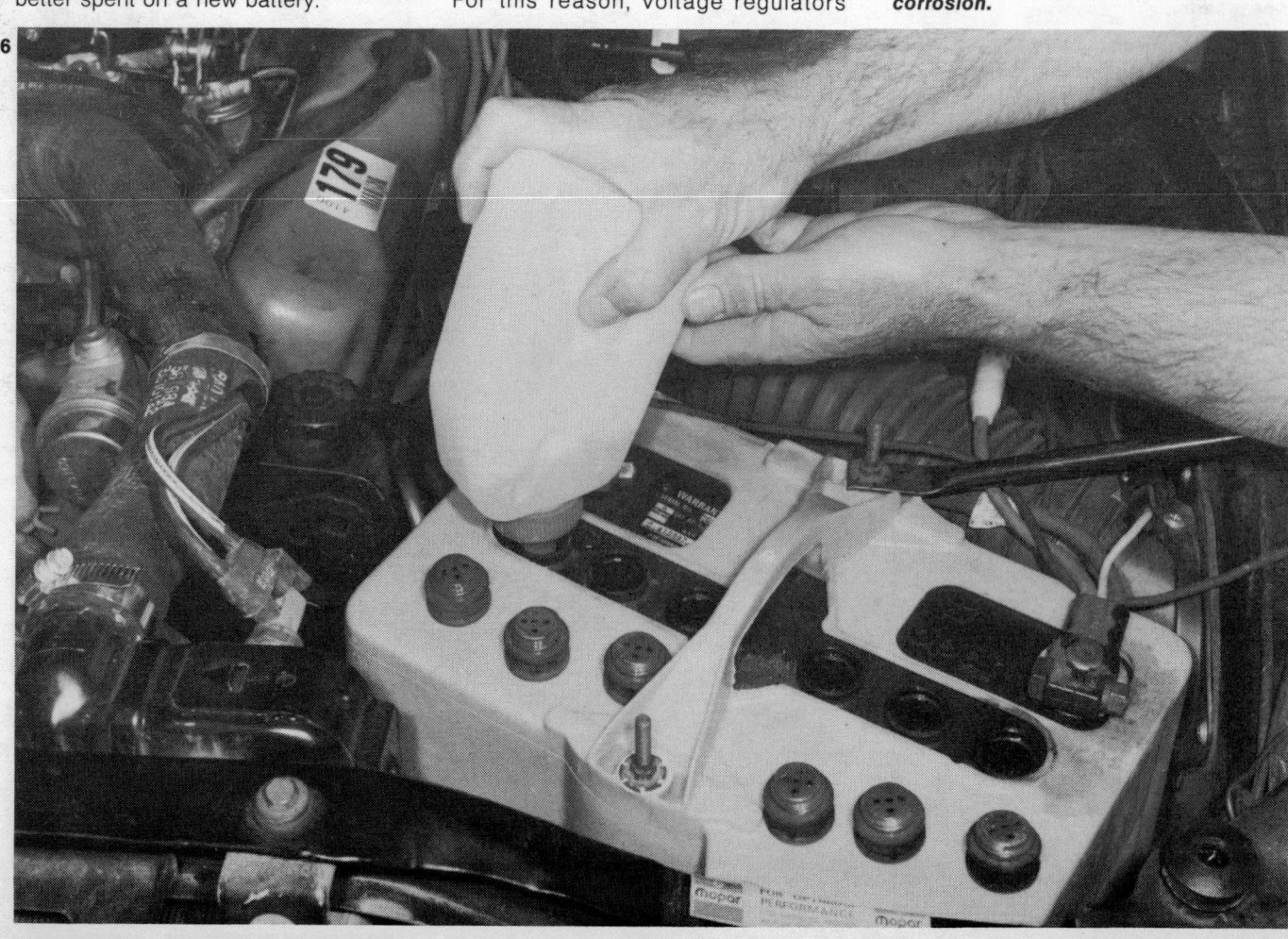

allowed to accumulate on the top of the battery, a conductive layer forms that puts a constant discharge drain on the cells. This condition may become so advanced that in damp weather it can completely discharge the battery overnight. Conductive salt growths often form on the battery posts, ruining their effective electrical contact with the cable terminals.

Give the battery a bath with a mixture of baking soda and water a couple times during the year to keep external battery losses at a minimum. After cleaning the battery, remove the cables and brighten the posts and terminals with a battery-cleaning tool or sandpaper. Once they are clamped firmly back into place, a light coating of petroleum jelly spread over the terminals will prevent future corrosion.

Corrosion of the cable terminals is a major cause of battery problems. The poor contact results in high resistance and greatly reduces the voltage delivered to the car's electrical system. Always use a battery terminal puller to

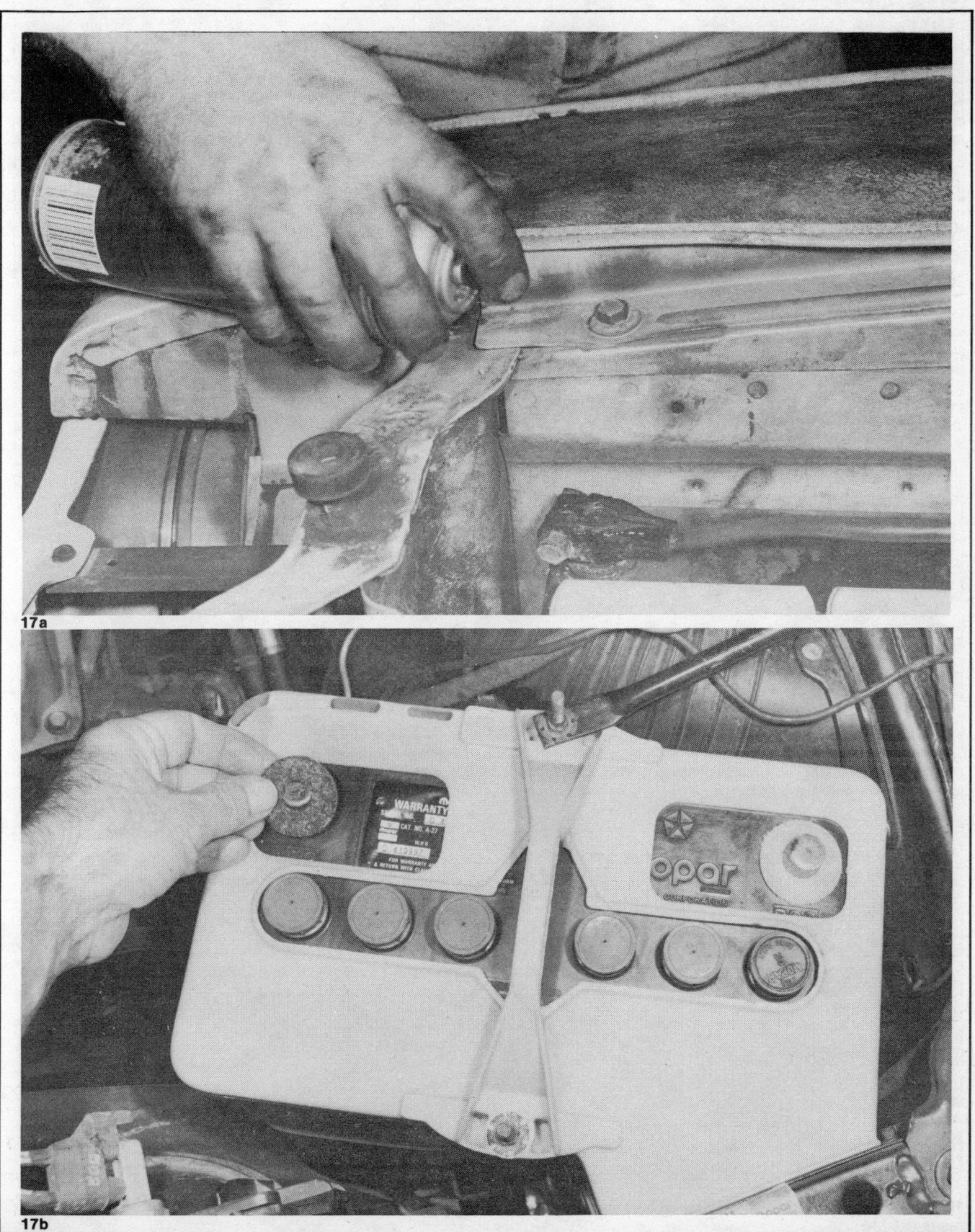

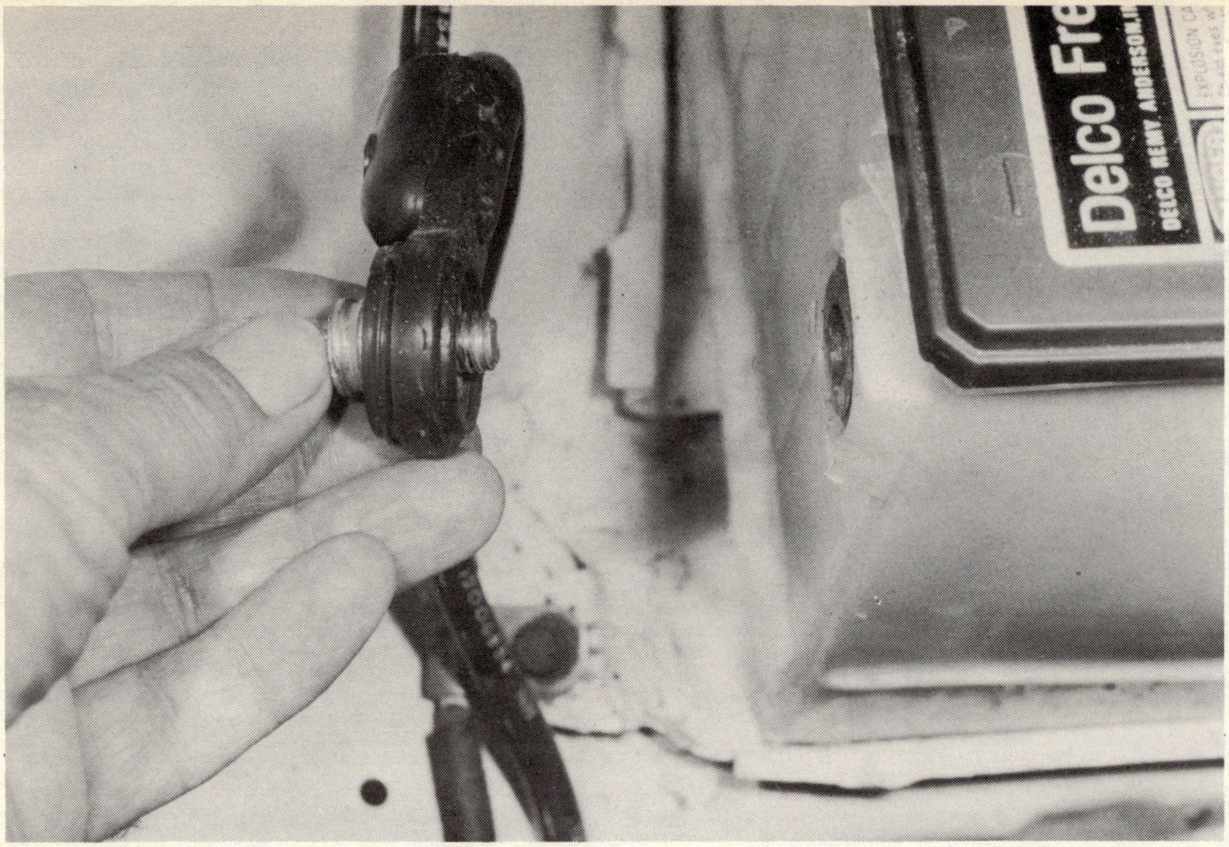

18a

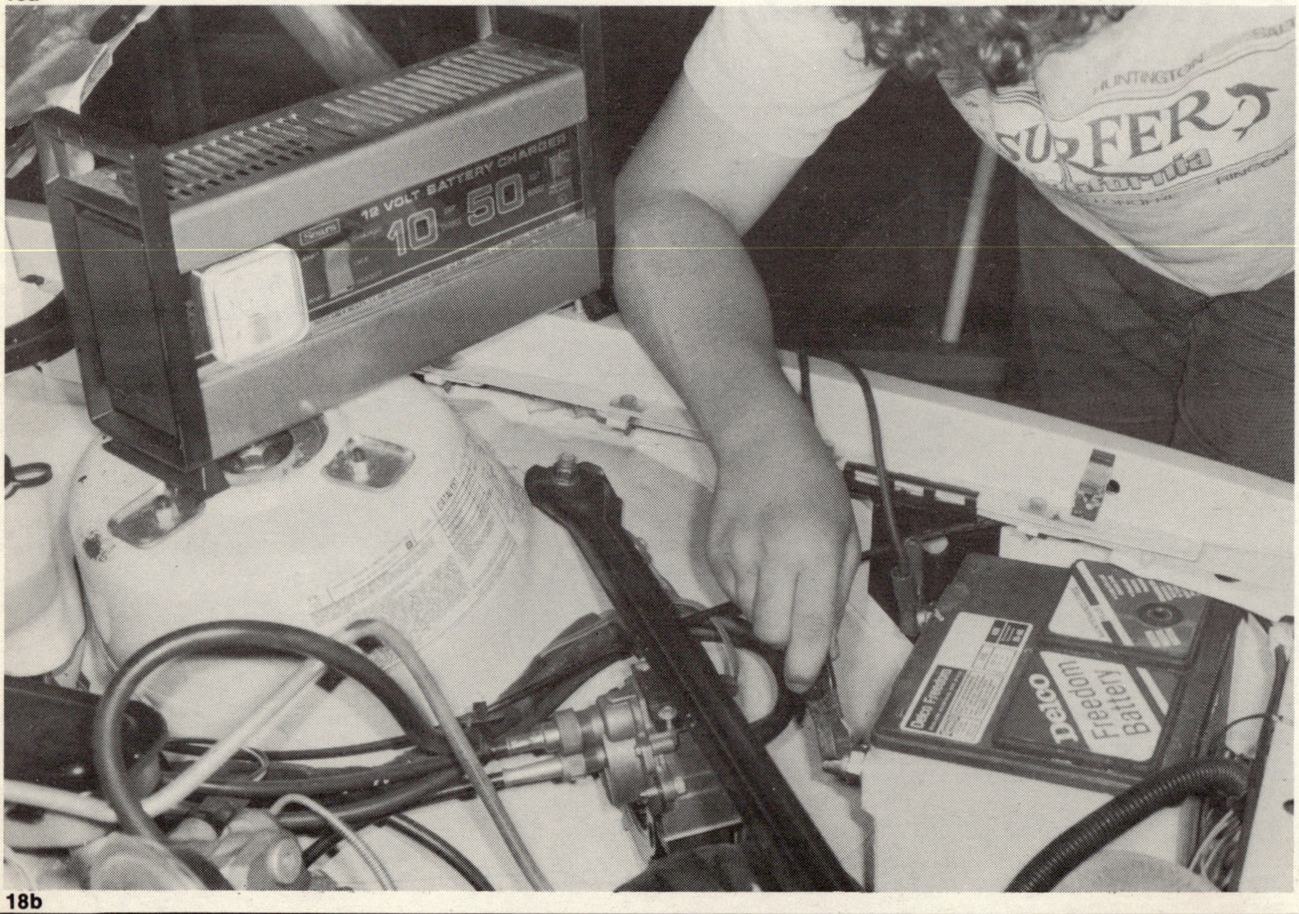

18b

18A and 18B. To charge a slide-terminal battery, you must remove the battery clamp (A) and install a pair of charging adapter posts (B).

remove the cable connectors from the battery posts. Pounding on the terminal, or prying and twisting cable connections away from the terminals, may break the battery post's internal bond with the plate connectors.

Acid corrosion leading to partial destruction of the cable also greatly reduces the current available to the starter from the battery. The cross section of the battery cables is determined by the amount of current flow they must carry. Current flow (amperage), not voltage, is what gives the starting motor the power to do its job. When cable strands are eaten away by corrosion, the cable loses its capacity to carry enough current. Overheating of the remaining strands further increases the cable's resistance to current flow. Proper cable and terminal care is as important as maintaining the battery itself, and on a cold morning, it can make the difference between a quick go and a no-start.

BATTERY JUMP-STARTING

When a car is jump-started, battery current is transferred from a charged battery to one that is discharged. The transfer is made through a set of battery jumper cables. Using cables is a simple matter, but certain precautions are required to avoid electrical damage. The first rule is to connect like terminals. Connect the positive to positive, and negative to negative—even if one car has a positive-ground system and the other a negative.

Always connect the ground terminals last and disconnect them first. This will avoid a shower of sparks which could explosively ignite a gasoline leak or a hydrogen gas leak from the battery. The battery supplying the charge should be close to the same capacity as the one being charged. To prevent alternator diode damage, disconnect the alternator leads before connecting the two batteries. In this way, if the batteries are improperly connected (always a possibility when done in the dark) alternator damage will be avoided.

Handle the cables carefully. Do not let them touch each other or another metal object, especially a fender, after connecting them to one battery. The car with the good battery should be left running whenever the cables are connected or both batteries will soon be dead. Jumper cables are very helpful, but can cause more trouble than the problem they're designed to solve if misused.

TROUBLESHOOTING THE BATTERY

Impending battery trouble gives few warnings. There may be nothing more than a few sluggish starts, which are usually ignored by most drivers, until turning the key results in nothing more than a clicking sound or a few slow attempts at starting that grow slower with each try. When this happens, you may be able to get started if you have a few basic tools at hand, such as a screwdriver, a pair of pliers, and maybe a spark-plug wrench.

The first problem is to determine if the battery is really at fault. Turn on the headlights; if they seem dim (along with the dash lights) during starting attempts, the battery is being discharged. Another indication may be a sick-sounding horn or one that doesn't work at all. Turn the headlights on again, raise the hood and check the cables and terminals for dirt, moisture, or corrosion. Insert a clean, dry screwdriver tip between the battery post and the cable end. Jiggle it around and if the lights grow brighter, the problem is dirty cables and posts.

If the lights grow brighter when you touch the screwdriver tip between the post and the cable end, but the car still will not start, remove the cables from the posts and scrape them both lightly with a screwdriver, penknife, or nail file until shiny. A corrosive film that's hardly noticeable accumulates on these contacts, and in time the film resists current flow. By scraping the outside of the battery post and the inside of the cable end, the resistance is reduced and metal-to-metal contact is restored.

There may still be sufficient charge in the battery to start the engine. Wait at least half an hour before trying again. Allowing a low battery to sit sometimes results in a partial rejuvenation. While waiting, clean and scrape the connections to the frame (usually overlooked as a source of poor contact) and the starter solenoid. You must lower both electrical and mechanical resistance as much as possible in order to increase current flow.

One cell that's low on electrolyte can bring the battery to a standstill. If water is available (rain water works well) and one or more cells are below the top of the battery plates, add water and let it mix with the remaining acid. There's a good possibility that the battery will put out sufficient juice to turn the engine over under these circumstances.

Engines are hardest to start in coldweather climates, especially those with high compression. The moving parts and thick oil resist movement. Pull a spark plug from every other cylinder in the firing order and place their cables where they will not be grounded or throw a spark. This not only reduces mechanical resistance and speeds up the engine's cranking speed, but also increases coil saturation enough to improve the spark noticeably.

Some engines are also very hard to start when hot because the pistons swell or the cylinders have become slightly egg-shaped because of uneven heating. If you have an engine that starts fine under all conditions except a hot restart, check the battery's cold cranking power rating. Many people will replace the original battery with one that's on sale, not realizing that the cold cranking power of the new battery is less than that recommended for the engine by the manufacturer. In such cases, the battery will be perfectly okay, but just doesn't kick out enough juice to turn the hot engine over. And if you continue to try and start the engine, you'll wear the battery down very quickly. In many cases, replacing the battery with one that has more output will solve the problem.

NEW BATTERIES

When you buy a new battery, make sure you select one of a size and amperage at least equal to that of the battery being replaced. The drain on a modern car battery can be very high when the engine is not running. Highcapacity alternators carry the electrical load when the engine is running, but a battery that's too small can be discharged so much by accessory use when the car is parked, or by leaving the parking lights on while shopping, that starting will be seriously impaired.

For these reasons, a battery that's oversize in its ability to deliver electricity is often highly desirable. Some battery stores will tell you to avoid this, as the extra power will burn up your wiring. Don't listen to them. An electrically oversize battery provides convenience and safety, lasts longer, and provides more starting power. Cars equipped with air-conditioning definitely require larger batteries, so go for a high-ampere-hour rating (or cold cranking capacity) even though it costs more than the smallercapacity batteries. The best advice is to purchase a battery that offers more capacity than you actually need. It costs more money initially, but saves money and gives more satisfaction and dependability in the long run.

HOW-TO: BATTERY CARE

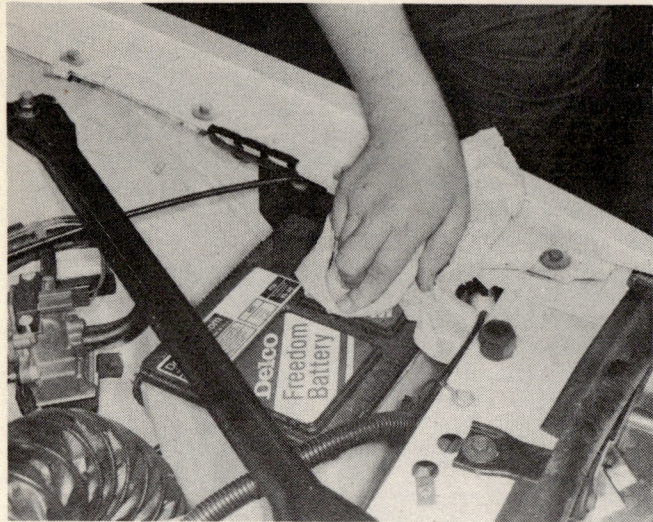

1. Battery case care is important. Check the case for cracks and wipe it off periodically to remove any surface dust and acid that can form a conductive charge.

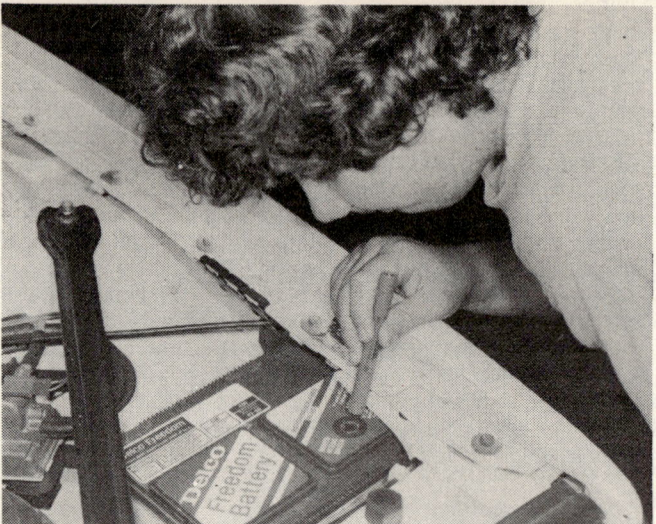

2. You may need a flashlight to check the built-in hydrometer, if so equipped. A green dot in the eye indicates a good battery; replace it if the center is clear or yellow.

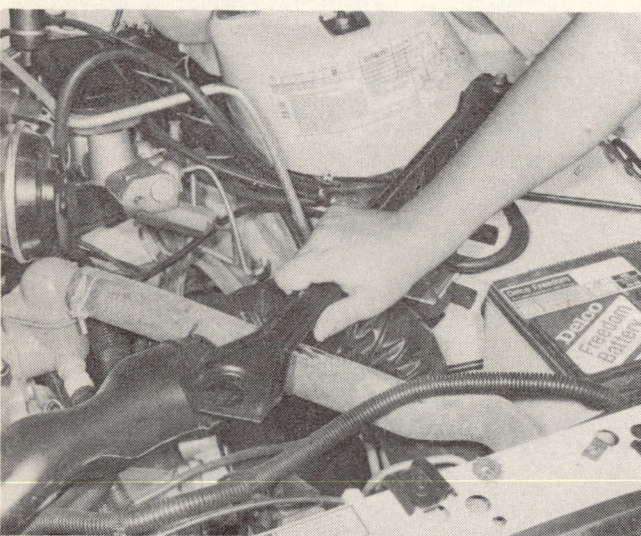

3. For access to the battery and its side terminals on our Citation, disconnect the fresh air duct tubing, remove crosspiece bolt and swing crosspiece to one side.

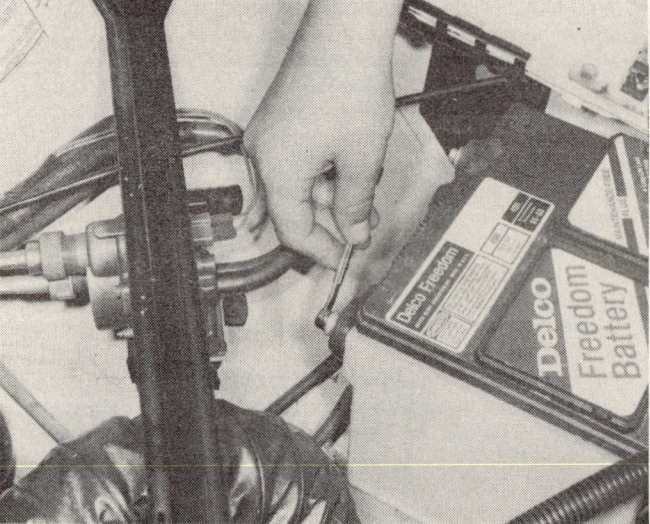

4. A 7mm wrench is used to remove or tighten side-mounted terminals on GM batteries. Don't overtighten or you may cause internal damage to the battery.

5. After removing the cable clamps from the battery terminals, clean the battery connection to remove any corrosion. A side-terminal cleaning brush does the job easily.

6. The reverse end of the terminal brush is used to clean the cable connection. When the connector is bright and shiny, you'll have a good electrical connection.

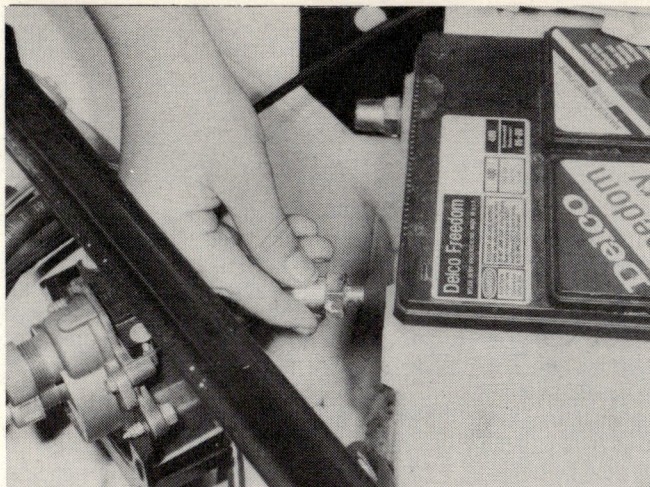

7. A set of screw-in battery posts comes in handy when side-terminal batteries need charging. These inexpensive accessories provide a good conductive surface for the charger leads.

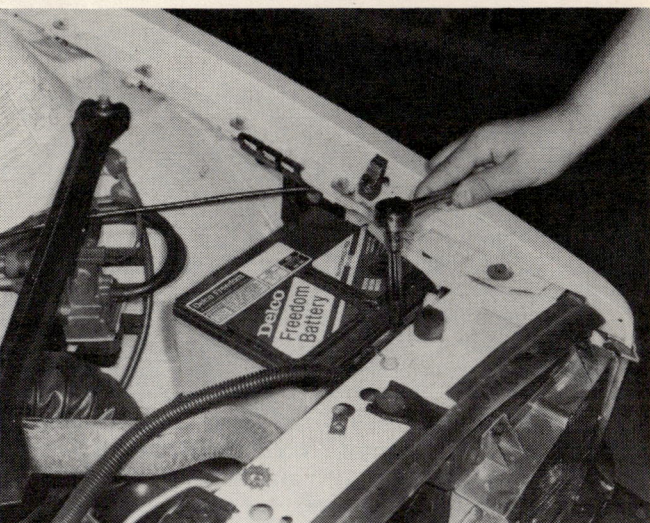

8. The battery hold-down on our Citation is at the front of the case and requires the use of a 12 to 14-inch socket extension. You'll be working by feel at this point.

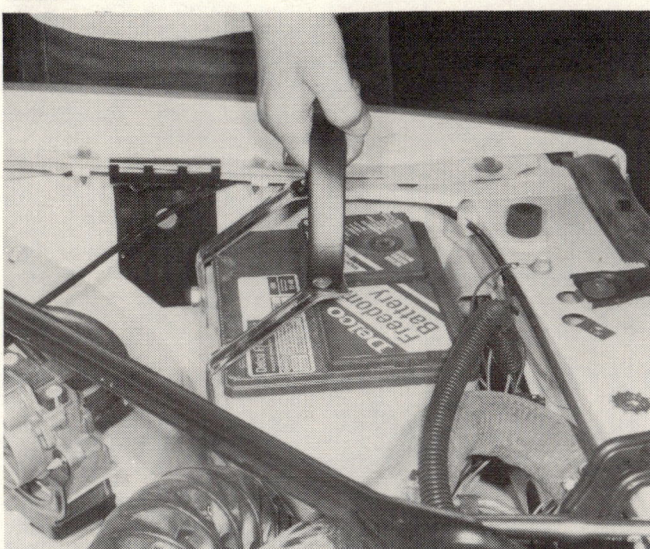

9. For easy removal, use a battery strap that screws into the side terminals to equalizes weight on the strap. Batteries are heavier than they look, so play it safe.

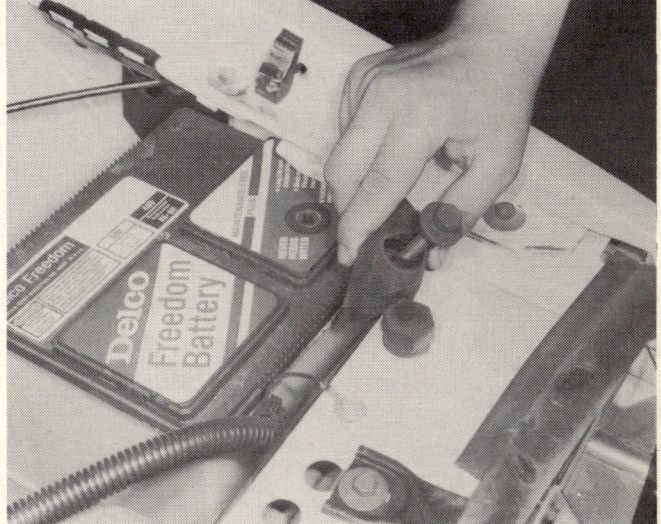

10. When replacing the battery in the car, install the hold-down block by hand, thread the bolt into the carrier hole and run it down snugly with the socket extension.

11. Pads impregnated with a corrosion inhibitor are not as messy as battery sprays. Use a set on the cable connectors to prevent corrosion and prolong battery life.

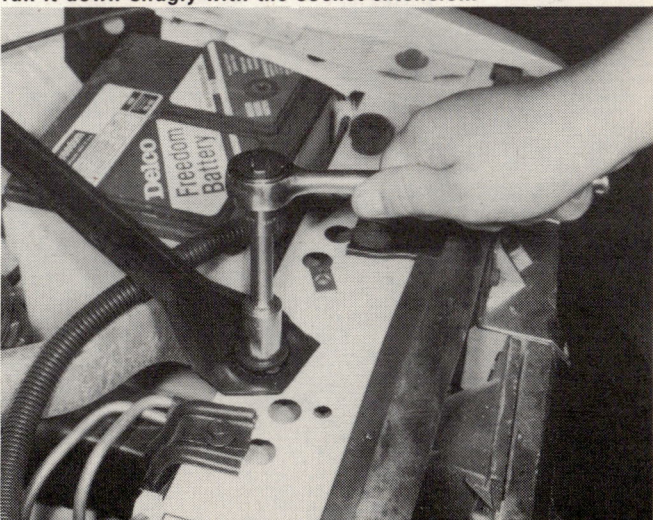

12. After making sure the battery is snugly in place and the connections secure, reinstall the crosspiece bolt and reconnect the fresh air ducting.

STARTERS

An automotive starting motor drives the engine's flywheel by means of a small pinion gear that engages a large ring gear fitted around the flywheel's circumference. Since the ratio between the starter pinion and the ring gear is something like 12:1 or 16:1, the starter would be driven in the neighborhood of 50,000 rpm if it were permanently coupled to an engine turning 4000 rpm. Obviously, this speed of rotation would cause the starter literally to explode from the developed inertia. For this reason, there is a device incorporated in the starter drive to disengage it as soon as the engine is operating under its own power.

STARTER DRIVES

The starter drive used in modern automobiles has a number of necessary duties to perform. First, it must couple the starting motor to the engine in such a way that starter operation will cause the engine's crankshaft to rotate fast enough to start the engine. It must also be able to absorb the shock of the sudden application of torque against the inert mass of the engine's movable parts. Last, it must uncouple the starting motor from the engine as soon as starting has been accomplished. Although other types of starter drives have been used over the years, there are basically two types in use today. Both have undergone a great deal of development since their introduction, and one has lost considerable ground to the other in the number of vehicles using it.

The first starter drive type is the so-called Bendix drive. It is also variously called an inertia drive, or self-engaging drive, as well as by various brand names, such as Folo-Thru. Bendix drives have been used on many English cars, and on older American Motors cars, Fords, Plymouths, and Studebakers. The most important feature of its operation is that the Bendix drive will engage itself with the engine's flywheel gear using no other power than that provided by its inertia against the sudden rotation of the starting motor. There is a spiral-cut sleeve fixed to the armature shaft of the starting motor. Around this is the pinion gear's driving sleeve, which engages the spiral grooves that turn with the starting motor shaft. A light spring keeps the pinion assembly pulled back from the flywheel when the starting motor is at rest, but when it is operated, the inertia of the pinion assembly's mass causes it to be thrust forward along the spiral splines before its rotation can catch up with that of the motor itself. By this time, the pinion teeth are engaged with the flywheel ring gear. There is also a very heavy spring—commonly called a Bendix spring—that serves to absorb the sudden impact and application of torque.

In the original form developed by Bendix, there was nothing more to the unit than is described above. As time passed, however, it became obvious that there were some definite shortcomings to the system. The foremost was that the heavy Bendix spring was asked to carry the entire load of the torque being applied by the starter. The result was that the spring fractured

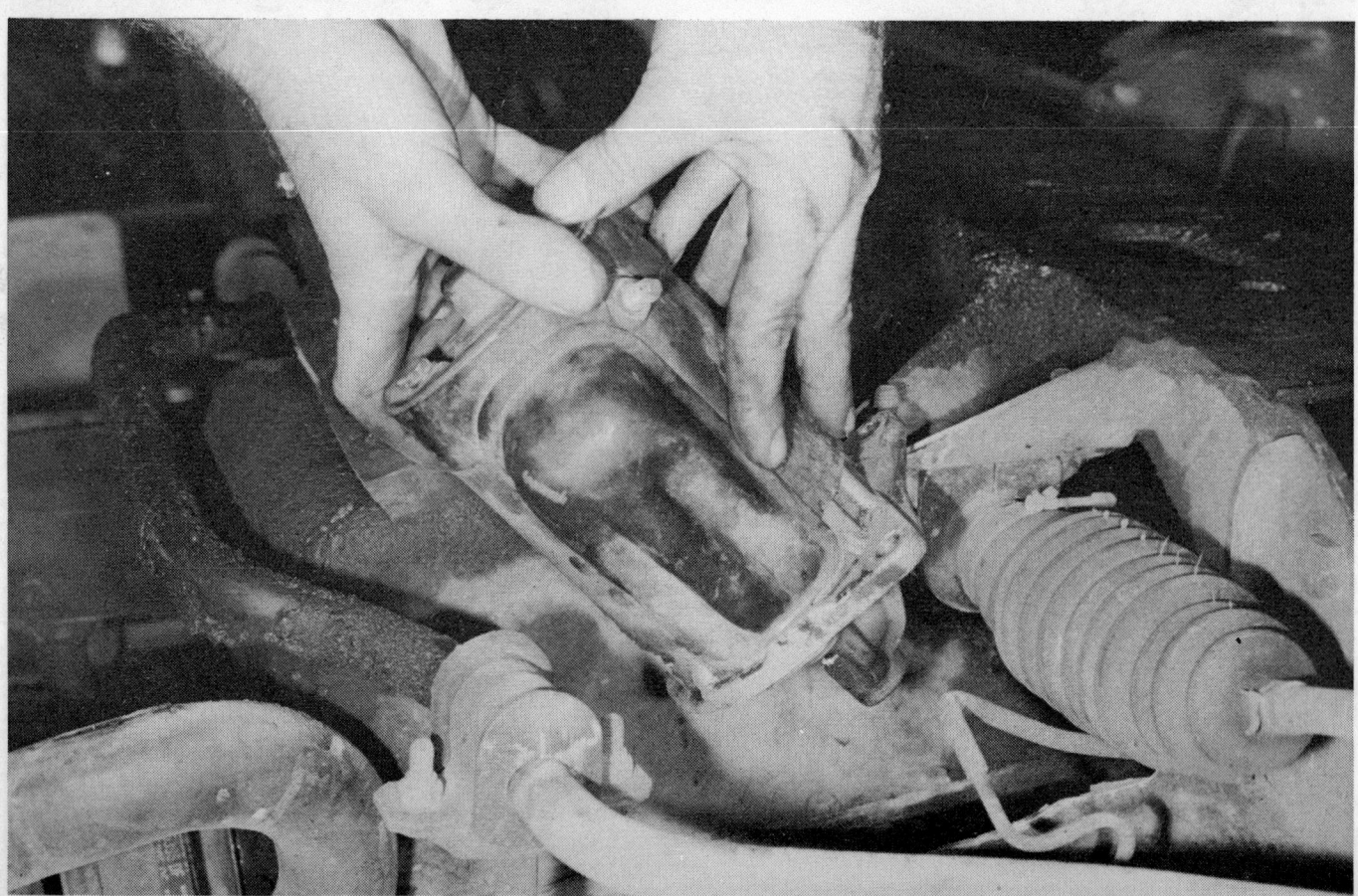

rather frequently, close to the bolts holding its "eyes" to the drive assembly. This was overcome by relieving the spring of its torque-transmitting duties except by the friction between itself and the drive. It still serves to absorb the impact of engagement.

Another annoying habit of Bendix drive starters was the tendency to disengage themselves the first time the engine fired, even though the engine was not yet ready to run under its own power. It is often necessary for the starting motor to help the engine through several revolutions after the cylinders have started to fire—particularly during a cold-weather start. With some of the older Bendix drives, even a very small increase in crankshaft speed was sufficient to reverse the pinion on its splines and disconnect the starter. The problem was solved by adding a lock pin that slipped into a detent cut into the spiral sleeve. The lock pin is loaded by a carefully calibrated spring that holds it in the detent until crankshaft speed reaches a level sufficient to keep the engine running under its own power.

A backfire, or accidental engagement of the starting motor while the engine was running, could still make mincemeat out of the flywheel gear or the starter drive. Perhaps one reason Ford continued to use this type of starter drive for so long is that its Folo-Thru unit completely overcame all the problems inherent in the original concept of the design. The latest Folo-Thru starter drives incorporate an overrunning clutch and a sealed-in rubber cushion that serves to protect the drive and flywheel gears from damage under conditions of malfunction or inept operation.

The other type of starter drive found on modern autos is the overrunning clutch, or positive-engagement system. Since the starter drive is held in engagement electrically, it will not be disengaged until the driver releases the key. To keep the running engine from overspeeding the starting motor, an overrunning clutch is an indispensable means of preventing damage to the starting motor. The overrunning clutch allows the starter gear to turn freely on its shaft when being driven by the engine's flywheel, yet locks up solidly when the starting motor is cranking the engine. As soon as the driver releases the key, the drive gear is disengaged by a spring.

The positive-engagement starting motor is more suitable for cranking high-powered engines because it provides an extra bearing for the starter shaft beyond the drive assembly. This serves to take much of the cranking load off the starting motor's bearings. However, the Bendix drive starters used by American Motors incorporated this feature into their design as well. Nonetheless, this unit

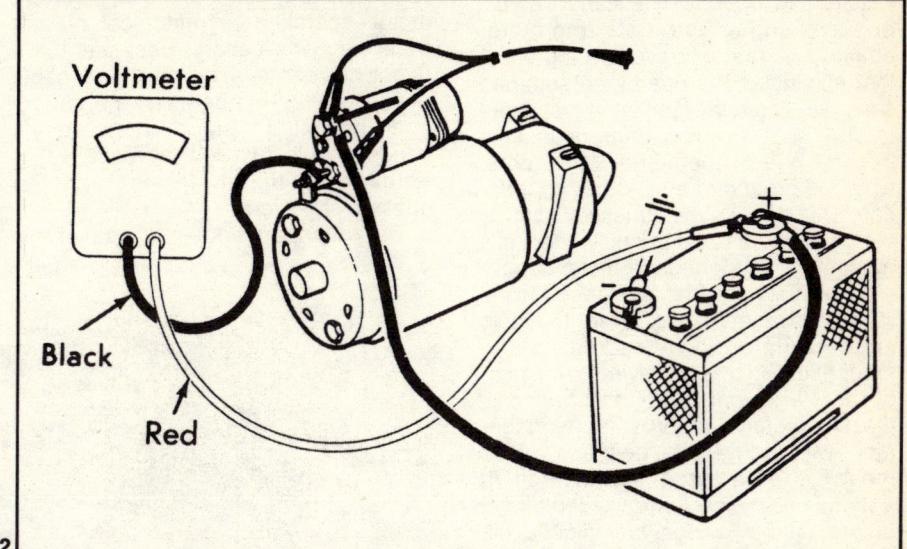

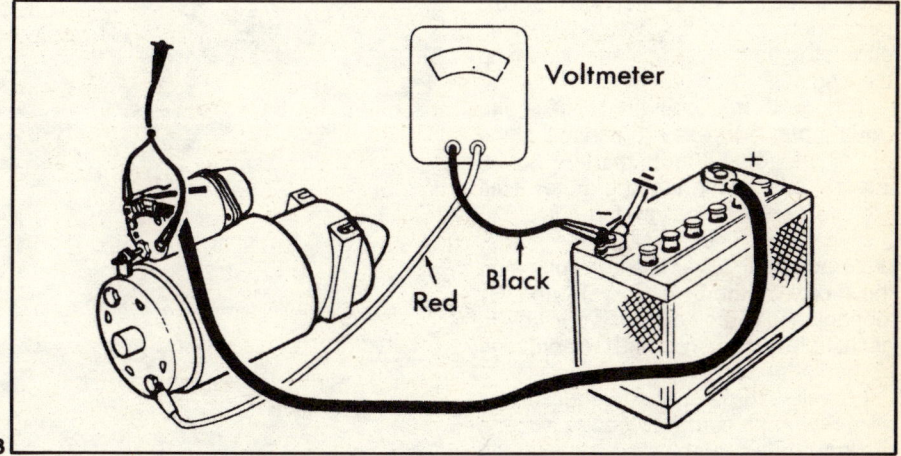

1. With today's crowded engine compartments, most starters must be serviced from underneath the car. They're heavy units, so be careful not to let one slip from your grasp.

2. Battery cable-to-starter test on Delco-Remy system. Gadget hooked to solenoid is an auxiliary start button. Be very careful when making voltage drop tests. Switch to the low scale only when the engine is cranking, then back to the high scale before the cranking stops.

3. Ground circuit test on a Delco-Remy system. It's a good idea to take your first readings on the voltmeter's high scale.

4. The Prestolite starter used on older AMC engines is similar to the Delco design, with an overruning clutch.

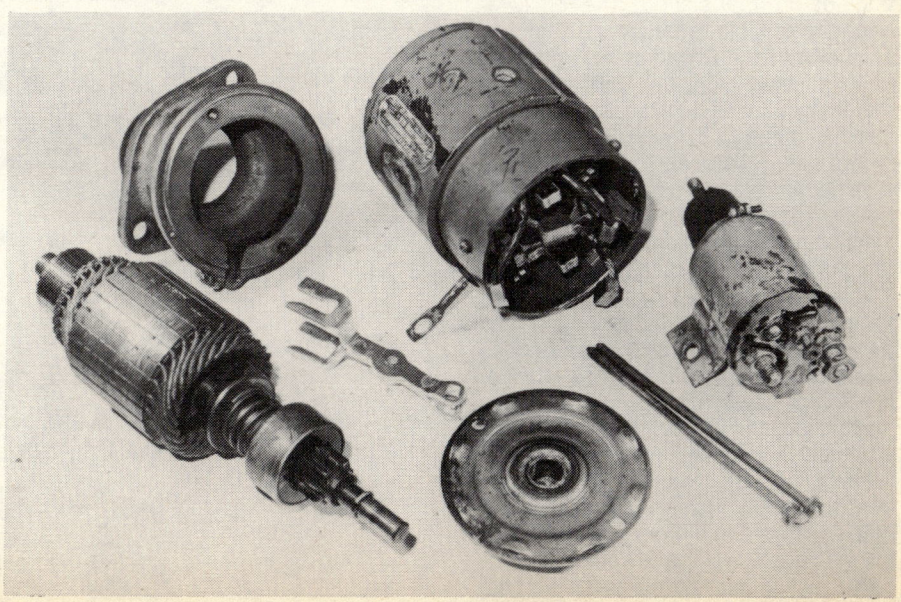

IGNITION & ELECTRICAL SYSTEMS/107

STARTERS

was dropped several years ago from AMC cars in favor of the Delco and Autolite positive-engagement starting motors.

The solenoid used on most positive-engagement, overrunning-clutch starting motors does increase the voltage required to operate the starter. Ford's positive-engagement starting motor employs a rather clever arrangement that eliminates the need for a separate solenoid. When the ignition key is turned to the start position, current is sent through one of the starter's field coils, which is grounded at its other connection. This causes a magnetic field to be set up in and around the coil. There is a movable iron pole-shoe-mounted beside this field coil that is attached to the starter drive actuating lever. The pole shoe is naturally attracted by the magnetic field and is drawn into the core of the starter coil. When this happens, the starter drive is thrust into engagement with the flywheel gear and, as the movable pole shoe seats itself, it switches on the current to the remainder of the field windings and places the starter in normal operation. A small holding coil is used to keep the movable pole shoe in the fully seated position during the time that the starter is turning the engine.

This unit has proved to be quite trouble-free and easy to service, since the only electrical parts that are not an integral part of the starting motor itself are the contacts that switch current to the windings. The cover for the starter drive actuating lever is held in place on the motor by the brush cover band. By loosening just one screw, it is possible to get at both the brushes and the actuating contacts for servicing or testing.

Chrysler Corp. dropped Bendix drives from Plymouth starters when its existing design proved unable to cope with the demands of its newer, more powerful engines in the sixties. The positive-engagement starter used on Chrysler cars other than Plymouth was different only in detail from the Delco starting motors used on GM cars. In addition, a special positive-engagement starting motor was developed that incorporates a reduction gear for use on models having more powerful engines. In this starting motor, the bearings are spared the punishment of carrying part of the load of sudden drive engagement. Since there is also about a 4:1 reduction ratio between the motor shaft and the shaft on which the drive mechanism is mounted, the motor turns more freely and at a higher rpm. Since motors draw more electrical energy when turning slowly, the windings are not as likely to become overheated, and less current is demanded from the battery. Unfortunately, the design is bulky and rather complicated, which did not make it one of the all-time favorites with service personnel in the days when starters were repaired instead of replaced. Other than the unique use of reduction gears, however, the drive mechanism is quite similar to that of any other overrunning-clutch type.

STARTING MOTOR

The starting motor is a direct-current motor operating on electrical current from the car's battery. Because it is a direct-current design, only one cable need be attached between the battery and the motor, since the battery's opposite pole (usually the negative) is coupled to the motor through the chassis of the car.

The outer part of the starting motor is known as its frame. On the outside of the frame, you'll see four screws which are quite large. These screw heads are slotted in the ordinary way on some starters, but others have square recesses in the heads. These are the pole-shoe screws, which hold the heavy iron pole shoes in place around the inside of the starter housing. Some light-duty starting motors used on GM cars since 1978 have field coils and pole shoes permanently mounted to the frame. Around the pole shoes are the field windings. When electrical current passes through the field windings, a magnetic field is produced which converts the pole shoes into powerful magnets.

The armature is mounted on the starting motor shaft. This is a round

5

6

assembly consisting of soft iron laminations wound with heavy copper wire. At one end of the armature windings is the commutator, made of brass segments to which the wires forming the armature windings are soldered. The brushes ride against the commutator providing current for the armature windings while in motion.

Each pair of pole shoes is directly opposite the other in the starter frame. When current flows through the field windings, one of these becomes a north pole magnet and the opposite one a south pole magnet. One of the principles of magnetism is that north poles are attracted to south poles, and vice versa, while like poles tend to repel each other. The armature windings are arranged in such a way that it too becomes a magnet. Its north pole is attracted to the south pole of the field, while being repelled by the field's north pole. The armature's south pole is similarly

5. To remove the solenoid from a Prestolite starter, disconnect the shift pin at the front end, then the lead at the other and remove the mounting bolts.

6. The right shift fork is definitely bad—one side is almost completely worn away. Compare it to the new fork at the left.

7. Once the armature is out on Delco or Prestolite starters, drive the collar back with a socket to expose the locking ring.

affected by the other field poles, but in the opposite manner. As a result, the armature turns on its shaft in the direction of magnetic attraction. But before the poles of the armature can align themselves with the poles of the motor's field, the motion of the commutator has cut off current to that part of the armature's windings, and has routed it to the next set of windings. The magnetic field of the armature thus remains almost stationary—in a constant state of attraction to the field poles—while the armature itself is made to rotate.

There are two basic types of direct-current motors and several derivatives that result from combinations of the two principles. The first is the shunt-wound motor, which is used in wiper motors, and other types that operate at a steady and controlled rate of speed. The other is the series-wound motor. This is the type used for automobile starters.

STARTING CIRCUITS

Each make of car has its own typical layout for the starting system. This is largely determined by the type of starting motor and drive used, but is also partly determined by the car maker's design philosophy, and may be further influenced by the type of transmission used and the optional accessories offered.

General Motors has used the same basic Delco starting motor for many years now, and the system has generally become a fixed concept that shows few changes from year to year. The solenoid on Delco starting motors is mounted directly on top of the motor itself, and serves not only to engage the starter

drive but also to close the internal contacts that make the final connection between the battery's positive pole and the starter windings.

On the end of the solenoid's dust cover are three terminals. The largest of these is connected directly to the battery by a heavy cable. In addition, there are two smaller terminals. One of these is connected to the ignition switch and actuates the starting motor when the key is turned to the start position. The other is the ignition terminal. The resistance wire used as ballast in the ignition system connects between the ignition switch and the coil, with a spliced wire running to this terminal on the solenoid. When the starter is operated, the solenoid contacts send full battery voltage to the coil via the spliced wire—current that is picked up directly from the large cable connecting the starting motor to the battery itself. On cars using HEI ignitions, the solenoid's "R" terminal has been removed, since there is no requirement for an electrical lead from the solenoid to the coil.

After the engine has started, the solenoid disengages the starting motor and cuts off the current flow from the battery. Current for the ignition system must then flow from the ignition switch by way of the resistance wire. Connections between the resistance wire and the plain wire have been handled differently through the years. Some cars run two wires to the coil, one being the resistance wire from the ignition switch and the other the plain wire from the starter solenoid. In later models, it is easier to make the wire harness if the resistance wire ends at or near the

STARTERS

starting motor, and a single plain wire runs from there to the coil. When doing any repairs to wiring, you must have the proper wiring diagram for the car, as furnished in the factory shop manual or by an independent publisher.

All later-model GM cars have two cables connected to the battery's positive pole. The larger of the two serves only the starting motor, and the smaller cable supplies the remainder of the car's electrical system. This small cable passes first to the horn relay, from which radiate the wires that conduct electricity to other parts of the system, including the ignition switch. Since some Ford trucks and the majority of American Motors 6-cylinder engines use the Delco starter, there is some similarity in the appearance of their starting systems to that of a GM car. However, the circuits serving these are often quite different from those used at General Motors, so it's always wise to check the wiring diagram for the particular make and model before doing any modifications, troubleshooting, or repair.

Since no current Ford passenger cars employ a solenoid-operated starter drive, there is no need to mount the starter relay (also called a solenoid or magnetic switch) on the starting motor. The starter relay on Ford products is thus a separate sealed unit mounted in most cases of the firewall or fender housing inside the engine compartment. There is just one heavy cable between the relay and the positive terminal of the battery that supplies both the starter and the remainder of the electrical system.

The FoMoCo starter relay has two large terminals and two small ones. The cable from the battery's positive pole is connected to one of the large terminals, and a similar cable connecting the relay to the starting motor is connected to the other. One of the small terminals is connected to the ignition switch, and when the key is turned to the start position, current is directed from the ignition switch to the relay, causing it to close the main circuit between the battery and the starting motor. Current to the ignition switch, as well as to the rest of the car's electrical system, is drawn from a wire attached to the large terminal on the relay to which the battery cable is connected. The other small terminal on the relay is the ignition terminal, which supplies full unballasted battery current to the ignition coil during starting.

As we've seen, GM starting systems have a solenoid at the starter, whereas FoMoCo products have their starting relays located elsewhere. Chrysler Corp. goes a step further and places a solenoid on the starter, in addition to a remotely located relay. The solenoid has just one job to do and that's to operate the starting motor. Also, the relay is not asked to carry the heavy starting current load in addition to the rest of the car's current demands.

When the ignition key is turned to the start position, the starter relay bypasses the ignition ballast and energizes the solenoid on the starting motor. Current for the entire electrical system is drawn from a terminal on the starter relay which has its own connection with the positive pole of the battery. The solenoid at the starting motor merely couples the motor to the heavy cable that leads to the battery's positive pole. After the engine has started, the ignition key is returned to the on position and the relay no longer supplies the ignition system—although the remainder of the electrical system does continue to draw current from the BAT terminal of the relay. The ignition now takes its power through the ballast resistor, which receives its electrical energy from the IGN terminal on the alternator regulator.

Although American Motors has used Delco and Prestolite (Chrysler) starting motors in recent years, the majority of its current output is equipped with the Ford-

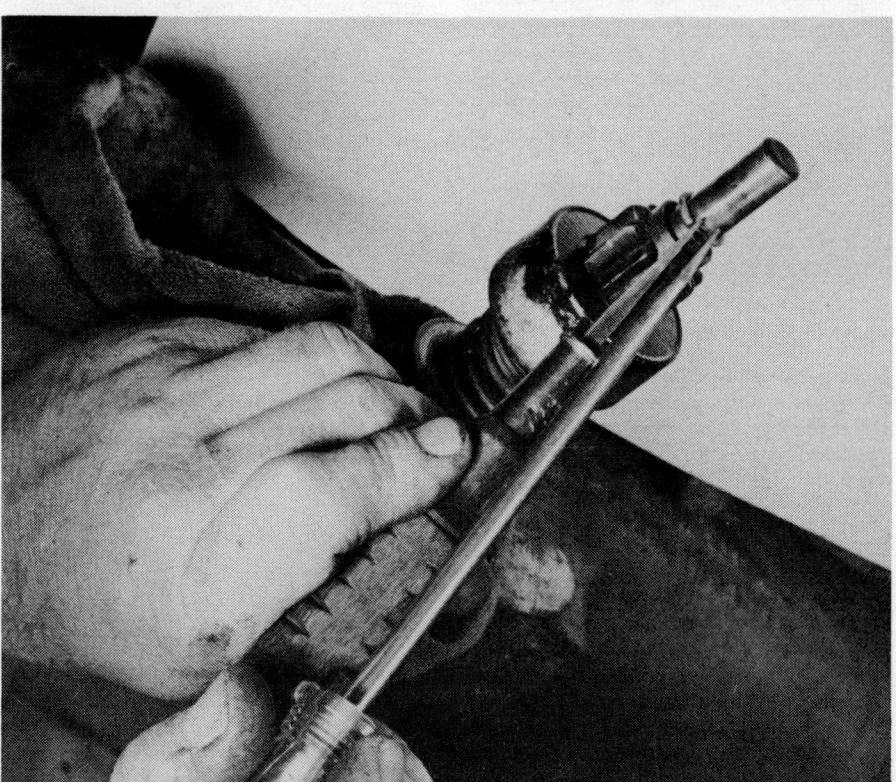

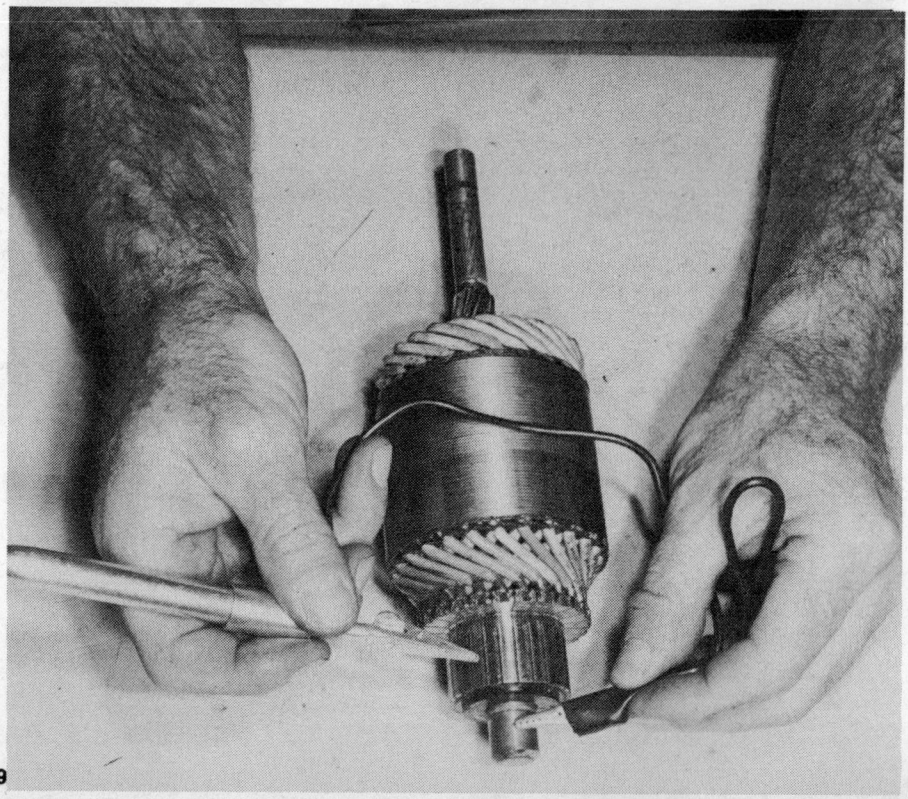

Autolite positive-engagement starting motor, described in detail earlier. The circuitry for this system is almost exactly like that described for FoMoCo products and should cause no special problems for those familiar with Ford starting motors.

STARTING SYSTEM TROUBLES

If the starting motor operates sluggishly, the chances are definitely in your favor that the trouble is in the battery or its connections, and not in the starter itself. However, even in cases where the starting motor does not turn the engine, the trouble often results from defects that are not in the motor. One of the quickest ways to locate a starting problem is to perform a simple series of headlight tests. But before doing so, the battery should be checked with a hydrometer to make sure that it is not the cause of your troubles. A weak battery will make any starting system test produce faulty or inconclusive results and prevent you from ever pinpointing the real cause of the trouble. Once you know that the battery is in good condition, switch on the headlights and try to operate the starter. The result will be one of three things: first, the lights may go out and the starter will not operate; second, the starter will make "working" sounds, but the lights will dim considerably and any actual cranking will be very slow; last, the headlights may remain bright but no cranking will take place.

If the lights go out when the starter is switched on, look for poor connections between the battery and the starting motor. Corroded battery terminals are the first suspect, but don't overlook the ground strap where it fastens to the engine block or car body. Some cars have the battery grounded to the body of the car and a separate ground strap between the body and the engine. This may be located under the car in the area of the transmission or starter mounting.

8. Getting the locking ring off can be a problem. Try not to bend it too much, as it will be reused.

9. Test the armature for grounded windings with one lead on the commutator and the other on the shaft. If the armature is good, the lamp should not light.

10. To test the field coil for grounded windings, connect one test lamp lead to the field insulated lead and the other to the frame. If the lamp lights, the field coils are grounded.

11. The Ford movable pole shoe starter is a little harder to disassemble. Brushes must be removed from their holders through the frame slot openings.

A loose bolt here can kill the voltage available to the starter just as quickly as a loose battery clamp. As more and more electronics are used under the hood, automakers are using an increasing number of ground straps to eliminate any excess magnetic fields or RFI signals that might affect computer operation. Thus, late-model cars may have several grounds instead of the one or two formerly used. Another rather offbeat cause of poor contact between starter and battery is paint—either between the starter motor and the engine's bellhousing, or under the ground strap mounting. This trouble is usually associated with new cars or rebuilt/renovated engines. The cure is simply to remove the paint layer with sandpaper and bolt everything back together tightly. All cables in the starting circuit must be secure and in good condition to provide an adequate supply of current for cranking the engine.

If the lights dim noticeably when you operate the starter, and cranking action is sluggish or unable to turn the engine over at all, something is throwing an unusually heavy load on the starter and imposing a high discharge rate on the battery. The most frequent cause of such trouble is too heavy an oil in the crankcase, a problem usually associated with cold weather. Newly assembled engines will sometimes place an undue drain on the battery because

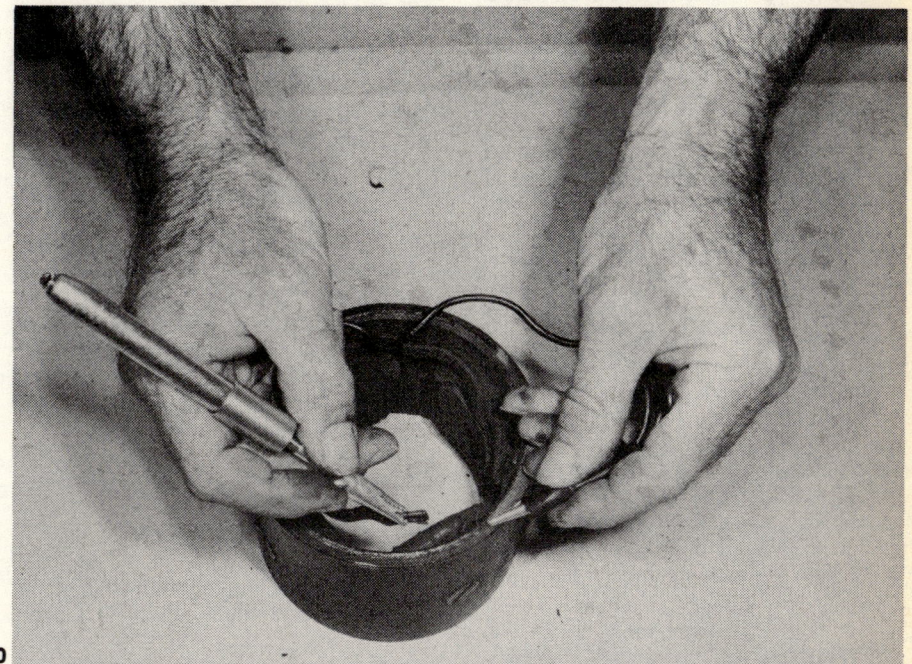

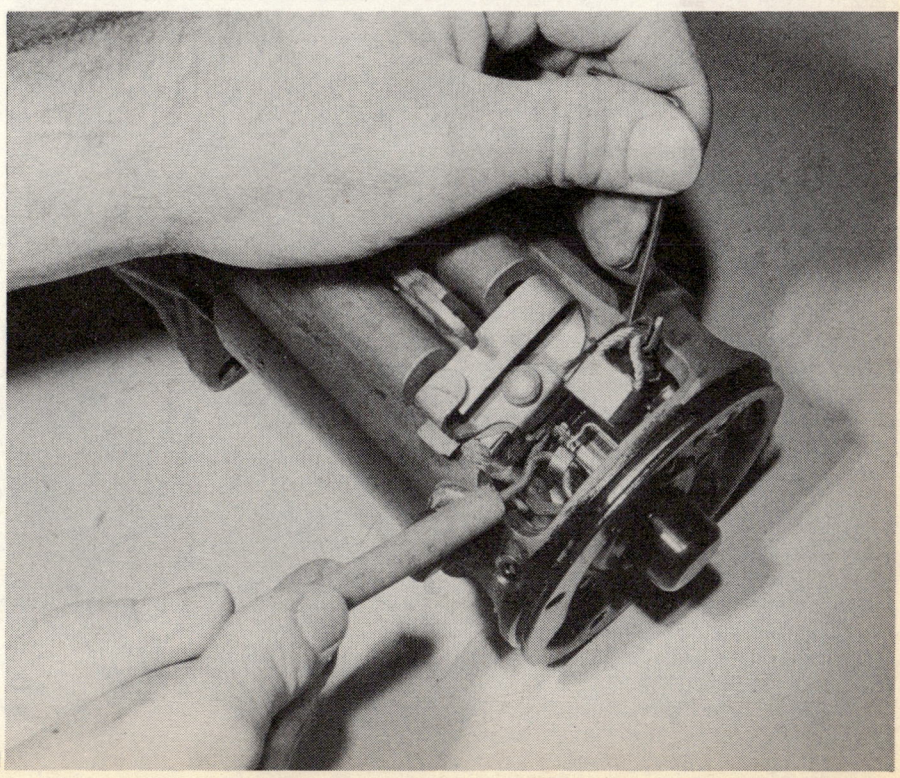

STARTERS

of tight clearances. It could also be a case of excessive spark advance. If the initial advance has been set too high or if the advance mechanism of the distributor is not working freely and correctly, the cylinders may be firing before the piston reaches the top of its stroke. The engine tries to run backward, fighting the action of the starter.

If the lights stay bright, but there is no response from the starter, there is an open circuit in the starting system. This could be in the starting motor itself (possibly worn-out brushes), in its wiring, the starter relay, or in the ignition switch and its wiring. The ignition switch gets a lot of wear and tear, since it is used at least twice every time you go somewhere, once starting up at home and again to get you back. This can add up to hundreds of "clicks" every month and in time, the internal contacts may become too badly worn to work properly. This is probably the first thing to check; it has chewed up a fair share of the new Delco 5MT starting motors since their introduction on 1978 GM cars. Here's what happens to this light-duty starter: once the engine is started, the starter drive overruns, but the solenoid does not disengage. The 5MT is thus allowed to run freely at very high rpm and the armature self-destructs as a result. If you encounter this problem with a late-model GM car fitted with this starting motor, be sure to check the ignition switch before installing a replacement starter or the new one may also self-destruct.

You can either make a small jumper cable to test the control circuit using 14-gauge wire and two alligator clips, or do it the hard way using a screwdriver. In either case, make contact between the main (large) terminal on the starter relay or solenoid and the small terminal that receives the wire from the ignition switch's starter control. If the starter runs, the trouble is in the ignition switch or its wiring.

On cars with automatic transmissions, there is a neutral safety switch that allows the ignition key to actuate the starter relay only when the transmission selector is in the park or neutral positions. This might also be causing your trouble on cars with an automatic. Locate the switch and bypass it with the jumper wire after making sure that the transmission is in neutral. If the ignition key will now operate the starter, the trouble is in the neutral safety switch. Chrysler Corp. automatics have a neutral safety switch that grounds the starting circuit whenever the transmission is in neutral. These switches have only one terminal and can be bypassed by simply grounding the wire.

If these tests of the control circuit fail to provoke any action from the starter, try connecting a heavy booster cable jumper directly from the battery's hot side to the starter motor terminal. If this causes the starter to operate, the trouble is in the solenoid or starter relay. If the starter does not run when the booster cable is connected, the trouble is in the starting motor itself.

If the relay or solenoid makes a clicking sound when the key is turned to start, and the starter does not run, but does run with the booster cable in place, it is not necessarily an indication that the relay or solenoid is good. In many cases, the internal contacts may be burned, making it impossible for the solenoid to switch on the heavy starter current. Some solenoids can be repaired, but in the majority of cases, this problem calls for a replacement.

If you have a voltmeter, you can do a better job of checking your starting system. The first thing to do is to check cranking voltage. Just hook the voltmeter to the battery in correct polarity and crank the engine in the normal way. Battery voltage should not fall under 9.0 volts on a 12-volt system (4.5 volts on a 6-volt system). While the engine is cranking, check the cranking speed, either by listening to it or with a tachometer. Cranking speed on most 12-volt systems is about 180 rpm or more. On a 6-volt system, it is about 125 to 150 rpm. Your ear is really the best judge of whether an engine is turning over fast enough. If it sounds sluggish, you have problems.

The battery must be not only in good condition, but capable of the job as well. You can't start a 400-cubic-inch engine with a $20 battery—at least not very often. Be sure the battery is in good shape and powerful enough to do the job.

If the trouble is indicated by low voltage during cranking or a slow cranking speed, make voltage drop tests. These check only the wiring and connections, but are necessary to eliminate those sources of trouble. Voltage drop tests indicate the amount of electricity being used in the portion of the circuit you're checking. Any time you check a switch, a wire, or a connection, you should get a very low reading. In theory, you should get a zero reading because a switch or wire should be a perfect connection and use no electricity at all. But every conductor has a little resistance to the flow of current, so it uses up some electricity. Approximately one- or two-tenths of a volt is a normal reading on each connection or short length of wire. Through experience, you'll find that some connections always draw more than they should, but that is normal for that particular model car. You may get high readings on some voltage drop tests when the starter is bad and is drawing an extra heavy load from the battery. In that case, you will probably find that the wires and connections are getting hot from carrying so much load.

If the voltage drop test doesn't pinpoint anything and you know the battery is good, then the trouble must be in the starter. Remove the starter, take it apart, and you will probably be able to see the trouble just by looking. Starting motors take a tremendous load, and their bearings can easily wear enough to let the armature drag on the field pole shoes. When that happens, the starter is fighting itself and pulls large amounts of current out of the battery. Burned segments on the commutator are a possible sign of faulty windings in the armature—providing that the segments on either side of the burned one appear normal. Sloppy fitting bearings should also be an obvious fault. One sure sign of miseries is a ring of molten lead that has solidified on the inside of the brush inspection band. This may be accom-

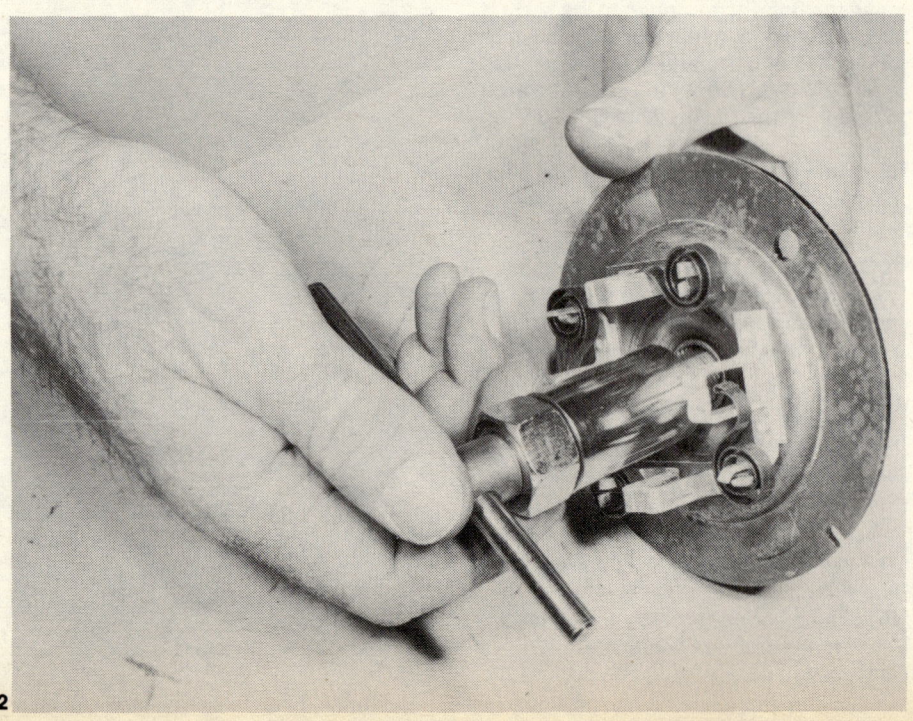

panied by one or more loose wires on the commutator, since the molten lead is the solder that once held them in place. Charged-appearing insulation on the field windings should also be grounds for immediate replacement.

For just about any starter motor trouble other than worn brushes, it is wise to replace the entire unit with a new or rebuilt starter. This is particularly true if the trouble appears to be a combination of several different and growing defects. On a brand-new car, it may pay to replace only the armature or the field windings if these prove to be faulty, but in older motors, it's likely that the brushes, bearings, brush springs, and internal insulation are also just about on their last legs.

Actually, the starting motor is a very reliable and rugged part and is seldom a troublemaker. When something goes wrong internally, it is usually the result of placing abnormal demands on the starting system. Cars that are chronic hard starters because of a poorly maintained ignition system can be death on a starter. If the starter has to work three times as long as it really should have to each time the engine is started, it's obvious that its useful life will be shortened considerably. In actual practice, its life is reduced even more because of the damaging effects of excessive heat buildup that may eventually break down the internal insulation.

OTHER TROUBLES

An engine will occasionally refuse to turn over even though the starter is making obvious working sounds. The trouble could be hydrostatic lock, which occurs when one or more of the cylinders become partially filled with some liquid. If a leaking head gasket or a stuck carburetor float has filled a cylinder with enough coolant or fuel, the starter will not budge the crankshaft. Should this seem a possible source of your trouble, pull out the spark plugs and try the starter again. If the engine turns over normally and there's a gush of liquid from one of the plug holes, you're a victim of hydrostatic lock.

Acute oil rundown can cause similar troubles. This frequently happens when poor-quality or over-age oil is used in a car being operated at high speeds on a hot day. Many motorists on the open road will find that after stopping for fuel, their car's starter can only turn the engine very slowly. At first sight, it appears to be a case of a weak starting system, but in reality, the engine has lost its lubrication, making it almost impossible to turn over. What's left of the oil will run off the cylinder walls of the hot engine moments after the key has been turned off, leaving them dry. The solution is to change oil right then and there, but that's not always possible. To get going again, remove the air cleaner and pour some SAE 10 motor oil slowly into the carburetor intake while someone attempts to start the engine. The cranking action should quickly speed up and the engine will start.

Another cause of slow cranking on a hot engine can be the cooling system. Many a starter has been changed in a desperate attempt to fix a starting system that actually had nothing wrong with it. The cooling system was the problem. After a few thousand miles, rust deposits can pile up around the cylinders, particularly around the rear cylinders where there may be poor coolant circulation. The accumulation of rust and sludge allows hot spots to develop in the cylinder walls. When the engine is shut off after a hot run, those hot spots grab and hold a piston skirt. Clean the cooling system thoroughly

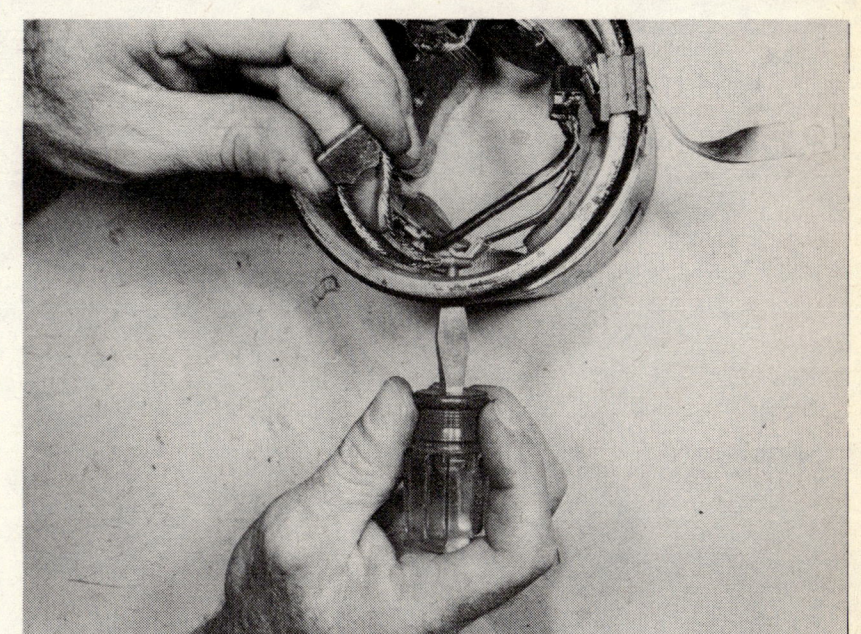

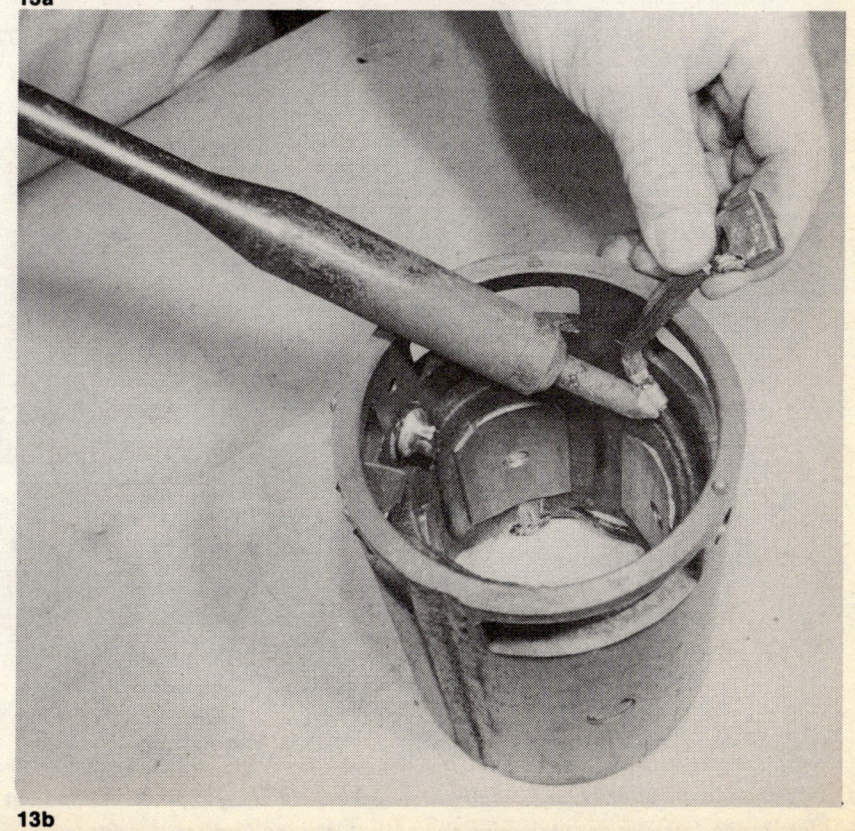

12. After the brushes are out, the through bolts can be unscrewed and the end plate will come off. Check the bushing for wear and replace if necessary.

13A and 13B. The brushes in some starter designs are held in place by retaining screws (A) while others must be cut off and a replacement soldered to the lead (B).

14

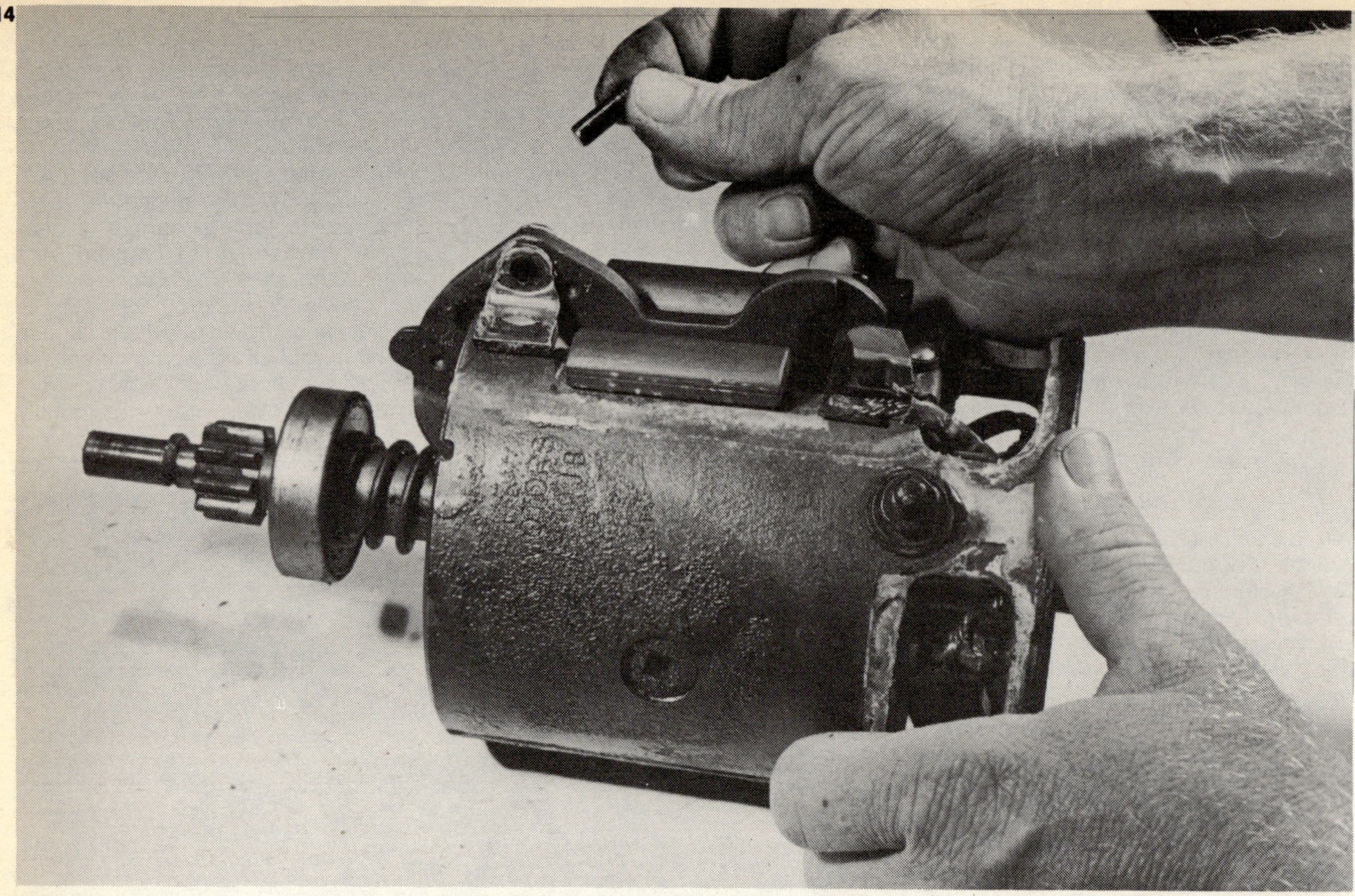

15

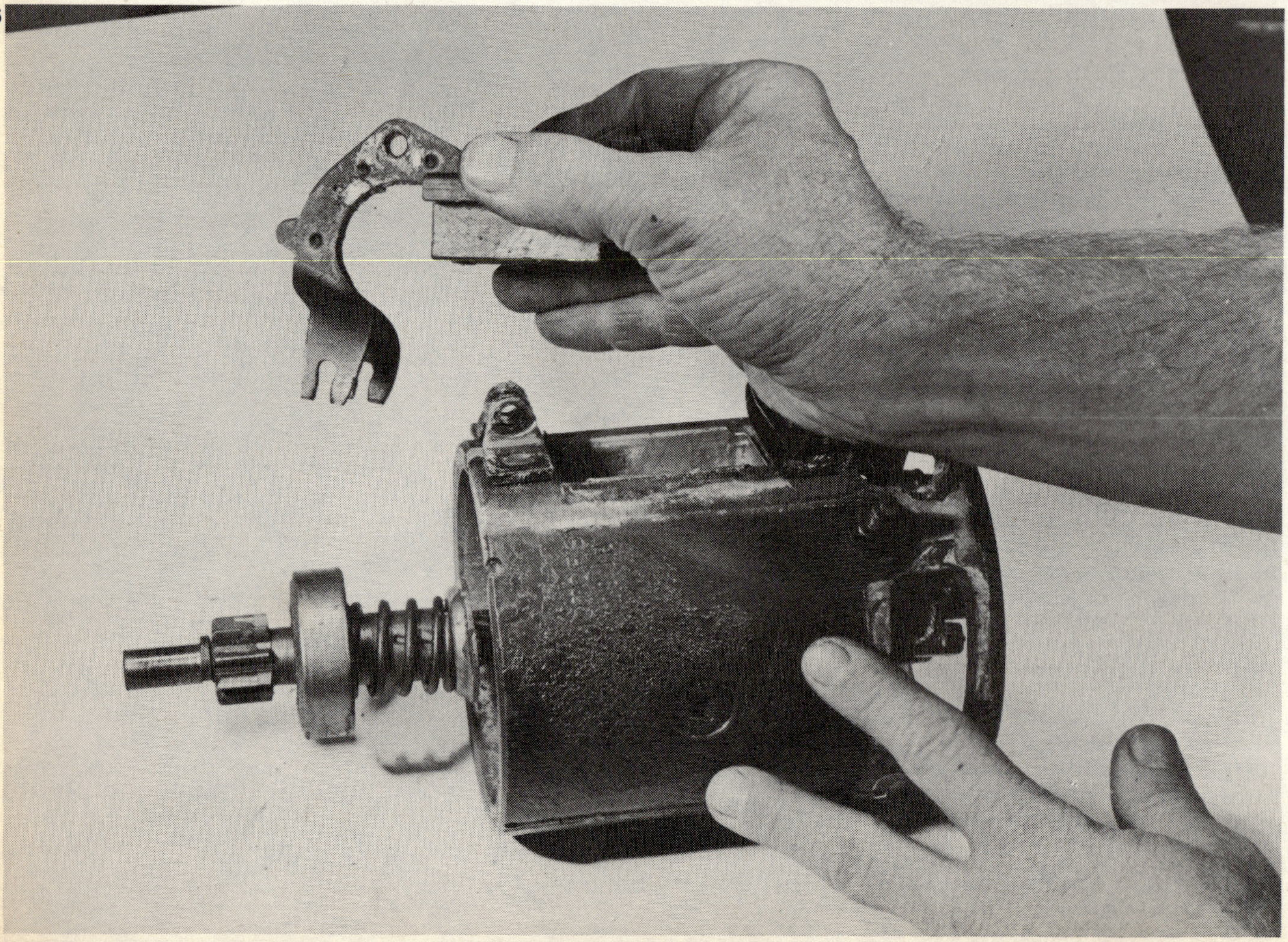

14. This pivot pin is all that holds the Ford movable pole shoe in place. It slips out easily, so don't lose it.

15. Slots in the fork slip over the drive and shift it into the flywheel ring gear.

and such starting difficulties will disappear.

Seeping antifreeze can cause another brand of cooling system starting problem. Ethylene glycol in oil causes high friction, and can seize an engine so tight you will think the crank is welded to the block. In mild cases, the seeping antifreeze will cause only one or two pistons to stick a little. If your engine starts sluggishly after sitting for several hours, it may be because the long rest has allowed antifreeze to seep into the cylinders. Drain the cooling system and refill with pure water for a test. If starting improves, use a good stop-leak preparation and then put in new antifreeze.

DRIVE PROBLEMS

If the starter motor appears to run normally when the key is turned to start, but the engine does not crank over, there is probably something wrong with the drive mechanism. Similarly, if there are horrible grinding noises—with the starter either turning or failing to turn the crankshaft—the drive unit should be checked immediately. If you're lucky, the trouble might be only a broken overrunning clutch, pinion assembly, or spring. If the stars are against you, it might be a stripped flywheel ring gear—which means pulling the transmission, clutch, and flywheel.

The starter drive may occasionally jam in the engaged position, especially with Bendix drives. This is usually a car's way of telling you it's time to replace the drive unit, but you can generally free such jams (unless the car has an automatic transmission) by placing the transmission in high gear and rocking the car forward and backward—with the emphasis on backward. A lack of proper lubrication may be at the bottom of such a malfunction, and a thorough cleanup followed by an application of the specified lub could be all that's needed.

Some overrunning clutches, such as those used by GM and VW, have permanent lubricants packed into them at the factory. These units must not be cleaned in solvents, since this could destroy the lubrication. Most starter drives that are not factory-lubricated are either to be assembled without lube, or to be lubricated with engine oil. Car maker's specifications should always be noted before applying any greases or oils to starter drives.

Late-model General Motors starters with vertical mounting bolts sometimes have shims between the starting motor and the clock. Those shims determine the mesh of the pinion teeth with the flywheel. If left out, the pinion will end up too close and may jam in the engaged position. If shims are put in when they aren't needed, the pinion will be too far from the flywheel and will make horrible noises as the pinion teeth skip over the flywheel teeth, resulting in destruction of either the pinion or the flywheel ring gear. Before removing any starter with vertical bolts, make a check of the pinion-teeth-to-ring-gear clearance. Engage the drive by disconnecting the battery and running a wire to the solenoid only. Be sure that the new or rebuilt starter goes on with the same pinion-teeth clearance as the old starter had.

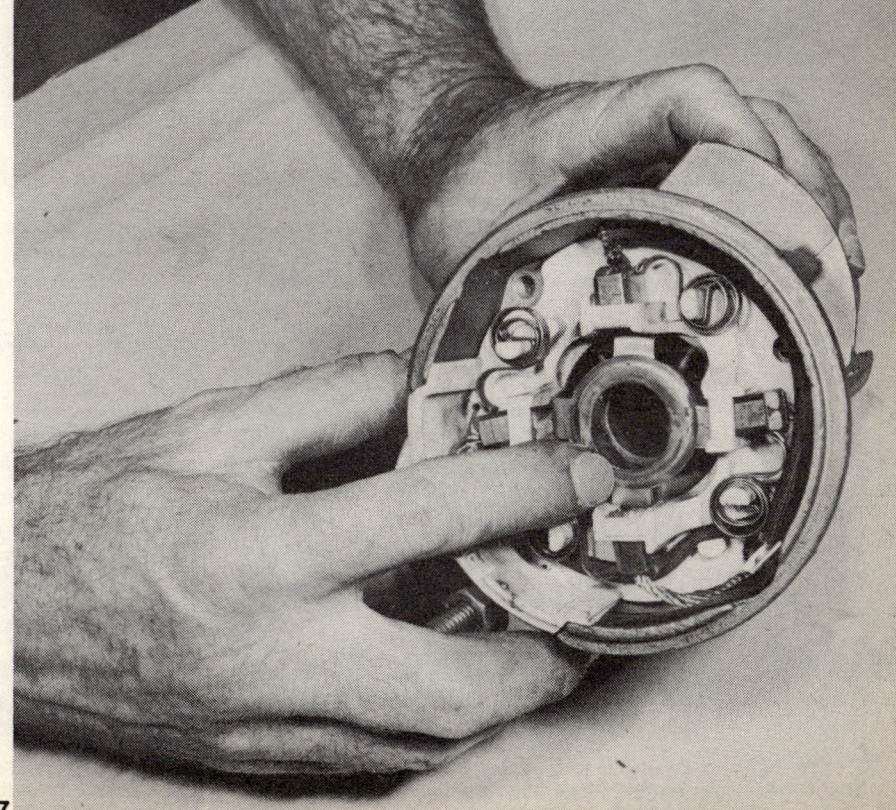

16. An armature lathe is used to renew the commutator. The small wheel (arrow) is used to undercut the mica.

17. If a starter uses a brush plate or holder, be sure to check it for defects before reassembling the starter.

Ignition Conversions

HOW-TO: STARTER REBUILD

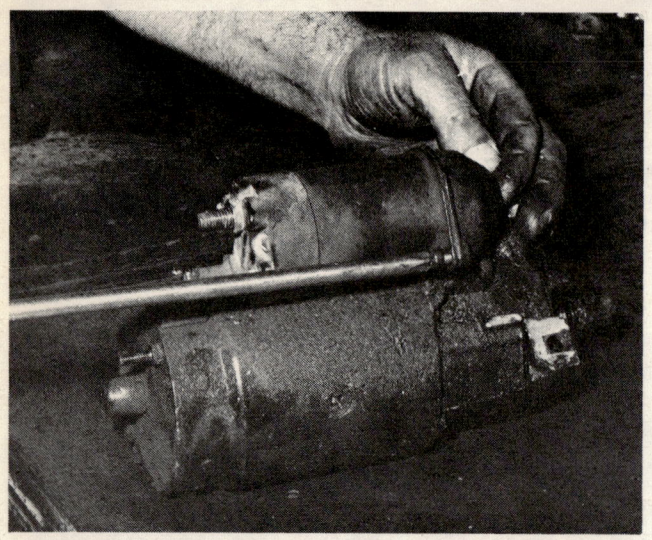

1. Working at Ivan's Generator Exchange in Hollywood, Calif., we begin the starter overhaul by attacking the solenoid first.

2. After removing all its screws, the solenoid is twisted slightly to unlock a flange that attaches it to the starter case.

3. Next, unbolt the long through-bolts. The armature can then be slid out of the case. Watch out for the big solenoid spring.

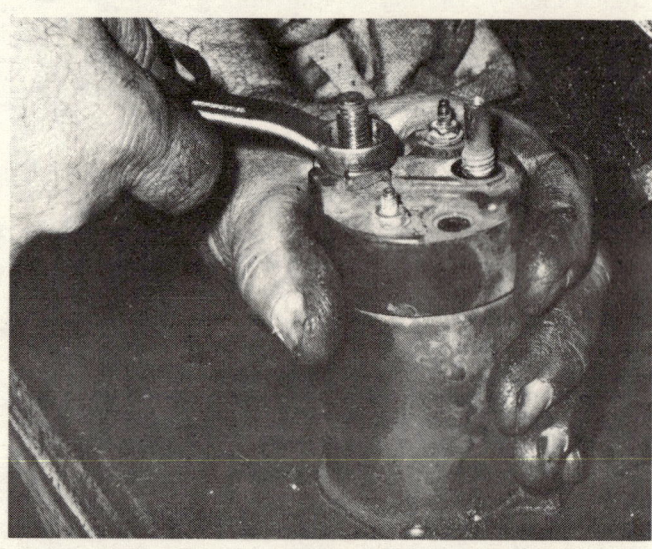

4. Removing two screws and these two terminal nuts allows access to the electrical components of the solenoid.

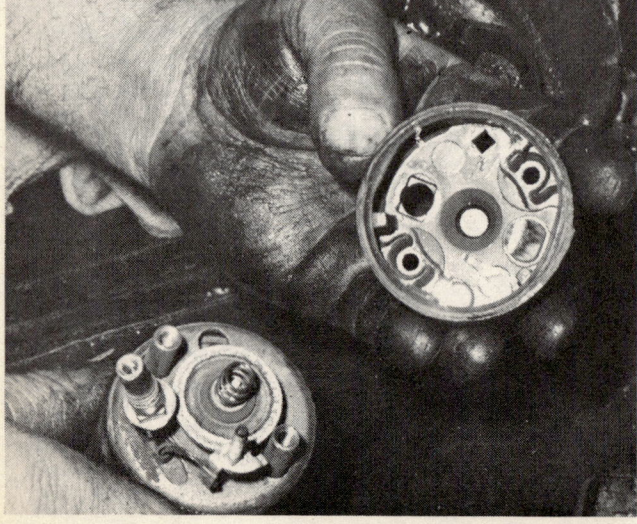

5. The solenoid operates by pushing back the round copper disc so that it contacts the two square copper bolt heads.

6. If in good shape, the copper disc and bolts are cleaned up and reused. If badly burned or pitted, they are replaced.

7. Here are the refurbished components of the solenoid. Reassemble them and set them aside until later.

8. Now let's look at the armature. The Bendix assembly can be slid off the shaft once this snap ring has been removed.

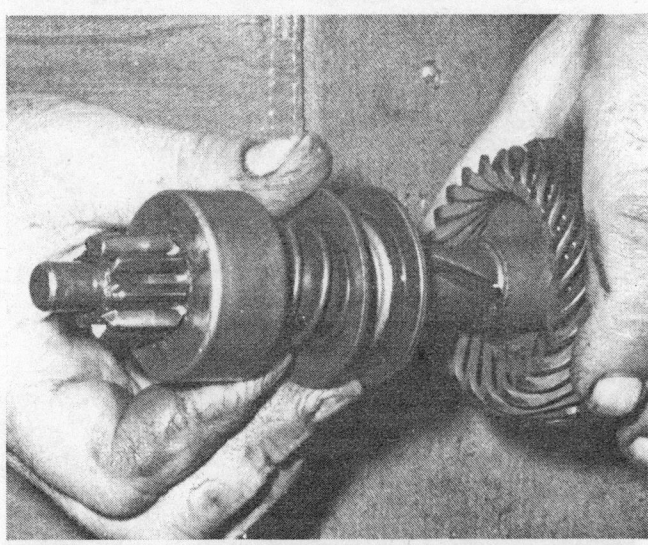

9. Off comes the Bendix assembly. First a spacer and a retaining sleeve have to be removed, after snap ring comes off.

10. The armature's commutator is then lightly turned down on a lathe. This one is useless; note the broken commutator bar.

11. After being turned down, the commutator's insulators must be carefully undercut so that they do not foul the brushes.

12. To make sure that all commutator connections are soldered, the end is carefully dipped into a pot of molten solder.

Ignition Conversions

HOW-TO: STARTER REBUILD

13. The armature is then checked on a growler machine to determine its electrical continuity and magnetic flux continuity.

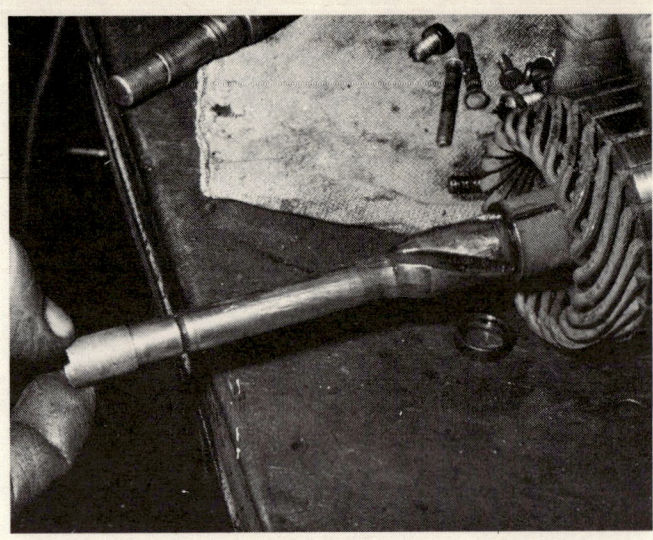
14. After tapping out the old bushing from the Bendix nose housing, the new bushing is test-fitted to the armature shaft.

15. Using a shouldered drift punch of exactly the right size, the new bushing is tapped into the Bendix nose housing.

16. The copper bushing in the front cover is also replaced. Then the Bendix unit is replaced. A new snap ring is included.

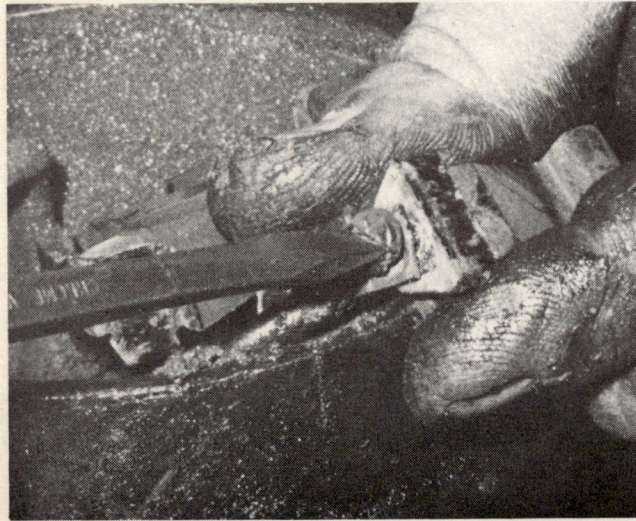
17. Remove the small screws that hold the brushes in brush holders. Next, field windings are checked for continuity.

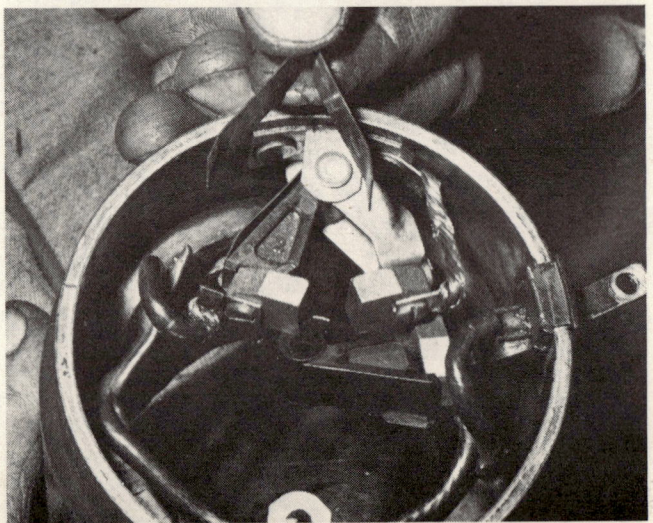
18. If you removed the V-shaped brush springs, they must be replaced behind new brushes. This is tricky—be careful.

19. A pivot pin holds each spring and brush holder. Make sure electrical leads do not interfere with brush movement.

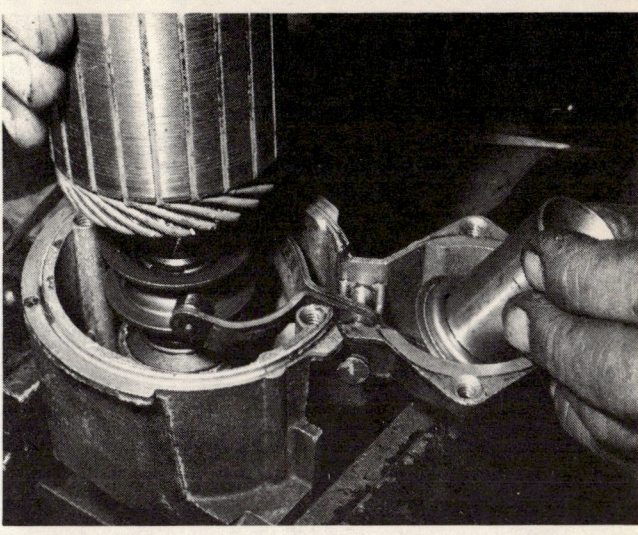
20. With its Bendix side down, the armature is fitted into the nose housing. The Bendix clevis must engage the collar.

21. These fiber washers have to be fitted at the commutator end of the armature before slipping on the case.

22. With thumbs holding the brushes apart so that they will slip over the commutator, case is lowered over the armature.

23. The front end of the starter looks like this before the cover is bolted back on. Now install the rebuilt solenoid.

24. Ivan's adds this final nicety: a dressing stone touches up the commutator while the starter is spun with external power.

IGNITION & ELECTRICAL SYSTEMS/119

SOLENOIDS AND SWITCHES

All large electromagnetic switches that control the flow of battery current to the starter motor are commonly called solenoids, yet, in the strictest sense of the word, a few are not solenoids at all. To make things more involved, the car manufacturers' service publications sometimes use other terms for electrical devices that are really solenoids. For the purpose of our discussion, we'll consider starter circuit controls under two specific names—solenoids and relays. Whether trying to understand a service manual or just communicate with a mechanic, a discussion of these will help you understand what they're talking about.

ELECTROMAGNETIC ATTRACTION

When electrical current is passed through a solenoid, an extremely powerful magnetic attraction is exerted upon a piece of iron placed partially within the coil. The iron is drawn suddenly and powerfully along the parallel lines of force until it rests within the strongest part of the magnetic field. Such arrangements have the ability to exert leverage and do mechanical work at the push of a button.

The starter solenoid found in GM and Chrysler starter circuits consists of such a solenoid coil with a spring-retracted iron plunger resting partially inside the core of the windings. When the ignition key is turned to the start position, current is directed to the solenoid windings. The resulting magnetic field draws the plunger home, engaging the starter drive mechanism and closing the heavy contacts that complete the circuit between the battery and the starter motor.

The term *relay* can be properly applied to a solenoid—since a relay is any electromechanical device used to switch current on and off at a point remote from the operator. However, not all relays are solenoids, since the term *solenoid* applies only to electromagnetic coils wound in a cylindrical pattern. For example, the drive-engagement unit on a Ford positive-engagement starter cannot be properly called a solenoid, since the windings are circular in pattern rather than cylindrical.

A cylindrical coil wound about an iron bar—which in turn is used to produce a magnetic attraction between the magnetized core and a movable armature that serves to close a set of electrical contacts—would appear to be justifiably called a solenoid. However, since the coil is not being employed as a solenoid coil, but simply as a means of magnetizing a fixed iron core, it is really an electromagnetic relay. Such relays are used in the control circuit of Chrysler Corporation starting systems. To be absolutely proper, devices with a fixed core and movable armature are relays, whereas those with a cylindrical coil having a movable iron core to do the work are solenoids.

SOLENOID & RELAY CONSTRUCTION

The movable iron plunger in starter-mounted solenoids pulls the starter drive into engagement. In addition, as the plunger is pulled into the solenoid's core, it strikes a rod that projects into the solenoid from the opposite direction. This rod passes through the closed end of the solenoid housing to provide the movement required to switch battery current into the starter motor windings. An insulated contact disc is attached to the end of the rod and as the rod is moved outward by the striking action of the solenoid plunger, presses the disc into contact with two large brass terminals set into the bakelite cover of the solenoid assembly. One of these terminals is connected to the heavy "hot" cable coming from the battery, the other to the windings of the starter motor itself.

Ford automobiles and AMC cars using FoMoCo starters are the only domestic makes currently employing remote relays for switching the starting current. These units can quite properly be called solenoids because of their construction, yet Ford service publications quite properly called them relays. FoMoCo relays are sealed assemblies which can be serviced only by replacement. In construction, they all employ a rather short solenoid of small diameter. The iron plunger that is drawn by magnetic attraction into the core of the solenoid has an insulated contact disc affixed directly to it. This bridges the gap between the relay's heavy internal terminal contacts. An additional terminal on 12-volt relays draws current directly from the contact disc to supply the ignition coil with unballasted current

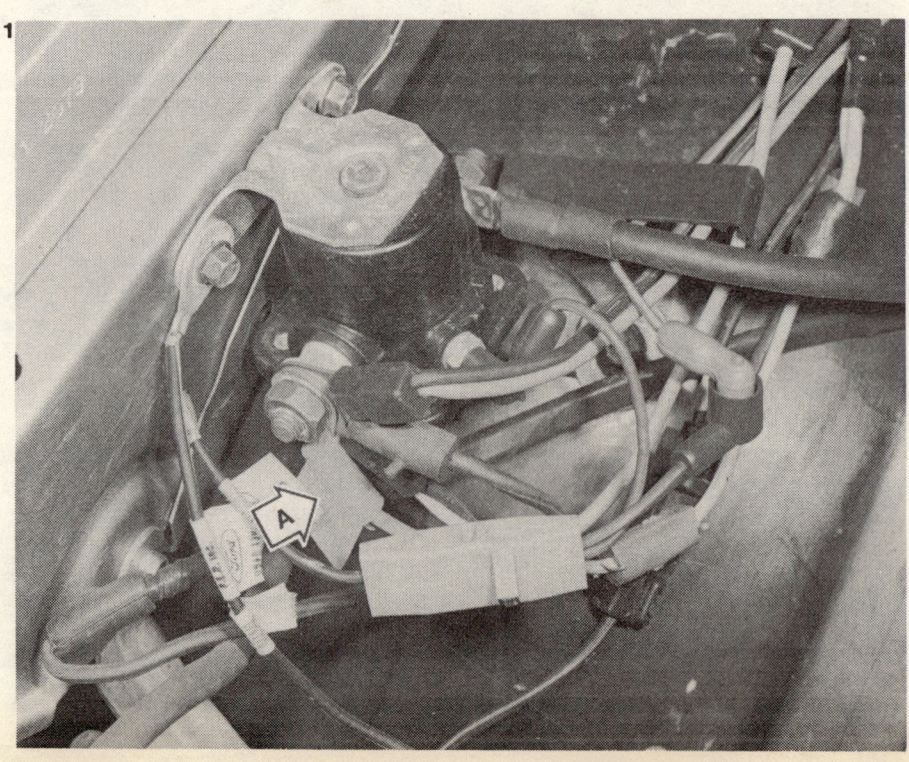

during starting. On Ford units, this terminal is marked "I" for "ignition." A similar small terminal marked "S" (for "start") receives the solenoid-energizing current supplied by the ignition switch when it is turned to the start position.

The starter relay used on Chrysler Corporation cars is a simple electromagnetic relay—not a solenoid. It does not need to handle heavy battery current since there is a drive-engagement solenoid mounted on the starter for this purpose. The relay consists of a coil of light-gauge wire wrapped around an iron core. When the ignition key is turned to the start position, it energizes the coil. This in turn causes the iron core to become a magnet. A flat movable iron armature is attracted toward the magnetized core, closing a set of contacts in the process. These contacts control both the current used to energize the starter solenoid and the unballasted voltage delivered to the ignition system during starting.

WHY RELAYS ARE NECESSARY

The contacts in the ignition switch would be quickly burned out by a current only one-tenth as strong as that needed to operate the starter motor. An extremely heavy switch is thus required to handle the 150-200-amp current which the starter motor may draw from the battery under cold-weather starting conditions. The low-amperage current from the starter/ignition switch is thus used simply to energize a solenoid, which in turn can do the job of closing the heavy switch and engaging the starter drive. It would seem that the task of engaging the starter drive alone would be too great a load to place on the ignition switch and its wiring. This would probably be true if a simple electromagnet were used. However, the electromagnetic principles governing operation of a solenoid and plunger come to the rescue, multiplying the power produced by the electrical energy supplied by the starter's ignition switch control.

A solenoid and plunger take advantage of amperian circuits (electron movement in a magnetic field) and the currents they generate to multiply the strength of the basic magnetic field set up by energizing the windings of the solenoid. When the ignition switch is turned to its start position by the driver, the solenoid establishes an initial magnetic field that attracts the iron plunger. In the process, the magnetic field transforms the plunger into a magnet. The important thing is that the electron spins in the plunger produce amperian circuits that imitate those in the solenoid windings. The plunger, therefore, becomes the equivalent of another solenoid.

The electron currents in the plunger are the same as those in the nearest part of the solenoid windings. Since like currents tend to flow parallel and in the same direction, the plunger is drawn into the solenoid. This motion closes the starter switch, and in most cases is also used to engage the starter drive. As this happens, the amperian currents in the plunger become progressively more coincident with the current in the solenoid. As a result, the cooperation of the currents in the plunger and the solenoid increase, greatly multiplying the attraction that would be possible because of the battery-supplied current alone. A solenoid and plunger, therefore, exert a considerably greater force in relation to the current supplied them than does a simple electromagnetic relay. Without the principle just described, we'd still be saying, "Step on the starter."

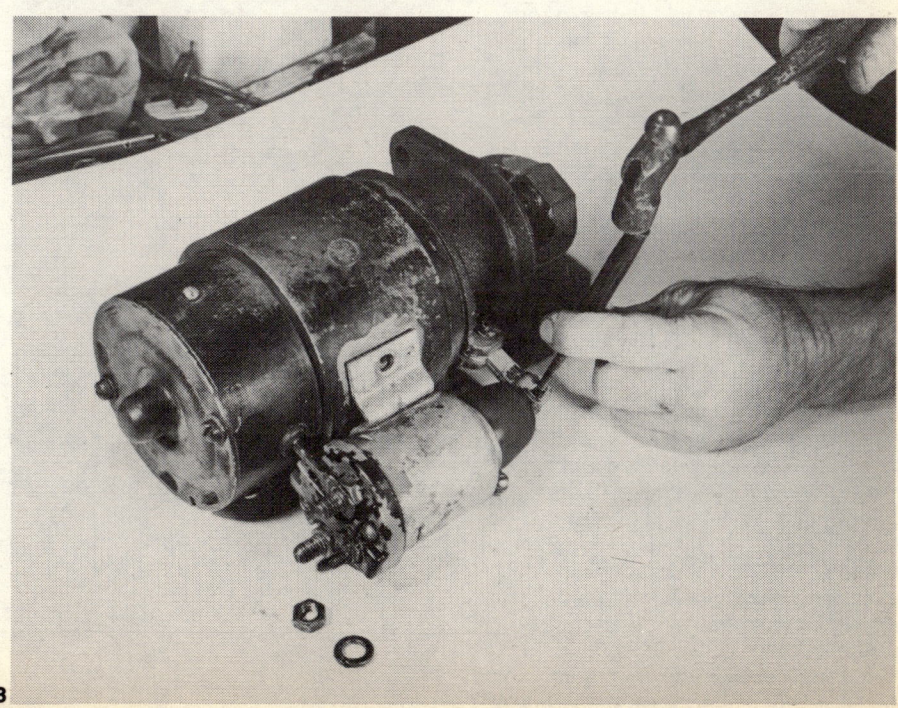

1. Ford starter relays are not repairable. The small terminals are marked "I" for ignition and "S" for start. Fusible links (A) are installed at the relay.

2. Starter solenoids used to be repairable, but are serviced by replacement these days.

3. Prestolite starter with exposed shift lever. Solenoid removal is easy but in most cases, there isn't room to do it in the car. You have to remove the entire starter.

SOLENOIDS & SWITCHES

MAINTENANCE & REPLACEMENT

The prime maintenance consideration in caring for starter-mounted solenoids is cleanliness. Many solenoids are put out of commission by oil leaks that allow engine oil to coat and saturate the solenoid and starter. Oil seeping into the windings or onto the electrical contacts will eventually break down the insulation and promote burning of the electrical contacts. Also, any dust settling in the oil is retained, and in severe cases, such a heavy accumulation of sludgy grime develops that the plunger becomes jammed or the switching mechanism no longer makes proper electrical contact.

In the natural course of everyday use, a solenoid may begin to give trouble. In nearly all such cases, it's the result of wear, burning, or pitting of the main contacts and contact disc. You can often get by "on the cheap" with older solenoids by simply rearranging the position of the various electrical contacts. The battery terminal contact is usually the one that receives the most wear and tear. By loosening the nut that holds it in place in the solenoid end cover, it can be turned 180 degrees to place its unused side under the contact disc. The motor connector strap's terminal is sometimes welded to the solenoid winding's lead-in wire and cannot be turned. But since wear at this point is generally less, it can often be filed smooth and left as is. Similarly, the contact disc can be removed from the plunger rod and turned over to place its new side toward the terminal contacts. Late-model solenoids (from about 1970 on) are not serviceable in this manner, and require replacement of the entire solenoid when the battery terminal contact is excessively worn.

As mentioned earlier, most relays located remotely from the starter are sealed units that are not supposed to be serviced but require replacement. This depends in many cases upon just how determined you are. By removing the four rivets holding the bottom cover on the FoMoCo relay, it is possible to restore the contacts in the main circuit rather easily. The cover can then be replaced with the help of four self-tapping screws obtained from any hardware store. The terminals in Ford-made units can be loosened and turned over to present their unused side to the contact disc, just as in starter-mounted solenoids. It's not out of the question to turn over the contact disc as well—even though this is riveted in place and requires more than a casual effort to perform.

If your problem is in the ignition terminal circuit, the cause of the failure will be immediately apparent upon taking the cover off the unit. Often, it is only corrosion, although a broken conductor is not out of the realm of probability. In an emergency, a bit of solder may produce a fix that might otherwise have had to wait until the car could be towed to a repair shop. If you're grounded at a time when the parts stores are close, it may be practical to attempt such a fix. If you destroy the unit in the process, you haven't lost a thing.

If the jumper cable or voltmeter tests described in the starter chapter seem to indicate that the solenoid winding is defective and is preventing the unit from being energized by current from the ignition switch, it does not necessarily mean that the assembly is beyond repair. By removing the solenoid's end cover, you can inspect the wire connecting the windings to their terminals. In some cases, what have appeared to be burned-out solenoid windings have been repaired simply by soldering a broken wire. If a broken wire is not evident, test the windings with a voltmeter or a battery-operated circuit testing lamp. These tests will sometimes reveal that the windings are intact but grounded. A careful inspection of all visible insulation may lead you to the source of the electrical problem.

When reassembling a solenoid or relay, it's very important to make sure that the plunger or contact shaft works smoothly and effortlessly. A stuck or binding contact can shut the solenoid down just as quickly as a burned-out winding. If you have left the drive-engaging plunger attached to the starter's shift arm, don't tighten the bolts holding the solenoid onto the side of the starter motor until it has been aligned to allow the plunger to move effortlessly. A starter relay can be bench-tested following repairs by connecting its start terminal to the hot side of the car's battery with a jumper cable, and grounding the relay case against the engine or frame. Starter-mounted solenoids, of course, must be tested on the starter. When the connection is made, there should be one click as the plunger moves into the contact position, and another click as the spring causes the plunger to retract when the connection is broken. If there is no click when battery voltage is applied, the windings are most likely defective and the relay or solenoid will have to be replaced. Since the solenoid case on Chrysler Corporation reduction-gear starters is a part of the drive housing casting, the windings

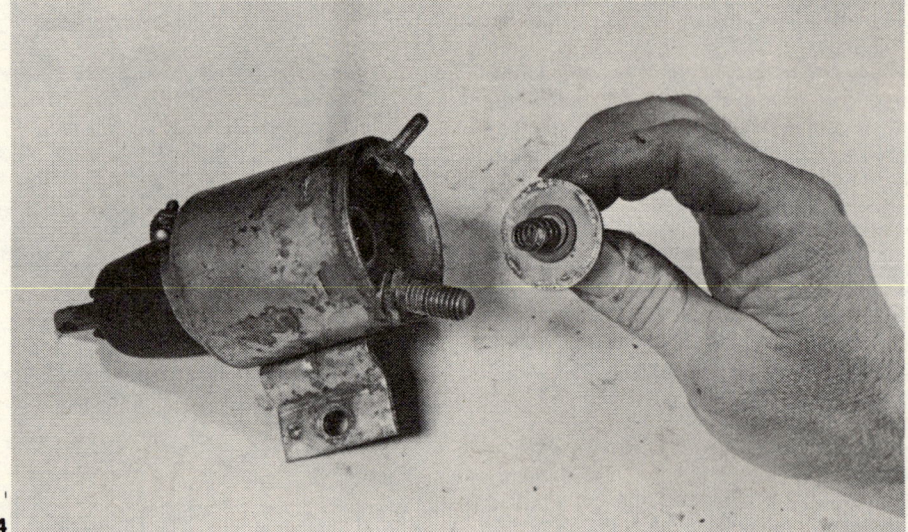

4

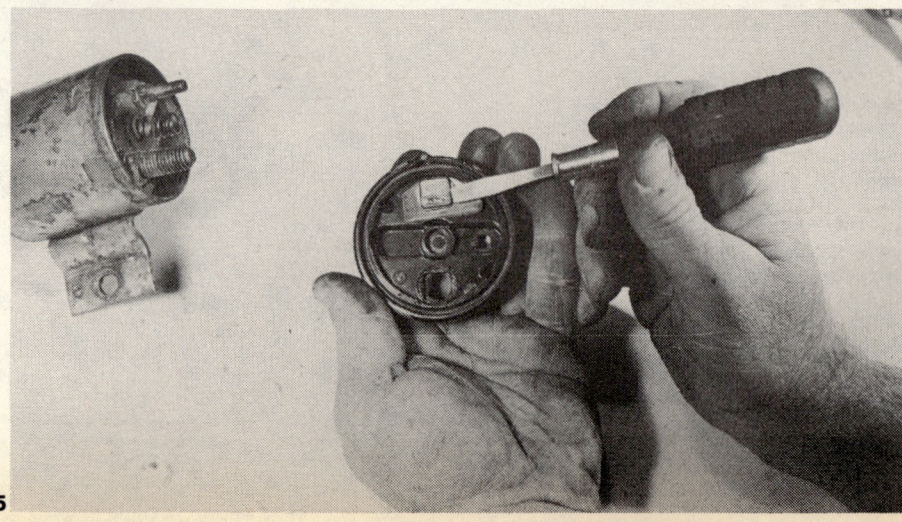

5

can be replaced separately.

Should the starter's control circuit relay give trouble on a Chrysler-built car, you may be able to repair the unit. If it clicks when current is applied to it, burned or dirty contacts are probably the cause of the malfunction. If no sound is heard, the windings are bad and will have to be replaced. Remove the cover to inspect the condition of the contacts. If they are burned or fouled, use crocus cloth or a small file to clean them. Replace the cover and apply battery voltage again to see if the relay works.

MISCELLANEOUS SWITCHES

Regardless of the term by which each is called—solenoid, relay, magnetic switch, toggle switch, or headlight switch—such devices are only a switch that turns something on or off. Switches are designed for most jobs according to the amount of current they will carry. Any time a switch is replaced, the new one must have sufficient capacity to carry the current. If not, it might burn out the minute you turn it on.

If a switch is made so it can be disassembled, all you have to do is look at the contacts to tell if they are in good shape. Most switches used these days, however, cannot be disassembled and will have to be tested with a voltmeter. The best way to test a switch is to have current flowing through it in actual operation. The battery supplies electricity to one side of the switch, and the electrical load (a light, motor, or whatever) is connected to the other side. Never connect a switch directly across a battery without a load or it will burn up instantly. Connecting solenoid or relay windings across a battery is okay, since those windings are an electrical load in themselves. But if you also connect the battery across the electrical contacts that the solenoid or relay operates, the switch is a goner. Whenever making any connection, stop and consider whether you have a load in the circuit.

With the switch connected between the battery and the load, it's a simple matter to connect a voltmeter across the switch terminals and read the voltage drop on the meter. The reading on the voltmeter indicates the amount of electricity you are losing because of resistance in the switch. If the switch was perfect, you wouldn't lose anything and the meter would read zero. Even the best switch has a little resistance, however, so we should expect the meter

4. You'll see a lot of these contact washers on older Delco or Prestolite solenoids. Note how the posts are pushed to one side so that the washer and plunger can be removed.

5. Electric contacts shown wear from a lot of starting. On older Delco units, the bolt can be turned and contact washer flipped over to provide a new surface.

6. This is what the underside of a headlight switch looks like. The circular coil (arrow) is part of the resistance unit that dims the instrument lights.

7. This rocker-type windshield wiper switch operates by opening and closing a pair of contacts (arrow).

SOLENOIDS & SWITCHES

to read something. Most switches will carry the amount of current they were designed for with only about two-tenths of a volt drop. If you get more than that on the meter, either the switch is making poor contact, or there is more current passing through it than it is supposed to carry.

When making voltage drop tests, do not connect the voltmeter to the switch until after you have turned it on. Remove the voltmeter before turning the switch off. These precautions will save your meter. Do it any other way and you'll put full battery voltage through the meter, which is okay if you're on the 12-volt scale, but not if the meter is set on the 1- or 3-volt scale.

Most small switches cannot be taken apart—they must be replaced if they go bad. Removing most such switches from the car is easy enough if you look for screwdriver slots or other obvious ways of getting the switch out of the instrument panel. Headlight switches, however, can be tricky on occasion. They usually have a button on the body of the switch behind the instrument panel. Depress the button with your finger, then gently pull the switch knob and shaft from the body of the switch with a turning motion. Once the knob and shaft are out, unscrew the bezel and the switch will fall out the back of the panel. When it does, it may blow all the fuses if you failed to disconnect the battery first. When testing, you have to use the battery for the test, but when disassembling or removing anything electrical—especially when working behind the instrument panel—always disconnect one cable from the battery, preferably the ground cable.

As with any sealed or encased electrical component, the starter solenoid or relay can seem like a first-class puzzle, but once you've taken one apart, the mystery disappears and its faulty operation is no longer cause for apprehension. You should have gained an understanding of the electrical principles behind the operation of such devices in this chapter, as well as confidence in dealing with them in repair situations. A basic understanding of solenoids can also give you the needed insight to get yourself going again should one of these indispensable bits of machinery let you down in the future. No matter how you look at it, fixing the problem yourself is always preferable to paying for an expensive tow and a repair bill.

IGNITION SWITCHES

The once simple ignition switch (it makes and breaks electrical contact—nothing more) has advanced in complexity over the years to become a sophisticated, multiterminal device that does a great deal more than just complete a single electrical circuit. In fact, today's "ignition switch" provides several mechanical actions in addition to routing current in several directions at once. It has up to five positions to which the ignition key can be turned and held—a far cry from the simple dash-mounted on/off ignition switch many of us remember so well.

Things began to get complicated for the ignition switch when manufacturers decided to mount it on the steering wheel column, where it was ostensibly easier for the driver to reach. This meant that all the wires running to and from the switch had to be encased inside the mast jacket (the steering column's outer tube). There the wires were virtually inaccessible in case of a broken wire or faulty insulation on a wire which might cause it to short against some grounded metal part.

The next advance came when manufacturers began designing switches that would not only direct electrical current, but also lock the steering shaft when the key was removed. This step was taken in the interests of preventing vehicle theft. The theory was that a thief would be foiled even if he shorted the ignition under the hood, since he couldn't turn the steering wheel to maneuver the car after he got it running. Lobbyists for the insurance companies had been behind this move, and in the late sixties, they further confounded Detroit engineers by making it mandatory that manual-shift cars be shifted into reverse before the key could be removed. This would theoretically prevent the car from being towed away by thieves unless the entire vehicle were lifted bodily off the ground by a derrick.

These "advancements," plus several others, served to change the lowly ignition switch from a simple make-and-break device to a complex assemblage of wires, terminals, and contacts, plus rods and linkage, all of which had to be routed down through the mast jacket and exit from the shaft on the engine side of the firewall. Let's look at one maker's example of an ignition switch system to gain some insight into the whys and wherefores of troubleshooting the mechanical and electrical portions of the modern car's ignition switch.

AN INSIDE LOOK

Like any other mechanical device, an

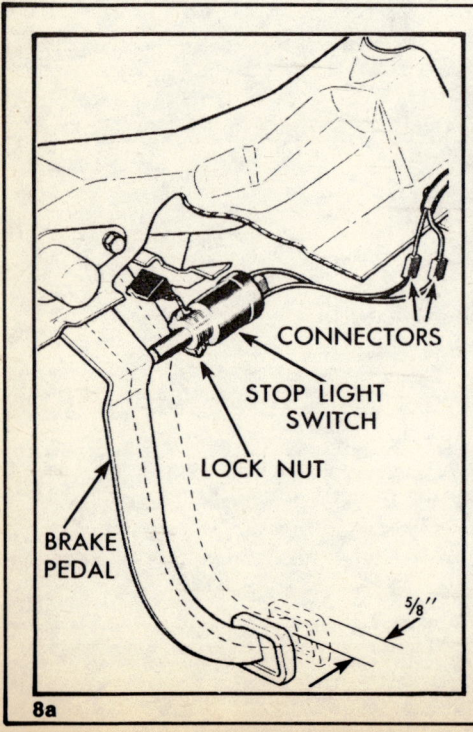

8a

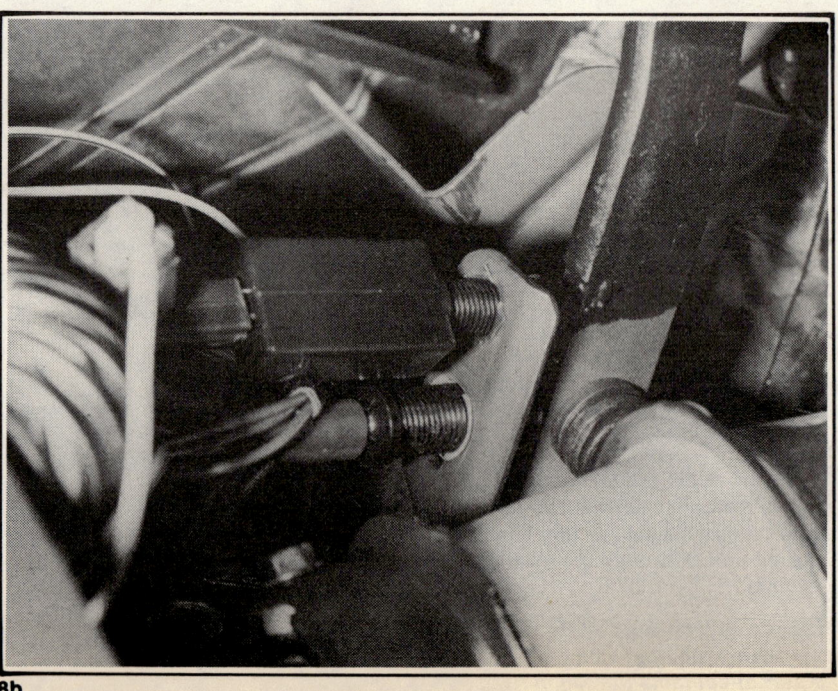

8b

ignition switch can go bad—usually just when it is needed the most. Such failure can occur when internal contacts within the switch body become corroded or damaged, or just wear out. The typical ignition switch has five key positions. These are usually labeled ACC (accessory-on position), LOCK, OFF, ON, and START. The key lock switch also controls the mechanism that provides a positive lock for the transmission linkage and steering shaft. On late-model Ford vehicles with an automatic transmission, the ignition key can be removed from the lock cylinder only when the shift lever is in the park position and the key is turned to the LOCK position. The ACC position operates while the steering and transmission systems remain locked, in case you want to shut off everything but the radio.

Turning the key to the OFF position shuts off battery current to the ignition coil *without* locking the transmission or steering. With manual transmissions and floorshift automatic transmissions, the pushbutton on the left side of the steering column must be pushed inward before the lock cylinder can be rotated to the LOCK position and the key removed. On many Ford-built models, the ignition switch is connected to the lock cylinder by an actuator rod, since the actual switch is located far down the mast jacket on the engine side of the firewall. This switch has blade-type terminals that engage with two multiple-connector plugs. They are held to the switch by snap-type locking tabs. These tabs must be disconnected before unplugging the connectors.

To troubleshoot this kind of ignition switch, disconnect its multiple-plug connectors by lifting up on the retaining or locking tabs while pulling the connector off the switch itself. Connect a battery-powered test lamp or ohmmeter between the plug terminals for each switch position and test for electrical continuity through the switch. If the switch is faulty, or if for some reason the lock cylinder mechanism at the top of the mast jacket has to be replaced, some adjustment will be necessary to make sure that the actuating rod, the steering column and transmission lock assemblies, the ignition switch, and the lock cylinder itself work harmoniously.

**8A and 8B. Some stoplight switches have a locknut that sets the adjustment (A). Others are a friction or screw fit (B) and the switch is slid or screwed back and forth to adjust it.
9. This Chrysler air conditioning control panel uses electric switches instead of vacuum controls. The fan switch (A) can be replaced separately.
10. You may not think of this as a switch, but it is. Vacuum flow is controlled by changes in internal resistance. Its operation can be tested by determining the cold/hot resistance values with an ohmmeter and comparing your reading to specifications.**

To adjust the position of the ignition switch, rotate the ignition key back and forth to either side of the LOCK position until you can insert a drill bit through the locking pin hole to a minimum of ⅜-inch. Lock pin hole location and drill bit sizes vary according to design. On blade-type ignition switches with a plastic switch housing, the locking pin hole is on the top surface of the ignition switch between the terminals marked "Al" and "B." This hole accepts a 3/64-inch drill bit. Blade-type switches with a metal housing locate the lock pin hole next to the mast jacket on the right side of the switch. This one accepts a 5/64-inch drill bit. If the switch is the pigtail variety, the locking pin hole will be found at the uppermost part of the switch, at the junction between the metal and plastic parts of the assembly, and require a 3/32-inch drill bit.

With the switch locked, loosen the two ignition switch mounting nuts. Turn the key to LOCK—you'll feel the detent position—and remove the ignition key. Next, move the switch up and down on the steering column to locate the midpoint of rod lash (or free play) and tighten the mounting nuts. Remove the drill bit from the locking pin hole. Plug in all the electrical connectors, insert the key in its cylinder, and turn it through all of its positions while watching all the instruments, gauges, and, of course, engine-start and engine-running conditions.

Although other manufacturers have somewhat different versions of the ignition, all cars work in pretty much the same way. Even if looking at a factory service manual convinces you that you don't want to trace any malfunctions in the ignition switch and its related systems, at least you can understand why your dealer or local mechanic had your car torn apart for so long and why the job of fixing a simple switch cost so much.

As mentioned earlier, the simple ignition switch has come a long way over the years. As a result, the increased complexity of the switch functions means repair procedures more complex and time-consuming. But remember, no matter how complex a system may seem, it can still be reduced to just a few elementary mechanical and electrical functions. And don't forget, someone had to install the switch in the first place. If he could get it in, you can get it out and put it back.

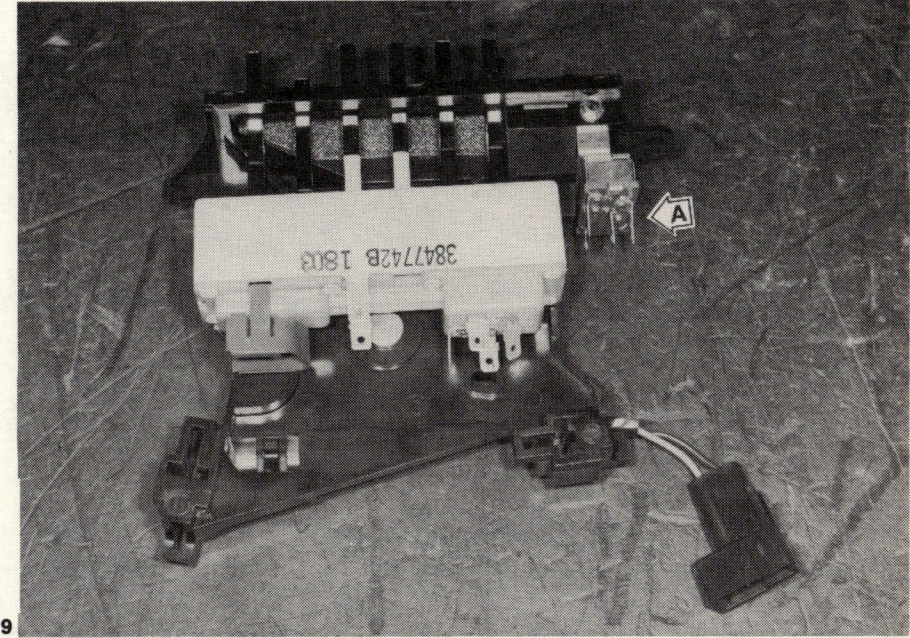

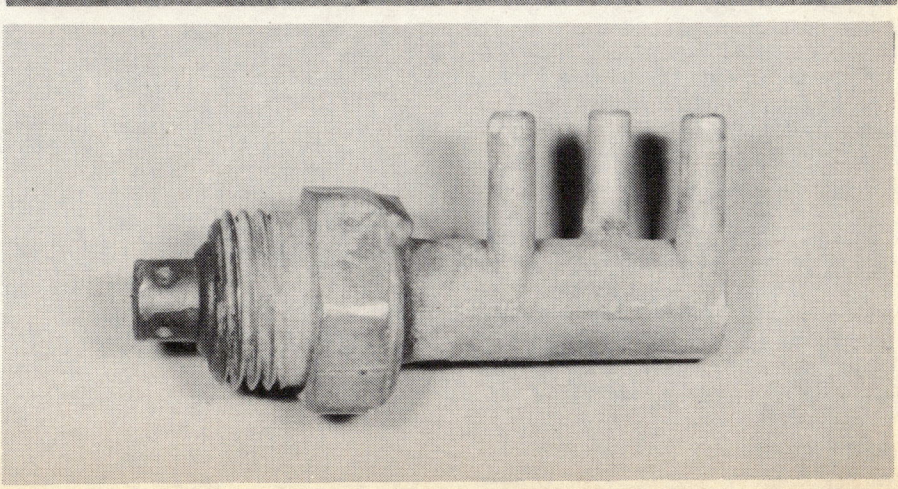

GENERATORS

The automotive generator is a highly refined device designed to convert a small part of the engine's mechanical power into electric power for the purpose of charging the car's battery. Its operation is based on the principle that an electric current can be produced in a coil of wire by rapidly changing the number of magnetic lines of flux linking the turns of its windings. For example, if you were to take a simple horseshoe magnet and place one side of a wire coil between the two poles, a sensitive voltmeter attached to the coil would register no current so long as the coil is held stationary. Yet, when the coil is moved deeper into the horseshoe, the voltmeter will register a current. When the coil is withdrawn, it also indicates a current, but one of the opposite polarity (positive or negative). The reason for this phenomenon? When the coil is in motion, the lines of flux extending through its windings are constantly changing. As a result, an induced electric current flows from the windings of the coil.

The generators used on standard production cars have all been shunt-wound, two-pole units. A shunt-wound field is one which is connected directly to the battery without having any common circuit with the windings of the armature. The generator is thus dependent upon current from the battery to operate it. The two large poles within the frame of the generator have circular windings wrapped about them. When battery current is fed through these windings, the iron pole shoes are converted into strong electromagnets. One pole shoe becomes a magnetic north pole and the other a magnetic south pole.

The generator's armature rotates in the space between the two pole shoes. The windings of the armature are thus subjected to a constant change of magnetic flux, which causes an electrical current to be induced within them. The current in the windings is alternating current—that is, it changes its direction of flow twice during each revolution of the armature. If a voltmeter were attached to the armature windings, the maximum voltage peaks recorded would be alternately positive and negative separated by periods of zero voltage as the windings aligned themselves momentarily in a position parallel to the magnetic field's lines of flux.

Alternating current, however, cannot be used to charge a battery. For this reason, the windings of the armature are attached to a segmented commutator in such a way that the ends of each coil connect to segments that are opposite one another on the shaft. Two brushes are kept in contact with the commutator, and located in such a position that each is in contact only with those segments producing straight positive or straight negative current. In actual practice, there are about 14 overlapping windings in most automotive generators, and about twice that number of commutator segments—one attaching to either end of each individual coil. The brushes, therefore, make contact only with those windings producing maximum voltage during each fractional degree of armature rotation.

The insulated brush picks up the current off the commutator. The current then goes to the armature terminal on the generator, which is connected to the various accessories and lights on the car, as well as to the battery. Everything that receives current, including the battery, is grounded. The current goes through the ground into the frame or body of the car, travels along until it comes to the generator frame, enters the ground brush, and completes the circuit to the armature.

1

2

Most car generators have only two poles, which means they only need two brushes to make a circuit for taking current off the armature. However, since the brushes are only picking up and delivering current to the armature for a very few degrees of armature rotation, it's possible to put more poles and more brushes around the armature to get more current. A generator can have four, six, or eight poles and brushes.

CURRENT CHARACTERISTICS

The voltage delivered by a direct-current generator increases with both its speed of rotation and the strength of the current supplied to its field windings. Since the generator is coupled directly to the car's engine, it goes through wild speed variations. Early generator-equipped cars would frequently burn out their headlights when the engine was revved too high. Not only was the constant variation of overcharge and undercharge harmful to the battery, the stronger the battery became, the higher the voltage it sent to the generator's field windings. As a result, generator output increased at the very time when the battery needed less voltage. It soon became apparent to automotive engineers that something would have to be done to the generator to limit the amount of voltage it could deliver to the battery.

GENERATOR CONSTRUCTION

The frame of most generators is cast iron. This is partly for strength and economy, and partly because in most generators the magnetic lines between the field poles pass in a return circuit through the unit's housing. The end pieces, on the other hand, are usually of some nonmagnetic material such as aluminum alloy. The pole shoes used in automotive generators are generally of mild steel and may retain a considerable degree of residual magnetism even when not energized by battery current. The pole shoes are held in place in the generator's frame by large screws similar to those found in starter motors. The steel plates from which the pole shoes are made are flanged at their outer edges, and that serves to hold the generator's field windings in place.

The coils surrounding the poles of an

1. Most late model generators have done away with the end slots and cover band. Brush inspection is a little more difficult, but can be done on most units with a small mirror.

2. Generators can be completely dismantled for inspection, cleaning and repair by removing the two long through-bolts that pass from one end of the unit through to the other.

3. A growler checks armatures for shorted coils. The better growlers have a meter for checking the armature loops individually for open circuits.

4. Large screws pass through the generator frame to hold the heavy pole shoes and their field windings in place inside the housing.

5. The position of the commutator is almost 90 degrees off from the windings to which the individual segments connect. Note that the wires are spiraled between the armature core and the commutator bars.

6. While most GM and Chrysler generators use an "A" circuit, this Ford generator is an exception, using a different wiring setup ("B" circuit). This is important when eliminating the regulator from the circuit for testing.

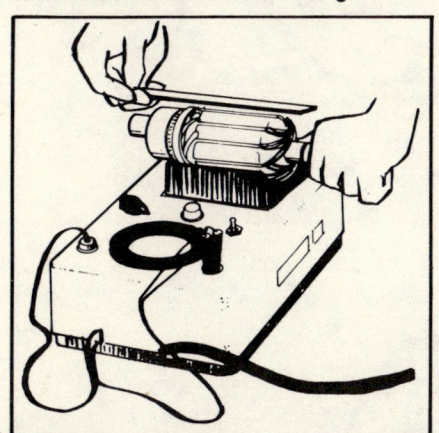

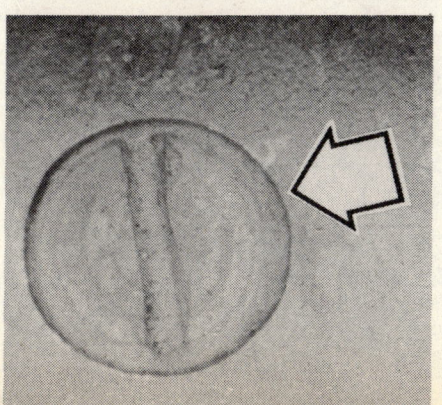

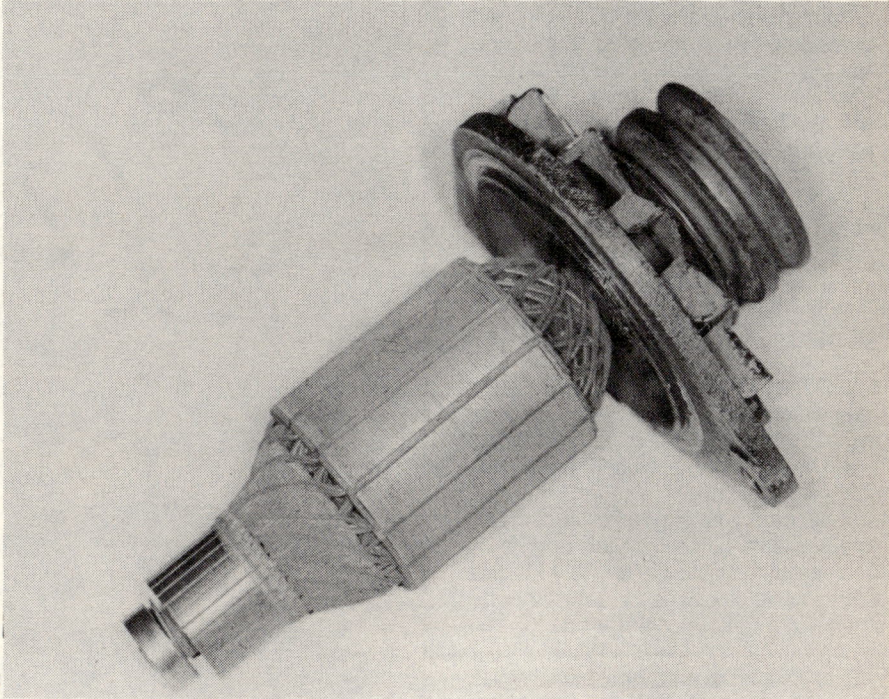

IGNITION & ELECTRICAL SYST

GENERATORS

automotive generator are interconnected so that current passes through first one coil and then the other. One end of the wire forming the field coils is attached to the "field" terminal on the outside of the generator housing. This terminal is insulated from the generator frame by a fiber insert and washer. In most cases, this terminal is marked "Fld." or "Field," with letters stamped into the generator housing. The wire leading from the generator's field terminal attaches to the "field" terminal on the voltage-regulator unit, which completes the circuit for battery current needed to energize the electromagnetic poles of the generator. When the car's engine is not in operation, no battery current is delivered to the field windings because the cutout unit in the voltage regulator breaks the circuit. This automatically shuts off the generator when the car is not in use.

The armature found in the majority of automotive generators is relatively long in proportion to its diameter. This design reduces the effect of inertia on the armature windings at high rpm. The core consists of 60 to 75 laminations stacked up on the armature's steel shaft. Each lamination is about 1/16-inch thick, although in some cases they are made even thinner. These laminations are of soft iron, which does not retain magnetism well, but does accept it temporarily.

Grooves cut into the surface of the armature core serve to retain the windings. The wires forming the windings are insulated to prevent their making contact electrically with one another or with the laminated core of the armature. They are wound back and forth through the grooves in the armature according to a precise and rather complex pattern so that the portion of their length exposed directly to the magnetic field between the generator's poles is parallel to the shaft of the armature.

Each coil of the armature's windings is connected at either end to two opposing segments on the commutator. The segments are insulated from each other (as well as from the armature shaft) by strips of mica or a synthetic substitute. Brass is generally used in the commutator's construction because of its superior conductive ability and its comparative resistance to corrosion. The armature windings are soldered in place on the commutator segments; however, the position of the commutator is almost 90 degrees off from the position of the related windings on the armature core. The brushes are therefore in electrical contact with those loops of wire in the coil traveling fastest in relation to the magnetic flux lines—that is, those midway in their semicircular course between the poles of the ᵌeld. It is these windings that are developing the maximum voltage at any given time.

The brushes that ride against the commutator in an automotive generator are of a design and material different from those found in auto starting motors. Starter brushes are cut from a metallic copper-based material, but those used in the generator are of carbon. Although carbon brushes could not carry the extreme current loads for very long in a starting motor, they have several virtues all their own. The primary one is their extremely long life when used in friction with a brass commutator. Generator brushes commonly last well over 50,000 miles, even though the generator is in constant operation. A starter, by contrast, is required to run only in short bursts and remains idle for the rest of the time.

One of the generator's brushes is connected to a terminal—usually in the end of the unit—which sends the current produced in the armature to the battery via the voltage regulator. This terminal may be marked "A" or "ARM" for armature, but in most cases, its location alone is sufficient to prevent confusion. The other brush is grounded directly to the frame of the generator. Polarity of the ground brush is the same as that of the grounded side of the battery. The charging system's circuit is therefore completed through the frame of the automobile.

The armature runs in bushings or bearings set into the end plates of the generator. In the past, these had to be oiled every thousand miles or so to prevent excessive friction and possible failure. Later generators are often equipped with ball or roller bearings—at least at the drive end—which are prepacked with a permanent lubricant at the factory, while the commutator end of the armature shaft still requires periodic oiling on many generators. Ruined generator bearings and broken drive pulleys are often the result of excessive

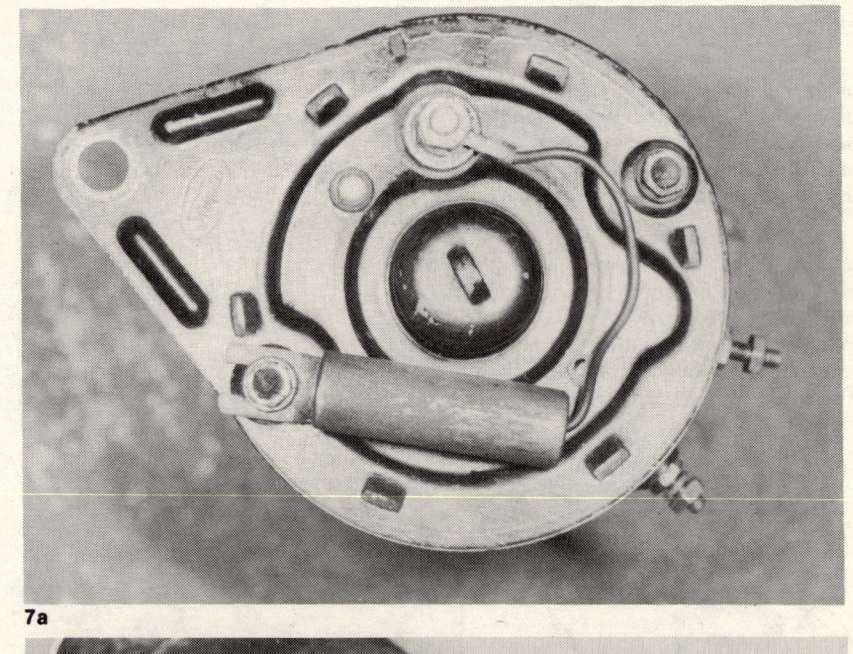
7a

7b

fan belt tension. Incorrect tension is always a prime suspect in cases where bearings fail in spite of proper lubrication.

QUICK-CHECK TROUBLESHOOTING

The generator on most contemporary V-8s (except Ford) is mounted high on the engine, making it easy to test or remove for repairs. Once off the engine, disassembly usually consists of nothing more than removing the drive pulley, unscrewing the brush wires, and taking out the two long bolts that retain the endplates on the generator frame. Before you start taking anything apart, however, it should be determined definitely whether the fault is in the generator or elsewhere.

Generator problems are much more easily detected if your car is equipped with a dashboard-mounted ammeter, although those types of trouble normally associated with the generator itself will usually be caught by even a warning light. Overcharging, low-charging, or a fluctuating charge are most likely the result of a malfunctioning voltage regulator. Intermittent charging and no charging are the troubles that most often originate in the generator itself.

Low-charging and no charging are generally the most common forms of charging system trouble. If the ammeter begins to register a constant and steady discharge while you're driving, or if the generator light comes on and stays on, the generator may be delivering no charge at all. Take a quick look at the water temperature gauge. If the cooling system's temperature is rising, the cause of the no-charge condition is probably nothing more than a broken fan belt.

7A. *A condenser is often seen attached to the generator's armature terminal to prevent radio noise. In an emergency, it can often be removed and used with the distributor should the ignition condenser fail.*

7B. *Heat is one of the generator's worst enemies, so the drive pulley incorporates a cooling fan to circulate air through the generator. Removing the large nut pemits pulley removal from shaft and allows bearing to be removed.*

8. *Generator brushes are mounted in the end cap on Ford generators.*

9. *This Delco design shows the brush location after the end cap is removed. Brushes are attached to the generator terminal by means of a wire and screw, making replacement easy.*

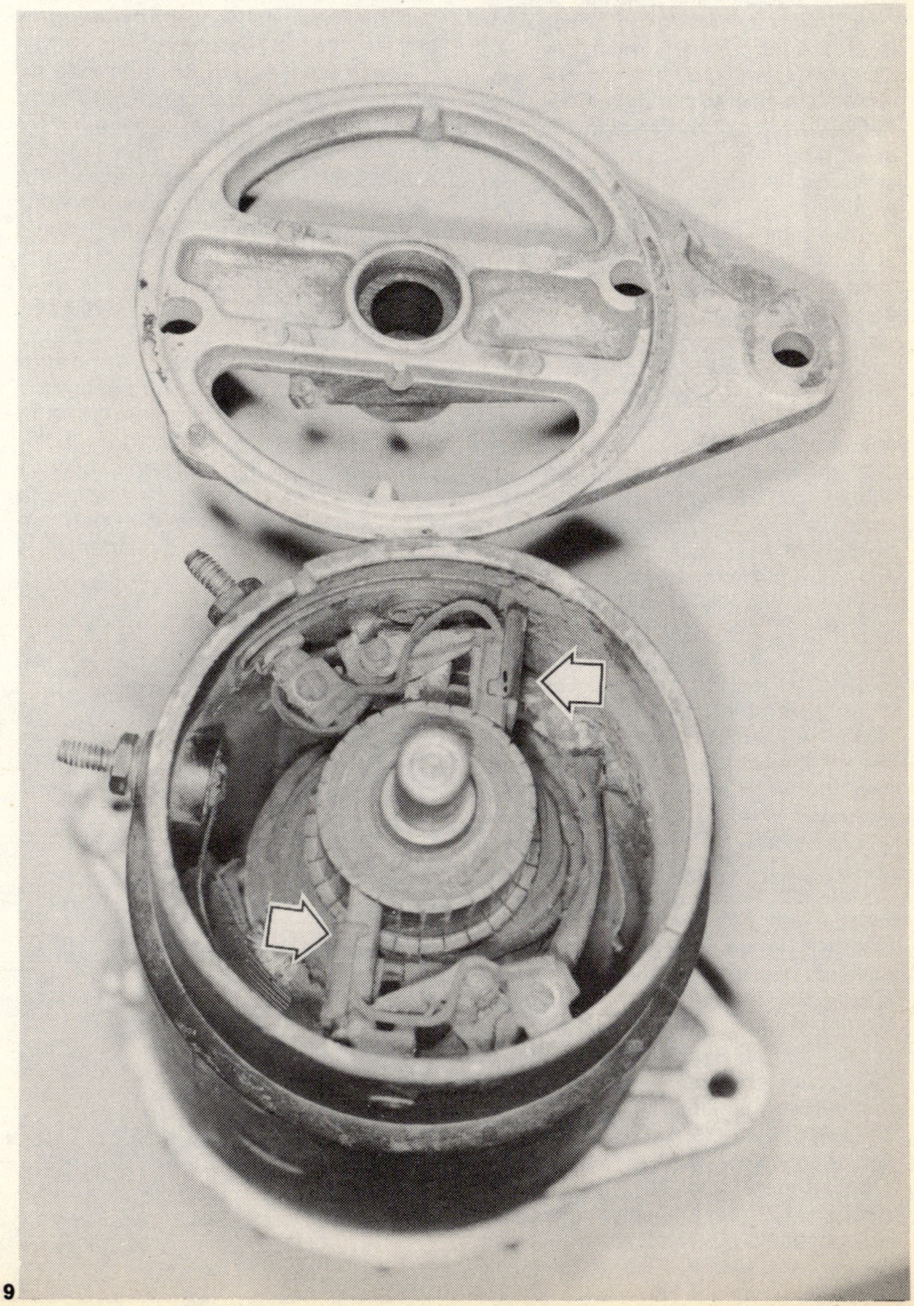

GENERATORS

Your attention may be attracted by an ammeter needle that dips suddenly into the discharge zone and then returns an instant later to a reading well up in the charge range—even at a steady engine speed. This is an indication that charging is taking place only part of the time. A winking warning light can tip you off to the same problem. Troubles such as this—as well as those discussed in the preceding paragraph—are the types normally produced by generator defects. But before attacking the generator, check the condition of the battery and its connections. A loose battery connection that is making poor or intermittent contact can also cause the generator light to flicker or the ammeter needle to take dips.

The next step is to determine if the defect lies in the generator or in the voltage-regulator unit. This can be done quite simply by eliminating the regulator from the circuit. On most GM and Chrysler Corp. cars ("A" circuit systems), you can do this by removing the field wire from the regulator, then grounding the field terminal at the generator. If you don't remove the field wire, you'll burn up the regulator if it is the double-point kind. Ford uses a different wiring arrangement ("B" circuit system), so you must run a jumper wire from the armature terminal to the field terminal, either at the generator or at the regulator, and it's not necessary to remove the field wire.

You can perform this test in emergencies with the blade of a screwdriver. The engine must be running and you should take precautions to keep your hands or tools away from the moving fan blades. If eliminating the regulator increases the ammeter reading to a high level, the trouble lies in the voltage regulator. But if it does not increase the output, the generator is at fault. When making this test, be sure that everything in the car is turned off except the ignition. Run the engine just fast enough to see if the generator is going to put out, then turn the engine off. An uncontrolled generator puts out a lot of voltage and you can blow a stereo or radio, or even a dome light if it happens to be on.

Many drivers think that the generator is charging only when the ammeter needle is on the charge side of the zero position. This is not true—the ammeter is hooked into the circuit so that any time the needle is on the plus side of zero, it shows the amount of charge that is going into the battery, not the amount that is coming out of the generator. You can test this yourself by turning on lights and accessories with the engine at idle. The ammeter needle will show a discharge of the amount of electricity being used from the battery. As you bring the engine speed up, the generator will supply electricity to run the things you have turned on, and the needle will move toward zero. The generator is putting out enough electricity to take over operation of the lights and accessories from the battery. If you run the engine faster and the generator has any output left over, the needle will move to the plus side of zero. That means the generator is running all the lights and accessories, and putting some electricity into the battery besides. Just because you see a zero reading on the ammeter, it doesn't mean the generator is not charging.

Worn-out generator brushes are the cause of most no-charge generator problems. If you're lucky enough to have a generator with a removable inspection band at one end, it can be snapped off for the purpose of checking the brushes. Of course, if your particular generator does not have a removable inspection band, the unit will have to be taken apart or a mirror used to check the condition of the brushes. Should inspection reveal that the brushes have worn to less than half their original length, they are in definite need of replacement.

In some cases, the brushes may be simply sticking in their holders. This is particularly true if the generator has become very dirty and perhaps oil-soaked. Sticking brushes usually call for nothing more than a good cleaning, but if the commutator has become burned and glazed because of the effects of the poor electrical contact, the unit should probably have the brushes and commutator renovated as a precaution against further trouble. Whenever brushes are replaced, the commutator should always be turned in a lathe to make sure that it is concentric with the shaft and that the segments have a smooth, level surface for the brushes to ride against. The mica between the commutator bars should be undercut so it won't interfere with the brushes. New brushes should be sanded after they are in place in the generator to ensure proper contact, which can be done by drawing a strip of fine sandpaper between the commutator and the brushes with the abrasive side against the contact area of the brush. The sandpaper should be pulled through four or five times in the direction of armature rotation to make a good job of it.

The presence of individual burned commutator segments means open circuits in the armature. This and other troubles involving the wiring of the generator are probably best left to a shop with the proper equipment for quickly determining the extent of the trouble with the unit. If it's a relatively new generator, it may be less expensive to replace individual parts such as the armature, endplates, or field windings. In the case of older units, any trouble more serious than worn brushes is often just the first in a series of failures that may be logically expected. Before investing any money in the repair or an older generator, have it checked out by a competent automotive electrical shop and if a rebuilt or replacement unit is recommended, you'll be better off in the long run by following that advice.

Generator testing is done pretty much the same as starter testing. Of course, the first thing you have to be sure of is that the generator is bad. In most cases, you can do this on the car, either by electrical testing or by looking into the generator with a small inspection mirror. When the generator is disassembled, look first for signs of the armature hitting the field coils or the pole shoes. If hitting is evident, it's a sure sign that a bearing or bushing is bad. If the bearing is causing the trouble, replace it by removing the pulley and any dust shields

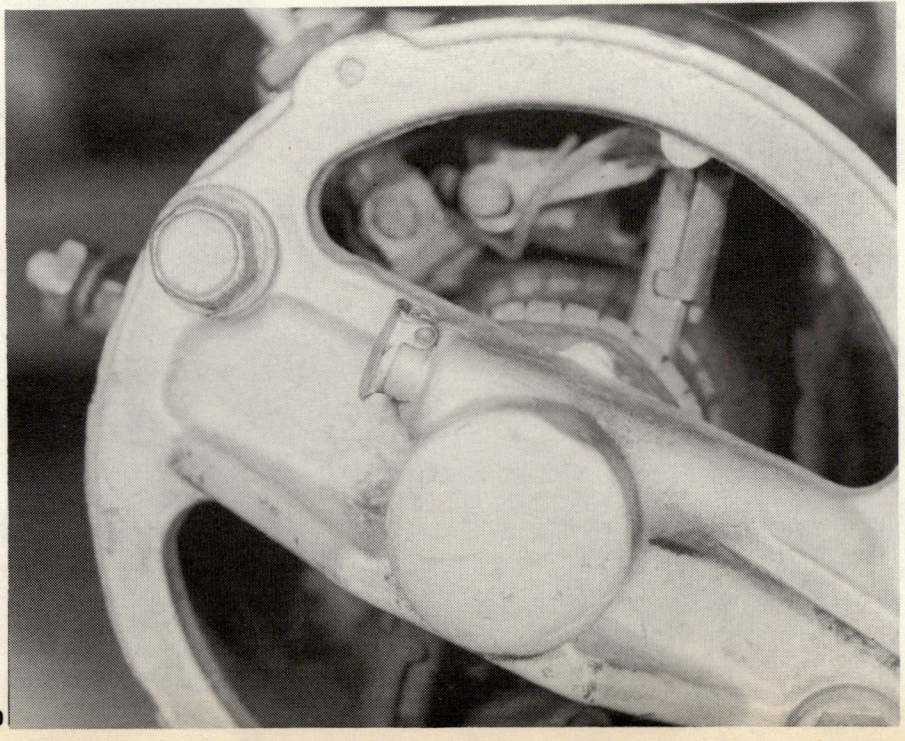

or plates. If the bushing is bad, it's more of a problem because the hole in the endplate does not extend completely through. Some garages stock endplates that have new bushings already installed. You will even find a few shops that have the tools to remove the old bushing. In most cases, however, you're best off going directly to a rebuilder for such work, as he's most likely to have the parts and equipment on hand to do the job. Few garages and fewer dealerships have much of a call these days for generator parts and service.

Armatures should be tested for grounds, shorts, and open windings. Grounds are detected by using a battery or power-operated test lamp and touching the test leads to the commutator and the armature shaft at the same time. If the light goes on, the armature is grounded, which it shouldn't be since its electrical parts are supposed to be insulated from the armature shaft.

To test armatures for a shorted winding, put them on a growler and hold a steel strip such as a hacksaw blade lengthwise over the armature. Rotate the armature in the growler at the same time. If you feel any vibration or attraction of the steel strip, the armature is definitely bad.

Testing an armature for open windings is best done with the type of growler that has a meter. When used according to directions, the meter measures the induced voltage in the armature, one winding at a time. If some windings give a low reading, they're probably open or have a bad connection where they're soldered into the commutator bars. Another way to check for an open winding is with a test light or high-frequency current on adjacent commutator bars. Any variation in the brightness of the light or arcing of the high-frequency current indicates a bad connection or a break in one of the windings.

Brushes and armatures cause most generator troubles, but that doesn't mean you should ignore the fields and other parts. Check field coils to see if they are grounded, shorted, or open. If the field is grounded in the generator, as on Fords, you'll have to disconnect the ground wire before using the test light. To check for a short or an open, use a low-reading ammeter with battery voltage to see how much current the fields will draw. If they draw too much and burn up the ammeter, you can be pretty sure they're shorted.

To finish up your generator testing, check the insulated brush holder with a test light to see if it is grounded. Then clean the endplate with solvent—not gasoline. Be very careful around the fields with solvent—they soak it up like a sponge and it could cause a short later one. The generator frame and fields are best cleaned with a dry brush. With the high cost of labor today, automotive servicemen do very little electrical testing. It's much easier and faster to throw a bad generator away and install a new or rebuilt one than to waste time with a lot of testing. This is where the do-it-yourself approach can save you considerable money.

POLARIZING THE GENERATOR

After assembling the generator, you must polarize it—*before* it is started up. Polarizing can be done before or after the generator is installed on the engine, but it must be done before the engine is started. It is possible that while installing the generator, a couple of wires may have been crossed for an instant, giving the generator reverse polarity. For that reason, polarizing is best done after everything is reconnected, before starting the engine. To polarize the generator, just touch the jumper wire between the battery terminal and the armature terminal. Remember, it only requires a touch of the jumper wire between these two terminals. If you leave it connected for more than a fraction of a second, you may very well burn up the regulator. Always polarize a direct-current generator after installing either it or a regulator.

Most of the generators supplied on late-model American cars before the alternator came into favor have an output in the neighborhood of 32 to 35 amps. This output is controlled by the regulator unit so that only the amount of current that the generator can safely put out will be produced at any given time. Under normal circumstances, the generator is seldom required to produce a charge greater than about 7 to 10 amps in a 12-volt system. This places no great physical strain on the generator and for this reason, it seldom offers trouble in the well-cared-for automobile. On the other hand, neglected batteries and malfunctioning voltage regulators can place upon the car's generator a load that far exceeds the capacity of its normal charging rate. When a generator is called upon to operate almost constantly at its highest possible level, its useful lifetime may be greatly shortened.

Very often the combination of high summer temperatures, high speeds, and an improperly functioning regulator will spell death not only for the car's battery, but for the generator as well. A cool generator is an efficient, happy generator. The air vents in the endplates and the fan built into the drive pulley have a vital job to perform. If the air vents are allowed to become clogged with grime, or if the fan vanes are bent or broken, expect a rather drastic reduction in the unit's service life.

Overcharging, with its resultant destructive effect on both battery and generator, should be considered one of the most serious of possible charging system malfunctions. If your car has only a warning light, one of the best investments you can make is the addition of an ammeter to your car's instrument panel. Extreme accuracy is not important; a gauge that gives you an indication of excessive charging or an abnormal charge rate that progresses up and down the ampere scale in direct proportion to engine rpm is all that's really necessary. That little red light won't tip you off to either of those conditions—ever. You'll never know anything's wrong until it's too late.

10. Most generators have small "flip-top" oil cups which should be given a few drops of oil periodically. Late models had permanently lubricated drive end bearings.

11. Although somewhat simplified, this is a typical battery-generator circuit.

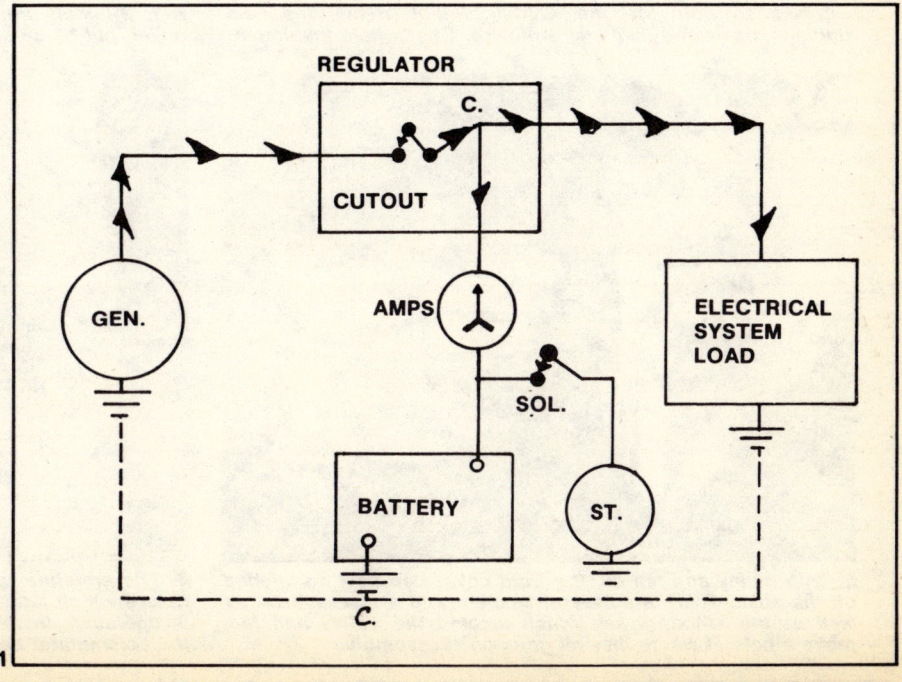

Generators

HOW-TO: GENERATOR OVERHAUL

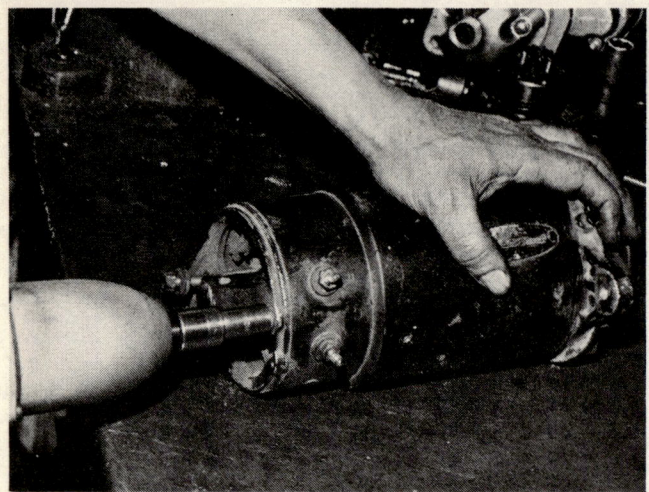

1. A Delco-Remy generator overhaul is old hat to a shop like Ivan's Generator Exchange, located in Hollywood, Calif. Disassembly begins by removing the two long bolts which extend through the case and attach the front cover to the rear cover.

2. The rear cover will now drop off. Grasp the front cover and pull it forward, carefully withdrawing the armature and commutator. Slight tapping with a plastic hammer may be necessary here. The brushes and field windings remain in the case.

3. Field coils are checked by passing current through them. A common problem in old generators is that the rear bushing becomes so worn that the whirling armature hits the field windings, damaging field and armature. Check field insulation.

4. After removing the nut on the front end of the shaft, the pulley and fan must be removed. The best way to do this is with a bench press, shown here. You can use a small gear puller, but be careful not to damage the fan or belt pulley.

5. With pulley and fan off, the front cover can now be slipped off the shaft. There are several spacers and a sleeve here, as well as the Woodruff key which located the pulley and fan; make a note of where they all go upon reassembly.

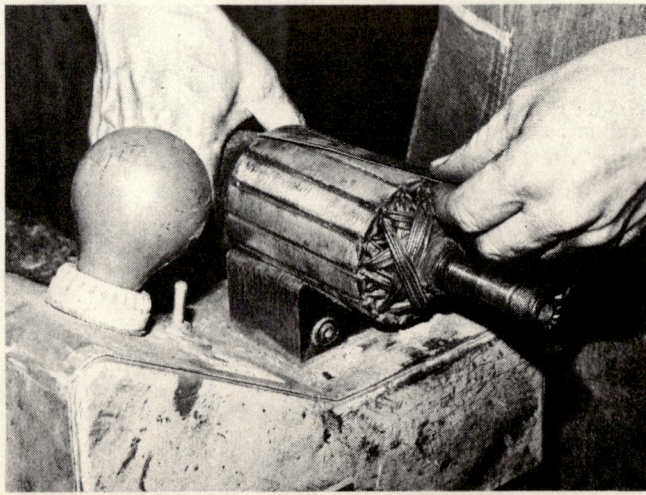

6. The armature is checked for shorts on a "growler," a test fixture which lights up and really does emit a growling noise in operation. Inspect the wire connections around the base of the commutator bars; they must be resoldered if loose.

7. The surface of the commutator should be clean and perfectly round, so it is customary to take a light cut off the surface with a lathe. Commutator bars are of thick copper and can take many light cuts before a new armature is needed.

8. After a light cutting on the commutator, the mica insulators between the commutator bars must be cut down below the level of the commutator. Otherwise they will touch the brushes and prevent proper conversion of AC current into DC.

9. Getting the old shaft bushing out of the rear cover can be a real problem, because it's fitted in a blind hole. Ivan's has a special bushing puller, but you'll have to use a hammer, drift pin and a cold chisel, preferably a diamond-point chisel.

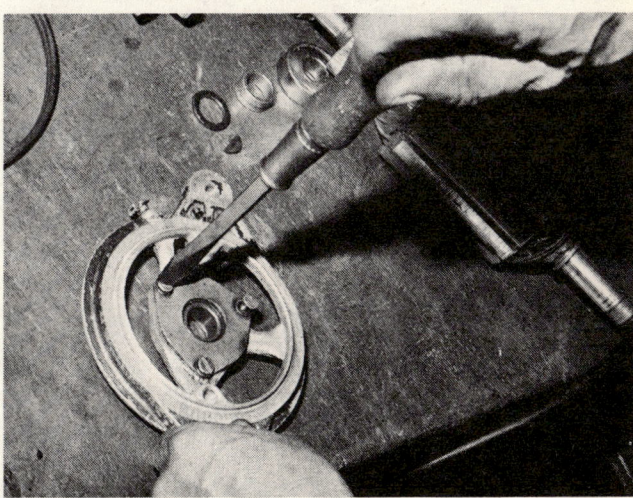

10. The new rear bushing is pushed into the cover with a press. Now don't you wish you had let Ivan rebuild the generator? Removing these three screws and the retainer plate allows access to the front bearing, which must be tapped out.

11. Before installing the new front ball bearing, put in this felt washer and metal shim first. Then press in the new bearing. Be careful to get it in straight, not cocked. Next, replace the retainer plate and the three screws.

12. Install new brushes. Replace the front cover on the armature shaft, then the fan and pulley. Don't forget the Woodruff key. Carefully slide the armature into the case, pulling the brushes aside. Then the rear cover bolts back on.

ALTERNATORS

The alternator has become a practical replacement for the DC automotive generator in recent years mainly because of the revolutionary developments that have been made in solid-state electronics. The modern automotive alternator employs a number of positive-negative diodes—a basic form of transistor—to rectify its alternating-current output into direct current. These diodes are relatively durable and are produced in quantity at low cost by many solid-state electronic component manufacturers.

As a device for converting mechanical power into electrical power, the alternator has certain distinct advantages over the generator both in efficiency and durability. The same principles of magnetism employed in magnetos and generators are also used in alternators, but there are certain very noticeable differences in their actual construction. As we discussed in the previous chapter on generators, it is possible to induce an electrical current in a coil of wire either by moving the coil and allowing the magnetic field to remain stationary, or by leaving the coil stationary and moving the magnetic field. The important thing is that some means must be employed to change the number of magnetic flux lines passing through the coil windings.

In the generator, the magnetic field remained stationary while the armature's coils were rotated. This is the most practical way of designing a direct-current unit that must be made compact, since many coils are needed to produce a steady supply of direct current. Direct-current generators thus require a segmented commutator so that voltage of the right polarity can be picked up from whichever coil in the windings is developing the most power. If alternating current is desired, the current produced in all the windings at all times is acceptable for use. In an alternator, the aim is not merely to tap the maximum voltage of one particular polarity, but to use the entire output—regardless of the fluctuating voltage. To obtain a sufficiently high average voltage, however, a greater number of cycles must be generated.

An alternating-current cycle is the length of time that it takes for the current output to rise from zero voltage to maximum positive voltage, return to zero voltage, proceed to maximum negative voltage, and again fall to zero. Normal house current is said to be 60-cycle AC, which means that it completes this cycle pattern 60 times per second, giving 120 voltage peaks that are alternately positive and negative.

Current flow alternates in the windings of a direct-current generator's armature, but the brushes pick up only the current from those coils having the correct polarity at any given time. The alternating current in the individual coils of an automotive DC generator changes direction twice with each turn of the armature. This means that if such a two-pole machine were used as a source of alternating current, it would only produce one cycle for each turn of the armature. The automotive alternator usually has about 14 magnetic field poles and produces seven AC cycles for each rotation of the shaft. The most important fundamental difference between the automotive DC generator and its AC successor is that the field magnets rotate in the alternator while the current-producing windings stand still.

To avoid confusion, different terms are commonly used to describe the same parts of the alternator and the DC generator. The rotating part of an automotive generator is called the armature. The rotating part of an alternator is called its rotor. The rotor contains the magnetic field coil in an alternator. The stationary windings of the alternator, which correspond to the armature windings in a generator, are called the stator. Since the rotor forms the magnetic field in an alternator, it only needs to be supplied with a steady source of direct current from the battery. It has no segmented commutator such as that found in generators, but only two smooth brass slip rings. The slip rings have brushes riding against them—one supplying the field coil with current of positive polarity and the other providing a negative ground connection. The voltage output of the automotive alternator is quite low and does not present the danger of flash-over between the slip rings.

Since the windings in the stator are producing alternating current, and direct current is needed to charge the battery, a means of rectifying the current output is necessary. It is much simpler to couple the stator windings to the rectifying diodes than it would be to connect diodes to the rotating windings by means of multiple brushes.

CURRENT CHARACTERISTICS

Alternating current can be transmitted over a single wire and used in conjunction with a common ground, whereas direct current requires two conductors of opposite polarity. Since the electrical

power results from a constant reversal of flow and polarity rather than from the unidirectional flow of direct current, the alternator's stator coils need only one wire between them and each pair of diodes.

For maximum efficiency, it is desirable that the wave form of AC voltage be a sine wave—the voltage pattern giving the smoothest transition, fastest rise, and longest peak possible from the alternator's rotary motion. Wave form is controlled by the spacing and winding lengths of the stator coils and by the air gap between the poles of the stator and rotor. Commercial power generators normally produce 60 cycles per second, which is still rather "peaky" in its voltage levels for maximum power. Automotive alternators are of single-phase construction since they produce current in the neighborhood of 3000–3500 cycles per second, even at idle speeds. This may increase to as much as 50,000 cycles at top engine rpm. With this number of voltage peaks being reached each second, ample power is available to handle the electrical system's demands.

The use of the alternator has also made it possible greatly to simplify the regulator. Although alternator voltage output is, like that of the generator, proportional to rpm and field strength, its current output (amperage) is much more stable. In addition, since it produces nearly maximum current at low speeds, the voltage-regulating function has a more uniform requirement throughout the engine's speed range. Some of the first alternator systems employed a regulator not very different from those used with DC generator systems, but developments in both alternator design and regulator construction have served to simplify and miniaturize the regulator to the point that many cars no longer even have a separate regulator, but only a small transistorized regulating device incorporated into the alternator itself. Now that solid-state electronic components have become an economical alternative to electromagnetic relays, transistorized regulating circuits have grown in popularity with car makers. In a properly maintained electrical system, such units have an indefinite service life, whereas all-relay-type regulators sooner or later begin to suffer from burning and deterioration of their contact points.

Unfortunately, some transistorized regulators can't stand booster-battery starts. When a booster battery is removed after starting a car with a dead battery, the voltage will shoot up to such a high value that it kills the transistor in the regulator. This can be avoided by turning on all the accessories and lights in the car before disconnecting the booster battery, but very few drivers and fewer emergency road servicemen know this.

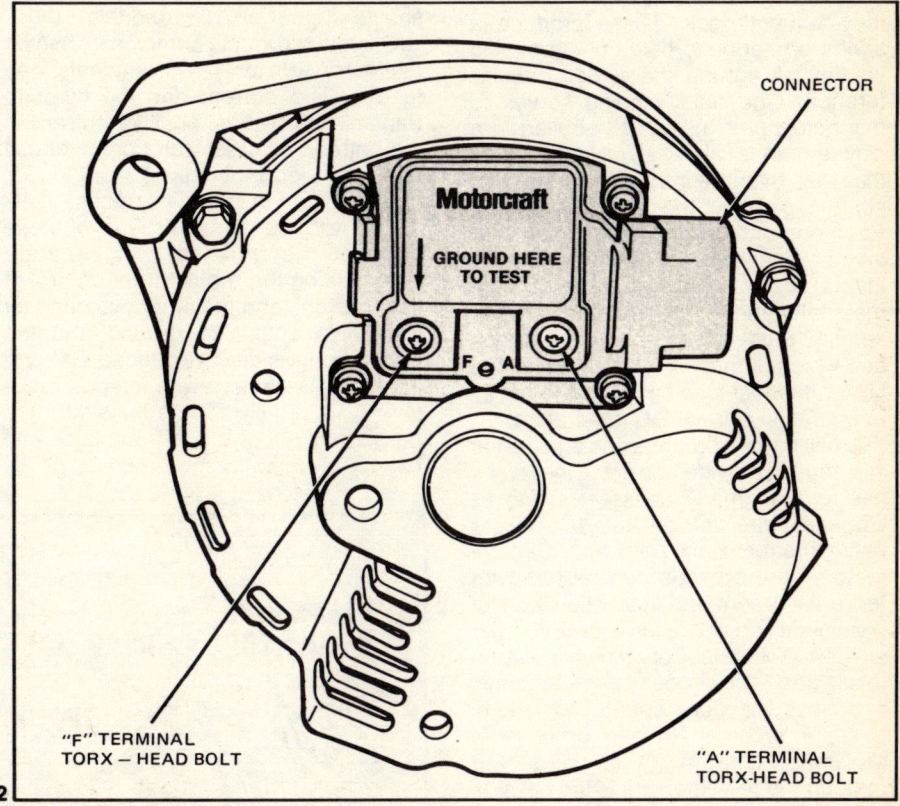

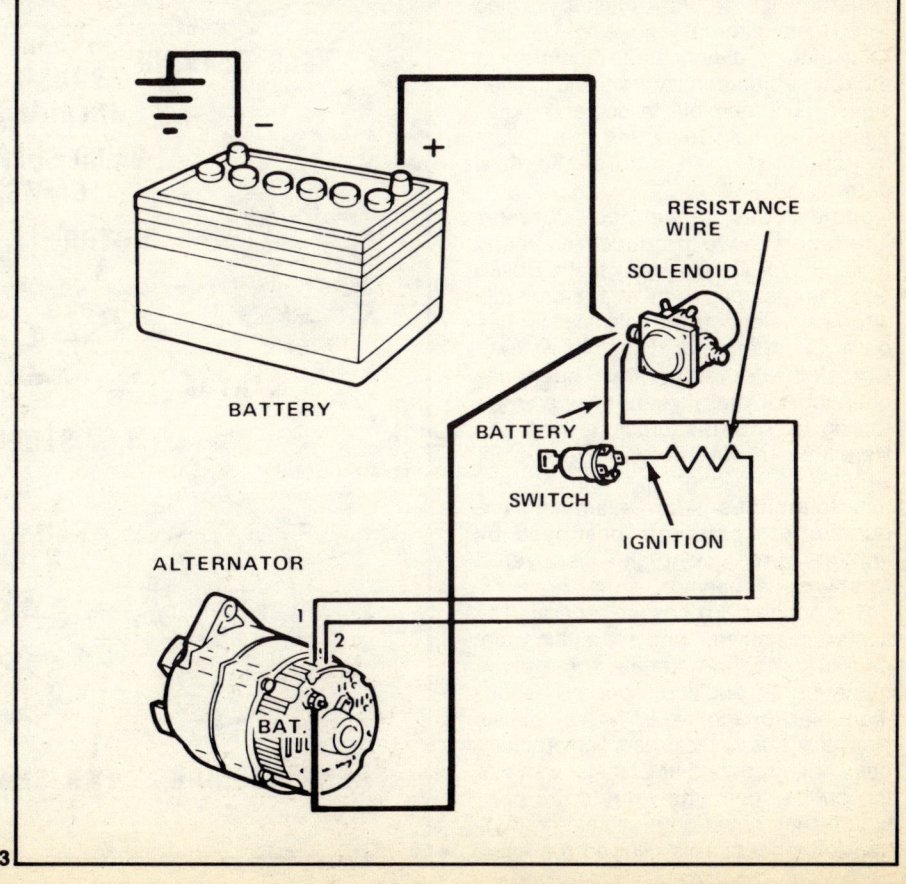

1. Alternators used with air conditioned Escort/Lynx 1.6L engines use an air duct to keep the diodes cool. Note the fan shield (arrow) at the front of the unit—one of Ford's "better ideas" to keep your fingers intact.

2. Ford made the move to an alternator-mounted regulator on air conditioned 1984 2.3L engines installed in Tempo/Topaz models. The "F" terminal is grounded to full-field the alternator. Note the use of Torx-head bolts. These require a special Torx driver for removal.

3. The AMC version of GM's charging system runs the No. 2 lead through a Ford starter solenoid.

ALTERNATORS

CONSTRUCTION

One of the most striking features of alternator construction is the simplicity of the rotor. The field poles are two—usually identical—starlike pieces of mild steel having their points bent over so that they will interlock. These produce a series of magnetic poles of alternating polarity all around the rotor's circumference. One field winding serves to magnetize both poles. It is coiled in a simple manner about an insulated spool that slips over the iron core on the rotor shaft separating the two pole pieces. Each end of the rotor's coil attaches to an individual slip ring, both of which are insulated from the rotor shaft. The materials and their layout in the assembly produce an extremely strong unit which is much better able to stand high rotational loadings than the armature used in normal DC generators.

Small carbon brushes ride against the slip rings to provide current to the rotor's field coil. In many units—including all Chrysler alternators and the larger options offered by Ford and General Motors—the brushes can be removed for replacement and inspection without disassembling the alternator. Even the smaller GM Delcotron, which must be taken apart for access to the brushes, has these vital components mounted in a separate brush holder for ease in servicing. One brush is connected through the regulator unit to the hot side of the battery. The other is placed in contact with ground—often by being wired to the alternator housing. The field relay in the regulator shuts off current to the rotor automatically when the ignition switch is turned off. In some designs, there is no field relay and the ignition switch must then control the field current.

Incidentally, late-model Chrysler alternators have produced so many problems for the company that a Bosch alternator is used in most 1984 models while Chrysler puts the finishing touches on a new alternator design of its own. Chrysler alternators have been unchanged for many years now, and the tooling used to manufacture them has literally worn out—at least to the point where it can no longer maintain satisfactory tolerances. After examining the number of computers destroyed by voltage surges, Chrysler discovered what was happening.

The copper slip rings are separated by a plastic insulator and the cutting tool cannot cut both materials to the same tolerance. In addition, copper is softer than plastic and wears more readily. Normally, this would present no problem, but what happened at Chrysler was that the cutting tools had worn to the point where they could not maintain production tolerances. This allowed the alternator brushes to ride partially on the copper slip ring and partially on the plastic. As the rotor turned, the brushes would "chatter" or bounce, causing momentary voltage arcing or "spikes." This brief but hot shot could affect the computer's operation in some cases and wipe it out in others. Rather than simply retool, Chrysler opted to design a new and more efficient alternator, which should appear on 1985 models.

Chrysler products commonly have an alternator with only two terminals, one for the field current and the other to transmit the diodes' positive current to the battery. All other parts of the circuit are grounded internally. Ford and GM cars employ, in most instances, alternators with four terminals. Two of these connect the brushes with separate terminals on the regulator for control of field current, and the other two connect the unit's output to ground and the battery's hot side. Even those GM and FoMoCo alternators with integral regulator units require four terminals for the purpose of supplying the regulator with battery current.

Like the armature of the DC automotive generator, the stator of most alternators is built up from many laminations, which in turn hold the windings in place. Although the stator windings appear to be complex, they're really nothing but coils overlapping one another in a simple chain pattern. At the present time, all common automotive alternators have their stator coils in multiples of three, such as 12, 18, 24, etc. These are linked together into three basic interconnected circuits which feed current from their juncture points to the three rectifier diode pairs.

Since the frame—or housing—of the alternator has no function in the magnetic field of the unit, it's not necessary to construct it of a ferrous metal. Aluminum, lightweight sheet metal, and various other light alloys are commonly used for this purpose. This tends to make the comparative weight of an alternator much less than that of a DC generator. The housing serves principally to hold the stator in place, provide a mounting point for the unit, and supply bearing support for the rotor. As with the

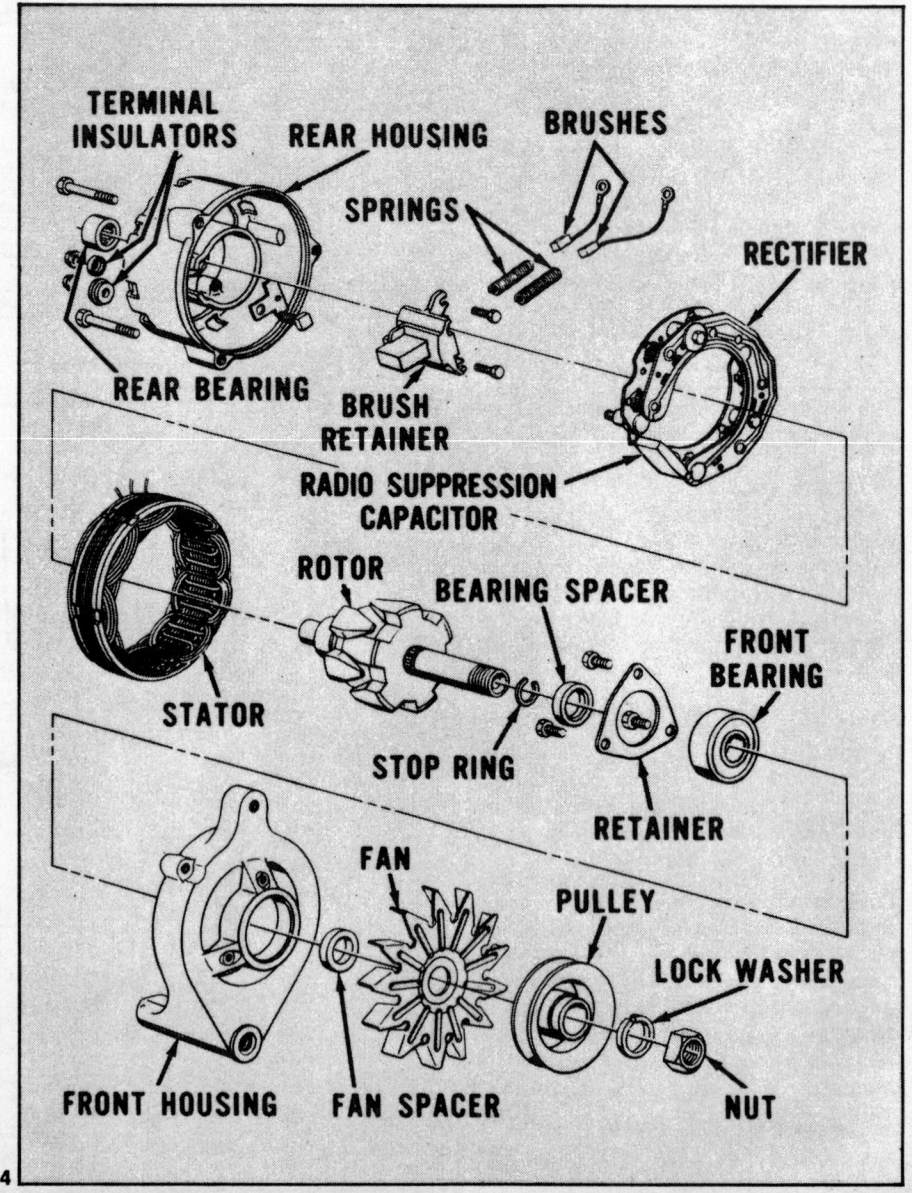

136/IGNITION & ELECTRICAL SYSTEMS

generator, ample openings are allowed for the passage of cooling air and a fan is incorporated into the rotor and shaft assembly to improve its circulation. The bearings which support the rotor shaft are of the permanently lubricated ball bearing type in most cases, although plain or needle bearings prepacked with lubricant are common on the smaller units at the brush end. This serves to make the alternator virtually service-free and is in keeping with the trend toward longer service intervals for passenger cars.

Perhaps the only unique factor in automotive alternator design is the use of rectifying diodes that are self-contained parts of the unit. Rectifying diodes are a simple type of transistor that have the unique property of permitting electrical current to flow through them in only one direction. As mentioned in another chapter, such a diode was commonly used in early transistorized ignition systems to prevent current backflow from arcing across the breaker points or damaging the switching transistor. The Motorola alternator formerly supplied on American Motors cars had an additional "isolating" diode for similar reasons and was not necessary to the production of an electrical current.

There are six rectifying diodes in the alternator that are supplied with alternating current from the stator windings. Three of these diodes permit the passage of negative polarity current and three allow only positive current to pass. Alternating current leaves the alternator windings and goes directly to the six diodes. Three of the diodes feed current to the battery and electrical parts of the car. The other three diodes are grounded in the alternator, and act as a return path for the electricity that has done its work at the battery, lights, and accessories.

The windings of the stator overlap and the voltage peaks produced by the three diode pairs also overlap. However, their output is fed into a common wire so that the end result is either positive or negative current of relatively uniform voltage. Much has been made of diodes as the weak point in an alternator system, but there is no reason to regard them as such—ignorance is usually responsible when they are damaged. The two conditions to which diodes are most susceptible are heat and reversed polarity.

To protect them against excessively high temperatures, diodes are generally mounted in some type of heat sink. This is usually an aluminum casting—often one that is finned for better heat dissipation—which is mounted by a thin "neck" that allows little heat to be conducted to the diodes from other parts of the alternator. A far more damaging source of heat results if improper procedures are used when the lead wires of new diodes are soldered into place. To solder safely the diode leads, a heat dam (a small metal clamp that absorbs excess heat) must be clipped onto the diode wire during the soldering operation. This is seldom a problem with the unit in normal service, but in cases where mechanics have attempted to remove a bad diode by hammering rather than by pressing it out of the case, the shock of the blows will often destroy the other diodes in the assembly as well. In all fairness, alternators present far fewer troubles than generators ever did.

As a final word of caution, never continue to drive a car that has an evident charging system trouble. Should the problem be a loose connection that opens the charging circuit, unregulated current of the wrong polarity may be allowed to enter the battery or the alternator diodes. Nor should you ever short across or ground any of the terminals on a regulator or an alternator—even though such practices are part of the troubleshooting routine used with generator systems.

QUICK-CHECK TROUBLESHOOTING

Brushes last a good deal longer on an alternator than on a generator, but they can wear out eventually. The quickest way to check for this trouble is to pull the field connection off, since it is usually in

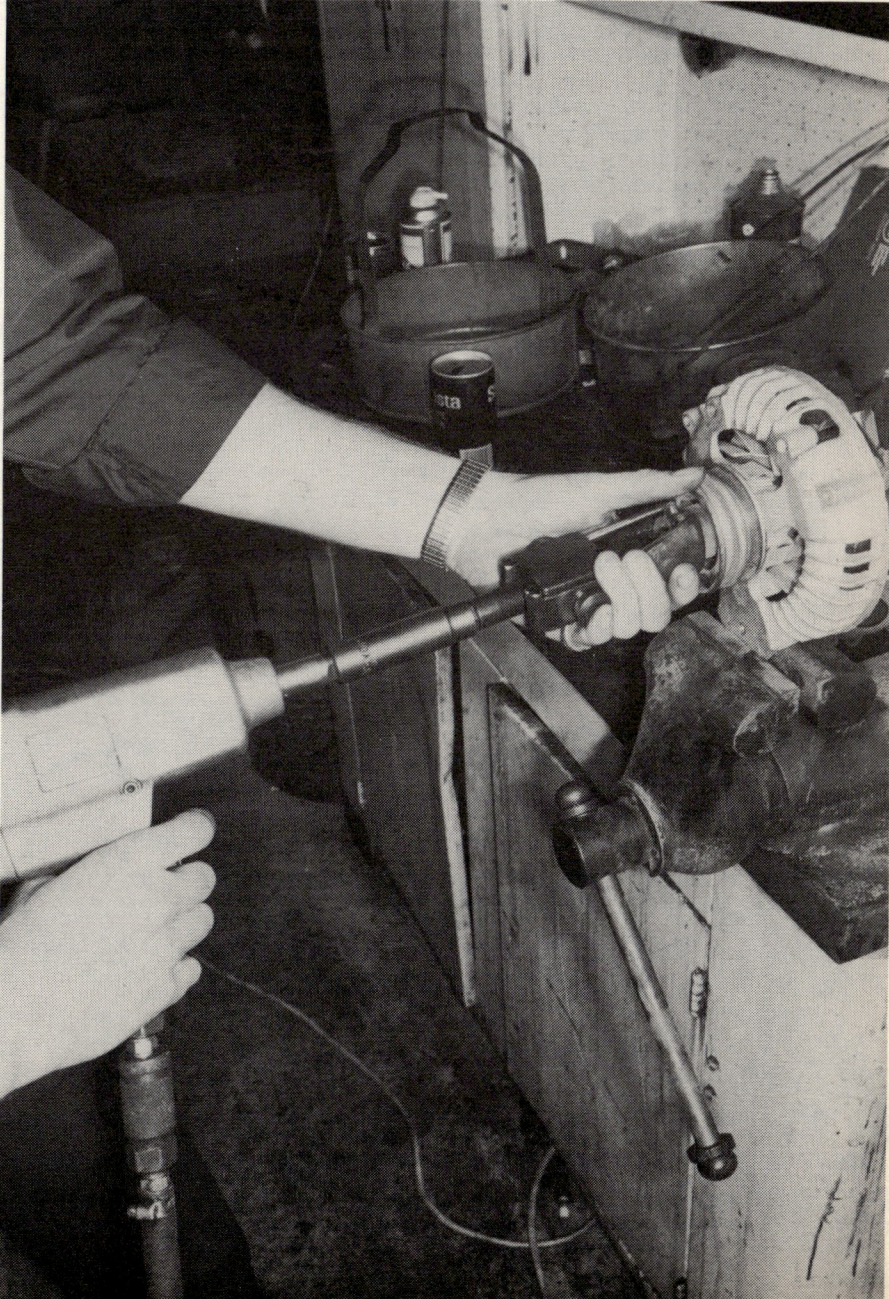

4. A mid-Seventies Ford alternator uses brushes that are separate from the diode (rectifier) plate. If one diode burns out, replace them all.

5. Alternator pulley removal is a real chore on Chrysler units, requiring the use of a special puller.

ALTERNATORS

the form of a plug connector. The "F" terminal, uncovered by pulling the plug, is the one leading to the insulated brush. Using an ohmmeter with the selector set on the X10 position—or a 110-volt bulb with two test probes—it's possible to check the circuit through the brushes and field windings for continuity, with the engine off. Touch the test probes to the field terminal and ground, and the ohmmeter should register little measurable resistance (or the test lamp should light). If considerable resistance or a reading of infinity is indicated, or if the bulb fails to light at all, there is probably poor contact between the brushes and the slip rings. Actual resistance of the field winding can be as high as 12 ohms, depending upon the design. However, you're not interested in the resistance value as much as in finding a bad connection or broken wire, which would be indicated by a very high reading on the ohmmeter.

On some of the alternators used by Chrysler, it's possible to remove the brush holders individually. Sometimes the unit can be made to charge temporarily by wiggling the brush holders with the engine running. When this happens, it's a sure indicator that the brushes need attention. On most other alternators, the housing will have to come apart to get at the brushes should an initial ohmmeter check indicate potential poor contact. Once this is done, it's possible to duplicate the test at the slip rings. If the windings are intact, the trouble has to be caused by worn-out or sticking brushes.

If the brushes are making good contact and the rotor windings are also okay, the diodes should be tested. This is not difficult once the housing is apart, but the diode leads must be disconnected. The diodes can then be tested either with a 3-volt battery-powered test light, or an ohmmeter or "VOM" containing a 1.5-volt battery. Higher voltage should never be used since it will ruin the diodes. The test lead probes are touched to the wire and the case of each disconnected diode, and then reversed to check current flow in the opposite direction. A good diode will light the lamp or produce a low resistance reading in one direction, but not in the other. If both readings are about equal—high or low—or if the light will (or will not) light in either direction, the diode is definitely bad.

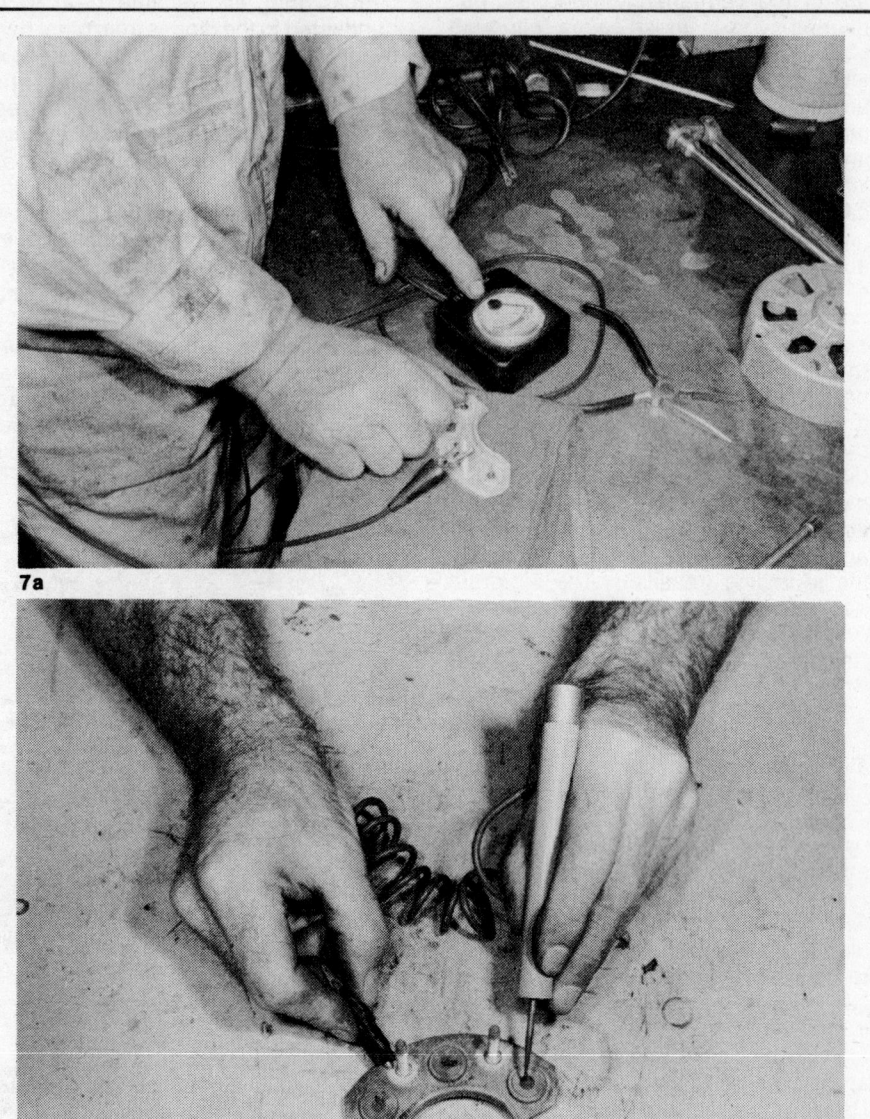

7a

7b

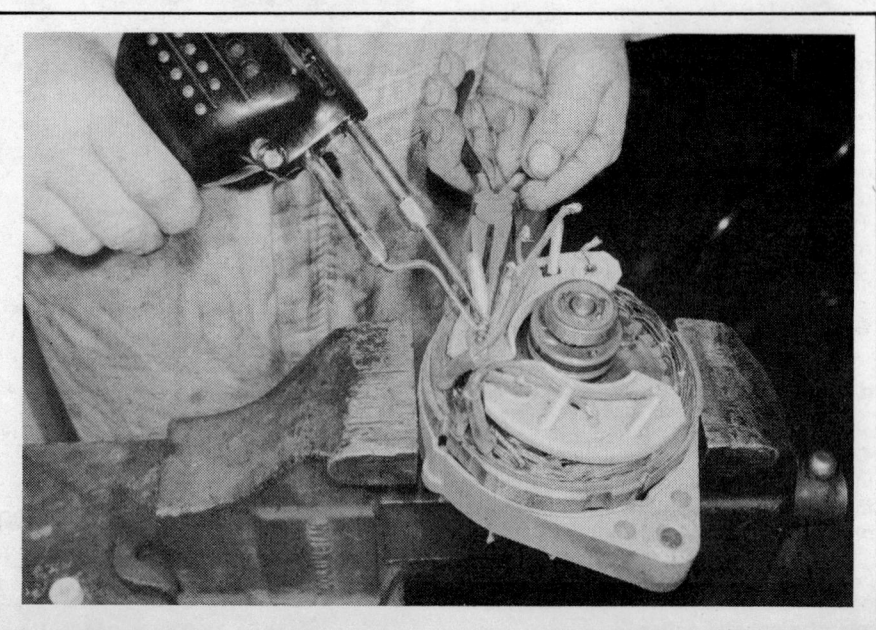

6

8

138/IGNITION & ELECTRICAL SYSTEMS

Individual diodes can be replaced in some cases, but it's often more practical (and in some cases, mandatory) to replace the entire heat sink in which the diodes are mounted.

An even faster on-the-car check can be carried out by disconnecting the battery ground cable and taking ohmmeter readings in both directions across the output and ground terminals of the unit. Test results will be similar to tests of individual diodes, but will not pinpoint which diodes are faulty. In the case of late-model alternators that require replacement of the entire diode trio, it is necessary to pinpoint not the exact diode that's faulty, but simply the trio that is not working properly. Many garages have a diode tester. This is a small unit that tests the diodes after the alternator is taken apart, but without disconnecting the individual diode leads.

There is also the possibility that the rotor has developed serious problems. Grounded windings can be detected merely by testing between the slip rings and the rotor shaft. There must be absolutely no electrical contact between these parts. Grounds in the stator windings can be found only by disconnecting the coil leads from the diode terminals and testing between one of the wires and the stator frame. A higher voltage is necessary for this, and most electrical shops use 110-volt house current and a regular light bulb for such testing. If the lamp lights when the test leads are applied, the stator windings are grounded. Shorts in the stator are difficult to detect, unless you have special equipment. However, if everything is okay and alternator output still remains low, shorted stator windings are probably at the root of the problem. Some alternators have a condenser

6. Here's how you remove the rotor bearing without damaging the rotor shaft.

7A and 7B. Diodes can be checked either with a diode tester (A) or a self-powered test lamp (B). In either case, they should pass current in one direction only.

8. If any heat must be applied near the diodes, as when connecting/disconnecting the leads with a soldering gun, use pliers as a heat sink to avoid diode damage.

9A and 9B. The diode trio used in Motorola positive diode plates (A) can burn out. When it does, here's what you'll find after removing the plate from the alternator (B).

10. Drive belt tension is important. Too much tension and you'll wear the bearing out prematurely; too little and the battery won't charge properly.

11. It's a good idea to periodically check drive belt condition. Replace any that look like this and you'll avoid an expensive and possibly damaging breakdown on the road.

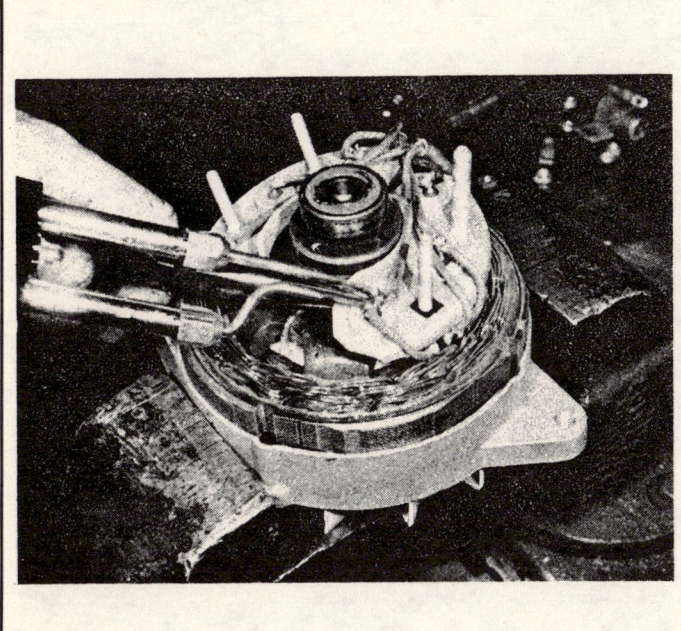
9a

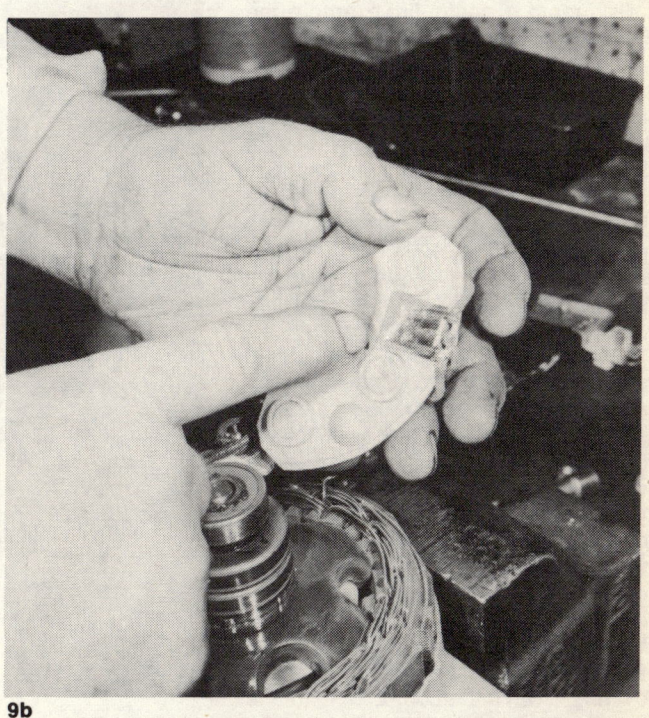
9b

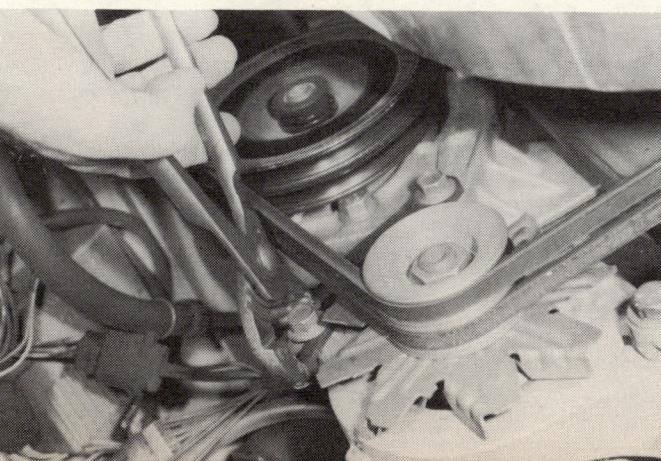
10

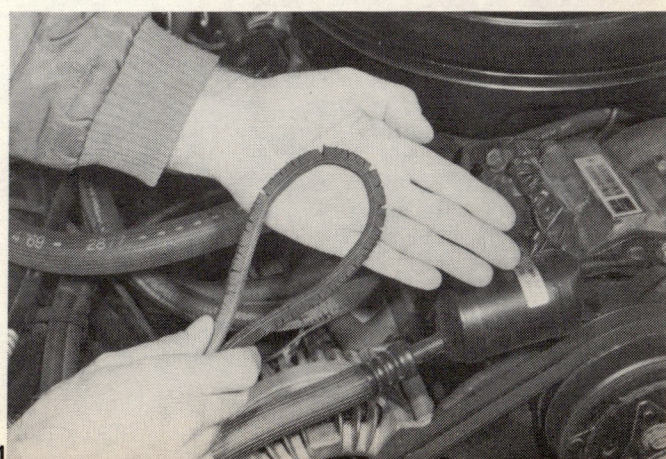
11

which can cause problems, but this can be tested with a condenser tester.

ALTERNATOR FACTS

With the trend in recent years toward loading the electrical system with more and more current-consuming accessories, the drain on the battery can become acute in city traffic, where a great deal of time is spent with the engine idling at traffic signals, and speeds are generally below 25 miles per hour. Even without such electrical extras as tape decks, power windows, and four-way seats, an alternator is almost a must under such driving conditions, unless the driver forgoes the pleasures of radio music and air-conditioning.

The alternator's greatest virtue is the fact that it can charge at idle. Furthermore, extra-high-output alternators can be supplied as options on "loaded" cars. Such heavy-duty alternators will fit into just about the same amount of space as the standard dynamo. For example, the standard 40- and 42-amp alternators supplied on Fords and Mercurys can be replaced with a 60- or 65-amp unit to handle extra electrical equipment. The standard 37-amp Delcotron on GM cars can be replaced with units of 42- or 62-amp ratings for more heavily laden electrical systems. Chrysler products are generally equipped with alternators ranging from little 26-amp units on stripped models to 40-amp or larger jobs on special-equipment models.

When building a hot rod or adding custom electrical accessories to any car, you should consider upgrading the charging system for the sake of increased capacity. This is basically a three-part undertaking. The first step is to obtain a higher-rated battery, which is an absolute must if you expect to gain the full value of the charging system improvements. As a second step, the alternator must not only be switched for one of greater output, but also be exchanged for one that matches the new unit. Even if the components of the new system come from the same make and model car as yours, it will not always be possible merely to switch the two major components, since the wiring between them may differ. This is particularly true of Ford products that use Ford-built alternators for most standard models, and Leece-Neville 42-, 60-, and 65-amp units on special-equipment models. The regulators have a different number of terminals and are wired into the electrical system in different ways. The only way the job can be done is to consult the electrical schematic diagrams in factory service manuals. If the systems differ significantly, you must plan on rewiring the connections to suit the plan for the larger unit.

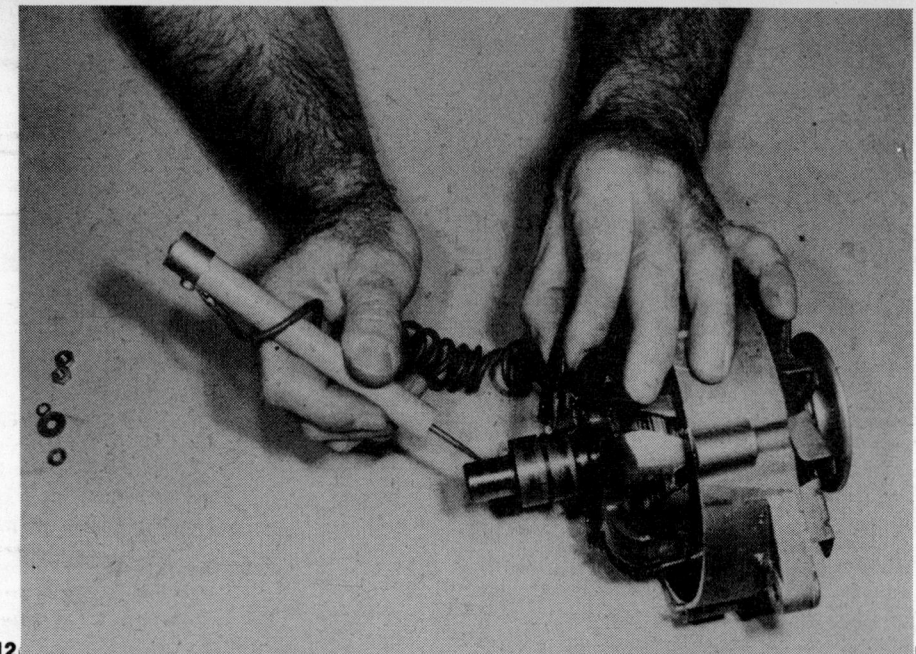
12

13

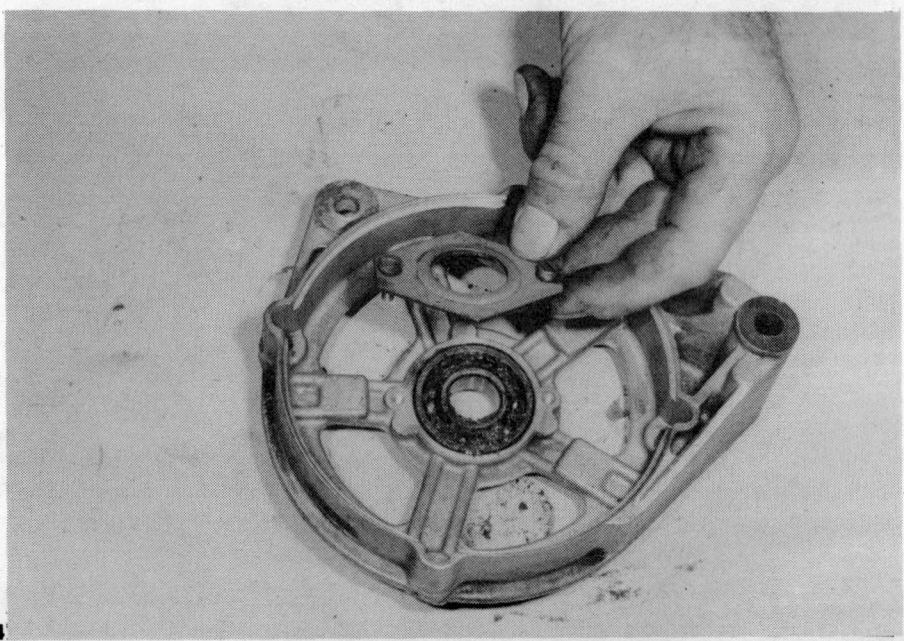
14

If most of your driving is done in the warmer areas of the country, the standard charging system is probably adequate, even if you add quite a few accessories—at least on the average domestic car. Your battery won't be fighting the debilitating cold or suffering the rigors of winter starting, and you probably won't be using the heater very much either. It's when you add several voltage-consuming extras that a revamping of the charging system will very likely pay off.

On the whole, the alternator is a much more satisfactory piece of hardware than the generator, and nobody should long for the "good old days." The increased electrical system reliability alone is well worth any changes in service procedures that mechanics have had to learn, and alternators have been with us long enough now for every shop to understand them fully. The most interesting thing is not that the DC generator has disappeared from the automotive scene, but that it didn't happen sooner.

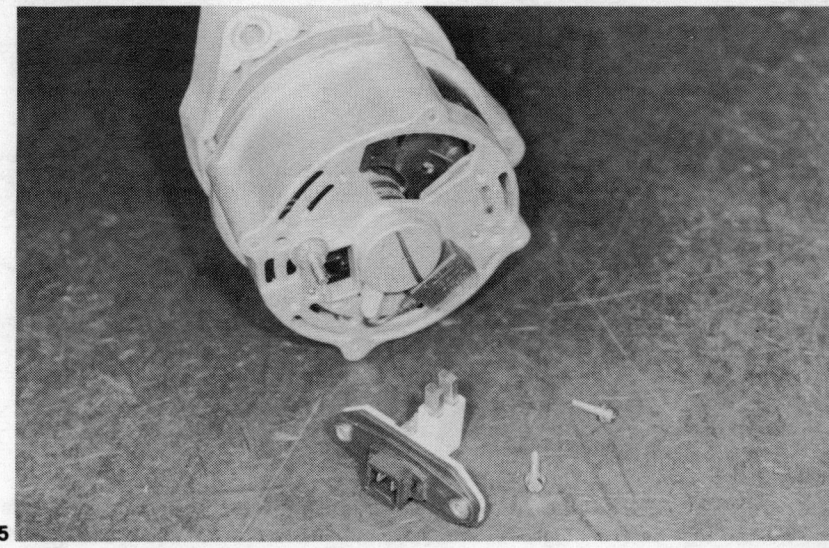

12. Continuity test for a rotor. The light should come on. Also make a ground and current draw test to be sure the rotor is good.

13. Check each stator lead combination as shown to determine if the windings are open or grounded, then connect each stator lead to the frame through the test lamp to check for grounds.

14. End frame bearings can be pressed out and replaced with new ones on some alternators. Newest models require the purchase of a new end frame if the bearing is bad.

15. The Bosch alternator used on Volkswagens has found its way to 1984 Chrysler products. Brush holder comes out from the rear by removing two screws.

16. Brushes in the GM SI alternator design fit into a holder installed over the regulator and require partial alternator disassembly to replace. Be sure to install insulator screws as shown.

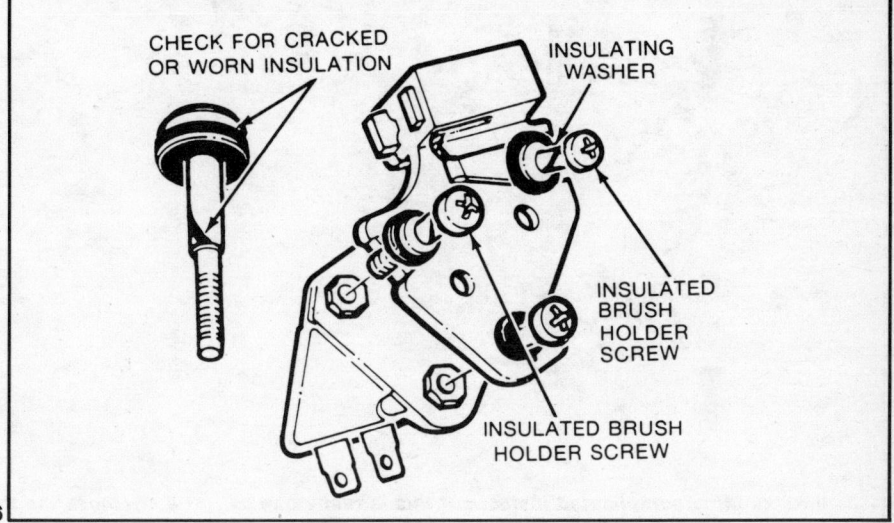

HOW-TO: ALTERNATOR OVERHAUL

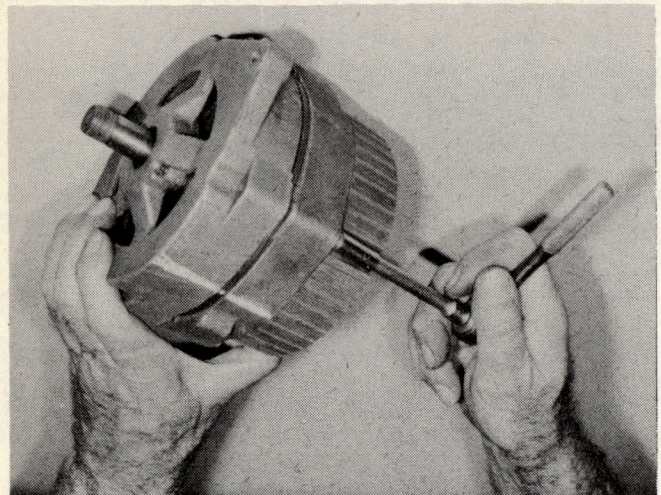

1. The 10-SI Delcrotron is typical of GM alternators used in the past decade. Begin overhaul by scribing a reference mark across the end frames and then remove the through-bolts.

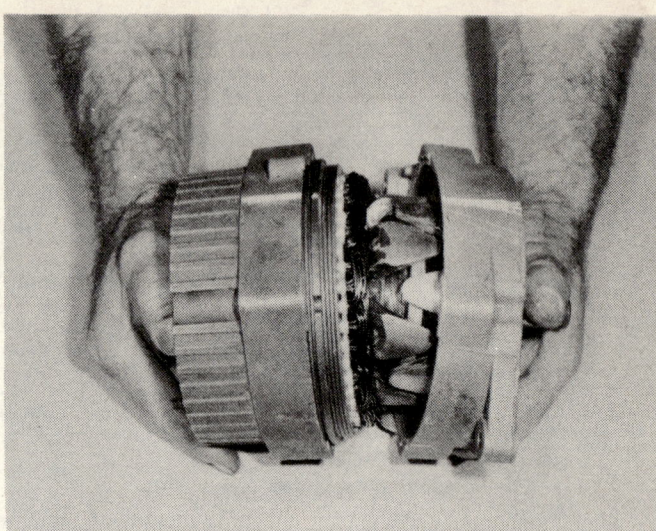

2. The slip ring end frame and stator should separate easily from the rotor end frame. If not, insert a screwdriver at each side of the stator slot and pry apart carefully.

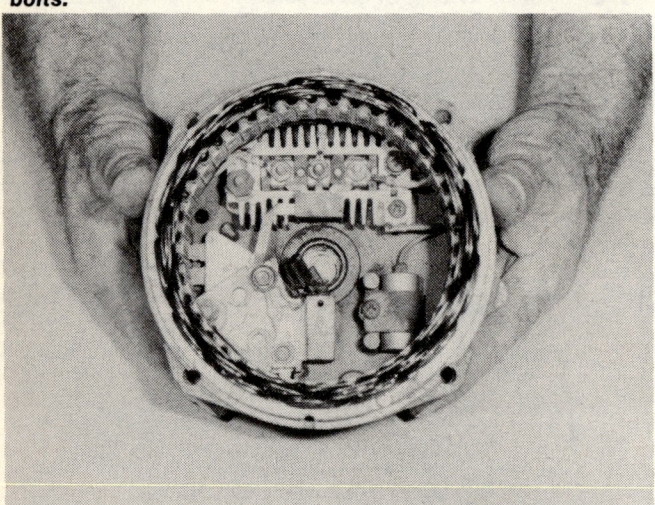

3. It looks fairly complicated inside, but this is really one of the easiest alternators to work on. Use this photo as a reference to check your work when reassembly is completed.

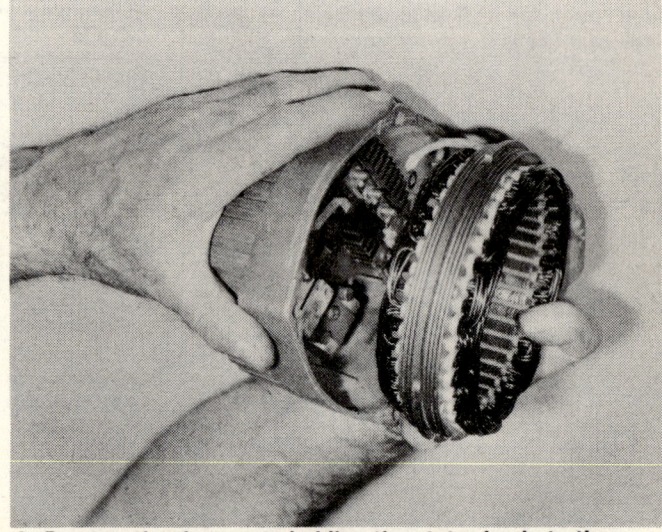

4. Remove the three nuts holding the stator leads to the heat sink; then lift the stator off the end frame and place to one side on a solid surface for testing.

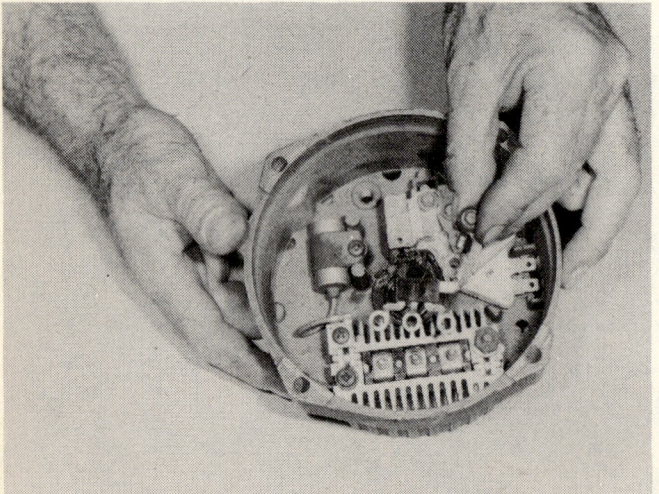

5. Remove the screw holding the diode trio to the brush holder assembly and remove trio from end frame. Diode trio can be checked for a grounded brush lead clip at this time.

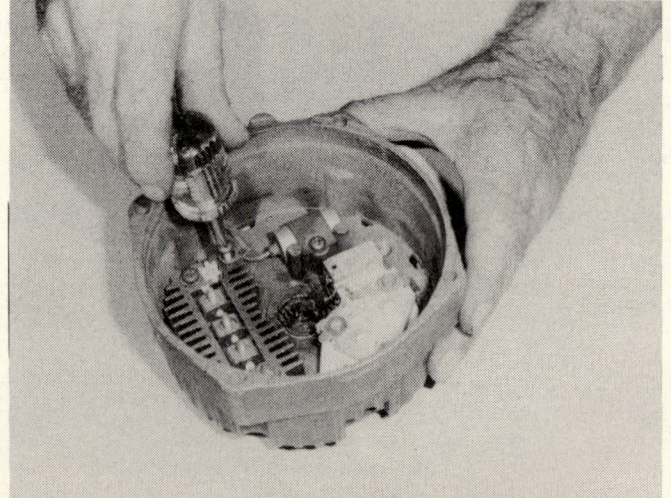

6. Disconnect the capacitor lead from the heat sink and then remove the capacitor. The capacitor should be tested before reinstallation in the end frame.

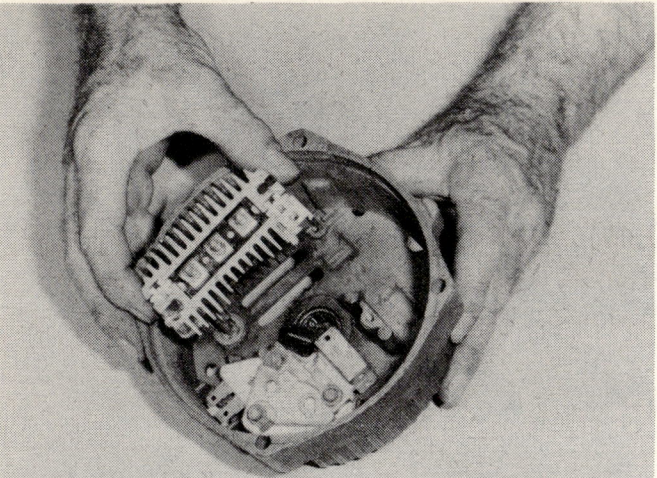

7. Now remove the rectifier bridge attaching screw and the BAT terminal screw, lifting the rectifier bridge from the end frame. Keep track of the different screws as they are removed.

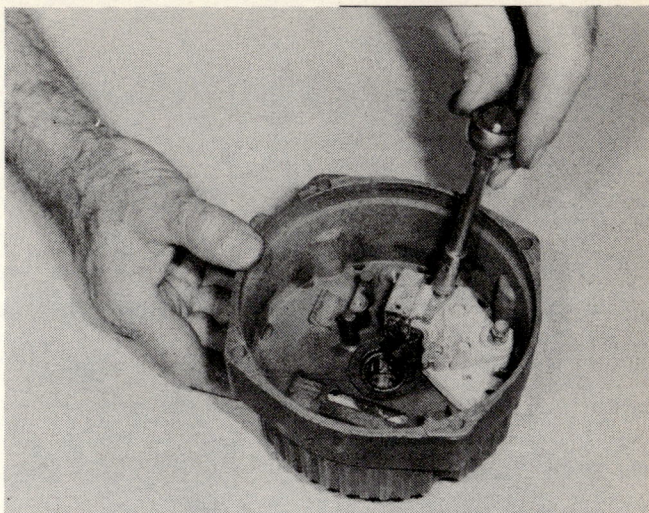

8. Remove two screws holding the brush holder and integral regulator assembly. Two insulators are assembled over the top of the brush retaining clips; the screws have sleeves.

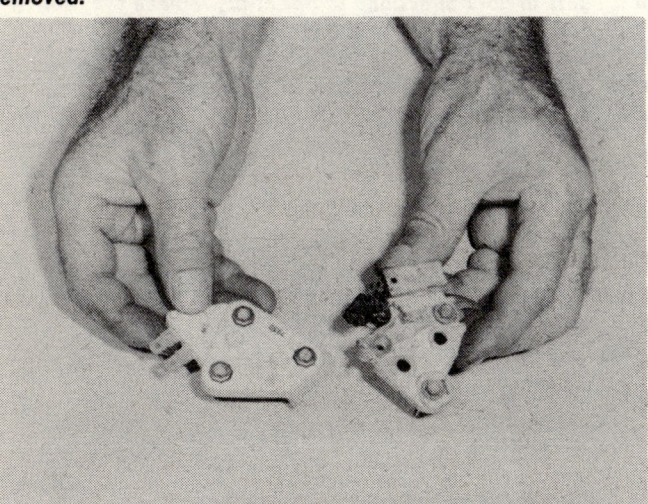

9. Separate the regulator from the brush holder. Remove brush springs and set them aside. Inspect brushes for excessive wear and replace if necessary. Always replace in pairs.

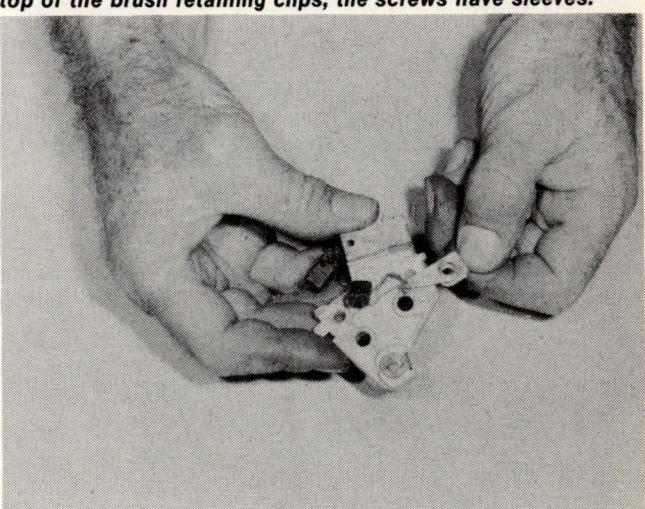

10. Both brush assemblies are identical and simply slip off the holder. Brush leads are connected to brush assemblies and the entire unit is replaced by slipping a new one in place.

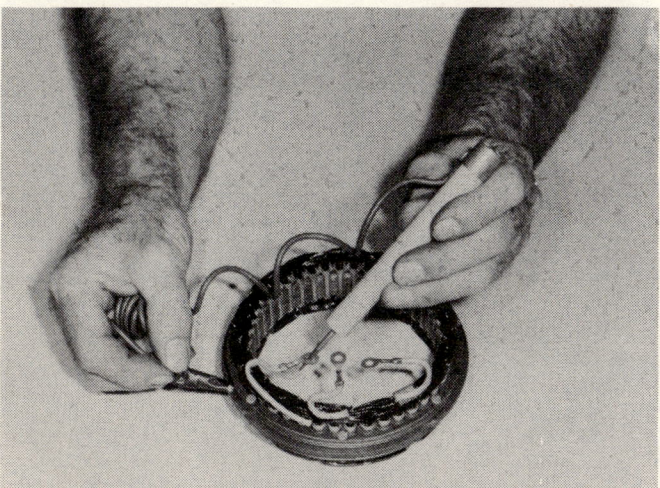

11. Test stator for ground by touching one lead of test lamp or ohmmeter to stator frame and other lead to one stator lead. If lamp lights or ohmmeter reads low, discard the stator.

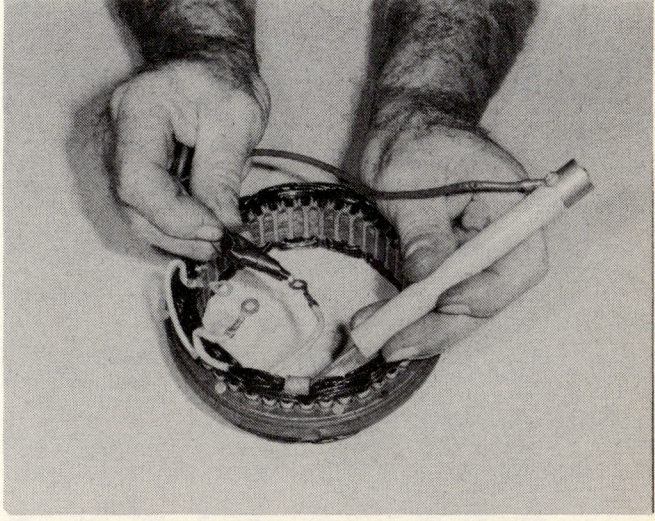

12. Test the stator for opens as shown here, moving alligator clip from one lead to another. If lamp lights or ohmmeter reads low, discard the stator.

IGNITION & ELECTRICAL SYSTEMS/143

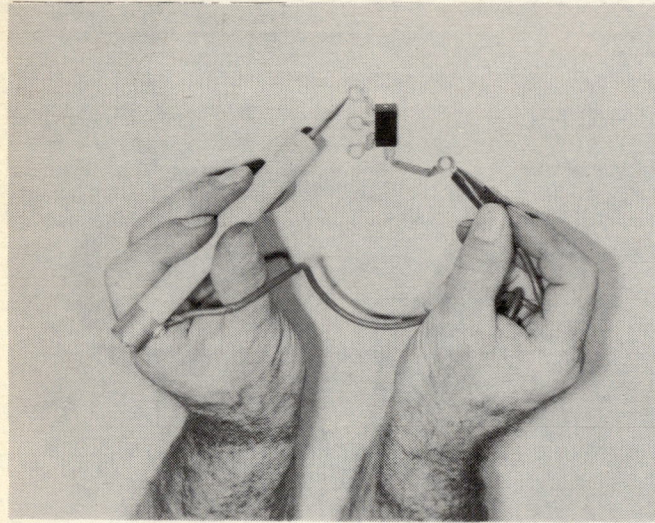

13. To test diode trio, connect one test lamp lead to the single connector and the other lead to any one of the three connectors. Note whether or not lamp lights.

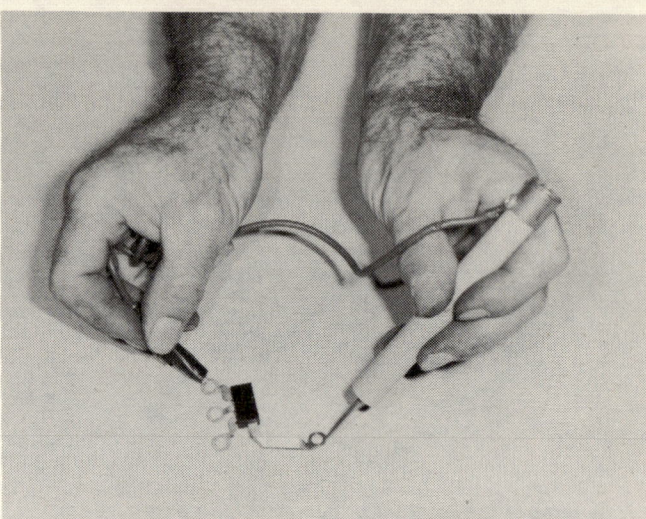

14. Reverse test leads on same connectors and note lamp reaction. It should light in one direction only if trio is good. If it lights in both directions or not at all, replace the trio.

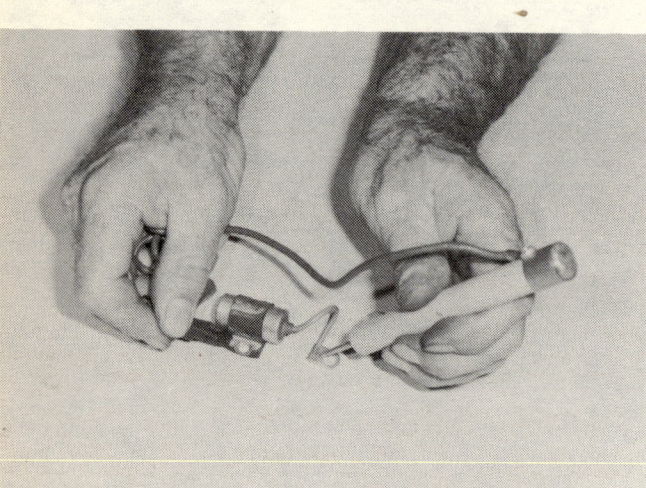

15. The capacitor can also be tested with the same test lamp. It should not light if the unit is satisfactory. If lamp does light, capacitor is shorted and should be replaced.

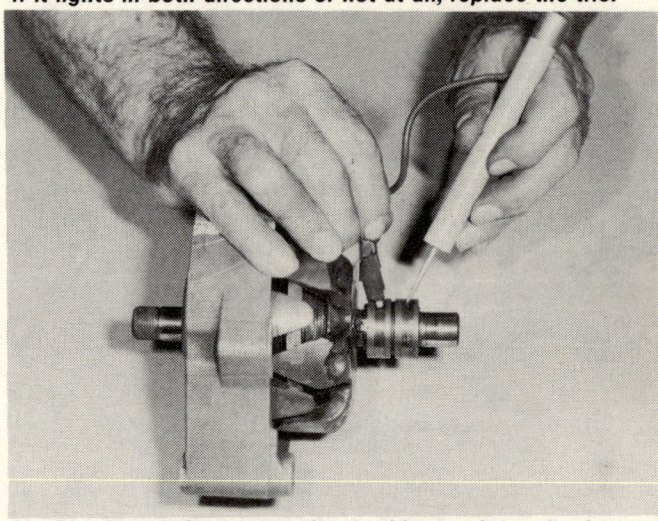

16. Check rotor for an open by touching each test lead to the slip rings as shown. The test lamp will light if windings are good. If an ohmmeter is used, it should give a high reading.

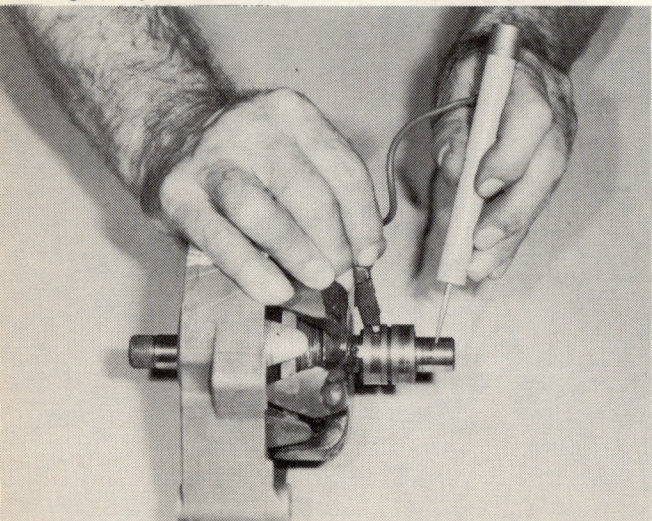

17. Test rotor for grounds by connecting the test lamp leads as shown. If ground is good, lamp will light. If slip rings require cleaning, use a fine polishing cloth and blow dry.

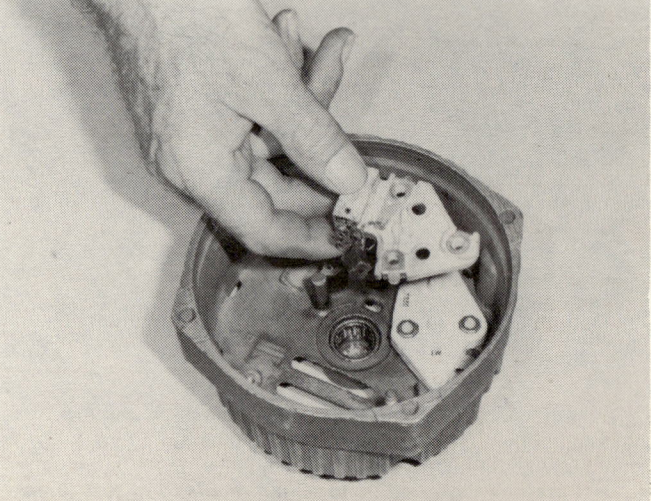

18. Begin reassembly by reinstalling regulator and brush holder. Regulator slips into position in end frame holder; two holes in brush holder fit over regulator studs.

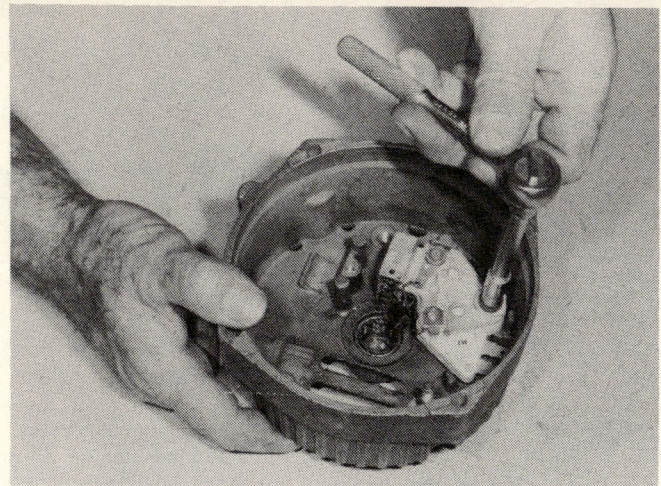

19. Before replacing brush holder screws, check insulating sleeves on each; be sure they're not cracked or damaged. The screw shown here may or may not have an insulating washer.

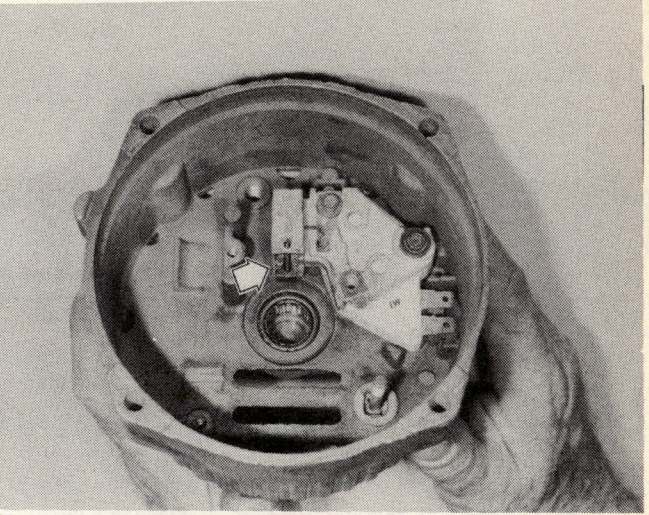

20. Install brush springs and fit brushes in holder. Insert a small drill bit or piece of stiff wire through a hole in the end frame (arrow) to keep the brushes in place.

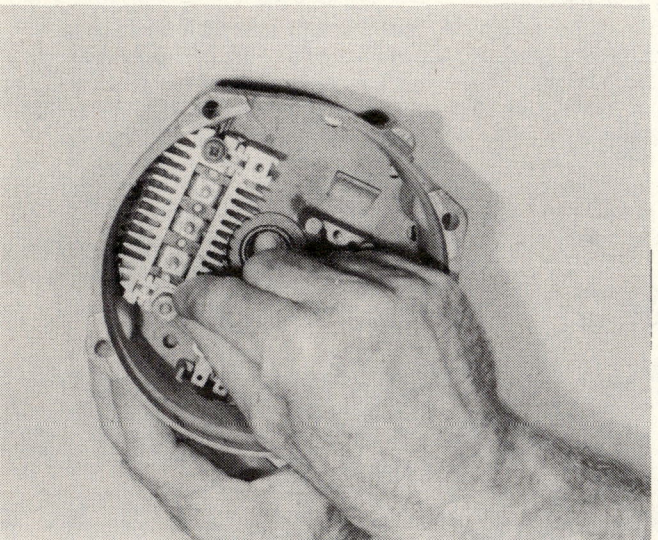

21. Install BAT terminal from rear, fit rectifier bridge over it and install retaining screw with insulator at the other end. Replace nut on BAT terminal, which holds left side of bridge.

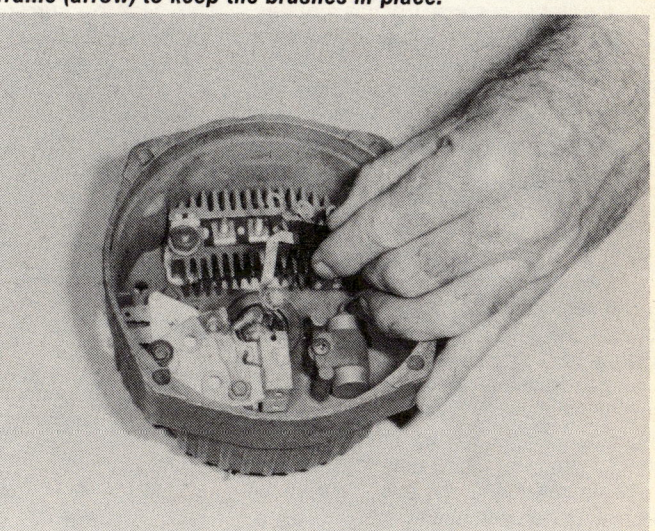

22. Reinstall capacitor, connect its lead to rectifier bridge and replace diode trio. Trio attaching screw must have an insulating sleeve. Trio leads fit over rectifier bridge terminals.

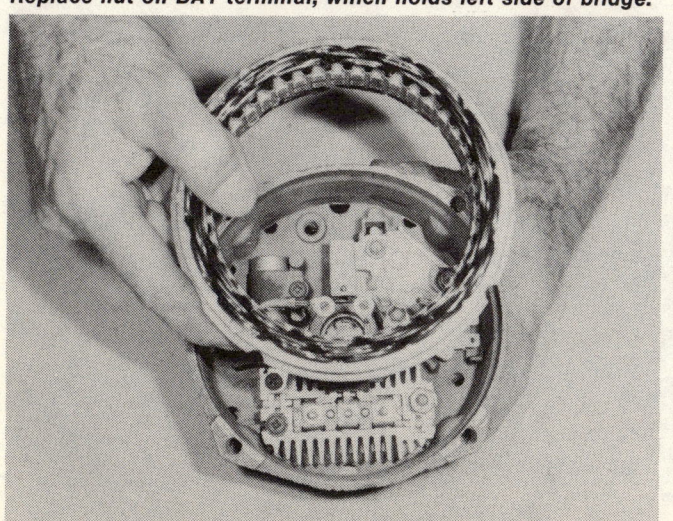

23. Stator is the final part to be replaced. Fit its leads over the rectifier bridge terminals and then seat the stator. Reinstall terminal attaching nuts.

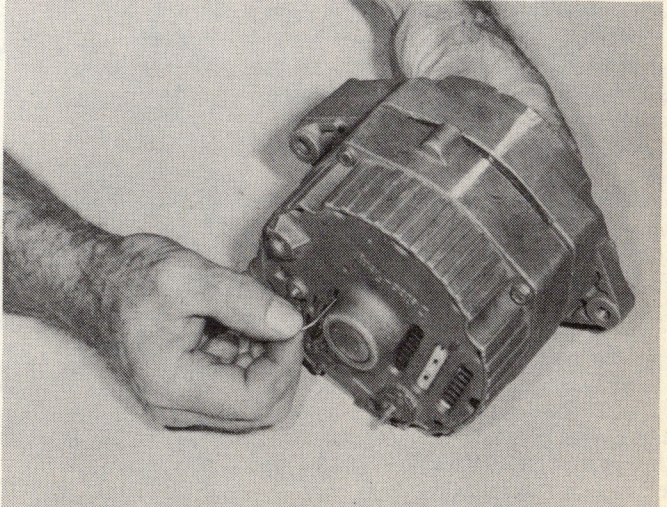

24. Align end frames according to scribed mark, fit together and install through-bolts. Remove drill bit or wire to allow brushes to contact slip rings. Your overhaul is complete.

REGULATORS

Fed a steady diet of raw current from the alternator, a battery would boil one moment from an overcharge and die the next under the burden of the electrical system's entire current load. When alternator output is adequate, the main load of the electrical system is carried solely by the generated current, with only the "surplus" being used to charge the battery—providing it needs it. It's only when the alternator output falls below the demands of the electrical system—or when the starter is in use—that the battery becomes the prime source of the car's electrical power. All of this requires a fine balance between charging system output and current demand. Making sure that the dynamo is neither putting out too much power nor draining the battery dry is the job of your automobile's regulator.

BATTERY-ALTERNATOR CIRCUITS

An alternator or generator alone would be an extremely poor power source for the automotive electrical system. First of all, it would not be able to provide current for starting, since electrical power is not produced unless the engine is already running. Even if it could generate electricity without the engine's mechanical power to turn it, such a generator would have to be a huge affair to supply the immense current demands of the starter motor. A battery alone would be a far better power source for an automotive electrical system than just an alternator, but the battery would have to be recharged quite frequently from some outside source. The ideal arrangement is for the battery and alternator to work together as partners, the battery carrying the load when the engine is not running, or running very slowly, and the charging system taking over the job as engine speed builds up.

Our accompanying diagrams show only the battery-alternator circuit. The details of the car's starting and electrical systems have been eliminated in the interests of clarity. The basic wiring diagram and circuit diagram show a General Motors system in which the regulator is built into the alternator housing. To add to the confusion of today's technical terms, GM refers to its alternator as an "AC Generator." The basic system is the same for all cars, even though Ford and Chrysler products have the regulator mounted separately from the alternator and call the alternator by its rightful name.

We show a system using a warning light, since most cars are unfortunately equipped that way today. When the system is turned on with the ignition switch, current from the battery flows through the light to the number one terminal on the alternator. This is part of the regulator circuit, and current flows through resistor R1, diode D1, and the base of transistor TR1 on its way back to the battery through the ground connection. This current flow turns the transistor on, allowing current to flow through the alternator field coil and the other side of TR1 before flowing back to the battery. A resistor in parallel with the indicator lamp reduces the total circuit resistance to provide a higher field current for initial voltage buildup when the engine starts. The powerful battery current that goes to the starter does not appear on either diagram, since it is electrically outside the charging circuit.

Once the engine is running and the alternator turning, AC voltages are produced in the stator winding in proportion to the movement of the rotor. The diodes in the rectifier change the alternating current across the BAT terminal and ground. As alternator speed increases, more voltage is provided for charging the battery and operating accessories.

With the alternator operating, the same voltage appears across the BAT terminal and the No. 1 terminal, and the indicator lamp goes out, showing that the alternator is producing voltage. The No. 2 terminal is also connected to the battery, but the high resistance of R2 and R3 limit the discharge current. As the speed of the alternator increases, and the voltage output increases, the increased voltage between R2 and R3 allows zener diode D2 to conduct, turning on transistor TR2. With TR1 off, system voltage decreases, until TR2 turns off again and TR1 turns back on, increasing the voltage again. This cycle repeats many times per second, keeping output voltage to a predetermined value.

The other elements of the system shown include a capacitor to smooth out

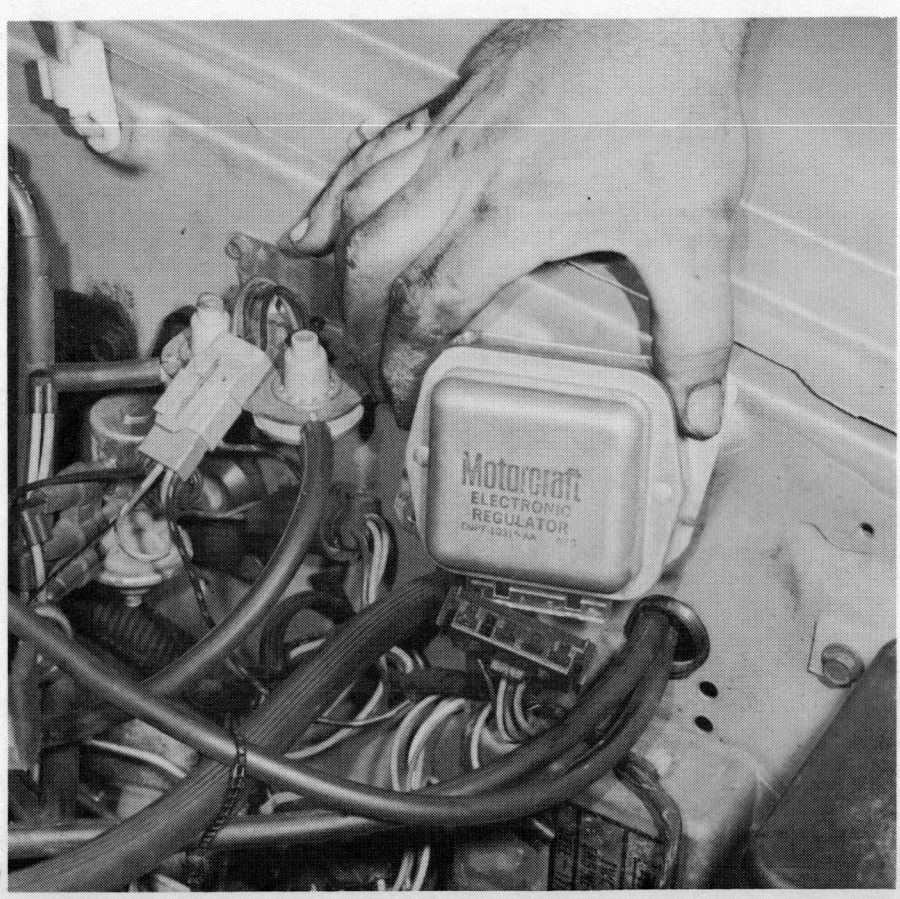

1

the voltage across R3, a resistor to limit the current through TR1 at high temperatures, and a diode that prevents high induced currents in the field windings when TR1 turns off. To summarize, the regulator in an alternator controls the voltage allowed into the system at all times, protects the battery from an overcharge, and keeps battery current from flowing into the stator during periods of low output.

BATTERY-GENERATOR CIRCUITS

At first glance, the generator system looks much simpler in the diagrams. It can be simplified more and has fewer components, but actually it is prone to more troubles—one major reason car makers dropped it for the alternator system with full electronic control.

In our simplified diagram, the engine is started by turning on the ignition (part of the electrical system load) and operating the starter by closing switch "Sol." The generator relay shown in the simplified regulator remains open, since there is not yet sufficient current being produced by the generator to operate the relay that controls it. Therefore, the powerful battery current directed to the starter ("St.") will not be shown on the ammeter ("Amps") since it is outside the starting circuit electrically. There will be some deflection of the ammeter needle, however, since the solenoid (also part of the electrical system load) requires some current to operate.

Once the engine is running, the generator action increases with engine rpm until it begins to put out current. This causes the regulator relay to energize and close the cutout contacts, so that current flows through the ammeter into the battery. The reversal of current flow through the ammeter causes the needle

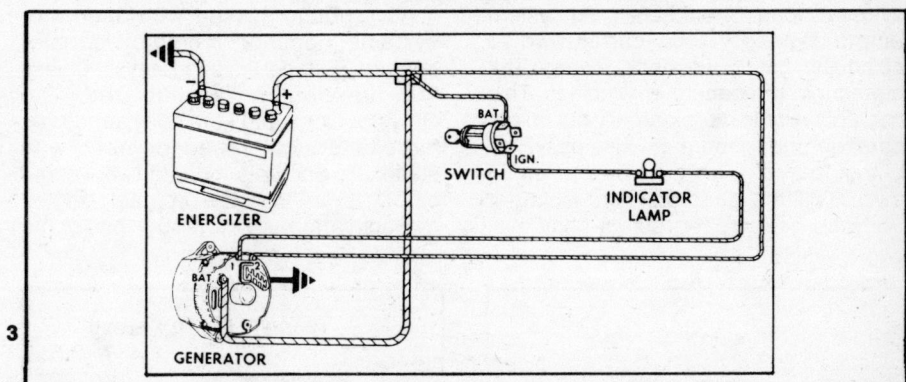

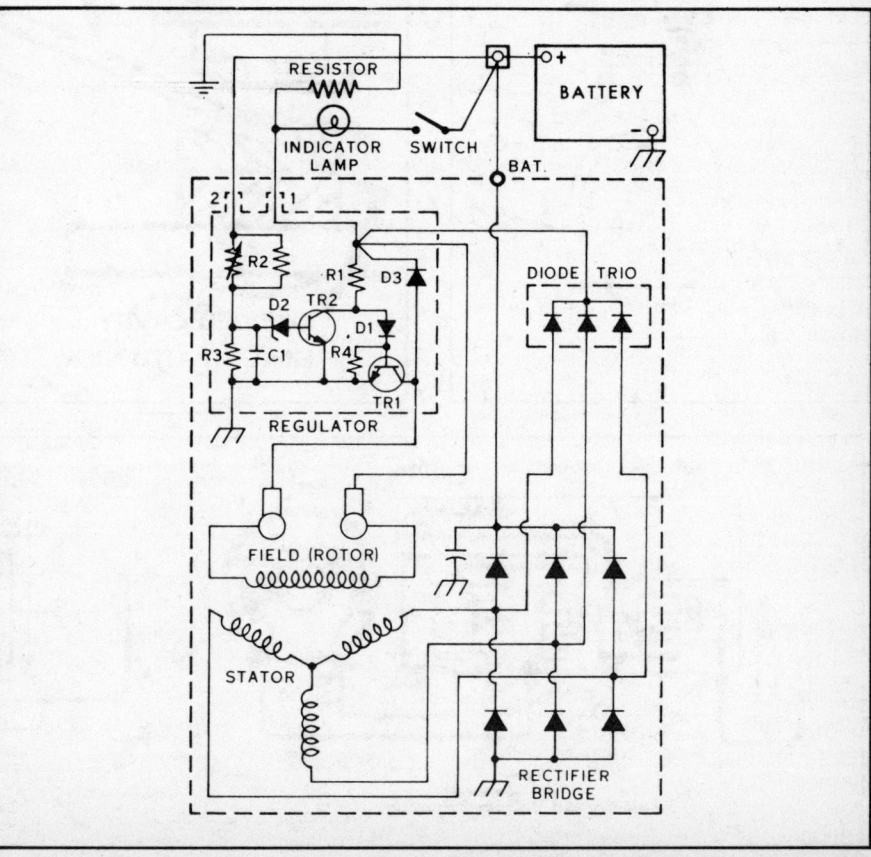

1. Ford's most recent regulator is a non-adjustable solid-state unit and is mounted to the fender apron to provide a ground. Always disconnect the regulator plug with the ignition Off before removing the unit.

2. GM uses a solid-state integral regulator found inside the alternator. It's serviced by replacement only.

3. This simplified charging circuit shows the relationship of the main components in a current GM charging circuit. GM calls its alternator a "Delcotron" and refers to it as an "AC generator."

4. This schematic wiring diagram shows the components which make up the circuit of an alternator/transistorized regulator system. Everything within the dashed lines is inside the alternator housing.

REGULATORS

to swing from the discharge zone (battery doing the work) to the charge zone (charging system doing the work). Once the charging system has taken over, current is driven not only through the ignition and other components included in the electrical system load, but also through the battery. The current flow therefore divides at connection C1—as the arrowheads indicate—and rejoins at connection C2, the battery ground.

If the engine is slowed down, the charging system output weakens and the ammeter needle gradually returns to "zero"—the point where the charging system is just meeting the needs of the electrical system load and no more. If the engine is allowed to idle—especially when several electrical accessories are in operation—the ammeter needle will swing down into the discharge zone, indicating that the current flow has reversed and that the battery has assumed some (or all) of the electrical system's load. Should charging system output fall very low, current would obviously be drawn back through the cutout into the generator windings. This not only would be wasteful, but might damage the generator windings. The cutout relay prevents this by opening to switch off the generator and isolate it from the battery. The cutout relay has, therefore, two basic functions: (1) When the engine is not operating, the contact points are held open by spring tension to prevent battery current from flowing to the generator windings. (2) It switches the generator output "on the line" when the voltage being produced is slightly above 12 volts, or 6 volts in a 6-volt system.

ALTERNATOR SYSTEMS

Most cars produced in recent years use alternator systems with transistorized regulators, as described above. These systems allow no adjustments of the regulator, or at most only an adjustment for maximum voltage. If the regulator proves bad, you throw it away and buy a new one, and that's that. Older cars, however, used a conventional electromechanical regulator in conjunction with their alternators, and before that, with their generators. Many cars still on the road have this system, and there is considerable leeway for repair or any necessary adjustments.

All regulators used with alternator systems commonly employ double-contact, voltage-limiting relays—unless this function is transistorized. The Chrysler Corp. and Ford relay armatures have a double-faced contact with stationary contacts mounted above and below it so that the contact on the movable armature may touch one or the other of these, depending upon the armature's position. When the upper contacts are closed, full voltage is supplied to the field windings, and the alternator is permitted to produce its maximum output. If the resultant voltage exceeds the demands of the electrical system, the relay core begins to build up a magnetic field, thereby attracting the relay's armature. When the armature floats between the upper and lower contacts, the field current is lowered by forcing it to flow through a resistor located under the regulator's base. If the magnetic attraction is strong enough to pull the armature even further against its controlling spring tension, the lower contacts are brought together. When this happens, no current is sent to the field windings, and alternator output ceases.

Each progressive movement of the movable contact results in lowered output of the alternator, which means that the coil controlling the regulator armature puts out less magnetic force. Less magnetic force means that the movable contact will move up to its previous position. When it gets back to that position, the regulator coil gains strength, so the movable point goes down again.

Delco voltage regulator relays are constructed opposite to those used by Chrysler and Ford. In the Delco design, the double points are on the armature, and the single double-faced point is stationary. The coil and spring arrangement is also different. The result is that

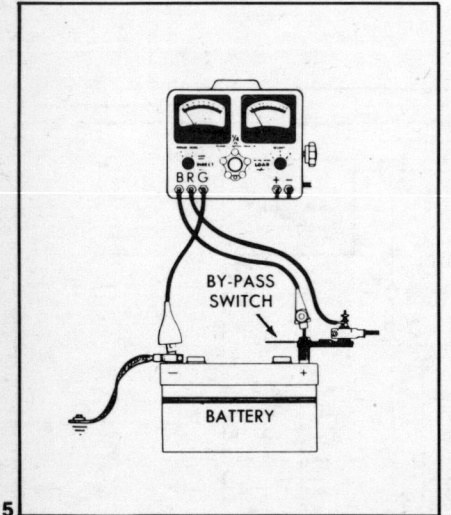

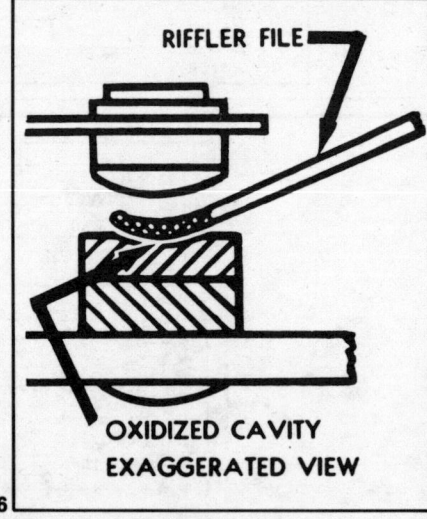

5. A terminal by-pass switch makes it possible to test the charge/discharge rate of the battery while the engine is running. This is a must for checking voltage regulator operation.

6. Here's what we mean when we mention cleaning the regulator points with a riffler file. The tip of the file digs all of the contamination from the points so they'll work properly.

7. Basic Delco-Remy generator circuits with single- and double-contact regulators. Note that the field windings are grounded in the regulator in both circuits.

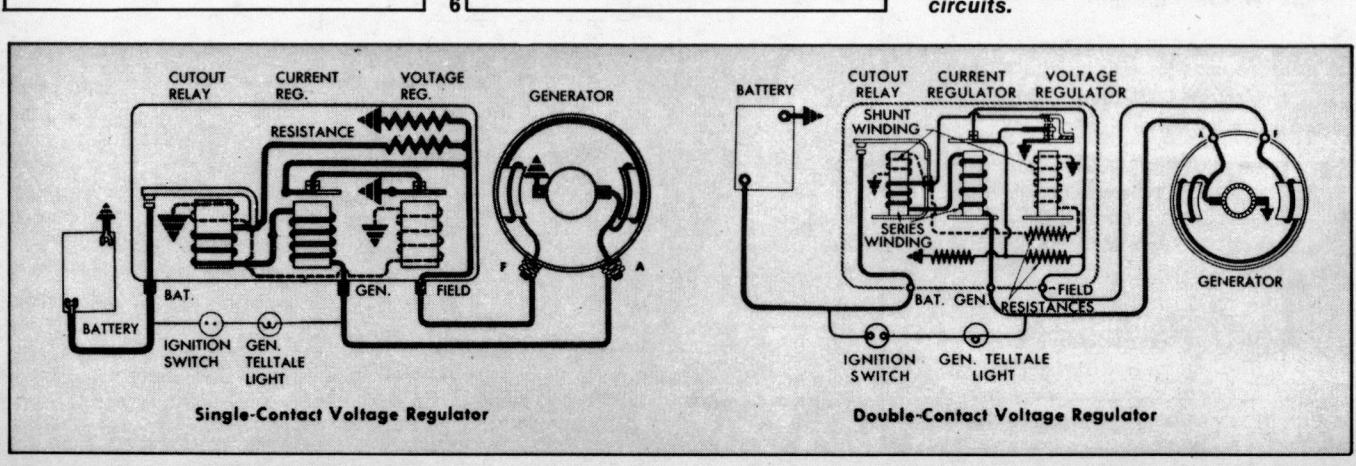

the resistor contact is the lower one, and the shorting contact the upper one. In any case, the effect on the alternator or generator is the same with either design.

These contacts seldom ever come completely at rest in any one position, but are in constant vibratory motion. When there is a fair electrical system load, and the engine is running slowly, the armature vibrates against the resistor contact. In doing so, it alternately sends full current and resistor-reduced current to the field coil. The varying proportion of one to the other determines the strength of the rotor's magnetic field, and hence the alternator's output. Since the voltage limiter's coil is sensitive to electrical system load, it varies the rate of vibration to change the alternator's field strength in direct proportion to the electrical system's load. If engine speed is high and there is only a light electrical system load, more current is made available to the relay windings, and the armature begins to vibrate against the shorting contact. This means that it will be alternately supplying resistor-reduced voltage and "zero" voltage to the alternator field. The alternator's output is thus reduced considerably for the protection of the battery, lights and various accessories. To prevent the regulator from being subjected to electrical surges while the limiter relay is vibrating, a resistor of about 50 ohms is connected from the regulator's field terminal to ground.

On Delco-Remy circuits that use an indicator light without a separate relay, the electrical path becomes more complex. Instead of using current from the ignition switch to close the field relay, actual charge current from the alternator is used. When the ignition is switched on, battery current flows through the indicator lamp and a low-ohm resistor wired in parallel with it. From here, it proceeds through the relay contacts of the voltage regulator to the field coil of the alternator. This small current is adequate to magnetize lightly the field poles of the rotor and initiate the production of electrical current. The low-powered current that results serves only to close the field relay, which then allows the voltage limiter to supply full battery current to the alternator's field windings. Since the main load of the charging system's field current is now being transmitted through the regulator from the battery, the charge indicator light consequently goes out.

To compensate for temperature variations that affect the charging requirements of the battery, the alternator's regulator uses bimetal hinges and/or springs. When checking or adjusting the voltage setting of the regulator, the temperature of the air one-quarter inch from the regulator cover should be recorded with a thermometer. The manufacturer's specifications will provide a temperature allowance accordingly, and this should be followed in making the final adjustments.

TRANSISTORIZED & ELECTRONIC REGULATORS

The use of transistors to control the limiting circuits in alternator system regulators began with General Motors and its introduction of a regulator containing twin diodes. This device still relied on the use of electromagnetic relays to carry out the actual voltage-regulating and field-control operations. The diodes were incorporated solely to prevent current backflow. They were in effect merely solid-state switches. The trend in recent years has been to make even conventional regulators "sealed" units that are to be not adjusted, but only replaced in the event of malfunction. More recent transistorized regulators also follow this pattern, but those used by Ford in the late seventies had an adjusting screw that makes it possible to control voltage output.

Electronic regulators have no moving parts, require no adjustments after being set at the factory, and can be serviced only by replacement. Whether mounted inside the alternator housing or externally, the electronic regulator contains

8. A typical regulator design for generator-based systems.

9. The earliest GM transistorized regulators (circa 1963) still had two functions carried out through the use of mechanical relays; single transistor carries out part of the voltage limiting function.

10. The entire voltage limiting function is transistorized in intermediate versions of the GM transistorized regulator; the relay controls only field current.

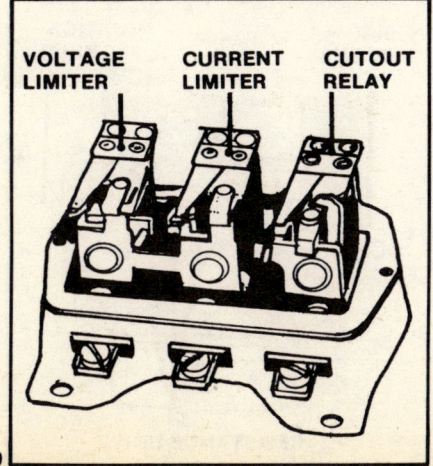

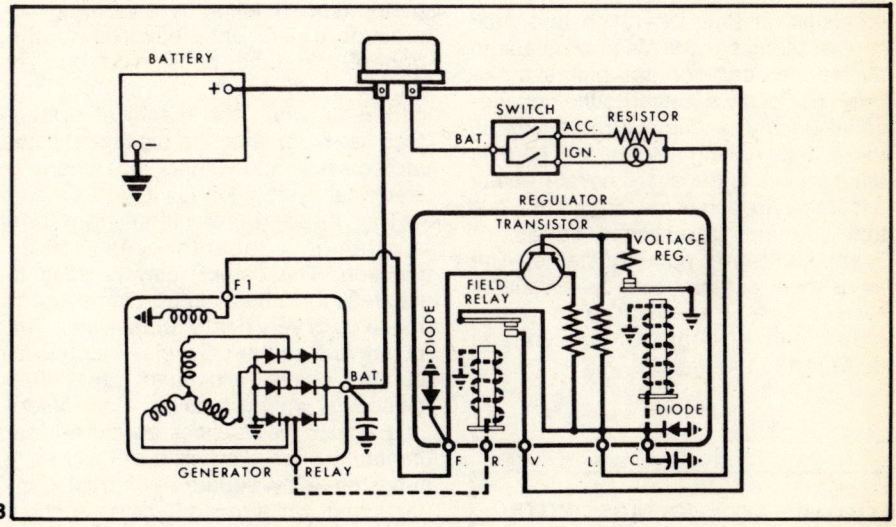

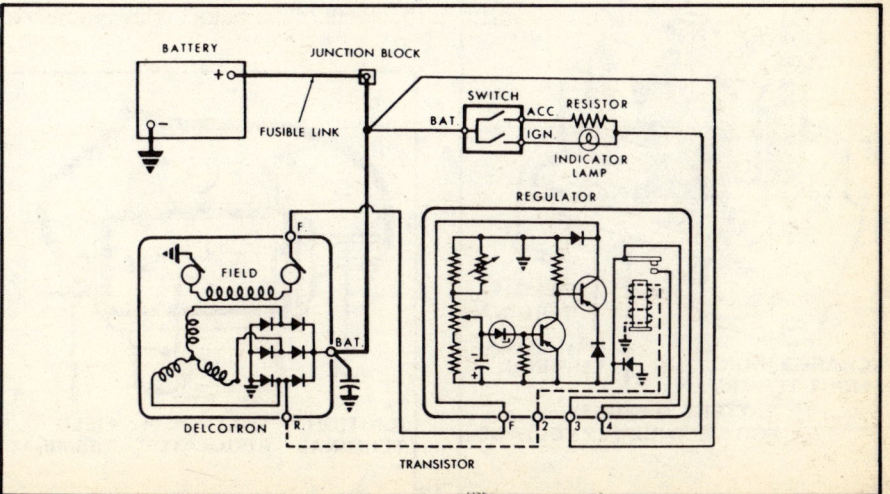

REGULATORS

semiconductors, transistors, diodes, resistors, and a capacitor. This reliance on electronic components greatly reduces the size of the unit. The most recent electronic regulator designs incorporate temperature compensation, which causes the charging voltage to vary according to temperature. When testing such regulators, the temperature around the rear bracket of the alternator must be measured and the charging voltage corrected to the specified temperature according to a factor provided by the manufacturer.

Since there is no way to take transistorized or electronic regulators apart to work on them, there is little to be gained from delving too deeply into precisely how their circuits function. However, there are two or three general points that should be considered. The first is that the circuits between this type of regulator and the alternator are exactly the same as those associated with conventional relay-controlled regulator units.

Second, the transistors controlling the field current strength are generally triodes that can vary the electrical flow through two of their connections in proportion to the strength of the current fed into their third connection. The precision of their operation and their inherent long service life in comparison to mechanical contact points make them obviously superior to the conventional electromechanical devices. Last, in those units having a screw that permits adjustments to the charging rate, do not assume—as some mechanics have—that you are "adjusting a transistor." Transistors are not adjustable. The adjustment actually controls a variable resistance—or rheostat—that determines the strength of the voltage delivered to the triodes.

GENERATOR SYSTEMS

In actual practice, there is considerably more to the voltage regulator than the simple cutout relay shown—at least in this day and age. Generator systems commonly have regulators containing two other additional relays as well. These are designed to correct various other conditions that might be harmful to either the battery or the generator. As pointed out in the chapter on generators, charging system output increases with engine speed. For this reason, there is another relay that limits the unit's total voltage output. This voltage-limiter relay keeps the generator's output below a predetermined level by controlling the amount of electricity supplied to the field coils. When the charging system output begins to approach higher voltages than are healthy for the car's light bulbs, battery, and other accessories, the voltage-limiter relay must "apply the brakes" on the generator's production capacity.

There is also a current-limiter relay in regulators used with generator-based charging systems. Its job is to protect the generator's armature windings by limiting the maximum amount of the electrical system's load that can be assumed by the generator. Like the voltage limiter, the current limiter performs its function by controlling the amount of current delivered to the generator's field coils. The current limiter thus serves to protect the generator when the electrical system load is high, and the voltage limiter protects the battery, lights, etc., when the electrical system load is low.

The three relays differ from one another in appearance as well as function. The cutout relay is easy to locate since it has a large-diameter coil made up of very heavy copper wire. The cutout is also the only relay that has its contact points held open rather than closed by spring tension. Most cutout relays also have either an extra-large contact—often consisting of two heavy tungsten alloy squares—or dual contacts that, while round in cross section, are quite large in diameter. The heavier contacts of the cutout relay are necessary since they must carry the generator's entire output to the battery and electrical system.

A more detailed examination of the cutout relay will show that there is also a fine wire leading to its coil. The reason is that there is another smaller coil made up of fine windings concealed beneath the heavy copper wire of the exterior coil. The smaller coil is connected from generator output to ground. When the generator starts to charge, no current can go through the large coil because the cutout points are open. But current can go through the small coil to ground, and it is the magnetism from this small coil that closes the cutout. When the cutout closes, current flows through the large coil, and its magnetism is added to that of the small coil, holding the points closed that much tighter. If the engine is idled or shut off, battery current will start to flow back into the generator because it is not turning enough to put out. When the current flows in a reverse direction through the heavy coil, the magnetism reverses, and the cutout is kicked open.

The current-limiter relay is wound only with large-diameter copper wire, whereas the voltage relay has many turns of fine wire about its core. Both relays have relatively small contacts which are more than able to handle the field current delivered to the generator's stationary coils through them. Some regulators have a fusible wire connecting the field contacts of these two relays to prevent the generator windings from damage in the event that one of the limiters' contacts "weld" together. The contacts of both the voltage limiters are in almost constant vibration. By this action, they control the amount of current available to the generator's field. A resistance between the regulator's field terminal and ground "damps out" the electrical surges produced by these vibrations, to protect further the system from any damage.

Note that the flat springs and/or hinges used in the relay armatures (their movable parts) are stamped with words, letters, numbers, or abbreviations. These are metallurgical indications of the type of material from which the

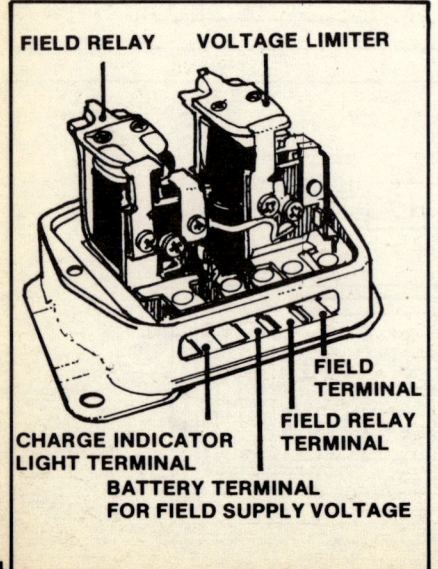

11 FIELD RELAY / VOLTAGE LIMITER / FIELD TERMINAL / FIELD RELAY TERMINAL / CHARGE INDICATOR LIGHT TERMINAL / BATTERY TERMINAL FOR FIELD SUPPLY VOLTAGE

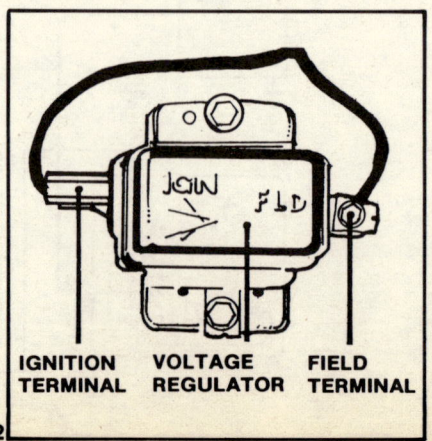

12 IGNITION TERMINAL / VOLTAGE REGULATOR / FIELD TERMINAL

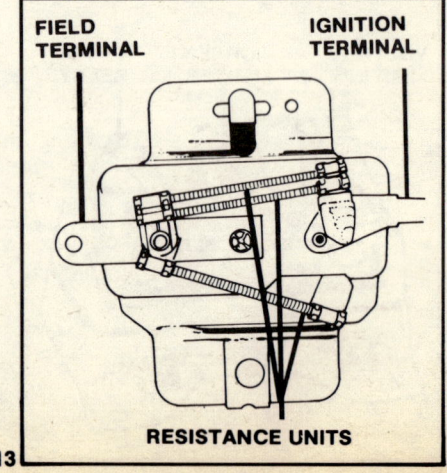

13 FIELD TERMINAL / IGNITION TERMINAL / RESISTANCE UNITS

springs and hinges are made. Generator regulators are designed to provide automatic compensation for temperature variations as well as for changes in electrical conditions. The springs and/or hinges are thus cut from a bimetal plate that changes its degree of tension in precise relation to ambient temperature. As observed in the battery chapter, a higher-charging system output is required to handle the car's electrical system and battery-charging load in cold weather, whereas a corresponding reduction of the charge is dictated by a return to warmer temperatures.

It is very important that any warm-weather overcharging be prevented for the sake of the battery. Whenever voltage regulators are readjusted, the unit must first be warmed up until its temperature has stabilized at a normal level. Most car makers specify that the unit's prescribed voltage output be achieved at a temperature from 70 to 80 degrees Fahrenheit. Further, it will usually require at least one-half hour of operation for the regulator to reach its own stable operating temperature. If attempts are made to adjust the regulator without taking temperature into consideration, it is impossible to expect the battery to receive the proper amount of current under all sorts of varying temperature conditions.

TROUBLESHOOTING & ADJUSTMENTS

Unless the field circuit and brush tests described in the alternator and generator chapters turn up an obvious source of trouble, it is advisable to give the regulator at least a casual inspection before bothering to remove and disassemble the generator or alternator itself. Certain other troubles that definitely indicate regulator malfunctions can often be spotted by the behavior of the instrument panel ammeter. One of the most common symptoms is an ammeter needle that proceeds up and down the scale from a high charge rate to a low discharge in direct proportion to engine speed. This condition is very harmful to the battery and should be corrected immediately. Since the cause is usually either a burned-out resistance in the regulator or a faulty relay winding, the only practical cure is to install a new regulator. Actually, the only regulator troubles that you should attempt to correct by repair and/or adjustment are those involving incorrect charge rates, or a no-charge condition. If this is the case, the regulator should be calibrated exactly to the car maker's specifications and if such adjustment proves impossible, scrap the unit in favor of a new one.

A no-charge condition—if caused by the regulator—is limited to two possibilities. First, the contacts controlling current to the alternator or generator field may not be making contact. An inspection of the contacts' condition will usually verify if this is the case. Second, the regulator may contain fusible wires that are designed to melt under an abnormally high charging condition for the protection of the alternator/generator. The regulator should be checked visually to see if it has fusible wires, and if so, if they have separated. The cause of a burned-out fusible wire probably lies in the regulator itself, so it is a must that it be tested according to the car maker's instructions before renewing the fusible wires and returning the regulator to service. For the protection of the alternator, these wires must be replaced with fusible wire of the proper rating and material.

A low-charging system output, usually accompanied by a low battery, probably results from improper calibration of the regulator. The unit's charge rate should thus be readjusted to bring it within the manufacturer's specifications. A low, unsteady charging rate is generally caused by a high resistance somewhere in the charging system or its connections—including the battery posts and terminals. In some instances, this may result from the formation of oxidation deposits on the regulator contacts. Incidentally, a sooty or discolored condition of the contacts after a relatively short period of operation is perfectly normal and should not be taken as an indication that cleaning is necessary. When needed, the relays can normally be cleaned and the contacts lightly burnished with a "riffler" file without upsetting the unit's basic adjustment.

An excessive charge rate is the most dangerous condition that can develop in the electrical system. In some cases, the regulator may be set too high. This could result from recalibrating the unit without first bringing it to the proper operating temperature. It can also stem from nonfunctioning relays or regulator contacts that have stuck or welded together. Both conditions call for replacement of the regulator. Another common cause of excessive charge rates is a poorly grounded regulator. Some cars do not have a separate ground connection for the regulator, which must then depend on having its base in good electrical contact with the

11. Mechanical regulators are usually adjusted by bending the tabs holding the relay springs and gap limiters. Adjustments should be made according to the procedures specified in the manufacturer's service manual.

12. Most early Chrysler products with alternators use single-relay regulators. The unit draws battery current from the ignition and controls voltage by regulating the field current.

13. Resistors under the regulator base prevent electrical surges which can result from regulator functioning.

14. Ford's electronic regulator is non-adjustable, but its earlier transistorized regulator can be adjusted as shown.

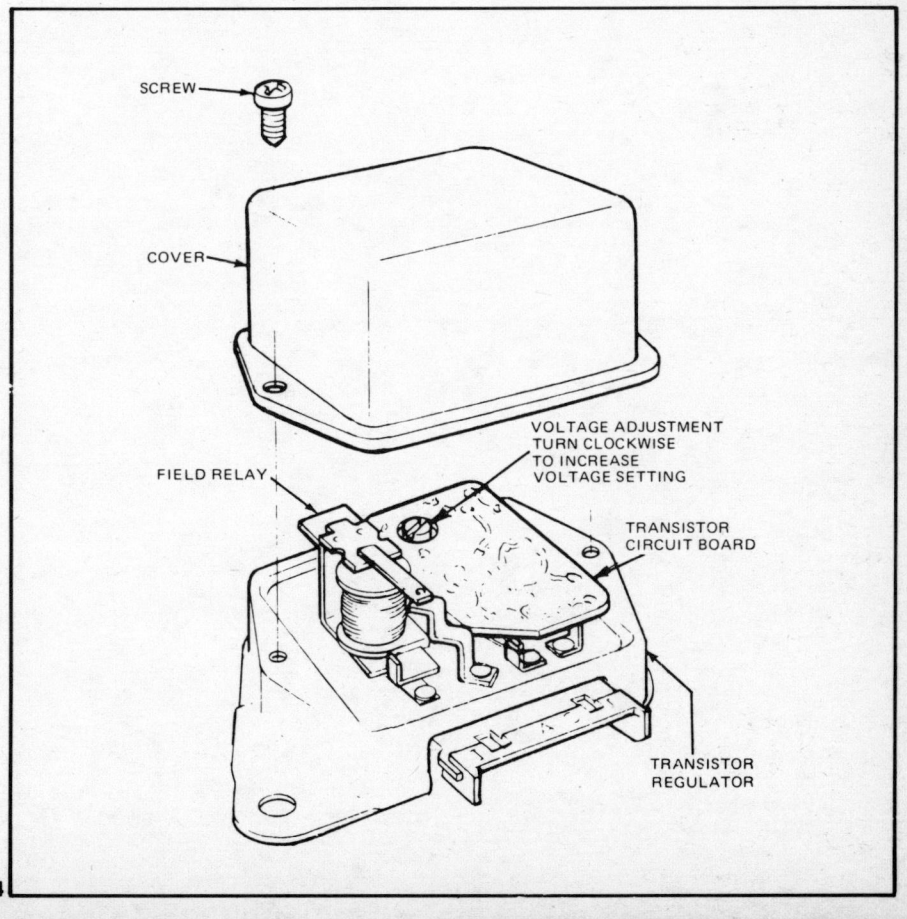

REGULATORS

body of the car. Try connecting a jumper wire between the regulator base and a clean spot on the car's body or chassis. If the charge rate then becomes normal, it's a simple matter to correct the regulator's contact with ground.

When installing a new regulator on a generator-equipped car, the generator must be polarized *before* starting the engine. If this is not done, either the generator or the regulator will burn out in the first few minutes of operation. This is especially important with cars that have only a warning light. An ammeter will show a no-charge condition when the engine is started without first polarizing the system—the light may not. Should you accidentally reverse the system's polarity and start the engine, remove the battery ground cable before shutting off the motor to save the generator from potential damage because of unregulated battery current flowing "backward" into the windings. When making an engine swap, polarizing the generator and regulator is sometimes overlooked in the confusion of taking care of so many other important details. Don't neglect this important step before firing up for the first time.

The generator must be polarized before starting the engine. To do so, touch a jumper wire momentarily between the generator (Arm. or Gen.) terminal and the battery terminal of the regulator. The jumper should only be connected for a fraction of a second. If you leave it connected any longer, you'll burn up the points in the voltage regulator on some double-contact regulators. To be 100 percent safe, remove the field lead from the regulator and ground it, then flash between the armature and battery terminals to polarize any generator with an "A" circuit.

An "A" field circuit is one that has the field grounded at the regulator. A "B" circuit has the field grounded at the generator. As a general rule, all generators are "A" circuit except those used by Ford, which are "B" circuit. All alternators are "B" circuit, except the integral regulator types, which are usually "A" circuit. You must know which is which so you can hot-wire current to the fields when making tests on either alternators or generators, or when polarizing generators.

Alternator systems are never polarized. They do not depend upon residual magnetism in the field. Since the alternator's polarity cannot be lost or changed, any attempt to polarize it can result in damage to the diodes, wiring harness, and/or other system components. If you have any doubt about the polarity of a given alternator, connect a battery to the field circuit only and a voltmeter between the insulated and ground terminals of the alternator. Rotate the rotor slowly in either direction and note the polarity of the voltage as shown by the voltmeter.

As a final word, the regulator is an amazing little device that probably does more to keep the electrical system functioning properly than any other single component. Keeping a check on its operation is the best insurance you can have against premature battery or electrical system failure.

LIGHTS

Until recently, the changes that had taken place in automobile headlights since World War II were limited to a few lens modifications, a modest increase of 3000 candlepower in 1955, the switchover to four-light systems on large domestic cars beginning in 1958, and the sudden shift to rectangular headlamp styling pioneered by GM for 1975. Over the years, various state legislatures had passed laws limiting the power and type of headlights, as well as specifying the permissible number and legal aim for auxiliary lights—sometimes banning them altogether.

It took tremendous effort on the part of the industry just to get all the states to approve the four-light systems—which have some disadvantages as well as advantages in comparison with two-light installations. Detroit had played around with rectangular sealed-beam units for years, primarily on its advanced-concept or "dream" cars, but buggy-era regulations eliminated their use on production vehicles. It took the clout of GM to obtain the go-ahead for the use of rectangular units on some of its cars in 1975.

However, it's interesting to note that the corporation promised the bureaucrats to discontinue use of the lights if car buyers frowned on them for any reason, or if they created service problems at dealership levels. Thus was born the greatest change in headlighting in many decades, thanks to the stylists who insisted on the new shape in order to design "tighter" front-end sheetmetal with lower hoodlines. Rectangular lights are now very nearly the universal choice of our domestic car industry. Yet, only the shape of the sealed-beam lights had changed. Candlepower limits were the same as before, but because of the units' smaller sizes (in total area), their illuminating beams had actually been *reduced*.

The most revolutionary improvement in nighttime driving came as the result of action taken by the National Highway Traffic and Safety Administration (NHTSA) in July 1978. With a stroke of a pen, the agency increased the permissible light output of auto headlamps from 75,000 to 150,000 candlepower, thus paving the way for use of the halogen headlamps, which are beginning to appear as standard equipment on domestic cars.

Halogen lamps use about 30 percent less power than conventional headlamps, but produce a brighter (and whiter) light because the tungsten filament encased in the halogen-filled bulb burns at a higher temperature than the filament of a conventional incandescent lamp. Since the circuitry in a

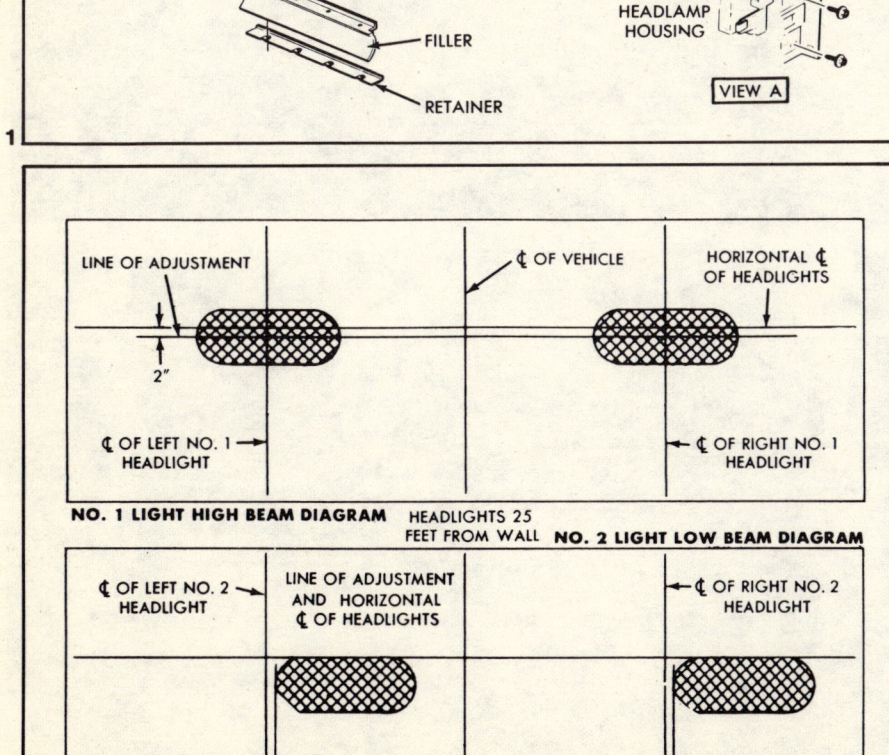

1. The once-simple headlight became a complex system of dual headlamps, parking lights and turn signal lamps in the Seventies. All were located in a huge housing with a bezel and other retainers to hold the assembly together. This is a 1977 Seville.

2. Draw this diagram on your garage door and you can do your own headlight adjusting right in your own driveway—providing the pavement is level.

IGNITION & ELECTRICAL SYSTEMS/153

LIGHTS

halogen lamp system is designed specifically for its power requirement, you should not replace a burned-out halogen lamp with a conventional headlamp, as it will drain the battery rapidly in slow-driving situations.

Regardless of shape or location, headlights function much as they always have, and changing a bulb is pretty much the same now as it was when sealed-beam units first came along. One caution is in order, however, when installing halogen lamps. You should not touch the quartz surface on the lamp with your bare hands, as this can cause it to stain and result in premature lamp failure. Keep the lamp in its protective cover until it is installed. If you should touch the quartz surface accidentally, clean it immediately with a soft cloth that has been moistened with alcohol.

HEADLIGHTS

The headlights supplied on two-light cars have a twin-filament system for dimming. Four-light systems have two sealed beams with both high- and low-beam filaments, plus two additional sealed beams with high-beam filaments only. These last two units go out completely when the headlights are dimmed, and since the diameter of the remaining two lamps is less than that of the 7-inch sealed-beam units on two-headlight cars, the result is poorer visibility with the lights dimmed than is offered by the two-unit setup in the same mode.

Many states deny the car owner the right to aim his own headlights, although there are still parts of the country where this work can be done at home. Shops specializing in headlight aiming generally use a headlight aimer that attaches directly to the lens of the sealed-beam units. It does not require the use of a wall screen, except for calibration. These devices are quick, compact, and require little shop space for their use. But unless the mechanic using them understands their operation thoroughly and takes the time to perform a conscientious job, the results are often none too accurate. Halogen lights can pose a problem when an optical or visual aimer is used. Unless a filter screen is installed in the aimer system, the bright light can damage the photo cells of the aimer.

If you plan on aiming your own headlamps, an improvised aiming screen is probably the best way to go. The most important factor is having available an area that allows the car to sit absolutely level, with the headlight faces at a distance of 25 feet from the screen. The screen should have four lines drawn upon it. First, make a horizontal line across the screen that's parallel to the ground and at exactly the same height as the centers of the car's headlights. Now draw three vertical lines across it. One vertical line should be in the exact center of the horizontal line, and the two others equidistant from it at an included width equal to the distance between the car's headlight centers. If the car has a four-unit headlight system, a separate set of lines should be drawn for each pair of lights.

The sealed beams used on cars with two-light systems, as well as the combination high-beam, low-beam sealed beams used with four-light systems, are designated as Type 2 units. These are generally identified by a numeral "2" molded into their lens. The high-beam-only sealed beams used for two of the lamps in four-light systems are called Type 1 units and are correspondingly marked. Type 2 sealed beams can also be recognized by the fact that they have three terminals on the back, whereas Type 1 units have only two.

To aim the headlights, the car must be positioned 25 feet from the aiming screen so that the center vertical line on the screen is exactly in line with the center of the car. The quickest way to do this is to shift the screen from side to side until it is lined up with the center of the car's hood. If the car has no distinct line at the center of the sheet metal, you can locate the center by using a tape measure and then placing a small suction cup at that point for a "front sight." The "rear sight" can be the joint in the middle of the rear window molding, or a yardstick held straight up from the trunk lock. The car should be rocked from side to side several times and allowed to settle into its normal position before making the adjustments.

The Type 2 units are adjusted on low beams only. This ensures adequate illumination with the lights dimmed, and the built-in angle between the high and low beams takes care of the aiming for the high beam. Type 1 units are aimed separately in reference to their own lines

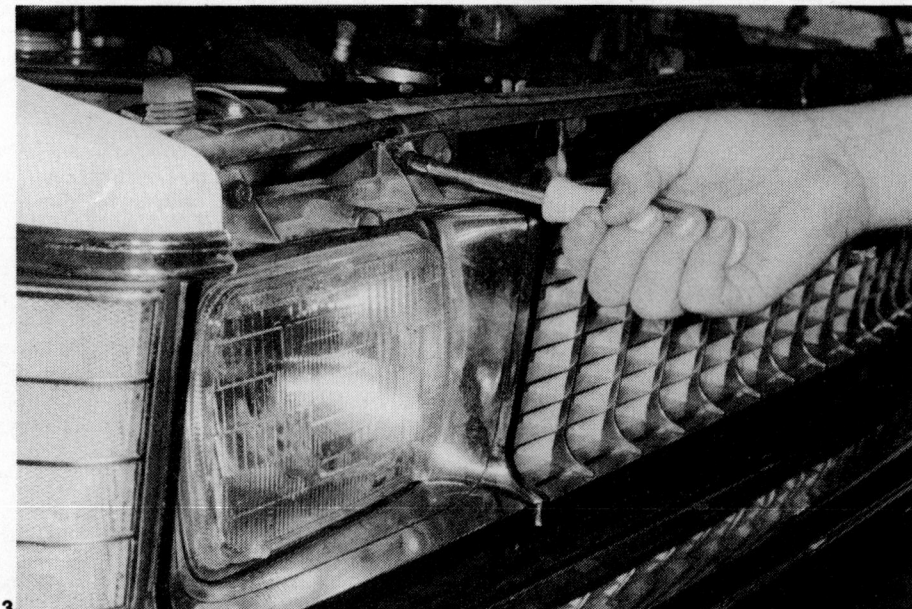

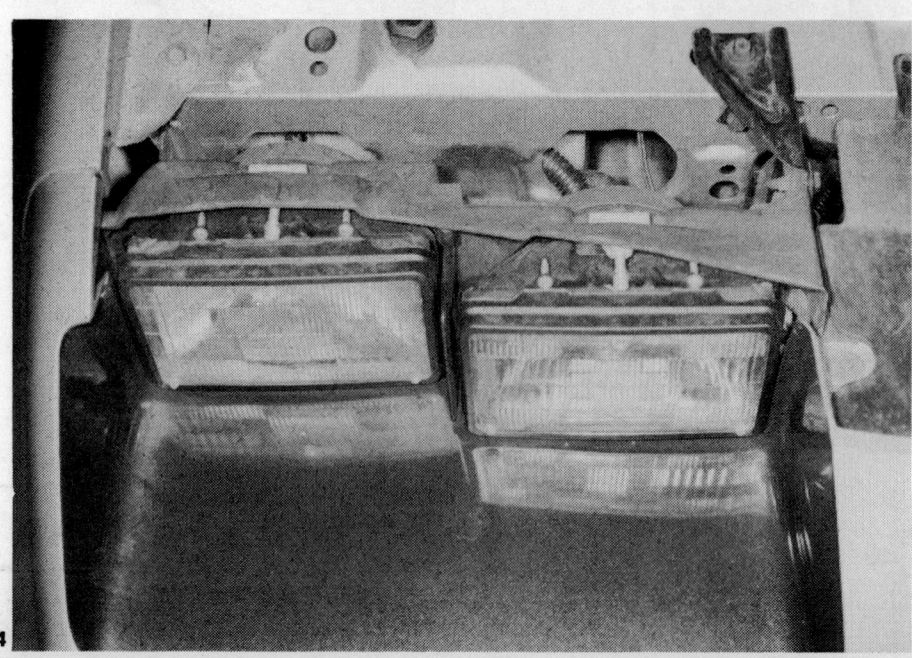

on the screen. Only the light to be adjusted should be allowed to shine on the screen; the other should be covered to prevent their interfering with your work. To ensure a good job, have the tires properly inflated and make sure that all grille, fender, and headlight assembly bolts are tight. Some car makers specify that the lights be aimed with a half-tank of gas and a person in the driver's seat. Others say a full tank and no one in the car, but all agree that there should be nothing in the trunk, and no passengers in the vehicle. The aiming charts appearing in the illustrations show where the light beams should fall relative to the lines on the aiming screen.

Older cars using the two-headlight systems had 5000-series bulbs, which may still be seen in some areas. They're most easily recognized by a lack of the three points around the rim, which all later bulbs have for use with mechanical aimers. The 5000-series bulbs are aimed so that the hot spot of the light hits the aiming screen exactly in front of the light, but with a two-inch drop at 25 feet. Some states may require more drop. Aiming the high beams in that manner automatically takes care of the low beams. That's exactly opposite to the later Type 2 units, which will fit in place of the 5000 series. If your car has one of each bulb, aim each one according to its own particular specifications.

OTHER LAMPS

When you turn on the headlights, a number of other lamps light up as well. These include parking lights, side lights, tail lights, and the bulbs that illuminate the instrument panel. A look at the average main light switch assembly on most domestic cars will show that this little piece of equipment is quite complicated. It controls more individual circuits and performs more varied tasks than any other electrical component on the car. When pulled out to its first detent, it switches on the parking lights, instrument panel lights, and other small bulbs. Pull it out to the second detent and the headlights come on. If it's turned from side to side, a rheostat dims or raises the intensity of the instrument panel bulbs. Turned all the way clockwise, it turns on the passenger compartment dome light.

In many cars, the headlight switch also contains a circuit breaker that replaces the headlight circuit fuses that were used on many older cars. If there is a short in the lighting system, the circuit breaker cuts out momentarily. Should any function of the headlight switch cease operation, the entire switch must be replaced. Car makers have made exchanging the light switch an easy task. Most late-model cars have a pushbutton on the switch that, when depressed, frees the control knob so that it can be pulled out of the dash. Then you simply unplug the multiple connector and unscrew the mounting ring nut. Incidentally, whenever you're working on this or any other part of the lighting system, always disconnect the ground cable at the battery.

The headlight beam selector switch mounted on the floorboard also has a multiple connector on most late-model cars. Headlights that "mysteriously" become inoperative are frequently the result of this connector being kicked loose, or becoming corroded by water or snow from the driver's shoes. As in the case of the main headlight switch, the dimmer pedal switch can be replaced,

5

6

3. Most cars, whether fitted with one or two pairs of either round or rectangular headlamps, require that the bezel or surrounding trim be removed to gain access to lamp adjustment screws, or in the case of bulb replacement, the retaining screws.

4. The 1982 Camaro design permits headlamp removal by simply lifting the hood.

5. With the emphasis on small cars these days, headlamps can be unplugged from inside the engine compartment, as on this 1983 Renault Alliance.

6. Cars with concealed headlamps, such as the 1983 Pontiac Firebird and 1984 Corvette, generally have a manual knob which can be used to raise or lower the headlamps should the motor or electrical circuit develop problems.

LIGHTS

but not repaired.

The dimmer switch has three terminals. One receives battery current from the headlight switch when it is turned on; the two other terminals are connected to the headlights. One goes to a terminal on both the Type 1 and Type 2 sealed beams and provides current for the high beams. The other connects to the low-beam filament terminals on the Type 2 units only. The remaining terminals on the sealed beams connect the filaments to ground. Whenever the driver depresses the dimmer switch, it redirects battery current from one set of lamp filaments to the other.

In the last few years domestic car makers have adopted the European/Japanese concept of column-mounted multifunction switches, commonly called stalk-mounted controls. This concept combines the operation of several electrical features, such as headlight dimmer, horn, hazard warning, etc., with the normal function of the turn-signal-indicator lever. In addition to the up-down movement of the lever, stalk-mounted controls require a forward/backward motion of the lever to control the headlights. Horn operation usually results when the end of the lever is pressed inward toward the column.

The multifunction switch is located at the top of the steering column under the shrouds, and is often attached to the lock cylinder housing with a pair of self-tapping screws. This is the second most complicated electrical switch in a modern automobile, and like the headlamp switch, it must be replaced whenever one function goes bad. The multifunction switch can be tested with a self-powered test lamp, but you'll need the manufacturer's test connection pattern to do so. This is usually found in the factory service manual for the car in question, and specifies where continuity should be found. No continuity indicates an open, whereas continuity not specified means a short in the switch.

SECONDARY LIGHTING SYSTEMS

Besides those circuits controlled by the main headlight switch, there are circuits for the turn signals, stop lights, backup lights, four-way flashers, and courtesy lights—all operating independently. Each of these systems has its own switches, its own particular type of bulbs, and is generally protected by its own individual fuse. On some cars only the headlights themselves are wired through the circuit breaker; all other circuits—including the taillights and parking lights—have fuses. Some newer cars have dropped fuses entirely in favor of circuit breakers, but there seems to be a move back to the use of independent fuses for the circuits.

The switches controlling the various secondary lighting systems are nearly always completely different from one another in their construction, location, and manner of operation. In addition, turn signal and four-way flasher circuits have a relay in them that switches the current delivered to the lamps on and off automatically.

Flasher and turn-signal relays are small electromagnetic switches that operate on thermoelectric principles. When the turn signal or four-way flasher switch is closed by the driver, current is sent through a fine wire inside the relay housing. Since the fine wire produces a short circuit, it begins to heat up. As with any other metal object, the heat causes the wire to expand and lengthen. A set of spring-loaded contact points is anchored open by this wire, and as the wire expands, the points are allowed to come together. This permits battery current to pass through the windings of the relay, rather than through the fine wire. The relay energizes, drawing a second set of contacts together which route current through the signal bulbs. However, once the current load is no longer on the fine wire, it begins to cool and contract, opening the points and deenergizing the relay. This causes the signal lamps to go off again. The fine wire once again receives battery current and starts to heat up. The entire cycle has begun all over. Nearly 100 percent of flasher failures result from the fine control wire burning or breaking off.

When replacing a faulty flasher unit, you'll find that most parts stores carry both "standard" and "heavy-duty" flasher relays. The heavy-duty type is intended primarily for trucks and other vehicles which have many high-wattage bulbs in the flasher or signal circuit. On most cars, the load is too light for these units and the fine control wire does not cool sufficiently to release the relay. The signals will simply go on and stay on without flashing. If you have a trailer that is equipped with stop lights, turn signals, flashers, and taillights which are coupled into the front circuits of the tow car, you may find that the flashes produced with a standard flasher are of very short duration and quite widely spaced. Since

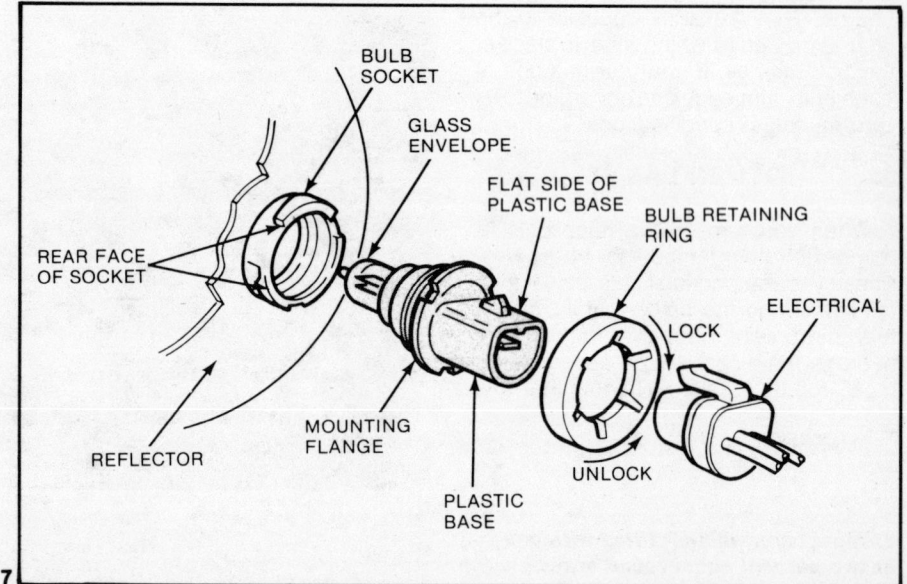

7

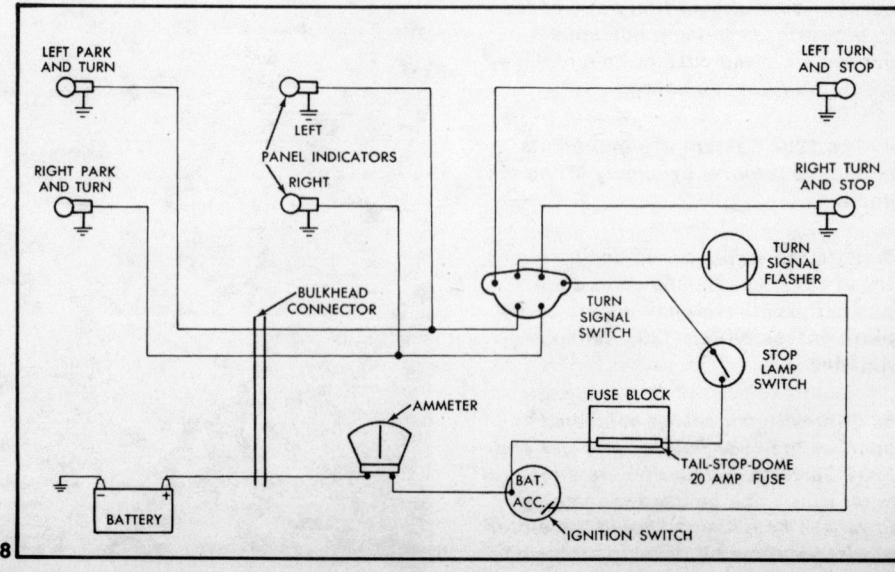

8

the heavy-duty flasher relays have the same terminal arrangement as the standard-duty type, it's a simple job to unplug one and insert the other when either towing or driving without the trailer.

In most instances where turn signals go on and stay on without flashing, the cause is a burned-out bulb. Since the flasher relay control wire is coupled in series with the signal lamps, it depends on their resistance to absorb the current and allow the control wire to cool. If the balance in the system is very critical, a burned-out dash indicator bulb may cause the signals to go on and stay on, or—depending on the circuitry—transform the signals into four-way flashers.

Stop lights and backup lights are commonly operated by mechanical switches, although a few cars still retain the hydraulically operated type common on American cars after World War II. Before the advent of suspended brake pedals, mechanical stop-light switches were a constant source of trouble since they had to be located under the car where they soon became rusted or water-soaked by spray thrown from the wheels. Now, with the stop-light switch located inside the car on the pedal-mounting assembly, it is practically trouble-free. Hydraulic switches were never subjected to the water and corrosion problems, but they're still a headache to change, as the brake system must be bled after a new switch is installed.

Backup-light switches—even those screwed directly into automatic transmission—are all mechanically operated. Their location varies from make to make, but the majority are mounted somewhere on the shift lever linkage. Those that are screwed into the transmission are actuated by an internal cam that moves whenever the driver puts the transmission into reverse.

7. Government regulations have been changed to allow the use of replaceable halogen headlamp bulbs on 1984 models. This will eventually spell the overdue end of the sealed beam unit. Incidentally, if the headlamp is properly aimed to begin with, replacement of the bulb inside the lamp housing means that the unit does not have to be re-aimed after installation.

8. A typical turn signal circuit. When the rear turn light is blinking, the stop lamp on that side is disconnected from the stop lamp switch by the turn signal switch.

9. Access to the rear lamps is made easier on newer cars. Just remove a few screws from a housing such as this and take the housing off to expose all of the lamp connections.

10. A fuse block that mounts under the edge of the instrument panel offers good protection against accidental shorting, as the clips and fuses are sunk in little wells.

AUXILIARY LIGHTS

Driving lights are not only extremely practical pieces of equipment, but also a great custom touch for any car. They're available in various power outputs ranging from about 35,000 candlepower to as much as 300,000. Most of these units are of overseas manufacture and can be had with sealed beams, regular incandescent bulbs, or quartz-iodine/halogen elements.

When it comes to what's legal and what isn't, things are still rather confused. Those states that have laws limiting the type of driving lights that can be used usually require that the manufacturer seek state certification for his product before it can become a legal accessory. However, many areas have no specific requirements for driving lights. Some states permit two driving lights, others allow only one. None permits them to be mounted above 42 inches, but the minimum mounting height varies from 12 to 24 inches—although, again, some states do not specify standards.

Foglights are a handy accessory during rain, snow, and foggy driving conditions. They're also quite useful for "balancing" a driving light in appearance in states that limit vehicles to only one such fixture. Nearly all manufac-

LIGHTS

turers of driving lights make a matching foglight for such installations. Foglights and driving lights come in various shapes and thicknesses to permit convenient mounting on most cars. Placing their centers at about 24 inches above the road will usually protect them from damage in parking lot encounters much better than mounting them just above bumper height.

When mounting auxiliary lights, it's a good idea to do so by drilling the minimum number of holes possible. Unless you plan to sell the lights when you trade the car, you'll find that open holes bored into the bodywork won't add a penny to its resale value. It may be possible to mount your lights on a through-the-grille bracket. This is usually designed to anchor to the grille or radiator bolts so that no drilling is required.

When wiring auxiliary lights, there are several important things to be considered. First, driving lights are meant to be used with high beams only, and most states specify that they switch off automatically when the headlights are dimmed. For this reason, it's necessary that they draw current from the wiring that leads to the car's high-beam units. A separate switch should always be incorporated in the wiring for the driving light(s) so that the driver can completely deactivate it when desired.

Foglights are generally used with the headlights on low beam to minimize reflections from snow, rain, or fog. It's unnecessary to wire them into the headlight circuit, but it is desirable to pick up current for them from either the headlight switch or the ignition switch. This will prevent the possibility of leaving them on accidentally when they're not necessary.

Anytime that an auxiliary light is wired to a power source other than the headlight circuit, it should be provided with a fuse or circuit breaker to prevent fires in the event that the unit becomes shorted for any reason. Most production vehicles have a blank space or two in their fuse panel, and you may find it possible to wire the light(s) through one of these. Inline fuseholders are also available when you wish to fuse such circuits individually.

A combination installation of fog and driving lights will assure you of having the best available illumination regardless of weather conditions. In all probability, auxiliary lights will receive increasing emphasis in the next few years. You can get ahead of the game by updating your lighting system now, but regardless of the type of installation you decide upon, be sure you follow the laws of your state.

11.

11. Detroit has come up with another good idea on recent cars. This type of fuse block eliminates the usual hassle of checking fuses, since it swings down from the dash. Note that spare fuses are located in the cover.

158/IGNITION & ELECTRICAL SYSTEMS

INSTRUMENTS

The instrument panel is a driver's main line of communication with his car's engine and electrical system. Anyone who has not learned the importance of instruments, or who does not make it a practice periodically to scan their readings, is one who's going to be surprised by sudden failures and malfunctions. When somebody tells you that his car's alternator or regulator has burned out "for no reason at all," or that its engine has incurred major damage "without warning" because of overheating or lack of lubrication, you know that he has not formed the basic good driving habit of keeping a constant check on the instrument panel gauges.

In past years, mechanical gauges of one sort or another were used for indicating fuel level, oil pressure, water temperature, and engine rpm. Although such instruments are not completely unknown today, these common types have been converted to electrical operation for convenience and reliability. The electrical instruments used in production automobiles are not highly accurate, but their indications are nonetheless relatively precise, considering their simplicity and low cost. They are designed so that their readings change in proportion to the resistance in an electrical circuit that is wired through them. To prevent the fluctuations in their readings that might be induced by changes in the electrical system load, a voltage-limiting device is incorporated into the system and it ensures the gauges a stable source of electricity. Currently, most gauges are of the thermal type; they react slowly to current changes and produce more steady "average" readings.

VOLTAGE LIMITERS

The voltage limiter keeps the current delivered to the instruments at a steady level. Actually, its output fluctuates between 0 and 7 (sometimes 10) volts, but since the instruments react slowly, the effect is the same as constant current of approximately 5 volts. The voltage delivered to the instruments is

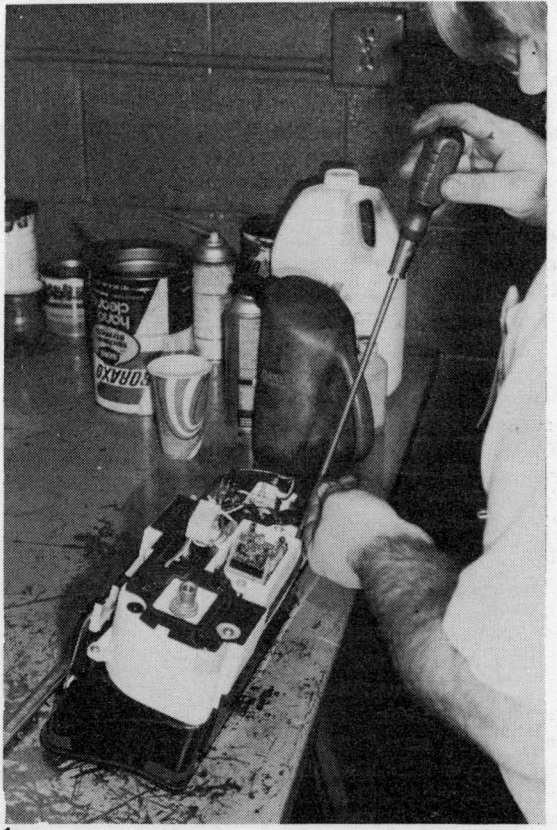

1A, 1B and 1C. Replacing instruments on today's cars is not difficult. The biggest problem comes in getting the instrument cluster out of the dash (A). Once that's done, simply unplug the connectors (B) and disassemble the cluster far enough to remove the defective unit (C).

INSTRUMENTS

kept well below the 12 volts at which the battery is rated. That way, when voltage in the electrical system drops because of the burden of lighting and accessory loads, it is still well above the minimum figure that's required to operate the necessary gauges accurately.

The voltage limiter is controlled by a bimetallic arm that flexes when heated, opening a set of contact points. Surrounding the bimetal strip is a coil of fine wire that receives battery current as long as the contact points are together. When the ignition switch is turned on, current is sent through the contacts and the fine-wire heating coil. When the coil has raised the temperature of the bimetallic strip to a precise level, the strip bends to open the contacts. This cuts off current to the heating coil as well as to the instruments. As the strip cools, the contacts come together once again and the cycle is repeated. When the car is first started, it sometimes takes a bit longer for the bimetal strip to reach its cutout temperature, so the gauges ascend to an abnormally high reading for a few seconds before returning to their correct level.

Cars equipped with only a fuel gauge commonly have the voltage limiter built right into the gauge itself. Those with additional instruments occasionally use the gas-gauge limiter to supply stable current to the other dials as well, but in most cases, multiple gauges are served by a common voltage limiter that is a unit by itself.

THERMAL GAUGES

The thermal gauges used for fuel, water temperature, and oil pressure are usually identical in construction, but have different faces and sending units. Their operation is similar to that of the voltage limiter itself, being controlled by a bimetallic strip which flexes in proportion to the heat it receives. Here, however, the strip does not operate a set of contacts, but is coupled directly to the gauge's indicator needle. The reading produced by the needle is directly proportional to the degree of flex in the bimetal strip. The sending units for the gauges vary the resistance of each control circuit in precise relation to whatever is being measured. Current passing through the gauges' heating elements is thus varied according to the condition sensed by the sending units.

In the case of the fuel gauge, a movable float located in the fuel tank controls the position of a wiping contact against a semicircular resistance coil. This is actually a simple rheostat. When the fuel level falls, the resistance is increased, allowing less current to flow from the voltage to the sending unit's ground connection. Since this reduced current also passes through the gauge, its bimetal strip cools proportionately and moves the needle to a lower reading on the dial. Resistance is lowest when the tank is full, and the resultant increase in current flow heats the gauge's bimetallic strip to produce the maximum reading.

The oil pressure gauges once installed on automobiles were operated mechanically by an oil line attached to the engine's lubrication system. However, production cars now universally use electric oil pressure gauges. Electric oil pressure gauge sending units generally consist of a small sealed cylinder that has inside a diaphragm or piston against which engine oil can bear when under pressure. The piston is spring-loaded and connected to a variable resistance that functions in a manner similar to that of the fuel tank sending unit. The greater the oil pressure, the lower the electrical resistance and the higher the gauge's reading.

Water temperature gauges use a different sort of sending unit, since the quantity being measured (heat) cannot be converted directly into mechanical motion, as can fuel level and oil pressure. The means of varying the

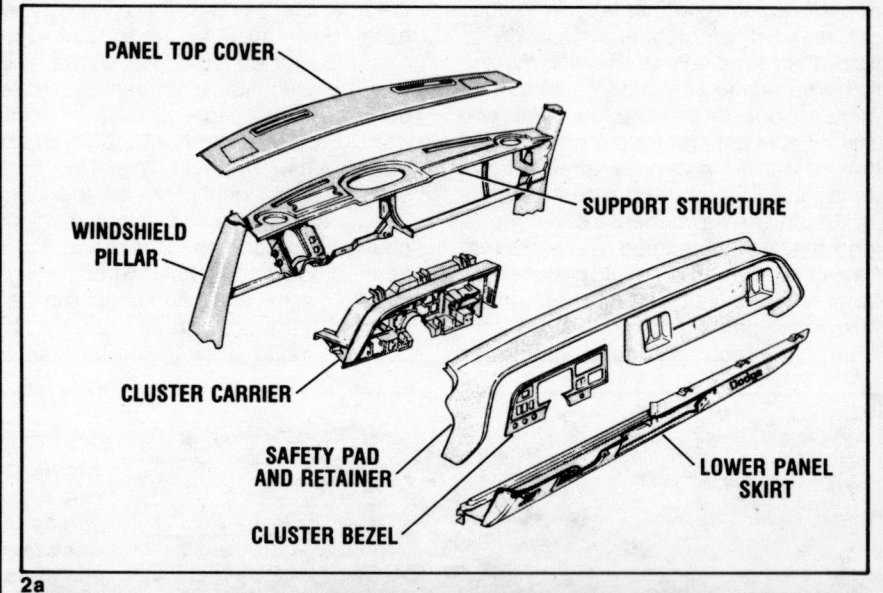
2a

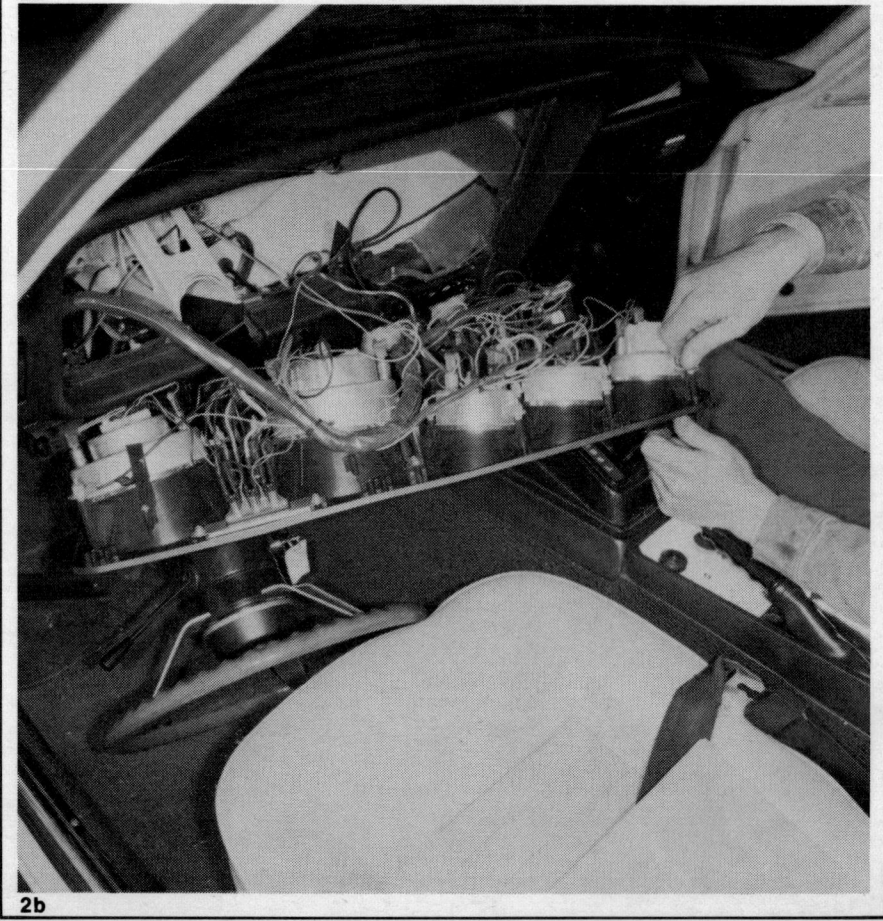
2b

2A and 2B. *Old cars had a nearly flat panel that formed the dash, and the gauges came out from the back side after undoing hard-to-reach screws or nuts buried in the wiring jungle (A). Engineers have helped the at-home tinkerer by making most dials and gauges accessible after removal of trim panels and the cluster bezel (B). This allows gauge access within the cluster carrier.*

3. *The back of this temperature gauge requires that insulating washers be placed over the studs to keep the terminals from touching the case. The terminal at the back of this gauge is upside down, producing a direct short to ground that will probably ruin something.*

4. *The fuel warning light on the dash connects to the sending unit (top arrow). When the unit is covered with fuel, the light remains off. The lower arrow shows the filter location.*

5A and 5B. *Mechanical voltage limiters containing a bimetallic strip (A) have been replaced in recent years by solid-state devices that perform the same function more reliably.*

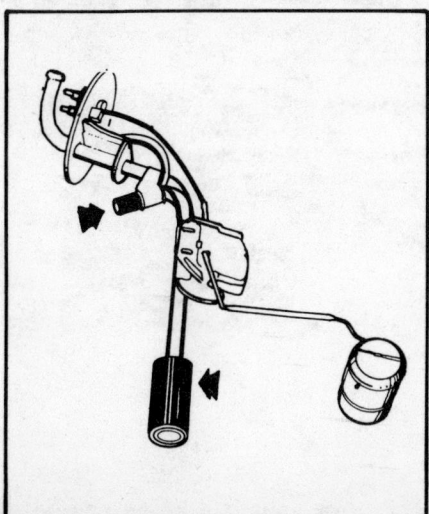

resistance in the water temperature unit must therefore be different. A disc of heat-sensitive material is incorporated in the temperature sending unit and changes its level of conductivity in proportion to its temperature. When the engine is cold, the resistance of the disc is high and little or no current is allowed to pass through the gauge circuit. As engine temperature increases, the disc becomes more and more conductive, permitting a greater current to pass through it to ground so that the flow through the dash gauge is strengthened.

Many older American cars, as well as some recent foreign imports, have a mechanical temperature gauge that employs a copper tube to couple the engine with the gauge. There is a sealed bulb containing a volatile liquid suspended in the cooling system, and as the temperature increases, the liquid begins to expand and fill a metal bellows that moves the indicator needle on the gauge. Vibration will often cause the copper tube eventually to break; thus the change to electric temperature gauges on domestic cars.

AMMETERS & WARNING LIGHTS

Of the common instrument panel gauges, the ammeter alone is different in its operation from all the others. Most ammeters used in sensitive electronic equipment applications have an electromagnetic coil that moves a piece of iron attached to the indicator needle. In other designs, a movable coil is deflected when its magnetic field reacts to a fixed magnet or piece of iron. The

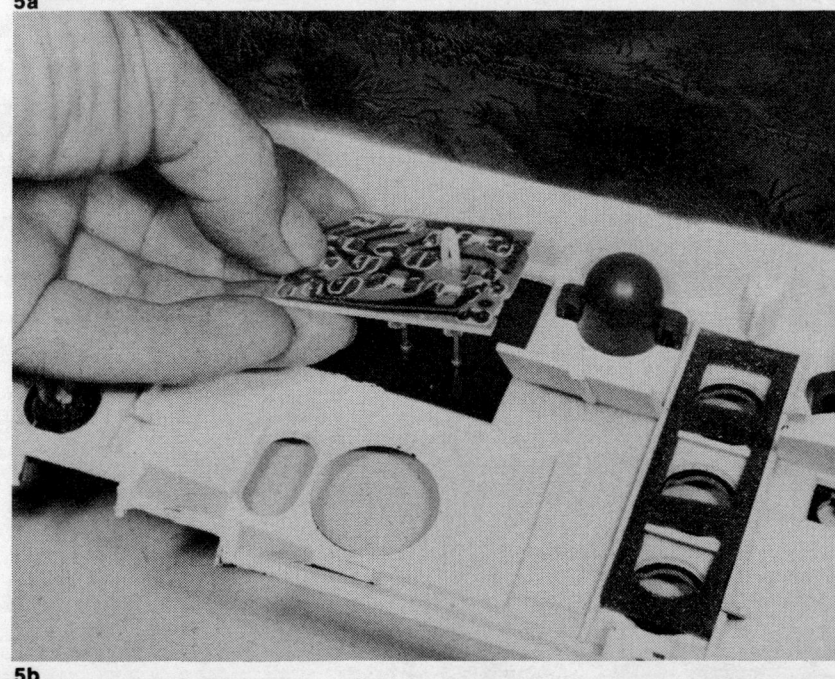

INSTRUMENTS

ammeter on your instrument panel comes closest to being of the movable iron type, but it is very simplified. The wire serving the ammeter in most cars is not connected electrically to the meter, but merely passes through a loop by the back of the instrument. A small magnet inside the gauge is affected by the passage of current through the wire. When current is flowing from the charging system into the battery, the magnet moves the pointer in the "charge" direction. When the battery takes over the electrical system's load, current flows in the opposite direction and the pointer is drawn into the "discharge" zone.

Indicator lights are often used in conjunction with gauges for the purpose of attracting the driver's attention when something abnormal is taking place so that he'll take time to check the dials and find out what's wrong. The only flaw in this idea is that drivers who do not bother to check their gauges are just as unlikely to look for little winking lights. Even if the light does draw his glance toward the instruments, it's not likely that he'll understand what they're telling him anyway. If he did, he'd have been watching the gauges in the first place.

Cars with only warning lights for oil pressure, coolant temperature, and battery charge place the driver in a very poor position for anything other than normal, conservative driving. Even regular high-speed freeway driving can create conditions that may completely wreck an engine or electrical system before the lights tell you anything at all. For example, some warning lights do not even begin to glow until the battery is being discharged at a rate of 10 to 15 amps. Worse yet, none of them will warn the driver of overcharging. Regulator failures that can destroy the battery often go undetected at high speeds until it's too late to make any difference.

Oil pressure warning lights are often set to stay off until pressure has dropped to less than 7 psi. A bearing that has started to go, or an oil pump that's losing its bite, will not show up on such a gauge. If you happen to be cruising the turnpike at 55 mph, you'll probably be in the market for a complete engine rebuild long before the light comes on.

Temperature indicators are generally more satisfactory—providing they indicate both hot and cold conditions. But even so, an overheating condition may already have become critical long before you're aware that anything is wrong.

MAGNETIC GAUGES

Chrysler introduced magnetic gauges on some of its 1983 front-wheel-drive models and extended their use to all 1984 FWD vehicles. In this type of gauge, a varying electric signal is sent to the gauge from its sensor or sending unit. This signal causes a pivoting permanent magnet to move proportionate to the strength of the signal. Since the gauge pointer is attached to the magnet, it also moves.

Magnetic gauges are more accurate, not affected by temperature extremes, and do not create RFI (radio-frequency interference) signals. They will give a reading when the ignition switch is off, but it is not accurate and has no meaning. Incidentally, they require no voltage limiter.

To test this type of gauge, simply disconnect and ground the sending unit lead. Turn the ignition switch on and read the gauge. If the gauge reading is at its maximum, replace the sending unit. If the reading is less than maximum, check the wiring between the gauge and the sending unit. If this is satisfactory, replace the gauge.

DIGITAL OR ELECTRONIC DISPLAYS

The digital or electronic displays that are taking the place of traditional instruments in late-model cars provide readouts via LEDs (light-emitting diodes) or multicolor vacuum fluorescent readings. These are expensive sealed units and should not be tampered with. If any display or reading malfunctions, the entire assembly is replaced, at this writing.

AFTERMARKET GAUGES

Keeping the above in mind, you will not be surprised that ammeters and oil pressure gauges are among the hottest-selling accessory lines on the auto market. Additional instruments are available from new-car dealers, parts stores, speed shops, mail-order companies, discount stores, etc. Prices can range from about $35 for an inexpensive three-dial ammeter, oil pressure, and water temp combination to almost the same amount for individual gauges. The difference in price from the least expensive to the most expensive instruments reflects variations in both appearance and construction. The lower-priced units are comparable in quality to those supplied by car makers as original equipment and are accurate enough for highway use, even if their appearance is generally none too elegant.

The more expensive gauges are usually more accurate. Some are of a quality suitable for such precision work as calibrating the voltage regulator or adjusting oil pressure bypass valves. Many of the more refined instruments are electromagnetic rather than thermal in operation, and have a small rotating armature that is controlled by a magnetic field. These units generally include a damper mechanism to prevent erratic pointer movement.

For the most part, the difference in price between one set of instruments and another is strictly a matter of price

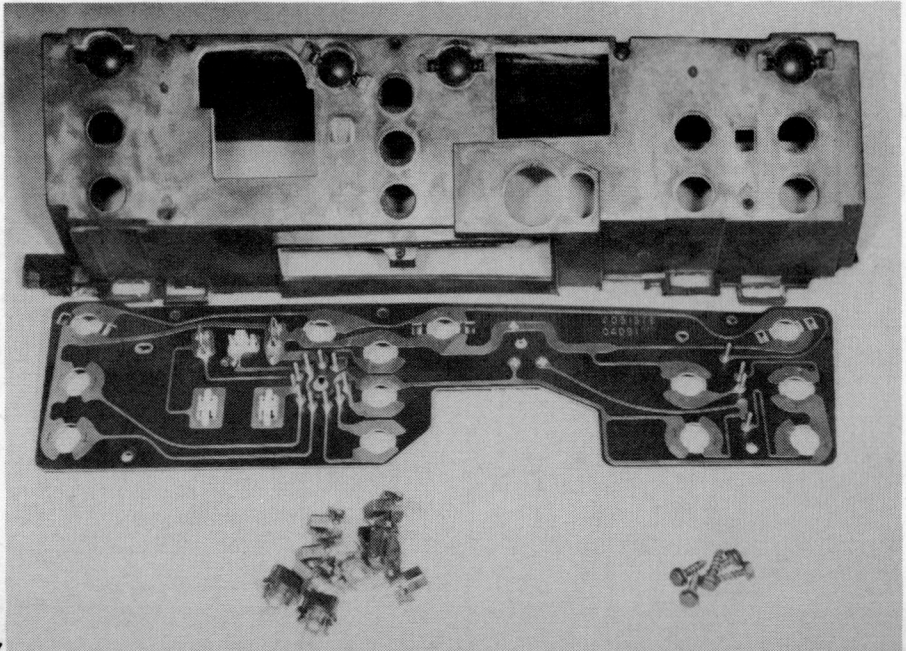

versus engineering. Pay a little more and you'll get a little more in the way of accuracy. If you're just looking for reasonably accurate and attractive instruments that can be added to a stock passenger car to replace or supplement the warning lights, the lower-priced models should be satisfactory. After a couple of years, you won't feel so bad about trading them with the car; getting around to removing them always seems to take more effort than their installation did. Find a set that offers fairly neat appearance at a modest price and you'll discover that their accuracy is more than adequate for highway driving.

Many of the inexpensive gauge sets come installed in small panels suitable for under-the-dash mounting. The location makes them a bit difficult to see, but the instrument panels on most production cars do not readily lend themselves to in-the-dash mounting. There are a number of complete instrument panels available for custom installation, and these are definitely worth the car owner's consideration. However, many attractive custom mountings are also made possible by some of the accessories sold for use with standard 2 1/16- and 2 5/8-inch gauges. These include recessed mountings and angle-mount bezels.

For the really mechanically minded driver, there are additional instruments not normally thought of as standard on auto instrument panels. Some, such as altimeters, inside/outside thermometers, accelerometers, and air-speed indicators, are of limited use in a car, but are nevertheless sometimes installed for appearance or for the sheer love of gimmickry. However, voltmeters, transmission or differential temperature gauges, and vacuum gauges can be of definite value to any driver.

A voltmeter, for example, tells the driver more about the condition of his car's electrical system than an ammeter does. The ammeter merely indicates whether the battery or the generator is doing more of the work in the electrical system. It also tells the driver whether the charging system is functioning normally. It does not really give a very good picture of the actual condition of the battery as to its power—a voltmeter does. When the voltmeter begins to indicate lower-than-normal "pressure" in the system, it is time to check the battery and voltage regulator. Battery failures can be avoided by paying close attention to a dash-mounted voltmeter.

TACHOMETERS

One of the most useful instruments you can add to a car is a tachometer. Tachs are offered either as options or as standard equipment on many sporty models, but these factory-supplied instruments are sometimes of very dubious quality. Worse yet, they are usually sealed units that cannot be repaired when they stop working properly. If you want a tach, check those available at nearby specialty equipment shops. You'll find that even superlative instruments sell for less than most of the factory-installed options. Furthermore, you'll probably get a worthwhile guaran-

6. Today's speedometer is a very simple device, but setting it back to take mileage off the car is still against the law in most states.

7. Modern instrument panel clusters use a solid-state design with printed circuit board. The board cannot be tested. If all else fails to correct the problem, replace the board with one known to be good.

8. Gauge design and construction vary with the job to be done. With mechanical oil pressure gauges (A and B), the application of pressure to the center of the offset lever operates the spring-loaded indicator needle.

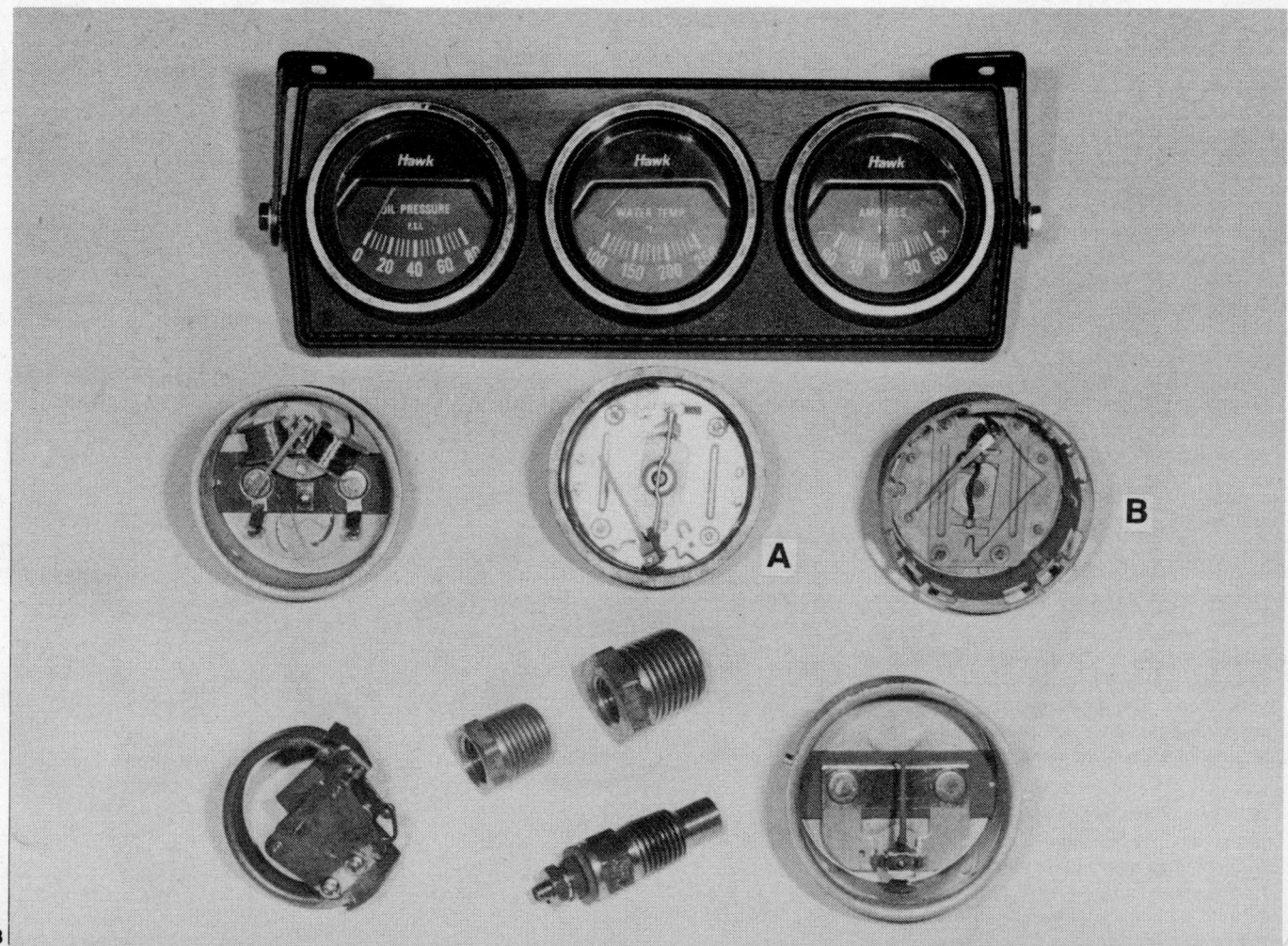

INSTRUMENTS

tee if you shop for a brand name. Find out if the unit can be serviced, either by returning it to the factory or by turning it over to a shop specializing in such repairs.

There are dozens of tachometers on the market, and some of them are none too good for either durability or accuracy. It doesn't help you very much to find a brand that's $10 cheaper than the one you would really like to have, if the cheaper model turns out to be a short-lived unit that cannot be fixed. Tachometer dial layouts receive much attention in the instrument makers' advertising, but often get too little from prospective buyers. The greater the needle sweep, the farther apart the dial calibrations can be, making for greater accuracy and ease in reading. However, some units that advertise a 250- to 270-degree sweep can do so only because their scale extends to 10,000 rpm. This means that on the average passenger car—which is all used up at about 5000 rpm—half the scale will be useless. You'll really have only a 125- or 135-degree sweep instrument. A wide sweep of about 250 degrees on a 7000-rpm scale is really needed for most ordinary cars.

REPAIRING/RECALIBRATING GAUGES

If you check most of the official service manuals, you'll find that nothing is said about repairing or recalibrating gauges. Frankly, it's neither simple nor advisable to attempt adjusting them in some cases. The basic reason that the car manufacturers advise replacement rather than repair is that it would cost in labor more to adjust a set of damaged gauges than to replace them. In the majority of cases in which the gauges have stopped working altogether, the problem is somewhere in the wiring. Usually, a wire has broken or there is corrosion under the terminal nut on the sending unit. Thermal gauges simply don't contain many parts that can go bad.

Instruments mounted in plastic instrument panels are sometimes damaged by losing their ground contact. Ground is often provided for the instrument panel via one of the wires leading to a dial-illuminating lamp. If this is pulled out to replace a bulb with the ignition turned on, or if it falls out while driving, the voltage limiter is no longer grounded. It therefore sends full battery current to all the instruments it serves. Their pointers are then forced far above the normal scale and the bimetallic strips that control them may be deformed permanently to some degree. After proper ground has been restored, the damaged instruments will record readings that are far from normal, usually quite a bit lower than they actually should be indicating.

Most gauges have to be calibrated at the factory before they are installed. For this reason, there is usually some means of adjusting the pointer position. It may be that a metal tab must be bent, or the gauge assembly may have a gear-toothed rack or screwdriver slot for this purpose. Their manufacturer adjusts them by coupling the gauge to a known output source and turning or bending the adjustment provision until the pointer indicates the correct figure. If your gauges have become accidentally damaged so that their readings are no longer accurate, take them out and inspect them. It may be possible to correct the condition yourself.

The best procedure is to set the pointers at zero and then attach them to the car's wiring once again without actually installing them in the dash. Operate the engine until it is thoroughly warmed up and check the gauge readings. They can then be readjusted slightly until they once again register the figures that you have learned are their normal reading. For more precise recalibration, you can adjust their pointers to match the figure recorded on a shop-tested ammeter or oil pressure gauge.

Since gauges rely on a precise amount of heat to make them function properly, their fronts must be covered by the glass or plastic lenses just as they are when the instruments are installed in the dash. Otherwise, heat will escape, lowering the readings. The gauges must also be held in an upright position and properly grounded. Fuel-level gauges can be set to indicate just barely a full tank immediately after filling the tank with gasoline. This will allow you a safe margin for error when approaching the empty position. When fuel gauges stick or give consistently misleading or incorrect readings, the trouble is generally in the sending unit rather than the gauge.

9. This example of a magnetic gauge uses two tiny wire coils mounted on pole shoes. The electromagnet exerting the strongest force will draw the indicator needle in its direction.

10. Typical of the thermal-electric gauge design, the needle moves as the bimetal strip expands or contracts. You're more likely to have problems with its sending unit than with the gauge itself.

Wiring

Automobile wiring diagrams currently provided by car makers are relatively easy to read and understand, compared to what they used to be, but the average person may still find them baffling. There are a number of traditional symbols commonly used by engineers when drawing up electrical system blueprints, and at one time, the wiring diagrams furnished in factory shop manuals were simply copies of such blueprints.

Unfortunately, most mechanics found such diagrams more confusing than helpful. The wiring diagrams supplied by some foreign car manufacturers still retain many of the symbols used by electrical engineers. For the most part, domestic car makers have adopted a more pictorial approach for the benefit of the mechanic who has a car to fix right now and can't take time out for a crash course in electrical engineering.

The most noticeable difference between engineering blueprints and factory shop manual wiring diagrams is that components—like switches, batteries, generators, gauges, etc.—are represented in auto diagrams by drawings of the part itself rather than by a schematic rendering of its circuitry. Simple drawings of an alternator can be understood at a glance, whereas a collection of looped lines and little arrows (the windings and diodes) may mean almost nothing to the mechanic who's interested only in determining which connection is the field terminal.

Still, certain engineering symbols are indispensable, regardless of how realistic you try to make a wiring diagram. There are times, for example, when the actual circuits of some electrical system component must be shown in more detail. When trying to show exactly how a voltage regulator works, a straight blueprint presentation of the coils, contacts, diodes, and resistances shows their relationship much more clearly than a drawing of the actual regulator would. A double-wound relay coil and its core could not be presented as an ordinary picture. You just wouldn't be able to tell for certain whether it had a hidden internal winding. Yet this precision is not normally required in an ordinary diagram of a standard wiring system.

The most common symbol found in automotive wiring diagrams is the one used to represent ground. Obviously, it would be very confusing if wires that are connected to the car's chassis were shown in the diagram as merely screwed to an undistinguishable hunk of metal. The ground symbol can be seen throughout automotive wiring schematics. It indicates wires that are in contact with the grounded side of the electrical

1. This Ford lighting and wiring diagram is for use in following the hypothetical tests described in the text.

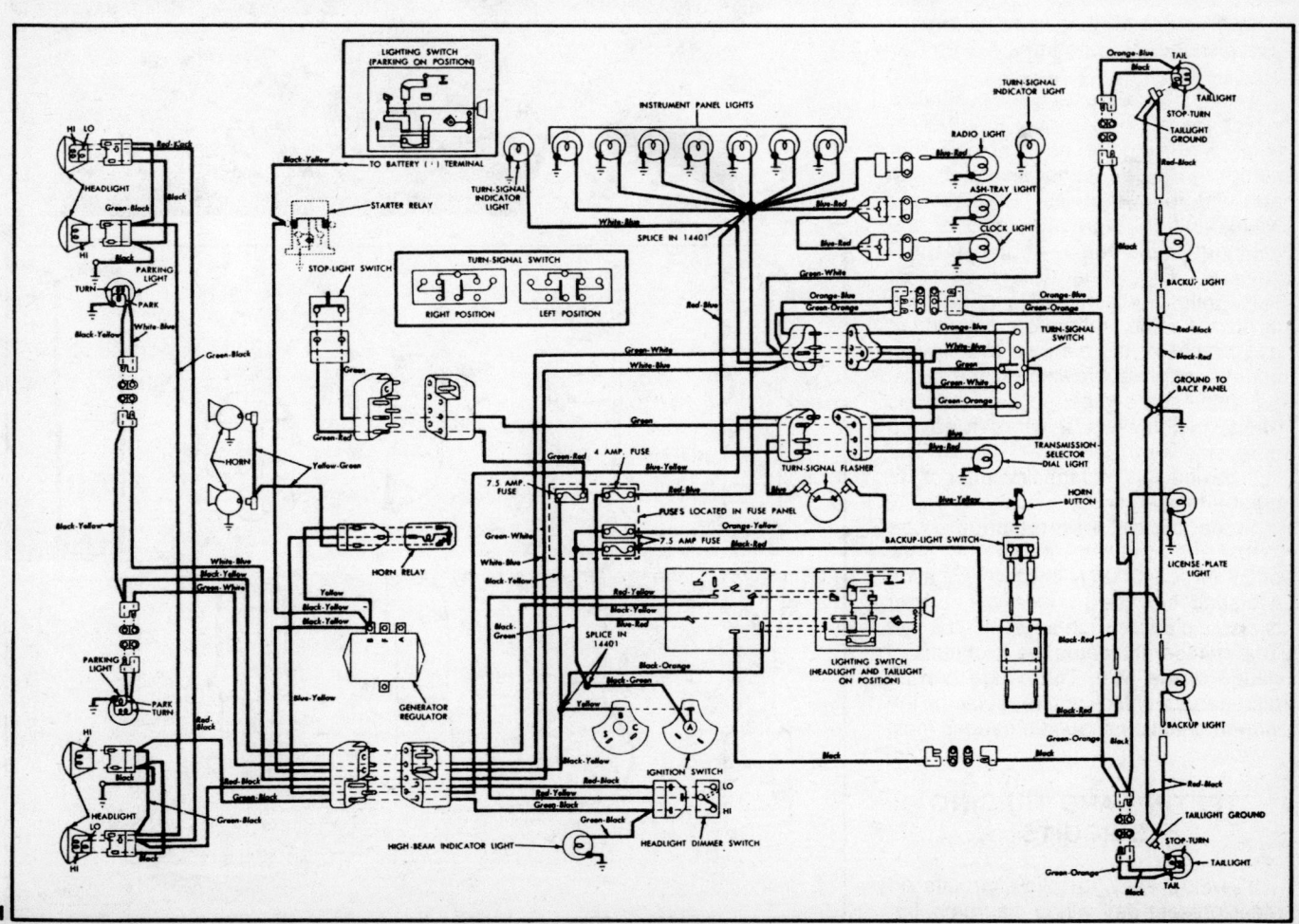

IGNITION & ELECTRICAL SYSTEMS/165

WIRING

system via the chassis of the car.

The symbols for positive (+) and negative (−) are generally known, but when presented at either end of something that looks like a clump of lines, it may be difficult for the uninitiated to grasp exactly what is meant. Actually, it's only a battery. Most service manual wiring diagrams have an actual picture of the battery, but sometimes—especially where space is limited or where the battery does not play an important part in the circuit—the symbol for a battery is used instead of a picture.

Lights are normally shown as simple loops in blueprints, but shop manual wiring diagrams usually modify this by adding a circle for bulbs and a pictorial approximation for sealed beams. The symbol for a switch is nearly always omitted in favor of a drawing of the actual unit. Ford Motor Company manuals contain the most traditional wiring diagrams and symbols. Chrysler, GM, and American Motors manuals are much more pictorial in their approach to the subject.

To help mechanics locate the various wires that are shown in diagrams on the actual automobiles, the wires are color-coded. You may have noticed that the insulation on the wires in your car comes in many different colors. Some wires are sheathed in solid colors, whereas others are combinations of two or more hues. Textile-covered wiring may have various distinguishing patterns woven into the outer sheath.

Even a casual look at a representative wiring diagram will show that beside each wire, a color or combination of colors is listed. Some diagrams use abbreviations such as "BW" (black-white) and "G" (green). However, the mechanic probably could not tell whether "BW" meant black-white or blue-white, or whether "G" meant green or gold. A table is therefore included in one corner of the diagram to tell what color(s) each abbreviation represents. Sometimes, a symbol such as "LW" is used for blue-white wires to avoid confusion with "BW" (black-white). The "L," obviously, is not the first letter of the color it indicates.

Some of the newer manuals use longer abbreviations such as BLK, BRN, or DK GRN, LT GRN—the last indicating two shades of green. Usually, a number is also included, such as 14, 16, 18, etc. This number indicates the thickness or gauge of the wire. The gauge can be disregarded unless you're replacing the wire in question; if so, the gauges must match.

TESTING AND TRACING CIRCUITS

It's fairly easy to follow circuits on most present-day wiring diagrams, but things can become a bit confusing where the wires are shown to pass through an intermediate switch or accessory before reaching their ultimate destination. The following example will serve to illustrate this problem. Let's assume that all four of your car's headlights have stopped working and you have no idea at all where the trouble is. Trying to find the source of the malfunction by simply checking over the car itself could be a long, involved job. If you inspect the wires coming from the headlight switch, you may discover that their color does not match any of those that you can see attached to the headlights. To confuse the situation further, the wires between these two points are encased in a harness that appears to lead to and from a great many interconnected components. You could spend many hours trying to make sense of this situation.

The solution to your problem is to consult a wiring diagram. It's amazing how easily you can figure out which wire goes where by spending a few minutes checking the chart. Let's refer to the Ford lighting and horn diagram and assume that this is the diagram for your car. Since all four headlights are inoperative, you can rule out a loose ground connection at the lamps. Starting at the headlights, you can see that only two wires serve the four sealed-beam units—a red-black and a green-black. Tracing these from the lights backward into the electrical system, we see that they pass through a multiple connector—one potential trouble spot. Looking beyond the connector, we find that the red-black and green-black wires both

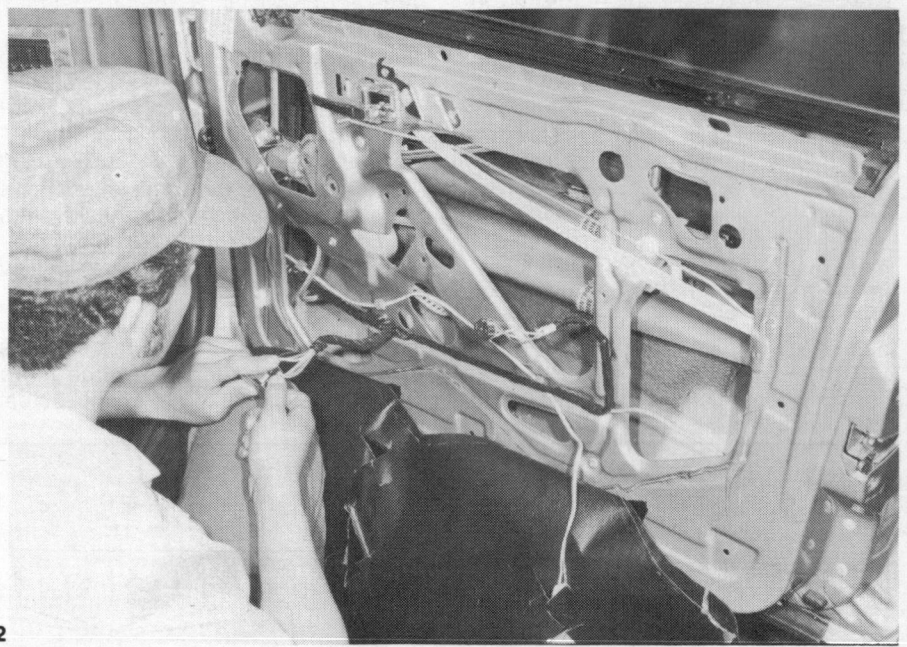

2

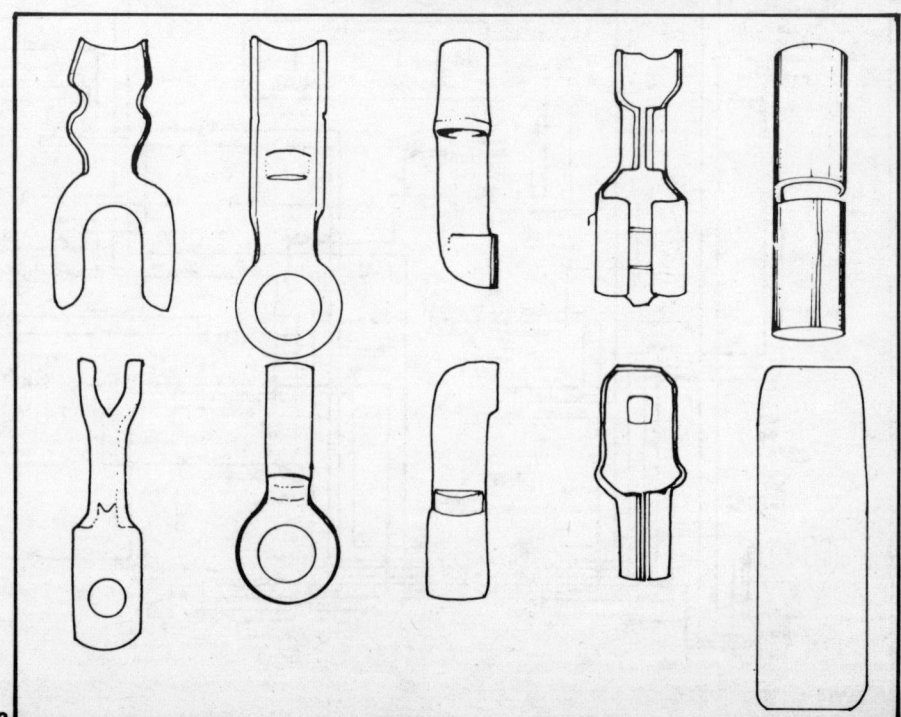

3

lead to the dimmer switch, still another potential trouble area. The only other wire leaving the dimmer switch is a red-yellow one, which leads right to the headlight switch.

The first step is to find out whether current is reaching the multiple connector on the firewall. Pull out the connector and turn on the headlight switch. By inserting a test light or voltmeter probe into the indicated holes in the female connector, you can determine whether current is reaching this point. If it is, then the trouble is in the connector plug (which may be misaligned or corroded) or in the wiring to the lights (although it's highly unlikely that both wires would break at the same time).

If no current is reaching the multiple connector, move your point of investigation to the dimmer switch. If current is reaching the switch by way of the red-yellow wire but none is leaving via the red-black or green-black wire, the switch is defective. Here again, the problem may be a misaligned or corroded connector. If no current is being delivered from the main headlight switch, take a look at the taillights. If they're burning normally, the trouble is probably a worn contact in the headlight switch. Another possibility is a break in the red-yellow wire that connects to the switch.

If the taillights are not working either, check the diagram to find the color code of the wire coming from the battery to the headlight switch. You'll see that it's a black-yellow. You can follow this wire all the way from the battery to the starter relay, the generator regulator, the multiple connector, and right up to a splice where it changes to black-orange and goes into the headlight switch itself. Using the diagram, you'll know where to make your tests. Without it, you'd have to do a good bit of head scratching before you were even able to figure out where to hook up the voltmeter.

However, if both the headlights *and* taillights are not working, yet the instrument panel lights are, the problem is most likely a defective main light switch or corroded terminals. Examine, clean, and tighten all terminals and check the lights once again. If this does not solve the problem, you'll have to replace the switch.

There may be times when either you are far from home and your wiring diagram (a good reason for carrying it in the car) or you simply have no wiring diagram to consult. There's no really quick and easy way to determine exactly which wires serve the circuit that's not working properly. In the case of the example just discussed, you could check the more common lighting system trouble spots, such as the dimmer switch and the multiple connector. But what if the failure happens to be in the dome light, backup light, or some other obscure circuit?

Probably the best way to find the correct wire when you don't have a diagram to work with is to trace the circuits with a test light. The test light should be equipped with alligator clips that can be snapped onto a ground or the component being checked. Let's suppose you're trying to locate the wire under the instrument panel that conducts electricity to the backup lights. The lights don't work and a voltmeter or test light check at the switch or the transmission shows that no current is reaching that point. The circuit's fuse is all right, but no current seems to be reaching it either. Logic should tell you that the trouble is between the fuse block and the current source, but no wire leaving the fuses corresponds in color to the one leading to the backup light switch. Without a diagram to guide you, you don't know which wire to trace from the fuse block back to the battery.

With the ignition switch and headlight switch off, and the transmission in neutral, clip the positive lead of a test light to a good ground somewhere nearby. Now take a short jumper wire that has a large pin or needle soldered to one end and an alligator clip to the other.

4

5

2. The modern car contains far more electrical wiring and circuits than those of just a decade ago. The ability to read and follow a wiring diagram is essential in electrical troubleshooting today.

3. Here's a small sample of the many types of electrical connectors used in automotive wiring.

4. The old reliable non-powered test light is almost indispensible. The light bulb inside the handle can be easily changed when it burns out. To use, ground the clip, then touch the point to any terminal to see if it's hot.

5. Heat damaged or deteriorated insulation can create hard-to-locate electrical problems. When troubleshooting electrical problems, don't overlook this basic fact of life.

WIRING

Attach the clip to ground. The needle of the jumper wire can then be used to probe the wires leading to the fuse block. When you probe the correct wire, the test lamp will light. At this point, you'll know which wire to trace from the fuse block to the source of battery current.

If you're using this method to find a wire that may be continuously connected to the car's battery, or if you're going to have to touch some "hot" wires in the process of elimination, remove the car's battery connections. If the wires being checked have inline connectors, these can be pulled apart and touched with the needle so that you won't have to force the probe through the insulation.

Simply speaking, tests made with a test light and a jumper allow you to apply current to a known part of a circuit so that you can find the same circuit elsewhere. By eliminating the car's battery, you can be certain that only one circuit has current in it. Another method of circuit testing uses a nonpowered test light. These test lights have a light bulb in the handle, a sharp probe at one end, and an alligator clip at the end of a wire on the other end. With the car's battery, energize the circuit you wish to find. Attach the test light's clip to a good ground. When the probe's point finds a "hot" circuit, the test light will come on. When examining a light circuit, always work backward from the nonfunctional light bulb; that is, toward the car's battery.

WIRING CIRCUIT TERMS

The terms *series* and *parallel* are easy to understand if you think of them as describing, like a roadmap, how the current is going to travel. For example, if you talk about connecting one electrical unit to a battery, it's just as if you were describing a road between Kansas and California. The electrical unit is simply connected to the battery, and that's really all there is to say about it. But when you connect a second electrical unit to the battery, you must consider whether you're connecting it in series or parallel. Suppose our second unit is Nevada, and we connect it so that it's on the same road that we originally had running to California. To get to California on that road, we now have to go through Nevada, so we can say that Nevada is in series with California. The current that operates our first electrical unit, California, now has to pass through Nevada before it can reach California.

In the process, the electricity becomes slightly tired as it goes through Nevada, so that when it reaches California, it doesn't have enough push left to do the job it's supposed to do. To enable our electricity to do its job better, we'll build a second road from Kansas directly to Nevada, and route our first road so that it bypasses Nevada and goes directly to California. Now we have a parallel circuit. Electricity can go directly from Kansas to California without the exhausting experience of passing through Nevada. And our Nevada unit receives electricity directly from the battery also. The result is plenty of electricity to operate both electrical units without one disturbing the other.

Regardless of how many electrical units there are, all are connected to the power source either in series or parallel when considered in relation to another unit. How about the relation between the two headlights? They're in parallel. The headlights and taillights? Parallel. All four turn signals? Parallel again. What about the headlight switch and the headlights? That's a series connection, since the electricity goes through the headlight switch before it gets to the headlights.

Switches are always wired in series with the load they control. The word "load" means anything that uses up electricity, such as a light bulb, relay, resistance, electric motor, or anything that does work. A switch is not a load. It's supposed to pass on the electricity without any losses. If it doesn't, it starts to heat up, which means that it's using electricity because it doesn't have enough capacity for the load it's feeding. Dirty contacts or a switch that's too small for the job makes the switch heat up.

The word "shunt" is another way of describing a parallel circuit. A shunt is a branch from a wire feeding some other unit. Suppose there's a wire feeding the taillights. We break into that wire somewhere in the vicinity of the trunk and connect an additional wire to an auxiliary taillight. Electricity now goes through both taillights to ground. It's correct to say that the taillights are wired

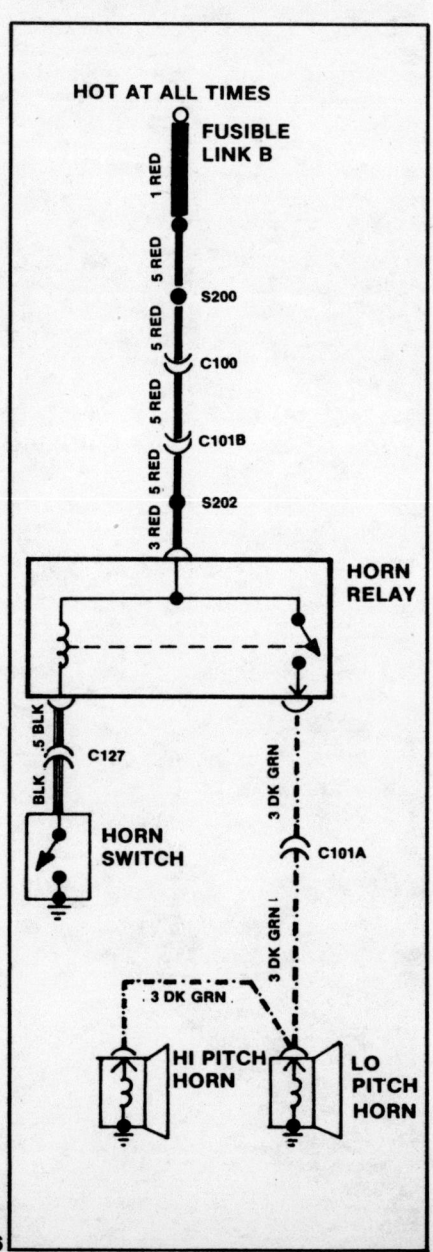

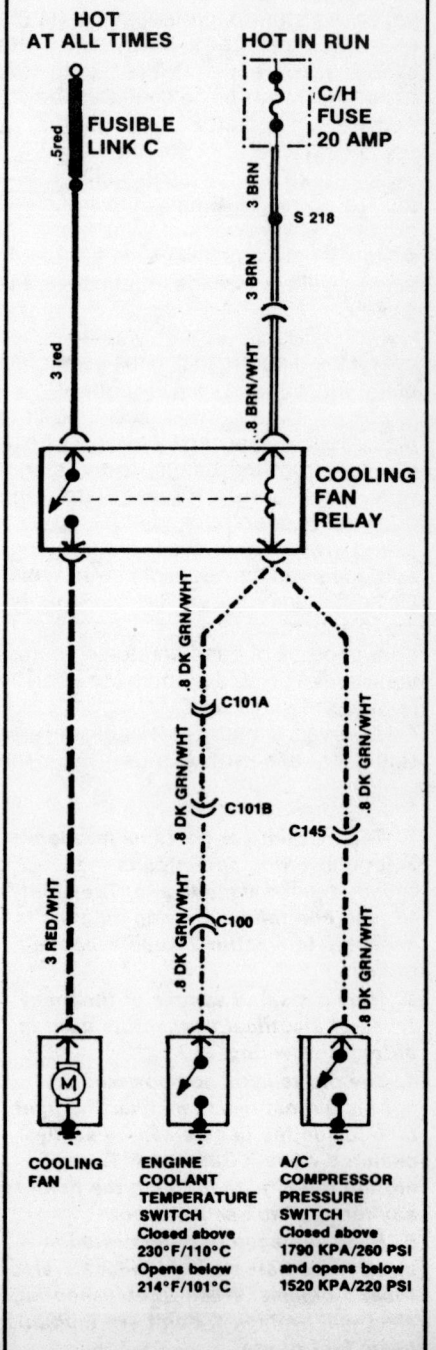

in parallel, but because we tapped into the original taillight wire instead of coming directly from the battery, our auxiliary taillight is actually shunt-wired. Both stock taillights work in parallel, each receiving an equal supply of electricity, but we have increased the load by adding a light to the original wiring. If the original wire is not large enough to carry the added current, both taillights may burn too dimly because they're starved for electricity. By the way, taillights have a tendency to fill with water during heavy storms or while passing through a carwash. This will cause the bases of the bulbs and sockets to corrode, resulting in a poor ground.

A ground is nothing more than a return path for the electricity after it has done its job. The ground strap on the engine provides a return path for the ignition and starting current on an engine that is rubber-mounted. If you think of electricity and wiring as similar to cars traveling a road, you'll be a long way along your own road to understanding wiring.

WORKING WITH ELECTRICAL WIRING

One of the most frequent mistakes made by car owners is to add electrical accessories without giving careful thought to where to pick up the current to operate them. In some cases, the car's battery and generating system may be just barely adequate to supply the electrical system's original current needs. Even the addition of a pair of driving lights can sometimes put an overload on the charging system. In a few cases, the charging system may not be able to keep up with the added current demands at all, which means that the battery will be under a steady discharge.

Before adding any really big current consumers, it's a good idea to take a voltmeter reading of the entire electrical system with all existing lights and electrical accessories in operation. First, make sure that your battery is fully charged. Then with the engine dead, turn everything on and see how much the load drags the battery down. If the reading is 11.5 volts or less, you'd probably better think twice before wiring in anything else. An even better test is to insert a test resistance equal to the load of the proposed accessory into the circuit and then make a check of the charging system's ampere output with everything in operation. If the load is continuously above the factory specs for the generator or alternator, you'll need a higher-output charging system to handle the proposed load. For this reason, new cars destined for trailer towing are factory-equipped with heavy-duty electrical systems. Alternators in such systems have almost double the usual amperage output. The on-board battery and clearance lights of a trailer or

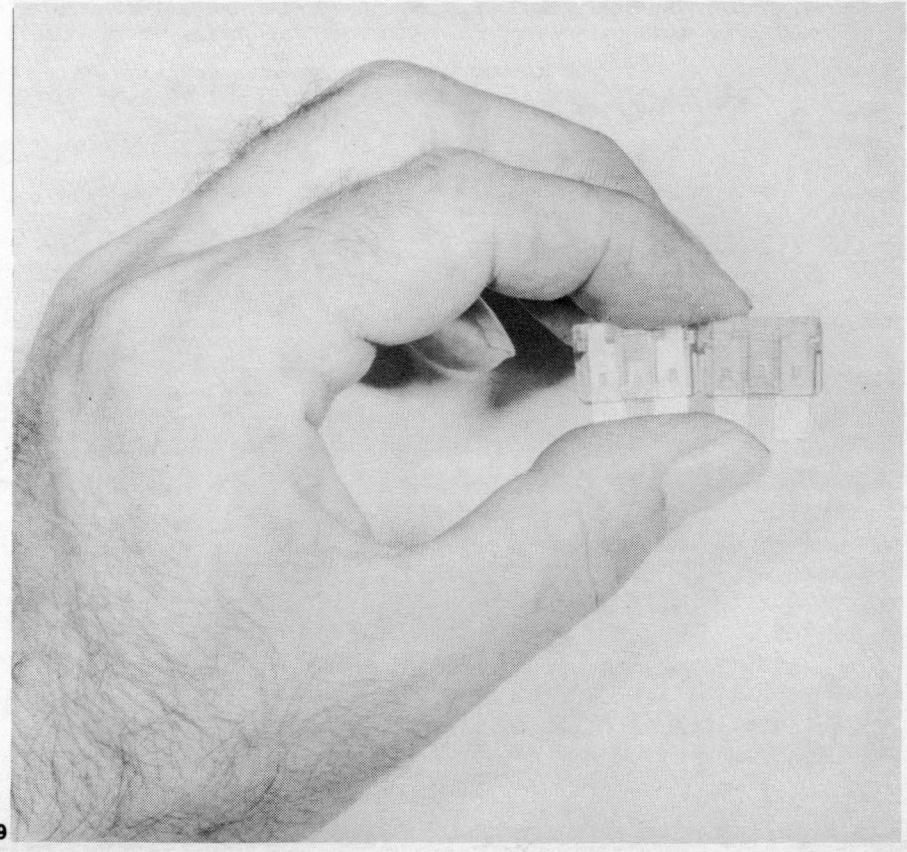

6. Automotive horns require a relatively heavy current for their operation. While some cars use the horn button electrical contacts to send current directly to the horn, most American cars use a horn relay. Pressing the horn button closes the relay contacts and send battery voltage to the horn, regardless of how many other accessories are in use at the time.

7. Electric cooling fans on transverse-mounted engines use a relay with an engine coolant temperature switch and an air conditioning compressor pressure switch wired into the circuit.

8. The auto industry gradually changed over to plastic mini- or blade-type fuses in the late Seventies. Color-coded according to its amperage value, the mini-fuse is far easier to replace.

9. The mini-fuse consists of two blade terminals connected by a wire loop. Current enters through one terminal, passes across the loop and out the other blade, unless the loop is blown. The end of each blade protrudes through the plastic housing to provide test terminals without removing the fuse.

WIRING

camper can quickly overtax a standard generator or alternator system.

You should also give careful thought to where the new accessory will connect in your car's wiring. If you hook it into a circuit that's already serving another electrical component, you may overload its fuse or circuit breaker. Worse yet, you may overload the wiring. Wire sizes are measured by the gauge system—the higher the number, the smaller the wire. Eighteen-gauge wire is the lightest type used in automobiles, generally for such things as instrument panel illuminating bulbs. The heaviest is usually 10 gauge, which is reserved for main charging system connections and the current supply to the headlight switch and fuse panel.

In some circuits, you'll find 12-gauge wire used for some of the charging system connections, but 12 gauge is most frequently installed between the fuse block and the more current-hungry lights and accessories. Fourteen-gauge wire generally serves such things as the headlights, radio, horn, and cigarette lighter. Taillights, brake lights, parking lights, and other small bulbs are normally provided with 16-gauge wire, as are the gauges, heater, and interior lighting.

In all such wiring applications, the fuse size corresponds closely to the size of the wire. There are light-duty fuses for light-gauge wire, and higher-amperage-capacity fuses for heavier-gauge wire. The greater the current demand of the electrical component being served, the heavier the wiring and fusing must be.

The most common wear points in automotive wiring systems are at the terminals and where wires are exposed to weather or to mechanical abrasion. Terminals that are loose tend to erode because of both corrosion and the arcing of electrical current. Very often, wire flexing induced by mechanical vibration is greatest where the terminal joins the wire, causing it to break at that point. If the rest of the wire is in good shape, a new terminal can be added. If the wire has broken somewhere in the middle, it's possible to make a good permanent splice.

New terminals in various styles and sizes are sold at all auto-supply stores. Some are of the crimp-on variety, and are available in kits including the special plierlike tool used to install them. Others slip onto the wire and are already tinned so that they can be quickly soldered into place. The better terminals have short pieces of plastic tubing slipped onto them which can be slid down to cover the exposed portion of the terminal's stem as well as slightly overlapping the wire's insulation.

Beginning with its 1980 X-cars, General Motors introduced a special type of terminal designed to overcome many of the problems presented by ordinary terminals/connectors. Called a Weather-Pack terminal/connector, it is a molded unit with a secondary lock hinge which retains the terminal in the connector even if the small terminal lock tangs are not properly positioned. As much as possible, the Weather-Pack design is an environmentally protected connection; that is, it prevents heat, moisture, dirt, and other environmental conditions from affecting the terminal connection. Because of its unique design, a special tool (GM P/N J-28742) is needed to remove the pin/sleeve terminals. Attempting removal with ordinary tools will deform the terminal, which cannot be straightened once it's bent. When a Weather-Pack terminal is defective and must be replaced, it is necessary to splice a whole new connector assembly into the wiring harness. Such connectors do not, however, prevent terminal oxidation, and GM recommends that you wiggle a connector suspected of an open-circuit condition to see if it corrects the problem before replacing the connector.

When breaks occur in the middle of a wire, the first thing you must decide is whether to replace the entire wire, or just repair the break itself. The wire can probably be kept in service if the insulation is not soft and spongy, or hard and cracked. If its general condition is poor, it is wise to remove it and install a new piece.

Broken wire ends should not merely be twisted together, since vibration and corrosion will ultimately turn this makeshift joint into a high-resistance one. The wire should be spliced either with solder or with a crimped-on sleeve. Soldering is the neatest and most practical method of splicing the multistrand wire used in car wiring. Brighten the strands lightly by pulling a piece of fine emery cloth over them a few times, then intersperse them and give a twist or two. Apply a small amount of solder to the tip of the soldering iron and touch the iron to the joint. As soon as the solder has flowed into the wire strands, remove the iron. Overheating the joint damages the surrounding insulation.

Although soldering is a good way to splice two wires together, the existing joint must be protected with some form of insulation. Plastic electrical tape is

170/IGNITION & ELECTRICAL SYSTEMS

commonly used, but it's not a good practice. Exposed to heat, oil, weather, and gasoline fumes as they are, these tapes tend either to harden and crack, or to become soft and gummy, sliding away from the joint they were intended to protect.

What is recommended is the use of electrical shrink tubing, a material widely used by wiring specialists but little known by the general public. A strip of shrink tubing long enough to cover the entire splice (or shank of a wire end terminal) and a reasonable section of wire insulation at either end protects the splice from possible shorts. First slip a piece of shrink tubing over a splice or terminal end, then heat it with a match or hair dryer. The heat makes the material shrink, creating an extremely tight fit over the splice or terminal end.

The use of a crimped-on sleeve is an alternative to soldering a wire splice. Actually, there is a choice here too. One type known as a butt connector is plain and crimps onto wires butted together in its open ends. A shrink tube must be used to protect this butt connector. You can also buy butt connectors that are preinsulated. Finally, you can buy crimp-on bullets that fit onto the wire ends. These plug into insulated connectors and offer the advantage of being able to disconnect the "splice" at any time by simply pulling one bullet or the other from its end of the connector.

A wiring system in good condition is like a healthy circulatory system. If the wires are of the correct capacity, properly fused, and have tight, well-insulated joints and terminals, your car should enjoy a long and efficient electrical lifetime. One thing bears mentioning here: you can always use wires of a larger gauge than necessary in any wiring circuit—nothing can be hurt by it and the added cost for the wiring is minimal. But never try to skimp on your wiring by going to a wire gauge one size or more smaller than specified and attempt to justify this by saying that the circuit won't be used very much. If you reduce the wire size, you increase the load on the wire—and that's how fires start. So if you're going to wire your car, do it the right way. Otherwise you'll have the time of your life trying to locate shorts and other hidden problems, problems you built into your car's wiring by negligence.

10. Some foreign cars still use the ceramic-type fuses found on VWs until recently. Although they are also color-coded, they are less convenient to test and replace.
11. Automakers have spent fortunes attempting to devise a foolproof wire connector that (a) is waterproof, (b) will not corrode and (c) protects the wires against those who insist on yanking the connector apart. This Ford connector is typical, but the desired design continues to elude everyone.

ELECTRICAL TROUBLESHOOTING

For many drivers, troubleshooting electrical problems on a car proves to be such a frustrating experience that they eventually throw up their hands and turn the problem over to their corner garage or dealer to solve. The cost for such a solution can be far in excess of its true worth, especially if the problem is only a burned-out bulb and the service agency sharpened its pencil when you walked through the door. It's true that you'll occasionally encounter an electrical problem that seems to defy all reasonable attempts to find the solution, but for the most part, troubleshooting any electrical failure or problem requires only patience and a systematic procedure.

Once you know what's wrong, refer to the proper wiring diagram to get your bearings and figure out how the circuit should work. Then apply logic to the situation and go to work. With the many different circuit designs used in automobiles, it's just not possible to formulate a single problem-solving procedure that will work in every case, every time. But there are two general principles you can use to apply a systematic approach to troubleshooting any electrical problem:

1. If a single component in a multiple-component circuit will not work, start your test procedure at that point. Translated to a lighting circuit where only one of the bulbs in the circuit does not work, you should begin your troubleshooting at the bulb and work backward into the circuit until you find what is causing the failure.

2. If none of the components in a multiple-component circuit works, begin troubleshooting at the point where the circuit receives its power. In the case of our lighting circuit, you would start by checking the battery's voltage output and then test each component and connection in sequence until you find the cause of the problem.

Basically, you'll be looking for one of four electrical failures:

1. Short Circuit—a connection (often copper to copper) that lets current bypass all or part of a given circuit.
2. Open Circuit—a break in the circuit that results in very high resistance and little or no current flow.
3. Grounded Circuit—a connection that bypasses part or all of the circuit from the insulated side to the ground side.
4. High-Resistance Circuit—a result of poor or corroded connections, or frayed/damaged wiring.

Each of these conditions creates excessive resistance that reduces current flow sufficiently to prevent the circuit from working properly.

In addition to a wiring diagram, you should have a voltmeter, an ammeter, and an ohmmeter (see "Electrical Test Equipment" chapter), as well as the three common electrical troubleshooting tools described below in detail.

12-VOLT TEST LIGHT

This is simply a 12-volt bulb with a set of test leads attached. It can be used to locate voltage or to find a short circuit. To find voltage, connect one lead of the test light to a known good ground and use the other lead to probe various points in the circuit. If the bulb lights, there is power to the circuit to that point. When you check for a short, one test lead is connected to a power source and the other used to probe various points in the circuit where a short is suspected. In this case, the bulb will only light if there is a short to ground.

This is a particularly useful test with late-model cars that use many plastic components or mount metal components on plastic. Such cars can develop many problems because of a poor ground. Some units, such as heater blowers, are often mounted on plastic and thus require an additional ground wire; others may develop high resistance from corrosion or loose mounting. If plastic is involved with the component or circuit you're checking, check the ground as one of your first troubleshooting steps.

CONTINUITY TESTER

This is also called a self-powered test

1

lamp, since it is a 12-volt bulb, a 1.5-volt dry-cell battery, and a pair of test leads wired in series. Because it contains its own power source, the continuity tester can be used to check for complete circuits, or for continuity between given points in a circuit. Because of its low available voltage, however, the self-powered test lamp cannot be used to check high-resistance components such as ignition cables.

When using a continuity tester, remove any battery voltage from the circuit by disconnecting the negative battery cable before connecting the tester across two points in the circuit. If the circuit is okay, the bulb should light. Failure of the bulb to light indicates that there is an open in the circuit.

You can also test switches, gauges, etc., on or off the car with a continuity tester to determine if they are functioning properly. When using a continuity tester with a simple on/off toggle switch, for example, the bulb should light when the switch is in the on position (circuit complete) and not light when the switch is in the off position (circuit open).

JUMPER LEAD

In most cases, this is simply a length of electrical wire (usually 14-gauge) with alligator clips soldered at each end. More sophisticated jumper leads may contain a 5-amp circuit breaker. The jumper lead is useful in bypassing switches and open circuits, but should never be used across any load or resistance circuit component. This will cause a direct battery short and may result in damage to circuit components, start a fire, or cause personal injury.

DIAGNOSTIC CONNECTORS

The crowded engine compartments in late-model cars have made it increasingly difficult to reach certain electrical test points. Since many electrical system components have a direct

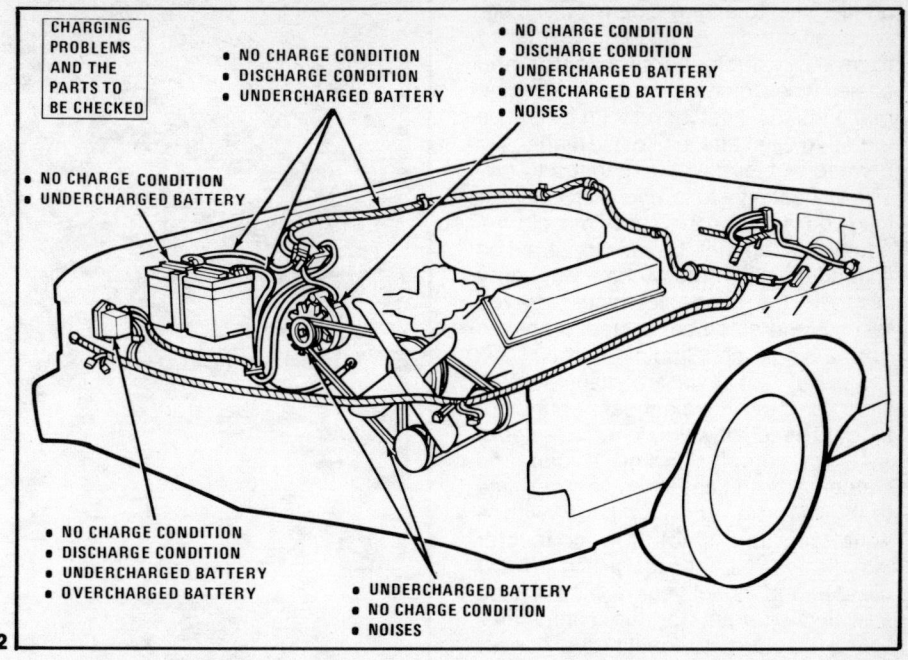

1. Troubleshooting can lead you to the general problem area but you may still have to disassemble a unit for further testing.

2. Before troubleshooting a specific problem, try to visualize the system involved and check out the most logical causes of the malfunction. This charging circuit diagram shows the potential trouble points that might lead to a flat battery.

3. The old reliable self-powered test lamp is a most useful and inexpensive tool for checking out circuit continuity. Be sure the battery inside the unit is good before accepting its results as gospel.

4. Most electrical troubleshooting should begin with a check of the fuse box. After that, inspect the fusible links to make sure they're good.

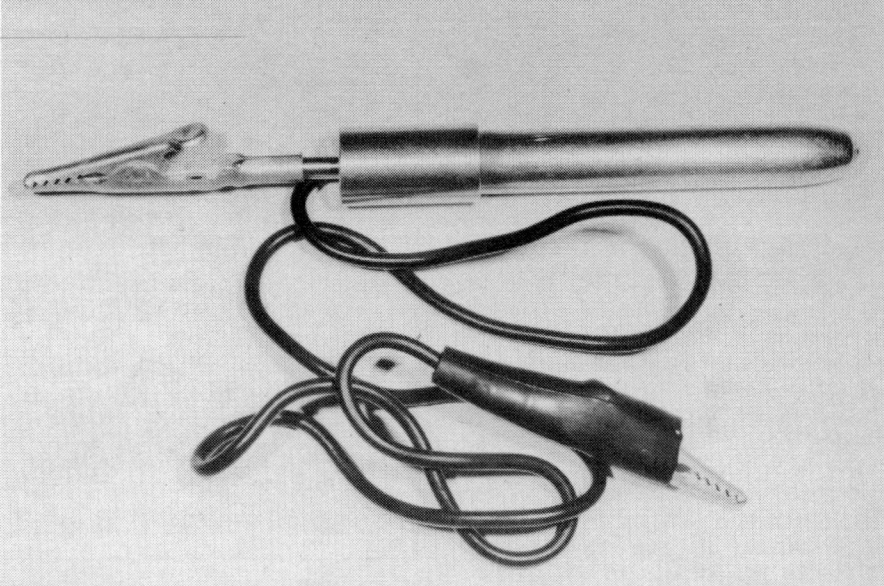

ELECTRICAL TROUBLESHOOTING

relationship to engine operation, a plug-in connector block has been developed to make troubleshooting faster and easier when diagnosing certain engine malfunctions. First introduced by GM on the 1976 Chevette, use of the diagnostic connector block was expanded to full-size GM cars the following year. Chrysler followed suit in 1979, but Ford did not adopt the concept. Usually mounted on a fenderwell where it can be easily reached, the connector block lets you test several electrical system problems from a single checkpoint.

Special test units are manufactured which plug into the diagnostic connector block. These allow you to run a series of tests by simply turning a dial and watching the indicator needle. The same tests can be accomplished with a voltmeter, but since the connector installations differ according to car marque and model year, you'll still need a wiring diagram (or the connector's wiring diagram) to identify the correct test points.

The same concept was applied to quick-check the air-conditioning system on GM cars; thus you'll find two connector blocks on the 1976 Chevette and 1977–80 full-size GM cars. Servicemen apparently did not care for the idea, and it was discontinued with the 1980 model year.

TROUBLESHOOTING ELECTRICAL CIRCUITS

Thus far, in this and other chapters, we've discussed electrical troubleshooting mainly of lighting circuits. To broaden the horizons of those drivers to whom electrical circuits are a deep mystery, let's take a look at two different kinds of circuits and see how we can apply our troubleshooting knowledge. We'll start with the horn circuit, since it probably provides more aggravation than any other electrical circuit for many drivers. If you've ever tapped the horn button and heard nothing, or couldn't shut the darned thing off once it started blasting, you know what we mean.

Horn circuits can be wired in two different ways. One is to use the horn button to complete the circuit from the battery to the horn. When the horn button is depressed, it closes a switch, completing the circuit and sending battery current to the horn. Such systems have a fuse or circuit breaker in the horn circuit.

The other method is to insert a relay between the horns with a direct connection from the battery to the relay through a fusible link (more on these later). When the relay coil is grounded by depressing the horn button, the relay contacts close to complete the circuit and current flows to the horn. Since this method is more commonly used by domestic car makers,

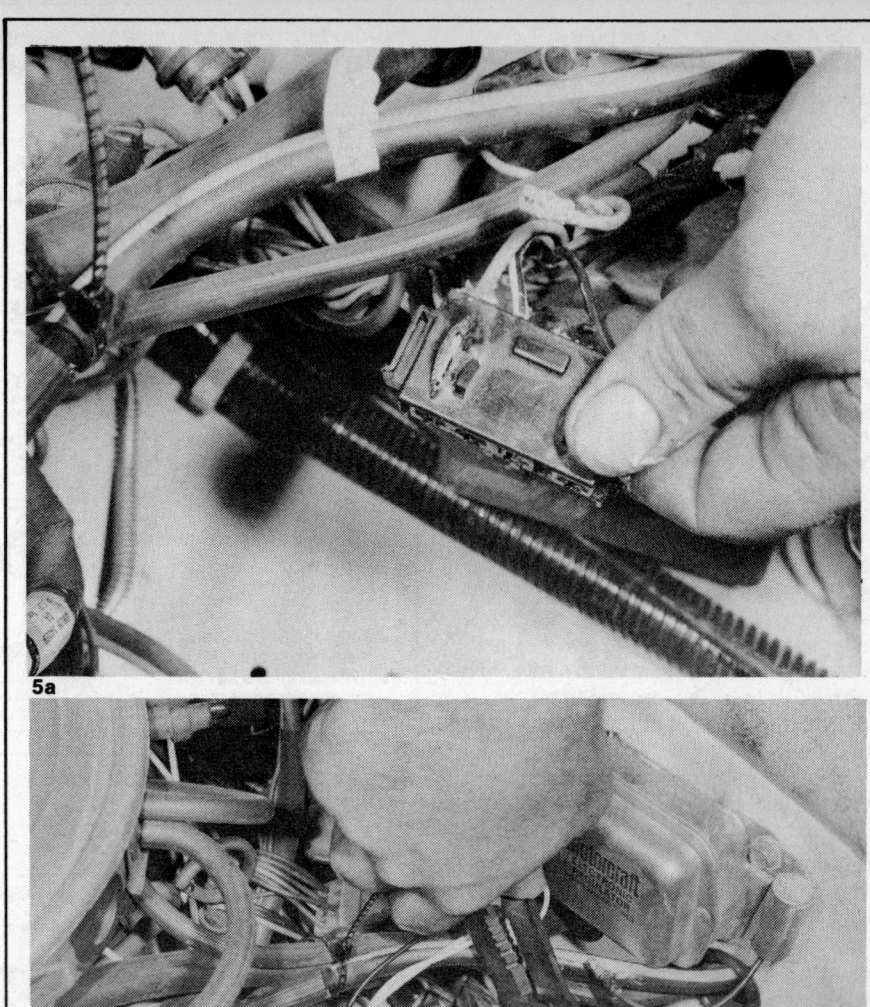

5a

5b

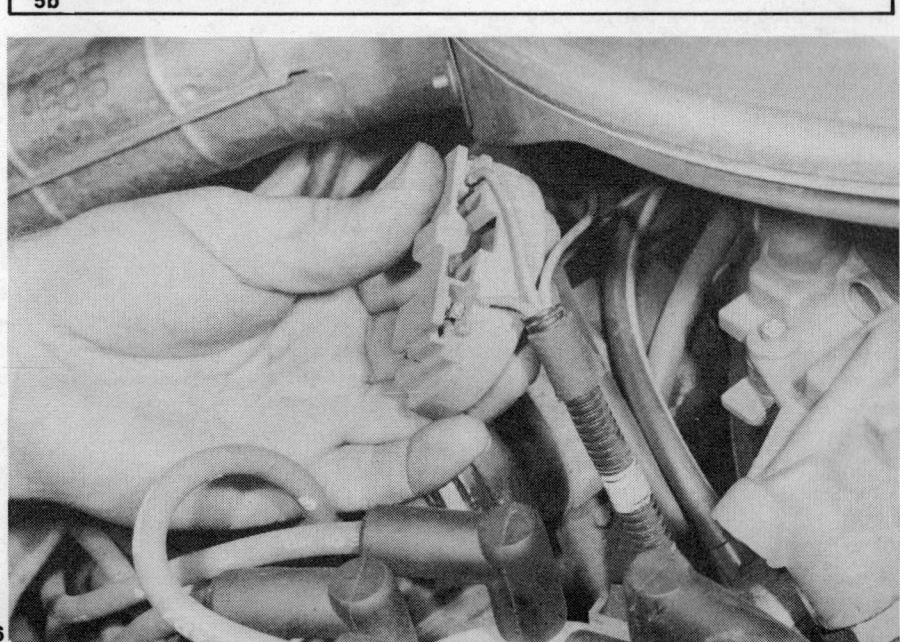

6

we've selected the circuitry of GM's X-car as a typical example. Here are the most common horn circuit problems and how to troubleshoot them.

One Horn Does Not Work

If one horn does not sound when the horn pad is depressed, connect your jumper lead between the horn terminal and the positive battery terminal. This will send full battery voltage directly to the horn; if it works, the problem can be found in the wire that connects the horn terminal to the hot circuit. In the X-car circuit diagram, we see that the problem is in either the dark green wire or the horn relay on the fuse block. When full battery voltage does not sound the horn, ground the black horn relay wire. If the horn still does not work, you need a new horn.

Both Horns Do Not Work

If neither horn sounds when the horn pad is depressed, check for a blown fuse in the fuse block. If the fuse is good, connect a test lamp across the fuse terminals to see if voltage is present. When power is available at the fuse block, check for a blown fusible link in the circuit. If the fusible link is good, connect a jumper lead between the battery and the horns. This should sound the horns, unless there's a problem with the horn switch.

Horns Sound at All Times

The most likely problem in this case is a faulty horn relay or a bad horn switch. Disconnect the 11-terminal connector at the base of the steering column. This disconnects the horn switch. If the horns stop operating, replace the switch. If they continue to sound, replace the relay.

Poor Tonal Quality

Some horns have an adjusting nut or screw that allows adjustment of the tone quality, although horns on many late-model cars lack this feature for reasons of economy—nonadjustable horns are less expensive. When the tonal quality of a horn is poor, it stems from either improper adjustment or high resistance in the circuit.

To determine the cause of the poor-quality sound, connect a voltmeter and an ammeter to the horn and battery to check the horn's current draw—it should be between 4 and 5 amps. If the current draw is not within this range, turn the adjusting nut or screw on the horn to bring it into range.

When high resistance is suspected, connect a voltmeter across the horn terminal and the positive battery terminal to check the voltage drop. Note the voltmeter reading, then depress the horn button and note the amount of voltage drop. If excessive, it indicates high resistance and you should check the circuit wiring to determine the cause—poor connections or high resistance in the wires.

Our second circuit is one many drivers are not familiar with, since the electrical cooling fan came into use with transverse-mounted engines. Again, we'll use the popular X-car as a typical example of the circuit and how to troubleshoot it. A look at the schematic tells us that the fan is operated by a normally open cooling fan relay whose contacts have voltage available con-

5A and 5B. A short inside this alternator regulator plug-in connector allowed the wires to overheat and burn a hole right through the plastic connector (A). When replacing the connector (B), make sure that your wire connections are properly made and insulated against grounding.

6. Here's an example of a hard-to-locate problem. The wire broke at the connector but because of its positioning and the tightness of the wire loom, it did not fully separate from the connector but caused an intermittent problem instead. Be sure to check all connections thoroughly when troubleshooting an electrical problem.

7. Some problems are caused by a simple failure such as properly snapping the connector halves together. Automakers have put snap-locks on such connectors but they're not foolproof.

8. Electrical problems are not restricted to the ignition, starting or charging circuits. If your carburetor is equipped with an electrical choke and the choke isn't working properly, check out the connection, voltage and resistance involved.

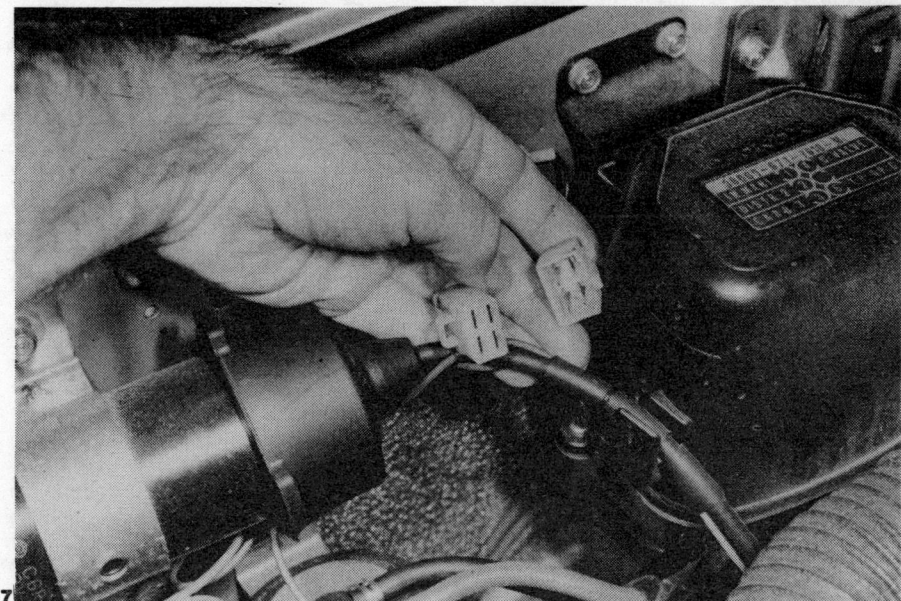

ELECTRICAL TROUBLESHOOTING

stantly through the fusible link and red wire. Whenever the ignition switch is in the Run position, voltage passes through the C/H fuse to the relay coil.

An engine-coolant temperature switch wired to the relay coil closes whenever the coolant exceeds 230° F, sending current to ground. This closes the relay contacts, which now allow current from the hot lead (fusible link/red wire) to reach the cooling fan motor. If the coolant temperature falls below 214° F, the temperature switch opens. This opens the relay contacts and shuts off current flow to the fan motor. An air-conditioning compressor pressure switch is also wired into the circuit to bring on the cooling fan whenever the air-conditioning is turned on, according to refrigerant pressure.

If the cooling fan does not operate at all, check the C/H fuse at the fuse block. If it's good, inspect the fusible link. If this is also good, unplug the connector at the coolant temperature switch. Ground the connector with a jumper lead and turn the ignition switch to Run. If the fan motor works, replace the coolant temperature switch.

But suppose nothing happens—you have either a bad relay or a defective fan motor. Run a jumper lead from the positive battery terminal directly to the fan motor. If the motor runs when it receives direct battery voltage, replace the relay; if it doesn't, replace the fan motor.

TESTING ALTERNATOR/STARTER COMPONENTS

Electrical test procedures have other uses than that of locating circuit problems. When you've determined that an alternator or a starter motor is defective, it's a tossup at today's prices whether you're ahead of the game by trying to pinpoint the problem and correct it, or simply replacing the defective unit with a rebuilt one. If you can afford the rebuilt unit, that's probably the easiest way to go, but not everyone's budget can stand such unexpected blows. And if you're dealing with a foreign car, a rebuilt unit may simply not be available for your make/model.

Alternator Testing

Once an alternator is disassembled, you can check out the internal parts with an ohmmeter or your self-powered test lamp. To test the rotor (field) winding for grounds, hold one test lamp lead on the end of the shaft. Touch the other test lead to each slip ring in turn. If the bulb lights when connected to either slip ring and the shaft, the winding is grounded. To check the winding for open or short circuits, connect your test lamp leads to both slip rings and the bulb should light. If it does not, the winding is open.

The stator windings can be checked for open circuits once they are disconnected from the end frame. The test lamp should light when connected between each pair of stator leads if the winding is good. If the bulb lights when connected from one stator lead to the stator frame, the winding is grounded.

Diodes can also be checked with your test lamp after they have been disconnected from the stator windings. Apply one test lead to the diode case and the other to the diode lead, then reverse the leads. If the bulb lights in both directions, or does not light in either direction, the diode is bad. Good diodes will light in only one direction.

Starter Testing

Testing starter components is a bit more difficult, since a growler is required to check the armature—and few service facilities today have a functioning growler on the premises. Most will simply install a new starter as a matter of course. You can, however, check the field windings for ground or an open. To check for a ground condition, disconnect the field winding ground connections. Connect one test lamp lead to the field frame and the other to the field connector terminal. If the bulb lights, the field windings are grounded. Field windings can be replaced on all automotive starters except the new 5MT starter motor used on late-model GM cars. To check for an open condition, connect the test lamp leads to the ends of the windings. If the bulb does not light, the field winding is open and current cannot pass through the circuit.

Brushes and their holders are also a common source of trouble with starters. You can quickly determine if they are the cause of your particular problem by using your test lamp. To check the insulated brush holders, touch one lead to the holder and the other lead to the frame. The bulb should not light. If all of the brush holders are insulated, the bulb should light when connected to opposite holders, but not when connected to adjacent ones, or from any holder to the frame.

FUSIBLE LINKS

These are short lengths of wire installed as protective devices in certain automotive electrical circuits not protected by circuit breakers or fuses. The wire used in a fusible link is several sizes smaller than the other wire in the circuit, and is covered with a special high-temperature, nonflammable insulation. Some car makers use a fusible link with a color-coded molded flag on the wire or terminal insulator. The color indicates the wire gauge used in the fusible link. When a circuit is overloaded, as when a

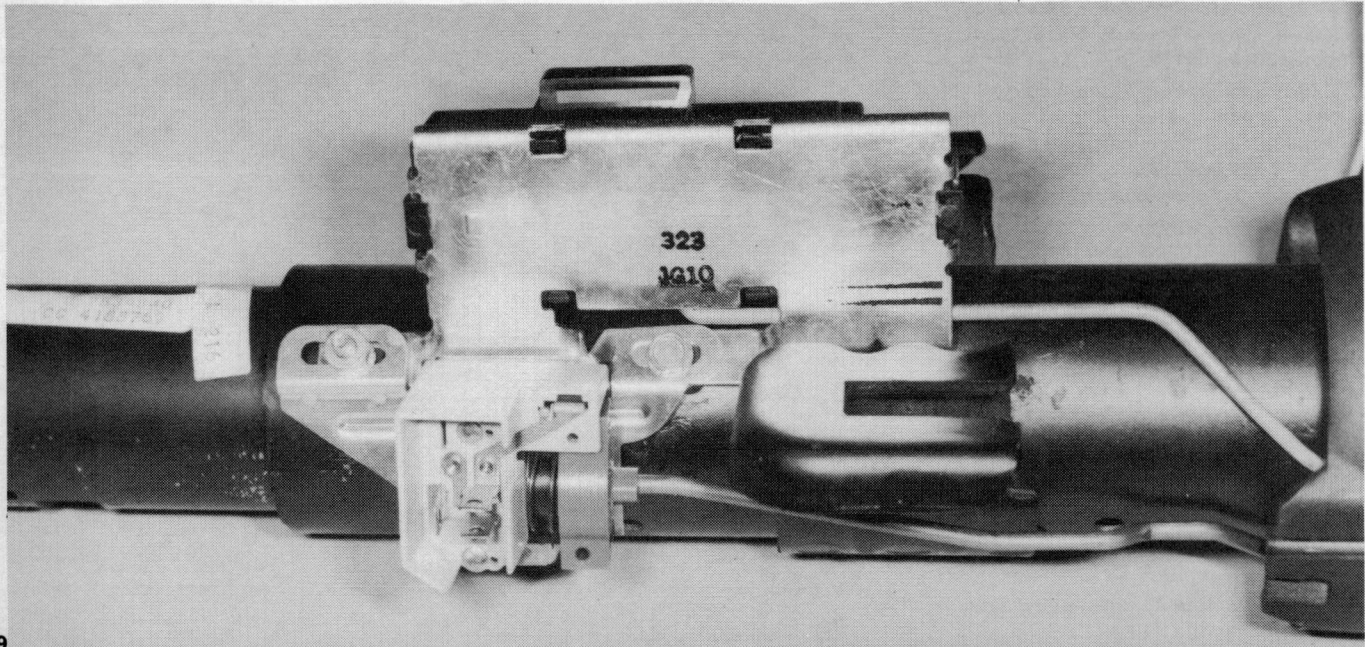

176/IGNITION & ELECTRICAL SYSTEMS

booster battery is connected incorrectly, or a short to ground occurs in the wiring harness, the fusible link will melt. This breaks the circuit and prevents damage to the rest of the wiring or to electrical components.

Damaged fusible links are usually easy to locate—look for blistered or melted insulation, or bare wire ends protruding from the insulation. In some cases, the link may burn out without affecting the insulation. If you think this is the case check the wiring containing the fusible link for continuity at the nearest points on either side of the link. When the link protects a specific component such as the alternator, you can use a voltmeter to check for voltage at its battery terminal—after making certain that the battery is okay. If you get no voltage reading, replace the link.

Simply replacing the blown link will not solve the problem. The cause of the overload must be located and corrected, or the link will blow again. Some fusible links are available as service replacement items; that is, they are prefabricated complete with any necessary terminal connections. Others are simply a piece of fusible wire cut from bulk reels by the dealer's parts department. Never replace a blown fusible link with standard wire, as this will remove all protection from the circuit.

To replace a blown fusible link, cut it out of the circuit at a point just behind where it's spliced into the wiring. New links can be installed with staking-type pliers and crimp joints, but the most satisfactory splice is made by soldering the link in place to ensure a good electrical connection. Remove about one inch of insulation from the end of the new fusible link and the same amount from the end of the harness wire to which it will be spliced. Wrap the two wires together and heat-splice with a soldering gun and rosin-core solder. When cool, insulate the soldered joint with at least three turns of electrical tape.

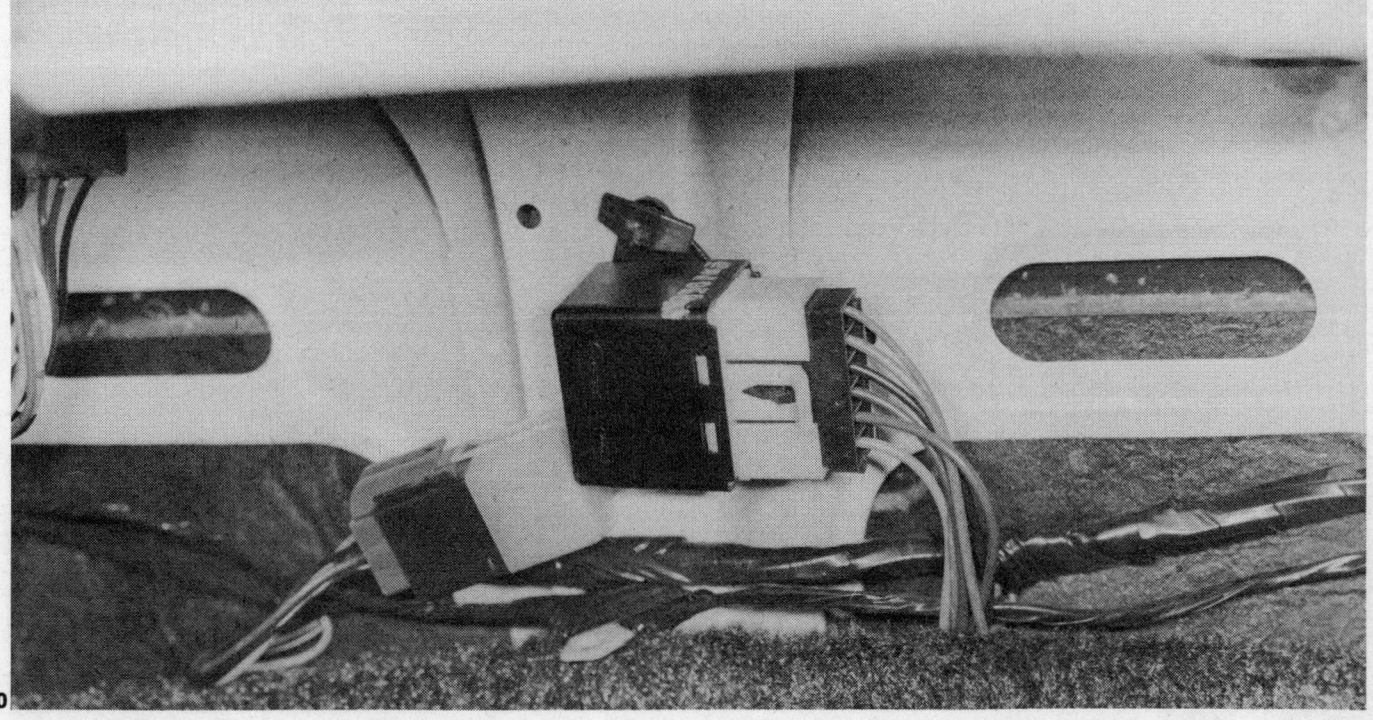

9. Troubleshooting ignition switches on modern cars is not as easy as it used to be. This Chrysler switch is column-mounted and the column may have to be removed from the car in some applications just to get at the switch terminals.

10. Today's fuel-injected vehicles from Ford have a fuel pump shutoff switch located in the trunk. If your car is tapped from behind in a parking lot, it may throw the switch and make it impossible to start the car when you return to it. Moral of the story? You MUST know the system involved, its components and what they do to troubleshoot a problem successfully.

ACCESSORIES

Modern automobiles contain a good deal of electrically operated gadgetry we take for granted. Electric door locks, self-raising radio antennas, automatic headlight dimmers, and speed-monitoring autopilots are only a few of the seldom-thought-of accessories that draw current from the car's electrical system. Some accessories, such as six-way power seats, convertible top lifters, and power windows are almost as complicated as the entire automobile of 50 years ago.

The fully loaded luxury car of today has a mass of accessories that would have brought the charging system of 1949 to its knees in a matter of minutes. With the small car and its four-cylinder engine taking over the road from the full-size vehicles, it's not difficult to understand the recent improvements in charging systems and batteries, nor why automakers show a continuing interest in developing them even further. Obviously, it would take an entire chapter to cover every function in detail, but in the few pages available, we'll set down the general engineering and construction features of each one and define their place in the many circuits of the electrical system.

MOTOR-DRIVEN ACCESSORIES

You may recall from our discussion of the starter that there are several types of direct-current motors that differ from one another in the way their windings are connected to battery current. Series-wound motors—such as those used in starters—have their field windings connected to the armature brushes so that current must pass through the field windings before reaching the armature. Such motors are best suited to moving heavy loads that have to be started slowly. They must, however, be kept under load to prevent their speed from building up to the point where they may damage themselves.

Shunt-wound motors provide current to the field windings independently from that supplied to the armature coils. This is the best type of motor for use where constant speed is required at varying loads.

Compound-wound motors have series windings as well as shunt windings. As we observed in the chapter on starters, most modern series-wound direct-current motors have at least one small shunt winding to keep them from running away if the load is suddenly removed. Units of this type are generally called lightly compounded motors. The ability of the compound motor to produce steady power at varying speeds makes it a natural for such auto accessories as windshield wipers. By controlling the armature and series-winding voltage with a rheostat, variable-speed wiper action can be obtained. Nearly all multispeed motor-driven automobile accessories are equipped with compound-wound motors.

Permanent magnet motors have no field windings, but rely on permanent magnets to provide this function. The torque characteristics of such motors are similar to that of a shunt-wound motor, and thus tend to be a bit weak at low speeds, since speed control is accomplished simply by varying the voltage delivered to the armature windings. This type of motor is sometimes used to operate various types of automotive accessories.

Direct-current motors have another valuable characteristic that AC motors do not possess. Their direction of rotation can be reversed simply by changing the polarity of the current delivered to them. This is frequently taken advantage of in the design of various motor-driven auto accessories, such as the self-raising/lowering radio antennas.

Windshield wipers are perhaps the most important motor-driven accessory on the car. Years ago, wipers were operated by engine manifold vacuum, but all wiper systems used today are motor-driven and wired to operate only when the ignition switch is in the on or ACC. position. There are, however, many details of windshield wiper construction that vary from one make of car to another. Each car maker has used at least one single-speed and one two-speed—or multispeed—wiper system. The single-speed units were standard equipment on base models and multispeed types were options, or standard on higher-priced models. Virtually all current designs are two-speed motors, even on the lower-priced "economy" cars. In the case of most domestic automobiles, the wiper motor is protected by a circuit breaker located in the fuse block. This prevents damage if the wipers are turned on while frozen to the glass, or in the event of a wiper circuit overload or electrical short.

Chrysler Corporation uses permanent-magnet motors on its two-speed systems, and compound-wound motors on its three-speed systems. Two different sets of brushes are used for the speed control in the two-speed units, and a resistance in the shunt field circuit controls speed on the three-speed units. The switch also has a provision for reversing the motor's polarity when the unit is turned off. This causes the motor

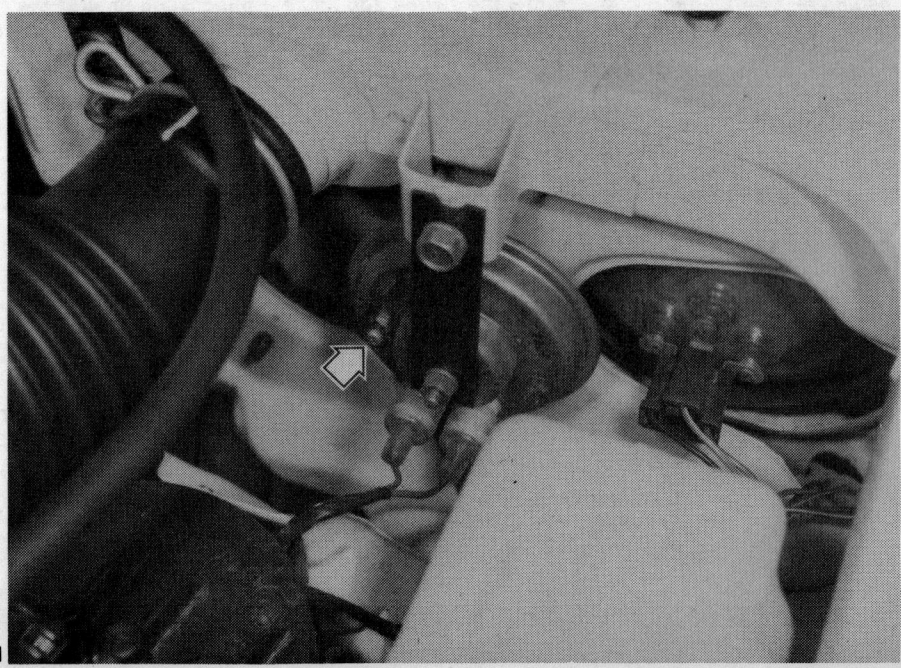

1

to run briefly backward to park the wipers in their lowest position before a cam-operated switch breaks the circuit completely to shut the current off.

GM uses a similar system for parking the wiper blades on many of its vehicles. Until recently, all were powered by compound-wound motors, and were two-speed on all models (except Cadillac). Heavier motors were used on Cadillacs and other models where the wipers are parked in a depressed position, out of the line of sight of the driver. The nondepressed parking units are provided with a flat-shaped motor instead of one with a round cross section.

GM began using a new Delco design in 1980. It uses a permanent magnet and is enclosed in an aluminum die-cast housing with a plastic cover. An RFI suppressor is located in the terminal connector on the wiper motor. When the wiper switch is turned off, the motor operates in low speed until the blades reach their park position. At that point, a cam on the gear opens the normally closed positive park switch to ground the motor. This results in what Delco calls a "positive park," and shuts off the wiper motor.

Ford uses a permanent-magnet motor on all models. Speed control on two-speed models is obtained by using different brushes on the motor. Parking is obtained by reversing the rotation of the motor, the same as with other makes.

Windshield washers are also usually motor-driven. In the case of General Motors cars, the wiper pump is screwed directly onto the windshield wiper motor and drive mechanism. When the "wash" button is depressed by the driver, a relay engages a cam drive that is turned by the wiper motor as it works the wind-

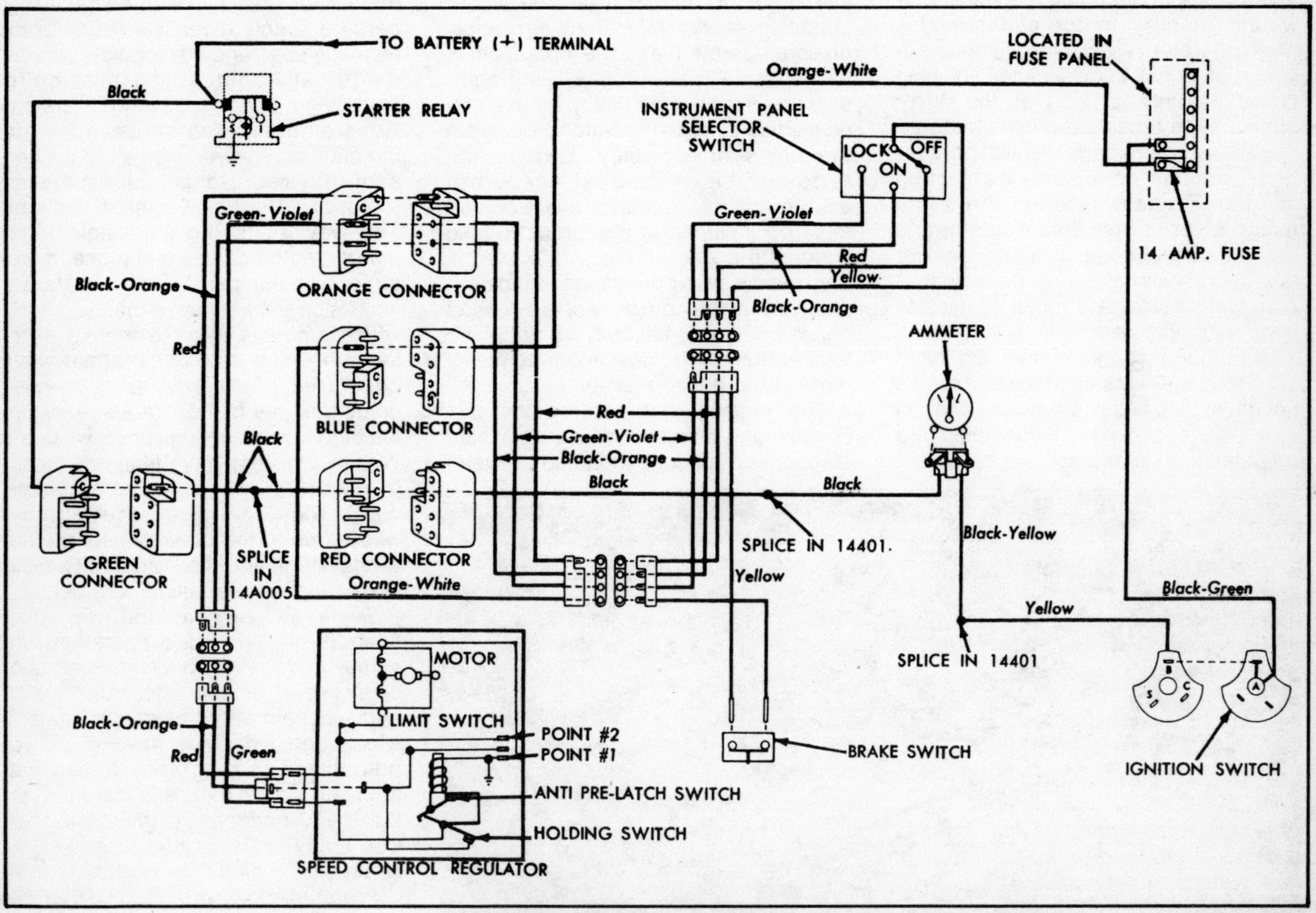

1. If your horn sounds strange, try adjusting the screw (arrow). On some horns, you must remove an end ball and adjust a nut. On others, you may have a set of points that require filing.

2. Here's a schematic of an electrical cruise control system. They can be repaired, but it takes time and patience. Early type cruise control unit had electrical motor to control throttle position. Current units use vacuum for the same application and are most reliable as well as less complex.

3. The blower motor on many car heaters or air conditioning units can be removed from the engine compartment without having to remove the entire heater/air conditioning unit.

ACCESSORIES

shield wipers. This cam operates a bellows-type pump that delivers water to the washer jets. The resulting flow is a series of pulselike squirts as each cam lobe passes under the pump unit's plunger. After one complete cam cycle, the washer mechanically disengages itself automatically.

Constant-delivery washer pumps, such as those used by Chrysler and other car makers, have a positive-displacement pump that functions somewhat like the engine's oil pump. This device is driven by a small shunt-wound electric motor and provides washing water whether the wipers are in operation or not. In most cases, washing continues only so long as the driver continues to press the control button.

Heaters, defrosters, ventilating systems, and air-conditioners are often integrated affairs sharing the same motor-driven blower. Sometimes there is a separate defroster or air-conditioner fan. In cars with a rear window wiper or defogger, a separate motor is used to control its operation.

Compound-wound motors are often used to power fans and blowers, but it's not unusual to find shunt-wound units as well. Their speed may be controlled by a rheostat that allows rpm to be varied over a wide band, or by a switch that provides two or three fixed speeds. This last system is more common today and consists of a number of resistors that can be cut into the blower motor's circuit at the driver's discretion. When the switch is in the low-speed position, more resistance is inserted into the motor circuit than when the intermediate speed is selected. High-speed operation is usually achieved by removing all resistors from the circuit.

In cars equipped with air-conditioning, the complexity of the ventilating system wiring becomes much greater. A switch and circuits must be included to provide low, medium, and high air-conditioner output, in addition to a fan-driven supply of unrefrigerated air. The operation of the air-conditioner's refrigerating compressor is also electrically initiated by energizing a magnetic clutch included in the unit's drive pulley. Further, the relatively heavy current needed to accomplish this demands that a control relay be included in the circuit to take some of the load off the control switch. This relay is also controlled thermostatically so that the compressor is switched on and off automatically to keep the temperature in the passenger compartment at the desired level.

The magnetic clutch on the air-conditioning compressor is a stationary electromagnetic coil mounted between the pulley and the compressor housing. To eliminate the need for brushes and slip rings, the coil is not allowed to revolve with the pulley—as is sometimes done in similar drive units—but is mounted rigidly onto the end of the compressor. It acts as a short solenoid, drawing the pulley and shaft-driving plate into engagement so that the car's engine will be able effectively to operate the air-conditioning compressor.

Power seats come in two varieties: two-way seats that provide movement fore and aft, and six-way seats that add up-and-down and tilting movements. General Motors uses series-wound motors for both types of seats in their cars—a simple reversible setup for the two-way seat, and a solenoid-operated, electrically shifted transmission for changing mode in the six-way versions. Reversing the motor changes the direction of movement on all seats. Ford and Chrysler use permanent-magnet motors in their power-seat systems. Two-way seats have a single motor connected by cables to the gear drives on each seat rail. Six-way seats use what is called a "three-armature" motor, which amounts to three motors in the same housing. One of the armatures is connected to the front edge up-down gears, another to the fore-aft gears, and the third to the rear edge up-down gears. With this system, more than one motion of the seat can be operated simultaneously. The GM system requires a six-wire cable to the controller for the six-way system, and the Ford and Chrysler systems require an eight-wire cable.

Some older cars have four-way power seats, but the principle of operation is the same, with a reversible motor operating sets of gears on both sides of the seat. In addition, some cars have split seats, in which one side may have a six-way adjuster and the other a two-way adjuster. All this means is that there are that many more parts to give trouble and that many more motors to add to the strain on the electrical system.

Power windows are wired so that they

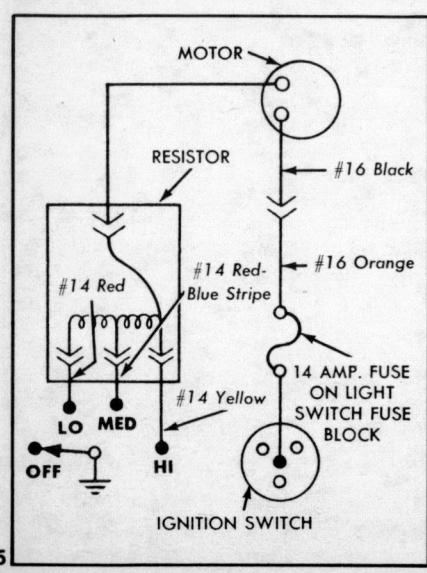

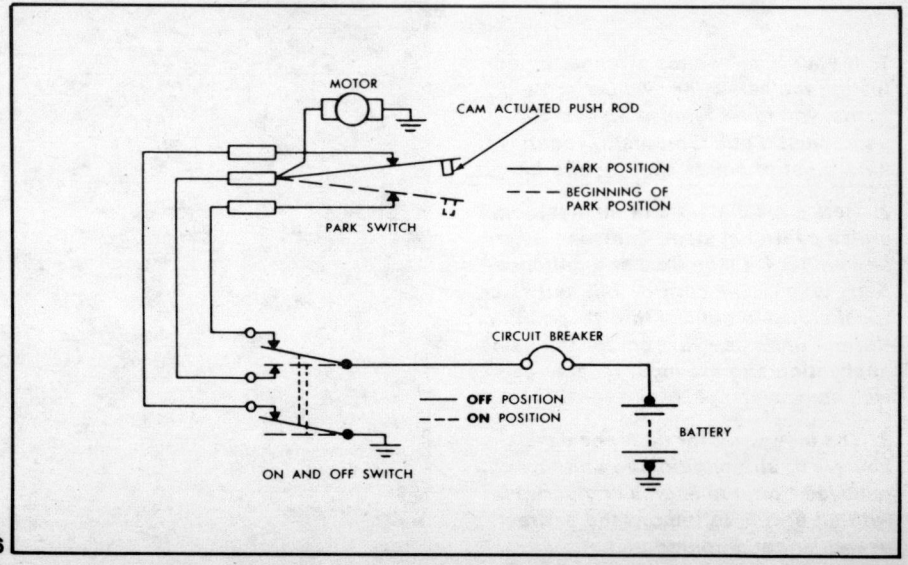

can be raised and lowered from the master control panel on the driver's door or by single switches located at the individual windows. Since initial loads may be high, series-wound motors are universally used. There is a separate motor at each window, and those used by GM have their own internal circuit breaker in addition to the one provided for the entire system. This prevents one stuck window from disabling the whole power-window system.

Each motor receives two wires. The position of the operating switch determines their polarity and therefore the direction of motor rotation. Although power-window motors draw only between 5 and 10 amps of current, the circuit breakers commonly have a capacity of about 30 amps. This is nice for forcing the windows loose when they're stuck by ice and snow, but not so nice if a child gets his fingers caught in one.

Convertible tops are raised and lowered by means of a hydraulic system having a motor-driven pump. The motor is a series-wound reversible unit and is part of an assembly that includes the motor, a pump, and the hydraulic fluid reservoir. Raising a convertible top puts a considerable draw on the motor despite the fact that the hydraulic system provides a tremendous mechanical advantage. Most draw about 35 amps of current, although this may reach 50 or more when almost stalled. The engine of the car must thus be

4. Blower motor resistors may be located under the dash, as in this Ford Escort, or right on the motor assembly under the hood.

5. Heater electrical circuit shows how resistors are arranged in the switch to provide different speed settings. Rheostats are seldom used in such applications today.

6. This simple circuit diagram shows how a typical single-speed wiper unit operates. A cam on the motor-driven pinion gear shuts off the motor when the blades have reached the park position.

7. The wiper reservoir supplies windshield solvent to the washer pump (arrow), which pumps it through hoses to nozzles to squirt the glass. Washer pump and wiper motor are built into the same unit, but can be repaired separately as long as motor works.

8. This exploded drawing of GM's new wiper motor assembly used on "J" cars and other recent models. Fortunately, wiper motors don't give all that much trouble.

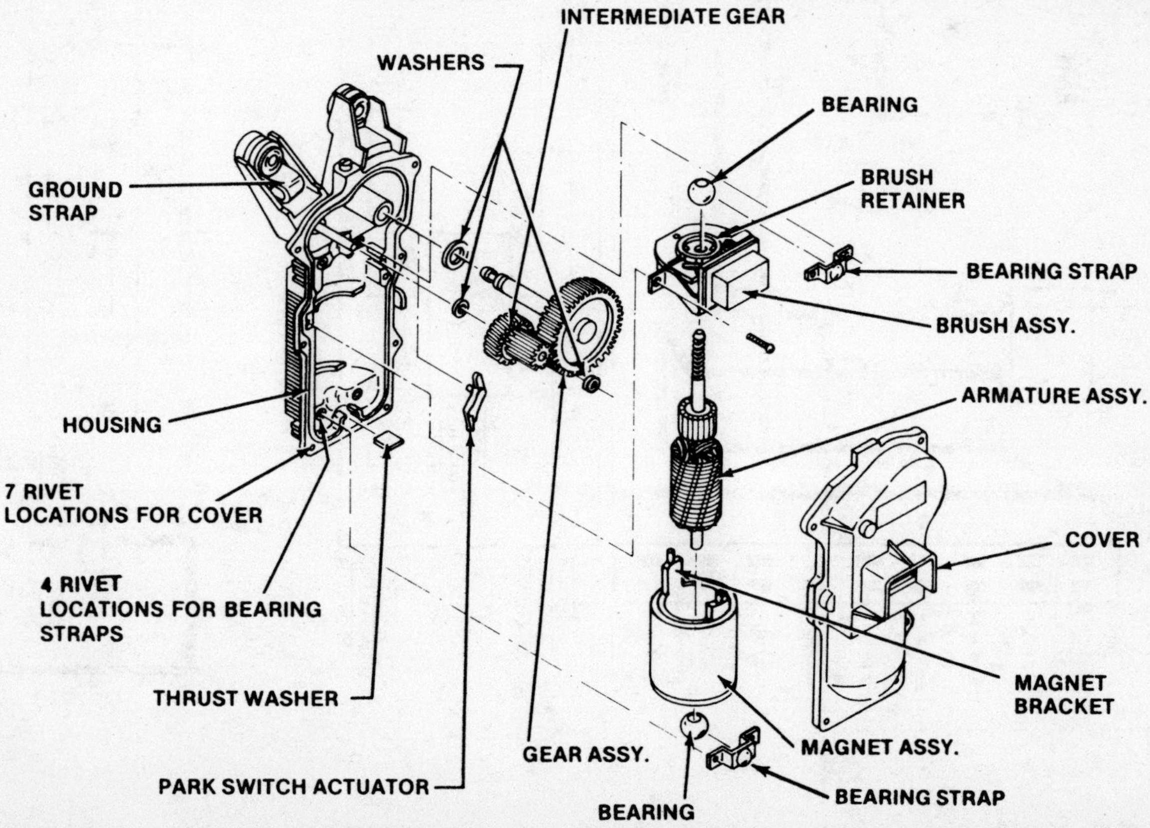

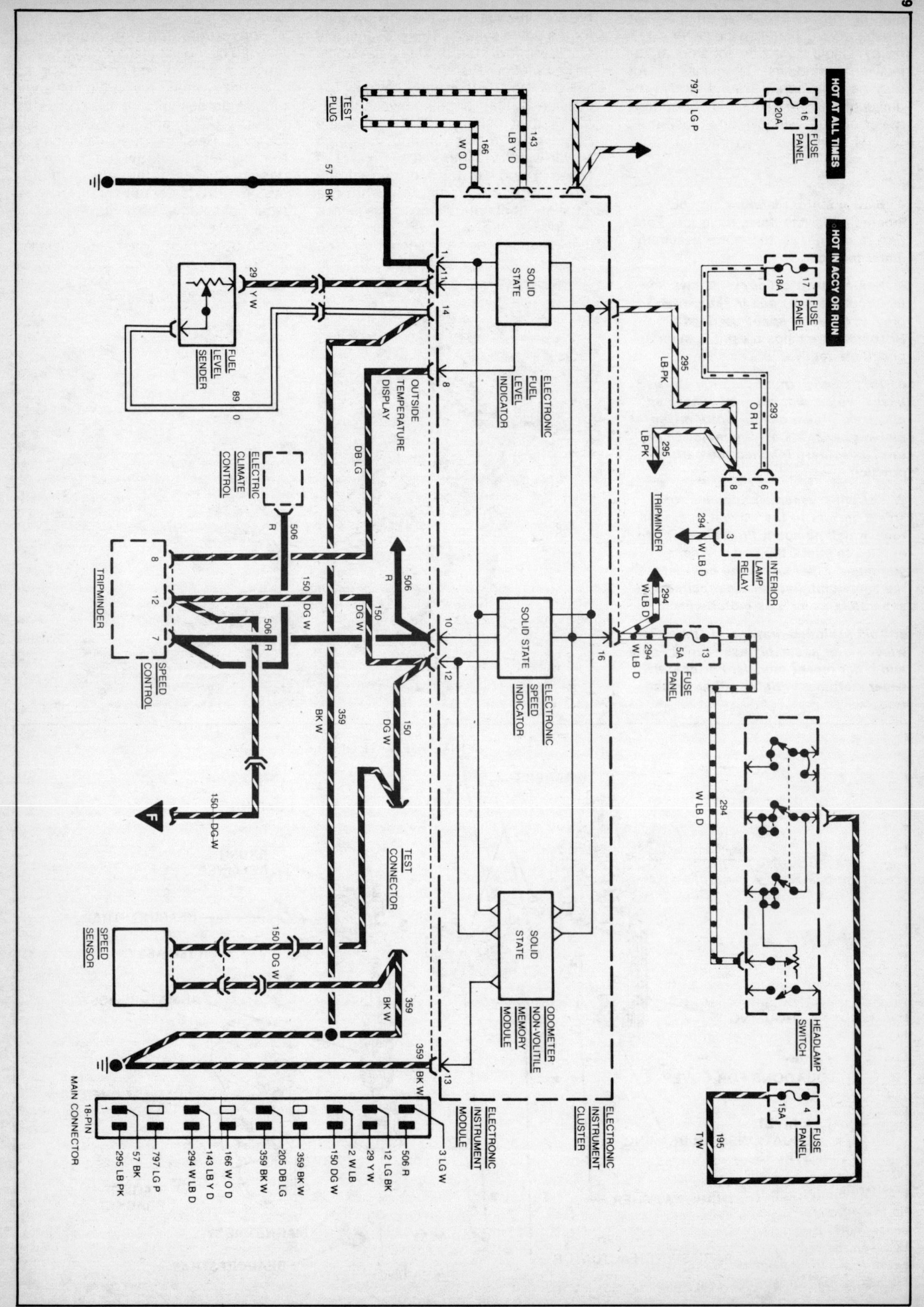

speeded up when raising the top so that the charging system can take over the added current demand. The motor is usually protected by its own circuit breaker, which cuts out at about 70 to 75 amps. Sliding sunroofs are available with electric power on some GM and Ford models. These are operated by a reversible motor mounted above the windshield header. A 25-amp breaker is part of the circuit.

Self-raising/lowering radio antennas are motor-driven units that usually operate automatically as soon as the radio is switched on or off. Series-wound motors are used for these, and their direction of rotation is reversed by changing the polarity of the battery current delivered to them.

In all, a car may have from 12 to 15 electric motors in addition to the starter. With the endless proliferation of power accessories, this number will likely continue to increase despite the almost overwhelming complexity it adds to the wiring of the electrical system as a whole. Electrical accessories do not stop with those operated by motors. Below are some other devices—electromagnetic and other—that also draw current from the battery and charging system.

Transmissions equipped with an overdrive unit are commonly controlled by means of a large, electrically operated solenoid. Essentially, an overdrive is just a two-speed planetary transmission—related to that found on the venerable Model T—that is bolted onto the back of a conventional three-speed box. Rather than use bands, like those found in automatic transmissions (and the Model T), overdrive units employ a pawl and balk ring to lock the ring gear, thereby stepping up the speed of the output shaft's rotation. It's the solenoid's job to engage the pawl when overdrive is needed, and disengage it when its operation is not desired. With the overdrive engaged, engine rpm is reduced by almost 30 percent over that required to drive the car at similar speeds without overdrive.

The electrical operation of the overdrive unit is controlled by a governor that is driven by the speedometer cable. This controls the action of the overdrive relay. When the car reaches a speed of approximately 28 mph (depending upon the particular unit), the governor contacts close, completing the relay's field

9. This little gem is the wiring diagram for Ford's 1984 electronic instrument module option on Continental and Mark VII models. Look for it to appear on the Ford/Mercury line in coming years. What it means is simple—as accessories become more sophisticated in what they will do, so does the circuitry—and the potential problems posed.

circuit to ground. Operation of the relay switches battery current to the solenoid, causing it to engage the pawl.

There is also a "kickdown" switch operated by the gas pedal that disengages the overdrive for faster acceleration. The kickdown switch not only breaks the circuit between the governor and the overdrive relay, causing it to shut off the current to the solenoid, but also grounds the ignition system momentarily. Grounding the ignition causes the engine to "cut out" for an instant to allow the overdrive pawl to retract.

The overdrive solenoid has two coils: one to move the plunger and a smaller one that holds the plunger once it is engaged. This prevents the solenoid unit from drawing excessive current while the overdrive is in operation. Overdrive transmissions offered since 1975 commonly achieve overdrive by means of a gear ratio that is less than 1:1 in top gear—a system that utilizes no solenoids and no electrical current.

Until recently, electric clocks were all solenoid-operated accessories. The type of electric clock found on your kitchen wall is driven by a synchronous motor that depends upon 60-cycle house current to keep it on time. Wired to 50-cycle house current, the same clock would require 72 seconds to record one minute. Since automobile electrical systems work on direct current, this type of clock motor would not run in your car. For this reason, car clocks are spring-driven, with a solenoid used to rewind the spring periodically. This explains why the clock makes a funny "zipping" noise every now and then. In recent years the electronically controlled digital clock has become a popular accessory. These generate their own frequency-controlled alternating current for their synchronous motors, and are designed to be replaceable rather than repairable. They also require a minimal amount of current draw.

Electric door locks are another accessory that makes use of solenoids. There is at each door a double-action solenoid that can be operated by the driver or by the passenger in the righthand front seat. They are controlled by a single-pole, double-throw switch that reverses the polarity of current to the solenoid with each change of direction. The reversing of the polarity changes the direction of current flow through the solenoid windings, causing the motion of the plunger to move in the opposite direction. All doors are locked or unlocked at once by this system.

Horns are electromagnetic, and usually require from 7 to 11 amps apiece to operate—relatively heavy current for a simple accessory. Although some cars use the electrical contacts in the horn button to send current directly to the horns, most domestic cars have a horn relay. The horn button merely energizes the relay's field, thereby drawing two contacts together that send full battery current directly to the horns. This ensures them the volts they need even when many other accessories are in operation. On General Motors cars, the horn relay is the main electrical path for all current flowing to and from the battery, with the exception of that used by the starter motor.

The voltage required for proper horn functioning is within a very narrow permissible band. Most horns are thus equipped with a current-adjusting nut to calibrate the horn so that it will sound properly. This control is quite sensitive and only a small fraction of a turn is usually all that's needed to put the horn back at full volume after age and wear have caused it to fall mute temporarily.

Radios are an item that could easily take an entire book to cover. Such accessories as tape recorders, record players, and televisions are also available either as dealer options or from independent sources. These specialized pieces of equipment are not really automotive circuits and their service and repair are usually farmed out by service departments to shops that specialize in this type of work.

All current automotive audio equipment is transistorized and there are several precautions that should be observed when installing or servicing either sound systems or their supplementary speakers. First, be very careful not to route current into them of the wrong polarity. Second, when installing extra speakers, be careful that the speaker or its mount does not come into contact with outside electrical sources, such as bare electrical system wires or their terminals. Soldering irons and electric drills used in their installation should be properly grounded. As a final warning, never operate a transistorized unit with its speaker(s) disconnected, as this will frequently damage or destroy the transistors.

Automatic headlight-dimmer systems rely on a photoelectric cell that triggers a relay controlling the high and low beams of the headlamps. The photoelectric cell used in these units is often of the vacuum tube type, since these react more quickly to changes in stimuli than do solid-state types.

Electrical antitheft devices are widely available both as factory-installed options and as add-on accessories. The simplest are the off-on switches that can be placed in the main battery cables or are wired into the ignition system's primary lead.

Audible alarm systems are sold by many companies. Some sound the horn when the car is moved or when a door or other switch-protected compartment is opened. Others disable the ignition or shut off the fuel supply in addition to activating the horn. Since many cars have their horns mounted where thieves can pull the connectors from them just by reaching through the grille opening with a long screwdriver, some of the

ACCESSORIES

audible systems come with an independent horn that can be mounted in a more inaccessible place.

Cigarette lighters and other minor gadgets are usually completely unsophisticated electrically. The lighter found on most cars is nothing more than a simple resistance wire coil that heats up when the unit is pushed into contact with battery current. A temperature-sensitive spring clip keeps it there until the spring becomes hot enough to flex and release the lighter.

Automotive electrical systems have so many circuits and subcircuits that it is difficult for even the dealers' service department to keep up with all of them. Their complexity far exceeds the wiring found in the average household, yet despite their involved layouts, only a few basic electrical principles are involved. Once you have grasped the workings of the ignition coil, the phenomenon of electromagnetism becomes understandable. This opens the way to learning about the operation of relays, solenoids, electric motors, and generators/alternators.

There's no reason to be timid when faced with a job involving the electrical system. If you've never done much electrical work before, your progress may be slow at first. But once you've handled some of the more routine phases of electrical troubleshooting and maintenance, you'll be surprised at the confidence you develop. Confidence and experience—these are the most important keys to becoming a real "pro."

WIRING GUIDE

GUIDE TO FUSIBLE LINKS*

Make	Location	Wire Color
AMC	Battery terminal of starter relay to main wire harness	Red
	Battery terminal of horn relay to main wire harness	Pink
	Accessory terminal of ignition switch to wire harness	Brown
	Battery terminal of starter relay to heated rear window relay	Red
	B-3 terminal of ignition switch to circuit breaker	Red
	I-3 terminal of ignition switch to circuit breaker	Yellow
	I-3 terminal of ignition switch (single wire at switch splits into two feed wires)	Yellow
	I-3 terminal of ignition switch to throttle stop solenoid	Yellow
	Engine compartment harness at AV terminal of dash connector	Dark Green
	SOL terminal of ignition switch to wire harness	Dark Green
CHRYSLER (Rear-Wheel-Drive Vehicles)	Rear of battery positive terminal in circuit leading to #10 cavity (hazard flasher circuit) of bulkhead disconnect	Orange
	Between alternator and wiring harness main splice R6	Black or Red
	Four links at rear of left front wheelhouse between wiring harness main splice R6 and bulkhead disconnect cavities 4, 38 (to ignition switch), 6 (to heated rear window), and 40 (to headlamp switch)	Gray (4, 38, 40) Dark Blue (6)
(Front-Wheel-Drive Vehicles)	Rear of battery positive terminal in circuit leading to #12 cavity (hazard flasher circuit) of bulkhead disconnect	Pink
	At left side shield between wiring harness main splice A1 and alternator	Red (65-amp alternator) Dark Blue (60-amp alternator)
	Four links at left side shield between wiring harness main splice A1 and bulkhead disconnect cavities 4, 37 (to ignition switch), 6 (to headlamp switch), and 35 (to heated rear window)	Gray (4, 6, 36) Orange (37)
FORD LINCOLN MERCURY	Between starter relay and alternator: All Mustang, Mustang II, Cougar through 1973, Mustang/Capri, Fairmont/Zephyr, Granada/Cougar with performance instrumentation from 1981	OEM links are Green or Black. Replacement links are color-coded according to wire gauge as follows:
	Looped outside wire harness between starter relay and alternator: 1974-76 Cougar, all T-Bird, Lincoln Continental, Mark IV/V through 1978, all 1979-80 Pinto/Bobcat with optional gauges, all escort/Lynx, ESP/LN-7 with optional gauges	
	Twin links—one between starter relay and alternator, and one between starter relay and vehicle equipment harness: All other FoMoCo cars through 1978, 1979-80 Pinto/Bobcat with standard warning lights, all escort/Lynx, ESP/LN-7 with warning lights, Fairmont/Zephyr from 1981	Blue—20 ga. Red—18 ga. Yellow—17 ga. Orange—16 ga. Green—14 ga.
	Triple links—one between starter relay and alternator, and two between starter relay and vehicle equipment harness: 1979-80 Granada/Monarch, all T-Bird/XR-7, Fairmont/Zephyr, Granada/Cougar with standard warning lights from 1981	
	Four links—one between starter relay and alternator, and three between starter relay and vehicle equipment harness: All Versailles	
GENERAL MOTORS Buick	At starter solenoid battery terminal	Black (except H & X-body) Red (H & X-body)
	To cooling fan relay, X-body	Red
Cadillac	One, two, or three links at starter solenoid battery terminal (depends upon model year/body style)	Black or Dark Green

GUIDE TO FUSIBLE LINKS*

Make	Location	Wire Color
Chevrolet	Single link at solenoid battery terminal	Brown
	Twin links at starter solenoid battery terminal	Red (gas vehicles)
		Black (diesel vehicles)
	To cooling fan relay, X-body	Red
	Molded splice at horn relay	Black
	Molded splice in voltage-regulator #3 terminal wire	Orange
	Molded splice in ammeter circuit (both sides of meter)	Orange
Oldsmobile	Single or twin links at starter solenoid battery terminal	Black or Brown (all except H & X-body)
		Red (H & X-body)
	To cooling fan relay, X-body	Red
Pontiac	Positive battery cable pigtail lead (requires entire cable replacement)	Brown
	At horn relay	Black
	Molded splice in circuit at junction block and horn relay (some single and some twin)	Orange
	Single or twin links at starter solenoid battery terminal	Black (all except H & X-body)
		Red (H & X-body)
	To cooling fan relay, X-body	Red

*Not all links are used on any one vehicle, unless otherwise specified. Colors and locations subject to change at manufacturer's discretion. Additional links may be added as running change during model year and not appear on vehicle wiring diagram for that year.

BELDEN AUTOMOTIVE PRIMARY WINDING SAFETY GUIDE

Total Approx. Circuit Amperes		Total Circuit Watts		Total Candlepower		Wire Gauge (For Length in Feet)											
6V	12V	6V	12V	6V	12V	3'	5'	7'	10'	15'	20'	25'	30'	40'	50'	75'	100'
0.5	1.0	3	12	3	6	18	18	18	18	18	18	18	18	18	18	18	18
0.75	1.5			5	10	18	18	18	18	18	18	18	18	18	18	18	18
1.0	2	6	24	8	16	18	18	18	18	18	18	18	18	18	18	16	16
1.5	3			12	24	18	18	18	18	18	18	18	18	18	18	14	14
2.0	4	12	48	15	30	18	18	18	18	18	18	18	18	16	16	12	12
2.5	5			20	40	18	18	18	18	18	18	18	16	16	14	12	12
3.0	6	18	72	25	50	18	18	18	18	18	18	16	16	16	14	12	10
3.5	7			30	60	18	18	18	18	18	18	16	16	14	14	10	10
4.0	8	24	96	35	70	18	18	18	18	18	16	16	16	14	12	10	10
5.0	10	30	120	40	80	18	18	18	18	16	16	16	14	12	12	10	10
5.5	11			45	90	18	18	18	18	16	16	14	14	12	12	10	8
6.0	12	36	144	50	100	18	18	18	18	16	16	14	14	12	12	10	8
7.5	15			60	120	18	18	18	18	14	14	12	12	12	10	8	8
9.0	18	54	216	70	140	18	18	16	16	14	14	12	12	10	10	8	8
10	20	60	240	80	160	18	18	16	16	14	12	10	10	10	10	8	6
11	22	66	264	90	180	18	18	16	16	12	12	10	10	8	6	6	6
12	24	72	288	100	200	18	18	16	16	12	12	10	10	10	8	6	6
15	30					18	16	16	14	10	10	10	10	10	6	4	4
20	40					18	16	14	12	10	10	8	8	6	6	4	2
25	50					16	14	12	12	10	10	8	8	6	6	2	2
50	100					12	12	10	10	6	6	4	4	4	2	1	0
75	150					10	10	8	8	4	4	2	2	2	1	00	00
100	200					10	8	8	6	4	4	2	2	1	0	4/0	4/0

*18 AWG indicated above this line could be 20 AWG electrically—18 AWG is recommended for mechanical strength.

NOTES